AA

GUIDE TO GOLF COURSES
in
BRITAIN
AND IRELAND

Produced by the Publishing Division of
The Automobile Association

Gazetteer compiled by the AA's
Information Research Unit, Information
Control.

Maps prepared by the Cartographic
Department of The Automobile
Association

© The Automobile Association 1992

Cover design The Paul Hampson
Partnership

Illustrations (black and white)
Steven Knight

Head of Advertisement Sales
Christopher Heard, Tel 0256 20123
(ex 21544)

Advertisement Production
Karen Weeks, Tel 0256 20123 (ext 21545)

Typeset, printed and bound in Great
Britain by William Clowes Limited,
Beccles and London

Colour section typeset by Microset
Graphics Limited, Basingstoke

Every effort is made to ensure accuracy, but
the publishers do not hold themselves
responsible for any consequences that may
arise from errors or omissions. While the
contents are believed correct at the time of
going to press, changes may have occurred
since that time or will occur during the
currency of this book.

© The Automobile Association April 1992

A CIP catalogue record for this book is
available from the British Library.

Published by The Automobile Association,
Fanum House, Basingstoke, Hampshire
RG21 2EA

ISBN 0 7495 0426 9

CONTENTS

BUDGET GUIDES

Britain • France • Italy

A brand new series of country guides for the independent traveller with detailed regional tours, outings off the beaten track, and packed with practical advice, tips on local specialities, money-saving hints and useful maps.

Price £6.99
Publication January 1992

Available from bookshops and AA shops

EVERY GOLFING NOMAD ENJOYS A TWO-UP START IN LIFE ...

John Ingham, regular contributor to 'Golf Monthly', takes a nostalgic look back through his rich golfing past to reveal the secrets of his favourite British courses.

The final hole for the Old course at Sunningdale.

The 11th and 7th greens at the home of golf, St Andrews. (inset) Bobby Jones, without question, the sports hero of his day.

Journalists quickly overcome the embarrassment about name-dropping. But, to be perfectly truthful, golf writers have few, if any, sporting heroes because we are too easily made aware that most superstars don't live in the real world and are almost overwhelmed with their own importance in a game which, because of publicity and raw cash, has become just another part of the entertainment industry.

What we love is the atmosphere. No golfer will ever really forget the first time tee-peg was pushed into turf. It was akin to one's first kiss. Anyway, while every golfer enjoys a two-up start in life, the ones who write about the royal and ancient sport take additional advantages for granted. When, for instance, in 1958 I was introduced to Bobby

Jones Jnr in the R&A clubhouse, I reckoned my walk through life's fairways would, from then on, be paved with similar golden moments.

So far, it has been. But no player since that time when I met Mr Jones, has compared with his quality. He appeared unaffected by adulation and was, apparently, never mean, boastful, arrogant or twisted in the way some of the 'stars' are today. He had the intellect to deal with anyone, and would have brought even tabloid pressmen round to his way of thinking. There would be no ghastly incidents.

As I helped Bobby Jones into an old black Humber, people watched with envy because to be associated in any way, however

humble, with a sports legend, somehow increased one's own self-esteem. Then to play on the course that he once played on years ago was, well, almost like walking in the spiked footsteps of a god.

But when you play the Old course St Andrews, things you have read about in books come flooding back because this birthplace of the game is filled with ghosts of great names past. When you stand on the first tee at St Andrews, in front of the daunting clubhouse and the window filled with a million eyes, you cannot remain unmoved. However tough. However professional. As golfers, we are all the same under the skin.

In selecting my favourite British courses, I have to bear in mind that they must be accessible to everyone. No golf course, in my view, should be out of bounds to the genuine golfer - but this is not the case. It distressed me that 1991 United States Open champion Payne Stewart found he could not gain entry to play Muirfield, arguably the finest championship golfing lay-out in these islands. Those privileged to act as guardians of a paradise like Muirfield, or Swinley Forest, or any other private and exclusive club, ought really to feel more comfortable with themselves if, say on a Monday, they allow visitors in the same way farm owners allow access to ancient walks that cross 'their' land.

Sadly, on the other side of the argument, some visitors spoil it for everyone by failing to

◆ ◆ 7

put back their divots, or ending the day with an overlong stay at the 19th hole.

Of all the democratic places to play, St Andrews undoubtedly heads the list and is memorable. Known as the headquarters of golf, all you need is to buy your ticket to play. You wait your turn and then stand on the first tee, in front of the clubhouse window.

Everyone takes their time and some overseas players take pictures as well. So don't expect a speedy round - and you won't be playing a manicured links. This is not Cypress

exposed to TV glare. That's when their shots find the Burn, or that infamous bunker at the 17th hole.

It is no co-incidence that the roll of honour of St Andrews winners includes such names as Jones, Sam Snead, Jack Nicklaus, Seve Ballesteros and Nick Faldo, not to mention Peter Thomson and Bobby Locke.

Possibly the only reason the great Ben Hogan never won at St Andrews was that the nearest fairway he ever walked was some fourteen miles away at Carnoustie, where he

Doug Sanders (left), with Billy Casper at Royal Birkdale in 1968, two years before that missed short putt cost him the 1970 Open title.

Almost home; the 17th green on St Andrews' notorious 'Road Hole', graced from afar by the R&A clubhouse.

Point. This is the home of golf and like many homes in the land, it is well-used and suffers re-turfed patches and the odd worm cast because of automatic watering. But you'll find it unchanged in design and none the worse for that. Hell Bunker is still there, so is the Valley of Sin.

Saturday golfers, playing a friendly, can find that on a calm day in the sun, the place is tranquil. Curtis Strange of America found it that way, once, and shot a record 62 in a Dunhill Cup. But normally the scene changes when the wind gets up, or the top players are

won the 1953 Open. Since those days, however, hotels and other creature comforts in Scotland, have improved. But Hogan never returned, nor did he ever play St Andrews. What a mistake.

The Old course can look innocent on a still day but, when the breeze gets going, it can change into a writhing, terrifying serpent so that players almost scurry back to the 18th which runs almost directly into the sheltered old grey town itself. Some golfers become

Golf enthusiast and famous statesman, Winston Churchill.

in 1946, he took 290 shots over the four rounds. When Nick Faldo collected the same trophy in 1990, he needed only 270 shots. Those with grey hair say conditions were different. Those without say equipment is better and claim Faldo worked harder at the game than Jones. Others point to that automatic watering which a former R&A captain, Roger Wethered, maintained had 'ruined' an otherwise great monument to the game. The extra water makes the greens greener, and backspin possible - hence lower scores.

"the game of

golf was

invented by

the devil"

To play the Old course with success probably needs a calm approach more than anything. And yet jolting moments can occur within minutes of the first tee. Who can forget Jack Nicklaus playing his second shot to the very first flagstick in the 1984 Open, and watching in horror as the ball fell short, into water! The same awful fate befell Ian Baker-Finch of Australia who, at the time, was championship leader.

And what about the unfortunate Doug Sanders of America? He arrived on the eighteenth tee in the last round needing a four to become 1970 champion. His caddie George Buss told him to knock it down the left, as usual, and stood away. The drive was fine. "But he was jumping like a cat" recalled George later. The second shot required a run-up, or loft; something decisive, anyway. In fact Sanders flew the ball in too fiercely and it shot miles past the hole. From that position three putts for the club player is very

frustrated at its basic traps which you can't see from the tee. Even Jones, on his first outing, tore up his card and allowed the pieces to blow away. Later, he came to love the place and there were tears of joy as he was made a Freeman of the City.

Whether Sir Winston Churchill actually said the game of golf was invented by the devil can never be proved. But as a would-be golfer himself, it is the sort of thing he might have said. And if the devil did invent it, then the Old course can be like the devil's playground. When Sam Snead won the Open

much on but not, surely, for a hardened US expert?

How well we remember the first putt, short by three feet six inches. We recall TV commentator Henry Longhurst groaning as Doug bent forward to move something between his ball and the cup. "O dear me ..." and the ball was eventually edged wide, right.

Sander's disaster let in Nicklaus, who predictably won the replay. So shattered Doug never won a major title, but is remembered for those few minutes when, surely, the devil *had* been let loose.

So how to play this course? In match-play, how about trying to ignore your opponent, and attack the card? So easy to say. How about concentrating, and going into a shell? But what happens when a crazy bounce wrecks the coolest introvert? Stay calm and aloof? But a banana skin has butchered the best here. If some are destined to win at St Andrews, maybe some are destined never to.

They say it pays to hook your way round, drawing the ball to the left. Certainly it causes less anxiety because, while you can slice out of bounds over the wall, or into the Old Course Hotel, it would be a remarkable stroke indeed that hooked off the course.

In 1991, Sean Connery a club member at St Andrews, won the Queen Victoria Jubilee Vase when he beat a dedicated journalist, Malcolm Campbell on the last green. Better known as secret agent 007, Connery loves his golf like we all do and that triumph will stay with him all his life. The club has other famous members. President George Bush was delighted to accept honorary membership, joining such names as the Duke of Edinburgh, the Duke of Kent, as well as professionals Arnold Palmer, Jack Nicklaus, Gene Sarazen, Kel Nagle, Peter Thomson and Roberto de Vicenzo from the Argentine. Even the Secretary, Michael Bonallack, won the Amateur Championship five times!

I select St Andrews despite many quirky things. Double greens are used by those on the outward nine holes, and those on the inward. The biggest green is the combination of the fifth and thirteenth, being a total of 5,555 square yards - or 1⅓ acres and it takes two

men an hour and a half to mow - and in so doing the cutters travel 3½ miles.

Anyway, you have to go to St Andrews before you die!

Having said all this, I admit that while most love the sea and splendid golf centres like Southport or St George's, plus Kent's unspoiled Deal nearby - not forgetting the staggering Ballybunion on Ireland's wind-lashed west coast - I really feel more at home on cushier inland courses like, say, Woodhall Spa where I once played in the Central England Mixed Foursomes with the then English champion, Jean Roberts. We lasted four rounds before my driving blew up.

Ballybunion Old, has long enjoyed the reputation of being amongst the world's finest courses.

"The great thing about golf is that you can play until they put you in the grave."

Think of silver birch, firm turf and a classic lay-out and you have Woodhall Spa in Lincolnshire. It should be high on anyone's list of favourites being as fine a place to enjoy shot-making as Sunningdale, another terrific English gift to the travelling player - providing you don't just walk in off the street, un-announced.

The secret about gaining access to a club is always to telephone first and ask whether it might be possible to play there sometime in the next few days, with a friend - or even three.

Clubs need additional revenue these days which means green fees, particularly in southern England, can be costly. For instance, a shock awaits those trying to play the new-look Wentworth, in Surrey, where £100 per person isn't enough for a day. When I competed in the English Amateur there in 1961, lunch was around £1, the clubhouse roof leaked, and my driving was too erratic to get me beyond the second round. Since then I've taken lessons, and prices have rocketed ...

Down the road from Wentworth are other gems, such as Berkshire and Sunningdale but some less famous courses exist which are absolute 'musts'. They are West Hill, Worplesdon, Woking and (still in Surrey) see if you can get yourself into New Zealand which, like Swinley Forest, is somewhat private, but very beautiful. Simply being there, on a sunny day, is memorable.

In my travels, I've encountered some great characters - and not all of them at the 19th hole. Playing the late Henry Longhurst at Gleneagles one evening before dinner (and before he put his clubs away in the attic for ever) I found he could get the ball round rather handily with what he called his Bedfordshire slice. In addition, of course, he was an excellent talker and could convince you that we were really among the heather and pine for fun, and not to worry about losing that ball, even though it was almost fresh out of the wrapper.

He won, or rather, I lost.

Our return clash at Troon, a links later bestowed with the 'Royal' title following the easy Arnold Palmer victory in the Open

♦ ♦ II

championship, provided more subtle words to un-hinge. According to Longhurst, *where* you hit your drive and on which line, was rather more important than how well you struck the ball. Immediately I tightened up.

Frankly Troon, over-flown by jets galore, could never be described as pretty or sympathetic to an inland-type golfer. It teases the temper. When I crashed my best drive, Henry (on intimate terms with every bump, or so he said) simply murmured "Wrong line".

Sure enough, when we got 200 yards down the fairway, my ball lay in a sandy trap more suitable for sleeping sheep than a golfer, while his ball was in position 'A'.

The 'Postage Stamp', par 3, 8th hole at Royal Troon, where Greg Norman's 64 is still the course record.

Henry Longhurst, who once won the German Amateur, rolled out winner and then, as I bought him whisky, was so entertaining that any suggestion of gamesmanship was quickly forgotten.

Another terrific personality whose company I would always seek for a quick interview or just a hilarious time was the eccentric Max Faulkner who won the Open once, in 1951, across one of the most beautiful stretches in the United Kingdom.

Before he teed off for that championship, Max claimed he signed an autograph "Max Faulkner, 1951 Open champion" and, despite a wobbly drive at the last hole, he did, in fact,

collect the old silver trophy. For the next ten years he assured us he would definitely win again. "No-one can stop me guv'nor" he'd say. But they did.

Max won his title at Royal Portrush, a coastal paradise less than 2 miles from the town, along the Bushmills Road. Although the Open has yet to return to this lovely place, it is, in my view, one of the finest in the land.

To describe Royal Portrush as spectacular is not an overstatement. It is one of the tightest driving courses and, if you're off the fairway, you'll find your ball nestling among wild roses which hug the ground to keep clear of off-sea breezes.

I recall that after a testing opening hole, a fine view of Islay and the Paps of Jura can appear on a clear day and later you can see the Giant's Causeway from the dog-leg downhill

5th hole. Anyone who hooks the ball will find one hole called 'Purgatory' but the course is much loved and experts will remind you that the late Fred Daly learned his golf there, and learned well enough to win the Open across the water, at Hoylake in Cheshire - another venue no longer on the regular championship rota.

Eccentric Max Faulkner, pictured here at the 1970 Open, once played for a season with a home-made wooden putter, created from a piece of driftwood and a snooker cue as a shaft.

Spectacular Royal Portrush is considered among the six best courses in the United Kingdom.

♦ ♦ 13

There are more than 2000 courses in Britain, certainly a *great* place for golf. Many more are under construction, some better in concept than others. However, why certain folk who call themselves Protectionists object when a golf course replaces a rubbish dump or swamp is beyond me and, I'm glad to report, beyond Viscount Whitelaw, a former deputy prime minister and golfer. Says the man, known in golf as Willie: "Throughout my career I have been frustrated by the blinkered views of people who, without thought it seems, air their views and raise objections to whatever is being proposed."

Viscount Whitelaw urges all golfers to lobby support for the construction of more courses on which to play, and nobody in my regular fourball would disagree with what he says as, today, overcrowding is causing golfers' to 'steal' rounds on other people's courses.

These intruders are known as 'pirates' by secretaries at private clubs, and the trend is causing worry even though the non-payers and uninvited guests cause no damage and, by and large, play other people's courses at off-peak times.

If you force me to say which is my favourite course in Britain, I greedily choose four. Winning the Sir Emsley Carr trophy years ago at Walton Heath (Surrey) may be an influence but I also recall enjoying the old Match-Play Championship with stars like Sir Henry Cotton, Dai Rees and Harry Weetman. So when I'm lucky enough to be invited there, memories come back as we walk across dry fairways, through heather and gorse.

Then, you must rate Sunningdale, both Old and New. Back in 1956 I watched Gary Player beating local professional Arthur Lees. Paired together in the last round, 21-year-old Gary called the wiley Yorkshireman "Mr Lees" throughout, making him feel as old as the hills - and just beat him to avenge a remark Lees had made when he first saw Gary swing a golf club: "He's absolutely no chance" Arthur had said.

The two other personal favourites are, of course, St Andrews, which is almost like a second home, and the eighteen holes closest to my own back garden - Royal Wimbledon.

I've been a member at Royal Wimbledon since 1952 and although it is only 9 miles from Piccadilly, each hole is delightfully isolated, thanks to tree-lined fairways plus gorse bushes which occasionally blaze into yellow flowers. Sadly we've lost our cock pheasants and partridges, but the badgers are still around and the rabbits and foxes which keep them in order decorate what, in my view, is a magnificent conservation area on the greenest belt you ever did see.

It was Ben Hogan who said what so many of us all feel: "The great thing about golf is that you can play until they put you in the grave." Undoubtedly it is the game of a lifetime and lucky indeed are those able to play, and those gifted enough to play well.

However, the game has a democratic duty. It should not be exploited by Corporations, or used merely as a vehicle to make money. Scotland gave the world democratic golf and is still a world leader in keeping it that way. But I fear that in the next few years many fine young players could be priced out because certain people insist on a 5-star clubhouse or selfishly keep out the one million nomadic golfers unable to join a club in Britain, but quite prepared to pay a green fee for the privilege of playing the most unspoiled sport in all the world.

John Ingham is a former golf correspondent of the London Evening Standard, magazine editor and feature writer.

He has ghost written columns with Arnold Palmer, Jack Nicklaus and with Peter Alliss, and covered Open championships won by Bobby Locke and Peter Thomson going back to the 1950s.

For the last 16 years John has written a column in every issue of Golf Monthly.

The highlight of his career, he says, is right now with the Dunhill Cup, the world team championship, which in the last 8 years has taken him all over the globe, including the People's Republic of China, Zimbabwe and Jamaica.

DEC 1991 £1.95

WOMEN & GOLF

ALFREDSSON
THE GREAT!

DOYLE FACES WOMEN'S TOUR CHALLENGE

RYDER CUP WIVES
PLAY THEIR PART

Available from Newsagents

BRITAIN'S ONLY WOMEN'S GOLF MAGAZINE

Pick-ups without hiccups.

SECURICOR
OMEGA
EXPRESS

☎ 0345 20 0345

securicor *communications*

The Securicor Communications division comprises five main business areas in which they have specialist knowledge and experience, they are as follows:

SECURICOR CELLULAR SERVICES

Securicor Cellular Services is a major retailer of cellular airtime and products. We support our customers with National Service and Installation Centres, a fleet of mobile workshops and a comprehensive range of value added services.

For further information ring 0800 181345

SECURICOR TELECOMS

Securicor Telecoms is a major supplier, installer and maintainer of office Telecommunications equipment. This includes the Rhapsody key telephones and small PABX's.

For further information ring 061 654 9990

SECURICOR DATATRAK

This is a unique automatic vehicle location and fleet management system available in the UK, accurate to better than 50 metres. The system automatically transmits the vehicle location and status including alarm to a fully computerised map display.

For further information ring 0800 378628

SECURICOR PMR SYSTEMS

A leading independent supplier of customised private mobile radio systems. With 30 years experience to meet customers specific requirements.

For further information ring 0761 413174

SECURICOR ELECTRONICS

Securicor Electronics specialise in the contract manufacturing of electronic systems to full BS5750 (Part 1) and ISO 90001 quality standards, including radio and security products.

For further information ring 0761 416035

securicor *security services*

Last year, Securicor carried enough money to fill the UK trade gap five times over. *In cash*.

£100 billion

Securicor's international fleet of more than 2,000 secure vehicles carries over £100 billion in cash alone every year.

An extraordinary endorsement of our expertise in cash transport.

But to us, it's just the most visible of an expanding range of activities. Our growth in the transport of cash and valuables itself demonstrates our on-going response to customer needs: *Business Link* for small businesses, *Community Link* for Local Authorities and *Safe Link* for secure overnight distribution.

Initiatives from our *Banking Support Services* such as Cash Processing for retailers, distribution of bulk cash and filled pay packs, and ATM cash dispenser replenishment continue to expand our role within banking and commerce.

As threats to business become more complex, technology plays an increasingly important role. The latest advances in electronics, telemetry and

computing have been incorporated into our *Genesis*
'intelligent' intruder alarm systems, their associated
nationwide signalling network and control centres. We monitor
all the vital areas of business property 24 hours a day,
including access control, CCTV, fire systems, access points
and outer fences.

But as well as being a leader in
technology, our reputation has always been
based on our people – especially the
reassuring sight of our uniformed personnel.
All our staff have to pass through rigorous
vetting and training procedures.

Our *Guarding Services* extend beyond
traditional on-site security services to
Special Events, Conference and Airport Security, Mobile
Patrols and the option of our unique integrated security
system, *Integra*.

And we apply our same high
standards of professionalism
to document and tape
storage, security shredding
and cleaning services.

What's more, Securicor is
one British company making a
positive contribution to closing
that trade gap.

securicor *security services*

Securicor Security Services Limited Sutton Park House 15 Carshalton Road Sutton Surrey SM1 4LD
Telephone 081-770 7000

securicor *business services*

The Business Services Division of Securicor consists of:–

SECURICOR VEHICLE SERVICES

Securicor Vehicle Services provides fleet maintenance to many nationally known customers.

THE RICHMOND GATE and **RICHMOND HILL HOTELS**

Two fine hotels high on Richmond Hill overlooking the Thames. Royal Mid-Surrey, Coombe Hill and many other famous golf courses are nearby.Golfing groups enjoy special rates. Richmond Hill Hotel AA***, Tel: 081 940 2247. Fax: 081 940 5424.

Richmond Gate Hotel, Tel: 081 940 0061. Fax: 081 332 0354.

HYLANDS HOTEL, COVENTRY

The Hylands Hotel is in the heart of Shakespeare's country. As well as golf courses, there are many other attractions nearby. Tel: 0203 501600. Fax: 0203 501027.

CONTRACT 2000

Contract 2000 is a recruitment services company, recruiting and supplying staff for temporary, permanent and contract assignments with a branch network covering London, Humberside, the South Coast, the South West and Wales. Tel: 081 770 7000. Fax: 081 770 1409.

BEDWAS BODYWORKS

Bedwas Bodyworks is one of the country's leading manufacturers of specialist bodywork on vehicles ranging from light commercial to heavy bespoke units. Both the home and overseas markets are served from its factories in Newport, Gwent and Chorley, Lancs. Tel: 0222 885781/868505. Fax: 0222 887313.

securicor parcels

SECURICOR OMEGA EXPRESS

Securicor Omega Express is the UK's largest privately-owned overnight express parcels carrier. With 25 years experience and a reputation for flexibility, Omega Express delivers on time, to anywhere your business takes you.

UK SERVICES

Omega 9: By 9am guaranteed delivery next working day throughout most of the United Kindgom, offering two sizes of free packaging.

Omega 12: By 12.00 noon delivery the next working day.

Omega Standard: For delivery before close of business the next working day.

Omega Economy: Delivery in 2–3 working days after the day of collection, at very competitive rates.

Warehousing: Secure storage with flexible delivery options.

INTERNATIONAL

World Premium: Desk to desk to international business destinations and to most major European cities by noon next day.

World Standard: For less urgent international parcel deliveries.

Mail Services: Worldwide mail and print distribution.

PONY EXPRESS

Pony Direct: Direct bike or van for collection and delivery between two or more points.

Pony Shuttle: Consolidated same day service between key towns and cities.

For a comprehensive information pack and service, call Omegaline on 0345 – 20 – 0345.

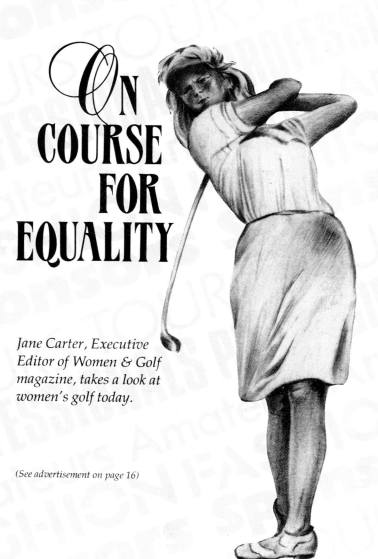

ON COURSE FOR EQUALITY

Jane Carter, Executive Editor of Women & Golf magazine, takes a look at women's golf today.

(See advertisement on page 16)

Women's Golf

Golf has been enjoying an incredible boom in popularity in recent years and nowhere is this more evident than in the massive growth in women's golf.

The membership of the Ladies' Golf Union (the official body governing women's amateur golf) now stands at some 175,000 and this does not include the 75,000 women golfers who are estimated to play at municipal courses. The growth of the Women's European Tour, with prize money at £1.6 million compared with £80,000 just a decade ago, speaks for itself and there seems no end to it all.

Fairway to success; Alison Nicholas, the 1987 British Open Champion.

People who spotted this massive growth rate in the early eighties are of course not surprised, but the sheer number of women taking up the game both at home and on the continent make it the fastest growing sector within the sport by miles.

Needless to say, golf equipment and clothing manufacturers have been quick off the mark and the number of women's clubs, shoes and clothing beginning to hit the market is a long way off from the times when they were lucky if a club professional even stocked ladies' gloves.

Companies such as Belle Golf, One Up Golf, On The Greens and Penguin are finding more and more women taking a special interest in looking good on as well as off the golf course, and the influence definitely seems to be continental.

Jean Loveridge of Belle Golf said: "Women golfers on the continent have always been very appearance conscious and now this seems to have caught on in England. New fashions coming from the continent and America have fired their imagination and we have been delighted with the response to our ranges."

*Long hitting
and popular; Laura Davies is
a former US and British Open Champion*

'It is now more likely that a club professional will stock ladies' clothing - and indeed that the professional may even be a lady herself.'

*Partners on tour;
Fanny Sunnesson,
Nick Faldo's Swedish
caddy, helps with the
putting line.*

It is now more likely that a club professional will stock ladies' clothing - and indeed that the professional may even be a lady herself. The Professional Golfer's Association has a growing women's section and more and more are entering the training scheme, with a handful of clubs already having appointed a woman club professional.

The fact that more and more people are reading about women's golf and going along to watch Europe's top professionals in action has helped. Britain's Laura Davies may not be quite a household name but she captured the imagination of everyone with her long hitting and victory in the US Women's Open in 1987, and proved that women's professional golf should be taken seriously in Europe. And taken seriously it is with sponsors such as Woolmark, Ford, Hennessy and Longines - the leading watch manufacturers - ploughing thousands of pounds into the game.

Gill Wilson, the PR and Marketing Consultant to the Women's Professional Golfers' European Tour based at The Tytherington Club, Macclesfield, said: "Companies who sell their products to women, whether it be cars, perfume or clothing, are realising the tremendous promotional vehicle women's golf can be.

"Women amateurs are now housewives with control of the purse strings and a big say in the household purchases or are career women with their own spending power, making them a valuable target for advertisers and sponsors."

With this growing interest in women's golf it was inevitable that a golf magazine would follow to cater for this massive market. "Women & Golf ' was launched in August of last year and defied all the sceptics who said it would never sell. With more than 200,000 playing the game it seemed ridiculous that they did not have a magazine of their own. The other titles paid little interest to the women's game and we set about redressing the balance.

We are delighted with the response so far and feel that our success demonstrates just how popular the game is with women and the move away from the traditional image of tweed skirt and brogues.

But what of the future? The growth in

'No Dogs, No Women signs are not yet being torn from their posts.'

Escape to glory; Scotland's Dale Reid has already passed the 20 victories in Europe barrier.

golf generally has to slow down eventually as the demand is met with the building of more and more courses. These new golf clubs are playing their own part in helping encourage women golfers with many of them offering the equal playing rights which have so often eluded women down the ages. It is hardly a tidal wave of change as some clubs will steadfastly refuse to change their ways and the 'No Dogs, No Women' signs are not yet being torn from their posts. However, a changing scene it is and women golfers whether professional or amateur are clearly a force to be reckoned with.

CountryWalks
in Britain

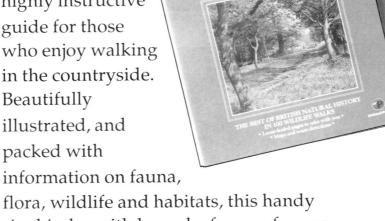

A practical and highly instructive guide for those who enjoy walking in the countryside. Beautifully illustrated, and packed with information on fauna, flora, wildlife and habitats, this handy ringbinder with loose-leaf pages for use en route describes 100 walks through the best of Britain's wild areas and reserves.

ABOUT THIS BOOK

The gazetteer contains around 2,000 of Britain and Ireland's golf courses, concentrating on those which welcome visiting golfers, and we have endeavoured to include all the information you would need to know before your visit. However, it is always a good idea to check in advance as details can change after we go to print. Some courses will always want advance notice, possibly also a letter of introduction from your own club, and, if this is the case, the gazetteer entry will include this information. We also tell you what kind of course you can expect, what club facilities are available, including catering and accommodation, any leisure facilities, and indicate the green fees you can expect to pay. It is particularly important to check on fees as they are liable to change during the currency of the guide.

For each course listed, we recommend a near-by AA appointed hotel, giving its classification, full name and address, telephone number and total number of bedrooms, including the number with private bath or shower. In some cases the hotel will be within the grounds of the golf course itself (see **Club Accommodation**).

HOW TO USE THE GAZETTEER

The gazetteer is arranged in country and county order and covers England, the Channel Islands and Isle of Man, Scotland, Wales, Northern Ireland and the Republic of Ireland. Within each county, the courses are in alphabetical order of the towns under which they are listed. If you are not sure where your chosen course may be, there is an alphabetical index of courses at the end of the book. Should you be travelling in an unfamiliar part of the country and want to know the choice of courses available to you, consult the atlas, also at the end of the book, where the locations of all courses listed in the guide are pin-pointed.

Those courses which are considered to be of particular merit or interest are printed in green within the gazetteer, a copy of their score card has been included in many cases and they have been further enhanced by the inclusion of a more detailed description. They may be very historic clubs or they may have been chosen because their courses are particularly testing or enjoyable to play; some have been included because they are in holiday areas and have proved popular with visiting golfers. Such a selection cannot be either exhaustive or totally objective and the courses included are not intended to represent any formal category on quality or other grounds. Championship courses have been given special treatment too, and appear with a full-page entry, including a selection of places to eat as well as stay.

A number of golf clubs have chosen not to have an entry in our gazetteer, usually because they do not have facilities for visitors or because they are private. If you know of any courses which do welcome visitors and which are not yet in our guide, we would be pleased to hear from you.

NB Although we make every effort to obtain up to date information from golf clubs, in some cases we have been unable to verify details with the club's management. Where this is the case, the course name is shown in **_bold italics_** and you would be strongly advised to check with the club in advance of your visit.

It should also be noted that where score card and gazetteer yardages vary, this represents the difference between tee marker positions.

Map References

To help you find the golf courses, each town heading is located on the atlas at the back of the book. After the town name there is a map reference, the first figure being the map page number, followed by the grid reference. Within the appropriate grid square, read the first figure across the map and the second vertically to find the town you are looking for.

Club Accommodation

Some courses offer accommodation at their club. Where this facility exists, the 'bed' symbol (🛏) will appear in the entry under club **facilities**. This has been listed as a further option for those who might wish to stay at the course. However, the only accommodation appointed by the AA is the star-rated hotel which appears at the foot of each entry.

In some instances, however, this may well be the club accommodation.

Republic of Ireland

In the Republic, green fees are quoted in Punts, indicated by the symbol **IR£**. The rates of exchange between pounds sterling and Punts is liable to fluctuate.

Area codes shown against telephone numbers are applicable within the Republic of Ireland only. Similarly, the area codes shown for entries in Great Britain and Northern Ireland cannot be used direct from the Republic. Check your telephone directory for details.

Symbols and Abbreviations

In order to maximise the space available, we have used certain symbols and abbreviations within the gazetteer entries and these are explained in the panel below:

04 TQ21	atlas page and grid reference
☎	telephone number
IR£	Irish Punts (Republic only)
✕	lunch
〉Ⅲ	dinner
🍴	bar snacks
🍺	tea/coffee
♀	bar open mid-day and evenings
🛏	accommodation at club
👔	changing rooms
🛍	well-stocked shop
⚑	clubs for hire
⌥	professional at club
★	hotel classification
✗	restaurant classification (applicable to championship course entry only)
❧	type of cooking (applicable to championship course entry only)

KEY TO HOTEL CLASSIFICATION

The AA System of star rating is the market leader in hotel classifications and has long been universally recognised as an accurate, objective indication of the facilities one can expect to find at any hotel in the AA scheme.

Hotels are classified with one to five stars, as follows:

★ Hotels generally of a small scale with good but often simple furnishings, facilities and food. This category sometimes includes private hotels where requirements for public access and full lunch service may be relaxed. Not all bedrooms will necessarily have en-suite facilities. These hotels are often managed by the proprietor and a more personal atmosphere may well prevail than in larger establishments.

★★ Small to medium sized hotels often offering more in the way of facilities such as telephones and televisions in bedrooms. Like one star hotels, this category can also include private hotels. At least half the bedrooms will have full en-suite facilities. Can be proprietor managed or group owned.

★★★ Medium sized hotels offering more spacious accommodation and a greater range of facilities and services. Generally these will include a full reception service as well as more formal restaurant and bar arrangements. You can expect all rooms to provide en-suite facilities, most of which will include a bath. Though often individually owned, this category encompasses a greater number of company owned properties.

★★★★ Generally large hotels with spacious accommodation including availability of private suites. This category of hotel normally provides a full range of formal hotel services including room service, reception and porterage and may well offer more than one dining operation. En-suite facilities in all rooms should include both bath and shower.

High standards of comfort and food are expected at this level.

★★★★★ Large luxury hotels offering the highest international standards of accommodation, facilities, services and cuisine.

⚫ This denotes a AA Country House hotel where a relaxed, informal atmosphere and personal welcome prevail. Some of the facilities may differ, however, from those found in urban hotels of the same classification. Country House hotels are often secluded and, though not always rurally situated, are quiet. Hotels attracting frequent conferences or functions are not normally granted this symbol.

Red Star Hotels

Red stars are the AA's highest accolade and are awarded, on an annual basis, only to hotels that AA inspectors consider to be of outstanding merit within their classification. You will find a warm welcome and a high standard of hospitality. They are indicated by the word 'red' after the star classification.

Percentage Ratings For Quality

The AA recently introduced a new assessment scheme whereby hotels are awarded a percentage score, within their particular star classification, based on quality. The percentage scores, printed immediately after the stars, are an indication of where each hotel stands in comparison to others within the same star classification. Hotels have been assessed for quality under a number of broad headings: hospitality, cleanliness, services, food, bedrooms, overall impression and the inspector's personal view. All hotels recognised by the AA may be expected to score at least 50%, and a score of around 61% is considered to be the average benchmark. Hotels with a higher percentage rating will have many extra touches, above what is normally required of an AA hotel of that particular star rating.

One hundred of England's best pubs are included, each at the half-way stage of a pleasant country walk. The round trip will average around five miles and the guide gives full directions for walkers, together with things to see on the way, places of interest nearby and, most important of all, a fine country pub to break the journey and enjoy a good bar meal and a pint of real ale.

Available at good bookshops and AA Centres

Another great guide from the AA

ENGLAND

AVON

BACKWELL   Map 03 ST46

Tall Pines ☎Lulsgate (0275) 472076
Parkland course with views over the Bristol Channel.
18 holes, 4600yds, Par 64, SSS 62.
Club membership 600.
Visitors	must contact in advance.
Societies	apply in writing.
Green Fees	£10 (£12.50 weekends).
Facilities	⊗ 🍴 🏌 ♀ ⛳ 🏠 ⊢ ⌂ Terry Murray.
Location	Cooks Bridle Path, Downside
Hotel	★★★61% Walton Park, Wellington Ter, CLEVEDON ☎(0272) 874253 38⇨🏚

BATH   Map 03 ST76

Bath ☎(0225) 463834
Considered to be one of the finest courses in the west, this is the site of Bath's oldest golf club. An interesting course situated on high ground overlooking the city and with splendid views over the surrounding countryside. The rocky ground supports good quality turf and there are many good holes. The 17th is a dog-leg right past, or over the corner of an out-of-bounds wall, and thence on to an undulating green.

SCORECARD: White Tees					
Hole	Yds	Par	Hole	Yds	Par
1	302	4	10	347	4
2	289	4	11	183	3
3	411	4	12	394	4
4	172	3	13	468	4
5	466	4	14	158	3
6	530	5	15	483	5
7	334	4	16	359	4
8	361	4	17	304	4
9	402	4	18	406	4
Out	3267	36	In	3102	35
			Totals	6369	71

18 holes, 6369yds, Par 71, SSS 70, Course record 65.
Club membership 675.
Visitors	must contact in advance and have an introduction from own club.
Societies	must apply in writing.
Green Fees	£21 per day (£25 weekends and bank holidays).
Facilities	⊗ 🍴 by prior arrangement 🏌 ♀ ⛳ 🏠 ⊢ ⌂ Peter J Hancox.
Location	Sham Castle, North Rd (1.5m SE city centre off A36)
Hotel	★★★62% Francis Hotel, Queen Square, BATH ☎(0225) 424257 94⇨

Lansdown ☎(0225) 425007
A flat parkland course in open situation.
18 holes, 6299yds, Par 71, SSS 70.
Club membership 725.
Visitors	must have a current handicap certificate. Must contact in advance.
Societies	must contact in advance.
Green Fees	not confirmed.
Facilities	⊗ 🍴 🏌 ♀ ⛳ 🏠 ⊢ ⌂ Terry Mercer.
Location	Lansdown (3m SW of exit 18 off M4)
Hotel	★★★68% Lansdown Grove Hotel, BATH ☎(0225) 315891 45⇨🏚

BRISTOL   Map 03 ST57

Bristol and Clifton ☎(0275) 393474
A downland course with splendid turf and fine tree-lined fairways. The 222- yard (par 3) 13th with the green well below, and the par 4 16th, with its second shot across an old quarry, are outstanding. There are splendid views over the Bristol Channel towards Wales.
18 holes, 6270yds, Par 70, SSS 70, Course record 64.
Club membership 835.
Visitors	must have a handicap certificate. Must contact in advance.
Societies	must book in advance.
Green Fees	£25 per day/round (£30 weekends and bank holidays).
Facilities	⊗ 🍴 by prior arrangement 🏌 🏠 ♀ ⛳ 🏠 ⊢ ⌂ Peter Mawson.
Leisure	snooker.
Location	Beggar Bush Ln, Failand (4m W on B3129 off A369)
Hotel	★★★69% Redwood Lodge Hotel & Country Club, Beggar Bush Ln, Failand, BRISTOL ☎(0275) 393901 112⇨🏚

Filton ☎(0272) 694169
Parkland course with a testing par 4 hole; 'dog-leg' 383 yds.
18 holes, 6042yds, Par 69, SSS 69, Course record 65.
Club membership 800.
Visitors	may not play at weekends. Must have an introduction from own club.
Societies	must contact in advance.
Green Fees	£25 per day; £18 per round.
Facilities	⊗ 🍴 🏌 & 🏠 by prior arrangement ♀ (ex Sun) ⛳ 🏠 ⊢ ⌂ Nicholas Lumb.
Location	Golf Course Ln, Filton (5m NW off A38)
Hotel	★★★67% Forte Crest Hotel, Filton Rd, Hambrook, BRISTOL ☎(0272) 564242 197⇨🏚

Henbury ☎(0272) 500044
A parkland course tree-lined and on two levels. The River Trym comes into play on the 7th drop-hole with its green set just over the stream. The last nine holes have the beautiful Blaise Castle woods for company.

SCORECARD: White Tees					
Hole	Yds	Par	Hole	Yds	Par
1	476	5	10	273	4
2	373	4	11	230	3
3	374	4	12	362	4
4	134	3	13	152	3
5	476	5	14	530	5
6	461	4	15	403	4
7	158	3	16	330	4
8	389	4	17	166	3
9	328	4	18	424	4
Out	3169	36	In	2870	34
			Totals	6039	70

18 holes, 6039yds, Par 70, SSS 70, Course record 62.
Club membership 800.
Visitors	with member only weekends. Must contact in advance and have an introduction from own club.
Societies	Tue & Fri only (minimum 20 players).
Green Fees	£19 per day.
Facilities	⊗ 🍴 by prior arrangement 🏌 🏠 ♀ ⛳ 🏠 ⌂ Nick Riley.
Location	Henbury Hill, Westbury-on-Trym (3m NW of city centre on B4055 off A4018)
Hotel	★★★51% St Vincent Rocks Hotel, Sion Hill, Clifton, BRISTOL ☎(0272) 739251 46⇨🏚

Knowle ☎(0272) 770660
A parkland course with nice turf but now somewhat naked after the loss of its fine elm trees. The first five holes climb up and down hill but the remainder are on a more even plane.
18 holes, 6016yds, Par 69, SSS 69.
Club membership 800.

SCORECARD: Medal Tees					
Hole	Yds	Par	Hole	Yds	Par
1	322	4	10	136	3
2	471	4	11	388	4
3	350	4	12	154	3
4	383	4	13	491	5
5	307	4	14	423	4
6	184	3	15	180	3
7	317	4	16	426	4
8	156	3	17	403	4
9	374	4	18	551	5
Out	2864	34	In	3152	35
			Totals	6016	69

Visitors   must have handicap certificate. Must play with member at weekends. Must contact in advance and have an introduction from own club.
Societies   Thu only. Must contact in advance.
Green Fees   not confirmed.
Facilities   ⊗ ⅷ 🍴 ♨ ♀ △ 🏠 (Gordon Brand.
Location   Brislington (3m SE of city centre off A379)
Hotel   ★★★(red)🏨 Hunstrete House Hotel, CHELWOOD ☎(0761) 490490 13⇨🏠Annexe11⇨🏠

Mangotsfield ☎(0272) 565501
An easy hilly parkland course. Caravan site.
18 holes, 5337yds, Par 68, SSS 66, Course record 65.
Club membership 500.
Visitors   may not play on competition days. Must contact in advance.
Societies   weekdays only, must contact 2 weeks in advance.
Green Fees   not confirmed.
Facilities   ⊗ 🍴 ♨ ♀ △ 🏠 ⫪ (Craig Trewin.
Location   Carsons Rd, Mangotsfield (6m NE of city centre off B4465)
Hotel   ★★★67% Forte Crest Hotel, Filton Rd, Hambrook, BRISTOL ☎(0272) 564242 197⇨🏠

Shirehampton Park ☎(0272) 822083
A lovely course in undulating parkland comprising two loops. There are views over the Portway beside the River Avon, where sliced balls at the opening hole are irretrievable.
18 holes, 5600yds, Par 67, SSS 67, Course record 61.
Club membership 600.
Visitors   with member only at weekends
Societies   Mon (if booked).
Green Fees   £20 per day.
Facilities   ⊗ 🍴 ♨ ♀ △ 🏠 (Brent Ellis.
Location   Park Hill, Shirehampton (4m W of city centre on A4)
Hotel   ★★★69% Redwood Lodge Hotel & Country Club, Beggar Bush Ln, Failand, BRISTOL ☎(0275) 393901 112⇨🏠

A golf-course name printed in ***bold italics*** means that we have been unable to verify information with the club's management for the current year

---

CHIPPING SODBURY   Map 03 ST78

Chipping Sodbury
☎(0454) 319042
A parkland course of Championship proportions. The whole course may be seen from the large opening tee by the clubhouse at the top of the hill. Two huge drainage dykes cut through the course and form a distinctive hazard on eleven holes.
New Course: 18 holes, 6912yds, Par 73, SSS 73, Course record 68.
Old Course: 9 holes, 6184yds, Par 70, SSS 69.
Club membership 770.

SCORECARD: White Tees					
Hole	Yds	Par	Hole	Yds	Par
1	423	4	10	334	4
2	533	5	11	527	5
3	450	4	12	437	4
4	352	4	13	402	4
5	525	5	14	152	3
6	166	3	15	381	4
7	407	4	16	517	5
8	158	3	17	400	4
9	368	4	18	380	4
Out	3382	36	In	3530	37
			Totals	6912	73

Visitors   must have a handicap certificate and may only play in the afternoons at weekends.
Societies   must contact in writing.
Green Fees   not confirmed.
Facilities   ⊗ ⅷ 🍴 ♨ ♀ △ 🏠 ⫪ (Mike Watts.
Location   .5m N
Hotel   ★★66% Cross Hands Hotel, OLD SODBURY ☎(0454) 313000 24rm(3⇨17🏠)

CLEVEDON   Map 03 ST47

Clevedon ☎Bristol (0272) 874057
Situated on the cliff-top overlooking the Severn estuary and with distant views of the Welsh coast. Excellent parkland course in first-class condition overlooking the Severn estuary. Magnificent scenery and some tremendous 'drop' holes. Strong winds.
18 holes, 5889yds, Par 69, SSS 69, Course record 62.
Club membership 750.
Visitors   must have a handicap certificate. Must contact in advance.
Societies   Tue only.
Green Fees   £20 per day/round (£30 weekends & bank holidays).
Facilities   ⊗ ⅷ 🍴 ♨ ♀ △ 🏠 ⫪ (Christine Langford.
Leisure   snooker.
Location   Castle Rd, Walton St Mary (1m NE of town centre)
Hotel   ★★★63% Commodore Hotel, Beach Rd, Sand Bay, Kewstoke, WESTON-SUPER-MARE ☎(0934) 415778 12⇨🏠Annexe7rm(4🏠)

KEYNSHAM   Map 03 ST66

Stockwood Vale ☎Bristol (0272) 866505
Undulating public course with interesting Par 3s and good views.
9 holes, 4010yds, Par 64, SSS 61.
Club membership 150.
Visitors   no restrictions, but booking system is available.
Societies   must contact in advance.
Green Fees   £9 per 18 holes, £4.50 per 9 holes (£11/£5.50 weekends).
Facilities   🏠 ⫪ (David Holder.

Location	Stockwood Ln
Hotel	★★72% Chelwood House Hotel, CHELWOOD ☎(0761) 490730 11⇨

LONG ASHTON   Map 03 ST57

Long Ashton ☎(0275) 392316
A high downland course with nice turf, some wooded areas and a spacious practice area. Good drainage ensures pleasant winter golf.
18 holes, 6051yds, Par 70, SSS 70, Course record 64.
Club membership 800.

Visitors	must contact in advance and have an introduction from own club.
Societies	must contact the secretary in advance.
Green Fees	£18 per day (£28 weekends).
Facilities	⊗)Ⅲ by prior arrangement ﾑ ■ ♀ ⚘ 🝙 ⚑ ℂ Denis Scanlan.
Leisure	snooker.
Location	The Clubhouse (.5m N on B3128)
Hotel	★★★69% Redwood Lodge Hotel & Country Club, Beggar Bush Ln, Failand, BRISTOL ☎(0275) 393901 112⇨

MIDSOMER NORTON   Map 03 ST65

Fosseway Country Club ☎(0761) 412214
Very attractive parkland course, not demanding but with lovely views.
9 holes, 4012yds, Par 62, SSS 65.
Club membership 340.

Visitors	may not play on Wed evenings, Sun mornings & competitions days
Societies	by arrangement.
Green Fees	£10 per day (£15 weekends & bank holidays).
Facilities	⊗)Ⅲ ﾑ ■ ♀ ⚘ 🖚
Leisure	heated indoor swimming pool, squash, snooker, sauna, outdoor bowling green.
Location	Charlton Ln (SE of town centre off A367)
Hotel	★★★68% Centurion Hotel, Charlton Ln, MIDSOMER NORTON ☎(0761) 417711 44⇨

SALTFORD   Map 03 ST66

Saltford ☎(0225) 32207
Parkland course with easy walking and panoramic views over the Avon Valley. The par 4, 2nd and 13th are notable.
18 holes, 6081yds, Par 69, SSS 69.
Club membership 800.

Visitors	must have a handicap certificate. Must contact in advance and have an introduction from own club.
Societies	Mon & Thu only.
Green Fees	£18.50 per round; £22.50 per day (weekends £25 per round).
Facilities	⊗)Ⅲ ﾑ ■ ♀ ⚘ 🝙 ⚑ ℂ Dudley Millenstead.
Location	Golf Club Ln (S side of village)
Hotel	★★★(red)⚑ Hunstrete House Hotel, CHELWOOD ☎(0761) 490490 13⇨ Annexe11⇨

We make every effort to ensure that our information is accurate but details may change after we go to print

WESTON-SUPER-MARE   Map 03 ST36

Weston-Super-Mare ☎(0934) 626968
A compact and interesting layout with the opening hole adjacent to the beach. The sandy, links-type course is slightly undulating and has beautifully maintained turf and greens. The 15th is a testing 455-yard, par 4.
18 holes, 6251yds, Par 70, SSS 70, Course record 70.
Club membership 900.

Visitors	may not play on competition days. Must contact in advance.
Societies	must contact in writing.
Green Fees	£20 per day (£28 weekends).
Facilities	⊗)Ⅲ by prior arrangement ﾑ ■ ♀ ⚘ 🝙 ℂ Terry Murray.
Leisure	snooker.
Location	Uphill Rd North (S side of town centre off A370)
Hotel	★★63% Beachlands Hotel, 17 Uphill Rd North, WESTON-SUPER-MARE ☎(0934) 621401 18⇨

Worlebury ☎(0934) 625789
Fairly easy walking and extensive views of the Severn estuary and Wales, on this seaside course situated on the ridge of Worlebury Hill.
18 holes, 5936yds, Par 70, SSS 69, Course record 68.
Club membership 600.

Visitors	must contact in advance.
Societies	must contact in writing.
Green Fees	£16 (£26 weekends).
Facilities	⊗)Ⅲ by prior arrangement ﾑ ■ ♀ ⚘ 🝙 ⚑ ℂ Gary Marks.

►

Leisure	snooker.
Location	Monks Hill (5m NE off A370)
Hotel	★★★53% Royal Pier Hotel, Birnbeck Rd, WESTON-SUPER-MARE ☎(0934) 626644 40rm(38⇄🛏)
Additional hotel	★★★63% Commodore Hotel, Beach Rd, Sand Bay, Kewstoke, WESTON-SUPER-MARE ☎(0934) 415778 12⇄🛏Annexe7rm(4🛏)

WICK   Map 03 ST77

Tracy Park ☎Abson (027582) 2251
This course, situated on the south-western escarpment of the Cotswolds, is undulating with fine views. The clubhouse dates back to 1600 and is a building of great beauty and elegance, set in the 220 acre estate of this golf and country club. Natural water hazards affect a number of holes.
27 holes, 6850yds, Par 72, SSS 73, Course record 66.
Club membership 1300.

Visitors	must contact in advance.
Societies	must contact in writing.
Green Fees	not confirmed.
Facilities	⊗ ⅢL ⅃ 🍺 ♀ 🛎 🖻 🆃 【 Grant & Kelvin Aitken.
Leisure	hard tennis courts, heated outdoor swimming pool, squash, snooker, croquet.
Location	Tracy Park, Bath Rd (S side of village off A420)
Hotel	★★★68% Lansdown Grove Hotel, BATH ☎(0225) 315891 45⇄🛏

BEDFORDSHIRE

ASPLEY GUISE   Map 04 SP93

Aspley Guise & Woburn Sands ☎Milton Keynes (0908) 583596
A fine undulating course in expansive heathland interspersed with many attractive clumps of gorse, broom and bracken. Some well-established silver birch are a feature. The 7th, 8th and 9th are really tough holes to complete the first half.
18 holes, 6248yds, Par 71, SSS 70, Course record 67.
Club membership 580.

	SCORECARD: White Tees				
Hole	Yds	Par	Hole	Yds	Par
1	294	4	10	182	3
2	505	5	11	349	4
3	304	4	12	399	4
4	164	3	13	147	3
5	429	4	14	503	5
6	347	4	15	195	3
7	223	3	16	358	4
8	526	5	17	386	4
9	424	4	18	513	5
Out	3216	36	In	3032	35
			Totals	6248	71

Visitors	with member only at weekends. Must have an introduction from own club.
Societies	normally booked 12 mths ahead.
Green Fees	£21 per day; £16 per round.
Facilities	⊗ & Ⅲ by prior arrangement L & ⅃ (limited on Mon & during winter) ♀ (limited in winter) 🛎 🖻 【 Trevor Hill.
Location	West Hill (2m W of M1 junc 13)
Hotel	★★62% Swan Revived Hotel, High St, NEWPORT PAGNELL ☎(0908) 610565 42rm(40⇄🛏)

BEDFORD   Map 04 TL04

Bedford & County ☎(0234) 352617
Pleasant parkland course with views over Bedford and surrounding countryside. The 15th is a testing par 4.
18 holes, 6347yds, Par 70, SSS 70.
Club membership 600.

Visitors	handicap certificate required, weekends with member only.
Societies	welcome Mon, Tue, Thu & Fri, telephone in advance.
Facilities	🛎 🖻 【 E Bullock.
Location	Green Ln, Clapham (2m N off A6)
Hotel	★★★78% Woodlands Manor Hotel, Green Ln, Clapham, BEDFORD ☎(0234) 363281 22⇄Annexe3⇄

Bedfordshire ☎(0234) 261669
Parkland course, tree hazards, easy walking.
18 holes, 6196yds, Par 70, SSS 69.
Club membership 600.

Visitors	may not play at weekends. Must contact in advance.
Societies	must telephone in advance.
Green Fees	not confirmed.
Facilities	⊗ Ⅲ by prior arrangement L ⅃ ♀ 🛎 🖻 【 Gary Buckle.
Location	Bromham Rd, Biddenham (1m W on A428)
Hotel	★★★78% Woodlands Manor Hotel, Green Ln, Clapham, BEDFORD ☎(0234) 363281 22⇄Annexe3⇄

Mowsbury ☎(0234) 771041
Parkland municipal course in rural surroundings. Long and testing. 14-bay driving range.
18 holes, 6514yds, Par 72, SSS 71.
Club membership 800.

Visitors	no restrictions.
Societies	apply in writing.
Green Fees	£5 (18 holes); £3.50 (9 holes). £8 (weekends).
Facilities	⊗ & Ⅲ by prior arrangement L ⅃ ♀ 🛎 🖻 🆃 【 J MacFarlane.
Leisure	squash.
Location	Cleat Hill, Kimbolton Rd (2m N of town centre on B660)
Hotel	★★★78% Woodlands Manor Hotel, Green Ln, Clapham, BEDFORD ☎(0234) 363281 22⇄Annexe3⇄

DUNSTABLE   Map 04 TL02

Dunstable Downs ☎(0582) 604472
A fine downland course set on two levels with far-reaching views and frequent sightings of graceful gliders. The 9th hole is one of the best short holes in the country. There is a modernised clubhouse.
18 holes, 6184yds, Par 70, SSS 70.
Club membership 600.

	SCORECARD				
Hole	Yds	Par	Hole	Yds	Par
1	484	5	10	411	4
2	167	3	11	454	4
3	531	5	12	458	4
4	343	4	13	328	4
5	161	3	14	308	4
6	355	4	15	340	4
7	352	4	16	440	4
8	448	4	17	317	4
9	123	3	18	164	3
Out	2964	35	In	3220	35
			Totals	6184	70

Visitors	weekends with member only. Must have an introduction from own club.
Societies	telephone in advance.
Green Fees	£25 per round/day.
Facilities	⊗ (ex Sat & Mon) ⅷ (ex Mon & Wed) ⓛ ⬛ ♀ △ 🏠 ⌀ Michael Weldon.
Location	Whipsnade Rd (2m S off B4541)
Hotel	★★★69% Old Palace Lodge Hotel, Church St, DUNSTABLE ☎(0582) 662201 49⇔

LEIGHTON BUZZARD   Map 04 SP92

Leighton Buzzard ☎(0525) 373811
Parkland course with easy walking.
18 holes, 6101yds, Par 71, SSS 70.
Club membership 595.

Visitors	may not play Tue pm. With member only weekends and bank holidays. Must contact in advance and have an introduction from own club.
Societies	apply in writing.
Green Fees	£25 per day; £18 per round.
Facilities	⊗ ⅷ ⓛ ⬛ ♀ △ 🏠 ⌀
Location	Plantation Rd (1.5N of town centre off A418)
Hotel	★★★72% Swan Hotel, High St, LEIGHTON BUZZARD ☎(0525) 372148 38⇔

LUTON   Map 04 TL02

South Beds ☎(0582) 591500
27-hole downland course, slightly undulating.
Galley Course: 18 holes, 6342yds, Par 71, SSS 71, Course record 67.
Warden Course: 9 holes, 2424yds, Par 32.
Club membership 960.

Visitors	restricted Tue. Must contact in advance and have an introduction from own club.
Societies	apply in writing.
Green Fees	Galley Course £24.50 per day; £15.30 per round. Warden Course £7.65-£10.20.
Facilities	⊗ ⅷ ⓛ ⬛ ♀ △ 🏠 ⌀ E Cogle.
Leisure	snooker.
Location	Warden Hill (3m N off A6)
Hotel	★★★67% Strathmore Thistle Hotel, Arndale Centre, LUTON ☎(0582) 34199 150⇔

Stockwood Park ☎(0582) 413704
Municpal parkland course.
18 holes, 5973yds, Par 69, SSS 69, Course record 66.
Club membership 750.

Visitors	no restrictions.
Societies	Mon-Thu only.
Green Fees	£5 (£7.50 weekends & bank holidays).
Facilities	⊗ ⅷ by prior arrangement ⓛ ⬛ ♀ (1100-2300) △ 🏠 ⌀ Glyn McCarthy.
Leisure	pool tables.
Location	London Rd (1m S on A6)
Hotel	★★★67% Forte Crest Hotel, Waller Av, Dunstable Rd, LUTON ☎(0582) 575911 93⇔

For a full list of golf courses included in the book, see the index at the end of the directory

MILLBROOK   Map 04 TL03

Millbrook ☎Ampthill (0525) 840252
Long parkland course, on rolling countryside high above the Bedfordshire plains, with several water hazards. Laid out on well-drained sandy soil with many fairways lined with silver birch, pine and larch.
18 holes, 6530yds, Par 74, SSS 71.
Club membership 550.

Visitors	welcome weekdays & with member at weekends.
Societies	weekdays except Thu.
Green Fees	not confirmed.
Facilities	⊗ ⅷ ⓛ ⬛ ♀ △ 🏠 ⌀ T K Devine.
Location	E side of village off A507
Hotel	★★★72% Flitwick Manor Hotel, Church Rd, FLITWICK ☎(0525) 712242 15⇔

SANDY   Map 04 TL14

John O'Gaunt ☎Potton (0767) 260360
Two tree-lined parkland courses.
18 holes, 6214yds, Par 71, SSS 71, Course record 64.
Carthagena Course: 18 holes, 5590yds, Par 69, SSS 67, Course record 62.
Club membership 1300.

Visitors	must have handicap certificate at weekends. Must contact in advance.
Societies	apply in writing.
Green Fees	£35 per day/round (£50 weekends).
Facilities	⊗ ⅷ ⓛ ⬛ ♀ △ 🏠 ⌀ Peter Round.
Location	Sutton Park (3m NE of Biggleswade on B1040)
Hotel	★★★78% Woodlands Manor Hotel, Green Ln, Clapham, BEDFORD ☎(0234) 363281 22⇔Annexe3⇔

SHEFFORD   Map 04 TL13

Beadlow Manor Hotel & Golf & Country Club ☎(0525) 60800
27 hole golf and leisure complex. Golf courses of undulating nature with water hazards on numerous holes.
18 holes, 6231yds, Par 71, SSS 70.
Club membership 750.

Visitors	must have an introduction from own club.
Green Fees	not confirmed.
Facilities	♀ △ 🏠 ⌀
Location	2m W on A507
Hotel	★★★72% Flitwick Manor Hotel, Church Rd, FLITWICK ☎(0525) 712242 15⇔

TILSWORTH   Map 04 SP92

Tilsworth ☎Leighton Buzzard (0525) 210721
A 9-hole parkland course. 30-bay floodlit driving range. New 18-hole course due to open Spring 1992.
9 holes, 5437yds, Par 70, SSS 67, Course record 64.
Club membership 350.

Visitors	may not play Sun mornings. Must contact in advance.
Societies	apply in writing.
Green Fees	£3.60-£4.10 for 9 holes. £5.15-£6.15 for 18 holes.
Facilities	⊗ ⅷ ⓛ ⬛ ♀ △ 🏠 ⌀ Nick Webb.

▶

Location	Dunstable Rd (.5m NE off A5)
Hotel	★★★69% Old Palace Lodge Hotel, Church St, DUNSTABLE ☎(0582) 662201 49⇨

WYBOSTON   Map 04 TL15

Wyboston Lakes ☎Huntingdon (0480) 219200
Parkland course, with narrow fairways, small greens, set around four lakes and a river.
18 holes, 5721yds, Par 69, SSS 69.
Club membership 300.

Visitors	must contact in advance at weekends.
Societies	must telephone in advance.
Green Fees	not confirmed.
Facilities	♀ ⚐ 🏠 ⛳ 🏨 (Paul Ashwell.
Leisure	fishing.
Location	NE side of village off A1
Hotel	★★★78% Woodlands Manor Hotel, Green Ln, Clapham, BEDFORD ☎(0234) 363281 22⇨Annexe3⇨

BERKSHIRE

ASCOT   Map 04 SU96

Berkshire ☎(0344) 21496
Two heathland courses with splendid tree-lined fairways.
Red Course : 18 holes, 6369yds, Par 72, SSS 70.
Blue Course : 18 holes, 6260yds, Par 71, SSS 70.
Club membership 950.

Visitors	must contact in advance and have an introduction from own club.
Societies	must telephone in advance.
Green Fees	£55 per day; £40 per round (weekdays).
Facilities	⊗ ⚐ ♥ ♀ ⚐ 🏠 ⛳ (K A MacDonald.
Location	Swinley Rd (2.5m NW of M3 jct 3 on A332)
Hotel	★★★★57% The Berystede, Bagshot Rd, Sunninghill, ASCOT ☎(0344) 23311 91⇨🏨

Lavender Park ☎(0344) 884074
Public parkland course. Driving range with 9-hole par 3 course, floodlit until 2200 hrs.
9 holes, 1102yds, Par 28, SSS 29, Course record 20.
Club membership 50.

Visitors	no restrictions.
Societies	welcome.
Green Fees	not confirmed.
Facilities	⊗ & ♥ (Mon-Fri) ♀ ⚐ ⛳ (T Bowers.
Leisure	snooker.
Location	Swinley Rd (3.5m SW on A332)
Hotel	★★★★57% The Berystede, Bagshot Rd, Sunninghill, ASCOT ☎(0344) 23311 91⇨🏨

Mill Ride ☎Winkfield Row (0344) 886777
A new course opened for play in 1991 and combining good golfing country and attractive surroundings with a challenging design. The holes require as much thinking as playing.
18 holes, 6639yds, Par 72, SSS 72.

Visitors	must contact in advance.
Societies	apply in writing.
Green Fees	£15 (£30 weekends & bank holidays).

Facilities	⊗ �♒ ⚑ ♥ ♀ ⚐ 🏠 ⛳ 🏨 (Suzy Baggs.
Leisure	sauna.
Location	Mill Ride Estate, North Ascot (1.5m NW of Ascot)
Hotel	★★★★57% The Berystede, Bagshot Rd, Sunninghill, ASCOT ☎(0344) 23311 91⇨🏨

Royal Ascot ☎(0344) 25175
Heathland course exposed to weather.
18 holes, 5653yds, Par 68, SSS 67.
Club membership 600.

Visitors	restricted weekends & bank holidays.
Societies	must telephone in advance.
Green Fees	not confirmed.
Facilities	⚐ 🏠 (
Location	Winkfield Rd (.5 N on A330)
Hotel	★★★★57% The Berystede, Bagshot Rd, Sunninghill, ASCOT ☎(0344) 23311 91⇨🏨

Swinley Forest
☎(0344) 20197
An attractive and immaculate course of heather and pine situated in the heart of Swinley Forest. The 17th is as good a short hole as will be found, with a bunkered plateau green. Course record holder is P. Alliss.
18 holes, 6001yds, Par 68, SSS 69, Course record 64.
Club membership 350.

		SCORECARD			
Hole	Yds	Par	Hole	Yds	Par
1	370	4	10	210	4
2	350	4	11	286	4
3	305	4	12	480	5
4	165	3	13	160	3
5	465	5	14	375	4
6	437	5	15	433	5
7	410	5	16	430	5
8	155	3	17	180	3
9	430	5	18	360	4
Out	3087	38	In	2914	36
			Totals	6001	74

Visitors	by invitation only. Must contact in advance.
Societies	must contact in writing.
Green Fees	£60 per day.
Facilities	⊗ ⚑ ♥ ♀ ⚐ 🏠 ⛳ (R C Parker.
Location	1.5m S, off A330
Hotel	★★★★57% The Berystede, Bagshot Rd, Sunninghill, ASCOT ☎(0344) 23311 91⇨🏨

CHADDLEWORTH   Map 04 SU47

West Berkshire ☎(04882) 574
Challenging and interesting downland course with testing 635 yds (par 5) 5th hole.
18 holes, 7069yds, Par 73, SSS 74.
Club membership 900.

Visitors	are restricted weekends. Must contact in advance.
Societies	by arrangement.
Green Fees	£22 per weekday..
Facilities	⊗ ⚑ ♥ ♀ ⚐ 🏠 (David Sheppard.
Location	1m S of village off A338
Hotel	★★★60% The Chequers, Oxford St, NEWBURY ☎(0635) 38000 56⇨

COOKHAM   Map 04 SU88

Winter Hill ☎Bourne End (0628) 527613
Parkland course set in a curve of the Thames with wonderful views across the Thames to Cliveden.
18 holes, 6408yds, Par 72, SSS 71, Course record 70.
Club membership 800.

Visitors	not permitted weekends. Must be accompanied by member and contact in advance.
Societies	must apply in writing.
Green Fees	£22 per day (Mon-Fri).
Facilities	⊗ ⅷ by prior arrangement ⮕ ■ ♀ △ 🏠 ƒ P Wedges.
Location	Grange Ln (1m NW off B4447)
Hotel	★★★★69% Compleat Angler Hotel, Marlow Bridge, MARLOW ☎(06284) 4444 due to change to (0628) 484444 46⇔

CROWTHORNE   Map 04 SU86

East Berkshire ☎(0344) 772041
An attractive heathland course with an abundance of heather and pine trees. Walking is easy and the greens are exceptionally good. Some fairways become tight where the heather encroaches on the line of play. The course is testing and demands great accuracy.
18 holes, 6345yds, Par 69, SSS 70, Course record 65.
Club membership 500.

Visitors	must have a handicap certificate and play with member at weekends & bank holidays. Must contact in advance and have an introduction from own club.
Societies	Thu & Fri only; must contact in advance.
Green Fees	not confirmed.
Facilities	⊗ ⅷ by prior arrangement ⮕ ■ (11am-4pm) ♀ △ 🏠 ⅋ ƒ Arthur Roe.
Location	Ravenswood Ave (W side of town centre off B3348)
Hotel	★★★★♨72% Pennyhill Park Hotel, London Rd, BAGSHOT ☎(0276) 71774 22⇔♦Annexe54⇔♦

DATCHET   Map 04 SU97

Datchet ☎(0753) 543887
Meadowland course, easy walking.
9 holes, 5978yds, Par 70, SSS 69, Course record 63.
Club membership 385.

Visitors	may play weekdays before 3pm.
Societies	Tue only.
Green Fees	£20 per day; £14 per round.
Facilities	⊗ ⮕ ■ ♀ △ 🏠 ƒ Andy Greig.
Location	Buccleuch Rd (NW side of Datchet off B470)
Hotel	★★54% The Manor Hotel, The Village Green, DATCHET ☎(0753) 43442 30⇔♦

HURLEY   Map 04 SU88

Temple ☎Maidenhead (0628) 824248
An open parkland course with many excellent, fast greens relying on natural slopes rather than heavy bunkering. On one 'blind' punchbowl hole there is actually a bunker on the green. Good drainage assures play when many other courses are closed.
18 holes, 6206yds, Par 70, SSS 70, Course record 62.
Club membership 650.

Visitors	must contact in advance.
Societies	must book one year in advance.
Green Fees	£35 per day; (£45 weekends).
Facilities	⊗ ⅷ ⮕ ■ ♀ △ 🏠 ⅋ ƒ Alan Dobbins.
Leisure	squash, putting green & practice ground.

Location	Henley Rd (1m SE on A432)
Hotel	★★★★69% Compleat Angler Hotel, Marlow Bridge, MARLOW ☎(06284) 4444 due to change to (0628) 484444 46⇔

MAIDENHEAD   Map 04 SU88

Maidenhead ☎(0628) 24693
A pleasant parkland course on level ground with easy walking to good greens. Perhaps a little short but there are many natural features and some first-rate short holes.
18 holes, 6348yds, Par 70, SSS 70, Course record 66.
Club membership 650.

Visitors	may not play after noon on Fri or at weekends. Must contact in advance and have an introduction from own club.
Societies	must contact in writing.
Green Fees	£27 per day.
Facilities	⊗ ⮕ ■ ♀ △ 🏠 ƒ Clive Dell.
Location	Shoppenhangers Rd (S side of town centre off A308)
Hotel	★★★★73% Fredrick's Hotel, Shoppenhangers Rd, MAIDENHEAD ☎(0628) 35934 37⇔♦

NEWBURY   Map 04 SU46

Donnington Valley ☎(0635) 551199
Undulating, short, but testing course with mature trees and elevated greens, some protected by water.
18 holes, 4002yds, Par 61, SSS 60, Course record 58.
Club membership 250.

Visitors	may not play at weekends. Must contact in advance.
Societies	booking required in advance for over 16 persons.
Green Fees	£14.
Facilities	⊗ ⅷ ⮕ ■ ♀ △ 🏠 ⅋ ⮀ ƒ Nick Mitchell.
Leisure	fishing, snooker.
Location	Old Oxford Rd, Donnington (2m N of Newbury)
Hotel	★★★72% Millwaters, London Rd, NEWBURY ☎(0635) 528838 32⇔♦

Newbury & Crookham ☎(0635) 40035
A well-laid out, attractive course running mostly through woodland, and giving more of a challenge than its length suggests.
18 holes, 5880yds, Par 68, SSS 68.
Club membership 800.

Visitors	must play with member on weekends & bank holidays. Must have an introduction from own club.
Societies	must contact in advance.
Green Fees	£25 per day/round; (£15 weekends).
Facilities	△ 🏠 ⅋ ƒ David Harris.
Location	Bury's Bank Rd, Greenham (2m SE off A34)
Hotel	★★★60% The Chequers, Oxford St, NEWBURY ☎(0635) 38000 56⇔

Opening times of bar and catering facilities vary from place to place. Please remember to check in advance of your visit

READING   Map 04 SU77

Calcot Park ☎(0734) 427124
A delightfully sporting parkland course just outside the town. Hazards include a lake and many trees. The 6th is the longest, 497 yard par 5, with the tee-shot hit downhill over cross-bunkers to a well-guarded green. The 13th (188 yards) requires a big carry over a gully to a plateau green.
18 holes, 6283yds, Par 70, SSS 70, Course record 66.
Club membership 735.

Visitors	must have handicap certificate, but may not play weekends & bank holidays. Must contact in advance.
Societies	must apply in writing.
Green Fees	not confirmed.
Facilities	⊗ ⊪ ⊾ ⚐ ♀ △ 🏠 ⫪ ⸙ Albert Mackenzie.
Location	Bath Rd, Calcot (2.5m W on A4)
Hotel	★★★67% The Copper Inn, Church Rd, PANGBOURNE ☎(0734) 842244 22⇨🎔

Reading ☎(0734) 472909
Tree-lined parkland course, part hilly and part flat.
18 holes, 6204yds, Par 70, SSS 70, Course record 67.
Club membership 700.

Visitors	must have handicap certificate. With member only Fri & weekends.
Societies	must book one year in advance.
Green Fees	£26 per weekday.
Facilities	⊗ ⊪ ⊾ ⚐ ♀ △ 🏠 ⸙ Tim Morrison.
Location	17 Kidmore End Rd, Emmer Green (2m N off B481)
Hotel	★★★★60% Ramada Hotel, Oxford Rd, READING ☎(0734) 586222 196⇨🎔

SINDLESHAM   Map 04 SU76

Bearwood ☎Arborfield Cross (0734) 760060
Flat parkland course with one water hazard - over part of a lake. Also 9-hole pitch and putt.
9 holes, 2802yds, Par 35.
Club membership 570.

Visitors	must have handicap certificate. With member only on weekends & bank holidays. Must have an introduction from own club.
Green Fees	£8 per round.
Facilities	⊗ (ex Mon) ⊾ ⚐ ♀ △ 🏠 ⸙ A Hanson.
Leisure	riding.
Location	Mole Rd (1m SW on B3030)
Hotel	★★60% Cantley House Hotel, Milton Rd, WOKINGHAM ☎(0734) 789912 29⇨🎔

SONNING   Map 04 SU77

Sonning ☎(0734) 693332
A quality parkland course and the scene of many county championships. Wide fairways, not overbunkered, and very good greens. Holes of changing character through wooded belts.
18 holes, 6366yds, Par 70, SSS 70, Course record 65.

Visitors	weekdays only. Must have an introduction from own club.
Societies	must apply in writing.

Green Fees	£26 per day.
Facilities	⊗ ⊪ by prior arrangement ⊾ ⚐ ♀ 🏠 ⸙
Location	Duffield Rd (1m S off A4)
Hotel	★★★★60% Ramada Hotel, Oxford Rd, READING ☎(0734) 586222 196⇨🎔

STREATLEY   Map 04 SU58

Goring & Streatley ☎Goring (0491) 873229
A parkland/moorland course that requires 'negotiating'. Four well-known first holes lead up to the heights of the 5th tee, to which there is a 300ft climb. Wide fairways, not overbunkered, with nice rewards on the way home down the last few holes.
18 holes, 6275yds, Par 71, SSS 70, Course record 65.
Club membership 750.

SCORECARD: White Tees					
Hole	Yds	Par	Hole	Yds	Par
1	369	4	10	382	4
2	425	4	11	324	4
3	344	4	12	152	3
4	139	3	13	363	4
5	485	5	14	300	4
6	392	4	15	511	5
7	452	4	16	206	3
8	377	4	17	496	5
9	149	3	18	420	4
Out	3132	35	In	3154	36
			Totals	6286	71

Visitors	with member only at weekends.
Societies	must telephone in advance.
Green Fees	not confirmed.
Facilities	⊗ ⊪ by prior arrangement ⊾ ⚐ ♀ △ 🏠 ⫪ ⸙ Roy Mason.
Location	Rectory Rd (N of village off A417)
Hotel	★★★★73% Swan Diplomat Hotel, High St, STREATLEY ☎(0491) 873737 46⇨🎔

SUNNINGDALE   Map 04 SU96

Sunningdale See page 43

Sunningdale Ladies ☎Ascot (0344) 20507
A short 18-hole heathland course designed for Ladies golf.
18 holes, 3616yds, Par 60, SSS 60.
Club membership 350.

Visitors	telephone in advance.
Societies	Ladies societies only.
Green Fees	not confirmed.
Facilities	⊗ (ex Sun and Mon) ⊾ ⚐ ♀ △
Location	Cross Rd (1m S off A30)
Hotel	★★★★57% The Berystede, Bagshot Rd, Sunninghill, ASCOT ☎(0344) 23311 91⇨🎔

WOKINGHAM   Map 04 SU86

Downshire ☎Bracknell (0344) 424066
Municipal parkland course with many water hazards, easy walking. Testing holes: 7th (par 4), 15th (par 4), 16th (par 3).
18 holes, 6382yds, Par 73, SSS 70.

Visitors	must contact in advance.
Societies	must apply in writing.
Green Fees	£9.70 per day (£11.30 weekends).
Facilities	⊗ ⊪ by prior arrangement ⊾ ⚐ ♀ △ 🏠 ⫪ ⸙ Geoffrey Legouix.
Location	Easthampstead Park (3m SW of Bracknell)
Hotel	★★★★57% The Berystede, Bagshot Rd, Sunninghill, ASCOT ☎(0344) 23311 91⇨🎔

This guide is updated annually – make sure that you use the up-to-date edition

SCORE CARD: Old Course					
Hole	Yds	Par	Hole	Yds	Par
1	370	4	10	318	4
2	411	4	11	172	3
3	352	4	12	316	4
4	419	4	13	398	4
5	514	5	14	523	5
6	374	4	15	401	4
7	359	4	16	351	4
8	166	3	17	461	4
9	307	4	18	354	4
Out	3272	36	In	3294	36
			Totals	6566	72

SUNNINGDALE   Map04SU96

Sunningdale ☎ Ascot (0344) 21681

John Ingham writes: Many famous golfers maintain that Sunningdale, on the borders of Berkshire, is the most attractive inland course in Britain. The great Bobby Jones once played the 'perfect' round of 66 made up of threes and fours on the Old Course. Later, Norman von Nida of Australia shot a 63 while the then professional at the club, Arthur Lees, scored a 62 to win a huge wager.

While the Old Course, with silver birch, heather and perfect turf, is lovely to behold, the New Course alongside is considered by many to be its equal. But just as golfers want to play the Old Course at St Andrews, and miss the redesigned Jubilee, so visitors to Sunningdale opt for the Old, and fail to realise what they are overlooking by not playing the New.

To become a member of this club takes years of waiting. Maybe it is the quality of the courses, maybe the clubhouse atmosphere and perhaps the excellence of the professionals shop has something to do with it; but added up it has to be the most desirable place to spend a day.

The classic Old Course is not long, measuring just 6341 yards, and because the greens are normally in excellent condition, anyone with a 'hot' putter can have an exciting day, providing they keep teeshots on the fairway and don't stray into the gorse and pine trees which lie in wait.

Founded some ninety years ago, the Old Course was designed by Willie Park, while H.S. Colt created the New Course in 1922. Most golfers will agree that there isn't one indifferent hole on either course and, on a sunny day, if you had to be anywhere in the world playing well, then we opt for the elevated tenth tee on the Old. What bliss.

36 holes. Old Course 18 holes, 6341 yds, Par 70, SSS 70. New Course 6676 yds, Par 70, SSS 72

Visitors	weekdays only. Must contact in advance, and have a letter of introduction from their own club along with a handicap certificate..
Societies	one year's notice required.
Green fees	£75 per day
Facilities	⊗ ⌕ ☎ ♀ ⚲ ☎ ʃ (Keith Maxwell)
Location	Ridgemount Rd (1m S of Sunningdale, off A30)

WHERE TO STAY AND EAT NEARBY

HOTELS:

ASCOT   ★★★★ 57% Berystede, Bagshot Rd, Sunninghill ☎ (0344) 23311. 91 ⌕♦ʃ . ♀ European cuisine.

★★ 65% Highclere, 19 Kings Rd, Sunninghill ☎ (0344) 25220. 12 ⌕♦ʃ . ♀ European cuisine.

BAGSHOT   ★★★★ ⚑ 72% Pennyhill Park, London Rd ☎ (0276) 71774. 22 ⌕♦ʃ , Annexe 54 ⌕♦ʃ . ♀ English & French cuisine.

RESTAURANTS:

BRAY   ✗✗✗✗ The Waterside, River Cottage, Ferry Road ☎ Maidenhead (0628) 20691 & 22941. ♀ French cuisine.

EGHAM   ✗✗ La Bonne Franquette, 5 High Street ☎ (0784) 439494. ♀ French cuisine.

BUCKINGHAMSHIRE

| Location | Tattenhoe Ln (W side of town centre on A421) |
| Hotel | ★★★72% Swan Hotel, High St, LEIGHTON BUZZARD ☎(0525) 372148 38⇨🏠 |

AYLESBURY   Map 04 SP81

Ellesborough ☎Wendover (0296) 622114

Once part of the property of Chequers, and under the shadow of the famous monument at the Wendover end of the Chilterns. A downland course, it is rather hilly with most holes enhanced by far-ranging views over the Aylesbury countryside.

18 holes, 6271yds, Par 70, SSS 70, Course record 66.
Club membership 780.

SCORECARD: White Tees					
Hole	Yds	Par	Hole	Yds	Par
1	353	4	10	141	3
2	515	5	11	310	4
3	414	4	12	331	4
4	378	4	13	393	4
5	189	3	14	559	5
6	405	4	15	128	3
7	395	4	16	262	4
8	180	3	17	441	4
9	391	4	18	486	5
Out	3220	35	In	3051	36
			Totals	6271	71

Visitors	must have a handicap certificate, but may not play Tue afternoons. With member only at weekends. Must contact in advance and have an introduction from own club.
Societies	Wed & Thu only.
Green Fees	£30 per day; £20 per round.
Facilities	⊗ ⅢⅡ 🏌 ⚑ ♀ ⚒ 🏠 ♪ Paul Warner.
Location	Butlers Cross (1m E of Ellesborough on B4010)
Hotel	★★★(red) Bell Inn, ASTON CLINTON ☎(0296) 630252 6⇨🏠Annexe15⇨🏠

BEACONSFIELD   Map 04 SU99

Beaconsfield ☎(0494) 676545

An interesting and, at times, testing tree-lined and parkland course which frequently plays longer than appears on the card. Each hole differs to a considerable degree and here lies the charm. Walking is easy, except perhaps to the 6th and 8th. Well bunkered.

18 holes, 6487yds, Par 72, SSS 71.
Club membership 862.

Visitors	with member only at weekends and bank holidays Must contact in advance and have an introduction from own club.
Societies	must contact in writing
Green Fees	£35 per day; £30 per round.
Facilities	♀ ⚒ 🏠 ♪ ♪ Michael Brothers.
Location	Seer Green (2m E, S of Seer Green)
Hotel	★★★68% Bellhouse Hotel, Oxford Rd, BEACONSFIELD ☎(0753) 887211 136⇨

BLETCHLEY   Map 04 SP83

Windmill Hill ☎Milton Keynes (0908) 648149

Long, open-parkland course designed by Henry Cotton and opened in 1972. Municipal.

18 holes, 6773yds, Par 73, SSS 72.
Club membership 600.

Visitors	no restrictions.
Societies	must contact in advance.
Green Fees	not confirmed.
Facilities	⊗ ⅢⅡ 🏌 & ⚑ by prior arrangement ♀ ⚒ 🏠 ♪ ♪ C Clingan.

BOW BRICKHILL   Map 04 SP93

Woburn ☎Milton Keynes (0908) 370756

These two 18-hole golf courses are set amid the beautiful surroundings of the Duke of Bedford's estate near Woburn, and are suitably named the Duke's and the Duchess.
Duke's Course: 18 holes, 6940yds, Par 72, SSS 74.
Duchess Course: 18 holes, 6641yds, Par 72, SSS 72.
Club membership 900.

SCORECARD: Duke's Course					
(White Tees)					
Hole	Yds	Par	Hole	Yds	Par
1	514	5	10	404	4
2	385	4	11	502	5
3	134	3	12	193	3
4	395	4	13	419	4
5	510	5	14	565	5
6	207	3	15	432	4
7	464	4	16	449	4
8	409	4	17	425	4
9	177	3	18	356	4
Out	3195	35	In	3745	37
			Totals	6940	72

Visitors	must play with member at weekends. Must contact in advance and have an introduction from own club.
Societies	must telephone in advance.
Green Fees	not confirmed.
Facilities	⊗ ⅢⅡ by prior arrangement (groups only) ⚑ ♀ ⚒ 🏠 ♪ A Hay.
Leisure	hard tennis courts.
Location	.5m E
Hotel	★★★🏳72% Flitwick Manor Hotel, Church Rd, FLITWICK ☎(0525) 712242 15⇨🏠

BUCKINGHAM   Map 04 SP63

Buckingham ☎(0280) 813282

Undulating parkland course cut by a stream.
18 holes, 5869yds, Par 70, SSS 69, Course record 67.
Club membership 680.

Visitors	with member only at weekends. Must contact in advance.
Societies	must contact by telephone.
Green Fees	£23.
Facilities	⊗ ⅢⅡ 🏌 ⚑ ♀ ⚒ 🏠 ♪ Tom Gates.
Leisure	snooker.
Location	Tingewick Rd (1.5m W on A421)
Hotel	★★★66% Buckingham Lodge Hotel, Ring Rd South, BUCKINGHAM ☎(0280) 822622 70⇨🏠

BURNHAM   Map 04 SU98

Burnham Beeches ☎(06286) 61448

In the centre of the lovely Burnham Beeches countryside. Wide fairways, carefully maintained greens, some hills, and some devious routes to a few holes. A good finish.

18 holes, 6449yds, Par 70, SSS 71.
Club membership 670.

Visitors	may play on weekdays only and must have a handicap certificate. Must contact in advance.
Societies	welcome
Green Fees	£34 per round.
Facilities	⚒ 🏠 ♪ ♪
Location	Green Ln (.5m NE)

Hotel	★★★63% Burnham Beeches Moat House, Grove Rd, BURNHAM ☎(0628) 603333 75⇨

CHALFONT ST GILES   Map 04 SU99

Harewood Downs ☎Little Chalfont (0494) 762184
A testing, undulating parkland course with sloping greens and plenty of trees.
18 holes, 5958yds, Par 69, SSS 69, Course record 65.
Club membership 750.

Visitors	must have a handicap certificate. Must contact in advance and have an introduction from own club.
Societies	must contact by letter.
Green Fees	£20 per round; £22 per day (£30 weekends).
Facilities	⊗ ⅢⅢ by prior arrangement ⤳ ⬛ ♀ ⚐ 🛅 ℓ G C Morris.
Location	Cokes Ln (2m N off A413)
Hotel	★★★68% Bellhouse Hotel, Oxford Rd, BEACONSFIELD ☎(0753) 887211 136⇨

CHARTRIDGE   Map 04 SP90

Chartridge Park ☎High Wycombe (0494) 791772
Parkland course set in idyllic surroundings. Currently the UK's longest 9-hole course.
9 holes, 6038yds, Par 68, SSS 69, Course record 68.
Club membership 500.

Visitors	may play mid-week only. Must contact in advance.
Societies	must telephone in advance.
Green Fees	£15 per 18 holes, £7.50 per 9 holes..
Facilities	⊗ ⅢⅢ (Thu) ⤳ ⬛ ♀ ⚐ 🛅 ⚐ ℓ Peter Gibbins.
Location	3m NW of Chesham
Hotel	★★62% The Crown Hotel, High St, AMERSHAM ☎(0494) 721541 23rm(13⇨1🐾)

CHESHAM   Map 04 SP90

Chesham & Ley Hill ☎(0494) 784541
Heathland course on hilltop with easy walking. Subject to wind.
9 holes, 5296yds, Par 67, SSS 66, Course record 64.
Club membership 430.

Visitors	may play Mon & Thu, Wed afternoon, Fri before 1.30pm.
Societies	subject to approval, Thu only.
Green Fees	not confirmed.
Facilities	⊗ & ⅢⅢ by prior arrangement ⤳ ⬛ ♀ ⚐
Location	Ley Hill Common (2m E)
Hotel	★★62% The Crown Hotel, High St, AMERSHAM ☎(0494) 721541 23rm(13⇨1🐾)

DAGNALL   Map 04 SP91

Whipsnade Park ☎(044284) 2330
Parkland course situated on downs overlooking the Chilterns adjoining Whipsnade Zoo. Easy walking, good views.
18 holes, 6800yds, Par 72, SSS 72, Course record 70.
Club membership 500.

Visitors	with member only at weekends. Must contact in advance.
Societies	must contact in advance.

Green Fees	£30 per day; £20 per round.
Facilities	♀ ⚐ 🛅 ⚐ ℓ Michael Lewendon.
Location	Studham Ln (1m E off B4506)
Hotel	★★★69% Old Palace Lodge Hotel, Church St, DUNSTABLE ☎(0582) 662201 49⇨

DENHAM   Map 04 TQ08

Denham ☎Uxbridge (0895) 832022
A beautifully maintained parkland/heathland course, home of many county champions. Slightly hilly and calling for good judgement of distance in the wooded areas.
18 holes, 6440yds, Par 70, SSS 71, Course record 66.
Club membership 550.

Visitors	must play with member Fri-Sun. Must contact in advance and have an introduction from own club.
Societies	must book 1 year in advance.
Green Fees	£42 per day; £28 per round.
Facilities	⊗ ⤳ ⬛ ♀ ⚐ 🛅 ⚐ ℓ John Sheridan.
Location	Tilehouse Ln (2m NW)
Hotel	★★61% Ethorpe Hotel, Packhorse Rd, GERRARDS CROSS ☎(0753) 882039 29⇨🐾

FLACKWELL HEATH   Map 04 SU89

Flackwell Heath ☎Bourne End (0628) 520027
Open heath and tree-lined course on hills overlooking Loudwater and the M40. Quick drying.
18 holes, 6207yds, Par 71, SSS 70, Course record 65.
Club membership 800.

Visitors	with member only at weekends. Must have an introduction from own club.
Societies	Wed & Thu only. Must contact in writing.
Green Fees	£22.50 per day.
Facilities	⊗ ⤳ ⬛ ♀ ⚐ 🛅 ℓ Stephen Bryan.
Location	Treadaway Rd, High Wycombe (NE side of town centre)
Hotel	★★★68% Bellhouse Hotel, Oxford Rd, BEACONSFIELD ☎(0753) 887211 136⇨

GERRARDS CROSS   Map 04 TQ08

Gerrards Cross ☎(0753) 883263
A wooded parkland course which has been modernised in recent years and is now a very pleasant circuit with infinite variety. The best part lies on the plateau above the clubhouse where there are some testing holes.
18 holes, 6295yds, Par 69, SSS 70.
Club membership 820.

Visitors	must have a letter of introduction from their club or a handicap certificate. Must contact in advance.
Societies	must book one year ahead.
Green Fees	£32 per day; £25 per round (weekdays only).
Facilities	♀ ⚐ 🛅 ℓ A P Barr.
Location	Chalfont Park (NE side of town centre off A413)
Hotel	★★★68% Bellhouse Hotel, Oxford Rd, BEACONSFIELD ☎(0753) 887211 136⇨

HALTON   Map 04 SP81

Chiltern Forest ☎Aylesbury (0296) 630899
Hilly, wooded parkland course on two levels. Currently 14
holes but will be extended to 18 during 1992.
18 holes, 5755yds, Par 70, SSS 69.
Club membership 570.

Visitors	must play with member at weekends.
Societies	must contact in advance.
Green Fees	£21 per day.
Facilities	⊗ 🎜 (summer only) 🔜 ➿ (no catering Tue and Thu) ♀ ⚲ 🏠 ⌈ C Skeet.
Location	Aston Hill (1m NE off A4011)
Hotel	★★65% Rose & Crown Hotel, High St, TRING ☎(044282) 4071 27⇦🐾

IVER   Map 04 TQ08

Iver ☎(0753) 655615
Pay and play parkland course; fairly flat.
9 holes, 2953yds, Par 72, SSS 69, Course record 68 or 3107yds,
Par 74, SSS 69.
Club membership 500.

Visitors	no restrictions.
Societies	must contact in advance.
Green Fees	£4.50 per 9 holes; £7.50 for 18 (£5.50 & £10 weekends).
Facilities	⊗ 🔜 ➿ ♀ ⚲ 🏠 ⌈ Terry Notley.
Leisure	Practice range.
Location	Hollow Hill Ln, Langley Park Rd (1.5m SW off B470)
Hotel	★★★★64% Holiday Inn Slough/Windsor, Ditton Road, Langley, SLOUGH ☎(0753) 544244 352⇦🐾

IVINGHOE   Map 04 SP91

Ivinghoe ☎Cheddington (0296) 668696
Testing parkland course with water on three holes. Easy
walking on rolling countryside.
9 holes, 4508yds, Par 62, SSS 62, Course record 61.
Club membership 250.

Visitors	may only play after 8am.
Societies	must contact in advance.
Green Fees	£6 per round (£8 weekends).
Facilities	⊗ 🎜 🔜 ➿ ♀ ⚲ 🏠 ⌈ Bill Garrad.
Location	Wellcroft (N side of village)
Hotel	★★★(red) Bell Inn, ASTON CLINTON ☎(0296) 630252 6⇦🐾Annexe15⇦🐾

LITTLE CHALFONT   Map 04 SU99

Little Chalfont ☎(0494) 764877
Gently undulating course surrounded by woods.
9 holes, 5852yds, Par 68, SSS 68, Course record 66.
Club membership 300.

Visitors	no restrictions.
Societies	must contact in advance.
Green Fees	£9 per round (£11 weekends).
Facilities	⊗ 🎜 🔜 ➿ ♀ ⚲ 🏠 ⌈ Leyton Cheyne.
Location	Lodge Ln (Between Little Chalfont & Chorley-wood)
Hotel	★★62% The Crown Hotel, High St, AMERSHAM ☎(0494) 721541 23rm(13⇦1🐾)

LOUDWATER   Map 04 SU89

Wycombe Heights Golf Centre ☎Penn (049481) 2862
A new course designed by the John Jacobs Partnership, and
including a 24-bay driving range.
18 holes, 6200yds, Par 70, SSS 72, Course record 69.
Club membership 1000.

Visitors	no restrictions.
Societies	apply in writing.
Green Fees	£9 (£12 weekends).
Facilities	⊗ 🎜 🔜 ➿ ♀ ⚲ 🏠 ⌈ Brian Plucknett.
Location	Rayners Ave
Hotel	★★★65% Forte Posthouse, Handy Cross, HIGH WYCOMBE ☎(0494) 442100 110⇦🐾

MILTON KEYNES   Map 04 SP83

Abbey Hill ☎(0908) 563845
Undulating municipal course within the new city. Tight
fairways and well-placed bunkers. Stream comes into play on
five holes. Also Par 3 course.
18 holes, 6177yds, Par 68, SSS 69, Course record 67.
Club membership 600.

Visitors	no restrictions
Societies	must telephone (0908) 562408 in advance
Green Fees	£6 per round.
Facilities	⊗ 🎜 🔜 ➿ ♀ ⚲ 🏠 ⌈ S Harlock.
Leisure	pool table and darts.
Location	Two Mile Ash (2m W of new town centre off A5)
Hotel	★★62% Swan Revived Hotel, High St, NEWPORT PAGNELL ☎(0908) 610565 42rm(40⇦🐾)

PRINCES RISBOROUGH   Map 04 SP80

Whiteleaf ☎(0844) 274058
Short, 9-hole parkland course requiring great accuracy, fine
views.
9 holes, 5391yds, Par 66, SSS 66, Course record 64.
Club membership 350.

Visitors	with member only at weekends. Must contact in advance.
Societies	must contact the secretary in advance.
Green Fees	not confirmed.
Facilities	⊗ 🎜 🔜 ➿ ♀ ⚲ 🏠 ⌈ K Ward.
Location	Whiteleaf (1m NE off A4010)
Hotel	★★★(red) Bell Inn, ASTON CLINTON ☎(0296) 630252 6⇦🐾Annexe15⇦🐾

STOKE POGES   Map 04 SU98

Farnham Park ☎(028814) 3332
Fine, public parkland course in pleasing setting.
18 holes, 5787yds, Par 69, SSS 68, Course record 68.
Club membership 900.

Visitors	no restrictions.
Societies	must contact in advance.
Green Fees	not confirmed.
Facilities	⊗ 🔜 ➿ ♀ ⚲ 🏠 ⌈ Paul Harrison.
Leisure	pool table, darts and satellite TV.
Location	Park Rd (W side of village off B416)

Hotel ★★★★64% Holiday Inn Slough/Windsor, Ditton Road, Langley, SLOUGH ☎(0753) 544244 352⇨🏋

Stoke Poges ☎Slough (0753) 26385

Judgement of the distance from the tee is all important on this first-class parkland course. There are many outstanding par 4's of around 440 yds, several calling for much thought. Fairways are wide and the challenge seemingly innocuous.

18 holes, 6654yds, Par 71, SSS 72, Course record 65.

Club membership 720.

SCORECARD: White Tees					
Hole	Yds	Par	Hole	Yds	Par
1	502	5	10	390	4
2	411	4	11	156	3
3	198	3	12	435	4
4	425	4	13	502	5
5	496	5	14	429	4
6	412	4	15	326	4
7	150	3	16	187	3
8	354	4	17	421	4
9	454	4	18	406	4
Out	3402	36	In	3252	35
			Totals	6654	71

Visitors may not play weekends and Tue mornings. Must contact in advance and have an introduction from own club.
Societies must contact in advance.
Green Fees £33 per day; £22 per round.
Facilities ⊗ & 🏋 by prior arrangement ⌶ 🍺 ♀ △ 🏠 🍴 ┃ Kim Thomas.
Leisure snooker, sauna.
Location Park Rd (1.5m W off B416)
Hotel ★★★★64% Holiday Inn Slough/Windsor, Ditton Road, Langley, SLOUGH ☎(0753) 544244 352⇨🏋

WAVENDON   Map 04 SP93

Wavendon Golf Centre ☎Milton Keynes (0908) 281811
Pleasant parkland course set in 96 acres of mature trees.
18 holes, 5361yds, Par 66, SSS 67, Course record 67.
Club membership 800.
Visitors must contact in advance.
Societies must contact in advance.
Green Fees £9 (£12 weekends).
Facilities ⊗ 🏋 ⌶ 🍺 ♀ △ 🏠 🍴 ┃ Nick Elmer.
Location Lower End Rd (just off A421)
Hotel ★★★71% Moore Place Hotel, The Square, ASPLEY GUISE ☎(0908) 282000 39⇨ Annexe15⇨

WESTON TURVILLE   Map 04 SP81

Weston Turville Golf & Squash Club
☎Aylesbury (0296) 24084
Parkland course, with views of the Chiltern Hills. Flat easy walking with water hazards.
18 holes, 6002yds, Par 69, SSS 69.
Club membership 600.
Visitors no restrictions.
Societies must contact in advance.
Green Fees not confirmed.
Facilities ⊗ 🏋 by prior arrangement ⌶ 🍺 ♀ △ 🏠 🍴 ┃ Tom Jones.
Leisure squash.
Location New Rd (.5m N off B4544)
Hotel ★★★(red) Bell Inn, ASTON CLINTON ☎(0296) 630252 6⇨🏋 Annexe15⇨🏋

WEXHAM STREET   Map 04 SU98

Wexham Park ☎(0753) 663271
Gently undulating parkland course. Two courses.
18 holes, 5836yds, Par 69, SSS 68 or 9 holes, 2283yds, Par 32, SSS 32.
Club membership 500.
Visitors no restrictions.
Societies may not play at weekends; must contact in advance.
Green Fees not confirmed.
Facilities ⊗ 🏋 by prior arrangement ⌶ 🍺 ♀ △ 🏠 🍴 ┃ David Morgan.
Location .5m S
Hotel ★★★★64% Holiday Inn Slough/Windsor, Ditton Road, Langley, SLOUGH ☎(0753) 544244 352⇨🏋

WING   Map 04 SP82

Aylesbury Vale ☎Leighton Buzzard (0525) 240196
New course, gently undulating and played over water, with five ponds. Clubhouse due for completion Spring 1992.
18 holes, 6800yds, Par 72, SSS 72.
Club membership 650.
Visitors must have handicap certificate & must contact in advance.
Societies telephone to book in advance.
Green Fees not confirmed.
Facilities ⊗ 🏋 ⌶ 🍺 ♀ △ 🏠 ┃ Lee Scarbrow.
Location Wing Rd (2m NW on unclassified Stewkley road)
Hotel ★★★72% Swan Hotel, High St, LEIGHTON BUZZARD ☎(0525) 372148 38⇨🏋

CAMBRIDGESHIRE

BRAMPTON   Map 04 TL27

Brampton Park ☎Huntingdon (0480) 811772
Set in truly attractive countryside, bounded by the River Great Ouse and bisected by the River Lane. Great variety with mature trees, lakes and water hazards. One of the most difficult holes is the 4th, a Par 3 island green, named 'Fowler's Folly'.
18 holes, 3245yds, Par 71, SSS 73.
Club membership 600.
Visitors must be accompanied by member and contact in advance.
Societies must telephone in advance.
Green Fees £24 (£36 weekend).
Facilities ⊗ 🏋 by prior arrangement ⌶ 🍺 ♀ △ 🏠 ┃ Michael Torrens.
Location Buckden Rd
Hotel ★★64% Grange Hotel, 115 High St, BRAMPTON ☎(0480) 459516 9rm(1⇨7🏋)

Opening times of bar and catering facilities vary from place to place. Please remember to check in advance of your visit

CAMBRIDGE
Map 05 TL45

Cambridgeshire Moat House ☎(0954) 780555
Undulating parkland course with lake and water hazards, easy walking. Many leisure facilities. Course record holders, Paul Way and Peter Townsend.
18 holes, 6734yds, Par 72, SSS 72, Course record 68.
Club membership 500.

Visitors	must contact in advance and have an introduction from own club.
Societies	must telephone in advance.
Green Fees	not confirmed.
Facilities	⊗ ⅏ ⅃ ⬤ ♀ △ 🏠 ⌐ 🏕 (Geoff Huggett.
Leisure	hard tennis courts, heated indoor swimming pool, squash, sauna, solarium, gymnasium.
Location	Moat House Hotel, Bar Hill (5m NW on A604)
Hotel	★★★62% Cambridgeshire Moat House, BAR HILL ☎(0954) 780555 100♣♠

Gog Magog ☎(0223) 247626
Situated just outside the centre of the university town, Gog Magog, established in 1901, is known as the nursery of Cambridge under-graduate golf. The course is on high ground, and it is said that if you stand on the highest point and could see far enough to the east the next highest ground would be the Ural Mountains! The courses (there are two of them) are open but there are enough trees and other hazards to provide plenty of problems. Views from the high parts are superb. The nature of the ground ensures good winter golf.
Old Course: 18 holes, 6354yds, Par 70, SSS 70, Course record 64.
New Course: 9 holes, 5833yds, Par 69, SSS 68.
Club membership 1100.

Visitors	must play with member at weekends. Must contact in advance and have an introduction from own club.
Societies	by reservation.
Green Fees	not confirmed.
Facilities	⊗ ⅏ by prior arrangement ⅃ ⬤ ♀ △ 🏠 (Ian Bamborough.
Location	Shelford Bottom (3m SE on A1307)
Hotel	★★★66% Gonville Hotel, Gonville Place, CAMBRIDGE ☎(0223) 66611 62♣♠

ELY
Map 05 TL58

Ely City ☎(0353) 662751
Parkland course slightly undulating with water hazards formed of lakes and natural dykes. Magnificent views of Cathedral. Joint course record holder Lee Trevino.
18 holes, 6602yds, Par 72, SSS 72, Course record 66.
Club membership 1000.

Visitors	must have handicap certificate. It is advisable to contact the club in advance.
Societies	must contact club in advance.
Green Fees	£22 per day (£30 weekends & bank holidays).
Facilities	⊗ ⅏ (ex Sun & Mon) ⅃ ⬤ ♀ △ 🏠 ⌐ (Fred Rowden.
Location	Cambridge Rd (SW side of city centre on A10)
Hotel	★★★60% Fenlands Lodge Hotel, Soham Rd, Stuntney, ELY ☎(0353) 667047 Annexe9♣♠

GIRTON
Map 05 TL46

Girton ☎Cambridge (0223) 276169
Flat, open parkland course with easy walking.
18 holes, 6088yds, Par 69, SSS 69.
Club membership 730.

Visitors	with member only at weekends. Must contact in advance.
Societies	by arrangement.
Green Fees	£23 per weekday (£18 with handicap certificate).
Facilities	⊗ ⅏ ⅃ ⬤ ♀ △ 🏠 ⌐ (S Thomson.
Location	Dodford Ln (NW side of village)
Hotel	★★★57% Forte Posthouse, Lakeview, Bridge Rd, Impington, CAMBRIDGE ☎(0223) 237000 115♣♠

PETERBOROUGH
Map 04 TL18

Orton Meadows ☎(0733) 237478
Municipal, parkland course on either side of the Nene Valley Railway, with lakes and water hazards. Also 12-hole pitch and putt course.
18 holes, 5800yds, Par 68, SSS 68, Course record 67.
Club membership 850.

Visitors	must contact in advance.
Societies	must telephone in advance.
Green Fees	£6.20 per round (£8.70 weekends & bank holidays).
Facilities	△ 🏠 ⌐ (Dennis & Roger Fitton.
Location	Ham Ln, Oundle Rd (3m W of town on A605)
Hotel	★★★66% The Haycock Hotel, WANSFORD ☎(0780) 782223 51♣♠

Peterborough Milton ☎(0733) 380489
Well-bunkered parkland course set in the grounds of the Earl Fitzwilliam's estate. Easy walking.
18 holes, 6221yds, Par 71, SSS 70.
Club membership 800.

Visitors	must have an introduction from own club.
Societies	must contact in advance.
Green Fees	£30 per day; £20 per round (£25 weekends).
Facilities	⊗ ⅏ ⅃ ⬤ ♀ △ 🏠 (Nigel Bundy.
Location	Milton Ferry (3m W on A47)
Hotel	★★★66% The Haycock Hotel, WANSFORD ☎(0780) 782223 51♣♠

Thorpe Wood ☎(0733) 267701
Gently undulating, municipal parkland course designed by Peter Alliss and Dave Thomas.
18 holes, 7086yds, Par 71, SSS 74, Course record 74.
Club membership 850.

Visitors	must contact in advance.
Societies	must telephone in advance.
Green Fees	£6.20 per round (£8.70 weekends & bank holidays).
Facilities	⊗ ⅏ ⅃ & ⬤ by prior arrangement ♀ △ 🏠 ⌐ (Dennis & Roger Fitton.
Location	Thorpe Wood (3m W of city centre on A47)
Hotel	★★★60% Bull Hotel, Westgate, PETERBOROUGH ☎(0733) 61364 112♣

For a full range of AA guides and maps, visit your local AA shop or any good bookshop

PIDLEY   Map 04 TL37

Lakeside Lodge ☎Ramsey (0487) 740540
A well designed, spacious course incorporating eight lakes
and a modern clubhouse. Also 9-hole Par 3 and 25-bay
driving range.
18 holes, 6600yds, Par 72.
Club membership 500.
Visitors   no restrictions.
Societies   must telephone in advance.
Green Fees   £4 per 9 holes, £7 per 18 holes; (£7/£14 weekends).
Facilities   ⊗ ╚ ⬛ ♀ △ 🏠 ⛳ (Alistair Headley.
Location   Fen Rd
Hotel   ★★★64% Slepe Hall Hotel, Ramsey Rd, ST
                  IVES ☎(0480) 63122 16rm(15⇆7♠)

RAMSEY   Map 04 TL28

Ramsey ☎(0487) 812600
Flat, parkland course with water hazards.
18 holes, 6133yds, Par 71, SSS 70.
Club membership 750.
Visitors   must have a handicap certificate; must play
                  with member at weekends & bank holidays.
Societies   must contact secretary in advance.
Green Fees   £20 per day/round.
Facilities   ⊗ ╠ by prior arrangement ╚ ⬛ ♀ △ 🏠 ⛳
                  (Stuart Scott.
Leisure   bowling green.
Location   4 Abbey Ter (S side of town)
Hotel   ★★★71% The Old Bridge Hotel,
                  HUNTINGDON ☎(0480) 52681 26⇆♠

ST IVES   Map 04 TL37

St Ives (Hunts) ☎(0480) 68392
Picturesque parkland course.
9 holes, 3302yds, Par 68, SSS 69.
Club membership 305.
Visitors   telephone for details.
Green Fees   not confirmed.
Facilities   ♀ △ 🏠
Location   Westwood Rd (W side of town centre off A1123)
Hotel   ★★★64% Slepe Hall Hotel, Ramsey Rd, ST
                  IVES ☎(0480) 63122 16rm(15⇆7♠)

ST NEOTS   Map 04 TL16

Abbotsley Golf & Squash Club ☎Huntingdon (0480) 215153
Attractive, parkland course surrounding moated country
house and hotel. Pleasant views. Floodlit, covered driving
range.
18 holes, 5829yds, Par 70, SSS 72.
Club membership 650.
Visitors   may not play before 10am at weekends.
Societies   must contact by telephone.
Green Fees   £14 per day (£20 weekends).
Facilities   ⊗ ╠ ╚ ⬛ ♀ △ 🏠 ⛳ ⋈ (Vivien Saunders.
Leisure   squash, snooker, sauna, solarium.
Location   2m SE off B1046
Hotel   ★★64% Grange Hotel, 115 High St,
                  BRAMPTON ☎(0480) 459516 9rm(1⇆7♠)

St Neots ☎(0480) 72363
Undulating parkland course with lake and water hazards,
close to the Kym and Great Ouse rivers. Easy, level walking.
18 holes, 6027yds, Par 69, SSS 69, Course record 65.
Club membership 600.
Visitors   must have handicap certificate. With member
                  only at weekends.
Societies   must contact in advance.
Green Fees   £25 per day; £18 per round.
Facilities   ⊗ ╠ ╚ ⬛ ♀ △ 🏠 (Graham Bithrey.
Leisure   snooker.
Location   Crosshall Rd (W side of town centre on A45)
Hotel   ★★64% Grange Hotel, 115 High St,
                  BRAMPTON ☎(0480) 459516 9rm(1⇆7♠)

CHESHIRE

ALDERLEY EDGE   Map 07 SJ87

Alderley Edge ☎(0625) 585583
Well-wooded, undulating parkland course. A stream crosses
7 of the 9 holes.
9 holes, 5828yds, Par 68, SSS 68, Course record 64.
Club membership 400.
Visitors   may not play Tue and Sat. Must have an
                  introduction from own club.
Societies   Thu only.
Green Fees   £16 per day; (£20 weekends).
Facilities   ⊗ ╠ ╚ ⬛ ♀ △ 🏠 ⛳ (A Sproston.
Leisure   snooker.
Location   Brook Ln (1m NW on B5085)
Hotel   ★★★73% Alderley Edge Hotel, Macclesfield
                  Rd, ALDERLEY EDGE ☎(0625) 583033 32⇆♠

ALSAGER   Map 07 H2

Alsager Golf & Country Club ☎(0270) 875700
An 18-hole parkland course situated in rolling Cheshire
countryside. Clubhouse is well appointed with good facilities
and a friendly atmosphere.
18 holes, 6206yds, Par 70, SSS 70, Course record 69.
Club membership 600.
Visitors   must play with member at weekends. Must
                  contact in advance.
Societies   Mon, Wed & Thu only; must contact in writing.
Green Fees   not confirmed.
Facilities   ⊗ ╠ ╚ ⬛ ♀ △ 🏠 ⛳ (Nick Rothe.
Leisure   snooker.
Location   Audley Rd (2m NE M6 junct 10)
Hotel   ★★★66% Manor House Hotel, Audley Rd,
                  ALSAGER ☎(0270) 884000 57⇆♠

CHESTER   Map 07 SJ46

Chester ☎(0244) 677760
Meadowland course on two levels contained within a loop of
the River Dee. The car park overlooks the racecourse across
the river, and the clubhouse stands just 1 mile S.W. of the
city centre.
18 holes, 6487yds, Par 72, SSS 71, Course record 66.
Club membership 700.
Visitors   must contact in advance.
Societies   must telephone in advance.

▶

Green Fees	not confirmed.
Facilities	⊗ ⫟ ⚑ 🍺 (no catering Mon) ⚑ 🏌 🏠 ⚑ ⚑
	G Parton.
Leisure	snooker.
Location	Curzon Park (1m SW of city centre)
Hotel	★★★★71% Chester International Hotel,
	Trinity St, CHESTER ☎(0244) 322330 150⇨

Upton-by-Chester ☎(0244) 381183
Pleasant, tree-lined, parkland course. Not easy for low-handicap players to score well. Testing holes are 2nd (par 4), 14th (par 4) and 15th (par 3).
18 holes, 5808yds, Par 69, SSS 68, Course record 62.
Club membership 700.

Visitors	restricted competition days Sat & Sun. Must
	contact in advance.
Societies	apply in writing.
Green Fees	£21 per day; £16 per round (£21 per round
	weekends).
Facilities	⊗ ⫟ ⚑ 🍺 ⚑ 🏌 🏠 ⚑ P A Gardner.
Leisure	snooker.
Location	Upton Ln, Upton-by-Chester (N side off A5116)
Hotel	★★★★65% Mollington Banastre Hotel,
	Parkgate Rd, CHESTER ☎(0244) 851471 64⇨

Vicars Cross ☎(0244) 335174
Tree-lined parkland course, with undulating terrain.
18 holes, 6238yds, Par 71, SSS 70.
Club membership 666.

Visitors	no casual visitors Fri-Sun & BH
Societies	contact in advance.
Green Fees	£17 per day.
Facilities	⊗ ⫟ & ⚑ (Tue-Thu) 🍺 ⚑ 🏠 ⚑ J A Forsythe.
Leisure	snooker.
Location	Tarvin Rd, Great Barrow (3m E on A51)
Hotel	★★★★65% Mollington Banastre Hotel,
	Parkgate Rd, CHESTER ☎(0244) 851471 64⇨

CONGLETON   Map 07 SJ86

Astbury ☎(0260) 272772
Parkland course in open countryside, bisected by a canal. Large practice area.
18 holes, 6269yds, Par 71, SSS 70, Course record 65.
Club membership 700.

Visitors	with member only at weekends. Must have an
	introduction from own club.
Societies	Thu by written request.
Green Fees	£25 per day.
Facilities	⊗ ⫟ by prior arrangement 🍺 ⚑ ⚑ 🏌 🏠
Leisure	snooker.
Location	Peel Ln, Astbury (1.5m S between A34 and A527)
Hotel	★★★62% Saxon Cross Hotel, Holmes Chapel
	Rd, SANDBACH ☎(0270) 763281 52⇨🐾

Congleton ☎(0260) 273540
Superbly-manicured parkland course with views over three counties from the balcony of the clubhouse.
9 holes, 5055yds, Par 68, SSS 65.
Club membership 400.

Visitors	may not play during competitions.
Green Fees	not confirmed.
Facilities	⊗ (ex Thu-Mon) ⫟ by prior arrangement 🍺 ⚑
	⚑ 🏌 🏠 ⚑ John Colclough.

Leisure	snooker.
Location	Biddulph Rd (1.5m SE on A527)
Hotel	★★★65% Chimney House Hotel, Congleton
	Rd, SANDBACH ☎(0270) 764141 50⇨

CREWE   Map 07 SJ75

Crewe ☎(0270) 584099
Undulating parkland course.
18 holes, 6229yds, Par 70, SSS 70, Course record 67.
Club membership 600.

Visitors	with member only weekends and bank holidays.
Societies	Tue only, telephone to arrange.
Green Fees	£21 per day; £16 after 1pm.
Facilities	⊗ ⫟ 🍺 ⚑ ⚑ 🏌 🏠 ⚑ R E Rimmer.
Leisure	snooker.
Location	Fields Rd, Haslington (2.25m NE off A534)
Hotel	★★★57% Crewe Arms Hotel, Nantwich Rd,
	CREWE ☎(0270) 213204 53⇨🐾

DELAMERE   Map 07 SJ56

Delamere Forest ☎Sandiway (0606) 882807
Played mostly on open heath, there is great charm in the way this course drops down into the occasional pine sheltered valley.
18 holes, 6305yds, Par 72, SSS 70, Course record 63.
Club membership 560.

Visitors	restricted weekends and bank holidays. Must
	contact in advance.
Societies	telephone to arrange.
Green Fees	£20/£30 for 18/36 holes (£25 for 18 holes
	weekends and bank holidays).
Facilities	⊗ & ⫟ (societies only) 🍺 ⚑ ⚑ 🏌 🏠 ⚑
	Ellis B Jones.
Location	Station Rd (1.5m N off B5152)
Hotel	★★★64% Hartford Hall Hotel, School Ln,
	Hartford, NORTHWICH ☎(0606) 75711
	21⇨

DISLEY   Map 07 SJ98

Disley ☎(0663) 62071
Parkland/moorland course with trees. Often breezy. Good views. Testing hole: 5th (par 5).
18 holes, 6015yds, Par 70, SSS 69, Course record 63.
Club membership 400.

Visitors	restricted Thu, Fri, weekends & bank holidays.
	Must have an introduction from own club.
Societies	must contact in advance.
Green Fees	not confirmed.
Facilities	⫟ 🍺 ⚑ ⚑ 🏌 🏠 ⚑ ⚑ A G Esplin.
Leisure	snooker.
Location	Stanley Hall Ln, Jacksons Edge (NW side of
	village off A6)
Hotel	★★★56% Alma Lodge Hotel, 149 Buxton Rd,
	STOCKPORT ☎061-483 4431 56rm(52⇨)

A golf-course name printed in ***bold italics*** means that we have been unable to verify information with the club's management for the current year

ECCLESTON   Map 07 SJ46

Eaton ☎(0244) 680474
A very testing, well-wooded parkland course.
18 holes, 6446yds, Par 72, SSS 71.
Club membership 530.

Visitors	must contact in advance and have an introduction from own club.
Societies	must contact in advance.
Green Fees	not confirmed.
Facilities	⊗ by prior arrangement ⅷ by prior arrangement ㄥ ➍ ♀ △ 🏠 ℂ A Mitchell.
Location	Eaton Park (1m S)
Hotel	★★★★(red) The Chester Grosvenor Hotel, Eastgate St, CHESTER ☎(0244) 324024 86⇨ฦ

ELLESMERE PORT   Map 07 SJ47

Ellesmere Port ☎051-339 7689
Municipal parkland course with natural hazards of woods, brook and ponds.
18 holes, 6384yds, Par 70, SSS 72, Course record 66.
Club membership 300.

Visitors	must contact in advance.
Societies	by arrangement with professional.
Green Fees	not confirmed.
Facilities	♀ △ 🏠 ⌐ⁿ ℂ David John Yates.
Leisure	squash.
Location	Chester Rd, Hooton (NW side of town centre on A41)
Hotel	★★62% Berni Royal, Childer Thornton, ELLESMERE PORT ☎051-339 8101 47⇨ฦ

HELSBY   Map 07 SJ47

Helsby ☎(0928) 722021
Quiet parkland course with natural hazards.
18 holes, 5906yds, Par 70, SSS 68.
Club membership 700.

Visitors	weekends and bank holidays with member only. Must contact in advance.
Societies	Tue & Thu.
Green Fees	£24 per day; £18 per round.
Facilities	⊗ ⅷ ㄥ ➍ ♀ △ 🏠 ⌐ⁿ ℂ Ian Wright.
Leisure	snooker.
Location	Towers Ln (1m S off A56)
Hotel	★★★★(red) The Chester Grosvenor Hotel, Eastgate St, CHESTER ☎(0244) 324024 86⇨ฦ

KNUTSFORD   Map 07 SJ77

Knutsford ☎(0565) 3355
Parkland course set in a beautiful old deer park. It demands some precise iron play.
9 holes, 6288yds, Par 70, SSS 70.
Club membership 230.

Visitors	are not permitted weekends and restricted Wed afternoons. Must contact in advance and have an introduction from own club.
Green Fees	£15 for 18 holes (£20 weekends and bank holidays).
Facilities	➍ (catering by prior arrangement) ♀ △

Location	Mereheath Ln (N side of town centre off A50)
Hotel	★★★61% The Swan Hotel, BUCKLOW HILL ☎(0565) 830295 70⇨ฦ

Mere Golf & County Club ☎Bucklow Hill (0565) 830155
A gracious parkland championship course designed by James Braid in the Cheshire sand belt, with several holes close to a lake. The round has a tight finish with four testing holes.
18 holes, 6817yds, Par 71, SSS 73, Course record 69.
Club membership 540.

Visitors	must contact in advance.
Societies	Mon, Tue & Thu only by prior arrangement.
Green Fees	£40 per day (£50 weekends).
Facilities	⊗ ⅷ ㄥ ➍ ♀ △ 🏠 ℂ Peter Eyre.
Leisure	hard tennis courts, heated indoor swimming pool, squash, fishing, snooker, sauna, solarium, gymnasium.
Location	Chester Rd, Mere (1m E of junc 19 of M6)
Hotel	★★★61% The Swan Hotel, BUCKLOW HILL ☎(0565) 830295 70⇨ฦ

LYMM   Map 07 SJ68

Lymm ☎(092575) 5020
First ten holes are gently undulating with the Manchester Ship Canal running alongside the 9th hole. The remaining holes are comparatively flat.
18 holes, 6304yds, Par 71, SSS 70, Course record 68.
Club membership 620.

Visitors	must have a handicap certificate, may not play on Thu mornings, weekends or bank holidays unless guest of member. Must contact in advance.
Societies	Wed only, must contact in writing.
Green Fees	£18.40.
Facilities	⊗ ⅷ ㄥ ➍ ♀ △ 🏠 ⌐ⁿ ℂ Steve McCarthy.
Leisure	snooker.
Location	Whitbarrow Rd (.5m N off A6144)
Hotel	★★★59% Lymm Hotel, Whitbarrow Rd, LYMM ☎(092575) 2233 22⇨ฦ Annexe47⇨ฦ

MACCLESFIELD   Map 07 SJ97

Macclesfield ☎(0625) 23227
Very hilly 9-hole heathland course situated on the edge of the Pennines. Excellent views. Currently being extended to 18-holes for 1993.
9 holes, 5220yds, Par 69, SSS 69, Course record 63.
Club membership 600.

Visitors	handicap certificate required.
Societies	by arrangement.
Green Fees	£15 per day (£17 weekends).
Facilities	⊗ ⅷ ㄥ ➍ ♀ △ 🏠 ℂ Tony Taylor.
Leisure	snooker.
Location	The Hollins (SE side of town centre off A523)
Hotel	★★62% Crofton Hotel, 22 Crompton Rd, MACCLESFIELD ☎(0625) 434113 8⇨ฦ

For an explanation of symbols and abbreviations, see page 32

Tytherington
☎(0625) 434562
Modern championship course in beautiful, mature parkland setting. Headquarters of the Women's European Tour and venue of the WPGET English Open and County matches. Country club facilities.
18 holes, 6737yds, Par 72, SSS 72, Course record 68.
Club membership 2000.

SCORECARD					
Hole	Yds	Par	Hole	Yds	Par
1	465	4	10	420	4
2	507	5	11	217	3
3	164	3	12	520	5
4	401	4	13	156	3
5	196	3	14	439	4
6	382	4	15	402	4
7	301	4	16	540	5
8	320	4	17	412	4
9	480	5	18	415	4
Out	3216	36	In	3521	36
			Totals	6737	72

Visitors   must contact in advance and have an introduction from own club.
Societies   apply in writing.
Green Fees   £22 per 18 hole weekdays.
Facilities   ⊗ ⊞ ⓛ ♚ ♀ ⌂ ⬠ ☂ ℂ Sandy Wilson.
Leisure   hard tennis courts, heated indoor swimming pool, squash, snooker, sauna, solarium, gymnasium, bowls, clay shot, creche..
Location   1m N of Macclesfield on A523
Hotel   ★★★★61% Shrigley Hall Golf & Country Club, Shrigley Park, POTT SHRIGLEY ☎(0625) 575757 58⇨

MOTTRAM ST ANDREWS   Map 07 SJ87

Mottram Hall ☎Macclesfield (0625) 828135
Championship course with flat parkland on the front nine and undulating woodland on the back. The hotel offers many leisure facilities.
18 holes, 6905yds, Par 72, SSS 72, Course record 66.
Club membership 450.
Visitors   must have current handicap certificate or letter of introduction from own club. Must contact in advance.
Societies   must contact in advance.
Green Fees   £25 (£30 weekends & bank holidays).
Facilities   ⓛ ♚ ♀ ⌂ ⬠ ☂ ⍓ ℂ Tim Rastall.
Leisure   hard tennis courts, heated indoor swimming pool, squash, fishing, snooker, sauna, solarium, gymnasium, jacuzzi.
Location   Wilmslow Rd
Hotel   ★★★70% Mottram Hall Hotel, Prestbury, MOTTRAM ST ANDREW ☎(0625) 828135 95⇨♠

POTT SHRIGLEY   Map 07 E8

Shrigley Hall Hotel ☎Bollington (0625) 575757
Parkland course set in 262-acre estate with breathtaking views over the Peak District and Cheshire Plain. Designed by Donald Steel, this championship course provides a real sporting challenge while the magnificent hotel offers a wealth of sporting facilities as well as accommodation and food.
18 holes, 6305yds, Par 71, SSS 71, Course record 68.
Visitors   must contact in advance.
Societies   contact in advance.
Green Fees   £20 (£30 weekends).
Facilities   ⊗ ⊞ ⓛ ♚ ♀ ⌂ ⬠ ☂ ⍓ ℂ Granville Ogden.

Leisure   hard tennis courts, heated indoor swimming pool, squash, fishing, snooker, sauna, solarium, gymnasium.
Location   Shrigley Park
Hotel   ★★★★61% Shrigley Hall Golf & Country Club, Shrigley Park, POTT SHRIGLEY ☎(0625) 575757 58⇨

POYNTON   Map 07 SJ98

Davenport ☎(0625) 876951
Undulating parkland course. Extensive view over Cheshire Plain from elevated 5th tee. Testing 17th hole, par 4.
18 holes, 6006yds, Par 69, SSS 69.
Club membership 750.
Visitors   no restrictions.
Societies   must contact in writing.
Green Fees   £24 per day/round (£30 per day/round Sun & bank holidays).
Facilities   ⊗ ⊞ ⓛ ♚ ♀ ⌂ ⬠ ☂ ℂ Wyn Harris.
Leisure   snooker.
Location   Worth Hall, Middlewood Rd (1m E off A523)
Hotel   ★★★56% Alma Lodge Hotel, 149 Buxton Rd, STOCKPORT ☎061-483 4431 56rm(52⇨)

PRESTBURY   Map 07 SJ97

Prestbury ☎(0625) 829388
Rather strenuous parkland course, undulating, with many plateau greens. Good views.
18 holes, 6143yds, Par 71, SSS 71, Course record 66.
Club membership 725.
Visitors   with member only weekends. Must contact in advance and have an introduction from own club.
Societies   Thu only, contact in advance.
Green Fees   £22 per day.
Facilities   ⌂ ☂ ℂ Nick Summerfield.
Leisure   snooker.
Location   Macclesfield Rd (S side of village off A538)
Hotel   ★★★70% Mottram Hall Hotel, Prestbury, MOTTRAM ST ANDREW ☎(0625) 828135 95⇨♠

RUNCORN   Map 07 SJ58

Runcorn ☎(0928) 572093
Parkland course with tree-lined fairways and easy walking. Fine views over Mersey and Weaver valleys. Testing holes: 7th par 5; 14th par 5; 17th par 4.
18 holes, 6035yds, Par 69, SSS 69, Course record 66.
Club membership 575.
Visitors   welcome except between 9-10am, noon-1.30pm and Tue afternoon. Must have an introduction from own club.
Societies   apply in writing.
Green Fees   not confirmed.
Facilities   ⊗ ⊞ ⓛ ♚ ♀ ⌂ ⬠ ℂ Ian Sephton.
Leisure   snooker.
Location   Clifton Rd (1.25m S of Runcorn Station)
Hotel   ★★★66% Forte Crest Hotel, Wood Ln, Beechwood, RUNCORN ☎(0928) 714000 134⇨♠

SANDBACH
Map 07 SJ76

Malkins Bank ☎Crewe (0270) 765931
Parkland course. Tight 13th hole with stream running through.
18 holes, 6071yds, Par 70, SSS 69.
Club membership 500.

Visitors	no restrictions.
Societies	apply for booking form
Green Fees	£4.40 per round (£5.40 weekends and bank holidays).
Facilities	⬚ ⬚ ♀ △ 🏠 ⚐ ⚑ David Wheeler.
Location	Betchton Rd, Malkins Bank (1.5m SE off A533)
Hotel	★★★62% Saxon Cross Hotel, Holmes Chapel Rd, SANDBACH ☎(0270) 763281 52⇆🐾

Sandbach ☎Crewe (0270) 21177
Meadowland, undulating course with easy walking.
9 holes, 5593yds, Par 68, SSS 67.
Club membership 570.

Visitors	weekdays except Tue, and with member only weekends & bank holidays. Must contact in advance.
Societies	apply by letter.
Green Fees	£12 per day/round.
Facilities	⊗ ⍫ ⬚ ♀ △
Location	Middlewich Rd (.5m W on A533)
Hotel	★★★62% Saxon Cross Hotel, Holmes Chapel Rd, SANDBACH ☎(0270) 763281 52⇆🐾

SANDIWAY
Map 07 SJ67

Sandiway ☎(0606) 883247
Delightful, undulating woodland and heath golf with long hills up to the 8th, 16th and 17th holes. Many dog-legged and tree-lined holes give opportunities for the deliberate fade or draw.
18 holes, 6435yds, Par 70, SSS 72.
Club membership 750.

SCORECARD					
Hole	Yds	Par	Hole	Yds	Par
1	405	4	10	467	4
2	523	5	11	219	3
3	193	3	12	446	4
4	502	5	13	138	3
5	416	4	14	441	4
6	151	3	15	362	4
7	413	4	16	519	5
8	357	4	17	305	4
9	396	4	18	182	3
Out	3356	36	In	3079	34
			Totals	6435	70

Visitors	must contact in advance and have an introduction from own club.
Societies	apply by letter.
Green Fees	£30-£35 per day (£35-£40 weekends).
Facilities	⊗ ⍫ ⬚ ⬚ ♀ △ 🏠 ⚐ ⚑ William Laird.
Location	1m E on A556
Hotel	★★★64% Hartford Hall Hotel, School Ln, Hartford, NORTHWICH ☎(0606) 75711 21⇆

TARPORLEY
Map 07 SJ56

Oaklands Golf & Country Club ☎(0829) 733884
New course with lovely views over Cheshire Plain. Many leisure facilities.
18 holes, 6169yds, Par 71, SSS 69.
Club membership 550.

Visitors	with member only at weekends.

Societies	must contact in advance.
Green Fees	£24 per day; £21 per round.
Facilities	⊗ ⍫ ⬚ ⬚ ♀ △ 🏠 ⚑ B Rimner, J Statham, P Murray..
Leisure	heated indoor swimming pool, snooker, sauna, gymnasium.
Location	Forest Rd
Hotel	★★⬤64% Willington Hall Hotel, Willington, TARPORLEY ☎(0829) 52321 10⇆🐾

Portal Golf Complex ☎(0829) 733933
New, mature, wooded parkland course with numerous water hazards and fine views over the Cheshire Plain. The 13th is just a short iron through trees, but its green is virtually an island surrounded by water.
18 holes, 7145yds, Par 73, SSS 74.

Visitors	no restrictions.
Societies	must contact at least 2 weeks in advance.
Green Fees	£25 per round (£30 weekends).
Facilities	⊗ ⬚ ⬚ ♀ △ 🏠 ⚑ David Clare.
Location	Cobbler's Cross Ln
Hotel	★★★69% The Wild Boar, Whitchurch Rd, Beeston, TARPORLEY ☎(0829) 260309 37⇆🐾

WARRINGTON
Map 07 SJ68

Birchwood ☎(0925) 818819
Very testing parkland course with natural water hazards. The 11th hole is particularly challenging.
18 holes, 6808yds, Par 71, SSS 73, Course record 64.
Club membership 1150.

▶

Visitors	welcome except Sun.
Societies	Mon-Thu only.
Green Fees	not confirmed.
Facilities	⊗ ⫼ ↳ ⬛ ♀ ⌂ ☂ ⍓ ℓ Derrick Cooper.
Leisure	snooker, sauna.
Location	Kelvin Close, Birchwood (4m NE on A574)
Hotel	★★★67% Forte Posthouse, Lodge Ln, Newton-Le-Willows, HAYDOCK ☎(0942) 717878 142⇨

Leigh ☎Culcheth (0925) 762943
A pleasant, well-wooded parkland course. Any discrepancy in length is compensated by the wide variety of golf offered here. The course is well maintained and there is a comfortable clubhouse.
18 holes, 5853yds, Par 69, SSS 68, Course record 64.
Club membership 750.

Visitors	may not play during competitions. Must have an introduction from own club.
Societies	must contact in writing.
Green Fees	£20 per day (£25 weekends & bank holidays).
Facilities	⊗ ⫼ ↳ ⬛ ♀ ⌂ ℓ Andrew Baguley.
Leisure	snooker.
Location	Kenyon Hall, Kenyon (5m NE off A579)
Hotel	★★★63% Fir Grove Hotel, Knutsford Old Rd, WARRINGTON ☎(0925) 67471 40⇨♠

Poulton Park ☎Padgate (0925) 812034
Tight, flat parkland course with good greens and many trees.
9 holes, 5379yds, Par 68, SSS 66, Course record 66.
Club membership 350.

Visitors	may not play between 5-6pm weekdays and noon-1.30pm Sat.
Societies	contact in writing.
Green Fees	£15 per day (£17 weekend & bank holidays).
Facilities	⊗ ⫼ ↳ & ⬛ (during bar hours) ♀ ⌂ ⌂ ℓ Steven McCarthy.
Location	Dig Ln, Cinnamon Brow, Padgate (3m from Warrington on A574).
Hotel	★★★63% Fir Grove Hotel, Knutsford Old Rd, WARRINGTON ☎(0925) 67471 40⇨♠

Walton Hall ☎(0925) 63061
Wooded, municipal parkland course on Walton Hall estate.
18 holes, 6843yds, Par 72, SSS 73, Course record 69.
Club membership 420.

Visitors	no restrictions.
Societies	must contact in writing.
Green Fees	not confirmed.
Facilities	↳ ⬛ ♀ ⌂ ⌂ ⍓
Location	Warrington Rd, Higher Walton (2.5m S off A56)
Hotel	★★★63% Fir Grove Hotel, Knutsford Old Rd, WARRINGTON ☎(0925) 67471 40⇨♠

Warrington ☎(0925) 65431
Meadowland, with varied terrain and natural hazards.
18 holes, 6305yds, Par 72, SSS 70.
Club membership 400.

Visitors	no restrictions.
Societies	apply in writing.
Green Fees	not confirmed.
Facilities	♀ ⌂ ⌂ ℓ

Location	The Hill Warren, London Rd, Appleton (2.5m S on A49)
Hotel	★★70% Rockfield Hotel, Alexandra Rd, Grappenhall, WARRINGTON ☎(0925) 62898 due to change to 262898 6⇨♠Annexe7rm(5⇨♠)

WIDNES Map 07 SJ58

St Michael Jubilee ☎051-424 6230
Recently extended, municipal parkland course, dominated by the 'Stewards Brook'. The old and the new sections are split by the main road and joined by an underpass.
18 holes, 2648yds, Par 69, SSS 68.

Visitors	must be accompanied by member, contact in advance and have an introduction from own club.
Societies	must contact in writing.
Green Fees	not confirmed.
Facilities	♀ ⌂ ⌂ ℓ
Leisure	snooker.
Location	Dunalk Rd (W side of town centre off A562)
Hotel	★58% Rockland Hotel, View Rd, RAINHILL ☎051-426 4603 10rm(9⇨)

Widnes ☎051-424 2440
Parkland course, easy walking.
18 holes, 5719yds, Par 69, SSS 68, Course record 65.
Club membership 300.

Visitors	may play after 9am & after 4pm on competition days. Must have an introduction from own club.
Societies	must contact in writing.
Green Fees	not confirmed.
Facilities	⌂ ⌂ ℓ Frank Robinson.
Leisure	snooker.
Location	Highfield Rd
Hotel	★58% Rockland Hotel, View Rd, RAINHILL ☎051-426 4603 10rm(9⇨)

WILMSLOW Map 07 SJ88

Wilmslow ☎(0565) 872148
A fine parkland championship course, of middle length, fair to all classes of player and almost in perfect condition.
18 holes, 6607yds, Par 72, SSS 72, Course record 64.
Club membership 896.

Visitors	restricted Wed & weekends. Must contact in advance.
Societies	must contact in advance.
Green Fees	On application.
Facilities	⊗ ⫼ ↳ ⬛ ♀ ⌂ ⌂ ℓ John Nowicki.
Location	Great Warford, Mobberley (2m SW off B5058)
Hotel	★★★★60% Belfry Hotel, Stanley Rd, HANDFORTH ☎061-437 0511 81⇨

WINSFORD Map 07 SJ66

Knights Grange ☎(0606) 552780
Municipal parkland course with water hazards.
9 holes, 2860yds, Par 35, SSS 68.
Club membership 100.

Visitors	no restrictions.
Societies	must contact in writing.

Green Fees	£2 (£2.60 weekends) for 9 holes; £2.80 (£3.60 weekends) for 18 holes.
Facilities	⬛ ♀ ⛳
Leisure	hard and grass tennis courts.
Location	Sports Complex (N side of town off A54)
Hotel	★★★64% Hartford Hall Hotel, School Ln, Hartford, NORTHWICH ☎(0606) 75711 21⇥

CLEVELAND

BILLINGHAM   Map 08 NZ42

Billingham ☎Stockton (0642) 554494
Parkland course on edge of urban-rural district, with hard walking and water hazards; testing 15th hole.
18 holes, 6460yds, Par 73, SSS 71, Course record 65.
Club membership 750.

Visitors	with member only at weekends & bank holidays. Must have an introduction from own club.
Societies	must contact in writing.
Green Fees	not confirmed.
Facilities	⊗ �🍽 by prior arrangement ⮢ ⬛ ♀ △ 🏠 (P S Bradley.
Leisure	snooker.
Location	Sandy Ln (1m W of town centre E of A19)
Hotel	★★★55% Billingham Arms Hotel, The Causeway, Billingham, STOCKTON-ON-TEES ☎(0642) 553661 & 360880 69⇥🐾

EAGLESCLIFFE   Map 08 NZ41

Eaglescliffe and District
☎(0642) 780098
This hilly course offers both pleasant and interesting golf to all classes of player. It lies in a delightful setting on a rolling plateau, shelving to the River Tees. There are fine views to the Cleveland Hills.
18 holes, 6275yds, Par 72, SSS 70, Course record 67.
Club membership 550.

	SCORECARD: White Tees				
Hole	Yds	Par	Hole	Yds	Par
1	333	4	10	478	5
2	383	4	11	200	3
3	467	4	12	534	5
4	182	3	13	482	5
5	281	4	14	449	4
6	352	4	15	162	3
7	498	5	16	349	4
8	348	4	17	160	3
9	318	4	18	299	4
Out	3162	36	In	3113	36
			Totals	6275	72

Visitors	restricted Tue, Thu, Fri & weekends.
Societies	must contact in advance.
Green Fees	£16 per day (£22 weekends & bank holidays).
Facilities	⊗ (ex Mon and Sat) 🍽 (ex Sun-Mon) ⮢ (ex Sun-Mon) ⬛ ♀ △ 🏠 (Nic Gilks.
Leisure	snooker.
Location	Yarm Rd (E side of village off A135)
Hotel	★★★★55% Swallow Hotel, 10 John Walker Square, STOCKTON-ON-TEES ☎(0642) 679721 124⇥🐾

HARTLEPOOL   Map 08 NZ53

Castle Eden & Peterlee ☎Wellfield (0429) 836510
Beautiful parkland course alongside a nature reserve. Hard walking, trees provide wind shelter.
18 holes, 6107yds, Par 70, SSS 69, Course record 66.
Club membership 750.

Visitors	with member only during 12-1.30pm & 4-6.30pm. Must contact in advance.
Societies	must contact in advance on (0429) 836689.
Green Fees	£18 per day (£24 weekends & bank holidays).
Facilities	⊗ 🍽 by prior arrangement ⮢ ⬛ ♀ △ 🏠 (Tim Jenkins.
Leisure	snooker.
Location	Castle Eden (2m S of Peterlee on B1281 off A19)
Hotel	★★★67% Hardwick Hall Hotel, SEDGEFIELD ☎(0740) 20253 17⇥🐾

Hartlepool ☎(0429) 274398
A seaside course, half links, overlooking the North Sea. A good test and equally enjoyable to all handicap players. The 10th, par 4, demands a precise second shot over a ridge and between sand dunes to a green down near the edge of the beach, alongside which several holes are played.
18 holes, 6255yds, Par 70, SSS 70.
Club membership 600.

Visitors	with member only on Sun.
Societies	must apply in writing.
Green Fees	£14 per day (£20 weekends).
Facilities	⊗ 🍽 ⮢ ⬛ ♀ △ 🏠 (Malcolm E Cole.
Leisure	snooker.
Location	Hart Warren (N side off King Oswy Drive)
Hotel	★★★67% Hardwick Hall Hotel, SEDGEFIELD ☎(0740) 20253 17⇥🐾

MIDDLESBROUGH   Map 08 NZ42

Middlesbrough ☎(0642) 311515
Undulating parkland course, prevailing winds. Testing 9th, 16th and 17th holes.
18 holes, 6111yds, Par 70, SSS 69, Course record 61.
Club membership 900.

Visitors	restricted Tue & Sat.
Societies	Wed, Thu & Fri only. Must contact the club in advance.
Green Fees	£18.50 per day (£23 weekends & bank holidays).
Facilities	⊗ 🍽 by prior arrangement ⮢ ⬛ ♀ △ 🏠 (Don Jones.
Leisure	snooker.
Location	Brass Castle Ln, Marton (5m S off A172)
Hotel	★★★50% Marton Way Toby Hotel, Marton Rd, MIDDLESBROUGH ☎(0642) 817651 53⇥

Middlesbrough Municipal ☎(0642) 315533
Parkland course with good views. The front nine holes have wide fairways and large, often well-guarded greens while the back nine demand shots over tree-lined water hazards and narrow entrances to subtley contoured greens. Driving range.
18 holes, 6314yds, Par 71, SSS 70, Course record 68.
Club membership 575.

Visitors	no restrictions.
Societies	by arrangement.
Green Fees	not confirmed.
Facilities	⊗ 🍽 by prior arrangement ⮢ (ex Sun & Mon evenings) ⬛ ♀ △ 🏠 ⛳ (
Location	Ladgate Ln (2.5m S of town centre on B1380 off A172)
Hotel	★★★50% Marton Way Toby Hotel, Marton Rd, MIDDLESBROUGH ☎(0642) 817651 53⇥

REDCAR
Map 08 NZ62

Cleveland ☎(0642) 471798
Links championship course.
18 holes, 6707yds, Par 72, SSS 72, Course record 68.
Club membership 890.

Visitors	may not play at weekends. Must contact in advance and have an introduction from own club.
Societies	must apply in writing.
Green Fees	£14.25 per day.
Facilities	⊗ ⅲ ㋥ ⬤ ♀ ⚲ 龠 ℓ D Masey.
Leisure	snooker.
Location	Queen St (8m E of Middlesborough on A19/ A172)
Hotel	★★★67% Park Hotel, Granville Ter, REDCAR ☎(0642) 490888 26⇨🐾

Wilton ☎(0642) 465265
Parkland course with some fine views.
18 holes, 6104yds, Par 70, SSS 69.
Club membership 750.

Visitors	restricted Sat.
Societies	must telephone in advance.
Green Fees	not confirmed.
Facilities	⊗ ⅲ by prior arrangement ㋥ ⬤ ♀ ⚲ 龠 ℓ R Smith.
Location	Wilton Castle (3m W on A174)
Hotel	★★★67% Park Hotel, Granville Ter, REDCAR ☎(0642) 490888 26⇨🐾

SALTBURN-BY-THE-SEA
Map 08 NZ62

Saltburn by the Sea ☎(0287) 22812
Undulating meadowland course surrounded by woodland.
Particularly attractive in autumn. There are fine views of the
Cleveland Hills and of Tees Bay.
18 holes, 5803yds, Par 70, SSS 68.
Club membership 850.

Visitors	must have an introduction from own club.
Societies	apply in writing.
Green Fees	not confirmed.
Facilities	♀ ⚲ 龠 ㋛
Location	Hob Hill, Guisborough Rd (S side of town centre on B1268).
Hotel	★★★50% Marton Way Toby Hotel, Marton Rd, MIDDLESBROUGH ☎(0642) 817651 53⇨

SEATON CAREW
Map 08 NZ52

Seaton Carew ☎Hartlepool (0429) 266249 A championship links course taking full advantage of its dunes, bents, whins and gorse. Renowed for its par 4 (17th); just enough fairway for an accurate drive followed by another precise shot to a pear-shaped, sloping green that is severly trapped. *The Old Course: 18 holes, 6604yds, Par 72.*	SCORECARD: Brabazon Course (White Tees)

Hole	Yds	Par	Hole	Yds	Par
1	363	4	10	394	4
2	555	5	11	477	5
3	172	3	12	390	4
4	399	4	13	537	5
5	385	4	14	512	5
6	165	3	15	208	3
7	358	4	16	434	4
8	349	4	17	413	4
9	363	4	18	375	4
Out	3109	35	In	3740	38
			Totals	6849	73

Brabazon Course : 18 holes, 6849yds, Par 73.
Club membership 650.

Visitors	no restrictions.
Societies	must apply in writing.
Green Fees	not confirmed.
Facilities	⊗ ⅲ ㋥ ⬤ ♀ ⚲ 龠 ℓ W Hector.
Leisure	snooker.
Location	Tees Rd (SE side of village off A178)
Hotel	★★★55% Billingham Arms Hotel, The Causeway, Billingham, STOCKTON-ON-TEES ☎(0642) 553661 & 360880 69⇨🐾

STOCKTON-ON-TEES
Map 08 NZ41

Norton ☎Stockton (0642) 676385
An extension to a 6, 100-yard, 18-hole course will be
completed by Spring 1992.
18 holes, 6100yds, Par 71, SSS 71.

Visitors	no restrictions.
Societies	large parties should telephone in advance.
Green Fees	£4.10 per 9 hole; £6.50 for new 18 hole course.
Facilities	⊗ ⅲ ㋥ ⬤ ♀ 龠
Location	Norton (at Norton 2m N off A19)
Hotel	★★★60% Forte Posthouse Teeside, Low Ln, Thornaby-on-Tees, STOCKTON-ON-TEES ☎(0642) 591213 135⇨🐾

Teesside ☎(0642) 676249
Flat parkland course, easy walking.
18 holes, 6472yds, Par 72, SSS 71, Course record 65.
Club membership 600.

Visitors	with member only weekdays after 4.30pm, weekends after 11am.
Societies	must contact in writing.
Green Fees	£15 per day (£20 weekends).
Facilities	⊗ ⅲ ㋥ ⬤ (no catering Mon) ♀ ⚲ 龠 ℓ Ken Hall.
Location	Acklam Rd, Thornaby (1.5m SE on A1130)
Hotel	★★★60% Forte Posthouse Teeside, Low Ln, Thornaby-on-Tees, STOCKTON-ON-TEES ☎(0642) 591213 135⇨🐾

CORNWALL & ISLES OF SCILLY

BODMIN
Map 02 C6

Bodmin Golf & Country Club ☎(0208) 73600 or 77325
Championship standard parkland/moorland course.
Picturesque but not hilly.
18 holes, 6142yds, Par 71, SSS 71.
Club membership 200.

Visitors	no restrictions.
Societies	must contact in advance.
Green Fees	£20 per day (£25 weekends).
Facilities	⊗ ⅲ ㋥ ⬤ ♀ ⚲ 龠 ㋛ ℓ J Madhvani.
Location	Lanhydrock (2m SE)
Hotel	★★58% Westberry Hotel, Rhind St, BODMIN ☎(0208) 72772 15rm(5⇨4🐾)Annexe8⇨🐾

For a full list of golf courses included in the
book, see the index at the end of the directory

BUDE
Map 02 SS20

Bude & North Cornwall ☎(0288) 352006
Seaside links course with natural sand bunkers, superb greens and breathtaking views. Club established in 1891.
18 holes, 6202yds, Par 71, SSS 70, Course record 70.
Club membership 900.

Visitors	restricted weekdays 9.30am-12.30pm, 2-5pm & from 6.30pm onwards. Closed Sat & Sun mornings. Must contact in advance and have an introduction from own club.
Societies	weekdays only by arrangement.
Green Fees	£20 per day (£25 weekends & bank holidays).
Facilities	⊗ Ⅲ ⌸ ♨ ♀ △ 🏠 (P J Yeo.
Leisure	snooker.
Location	Burn View (N side of town)
Hotel	★★64% Camelot Hotel, Downs View, BUDE ☎(0288) 352361 21⇔🅟

CAMBORNE
Map 02 SW64

Tehidy Park ☎Portreath (0209) 842208
A well-maintained parkland course providing good holiday golf.
18 holes, 6241yds, Par 72, SSS 70.
Club membership 1000.

Visitors	must have handicap certificate. Must contact in advance and have an introduction from own club.
Societies	must apply in writing.
Green Fees	£22 per day (£28 weekends).
Facilities	⊗ ⅢⅢ ⌸ ♨ ♀ △ 🏠 (James Dunbach.
Leisure	snooker.
Location	2m NE off A30
Hotel	★★★62% Penventon Hotel, REDRUTH ☎(0209) 214141 50⇔🅟

CARLYON BAY
Map 02 SX05

Carlyon Bay Hotel ☎(072681) 4228
Championship-length, cliff-top course moving into parkland. Magnificent views surpassed only by the quality of the course. The 230-yard (par 3) 18th with railway and road out-of-bounds, holds the player's interest to the end.
18 holes, 6501yds, Par 72, SSS 71.
Club membership 550.

Visitors	must contact in advance.
Societies	must contact in advance.
Green Fees	not confirmed.
Facilities	♀ △ 🏠 ♈ (
Location	2.5m E of St Austell off A3082
Hotel	★★★★61% Carlyon Bay Hotel, Sea Rd, Carlyon Bay, ST AUSTELL ☎(072681) 2304 73⇔🅟

See advertisement on page 59

For an explanation of symbols and abbreviations, see page 32

CONSTANTINE
Map 02 SW72

Trevose ☎Padstow (0841) 520208
A pleasant holiday seaside course with early holes close to the sea on excellent springy turf. It is a good and enjoyable test. Self-catering accommodation is available at the club.
18 holes, 6608yds, Par 71, SSS 71.
Short Course: 9 holes, 1360yds, Par 29, SSS 29.
Club membership 650.

SCORECARD:						
Championship Tees						
Hole	Yds	Par	Hole	Yds	Par	
1	443	4	10	467	4	
2	386	4	11	199	3	
3	166	3	12	448	4	
4	500	5	13	507	5	
5	461	4	14	317	4	
6	323	4	15	327	4	
7	428	4	16	225	3	
8	156	3	17	388	4	
9	451	5	18	416	4	
Out	3314	36	In	3294	35	
			Totals	6608	71	

Visitors	must have handicap certificate for main course. Must be accompanied by member, contact in advance and have an introduction from own club.
Societies	must apply in writing.
Green Fees	£20/£30 per round/day.
Facilities	⊗ ⅢⅢ ⌸ ♨ ♀ △ 🏠 ♈ ♨ (Gary Alliss.
Leisure	hard tennis courts, heated outdoor swimming pool, snooker.
Location	N side of village off B3276
Hotel	★★★76% Treglos Hotel, CONSTANTINE BAY ☎(0841) 520727 44⇔🅟

See advertisement on page 61

FALMOUTH
Map 02 SW83

Falmouth ☎(0326) 311262
Seaside/parkland course with outstanding coastal views. Sufficiently bunkered to punish any inaccurate shots. Five acres of practice grounds.
18 holes, 5680yds, Par 70, SSS 67, Course record 65.
Club membership 600.

Visitors	may not play on competition days. Must contact in advance.
Societies	must contact in advance.
Green Fees	£20 per day; £15 per round.
Facilities	⊗ ⅢⅢ by prior arrangement ⌸ ♨ ♀ △ 🏠 ♈ (David J Short.
Location	Swanpool Rd (SW side of town centre)
Hotel	★★★⚑76% Penmere Manor Hotel, Mongleath Rd, FALMOUTH ☎(0326) 211411 39⇔🅟 See advertisement on page 59
Additional hotel	★★61% Park Grove Hotel, Kimberley Park Rd, FALMOUTH ☎(0326) 313276 17rm(15🅟)

See advertisement on page 59

LAUNCESTON
Map 02 SX38

Launceston ☎(0566) 773442
Undulating parkland course with views over Tamar Valley to Dartmoor and Bodmin Moor. Dominated by 'The Hill' up which the 8th and 11th fairways rise, and on which the 8th, 9th, 11th and 12th greens sit.
18 holes, 6407yds, Par 70, SSS 71, Course record 64.
Club membership 800.

Visitors	with member only at weekends. Must contact in advance and have an introduction from own club.
Societies	must apply in writing.
Green Fees	£20 per weekday/round.

►

Facilities	⊗ 🖃 💺 ♀ 🛆 🏠 ᵞ 𝄢 J Tozer.
Location	St Stephens (NW side of town centre on B3254)
Hotel	★★★71% Arundell Arms, LIFTON ☎(0566) 84666 due to change to 784666 24➪🏠Annexe5➪🏠

LELANT   Map 02 SW53

West Cornwall ☎Penzance (0736) 753401					

A seaside links with sandhills and lovely turf adjacent to the Hayle estuary and St Ives Bay. A real test of the player's skill, especially 'Calamity Corner' starting at the 5th on the lower land by the River Hayle. A small (3 hole) course is available for practice.

18 holes, 5645yds, Par 69, SSS 67, Course record 64 or 56 holes.

SCORECARD: White Tees					
Hole	Yds	Par	Hole	Yds	Par
1	229	3	10	331	4
2	382	4	11	362	4
3	342	4	12	494	5
4	352	4	13	264	4
5	179	3	14	446	4
6	337	4	15	135	3
7	191	3	16	521	5
8	325	4	17	194	3
9	406	4	18	394	4
Out	2743	33	In	3141	36
			Totals	5884	69

Club membership 900.

Visitors	must have handicap certificate. Must have an introduction from own club.
Societies	must apply in writing.
Green Fees	£21 per day; £16 per round.
Facilities	🛆 🏠 𝄢 Paul Atherton.
Leisure	snooker.
Location	N side of village off A3074
Hotel	★★66% Boskerris Hotel, Boskerris Rd, Carbis Bay, ST IVES ☎(0736) 795295 13rm(11➪🏠)Annexe5➪🏠

LOOE   Map 02 SX25

Looe ☎Widegates (05034) 239
Exposed and somewhat windy course on high moorland; designed by Harry Vardon in 1934. Easy walking. Fine views over Looe coastline.
18 holes, 5940yds, Par 70, SSS 68.
Club membership 620.

Societies	must contact two weeks in advance.
Green Fees	£16 per round.
Facilities	⊗ 🍴 (Apr-Oct) 🖃 💺 ♀ 🛆 🏠 ᵞ 𝄢 Alistair Macdonald.
Location	Widegates (3.5m NE off B3253)
Hotel	★★★61% Hannafore Point Hotel, Marine Dr, Hannafore, LOOE ☎(05036) 3273 37➪🏠

LOSTWITHIEL   Map 02 C7

Lostwithiel Golf & Country Club ☎Bodmin (0208) 873550
An undulating, parkland course with water hazards. Overlooked by Restormel Castle and the River Fowey flows alongside the course. Driving range.
18 holes, 6098yds, Par 72, SSS 70.

Visitors	must have handicap certificate. Must contact in advance.
Societies	contact in advance.
Green Fees	£15 per round (£20 weekends & bank holidays).
Facilities	⊗ (Sun only) 🍴 🖃 💺 ♀ 🛆 🏠 ᵞ 🛏 𝄢 Martin Hammond.

Leisure	hard tennis courts, heated indoor swimming pool, fishing, snooker.
Location	Lower Polscoe (1m outside Lostwithiel off A390)
Hotel	★★68% Restormel Lodge Hotel, Hillside Gardens, LOSTWITHIEL ☎(0208) 872223 21➪🏠Annexe12➪

MAWNAN SMITH   Map 02 SW72

Budock Vean Hotel ☎Falmouth (0326) 250288
Undulating parkland course.
9 holes, 5007yds, Par 68, SSS 65.

Visitors	cannot play on bank holidays. Must contact in advance and have an introduction from own club.
Societies	welcome if resident in hotel.
Green Fees	£12 per round (weekends £15).
Facilities	⊗ 🍴 🖃 💺 ♀ 🛆 🏠 🛏 𝄢 David Short.
Leisure	hard tennis courts, heated indoor swimming pool, snooker.
Location	1.5m SW
Hotel	★★★70% Budock Vean Hotel, MAWNAN SMITH ☎(0326) 250288 59➪🏠

For a full range of AA guides and maps, visit your local AA shop or any good bookshop

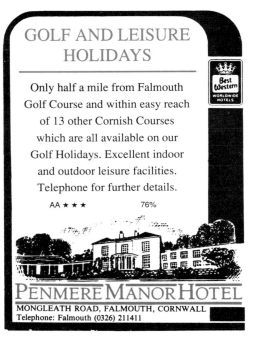

MULLION

Map 02 SW61

Mullion ☎(0326) 240685
Cliff top and links course with panoramic views over Mounts Bay. Well-known ravine hole (7th). Most southerly course in the British Isles.
18 holes, 6022yds, Par 69, SSS 67.
Club membership 825.
Visitors must have handicap certificate.
Societies must contact in advance.
Green Fees £16.50 per day/round (Apr-Sep); £12.50 (Oct-Mar).
Facilities ⊗ ⊪ ⅃ ⊒ (no catering Tue or Sun evenings) ♀ △ 🖻 ⫪ 𝄢 Robin Goodway.
Location Cury Cross Lanes (1.5m NW off A3083)
Hotel ★★★74% Polurrian Hotel, MULLION ☎(0326) 240421 40rm(38⇔🎝)

NEWQUAY

Map 02 SW86

Newquay ☎(0637) 872091
Seaside course close to the beach and open to wind.
18 holes, 6140yds, Par 69, SSS 69, Course record 63.
Club membership 500.
Visitors must have an introduction from own club.
Societies must contact in advance.
Green Fees £16 per day (£20 weekends & bank holidays).
Facilities ⊗ ⊪ ⅃ ⊒ ♀ △ 🖻 𝄢 Paul Muscroft.
Leisure hard tennis courts, snooker, gymnasium.
Location Tower Rd (W side of town)
Hotel ★★★57% Hotel Mordros, 4 Pentire Av, NEWQUAY ☎(0637) 876700 30⇔🎝

Treloy ☎(0637) 878554
A new Executive course constructed to American specifications. Large contoured and mounded greens. Offers an interesting round for all categories of player.
9 holes, 2143yds, Par 32, SSS 31.
Visitors must contact in advance.
Societies must contact in advance.
Green Fees £15 per day; £7.50 per round.
Facilities ⊒ △ 🖻 ⫪ 𝄢 Ian Welding.
Hotel ★★69% Whipsiderry Hotel, Trevelgue Road, Porth, NEWQUAY ☎(0637) 874777 24rm(5⇔14🎝)

PADSTOW

See **Constantine Bay**

PERRANPORTH

Map 02 SW75

Perranporth ☎Truro (0872) 572454
There are three testing par 5 holes on the links course (2nd, 5th, 11th) and a fine view over Perranporth Beach from all holes.
18 holes, 6286yds, Par 72, SSS 70.
Club membership 600.
Visitors restricted Sun mornings & competition days. Must contact in advance and have an introduction from own club.
Societies must apply in writing.
Green Fees £18 per day (£22 weekends & bank holidays).

Facilities ⊗ ⊪ ⅃ ⊒ ♀ △ 🖻 𝄢 D Michell.
Leisure snooker.
Location Budnick Hill (.75m NE on B3285)
Hotel ★65% Beach Dunes Hotel, Ramoth Way, Reen Sands, PERRANPORTH ☎(0872) 572263 7rm(3⇔🎝)Annexe3⇔🎝

PORTWRINKLE

Map 02 SX35

Whitsand Bay Hotel Golf & Country Club
☎St Germans (0503) 30276
Seaside course laid-out on cliffs overlooking Whitsand Bay. Easy walking after 1st hole. The par 3 (3rd) hole is well-known.
18 holes, 5850yds, Par 68, SSS 69, Course record 62.
Club membership 450.
Visitors must have handicap certificate.
Societies must contact in advance.
Green Fees £13.50 per day (£16 weekends).
Facilities ⊗ ⊪ ⅃ ⊒ ♀ △ 🖻 ⫪ 𝄢 S Poole.
Leisure heated indoor swimming pool, fishing, riding, sauna, solarium, gymnasium, games room.
Location E side of village off B3247
Hotel ★64% Whitsand Bay Hotel, Golf & Country Club, Portwrinkle, TORPOINT ☎(0503) 30276 30rm(28⇔)

PRAA SANDS

Map 02 SW52

Praa Sands ☎Penzance (0736) 763445
A beautiful parkland course with outstanding sea views from every tee and green.
9 holes, 4096yds, Par 62, SSS 60, Course record 59.
Club membership 300.
Visitors restricted Fri afternoon & Sun morning (May-Sep)
Societies must contact in advance.
Green Fees £11 per round.
Facilities ⊗ ⊪ ⅃ ⊒ ♀ △ 🖻 𝄢 Paul Atherton.
Leisure pool table & darts.
Location Germoe Cross Roads (N side of village on A394)
Hotel ★★▟70% Nansloe Manor Hotel, Meneage Rd, HELSTON ☎(0326) 574691 7⇔🎝

ROCK

Map 02 SW97

St Enodoc ☎Trebetherick (020886) 3216
Seaside course with natural hazards.
Church Course: 18 holes, 6207yds, Par 69, SSS 70, Course record 65.
Holywell Course: 18 holes, 4142yds, Par 63, SSS 61.
Club membership 1200.
Visitors may not play on bank holidays. Must have a handicap certificate for Church Course. Must contact in advance.
Societies must contact in writing.
Green Fees Church: £22 per round (£27 weekends); Holywell: £12 per round.
Facilities ⊗ ⊪ ⅃ ⊒ ♀ △ 🖻 ⫪ 𝄢 Nick Williams.
Leisure practice ground putting green.
Location W side of village
Hotel ★★67% St Enodoc Hotel, ROCK ☎(020886) 3394 13⇔🎝

St Austell   Map 02 SX05

St Austell ☎(0726) 72649
Very interesting, inland parkland course designed by James Braid. Undulating, well-covered with tree plantations and well-bunkered. Notable holes are 8th (par 4) and 16th (par 3).
18 holes, 6007yds, Par 69, SSS 69, Course record 70.
Club membership 800.

Visitors	must have handicap certificate.
Societies	must apply in writing.
Green Fees	not confirmed.
Facilities	⊗ ⅲ 🄻 ⬤ ♀ △ 🖾 Ʇ Mark Rowe.
Location	Tregongeeves Ln (1m SW off A390)
Hotel	★★★62% Porth Avallen Hotel, Carlyon Bay, ST AUSTELL ☎(072681) 2802 & 2183 23rm(18⇋1↖)

St Just (near Land's End)   Map 02 SW33

Cape Cornwall Golf & Country Club
☎Penzance (0736) 788611
Coastal parkland, walled course. The walls are an integral part of its design. Country club facilities.
18 holes, 5788yds, Par 72, SSS 68, Course record 75.
Club membership 740.

Visitors	may not play before 11.30am at weekends.
Societies	must contact in advance.
Green Fees	£14 per round (£15 weekends).
Facilities	⊗ ⅲ 🄻 ⬤ ♀ △ 🖾 ⱦ Ʇ R Hamilton.
Leisure	heated outdoor swimming pool, snooker, sauna, solarium, gymnasium.
Location	Cape Cornwall (1m W of St Just)
Hotel	★★★✦60% Higher Faugan Hotel, Newlyn, PENZANCE ☎(0736) 62076 11⇋↖

St Mary's

Isle of Scilly ☎(0720) 22692
Links course, glorious views.
9 holes, 2987yds, Par 36, SSS 69.
Club membership 300.

Visitors	no restrictions.
Green Fees	not confirmed.
Facilities	♀ △ ⱦ
Location	1m N of Hugh Town
Hotel	★★68% Tregarthens Hotel, Hugh Town, ST MARY'S ☎(0720) 22540 32rm(24⇋)Annexe1rm

Each golf-course entry has a recommended AA-appointed hotel. For a wider choice of places to stay, consult *AA Hotels and Restaurants in Britain and Ireland* and *AA Inspected Bed and Breakfast in Britain and Ireland*

St Mellion   Map 02 SX36

St Mellion International Golf & Country Club ☎Liskeard (0579) 50101
St Mellion is one of those fairly new, and delightful, resort courses which offers more than two 18 hole courses. Its Jack Nicklaus designed course has been featured on television - venue of the Benson and Hedges International Open.

SCORECARD: Nicklaus Course					
Hole	Yds	Par	Hole	Yds	Par
1	400	4	10	410	4
2	518	5	11	181	3
3	356	4	12	525	5
4	175	3	13	361	4
5	315	4	14	158	3
6	420	4	15	411	4
7	480	5	16	520	5
8	135	3	17	426	4
9	375	4	18	460	4
Out	3174	36	In	3452	36
			Totals	6626	72

Nicklaus Course: 18 holes, 6626yds, Par 72, SSS 72.
The Old Course: 18 holes, 5927yds, Par 70, SSS 68.
Club membership 4500.

Visitors	must have handicap certificate. Must contact in advance and have an introduction from own club.
Societies	must apply in writing.
Green Fees	not confirmed.
Facilities	⊗ ⅲ 🄻 ⬤ ♀ △ 🖾 ⱦ 🖛 Ʇ
Leisure	hard tennis courts, heated indoor swimming pool, squash, snooker, sauna, solarium, gymnasium, jacuzzi.
Location	.5m NW off A388
Hotel	★★★68% St Mellion Hotel, St Mellion Golf & County Club, ST MELLION ☎(0579) 50101 Annexe24⇋↖

TRURO
Map 02 SW84

Killiow Park ☎(0872) 70246
Picturesque parkland course with mature oaks and
woodland, and five holes played across or around water
hazards. Floodlit, all-weather driving range.
18 holes, 3542yds, Par 60.
Club membership 450.
Visitors   may not play until after 10.30am at weekends.
Must contact in advance.
Green Fees £8.50 per 18 holes; £5.50 per 9 holes (£10.50/
£6.50 weekends & bank holidays).
Facilities ⚑ ⚐ 🏌
Location   Killiow, Kea (3m SW of Truro, off A39)
Hotel   ★★★65% Brookdale Hotel, Tregolls Rd,
TRURO ☎(0872) 73513 & 79305 21⇨🐾

Truro ☎(0872) 72640
Undulating parkland course.
18 holes, 5347yds, Par 66, SSS 66, Course record 61.
Club membership 1000.
Visitors   must have handicap certificate. Must contact in
advance.
Societies   must apply in writing.
Green Fees £16 per day (£21 weekends & bank holidays).
Facilities ⊗ ⅲ by prior arrangement ⚑ ⚐ ♀ △ ⚐ 🏌
🏌 Nigel Bicknell.
Leisure   snooker.
Location   Treliske (1.5m W on A390)
Hotel   ★★★65% Brookdale Hotel, Tregolls Rd,
TRURO ☎(0872) 73513 & 79305 21⇨🐾

CUMBRIA

ALSTON
Map 12 NY74

Alston Moor ☎(0434) 381675
Parkland course with lush fairways and naturally interesting
greens.
9 holes, 5730yds, Par 66, SSS 66, Course record 67.
Club membership 180.
Visitors   no restrictions.
Societies   must contact in advance.
Green Fees £6 per day (£7.50 weekends).
Facilities ⊗ & ⅲ by prior arrangement ⚑ ⚐ ♀ △ 🏌
Location   The Hermitage (1.75m NE on B6277)
Hotel   ★63% Hillcrest Hotel, Townfoot, ALSTON
☎(0434) 381251 & 381444 9rm(3⇨)

APPLEBY-IN-WESTMORLAND
Map 12 NY62

Appleby ☎(07683) 51432
This remotely situated heather and moorland course offers
interesting golf with the rewarding bonus of several long
par-4 holes that will be remembered. There are superb
views.
18 holes, 5755yds, Par 68, SSS 68.
Club membership 760.
Visitors   restricted weekends and bank holidays.
Societies   must contact in advance by letter.
Green Fees £12-£16.
Facilities ⊗ & ⅲ by prior arrangement ⚑ ⚐ ♀ △
⚐
Leisure   snooker.
Location   Brackenber Moor (1m E of Appleby .5m off
A66)
Hotel   ★★★🔱70% Appleby Manor Country
House Hotel, Roman Rd, APPLEBY-IN-
WESTMORLAND ☎(07683) 51571
23⇨🐾 Annexe7⇨🐾

ASKAM-IN-FURNESS
Map 07 SD27

Dunnerholme ☎Dalton-in-Furness (0229) 62675
Unique 10-hole (18 tee) links course with view of Lakeland
hills, and a stream running through.
10 holes, 6181, Par 71, SSS 69.
Club membership 425.
Visitors   no restrictions.
Societies   must contact in advance.
Green Fees not confirmed.
Facilities ⚑ ⚐ ♀ △ ⚐
Location   Duddon Rd (1m N on A595)
Hotel   ★★62% Eccle Riggs Hotel, Foxfield Rd,
BROUGHTON IN FURNESS ☎(0229) 716398 &
716780 12⇨🐾

BARROW-IN-FURNESS
Map 07 SD17

Barrow ☎(0229) 825444
Pleasant course laid out on meadowland with extensive
views of the nearby Lakeland fells.
18 holes, 6209yds, Par 71, SSS 70, Course record 66.
Club membership 850.
Visitors   must be members of a recognised golf club.
Must contact in advance.
Societies   must contact in writing.
Green Fees £10 per round/day (£15 weekends).
Facilities ⊗ ⅲ by prior arrangement ⚑ ⚐ (catering
Wed-Sun only) ♀ △ ⚐ 🏌 🏌
Location   Rakesmoor Ln, Hawcoat (2m N off A590)
Hotel   ★★66% Lisdoonie Hotel, 307/309 Abbey Rd,
BARROW-IN-FURNESS ☎(0229) 27312 12⇨🐾

Furness ☎(0229) 41232
Links golf with a fairly flat first half but a much sterner
second nine played across subtle sloping ground. There are
good views of the Lakes, North Wales and the Isle of Man.
18 holes, 6363metres, Par 71, SSS 71, Course record 67.
Club membership 800.
Visitors   no restrictions.
Societies   must contact in writing.
Green Fees not confirmed.
Facilities ⊗ by prior arrangement ⅲ ⚑ ⚐ ♀ △ ⚐ 🏌
Leisure   snooker.
Location   Central Dr, Walney Island (1.75 E of town centre
off A590)
Hotel   ★★66% Lisdoonie Hotel, 307/309 Abbey Rd,
BARROW-IN-FURNESS ☎(0229) 27312 12⇨🐾

This guide is updated annually – make sure that
you use the up-to-date edition

BOWNESS-ON-WINDERMERE   Map 07 SD49

Windermere ☎Windermere (05394) 43123
Enjoyable holiday golf on a short, slightly hilly but sporting course in this delightful area of the Lake District National Park. Superb views of the mountains as the backcloth to the lake and the course.
18 holes, 5006yds, Par 67, SSS 65, Course record 58.
Club membership 943.

Visitors	must be a member of a recognised club with a handicap certificate. Must contact in advance.
Societies	must contact in writing.
Green Fees	£18 per day (£25 weekends & bank holidays).
Facilities	⊗ & ⫙ (ex Mon) ⏚ 🖢 ♀ △ 🏠 ⚲ (
Leisure	fishing, snooker.
Location	Cleabarrow (1m E on B5284)
Hotel	★★★70% Wild Boar Hotel, Crook, WINDERMERE ☎(05394) 45225 36⇔🐾 **See advertisement on page 65**

BRAMPTON   Map 12 NY56

Brampton ☎(06977) 2255
Challenging golf across glorious rolling fell country, demanding solid driving and many long second shots. A number of particularly fine holes, the pick of which may arguably be, the 3rd and 11th. The course offers unrivalled panoramic views from its hilly position.
18 holes, 6420yds, Par 72, SSS 71, Course record 67.
Club membership 750.

Visitors	some restrictions on Mon, Wed & Thu.
Societies	must contact in writing.
Green Fees	£14 per day (£18 weekends & bank holidays).
Facilities	⊗ ⫙ by prior arrangement ⏚ 🖢 ♀ △ 🏠 ⚲ (Stephen Harrisson.
Leisure	snooker.
Location	Talkin Tarn (1.5m SE of Brampton on B6413)
Hotel	★★69% Tarn End Hotel, Talkin Tarn, BRAMPTON ☎(06977) 2340 6⇔🐾

CARLISLE   Map 11 NY35

Carlisle ☎(0228) 513303
Majestic looking parkland course with great appeal. A complete but not too severe test of golf, with fine turf, natural hazards, a stream and many beautiful trees.
18 holes, 6080yds, Par 71, SSS 70, Course record 65.
Club membership 950.

Visitors	with member on Sat, restricted Tue afternoons and competition days. Must contact in advance and have an introduction from own club.
Societies	Mon, Wed & Fri.
Green Fees	£25 per day (Sun £30).
Facilities	⊗ ⫙ ⏚ 🖢 ♀ △ 🏠 ⚲ (John Smith More.
Leisure	snooker.
Location	Aglionby (On A69 1m E of M6 junc 43)
Hotel	★★★68% Cumbrian Hotel, Court Square, CARLISLE ☎(0228) 31951 70⇔🐾

For an explanation of symbols and abbreviations, see page 32

Stony Holme Municipal ☎(0228) 34856
Municipal parkland course, bounded on three sides by the River Eden.
18 holes, 5783yds, Par 69, SSS 68, Course record 68.
Club membership 350.

Visitors	must contact in advance.
Societies	must telephone in advance.
Green Fees	not confirmed.
Facilities	⊗ ⫙ ⏚ 🖢 ♀ △ 🏠 ⚲ (S Ling.
Location	St Aidans Rd (3m E off A69)
Hotel	★★★62% Forte Posthouse, Parkhouse Rd, Kingstown, CARLISLE ☎(0228) 31201 93⇔🐾

COCKERMOUTH   Map 11 NY13

Cockermouth ☎(07687) 76223
Fell-land course, fenced, with exceptional views and a hard climb on the 3rd and 11th holes. Testing holes: 10th and 16th (rearranged by James Braid).
18 holes, 5496yds, Par 69, SSS 67, Course record 65.
Club membership 586.

Visitors	restricted Wed, Sat & Sun.
Societies	must contact in advance.
Green Fees	£9 per day/round (£15 weekends & bank holidays).
Facilities	⏚ 🖢 ♀ △
Leisure	snooker.
Location	Embleton (3m E off A66)
Hotel	★★★63% The Trout Hotel, Crown St, COCKERMOUTH ☎(0900) 823591 23⇔🐾

GRANGE-OVER-SANDS   Map 07 SD47

Grange Fell ☎(05395) 32536
Hillside course with magnificent views over Morecambe
Bay and the surrounding Lakeland mountains.
9 holes, 4826mtrs, Par 70, SSS 67, Course record 68.
Club membership 300.
Visitors   may normally play Mon-Sat
Green Fees £10 per day (£15 weekends & bank holidays).
Facilities   ⬛ ♀ ⛳
Location   Fell Rd (1m W)
Hotel   ★★70% Netherwood Hotel, Lindale Rd,
                 GRANGE-OVER-SANDS ☎(05395) 32552
                 32rm(29⇨🏠)

Grange-over-Sands ☎(05395) 33180 or 33754
Parkland course with trees, ditches and easy walking.
18 holes, 5670yds, Par 69, SSS 68.
Club membership 525.
Visitors   may not play 8.30-9.30am & 11.45-1.15pm on
                 Sat & Sun.
Societies   must contact in writing.
Green Fees not confirmed.
Facilities   ⊗ ⛳ ⬛ ♀ ⛳ ⛳
Location   Meathop Rd (NW of town centre off B5277)
Hotel   ★★★65% Grange Hotel, Station Square,
                 GRANGE-OVER-SANDS ☎(05395) 33666
                 41⇨🏠

KENDAL   Map 07 SD59

Kendal ☎(0539) 724079
Elevated moorland course affording breathtaking views of
Lakeland fells and surrounding district.
18 holes, 5534yds, Par 66, SSS 67, Course record 60.
Club membership 700.
Visitors   must have a handicap certificate.
Societies   must contact in advance.
Green Fees £14 per day (£18 weekends & bank holidays).
Facilities   ⊗ ⛳ ⬛ (no catering Mon) ♀ ⛳ ⛳ ⛳ [D J
                 Turner.
Location   The Heights (W side of town centre)
Hotel   ★★★57% Woolpack Hotel, Stricklandgate,
                 KENDAL ☎(0539) 723852 54⇨🏠

KESWICK   Map 11 NY22

Keswick ☎Threlkeld (07687) 79324
Varied fell and tree-lined course with commanding views of
Lakeland scenery.
18 holes, 6175yds, Par 71, SSS 72, Course record 70.
Club membership 879.
Visitors   restricted on competition days. Must contact in
                 advance.
Societies   must contact in advance.
Green Fees £12 per day (£15 weekends & bank holidays).
Facilities   ⊗ ⛳ ⛳ ⬛ ♀ ⛳ ⛳
Leisure   fishing.
Location   Threlkeld Hall (4m E off A66)
Hotel   ★★★67% Borrowdale Hotel, BORROWDALE
                 ☎(07687) 77224 34⇨🏠

For a full range of AA guides and maps, visit
your local AA shop or any good bookshop

MARYPORT   Map 11 NY03

Maryport ☎(0900) 812605
A tight seaside links course exposed to Solway breezes. Fine
views across Solway Firth.
18 holes, 6272yds, Par 71, SSS 71, Course record 70.
Club membership 380.
Visitors   no restrictions.
Societies   must apply in writing.
Green Fees £10 per day/round.
Facilities   ⊗ ⛳ ⛳ & ⬛ by prior arrangement ♀ ⛳
Location   Bank End (1m N on B5300)
Hotel   ★★64% Ellenbank Hotel, Birkby, MARYPORT
                 ☎(0900) 815233 26⇨🏠

PENRITH   Map 12 NY53

Penrith ☎(0768) 62217
A beautiful and well-balanced course, always changing
direction, and demanding good length from the tee. It is
set on rolling moorland with occasional pine trees and
some fine views.
18 holes, 6026yds, Par 69, SSS 69, Course record 64.
Club membership 870.
Visitors   restricted at weekends. Must contact in
                 advance and have an introduction from own
                 club.
Societies   restricted at weekends.
Green Fees £15 per day (£20 weekends & bank holidays).
Facilities   ⊗ ⛳ & ⛳ by prior arrangement ⬛ ♀ ⛳
                 🏠 ⛳ [C B Thomson.
Leisure   snooker.
Location   Salkeld Rd (.75m N off A6)
Hotel   ★★64% George Hotel, Devonshire St,
                 PENRITH ☎(0768) 62696 31⇨🏠

ST BEES   Map 11 NX91

St Bees ☎(0946) 822695
Links course, down hill and dale, with sea views.
9 holes, 5082yds, Par 64, SSS 65.
Club membership 275.
Visitors   no restrictions.
Green Fees not confirmed.
Location   .5m W of village off B5345
Hotel   ★★★56% Blackbeck Bridge Inn, EGREMONT
                 ☎(094684) 661 22⇨🏠

SEASCALE   Map 06 NY00

Seascale ☎(09467) 28202
A tough links requiring length and control. The natural
terrain is used to give a variety of holes and considerable
character. Undulating greens add to the challenge. Fine
views over the Western Fells, the Irish Sea and Isle of
Man.
18 holes, 6419yds, Par 71, SSS 71, Course record 69.
Club membership 750.
Visitors   must contact in advance.
Societies   must contact in advance
Green Fees £18 per day (£22 weekends & bank holidays).

Facilities	⊗ (ex Mon-Tue) ℍ 📷 🍺 (all catering by prior arrangement) ♀ ⚘ 🏠 🛈
Location	The Banks (NW side of village off B5344)
Hotel	★★★56% Blackbeck Bridge Inn, EGREMONT ☎(094684) 661 22⇨🏕

SEDBERGH
Map 07 SD69

Sedbergh ☎(05396) 20993
New grassland course with superb scenery. Temporary greens during 1992.
9 holes, 2167yds, Par 70, SSS 61, Course record 64.
Club membership 300.

Visitors	must book to play on Sun. Must contact in advance.
Societies	must contact in advance.
Green Fees	£8 per day (£12 weekends & bank holidays).
Facilities	📷 ⚘
Location	Catholes, Abbot Holme (1m S off A683)
Hotel	★★69% Garden House Hotel, Fowl-ing Ln, KENDAL ☎(0539) 731131 10⇨🏕

SILECROFT
Map 06 SD18

Silecroft ☎Millom (0229) 774250
Seaside links course parallel to the coast of the Irish Sea. Often windy. Easy walking. Spectacular views inland of Lakeland hills.
9 holes, 5712yds, Par 68, SSS 68.
Club membership 365.

Visitors	restricted weekends.
Societies	must contact 14 days in advance.
Green Fees	£10 per day.
Facilities	⚘
Location	1m SW
Hotel	★★62% Eccle Riggs Hotel, Foxfield Rd, BROUGHTON IN FURNESS ☎(0229) 716398 & 716780 12⇨🏕

SILLOTH
Map 11 NY15

Silloth on Solway
☎(06973) 31304
Billowing dunes, narrow fairways, heather and gorse and the constant subtle problems of tactics and judgement make these superb links on the Solway an exhilarating and searching test. The 13th is a good long hole. Superb views.
18 holes, 6062yds, Par 72, SSS 71, Course record 64.
Club membership 600.

SCORECARD: Yellow Tees					
Hole	Yds	Par	Hole	Yds	Par
1	371	4	10	283	4
2	311	4	11	394	4
3	358	4	12	191	3
4	352	4	13	450	5
5	456	5	14	433	5
6	177	3	15	390	4
7	370	4	16	172	3
8	348	4	17	488	5
9	124	3	18	394	4
Out	2867	35	In	3195	37
			Totals	6062	72

Visitors	restricted Sat & Sun mornings. Must contact in advance and have an introduction from own club.
Societies	must contact in advance.
Green Fees	£18 (£23, one round only weekends & bank holidays).
Facilities	⊗ ℍ 📷 🍺 (no catering Mon) ♀ ⚘ 🏠 🛈 John Burns.
Leisure	snooker.

Location	S side of village off B5300
Hotel	★★66% Golf Hotel, Criffel St, SILLOTH ☎(06973) 31438 22⇨🏕

ULVERSTON
Map 07 SD27

Ulverston ☎(0229) 52824
Inland golf with many medium length holes on undulating parkland. The 17th is a testing par 4. Overlooking Morecambe Bay the course offers extensive views to the Lakeland Fells.
18 holes, 6142yds, Par 71, SSS 69, Course record 65.
Club membership 700.

Visitors	may not play on competition days. Must contact in advance and have an introduction from own club.
Societies	must apply in writing.
Green Fees	£16 per day (£20 weekends & bank holidays).
Facilities	⊗ ℍ 📷 🍺 (ex Mon) ♀ (ex Mon) ⚘ 🏠 🛈 M R Smith.
Location	Bardsea Park (2m S off A5087)
Hotel	★★62% Sefton House Hotel, Queen St, ULVERSTON ☎(0229) 52190 14rm(4⇨6🏕)

WINDERMERE
See **Bowness-on-Windermere**

A golf-course name printed in ***bold italics*** means that we have been unable to verify information with the club's management for the current year

WORKINGTON   Map 11 NX92

Workington ☎(0900) 603460
Meadowland course, undulating, with natural hazards
created by stream and trees. Good views of Solway Firth and
Lakeland Hills.
18 holes, 6200yds, Par 72, Course record 65.
Club membership 900.

Visitors	must have a handicap certificate. Must have an introduction from own club.
Societies	must contact in advance.
Green Fees	£15 per round/day (£20 weekends & bank holidays).
Facilities	⊗ ⫫ & ↳ (ex Mon) ■ ♀ ⌣ 🏠 ⚑ ʲ A Drabble.
Leisure	snooker.
Location	Branthwaite Rd (1.75m off A596)
Hotel	★★★68% Washington Central Hotel, Washington St, WORKINGTON ☎(0900) 65772 40⇔🕯

DERBYSHIRE

ALFRETON   Map 08 SK45

Alfreton ☎(O773) 832070
A small parkland course with tight fairways and many
natural hazards.
9 holes, 5074yds, Par 66, Course record 62.
Club membership 340.

Visitors	with member only Mon & weekends.
Societies	apply in writing.
Green Fees	£12 per day; £10 per round (18 holes).
Facilities	⊗ ⫫ ↳ & ■ by prior arrangement ♀ ⌣ 🏠
Location	Wingfield Rd, Oakerthorpe (1m W on A615)
Hotel	★★★69% Swallow Hotel, Carter Ln East, SOUTH NORMANTON ☎(0773) 812000 161⇔🕯

ASHBOURNE   Map 07 SK14

Ashbourne ☎(0335) 42078
Undulating parkland course.
9 holes, 5359yds, Par 66, SSS 66, Course record 61.
Club membership 350.

Visitors	may not play on competition days. With member only at weekends.
Societies	telephone in advance.
Green Fees	£10 for 18 holes.
Facilities	⌣
Leisure	snooker.
Location	Clifton (1.5m SW on A515)
Hotel	★★53% Meynell Arms Hotel, Ashbourne Rd, KIRK LANGLEY ☎(033124) 515 10rm(5⇔2🕯)

BAKEWELL   Map 08 SK26

Bakewell ☎(062981) 2307
Parkland course, hilly, with plenty of natural hazards to test
the golfer. Magnificent views across the Wye Valley.
9 holes, 5240yds, Par 68, SSS 66.
Club membership 400.

Visitors	no restrictions.
Societies	must contact in advance.
Facilities	♀ ⌣ 🏠 ʲ
Location	Station Rd (E side of town off A6)
Hotel	★★66% Milford House Hotel, Mill St, BAKEWELL ☎(0629) 812130 12⇔🕯

BAMFORD   Map 08 SK28

Sickleholme ☎Hope Valley (0443) 51306
Downland type course in the lovely Peak District. Fine
views.
18 holes, 6064yds, Par 69, SSS 69.
Club membership 600.

Visitors	restricted Wed mornings. Must contact in advance.
Societies	must contact in advance.
Green Fees	not confirmed.
Facilities	⊗ ⫫ ↳ ■ (all catering by prior arrangement) ♀ ⌣ 🏠 ʲ P H Taylor.
Location	Saltergate Ln (.75m S on A6013)
Hotel	★★★65% George Hotel, Main Rd, HATHERSAGE ☎(0433) 50436 18⇔🕯

BUXTON   Map 07 SK07

Buxton & High Peak ☎(0298) 23453
Bracing, well-drained meadowland course; the highest in
Derbyshire.
18 holes, 5980yds, Par 69, SSS 69, Course record 63.
Club membership 800.

Visitors	must contact in advance.
Societies	apply in writing to Mrs S Arnfield.
Green Fees	£16 (£20 weekends & bank holidays).
Facilities	⊗ ↳ ■ ♀ ⌣ 🏠 ʲ Andrew Hoyles.
Location	Town End (1m NE off A6)
Hotel	★★★60% Palace Hotel, Palace Rd, BUXTON ☎(0298) 22001 122⇔

Cavendish ☎(0298) 23494
This parkland/moorland
course with its comfortable
clubhouse nestles below the
rising hills. Generally open to
the prevailing west wind, it is
noted for its excellent surfaced
greens which contain many
deceptive subtleties. De-
signed by Dr Alastair Mackenzie, good holes include the
8th, 9th and 18th.
*18 holes, 5833yds, Par 68, SSS
68, Course record 65.*
Club membership 600.

SCORECARD: White Tees					
Hole	Yds	Par	Hole	Yds	Par
1	365	4	10	443	4
2	321	4	11	411	4
3	284	4	12	357	4
4	123	3	13	184	3
5	428	4	14	509	5
6	410	4	15	127	3
7	314	4	16	408	4
8	388	4	17	168	3
9	143	3	18	450	4
Out	2776	34	In	3057	34
			Totals	5833	68

Visitors	must contact in advance.
Societies	must contact in advance.
Green Fees	£20 per day (£30 per day weekends & bank holidays).
Facilities	⊗ & ⫫ by prior arrangement ↳ ■ ♀ ⌣ 🏠 ʲ ʲ John Nolan.
Leisure	snooker.
Location	Gadley Ln (.75m W of town centre off A53)
Hotel	★★★68% Lee Wood Hotel, 13 Manchester Rd, BUXTON ☎(0298) 23002 & 70421 36⇔🕯

CHAPEL-EN-LE-FRITH   Map 07 SK 08

Chapel-en-le-Frith ☎(0298) 812118
Scenic parkland course, with testing holes at the 15th (par 4) and 17th (517 yds), par 5. Good views.
18 holes, 6089yds, Par 70, SSS 69.
Club membership 685.

Visitors	must contact in advance.
Societies	apply in writing.
Green Fees	£15 per day (£25 weekends & bank holidays).
Facilities	⊗ ⅧⅢ by prior arrangement 🛍 🍺 ♀ 🛆 🛗 ♈ ⚑ D J Cullen.
Location	The Cockyard, Manchester Rd (1m W on A6)
Hotel	★★★68% Lee Wood Hotel, 13 Manchester Rd, BUXTON ☎(0298) 23002 & 70421 36⇨🌴

CHESTERFIELD   Map 08 SK 37

Chesterfield ☎(0246) 279256
A varied and interesting, undulating parkland course with trees picturesquely adding to the holes and the outlook alike. Stream hazard on back nine. Views over four counties.
18 holes, 6326yds, Par 71, SSS 70.
Club membership 500.

Visitors	may not play at weekends. A handicap certificate is required. Must contact in advance.
Societies	apply in writing.
Green Fees	not confirmed.
Facilities	⊗ ⅧⅢ 🛍 🍺 ♀ 🛆 🛗 ♈ M McLean.
Location	Walton (2m SW off A632)
Hotel	★★★64% Chesterfield Hotel, Malkin St, CHESTERFIELD ☎(0246) 271141 72⇨🌴

Stanedge ☎(0246) 566156
Moorland course in hilly situation open to strong winds. Some fairways are narrow. Accuracy is paramount.
9 holes, 4867yds, Par 64, SSS 64, Course record 64.
Club membership 300.

Visitors	with member only Sat & Sun, and may not play after 1400 weekdays.
Societies	apply in writing.
Green Fees	£10 weekdays before 1400.
Facilities	🍺 ♀ 🛆
Leisure	pool table.
Location	Walton Hay Farm, Walton (5m SW off B5057)
Hotel	★★★64% Chesterfield Hotel, Malkin St, CHESTERFIELD ☎(0246) 271141 72⇨🌴

Tapton Park ☎(0246) 239500
Municipal parkland course with some fairly hard walking. The 620 yd (par 5) 5th is a testing hole.
Tapton Main: 18 holes, 6013yds, Par 71, SSS 69, Course record 65.
Club membership 750.

Visitors	no caddies allowed. Must contact in advance.
Societies	telephone in advance.
Green Fees	Tapton Main £4.30 (£5.50 weekends). Dobbin Clough £2.20 (£3 weekends).
Facilities	⊗ ⅧⅢ 🛍 🍺 ♀ 🛆 🛗 ♈ ⚑ John Delaney.
Location	Murray House, Tapton (.5m E of Chesterfield Station)
Hotel	★★★64% Chesterfield Hotel, Malkin St, CHESTERFIELD ☎(0246) 271141 72⇨🌴

CODNOR   Map 08 SK 44

Ormonde Fields ☎Ripley (0773) 742987
Parkland course with undulating fairways and natural hazards. The par 4 (4th) and the par 3 (11th) are notable. There is a practice area.
18 holes, 6011yds, Par 69, SSS 69, Course record 70.
Club membership 500.

Visitors	restricted at weekends. Must contact in advance.
Societies	telephone in advance.
Green Fees	not confirmed.
Facilities	⊗ ⅧⅢ 🛍 🍺 ♀ 🛆 🛗 ♈
Location	Nottingham Rd (1m SE on A610)
Hotel	★★★58% Forte Posthouse Nottingham/ Derby, Bostocks Ln, SANDIACRE ☎(0602) 397800 97⇨🌴

DERBY   Map 08 SK 33

Allestree Park ☎(0332) 550616
Municipal parkland course in rather hilly country.
18 holes, 5749yds, Par 68, SSS 68, Course record 66.
Club membership 275.

Visitors	restricted weekends & bank holidays.
Societies	restricted at weekends & bank holidays.
Green Fees	£6.50 per round.
Facilities	⊗ & ⅧⅢ by prior arrangement 🛍 🍺 ♀ 🛆 🛗 ♈ ⚑ Colin Henderson.
Leisure	fishing.
Location	Allestree Hall (3m N on A6)

▶

This magnificent Victorian building, in the midst of the Peak District, overlooks the old spa town of Buxton. The hotel rooms have private facilities, hairdryers, trouser press and tea and coffee making equipment. Two completely different golf courses are within easy reach of the hotel. The Palace has an indoor swimming pool, gymnasia, sauna and sunbeds.

The Palace Hotel

PALACE ROAD, BUXTON, DERBYSHIRE SK17 6AG
TELEPHONE 0298 22001   FAX 0298 72131

Hotel ★★69% Kedleston Country House Hotel, Kedleston Rd, DERBY ☎(0332) 559202 & 556507 14⇔♠

Derby ☎(0332) 766323
Municipal parkland course. The front nine holes are rather difficult.
18 holes, 5618yds, Par 70, SSS 69, Course record 64.
Club membership 450.
Visitors	starting time must be booked at weekends. Must contact in advance.
Societies	apply in writing in advance.
Green Fees	not confirmed.
Facilities	⊗ ⦂ 🏌 ⦂ ♀ △ 🛋 ♈ ⦗ C T C Henderson.
Location	Shakespeare St, Sinfin (3.5m S of city centre)
Hotel	★★★59% International Hotel, Burton Rd (A5250), DERBY ☎(0332) 369321 41⇔Annexe21⇔

Mickleover ☎(0332) 518662
Undulating parkland course in pleasant setting.
18 holes, 5708yds, Par 68, SSS 68.
Club membership 650.
Visitors	must contact in advance.
Societies	telephone in advance.
Green Fees	£15 per day/round (£20 weekends).
Facilities	⊗ ⦂ 🏌 ⦂ ♀ △ 🛋 ⦗ Paul Wilson.
Location	Uttoxeter Rd, Mickleover (3m W off A516/B5020)
Hotel	★★★68% Forte Posthouse, Pasture Hill, Littleover, DERBY ☎(0332) 514933 62⇔

DRONFIELD Map 08 SK 37

Hallowes ☎(0246) 413734
Attractive moorland/meadowland course set in the Derbyshire hills. Several testing par 4's and splendid views.
18 holes, 6330yds, Par 71, SSS 70, Course record 66.
Club membership 600.
Visitors	may only play with member at weekends; restricted Wed. Must contact in advance and have an introduction from own club.
Societies	must contact in advance.
Green Fees	£22 per day; £18 per round.
Facilities	⊗ ⦂ by prior arrangement 🏌 ⦂ ♀ △ 🛋 ♈ ⦗ Martin Heggie.
Leisure	snooker.
Location	Hallowes Ln (S side of town)
Hotel	★★53% Manor Hotel, 10 High St, DRONFIELD ☎(0246) 413971 10⇔♠

DUFFIELD Map 08 SK 34

Chevin ☎(0332) 841864
A mixture of parkland and moorland, this course is rather hilly which makes for some hard walking. The 8th calls for a very hard drive, possibly the hardest in the area.
18 holes, 6057yds, Par 69, SSS 69, Course record 64.
Club membership 500.
Visitors	with member only weekends & bank holidays. Must have an introduction from own club.
Societies	contact in advance.
Green Fees	£22 per day.
Facilities	⊗ ⦂ 🏌 ⦂ ♀ △ 🛋 ♈ ⦗ Willie Bird.
Leisure	snooker.

Location Golf Ln (N side of town off A6)
Hotel ★★69% Kedleston Country House Hotel, Kedleston Rd, DERBY ☎(0332) 559202 & 556507 14⇔♠

GLOSSOP Map 07 SK 09

Glossop and District ☎(04574) 3117
Moorland course in good position, excellent natural hazards.
11 holes, 5723yds, Par 68, SSS 68.
Club membership 250.
Visitors	may not play on bank holidays.
Green Fees	not confirmed.
Facilities	♀ (ex Thu in winter) △ 🛋
Location	Hurst Ln, off Sheffield Rd (1m E off A57)
Hotel	★★70% York House Hotel, York Place, Richmond St, ASHTON-UNDER-LYNE ☎061-330 5899 24⇔♠Annexe10⇔

HORSLEY Map 08 SK 34

Horsley Lodge ☎Derby (0332) 780838
New course, opened in 1991, and set in 100 acres of Derbyshire countryside with some challenging holes. Also Par 3 course and floodlit driving range.
18 holes, 6434yds, Par 72, SSS 71, Course record 74.
Club membership 500.
Visitors	restricted during competitions.
Societies	must telephone in advance.
Green Fees	£20 per day; £15 per round (£10 per 9 holes).
Facilities	⊗ ⦂ (Thu-Sat) 🏌 (Tue & Wed evening) ⦂ ♀ △ 🛋 ⋈ ⦗
Leisure	fishing.
Location	Smalley Mill Rd (off A608 Derby-Heanor Rd)
Hotel	★★★72% Breadsall Priory Hotel, Golf & Country Club, Moor Rd, MORLEY ☎(0332) 832235 14⇔♠Annexe77⇔♠

KEDLESTON Map 08 SK 34

Kedleston Park ☎Derby (0332) 840035
The course is laid out in flat, mature parkland with fine trees and background views of historic Kedleston Hall (National Trust). Many testing holes are included in each nine and there is an excellent modern clubhouse.
18 holes, 6253yds, Par 70, SSS 70.
Club membership 978.

SCORECARD					
Hole	Yds	Par	Hole	Yds	Par
1	482	5	10	351	4
2	413	4	11	182	3
3	410	4	12	412	4
4	162	3	13	370	4
5	550	5	14	333	4
6	503	5	15	407	4
7	161	3	16	183	3
8	321	4	17	514	5
9	405	4	18	426	4
Out	3407	37	In	3178	35
			Totals	6585	72

Visitors	welcome weekdays. Must contact in advance and have an introduction from own club.
Societies	telephone in advance.
Green Fees	£25 per round.
Facilities	⊗ ⦂ 🏌 ⦂ ♀ △ 🛋 ♈ ⦗ Jim Hetherington.
Leisure	snooker, sauna.
Location	Kedleston Quarndon (2m SE)
Hotel	★★69% Kedleston Country House Hotel, Kedleston Rd, DERBY ☎(0332) 559202 & 556507 14⇔♠

MATLOCK   Map 08 SK 36

Matlock ☎(0629) 582191
Moorland course with fine views of the beautiful Peak
District.
18 holes, 5800yds, Par 70, SSS 68.
Club membership 650.
Visitors	with member only weekends & bank holidays.
Societies	telephone in advance.
Green Fees	£22 per day/round.
Facilities	⊗ & ⅢⅠ by prior arrangement ⅃ ■ ♀ △ 🖃 ⅂ (Mike Deeley.
Leisure	snooker.
Location	Chesterfield Rd (1m NE of Matlock on A632)
Hotel	★★★69% New Bath Hotel, New Bath Rd, MATLOCK ☎(0629) 583275 55⇨

MICKLEOVER   Map 08 SK 33

Pastures ☎Derby (0332) 513921 (ext 348)
Small course laid-out on undulating meadowland in the
grounds of a psychiatric hospital, with good views across the
Trent valley.
9 holes, 5005yds, Par 64, SSS 64, Course record 62.
Club membership 320.
Visitors	may not play on Sun. Must be accompanied by member and contact in advance.
Societies	must contact in advance.
Green Fees	£8 per day.
Facilities	⅃ & ■ (evenings & weekends) ♀ (evenings & Sat/Sun) △
Leisure	fishing, snooker, badminton, bowls, table tennis.
Location	Pastures Hospital (1m SW off A516)
Hotel	★★★51% St Vincent Rocks Hotel, Sion Hill, Clifton, BRISTOL ☎(0272) 739251 46⇨🕏

MORLEY   Map 08 SK 34

Breadsall Priory ☎Derby (0332) 832235
Set in 200 acres of mature parkland, the Old Course is built
on the site of a 13th-century priory. The new Moorland
Course, due to open in Spring 1992, will offer a complete
contrast, and the hotel provides a host of sports and leisure
facilities.
Old Course: 18 holes, 5844yds, Par 72, SSS 70, Course record 66.
Moorland (Due to opens Spring 1992): 18 holes, 6011yds.
Club membership 800.
Visitors	must contact in advance.
Societies	must contact in advance.
Green Fees	£35 per day; £25 per round (£28 per round weekends).
Facilities	⊗ ⅢⅠ ⅃ ■ ♀ △ 🖃 ⅂ ↤ (Andrew Smith.
Leisure	hard tennis courts, heated indoor swimming pool, squash, snooker, sauna, solarium, gymnasium, health & beauty salon.
Location	Moor Rd (.75m W)
Hotel	★★★72% Breadsall Priory Hotel, Golf & Country Club, Moor Rd, MORLEY ☎(0332) 832235 14⇨🕏Annexe77⇨🕏

If you know of a golf course which welcomes
visitors and is not already in this guide,
we should be grateful for information

NEW MILLS   Map 07 SK 08

New Mills ☎(0663) 743485
Moorland course with panoramic views and first-class
greens.
9 holes, 5633yds, Par 68, SSS 67, Course record 67.
Club membership 350.
Visitors	must play with member at weekends & special days. Must contact in advance.
Societies	must contact in advance.
Green Fees	not confirmed.
Facilities	⊗ & ⅢⅠ by prior arrangement ⅃ ■ ♀ △ 🖃 ⅂ (Andrew Hoyles.
Location	Shaw Marsh (.5m N off B6101)
Hotel	★★★56% Alma Lodge Hotel, 149 Buxton Rd, STOCKPORT ☎061-483 4431 56rm(52⇨)

RENISHAW   Map 08 SK 47

Renishaw Park ☎Eckington (0246) 432044
Part parkland and part meadowland with easy walking.
18 holes, 5949yds, Par 71, SSS 68.
Club membership 500.
Visitors	no restrictions.
Societies	apply in writing.
Green Fees	not confirmed.
Facilities	⊗ ⅢⅠ by prior arrangement ⅃ ■ ♀ △ 🖃 ⅂ (Simon Elliot.
Leisure	snooker.
Location	Golf House (.5m NW on A616)
Hotel	★★★61% Sitwell Arms Osprey Hotel, RENISHAW ☎(0246) 435226 30⇨🕏

SHIRLAND   Map 08 SK 35

Shirlands Golf & Squash Club ☎(0773) 834935
Rolling parkland and tree-lined course with extensive views
of Derbyshire countryside.
18 holes, 6072yds, Par 71, SSS 69, Course record 68.
Club membership 700.
Visitors	weekends by appointment. Must contact in advance.
Societies	contact Professional
Green Fees	£18 per day; £12 per round (£20 per round weekends).
Facilities	■ (catering by prior arrangement) △ 🖃 ⅂ (N B Hallam.
Leisure	pool table.
Location	Lower Delves (S side of village off A61)
Hotel	★★★69% Swallow Hotel, Carter Ln East, SOUTH NORMANTON ☎(0773) 812000 161⇨🕏

STANTON-BY-DALE   Map 08 SK 43

Erewash Valley ☎Sandiacre (0602) 323258
Parkland/meadowland course overlooking valley and M1.
Unique 4th and 5th in Victorian quarry bottom: 5th-testing
par 3.
18 holes, 6487yds, Par 72, SSS 71.
Club membership 860.
Visitors	may not play before 1200 weekends & bank holidays. Must contact in advance.
Societies	contact in writing.

▶

Green Fees £25 per day; £20 per round (£25 per round weekends & bank holidays..
Facilities ⊗ ⁓ by prior arrangement ≞ ⬤ ⌇ ⏚ 🏠 ⑂ ⑁ M J Ronan.
Leisure snooker, bowling green.
Location 1m W
Hotel ★★★58% Forte Posthouse Nottingham/ Derby, Bostocks Ln, SANDIACRE ☎(0602) 397800 97⇪🐾

DEVON

AXMOUTH   Map 03 SY29

Axe Cliff ☎Seaton (0297) 24371
Undulating links course with coastal views.
18 holes, 5057yds, Par 67, SSS 65.
Club membership 400.
Visitors may only play after 1pm on Sun. Must contact in advance.
Societies must contact in advance.
Green Fees not confirmed.
Facilities ⊗ ⁓ ≞ ⬤ ⌇ 🏠
Location .75m S on B3172
Hotel ★★61% Anchor Inn, BEER ☎(0297) 20386 9rm(2⇪2🐾)

BIGBURY-ON-SEA   Map 03 SX64

Bigbury ☎(0548) 810557
Heathland course with easy walking. Exposed to winds, but with fine views over the sea and River Avon.
18 holes, 5902yds, Par 69, SSS 68, Course record 67.
Club membership 850.
Visitors must have handicap certificate. Must contact in advance.
Societies must apply in writing.
Green Fees £20 per day.
Facilities ⊗ ⁓ by prior arrangement ≞ ⬤ ⌇ ⏚ 🏠 ⑂ ⑁ Simon Lloyd.
Location Kingsbridge (1m S on B3392)
Hotel ★69% Henley Hotel, BIGBURY-ON-SEA ☎(0548) 810240 8⇪🐾

BUDLEIGH SALTERTON   Map 03 SY08

East Devon ☎(03954) 3370
An interesting course with downland turf, much heather and gorse, and superb views over the bay. The early holes climb to the cliff edge. The downhill 17th, has a heather section in the fairway leaving a good second to the green.
18 holes, 6214yds, Par 70, SSS 70 or 18 holes, 5897yds, Par 70, SSS 68.
Club membership 850.
Visitors must contact in advance and have an introduction from own club.
Societies must contact in advance.

SCORECARD: White Tees					
Hole	Yds	Par	Hole	Yds	Par
1	343	4	10	155	3
2	341	4	11	337	4
3	414	4	12	483	5
4	151	3	13	143	3
5	361	4	14	404	4
6	524	5	15	301	4
7	392	4	16	402	4
8	206	3	17	453	4
9	464	4	18	340	4
Out	3196	35	In	3018	35
			Totals	6214	70

Green Fees £26 per day; £21 per round (£30 per day; £26 per round).
Facilities ⊗ ≞ ⬤ ⌇ ⏚ 🏠 ⑂ ⑁ Trevor Underwood.
Location North View Rd (W side of town centre off A376)
Hotel ★★★61% The Imperial, The Esplanade, EXMOUTH ☎(0395) 274761 57⇪🐾

CHITTLEHAMHOLT   Map 02 E5

Highbullen Hotel ☎(0769) 540561
Mature parkland course with water hazards and outstanding scenic views to Exmoor and Dartmoor. Excellent facilities offered by the hotel.
9 holes, 2210yds, Par 31, SSS 29.
Green Fees £8 per round.
Facilities ⊗ ⁓ ≞ ⬤ ⌇ ⏚ 🏠 ⑂ 🛶 ⑁ Paul Weston.
Leisure hard tennis courts, outdoor and indoor heated swimming pools, squash, snooker, sauna, solarium, gymnasium, indoor putting, steam room.
Hotel ★★★⚑74% Highbullen Hotel, CHITTLEHAMHOLT ☎(0769) 540561 12⇪Annexe23⇪

CHULMLEIGH   Map 03 SS61

Chulmleigh ☎(0769) 80519
Challenging par 3 courses on undulating meadowland.
18 holes, 1485yds, Par 54, SSS 54, Course record 52.
Club membership 150.
Societies must contact in advance.
Green Fees £4.50 per round.
Facilities ≞ ⬤ ⌇ ⏚ 🏠 ⑂ 🛶 ⑁ Michael Blackwell.
Leisure hard tennis courts.
Location Leigh Rd (SW side of village)
Hotel ★★⚑73% Marsh Hall Hotel, SOUTH MOLTON ☎(07695) 2666 7⇪🐾

CHURSTON FERRERS   Map 03 SX95

Churston ☎Churston (0803) 842751
A cliff-top downland course with splendid views over Brixham harbour and Tor Bay. There is some gorse in the wooded area inland. A variety of shot is called for, with particularly testing holes at the 3rd, 9th and 15th, all par 4.
18 holes, 6219yds, Par 70, SSS 70, Course record 64.
Club membership 700.
Visitors must be members of recognised golf club & have handicap certificate, play is restricted at times. Must contact in advance.
Societies must contact in advance.
Green Fees £20 per day/round (£25 weekends).

SCORECARD: White Tees					
Hole	Yds	Par	Hole	Yds	Par
1	242	3	10	296	4
2	378	4	11	354	4
3	437	4	12	412	4
4	173	3	13	296	4
5	558	5	14	519	5
6	473	4	15	345	4
7	341	4	16	326	4
8	168	3	17	175	3
9	387	4	18	339	4
Out	3157	34	In	3062	36
			Totals	6219	70

Facilities	⊗ 〣 ⤵ 🏌 ♀ 🛆 🏠 ⟨ Dick Penfold.
Location	NW side of village on A379
Hotel	★★62% Dainton Hotel, 95 Dartmouth Rd, Three Beaches, Goodrington, PAIGNTON ☎(0803) 550067 & 525901 11⇌🐾

CREDITON   Map 03 SS80

Downes Crediton ☎(03632) 3991 & 3025
Converted farmhouse course with lovely views. Parkland with hilly back nine.
18 holes, 5868yds, Par 69, SSS 68.
Club membership 700.

Visitors	restricted at weekends. Must contact in advance.
Societies	must contact in advance.
Green Fees	not confirmed.
Facilities	⊗ 〣 ⤵ 🏌 ♀ 🛆 🏠 ⟨ H Finch.
Location	Hookway (1.5m SE off A377)
Hotel	★★★68% Barton Cross Hotel & Restaurant, Huxham, STOKE CANON ☎(0392) 841245 & 841584 6⇌🐾

DAWLISH WARREN   Map 03 SX97

Warren ☎(0626) 862255
Typical flat, genuine links course lying on spit between sea and Exe estuary. Picturesque scenery, a few trees but much gorse. Testing in windy conditions. The 7th hole provides the opportunity to go for the green across a bay on the estuary.
18 holes, 5973yds, Par 69, SSS 69, Course record 65.
Club membership 700.

Visitors	must have handicap certificate. Must contact in advance.
Societies	telephone in advance.
Green Fees	£17 per day (£20 weekends & bank holidays).
Facilities	⊗ 〣 ⤵ 🏌 ♀ 🛆 🏠 ⟨ Geoff Wicks.
Location	W side of village
Hotel	★★★58% Langstone Cliff Hotel, Dawlish Warren, DAWLISH ☎(0626) 865155 64⇌🐾

EXETER   Map 03 SX99

Exeter ☎Topsham (039287) 4139
A sheltered parkland course with some very old trees, and known as the flattest course in Devon. 15th & 17th are testing par 4 holes.
18 holes, 6009yds, Par 69, SSS 69, Course record 64.
Club membership 850.

Visitors	must contact in advance and have an introduction from own club.
Societies	welcome Thu only, must telephone in advance.
Green Fees	£20 per day.
Facilities	⊗ 〣 (Fri & Sat evenings only) ⤵ 🏌 ♀ 🛆 🏠 ⟨
Leisure	hard tennis courts, outdoor and indoor heated swimming pools, squash, snooker, sauna, solarium, gymnasium, gym.
Location	Topsham Rd, Countess Wear (SE side of city centre off A379)
Hotel	★★★61% Countess Wear Lodge Hotel, Topsham Rd, Exeter Bypass, EXETER ☎(0392) 875441 44⇌🐾

HIGH BICKINGTON   Map 02 SS52

Libbaton ☎(0769) 60269
Parkland course on undulating land with no steep slopes. Floodlit driving range.
18 holes, 5812yds, Par 72, SSS 68.
Club membership 400.

Visitors	may not play during competitions, advisable to phone in advance.
Societies	must contact in advance.
Green Fees	£15 per day; £12 per round (£18/£15 bank holidays & weekends).
Facilities	⊗ 〣 ⤵ 🏌 ♀ 🛆 🏠 ⟨ John Phillips.
Hotel	★★★🏌74% Highbullen Hotel, CHITTLEHAMHOLT ☎(0769) 540561 12⇌Annexe23⇌

HOLSWORTHY   Map 02 SS30

Holsworthy ☎(0409) 253177
Pleasant parkland course.
18 holes, 6012yds, Par 70, SSS 69, Course record 66.
Club membership 530.

Visitors	may not play at weekends & on competition days.
Societies	must contact in writing.
Green Fees	not confirmed.
Facilities	⊗ 〣 ⤵ 🏌 ♀ 🛆 🏠 ⟨ Tim McSherry.
Location	Killatree (1.5m W on A3072)
Hotel	★★🏌70% Court Barn Country House Hotel, CLAWTON ☎(040927) 219 8rm(4⇌3🐾)

HONITON   Map 03 ST10

Honiton ☎(0404) 44422
Level parkland course on a plateau 850ft above sea level. Easy walking and good views. The 4th hole is a testing par 3. The club was founded in 1896.
18 holes, 5931yds, Par 68, SSS 68.
Club membership 800.

Visitors	must have handicap certificate. Must contact in advance and have an introduction from own club.
Societies	must contact in writing.
Green Fees	£16 per day (£20 weekends & bank holidays).
Facilities	⊗ 〣 & ⤵ (Mon-Sat during summer months only) 🏌 ♀ 🛆 🏠 ⟨ Adrian Cave.
Location	Middlehills (1.25m SE)
Hotel	★★66% Home Farm Hotel, Wilmington, HONITON ☎(040483) 278 7rm(3⇌)Annexe6⇌🐾

ILFRACOMBE   Map 02 SS54

Ilfracombe ☎(0271) 862176
A sporting, clifftop, heathland course with views over the Bristol Channel and moors from every tee and green.
18 holes, 5893yds, Par 70, SSS 68, Course record 66.
Club membership 636.

Visitors	must have handicap certificate, play is restricted at times.

▶

Societies	must contact in advance.
Green Fees	£16 per day (£18 weekends & bank holidays).
Facilities	⊗ ⊪ ⊪ ⚑ ♀ ⚲ 📷 ☂ 𝄢 David Hoare.
Leisure	pool T.V.
Location	Hele Bay (1.5m E off A399)
Hotel	★★67% Elmfield Hotel, Torrs Park, ILFRACOMBE ☎(0271) 863377 12rm(11🔥)

IVYBRIDGE   Map 02 SX65

Dinnaton Sporting & Country Club
☎Plymouth (0752) 892512
Currently a 9-hole, Par 3 course, but being extended to
provide four par 4 holes (late 1991). Floodlit driving range.
9 holes, 2552yds, Par 56, SSS 48, Course record 58.
Club membership 200.

Visitors	a handicap certificate is appreciated.
Societies	must telephone in advance.
Green Fees	£12.50 per day.
Facilities	⊗ ⊪ (Thu, Fri & Sat) ⚑ 🛒 ♀ ⚲ 📷 ☂ ⋈ 𝄢 Tom Elsey.
Leisure	heated indoor swimming pool, squash, snooker, sauna, solarium, gymnasium, badminton courts, volleyball courts..
Location	Blachford Rd
Hotel	★★♨74% Glazebrook House Hotel & Restaurant, SOUTH BRENT ☎(0364) 73322 11⇔🔥

MORETONHAMPSTEAD   Map 03 SX78

Manor House Hotel ☎(0647) 40355
This enjoyable parkland course is a sporting circuit with
just enough hazards (most of them natural) to make any
golfer think. The Rivers Bowden and Bovey meander
through the first eight holes. Driving range.
18 holes, 6016yds, Par 69, SSS 69, Course record 65.
Club membership 230.

Visitors	must pre-arrange starting times. Must contact in advance.
Societies	must contact in advance.
Green Fees	£25.50 per day (£31 weekends); £20.50 per round (£25.50 weekends).
Facilities	⊗ ⊪ ⚑ & 🛒 by prior arrangement ♀ ⚲ 📷 ☂ ⋈ 𝄢 Richard Lewis.
Leisure	hard tennis courts, squash, fishing, snooker, 3 hole pitch & putt.
Location	3m W off B3212
Hotel	★★★♨75% The Bel Alp House, HAYTOR ☎(0364) 661217 9⇔🔥

MORTEHOE   Map 02 SS44

Easewell Farm Holiday Park ☎Woolacombe (0271) 870225
New 9-hole course with good grass and providing a
challenge.
9 holes, 2148mtr, Par 33, Course record 31.
Club membership 200.

Visitors	no restrictions.
Societies	must telephone in advance.
Green Fees	£10 per day; £9 per 18 holes; £6 per 9 holes.
Facilities	⚑ 🛒 ♀ ⚲ 📷 ☂

Leisure	heated indoor swimming pool, camping & caravan site.
Hotel	★★★73% Watersmeet Hotel, Mortehoe, WOOLACOMBE ☎(0271) 870333 25rm(23⇔🔥)

NEWTON ABBOT   Map 03 SX87

Newton Abbot (Stover) ☎(0626) 52460
Wooded parkland course with a stream coming into play on
eight holes. Fairly flat.
18 holes, 5886yds, Par 69, SSS 68, Course record 63.
Club membership 877.

Visitors	must have proof of membership of recognised club. Must contact in advance and have an introduction from own club.
Societies	by arrangement on Thu only.
Green Fees	£21 per day.
Facilities	⊗ ⊪ by prior arrangement ⚑ 🛒 ♀ ⚲ 📷 𝄢 Malcolm Craig.
Location	Bovey Rd (3m N on A382)
Hotel	★★59% Queens Hotel, Queen St, NEWTON ABBOT ☎(0626) 63133 & 54106 24rm(20⇔🔥)

OKEHAMPTON   Map 02 SX59

Okehampton ☎(0837) 52113
Interesting and beautiful moorland course with true
Dartmoor turf.
18 holes, 5191yds, Par 68, SSS 67, Course record 62.
Club membership 550.

Visitors	must have handicap certificate. Must contact in advance.
Societies	must contact in writing.
Green Fees	not confirmed.
Facilities	⊗ ⊪ by prior arrangement ⚑ 🛒 ♀ ⚲ 📷 ☂ 𝄢 Phillip J Blundell.
Location	Tors Rd (1m S off A30)
Hotel	★★62% Oxenham Arms, SOUTH ZEAL ☎(0837) 840244 & 840577 8rm(7⇔🔥)

PLYMOUTH   Map 02 SX45

Elfordleigh ☎(0752) 336428
Charming, saucer-shaped parkland course with alternate tees
for 18 holes. Tree-lined fairways and three lakes. Fairly hard
walking.
9 holes, 5664yds, Par 68, SSS 68, Course record 68.
Club membership 350.

Visitors	must have handicap certificate. Must contact in advance.
Societies	by arrangement.
Green Fees	£15 per round (£20 weekends).
Facilities	⊗ ⊪ ⚑ 🛒 ♀ ⚲ 📷 ☂ ⋈ 𝄢
Leisure	hard tennis courts, outdoor and indoor heated swimming pools, squash, snooker, sauna, solarium, gymnasium, games room, jacuzzi, croquet.
Location	Plympton (8m NE off B3416)
Hotel	★★★58% Novotel Plymouth, Marsh Mills Roundabout, 270 Plymouth Rd, PLYMOUTH ☎(0752) 221422 100⇔🔥

Staddon Heights ☎(0752) 402475
Seaside course that can be windy. Walking easy.
18 holes, 5874yds, Par 68, SSS 68, Course record 59.
Club membership 750.

Visitors	cannot play Sun. Must have an introduction from own club.
Societies	must apply to the secretary.
Green Fees	£15 per day (£20 weekends & bank holidays).
Facilities	⊗ ⋔ ╚ ♨ ♀ ⚲ 🎒 ⎰ John Cox.
Leisure	snooker.
Location	Plymstock (5m SW)
Hotel	★★★65% Forte Crest, Cliff Rd, The Hoe, PLYMOUTH ☎(0752) 662828 106 ⇔

SAUNTON   Map 02 SS43

Saunton ☎Braunton (0271) 812436
Two traditional links courses (one championship). Windy,
with natural hazards.
East Course: 18 holes, 6703yds, Par 71, SSS 73, Course record 66.
West Course: 18 holes, 6356yds, Par 71, SSS 71, Course record 68.
Club membership 1180.

Visitors	must have handicap certificate. Must have an introduction from own club.
Societies	must apply in writing.
Green Fees	£21.50 (£26.50 weekends).
Facilities	⊗ ⋔ by prior arrangement ╚ ♨ ♀ ⚲ 🎒 ⎰ J McGhee.
Location	S side of village off B3231
Hotel	★★★★59% Saunton Sands Hotel, SAUNTON ☎(0271) 890212 92 ⇔ ♠
Additional hotel	★★64% Preston House Hotel, SAUNTON ☎(0271) 890472 15 ⇔ ♠

SIDMOUTH   Map 03 SY18

Sidmouth ☎(0395) 513451
Situated on the side of Peak Hill, offering beautiful coastal
views. Club founded in 1889.
18 holes, 5100yds, Par 66, SSS 65, Course record 59.
Club membership 700.

Visitors	must contact in advance.
Societies	must telephone in advance.
Green Fees	£18 per day.
Facilities	⊗ ⋔ ╚ (no catering Mon) ♨ ♀ ⚲ 🎒 ⍗ ⎰ Mervyn Kemp.
Location	Cotmaton Rd, Peak Hill (W side of town centre)
Hotel	★★★★65% Victoria Hotel, Esplanade, SIDMOUTH ☎(0395) 512651 61 ⇔ ♠

SOUTH BRENT   Map 03 SX66

Wrangaton (S Devon) ☎(0364) 73229
Moorland/parkland course within Dartmoor National Park.
Spectacular views towards sea and rugged terrain. Natural
fairways and hazards include bracken, sheep and ponies.
18 holes, 6040yds, Par 69, SSS 69, Course record 68.
Club membership 600.

Visitors	are restricted on competition days. Must contact in advance and have an introduction from own club.

▶

Societies	must give one months notice in writing.
Green Fees	£15 per day (£20 weekends & bank holidays).
Facilities	⊗ 🛒 ■ ♟ 🏌 🍴 (John Cox.
Location	Golf Links Rd, Wrangaton (2.25 m SW off A38)
Hotel	★★♨74% Glazebrook House Hotel & Restaurant, SOUTH BRENT ☎(0364) 73322 11⇨♠

TAVISTOCK   Map 02 SX47

Hurdwick ☎(0822) 612746
A new Executive parkland course with many bunkers and fine views. The idea of Executive golf originated in America and the concept is that a round should take no longer than 3 hours whilst offering solid challenge, thus suiting the busy business person.
18 holes, 4553yds, Par 67, SSS 62.
Club membership 150.

Visitors	no restrictions.
Societies	must contact in advance.
Green Fees	£14-£20 per day (£16-£25 weekends & bank holidays).
Facilities	🛒 ■ ♟ 🏌
Location	Tavistock Hamlets (1m N)
Hotel	★★★60% Bedford Hotel, Plymouth Rd, TAVISTOCK ☎(0822) 613221 31⇨♠

Tavistock ☎(0822) 612049
Set on Whitchurch Down in south-west Dartmoor with easy walking and magnificent views over rolling country-side into Cornwall. Downland turf with some heather, and interesting holes on undulating ground.
18 holes, 6250yds, Par 70, SSS 70.
Club membership 700.

Visitors	may not play on competition days. Must contact in advance and have an introduction from own club.
Societies	must apply in writing.
Green Fees	not confirmed.
Facilities	⊗ 🛒 🛒 ■ ♟ 🏌 🍴 🍴 (Reg Cade.
Leisure	snooker.
Location	Down Rd (1m SE)
Hotel	★★★60% Bedford Hotel, Plymouth Rd, TAVISTOCK ☎(0822) 613221 31⇨♠

TEDBURN ST MARY   Map 03 SX89

Fingle Glen ☎(0647) 61817
9-hole course containing six par 4's and three par 3's set in 52 acres of rolling countryside. Testing 4th, 5th and 9th holes. 12-bay floodlit driving range.
9 holes, 2466yds, Par 33, SSS 31.
Club membership 450.

Visitors	no restrictions.
Societies	must telephone two weeks in advance.
Green Fees	£12.50 per round/18 holes (£16.50 weekends).
Facilities	⊗ 🛒 🛒 ■ ♟ 🏌 🍴 🍴 ⛳ (Stephen Gould.
Location	5m from city centre on A30
Hotel	★★★61% Countess Wear Lodge Hotel, Topsham Rd, Exeter Bypass, EXETER ☎(0392) 875441 44⇨♠

TEIGNMOUTH   Map 03 SX97

Teignmouth ☎(0626) 774194
This fairly flat heathland course is high up with a fine seascape from the clubhouse. Good springy turf with some heather and an interesting layout makes for very enjoyable holiday golf.
18 holes, 5880yds, Par 70, SSS 68.
Club membership 900.

Visitors	must use yellow tees. Must contact in advance and have an introduction from own club.
Societies	must contact Secretary for details.
Green Fees	not confirmed.
Facilities	⊗ 🛒 by prior arrangement 🛒 ■ ♟ 🏌 🍴 🍴 (Peter Ward.
Location	Exeter Rd (2m NW off B3192)
Hotel	★★65% Ness House Hotel, Marine Dr, Shaldon, TEIGNMOUTH ☎(0626) 873480 7⇨♠Annexe5rm

THURLESTONE   Map 03 SX64

Thurlestone ☎Kingsbridge (0548) 560405
Situated on the edge of the cliffs with typical downland turf and good greens. The course, after an interesting opening hole, rises to higher land with fine seaviews, and finishes with an excellent 502-yard downhill hole to the clubhouse.
18 holes, 6303yds, Par 70, SSS 70, Course record 65.
Club membership 770.

SCORECARD: White Tees					
Hole	Yds	Par	Hole	Yds	Par
1	271	4	10	434	4
2	379	4	11	366	4
3	170	3	12	459	4
4	366	4	13	209	3
5	221	3	14	518	5
6	148	3	15	505	5
7	344	4	16	417	4
8	429	4	17	152	3
9	413	5	18	502	5
Out	2741	33	In	3562	37
			Totals	6303	70

Visitors	must have handicap certificate. Must contact in advance and have an introduction from own club.
Green Fees	£22 per round.
Facilities	⊗ 🛒 🛒 ■ ♟ 🏌 🍴 🍴 (Neville Whitley.
Leisure	hard and grass tennis courts.
Location	S side of village
Hotel	★★★★65% Thurlestone Hotel, THURLESTONE ☎(0548) 560382 68⇨♠

TIVERTON   Map 03 SS91

Tiverton ☎(0884) 252187
A parkland course where the many different species of tree are a feature and where the lush pastures ensure some of the finest fairways in the south-west. There are a number of interesting holes which visitors will find a real challenge.
18 holes, 6263yds, Par 71, SSS 71.
Club membership 930.

Visitors	must be member of a recognised golf club & have handicap certificate. Must contact in advance and have an introduction from own club.
Societies	must contact in advance.
Green Fees	£20 per day/round (£26 weekends & bank holidays).
Facilities	⊗ 🛒 🛒 ■ ♟ 🏌 🍴 (Robert Freeman.

Location	Post Hill
Hotel	★★58% Hartnoll Hotel, Bolham, TIVERTON ☎(0884) 252777 11⇔Annexe5♙

TORQUAY   Map 03 SX96

Torquay ☎(0803) 314591
Unusual combination of cliff and parkland golf, with wonderful views over the sea and Dartmoor.
18 holes, 6198yds, Par 69, SSS 69, Course record 66.
Club membership 700.

Visitors	must have handicap certificate. Must contact in advance and have an introduction from own club.
Societies	must apply in writing.
Green Fees	not confirmed.
Facilities	⊗ ⅷ (ex Mon) ⅼ ⬛ ♀ △ 🖻 ⌐ 〔 M Ruth.
Location	30 Petitor Rd, St Marychurch (1.25m N)
Hotel	★★55% Norcliffe Hotel, 7 Babbacombe Downs Rd, Babbacombe, TORQUAY ☎(0803) 328456 20⇔♙

TORRINGTON   Map 02 SS41

Torrington ☎Great Torrington (0805) 22229
Hard walking on hilly commonland course. Small greens and outstanding views.
9 holes, 4373yds, Par 64, SSS 62, Course record 64.
Club membership 429.

Visitors	cannot play Sun mornings & bank holidays. Must contact in advance.
Societies	by arrangement.
Green Fees	£9 per weekday/round.
Facilities	⊗ ⅷ ⅼ & ⬛ by prior arrangement ♀ △ 🖻
Location	Weare Trees, Great Torrington (1.25m NW)
Hotel	★★50% Beaconside Hotel, LANDCROSS ☎(02372) 77205 9rm(4⇔2♙)

WESTWARD HO!   Map 02 SS42

Royal North Devon ☎(02372) 73817
Links course with sea views.
18 holes, 6644yds, Par 71, SSS 72.
Club membership 550.

Visitors	no restrictions.
Green Fees	not confirmed.
Facilities	♀ △ 🖻 ⌐ 〔
Location	N side of village off B3236
Hotel	★★★63% Durrant House, Heywood Rd, Northam, BIDEFORD ☎(0237) 472361 120⇔♙
Additional hotel	★★62% Culloden House Hotel, Fosketh Hill, WESTWARD HO! ☎(0237) 479421 9rm(2⇔5♙)
Additional hotel	★★⚑57% Yeoldon Country House Hotel, Durrant Ln, Northam, BIDEFORD ☎(0237) 474400 10⇔♙

A golf-course name printed in **bold italics** means that we have been unable to verify information with the club's management for the current year

YELVERTON — Map 02 SX56

Yelverton ☎(0822) 852824
An excellent course on the moors with virtually no trees.
It is exposed to high winds. The fairways are tight but
there is plenty of room. The longest hole is the 8th, a 569-
yard, par 5. Outstanding views.
18 holes, 6293yds, Par 70, SSS 70.
Club membership 840.

Visitors	must be member of a club & have handicap certificate. Must contact in advance and have an introduction from own club.
Societies	by arrangement.
Green Fees	£15 per day (£20 weekends & bank holidays).
Facilities	⊗ ⌶ by prior arrangement ⮂ ▆ ♀ ⌂ ⌸ ℓ Iain Parker.
Leisure	snooker.
Location	Golf Links Rd (1m S off A386)
Hotel	★★★69% Moorland Links Hotel, YELVERTON ☎(0822) 852245 30⇥⚑

DORSET

BELCHALWELL — Map 03 ST70

Mid-Dorset ☎Blandford (0258) 861386
Set in an area of outstanding natural beauty, rich in wildlife,
which provides a picturesque backdrop to this stimulating,
undulating course. Modern clubhouse with magnificent
views.
18 holes, 5938mtrs, Par 70, SSS 71.
Club membership 350.

Visitors	no restrictions.
Societies	welcome by prior arrangement.
Green Fees	£20 per day (£25 weekends & bank holidays).
Facilities	⊗ ⌶ ⮂ ▆ ♀ ⌂ ⌸ ℓ Andrew Pakes.
Hotel	★★★66% Crown Hotel, 8 West St, BLANDFORD FORUM ☎(0258) 456626 32⇥

BLANDFORD FORUM — Map 03 ST80

Ashley Wood ☎(0258) 452253
Undulating downland course with superb views and
excellent drainage.
9 holes, 6630yds, Par 70, SSS 70, Course record 67.
Club membership 550.

Visitors	ladies only Tues mornings. Must contact in advance and have an introduction from own club.
Societies	contact in writing.
Green Fees	£17 per round.
Facilities	⊗ ⌶ ⮂ ▆ ♀ ⌂ ⌸ ℓ Spencer Taylor.
Leisure	practise ground & putting green.
Location	Wimborne Rd (2m E on B3082)
Hotel	★★★66% Crown Hotel, 8 West St, BLANDFORD FORUM ☎(0258) 456626 32⇥

Opening times of bar and catering facilities
vary from place to place. Please remember
to check in advance of your visit

BOURNEMOUTH — Map 04 SZ09

Knighton Heath ☎(0202) 572633
Undulating heathland course on high ground inland from
Bournemouth.
18 holes, 6120yds, Par 69, SSS 69, Course record 64.
Club membership 700.

Visitors	with member only weekends & bank holidays. Must have handicap certificate. Must contact in advance.
Societies	must book in advance.
Green Fees	£25 per day.
Facilities	⊗ ⌶ by prior arrangement ⮂ ▆ ♀ ⌂ ⌸ ℓ Jane Miles.
Location	Francis Av, West Howe (N side of town centre off A348)
Hotel	★★★61% Bournemouth Heathlands Hotel, 12 Grove Rd, East Cliff, BOURNEMOUTH ☎(0202) 553336 116⇥⚑

Queen's Park ☎(0202) 36198
Undulating parkland course of pine and heather, with
narrow, tree-lined fairways. Public course played over by
'Boscombe Golf Club' and 'Bournemouth Artisans Golf
Club'.
18 holes, 6505yds, Par 72, SSS 72.

Visitors	must contact in advance.
Societies	must contact in advance.
Green Fees	not confirmed.
Facilities	⊗ ⌶ ⮂ ▆ ♀ ⌂ ⌸ ℓ John Sharkey.
Location	Queens Park Dr West (2m NE of town centre off A338)
Hotel	★★61% Hotel Riviera, West Cliff Gardens, BOURNEMOUTH ☎(0202) 552845 34⇥⚑

BRIDPORT — Map 03 SY49

Bridport & West Dorset ☎(0308) 421095
Seaside links course on the top of the east cliff, with fine
views over Lyme Bay and surrounding countryside. At the
13th hole (par 3), the green is 70 ft below the tee.
18 holes, 5246yds, Par 67, SSS 66, Course record 61.
Club membership 800.

Visitors	may not play 8-9.30am & noon-2pm or on competition days.
Societies	must contact in advance.
Green Fees	£17 (£22 weekends & bank holidays).
Facilities	⊗ ⌶ ⮂ ▆ ♀ ⌂ ⌸ ℓ John Parish.
Location	East Cliff, West Bay (2m S)
Hotel	★★★61% Haddon House Hotel, West Bay, BRIDPORT ☎(0308) 23626 & 25323 13⇥⚑

BROADSTONE — Map 03 SZ09

Broadstone (Dorset) ☎(0202) 692595
Typical heathland course.
18 holes, 6183yds, Par 69, SSS 70, Course record 64.
Club membership 800.

Visitors	may not play weekends & bank holidays. Must have handicap certificate. Must contact in advance.
Societies	contact in advance.

Green Fees £30 per day; £25 per round.
Facilities ⊗ & ⅲ by prior arrangement 🍴 🍺 ♀ 🛆 🏠
ᵀ ℰ Nigel Tokely.
Location Wentworth Dr (N side of village off B3074)
Hotel ★★★61% King's Head Hotel, The Square,
WIMBORNE ☎(0202) 880101 27↩🐾

CHRISTCHURCH   Map 04 SZ19

Iford Bridge ☎(0202) 473817
Parkland course with the River Stour running through.
Driving range.
9 holes, 2377yds, Par 34, SSS 32, Course record 66.
Club membership 350.
Visitors   no restrictions.
Societies   must contact in advance.
Green Fees   £4.70 (£5.35 weekends & bank holidays) -18
              holes.
Facilities   🍴 🍺 ♀ 🏠 ᵀ ℰ Peter L Troth.
Leisure   hard and grass tennis courts, bowls.
Location   Barrack Rd (W side of town centre on A5)
Hotel   ★★★73% Waterford Lodge Hotel, 87 Bure Ln,
              Friars Cliff, Mudeford, CHRISTCHURCH
              ☎(0425) 272948 & 278801 20↩

DORCHESTER   Map 03 SY69

Came Down ☎(0305) 813494
Scene of the West of England Championships on several
occasions, this fine course lies on a high plateau
commanding glorious views over Portland. Three par 5
holes add interest to a round. The turf is of the springy,
downland type.
18 holes, 6244yds, Par 70, SSS 71.
Club membership 700.
Visitors   must have handicap certificate. Must contact
              in advance and have an introduction from
              own club.
Societies   by arrangement on Wed only.
Green Fees   not confirmed.
Facilities   ⊗ ⅲ 🍴 🍺 ♀ 🛆 🏠 ℰ R Preston.
Location   Came Down
Hotel   ★★★70% King's Arms Hotel,
              DORCHESTER ☎(0305) 265353 31↩

FERNDOWN   Map 04 SU00

Ferndown ☎(0202) 872022
Fairways are gently undulating amongst heather, gorse
and pine trees giving the
course a most attractive appearance. There are a number
of dog-leg holes, and, on a
clear day, there are views
across to the Isle of Wight.
Old Course: 18 holes, 6442yds,
Par 71, SSS 71.
New Course: 9 holes, 5604yds,
Par 70, SSS 68.
Club membership 700.

SCORECARD: Old Course (White Tees)					
Hole	Yds	Par	Hole	Yds	Par
1	396	4	10	485	5
2	175	3	11	438	4
3	398	4	12	186	3
4	395	4	13	488	5
5	206	3	14	152	3
6	409	4	15	398	4
7	480	5	16	305	4
8	304	4	17	397	4
9	427	4	18	403	4
Out	3190	35	In	3252	36
			Totals	6442	71

Visitors   not before 9.30am at weekends. Must contact
              in advance and have an introduction from
              own club.
Societies   welcome Tue & Fri only apply by letter.
Green Fees   Old Course £30 , New Course £15 (£35/£20
              weekends).
Facilities   ⊗ ⅲ by prior arrangement 🍴 🍺 ♀ 🛆
              🏠 ℰ D Sewell.
Location   119 Golf Links Rd (S side of town centre off
              A347)
Hotel   ★★★★65% Dormy Hotel, New Rd,
              FERNDOWN ☎(0202) 872121 130↩🐾

HIGHCLIFFE   Map 04 SZ29

Highcliffe Castle ☎(0425) 272210
Picturesque parkland course with easy walking.
18 holes, 4686yds, Par 64, SSS 63.
Club membership 500.
Visitors   must be a member of recognised club. Must
              have an introduction from own club.
Societies   Tue only.
Green Fees   £16.50 per day; (£25.50 weekends & bank
              holidays).
Facilities   ⊗ ⅲ by prior arrangement 🍴 🍺 ♀ 🛆 🏠 ℰ
              R E Crockford.
Location   107 Lymington Rd (SW side of town on A337)
Hotel   ★★★73% Waterford Lodge Hotel, 87 Bure Ln,
              Friars Cliff, Mudeford, CHRISTCHURCH
              ☎(0425) 272948 & 278801 20↩

LYME REGIS   Map 03 NY39

Lyme Regis ☎(0297) 442963
Undulating cliff-top course with magnificent views of
Golden Cap and Lyme Bay.
18 holes, 6220yds, Par 71, SSS 70, Course record 65.
Club membership 560.

Visitors	may not play on Thu & Sun mornings. Must contact in advance and have an introduction from own club.
Societies	Tue, Wed & Fri; must contact in writing.
Green Fees	£24 per day (£20 after 2pm).
Facilities	⊗ ⊪ ⓛ ⲙ ♀ ♨ 🛏 (Andrew Black.
Location	Timber Hill (1.5m N on A3052)
Hotel	★★★69% Alexandra Hotel, Pound St, LYME REGIS ☎(0297) 442010 & 443229 24⇨🐾

LYTCHETT MATRAVERS   Map 02 J5

Bulbury Woods ☎Morden (092945) 574
Parkland course in 40 acres of woodland, with extensive
views over the Purbecks, Poole Bay and Wareham Forest.
Not too hilly.
18 holes, 6020yds, Par 70, SSS 68, Course record 65.
Club membership 650.

Visitors	are advised to contact in advance.
Societies	must contact in advance.
Green Fees	£25 per day; £15 per round (£30/£18 weekends).
Facilities	⊗ ⓛ ⲙ ♀ 🛏 (John Sharkey.
Location	Halls Rd (2m W of Lytchett Minster)
Hotel	★★★78% Priory Hotel, Church Green, WAREHAM ☎(0929) 552772 & 551666 15⇨🐾Annexe4⇨🐾

POOLE   Map 04 SZ09

Parkstone ☎Canford Cliffs (0202) 707138
Very scenic heathland course with views of Poole Bay.
Club founded in 1910.
18 holes, 6250yds, Par 72, SSS 70, Course record 64.
Club membership 800.

Visitors	must have handicap certificate. Must contact in advance and have an introduction from own club.
Societies	by prior arrangement.
Green Fees	£30 per day; £24 per round (£40/£30 weekends).
Facilities	⊗ ⊪ ⓛ ⲙ ♀ ♨ 🛏 (Nigel Blenkarne.
Location	Links Rd, Parkstone (E side of town centre off A35)
Hotel	★★★76% Salterns Hotel, 38 Salterns Way, Lilliput, POOLE ☎(0202) 707321 16⇨

SHERBORNE   Map 03 ST61

Sherborne ☎(0935) 814431
A sporting course of first-class fairways with far-reaching
views over the lovely Blackmore Vale and the Vale of
Sparkford. Parkland in character, the course has many
well-placed bunkers. The dog-leg 2nd calls for an
accurately placed tee shot, and another testing hole is the
7th, a 194-yard, par 3. There is a practice area.
18 holes, 5949yds, Par 70, SSS 68.
Club membership 700.

Visitors	must contact in advance and have an introduction from own club.
Societies	must contact well in advance.
Green Fees	not confirmed.
Facilities	⊗ ⊪ ⓛ ⲙ ♀ ♨ 🛏 (Stewart Wright.
Location	Higher Clatcombe (2m N off B3145)
Hotel	★★★60% Forte Posthouse, Horsecastles Ln, SHERBORNE ☎(0935) 813191 60⇨🐾

SWANAGE   Map 04 SZ07

Isle of Purbeck ☎Studland (092944) 361
A heathland course sited on the Purbeck Hills with grand
views across Swanage, the Channel and Poole Harbour.
Holes of note include the 5th, 8th, 14th, 15th, and 16th
where trees, gorse and heather assert themselves. The
very attractive clubhouse is built of the local stone.
Purbeck : 18 holes, 6295yds, Par 70, SSS 71.
Dene : 9 holes, 4014yds, Par 60, SSS 63.
Club membership 600.

Visitors	no restrictions.
Societies	must contact in advance.
Green Fees	Purbeck £27 day; £20.50 round (£25/£32.50 weekends) Dene £8 (£10 weekends).
Facilities	⊗ ⊪ ⓛ ⲙ ♀ ♨ 🛏 ⚑ (Kevin Spurgeon.
Location	2.5m N on B3351
Hotel	★★★62% The Pines Hotel, Burlington Rd, SWANAGE ☎(0929) 425211 51rm(49⇨🐾)

WAREHAM   Map 03 SY98

East Dorset ☎Bere Regis (0929) 472244
Long 18-hole parkland course with natural water features.
The 9-hole course is set amongst trees and rhododendrons.
Alterations should be complete in July 1992. Floodlit 22-
bay driving range, club fitting centre, indoor putting area
and extensive golf shop.
Lakeland : 18 holes, 6640yds, Par 72.
Woodland : 9 holes, 2440yards, Par 33.
Club membership 800.

Visitors	must contact in advance and have an introduction from own club.
Societies	apply in writing.
Green Fees	£17 per day; £14 per round (£21/£17 weekends).
Facilities	⊗ ⊪ by prior arrangement ⓛ ⲙ ♀ ♨ 🛏 ⚑ (Graham Packer.
Location	Hyde (5m NW on unclass Puddletown Rd, off A352)
Hotel	★★69% Kemps Country House Hotel, East Stoke, WAREHAM ☎(0929) 462563 5rm(1⇨3🐾)Annexe10⇨🐾

Wareham ☎(0929) 554147
Heathland/parkland course. The club was founded in 1926.
18 holes, 5603yds, Par 69, SSS 67.
Club membership 550.

Visitors	must have a handicap certificate & should contact the club in advance. Must be accompanied by a member at weekends & bank holidays.
Societies	must contact in advance.

Green Fees £20 per day; £15 per round.
Facilities ⊗ ∭ by prior arrangement ⌾ ● ♀ ⌂
Location Sandford Rd
Hotel ★★★70% Springfield Country Hotel, Grange Road, Stoborough, WAREHAM ☏(0929) 552177 & 551785 32⇥🌢

WEYMOUTH   Map 03 SY67

Weymouth ☏(0305) 773981
Seaside parkland course. The 5th is played off an elevated green over copse.
18 holes, 6009yds, Par 70, SSS 69, Course record 63.
Club membership 730.
Visitors must have proof of membership or handicap certificate. Must contact in advance and have an introduction from own club.
Societies telephone in advance.
Green Fees £16 (£22 weekends & bank holidays).
Facilities ⊗ ∭ ⌾ ● ♀ ⌂ 🏠 (Des Lochrie.
Location Links Rd, Westham (N side of town centre off B3157)
Hotel ★★63% Hotel Rex, 29 The Esplanade, WEYMOUTH ☏(0305) 760400 31⇥🌢

CO DURHAM

BARNARD CASTLE   Map 12 NZ01

Barnard Castle ☏Teesdale (0833) 38355 Flat moorland course high above the River Tees and presenting fine views. A small stream runs in front of, or alongside, many of the holes adding challenge and enjoyment to the game. *18 holes, 5838yds, Par 71, SSS 68, Course record 63.* *Club membership 600.*	SCORECARD					
	Hole	Yds	Par	Hole	Yds	Par
	1	295	4	10	183	3
	2	480	5	11	480	5
	3	159	3	12	365	4
	4	488	5	13	363	4
	5	521	5	14	356	4
	6	311	4	15	129	3
	7	308	4	16	160	3
	8	142	3	17	349	4
	9	535	5	18	214	3
	Out	3239	38	In	2599	33
				Totals	5838	71

Visitors must be member of recognised club.
Societies by arrangement.
Green Fees £14 per day (£18 weekends).
Facilities ⊗ ∭ ⌾ & ● by prior arrangement ♀ ⌂ 🏠 ⚑ (J Harrison.
Leisure snooker.
Location Harmire Rd (.75m N on B6278)
Hotel ★★70% Rose & Crown Hotel, ROMALDKIRK ☏(0833) 50213 6⇥🌢Annexe5⇥🌢

BEAMISH   Map 12 NZ25

Beamish Park ☏091-370 1382
Parkland course. Designed by Henry Cotton and W Woodend.
18 holes, 6205yds, Par 71, SSS 70, Course record 67.
Club membership 520.
Visitors restricted except before 9am & 12.15-1.45pm.
Societies by arrangement.
Green Fees not confirmed.

Facilities ⊗ ∭ ⌾ ● ♀ ⌂ 🏠 (C Cole.
Location 1m NW off A693
Hotel ★★★66% Beamish Park Hotel, Beamish Burn Rd, MARLEY HILL ☏(0207) 230666 47⇥🌢

BISHOP AUCKLAND   Map 08 NZ22

Bishop Auckland ☏(0388) 602198 A rather hilly parkland course with many well-established trees offering a challenging round. A small ravine adds interest to several holes including the short 7th, from a raised tee to a green surrounded by a stream, gorse and bushes. Pleasant views down the Wear Valley. *18 holes, 6420yds, Par 72, SSS 71, Course record 65.* *Club membership 620.*	SCORECARD: Medal Tees					
	Hole	Yds	Par	Hole	Yds	Par
	1	286	4	10	193	3
	2	559	5	11	493	5
	3	529	5	12	221	3
	4	521	5	13	438	4
	5	214	3	14	386	4
	6	341	4	15	400	4
	7	143	3	16	370	4
	8	182	3	17	370	4
	9	494	5	18	280	4
	Out	3269	37	In	3151	35
				Totals	6420	72

Visitors may play on weekdays only. Must contact in advance and have an introduction from own club.
Societies weekdays only; must contact in advance.
Green Fees £20 per day; £16 per round (£20 per round weekends).
Facilities ⊗ ∭ by prior arrangement ⌾ (ex Mon) ● ♀ ⌂ 🏠 (David Skiffington.
Leisure snooker.
Location Durham Rd (1m NE on A689)
Hotel ★★70% Park Head Hotel, New Coundon, BISHOP AUCKLAND ☏(0388) 661727 8⇥🌢Annexe7⇥🌢

BURNOPFIELD   Map 12 NZ15

Hobson Municipal ☏(0207) 71605
Meadowland course opened in 1981.
18 holes, 6080yds, Par 71, SSS 69, Course record 68.
Club membership 600.
Visitors no restrictions.
Societies must contact in advance.
Green Fees £6.50 per round (£8.50 weekends).
Facilities ⊗ ∭ ⌾ ● ♀ ⌂ 🏠 ⚑ (Jack Ord.
Leisure practice area.
Location Hobson (.75m S on A692)
Hotel ★★★66% Swallow Hotel-Gateshead, High West St, GATESHEAD ☏091-477 1105 103⇥🌢

CHESTER-LE-STREET   Map 12 NZ25

Chester-le-Street ☏Durham (091) 3883218
Parkland course in castle grounds, good views, easy walking.
18 holes, 6054yds, Par 70, SSS 69, Course record 67.
Club membership 650.
Visitors restricted weekends & bank holidays. Must contact in advance and have an introduction from own club.
Societies must apply in writing.
Green Fees £25 per day; £18 per round (£30/£25 weekends & bank holidays).
Facilities ⊗ ∭ ⌾ ● ♀ ⌂ 🏠 ⚑ (A Hartley.
Leisure snooker, pool table.

▶ •

| Location | Lumley Park (.5m E off B1284) |
| Hotel | ★★★69% Ramside Hall Hotel, Carrville, DURHAM ☎091-386 5282 82⇨🏌 |

CONSETT   Map 12 NZ15

Consett & District ☎(0207) 502186
Undulating parkland/moorland course.
18 holes, 6011yds, Par 71, SSS 69, Course record 64.
Club membership 650.

Visitors	must contact in advance.
Societies	must contact in advance.
Green Fees	£15 (£25 weekends & bank holidays).
Facilities	⊗ & �🍴 (ex Mon) 🍺 ⬛ ♀ ⌂ 🏠 ⌢ S Corbally.
Location	Elmfield Rd (N side of town on A691)
Hotel	★★67% Lord Crewe Arms Hotel, BLANCHLAND ☎(0434675) 251 8⇨🏌 Annexe10⇨🏌

CROOK   Map 12 NZ13

Crook ☎Bishop Auckland (0388) 762429
Meadowland/parkland course in elevated position with natural hazards, varied holes and terrain. Panoramic views over Durham and Cleveland Hills.
18 holes, 6079yds, Par 68, SSS 69, Course record 62.
Club membership 430.

Visitors	welcome.
Societies	by arrangement.
Green Fees	£10 per day (£15 weekends).
Facilities	⊗ 🍴 & 🍺 ⬛ by prior arrangement ♀ ⌂
Location	Low Jobs Hill (.5m E off A690)
Hotel	★★70% Park Head Hotel, New Coundon, BISHOP AUCKLAND ☎(0388) 661727 8⇨🏌 Annexe7⇨

DARLINGTON   Map 08 NZ21

Blackwell Grange ☎(0325) 464464
Pleasant parkland course with good views, easy walking.
18 holes, 5621yds, Par 68, SSS 67, Course record 63.
Club membership 950.

Visitors	restricted Wed & Sun. Must have an introduction from own club.
Societies	must contact in writing.
Green Fees	not confirmed.
Facilities	⊗ 🍴 & 🍺 (Tue-Sat only) ⬛ (Mon-Sat mornings only) ♀ ⌂ 🏠 ⌢ ⌢ Ralph Givens.
Location	Briar Close (1m SW off A66)
Hotel	★★★★61% Blackwell Grange Moat House, Blackwell Grange, DARLINGTON ☎(0325) 380888 99⇨🏌

Darlington ☎(0325) 463936
Fairly flat parkland course with tree-lined fairways, and large first-class greens. Championship standard.
18 holes, 6032yds, Par 70, SSS 72, Course record 64.
Club membership 750.

Visitors	restricted weekends, bank holidays & competition days. Must contact in advance and have an introduction from own club.
Societies	must contact in advance.
Green Fees	£20.50 per day; £15.50 per round.

Facilities	⊗ & 🍴 by prior arrangement(ex Mon) 🍺 ⬛ ♀ ⌂ 🏠 ⌢ Ian Todd.
Leisure	snooker.
Location	Haughton Grange (N side of town centre off A1150)
Hotel	★★★61% Swallow King's Head Hotel, Priestgate, DARLINGTON ☎(0325) 380222 60⇨🏌

Stressholme ☎(0325) 461002
Picturesque municipal parkland course, long but wide, with 98 bunkers and a par 3 hole played over a river.
18 holes, 6511yds, Par 71, SSS 71, Course record 64.
Club membership 650.

Visitors	must contact in advance.
Societies	apply to the steward or professional.
Green Fees	£5.50 (£7.20 weekends).
Facilities	⊗ 🍺 ⬛ ♀ ⌂ 🏠 ⌢ ⌢
Location	Snipe Ln (SW side of town centre on A67)
Hotel	★★★★61% Blackwell Grange Moat House, Blackwell Grange, DARLINGTON ☎(0325) 380888 99⇨🏌

DURHAM   Map 12 NZ24

Brancepeth Castle ☎091-378 0075
Parkland course overlooked at the 9th hole by beautiful Brancepeth Castle.
18 holes, 6300yds, Par 70, SSS 70, Course record 64.
Club membership 780.

Visitors	may be restrictions at weekends for parties.
Societies	must contact in advance.
Green Fees	not confirmed.
Facilities	⊗ & 🍴 by prior arrangement 🍺 ⬛ ♀ ⌂ 🏠 ⌢ ⌢ D C Howdon.
Location	Brancepeth Village (4.5m SW on A690)
Hotel	★★★★68% Royal County Hotel, Old Elvet, DURHAM ☎091-386 6821 150⇨🏌

Durham City ☎091-378 0806
Undulating parkland course bordered on several holes by the River Browney.
18 holes, 6012yds, Par 71, SSS 70.
Club membership 700.

Visitors	restricted on competition days.
Societies	must contact in advance.
Green Fees	£14 per day (£18 weekends & bank holidays).
Facilities	⊗ 🍴 🍺 ⬛ ♀ ⌂ 🏠 ⌢ Steve Corbally.
Leisure	pool table.
Location	Littleburn, Langley Moor (1.5m S off A1050)
Hotel	★★★68% Three Tuns Hotel, New Elvet, DURHAM ☎091-386 4326 47⇨🏌

Mount Oswald ☎091-386 7527
Flat, wooded parkland course with Georgian clubhouse.
18 holes, 6101yds, Par 71, SSS 69, Course record 64.
Club membership 150.

Societies	must contact in advance.
Green Fees	£8 per round (£10 weekends & bank holidays).
Facilities	⊗ 🍴 🍺 ⬛ ♀ ⌂ ⌢
Location	Mount Oswald Manor, South Rd (1m S off A1050)
Hotel	★★62% Bridge Toby Hotel, Croxdale, DURHAM ☎091-378 0524 46⇨🏌

MIDDLETON ST GEORGE   Map 08 NZ31

Dinsdale Spa ☎Dinsdale (0325) 332297
A mainly flat, parkland course on high land above the River Tees with views of the Cleveland Hills. Water hazards front the 8th, 9th and 18th tees and the prevailing west wind affects the later holes. There is a practice area by the clubhouse.
18 holes, 6022yds, Par 70, SSS 69, Course record 64.
Club membership 850.

Visitors	restricted Tue & weekends. Must contact in advance and have an introduction from own club.
Societies	must contact in advance.
Green Fees	£18 per day; £15 per round.
Facilities	⊗ Ⅲ ﯼ ◖ ♀ △ 🏠 ⚐ ￥ D N Dodds.
Location	1.5m SW
Hotel	★★★64% St George Hotel, Middleton St George, TEES-SIDE AIRPORT ☎(0325) 332631 59⇨ 🏚

SEAHAM   Map 12 NZ44

Seaham ☎091-581 2354
Links course.
18 holes, 6017yds, Par 70, SSS 69, Course record 64.
Club membership 550.

Visitors	with member only weekends until 3.30pm.
Societies	must apply in writing.
Green Fees	£11 (£15 weekends).
Facilities	⊗ & Ⅲ by prior arrangement ﯼ ♀ △ 🏠
Leisure	snooker.
Location	Dawdon (S side of town centre)
Hotel	★★★72% Swallow Hotel, Queen's Pde, Seaburn, SUNDERLAND ☎091-529 2041 66⇨ 🏚

STANLEY   Map 12 NZ15

South Moor ☎(0207) 232848
Moorland course with natural hazards.
18 holes, 6445yds, Par 72, SSS 71, Course record 67.
Club membership 595.

Visitors	may not play competition days. Must contact in advance.
Societies	must telephone in advance.
Green Fees	not confirmed.
Facilities	⊗ Ⅲ ﯼ ◖ ♀ △ 🏠 ⚐ ￥
Leisure	snooker.
Location	The Middles, Craghead (1.5m SE on B6313)
Hotel	★★★66% Beamish Park Hotel, Beamish Burn Rd, MARLEY HILL ☎(0207) 230666 47⇨ 🏚

Each golf-course entry has a recommended AA-appointed hotel. For a wider choice of places to stay, consult *AA Hotels and Restaurants in Britain and Ireland* and *AA Inspected Bed and Breakfast in Britain and Ireland*

◦ EAST SUSSEX ◦

BEXHILL   Map 05 TQ70

Cooden Beach ☎Cooden (04243) 2040
The course is close by the sea, but is not real links in character. Despite that, it is dry and plays well throughout the year. There are some excellent holes such as the 4th, played to a built-up green, the short 12th, and three good holes to finish.
18 holes, 6450yds, Par 72, SSS 71, Course record 65.
Club membership 730.

Visitors	must have a handicap certificate. Restricted at weekends. Must contact in advance and have an introduction from own club.
Societies	must contact in advance.
Green Fees	not confirmed.
Facilities	⊗ Ⅲ ﯼ ◖ ♀ △ 🏠 🛏 ￥ Keith R Robson.
Leisure	snooker.
Location	Cooden (2m W on A259)
Hotel	★★★64% Cooden Resort Hotel, COODEN BEACH ☎(04243) 2281 40⇨ 🏚

Highwoods ☎Bexhill-on-Sea (0424) 212625
Undulating course.
18 holes, 6218yds, Par 70, SSS 70, Course record 66.
Club membership 820.

Visitors	must play with member on Sun. Must contact in advance and have an introduction from own club.
Societies	must contact 6 months in advance.
Green Fees	not confirmed.
Facilities	⊗ (Sun only) ﯼ (Mon-Sat 10am-2pm) ◖ ♀ △ 🏠 ￥ R McLean & M Andrews.
Leisure	snooker.
Location	Ellerslie Ln (1.5m NW)
Hotel	★★★61% Granville Hotel, Sea Rd, BEXHILL-ON-SEA ☎(0424) 215437 50⇨ 🏚

BRIGHTON & HOVE   Map 04 TQ30

Brighton & Hove ☎Brighton (0273) 556482
Downland course with sea views.
18 holes, 5722yds, Par 68, SSS 68.
Club membership 320.

Visitors	may not play Sun mornings. Must contact in advance.
Societies	must contact in advance.
Green Fees	not confirmed.
Facilities	⊗ Ⅲ ﯼ ◖ ♀ △ ￥ C Burgess.
Leisure	snooker.
Location	Dyke Rd (4m NW)
Hotel	★★★56% Courtlands Hotel, 19-27 The Drive, HOVE ☎(0273) 731055 53⇨ 🏚 Annexe5⇨

For a full list of golf courses included in the book, see the index at the end of the directory

Dyke ☎Brighton
(0273) 857296
This downland course has some glorious views both towards the sea and inland. The best hole on the course is probably the 17th; it is one of those teasing short holes of just over 200 yards, and is played across a gully to a high green.
18 holes, 6588yds, Par 72, SSS 71.
Club membership 700.

SCORECARD: White Tees					
Hole	Yds	Par	Hole	Yds	Par
1	502	5	10	412	4
2	503	5	11	539	5
3	334	4	12	362	4
4	499	5	13	388	4
5	191	3	14	161	3
6	446	4	15	365	4
7	340	4	16	457	4
8	163	3	17	204	3
9	403	4	18	319	4
Out	3381	37	In	3207	35
			Totals	6588	72

Visitors   restricted after 2pm on Sun
Societies   must contact in advance
Green Fees £21 per round; £31 per day (£31 per round weekends & bank holidays).
Facilities ⊗ ⊞ by prior arrangement ⬛ ♀ ⌂ 🏠 🕈 ℂ Paul Longmore.
Leisure   snooker.
Location   Dyke Rd (4m N between A23 & A27)
Hotel   ★★★56% Courtlands Hotel, 19-27 The Drive, HOVE ☎(0273) 731055 53⇥🏳Annexe5⇥

East Brighton ☎Brighton (0273) 604838
Undulating downland course, overlooking the sea. Windy.
18 holes, 6337yds, Par 72, SSS 70, Course record 64.
Club membership 700.
Visitors   may not play before 9am on weekdays. Must contact in advance and have an introduction from own club.
Societies   must contact at least 1 month in advance.
Green Fees £21 (£30 weekends).
Facilities ⊗ ⊞ ⮕ ⬛ (no catering Sun or Mon) ♀ ⌂ 🏠 ℂ W Street.
Leisure   snooker.
Location   Roedean Rd (E side of town centre on B2118)
Hotel   ★★★56% Courtlands Hotel, 19-27 The Drive, HOVE ☎(0273) 731055 53⇥🏳Annexe5⇥

Hollingbury Park ☎Brighton (0273) 552010
Municipal course in hilly situation on the Downs, overlooking the sea.
18 holes, 6500yds, Par 72, SSS 71, Course record 65.
Club membership 330.
Visitors   no restrictions
Societies   must book 1 month in advance
Green Fees £15.50 per day; £10 per round (£13 weekends & bank holidays).
Facilities ⊗ ⬛ ♀ ⌂ 🏠 🕈 ℂ P Brown.
Location   Ditchling Rd (2m N of town centre)
Hotel   ★★★56% Courtlands Hotel, 19-27 The Drive, HOVE ☎(0273) 731055 53⇥🏳Annexe5⇥

Waterhall ☎Brighton (0273) 508658
Hilly downland course with hard walking and open to the wind. Private club playing over municipal course.
18 holes, 5775yds, Par 69, SSS 68.
Club membership 420.
Visitors   may not play on competition days & before 10.30am at weekends.
Societies   must contact the secretary in writing.

Green Fees £15 per day; £10.50 per round (£13 per round weekends & bank holidays).
Facilities ⮕ ⬛ ♀ ⌂ 🏠 🕈 ℂ
Location   Seddlescombe Rd, (Off Devils Dyke Road) (3m N off A27)
Hotel   ★★★56% Courtlands Hotel, 19-27 The Drive, HOVE ☎(0273) 731055 53⇥🏳Annexe5⇥

CROWBOROUGH   Map 05 TQ53

Crowborough Beacon
☎(0892) 661511
A picturesque course in pleasant heathland. Though most fairways are wide and open, one or two are distinctly tight where a wayward shot results in a lost ball. By no means an easy course, with testing holes at the 2nd, 6th and 16th.
18 holes, 6318yds, Par 71, SSS 70.
Club membership 700.

SCORECARD: Medal Tees					
Hole	Yds	Par	Hole	Yds	Par
1	409	4	10	492	5
2	457	4	11	335	4
3	144	3	12	415	4
4	360	4	13	136	3
5	358	4	14	504	5
6	193	3	15	365	4
7	497	5	16	350	4
8	325	4	17	145	3
9	396	4	18	437	4
Out	3139	35	In	3179	36
			Totals	6318	71

Visitors   may not play at weekends. Must contact in advance and have an introduction from own club.
Societies   Mon Tues & Wed only.
Green Fees £34 per day; £22.50 per round.
Facilities ⊗ ⊞ by prior arrangement ⮕ ⬛ ♀ ⌂ 🏠 🕈 ℂ Dennis Newnham.
Location   Beacon Rd (1m SW on A26)
Hotel   ★★★76% Spa Hotel, Mount Ephraim, TUNBRIDGE WELLS ☎(0892) 20331 76⇥🏳

EASTBOURNE   Map 05 TV69

Eastbourne Downs ☎(0323) 20827
Downland/seaside course.
18 holes, 6635yds, Par 72, SSS 72.
Club membership 730.
Visitors   restricted after 1pm Sat & Sun.
Societies   must contact in advance.
Green Fees not confirmed.
Facilities ⊗ ⊞ ⮕ ⬛ ♀ ⌂ 🏠 🕈 ℂ T Marshall.
Location   East Dean Rd (1m W of town centre on A259)
Hotel   ★★★★62% Cavendish Hotel, Grand Pde, EASTBOURNE ☎(0323) 410222 114⇥🏳

Royal Eastbourne
☎(0323) 29738
A famous club which celebrated its centenary in 1987. The course plays longer than it measures. Testing holes are the 8th, a par 3 played to a high green and the 16th, a par 5 right-hand dog-leg.
Long Course: 18 holes, 6109yds, Par 70, SSS 69, Course record 62.
Short Course: 9 holes, 2147yds, Par 32, SSS 32.
Club membership 914.

SCORECARD: White Tees					
Hole	Yds	Par	Hole	Yds	Par
1	439	4	10	436	4
2	265	4	11	388	4
3	333	4	12	349	4
4	508	5	13	173	3
5	499	5	14	358	4
6	410	4	15	183	3
7	429	4	16	489	5
8	168	3	17	221	3
9	330	4	18	161	3
Out	3351	37	In	2758	33
			Totals	6109	70

Visitors	must have a handicap certificate for Long Course.
Societies	must telephone in advance.
Green Fees	£21.50 (£27.50 weekends).
Facilities	⊗ ⅢⅢ 🏌 ▬ ♀ 🏊 🏠 🍴 ⓕ Richard Wooler.
Leisure	snooker.
Location	Paradise Dr (.5m W of town centre)
Hotel	★★★71% Lansdowne Hotel, King Edward's Pde, EASTBOURNE ☎(0323) 25174 130⇌🏧
	See advertisement on page 85

Willingdon ☎(0323) 410981
Unique, hilly downland course set in oyster-shaped amphitheatre.
18 holes, 6049yds, Par 69, SSS 69, Course record 62.
Club membership 550.

Visitors	may play only with member on Sun. Must contact in advance and have an introduction from own club.
Societies	Mon-Fri only. Must contact in advance by telephone.
Green Fees	£24 per day/round (weekdays).
Facilities	🏊 🏠 🍴 ⓕ C J Patey.
Location	Southdown Rd (.5m N of town centre off A22)
Hotel	★★★63% The Wish Tower, King Edward's Pde, EASTBOURNE ☎(0323) 22676 67rm(59⇌)

FOREST ROW   Map 05 TQ43

Ashdown Forest Hotel ☎(0342) 824866
Natural heathland and woodland course cut out of the Ashdown Forest. The hotel specialises in catering for golf breaks and societies.
18 holes, 5510yds, Par 68, SSS 67.
Club membership 150.

Visitors	are advised to contact in advance.
Societies	apply in advance.
Green Fees	not confirmed.
Facilities	⊗ ⅢⅢ 🏌 ▬ ♀ 🏊 🏠 ⟷ ⓕ Martyn Landsborough.
Location	Chapel Ln (4m S of East Grinstead off A22 & B2110)

Royal Ashdown Forest ☎(0342) 822018
Undulating heathland course. Long carries off the tees and magnificent views over the Forest. Not a course for the high handicapper.
Old Course: 18 holes, 6477yds, Par 72, SSS 71.
Club membership 450.

Visitors	restricted weekends & Tue. Must have a handicap certificate. Must contact in advance and have an introduction from own club.
Societies	must contact in advance.
Green Fees	£31 per day (£36 weekends & bank holidays).
Facilities	⊗ 🏌 ▬ ♀ 🏊 🏠 🍴 ⓕ Martin Landsborough.
Location	Chapel Ln (SE side of village)
Hotel	★★★65% Roebuck Hotel, Wych Cross, FOREST ROW ☎(034282) 3811 28⇌🏧

This guide is updated annually – make sure that you use the up-to-date edition

HASTINGS & ST LEONARDS   Map 05 TQ80

Beauport Park ☎Hastings (0424) 52977
Played over Hastings Public Course. Undulating parkland with stream and fine views.
18 holes, 6033yds, Par 70, SSS 70.
Club membership 290.

Visitors	no restrictions.
Societies	must contact in writing.
Green Fees	not confirmed.
Facilities	♀ 🏊 🏠 🍴 ⓕ
Location	St Leonards-on-Sea (3m N of Hastings on A2100)
Hotel	★★★69% Beauport Park Hotel, Battle Rd, HASTINGS ☎(0424) 851222 23⇌🏧

LEWES   Map 05 TQ41

Lewes ☎(0273) 473245
Downland course. Fine views.
18 holes, 5951yds, Par 71, SSS 69, Course record 67.
Club membership 720.

Visitors	may not play at weekends after 2pm. Must contact in advance.
Societies	must contact in advance.
Green Fees	not confirmed.
Facilities	⊗ ⅢⅢ 🏌 ▬ ♀ 🏊 🏠 ⓕ Paul Dobson.
Location	Chapel Hill (E side of town centre off A26)
Hotel	★★★54% Shelleys, High St, LEWES ☎(0273) 472361 21⇌🏧

NEWHAVEN　　　　　　　　　　Map 05 TQ40

Peacehaven ☎(02739) 514049
Downland course, sometimes windy. Testing holes: 1st (par 3), 4th (par 4), 9th (par 3), 10th (par 3), 18th (par 3).
9 holes, 5235yds, Par 69, SSS 65.
Club membership 200.

Visitors	no restrictions.
Societies	must contact in writing.
Green Fees	not confirmed.
Facilities	♀ ♨ 🖼 ⛵
Location	Brighton Rd (.75m W on A259)
Hotel	★★★67% The Star, ALFRISTON ☎(0323) 870495 34⇨🏠

RYE　　　　　　　　　　Map 05 TQ92

Rye ☎(0797) 225241
Typical links course with superb greens and views.
Old Course: 18 holes, 6310yds, Par 68, SSS 71, Course record 64.
Jubilee Course: 9 holes, 6141yds, Par 71, SSS 70.
Club membership 1000.

Visitors	must be invited/introduced by a member. Must contact in advance.
Green Fees	£26 per round (£30 weekends); £39 per day (£42 weekends).
Facilities	⊗ ┗ ♨ ♀ ♨ 🖼 ⛵ Peter Marsh.
Location	Camber (2.75m SE off A259)
Hotel	★★68% George Hotel, High St, RYE ☎(0797) 222114 22⇨🏠

SEAFORD　　　　　　　　　　Map 05 TV49

Seaford ☎(0323) 892442
The great H. Taylor did not perhaps design as many courses as his friend and rival, James Braid, but Seaford's original design was Taylor's. It is a splendid downland course with magnificent views and some fine holes.
18 holes, 6233yds, Par 69, SSS 70.
Club membership 800.

SCORECARD: Medal Tees					
Hole	Yds	Par	Hole	Yds	Par
1	354	4	10	315	4
2	426	4	11	361	4
3	169	3	12	148	3
4	366	4	13	434	4
5	384	4	14	405	4
6	390	4	15	206	3
7	145	3	16	533	5
8	441	4	17	388	4
9	395	4	18	373	4
Out	3070	34	In	3163	35
			Totals	6233	69

Visitors	may play on weekdays only after 12pm (ex Tue). Must contact in advance.
Societies	must contact in advance.
Green Fees	£30 day; (£24 12-3pm, £14 after 3pm).
Facilities	⊗ ℳ ┗ ♨ ♀ ♨ 🖼 ⛵ Philip Stevens.
Leisure	snooker.
Location	Firle Rd, East Blatchington (1m N)
Hotel	★★★67% The Star, ALFRISTON ☎(0323) 870495 34⇨🏠

For a full list of golf courses included in the book, see the index at the end of the directory

TICEHURST　　　　　　　　　　Map 05 TQ63

Dale Hill ☎(0580) 200112
Picturesque course with woodland, water and gently undulating fairways. Hotel and leisure centre within grounds.
18 holes, 6066yds, Par 69, SSS 69, Course record 69.
Club membership 650.

Visitors	restricted mornings at weekends.
Societies	must contact in writing.
Green Fees	£17 per round (£24 weekends).
Facilities	⊗ ℳ ┗ ♨ ♀ ♨ 🖼 ⛵ 🏐 Ian Connelly.
Leisure	hard tennis courts, heated indoor swimming pool, fishing, snooker, sauna, solarium, gymnasium.
Location	N side of town off B2087
Hotel	★★65% Tudor Court Hotel, Rye Rd, HAWKHURST ☎(0580) 752312 18⇨🏠

UCKFIELD　　　　　　　　　　Map 05 TQ42

East Sussex National
☎(0825) 75577
Created with a £30 million budget, the East Sussex National, which runs round the elegant Horsted Place Hotel, is a wonderful creation for golfers and is planned to be one of the most luxurious golf clubs in the world. Its two courses have been created with tournaments in mind and the 18th green has been designed so that 50, 000 spectators can see.

SCORECARD: East Course (Gold Tees)					
Hole	Yds	Par	Hole	Yds	Par
1	361	4	10	510	5
2	517	5	11	394	4
3	448	4	12	386	4
4	216	3	13	194	3
5	460	4	14	559	5
6	309	4	15	471	4
7	573	5	16	178	3
8	149	3	17	450	4
9	466	4	18	440	4
Out	3499	36	In	3582	36
			Totals	7081	72

East Course: 18 holes, 7081yds, Par 72, SSS 74.
West Course: 18 holes, 7154yds, Par 72, SSS 74, Course record 64.

Visitors	may require a handicap certificate. Must contact in advance and have an introduction from own club.
Societies	must contact the Corporate Sales Executive in writing.
Green Fees	£80 per day; £60 per round.
Facilities	ℳ ┗ ♨ ♀ ♨ 🖼 ⛵ 🏐 Greg Dukart.
Leisure	hard tennis courts, heated indoor swimming pool, riding, croquet.
Location	Little Horsted (S on A22)
Hotel	★★★(red)🎖 Horsted Place Hotel, Little Horsted, UCKFIELD ☎(0825) 75581 17⇨🏠

Piltdown ☎Newick (082572) 2033
Natural heathland course with much heather and gorse. No bunkers, easy walking, fine views.
18 holes, 6059yds, Par 69, SSS 68.
Club membership 400.

Visitors	must telephone for details of restricted times. Must contact in advance and have an introduction from own club.
Societies	must contact in writing.
Green Fees	not confirmed.
Facilities	⊗ ℳ by prior arrangement ┗ ♨ ♀ ♨ 🖼 ⛵ 🏐 John Amos.

Horsted Place
★★★
(Red)

This delightful Victorian house offers the chance to play at the superb East Sussex National Golf Club, adjacent to the hotel.

These two excellent courses are complemented by the standard of comfort and service offered by this luxurious hotel.

The very best cuisine is served in the elegant Pugin Dining Room.

Other leisure facilities include a heated indoor swimming-pool, all weather tennis court and croquet lawn.

For more information please write to Horsted Place, Little Horsted, Nr. Uckfield, East Sussex TN22 5TS.
Tel: (0825) 75581 Fax: (0825) 75459
Telex: 95548

7 Courses to choose from!

Any 2 days – 12 January-31 December 1992

Your break includes 2 days' free golf (up to 36 holes each day), accommodation, newspaper (except Sunday), full English breakfast, light lunch at the golf club, with a 5 course Dinner and coffee at the hotel. Guaranteed tee-off times (ex Seaford Head Golf Club).

The Lansdowne has 130 en suite bedrooms.

The cost of your golf break from 12 Jan-29 Feb is £117; 1-31 Mar £128; 1 Apr-31 May £134; 1 Jun-30 Nov £138; 1-31 Dec £123. Extra days pro rata.

You may, subject to availability, play at a selection of 7 golf clubs (all 18-hole) in this lovely area.

Please write or telephone for our Golfing Break folder.

Lansdowne Hotel AA ★★★ *71%*

King Edward's Parade · Eastbourne BN21 4EE

Tel: (0323) 25174 · Telex: 878624 · Fax: (0323) 39721

Location 3m NW off A272
Hotel ★★66% Halland Forge Hotel, HALLAND ☎(0825) 840456 Annexe20

ESSEX

ABRIDGE — Map 05 TQ49

Abridge Golf and Country Club ☎Stapleford (04028) 396
A parkland course with easy walking. The quick drying course is by no means easy to play. This has been the venue of several professional tournaments. Abridge is a Golf and Country Club and has all the attendant facilities.
18 holes, 6703yds, Par 72, SSS 72.
Club membership 600.

Visitors must play with member at weekends. Must contact in advance and have an introduction from own club.
Societies Mon & Wed only; must contact in advance.
Green Fees on application.
Facilities Bernard Cooke.
Leisure heated outdoor swimming pool, snooker, sauna.
Location Epping Ln, Stapleford Tawney (1.75m NE)
Hotel ★★★62% Forte Posthouse, High Rd, Bell Common, EPPING ☎(0378) 73137 Annexe79

BASILDON — Map 05 TQ78

Basildon ☎(0268) 533297
Undulating municipal parkland course. Testing 13th hole (par 4).
18 holes, 6122yds, Par 70, SSS 69, Course record 63.
Club membership 300.

Visitors no restrictions.
Societies must contact in advance.
Green Fees not confirmed.
Facilities (weekdays only) by prior arrangement & (weekdays only) Graham Hill.
Location Clay Hill Ln, Kingswood (1m S off A176)
Hotel ★★★67% Forte Crest Hotel, Cranes Farm Rd, BASILDON ☎(0268) 533955 110

Pipps Hill Country Club ☎(0268) 27278
Flat course with ditches and pond.
9 holes, 2829yds, Par 34, SSS 34.
Club membership 400.

Visitors no restrictions.
Societies must contact in advance.
Green Fees not confirmed.
Facilities
Location Cranes Farm Rd (N side of town centre off A127)
Hotel ★★★67% Forte Crest Hotel, Cranes Farm Rd, BASILDON ☎(0268) 533955 110

For an explanation of symbols and abbreviations, see page 32

BENFLEET   Map 05 TQ78

Boyce Hill ☎(0268) 793625
Hilly parkland course with good views.
18 holes, 5377yds, Par 68, SSS 68, Course record 61.
Club membership 600.

Visitors	must have a handicap certificate. May only play with member at weekends.
Societies	Thu only
Green Fees	£26 per round; £30 per day.
Facilities	⊗ ⏶ by prior arrangement 🖿 ➡ ♀ ⚒ 🏠 ⚐ ℓ Graham Burroughs.
Location	Vicarage Hill, South Benfleet (.75m NE of Benfleet Station)
Hotel	★★★67% Forte Crest Hotel, Cranes Farm Rd, BASILDON ☎(0268) 533955 110⇨🏠

BRAINTREE   Map 05 TL72

Braintree ☎(0376) 46079
Parkland course with many rare trees.
18 holes, 6161yds, Par 70, SSS 69, Course record 65.
Club membership 750.

Visitors	may not play on Sun mornings. With member only Sat, Sun afternoon and bank holidays. Must contact in advance and have an introduction from own club.
Societies	must contact in advance.
Green Fees	£24 per day.
Facilities	⊗ ⏶ (by prior arrangement ex Sat & Sun) 🖿 (ex Sat & Sun) ➡ ♀ ⚒ 🏠 ℓ Tony Parcell.
Location	Kings Ln, Stisted (1m W off A120)
Hotel	★★55% The Saracen's Head, High St, GREAT DUNMOW ☎(0371) 873901 24⇨

Towerlands ☎(0376) 26802
Undulating, grassland course. Driving range.
9 holes, 2703yds, Par 34, SSS 66.
Club membership 300.

Visitors	must not play before 12.30pm Sat & Sun.
Societies	must contact in advance by telephone.
Green Fees	not confirmed.
Facilities	⊗ ⏶ 🖿 ➡ ♀ ⚒ 🏠 ℓ Andrew Boulter.
Leisure	squash, sports hall, indoor bowls.
Location	Panfield Rd (On B1053)
Hotel	★★68% White Hart Hotel, Bocking End, BRAINTREE ☎(0376) 21401 35⇨🏠

BRENTWOOD   Map 05 TQ59

Bentley ☎Coxtie Green (0277) 373179
Parkland course with water hazards.
18 holes, 6709yds, Par 72, SSS 72, Course record 68.
Club membership 550.

Visitors	may only play after 11am on bank holidays. Must contact in advance and have an introduction from own club.
Societies	must contact in advance.
Green Fees	£24 per day; £18.50 per round.
Facilities	⊗ ⏶ by prior arrangement 🖿 ➡ ♀ ⚒ 🏠 ℓ Keith Bridges.
Location	Ongar Rd (3m NW on A128)
Hotel	★★★67% Forte Posthouse, Brook St, BRENTWOOD ☎(0277) 260260 120⇨

Hartswood ☎(0277) 218850
Municipal parkland course, easy walking.
18 holes, 6160yds, Par 70, SSS 69, Course record 69.
Club membership 800.

Visitors	must contact in advance.
Societies	must contact in advance.
Green Fees	£6.15 per round (£9.20 weekends & bank holidays).
Facilities	Catering at the club by prior arrangement ♀ ⚒ 🏠 ⚐ ℓ John Stanion.
Location	King George's Playing Fields, Ingrave Rd (.75m SE on A128)
Hotel	★★★67% Forte Posthouse, Brook St, BRENTWOOD ☎(0277) 260260 120⇨

Warley Park ☎(0277) 224891
Parkland course with reasonable walking. Numerous water hazards. There is also a golf-practice ground.
27 holes, 3240yds, Par 36, SSS 71.
Club membership 650.

Visitors	must contact in advance and have an introduction from own club.
Societies	must contact in advance.
Green Fees	not confirmed.
Facilities	⊗ ⏶ 🖿 ➡ ♀ ⚒ 🏠 ⚐ ℓ P O'Connor.
Location	Magpie Ln, Little Warley (2.5m S off B186)
Hotel	★★★67% Forte Posthouse, Brook St, BRENTWOOD ☎(0277) 260260 120⇨

BULPHAN   Map 05 TQ68

Langdon Hills Golf & Country Club
☎Basildon (0268) 548444
The complex is the base of the European School of Golf. The course is of championship standard and will be extended to 27 holes in 1992 (summer). Practice facilities include a 22-bay covered floodlit driving range, short game practice area with greens and bunkers and three hole practice course.
18 holes, 6485yds, Par 72, SSS 71.
Club membership 700.

Visitors	must have a handicap certificate & must contact the club in advance.
Societies	must book in advance.
Green Fees	£17.50.
Facilities	⊗ ⏶ 🖿 ➡ ♀ ⚒ 🏠 ⚐ 🚗 ℓ J Slinger, H Arnott, B Lewis.
Location	Lower Dunton Rd
Hotel	★★★★65% Brentwood Moat House, London Rd, BRENTWOOD ☎(0277) 225252 3⇨🏠Annexe30⇨🏠

BURNHAM-ON-CROUCH   Map 05 TQ99

Burnham-on-Crouch ☎(0621) 782282
Undulating meadowland course, easy walking, windy.
9 holes, 5918yds, Par 68, SSS 68, Course record 66.
Club membership 400.

Visitors	may only play Mon-Wed & Fri 9am-2pm, Thu noon-2pm. Must contact in advance.
Societies	Tue only. Must contact in writing.
Green Fees	£18 per day/round.
Facilities	⏶ (Wed and Fri) 🖿 ➡ ♀ (Tue-Fri) ⚒ 🏠
Location	Ferry Rd, Creeksea (1.25m W off B1010)
Hotel	★★61% Blue Boar Hotel, Silver St, MALDON ☎(0621) 852681 20⇨🏠Annexe8⇨🏠

CHELMSFORD   Map 05 TL70

Channels ☎(0245) 440005
Built on land from reclaimed gravel pits, 18 very exciting holes with plenty of lakes providing an excellent test of golf.
18 holes, 5927yds, Par 70, SSS 69, Course record 65.
Club membership 750.
Visitors	must play with member at weekends. Must contact in advance.
Societies	must contact in advance.
Green Fees	£25 per day.
Facilities	⊗ ℳ ㎏ ■ ♀ ⌂ 🖼 (Ian Sinclair.
Leisure	fishing.
Location	Belstead Farm Ln, Little Waltham (3.5m NE off A130)
Hotel	★★★54% South Lodge Hotel, 196 New London Rd, CHELMSFORD ☎(0245) 264564 24⇨🖼Annexe17⇨

Chelmsford ☎(0245) 256483
An undulating parkland course, hilly in parts, with 3 holes in woods and four difficult par 4's. From the reconstructed clubhouse there are fine views over the course and the wooded hills beyond.
18 holes, 5944yds, Par 68, SSS 68.
Club membership 650.
Visitors	must play with member at weekends. Must contact in advance and have an introduction from own club.
Societies	must contact 9 months in advance.
Green Fees	£20 per round; £30 per day.
Facilities	⊗ ℳ (Fri and Sat only) ㎏ ■ ♀ ⌂ 🖼(D Bailey.
Location	Widford (1.5m S of town centre off A12)
Hotel	★★★54% South Lodge Hotel, 196 New London Rd, CHELMSFORD ☎(0245) 264564 24⇨🖼Annexe17⇨

CHIGWELL   Map 05 TQ49

Chigwell ☎081-500 2059
A course of high quality, mixing meadowland with parkland. For those who believe 'all Essex is flat' the undulating nature of Chigwell will be a refreshing surprise. The greens are excellent and the fairways tight with mature trees.

SCORECARD: White Tees					
Hole	Yds	Par	Hole	Yds	Par
1	466	4	10	163	3
2	187	3	11	387	4
3	476	5	12	383	4
4	379	4	13	364	4
5	478	5	14	191	3
6	137	3	15	460	4
7	363	4	16	312	4
8	309	4	17	332	4
9	354	4	18	538	5
Out	3149	36	In	3130	35
			Totals	6279	71

18 holes, 6279yds, Par 71, SSS 70, Course record 66.
Club membership 657.
Visitors	may play mid-week, but must be accompanied by member at weekends. Must contact in advance and have an introduction from own club.
Societies	must contact in writing
Green Fees	£35 per day; £28 per round.
Facilities	⊗ ℳ ㎏ ■ ♀ ⌂ 🖼🏴(R Beard.
Location	High Rd (.5m S on A113)
Hotel	★★59% Roebuck Hotel, North End, BUCKHURST HILL ☎081-505 4636 29⇨🖼

CHIGWELL ROW   Map 05 TQ49

Hainault Forest ☎081-500 0385
Club playing over Borough of Redbridge public courses; hilly parkland subject to wind. Two courses, driving range.
No 1 Course: 18 holes, 5744yds, Par 70, SSS 67, Course record 65.
No 2 Course: 18 holes, 6600yds, Par 71, SSS 71, Course record 68.
Club membership 600.
Visitors	no restrictions
Societies	must contact in writing
Green Fees	£7.50 (£10 weekends).
Facilities	⊗ ℳ by prior arrangement ㎏ ■ ♀ ⌂ 🖼🏴 (A E Frost.
Location	Romford Rd, Chigwell Row (.5m S on A113)
Hotel	★★★52% Woodford Bridge Hotel, Milton Damerel, HOLSWORTHY ☎(040926) 481 12⇨🖼

CLACTON-ON-SEA   Map 05 TM11

Clacton ☎(0255) 421919
Windy, seaside course.
18 holes, 6244yds, Par 70, SSS 68, Course record 65.
Club membership 630.
Visitors	must contact in advance.
Societies	must contact in writing.
Green Fees	not confirmed.
Facilities	⊗ ㎏ ■ ♀ ⌂ 🖼(S Levermore.
Location	West Rd (1.25m SW of town centre)
Hotel	★★65% Maplin Hotel, Esplanade, FRINTON-ON-SEA ☎(0255) 673832 12rm(9⇨1🖼)

COLCHESTER   Map 05 TL92

Birch Grove ☎Layer de la Haye (020634) 276
A pretty, undulating course surrounded by woodland - small but challenging with excellent greens.
9 holes, 4038yds, Par 62, SSS 60, Course record 61.
Club membership 250.
Visitors	restricted Sun mornings.
Societies	must contact in advance.
Green Fees	£9 (£11 weekends & bank holidays).
Facilities	⊗ ℳ ㎏ ■ ♀ ⌂ 🖼
Location	Layer Rd, Kingsford (2.5m S on B1026)
Hotel	★★65% Kings Ford Park Hotel, Layer Rd, Layer De La Haye, COLCHESTER ☎(0206) 34301 due to change to 734301 13⇨🖼

Colchester ☎(0206) 853396
A fairly flat parkland course.
18 holes, 6319yds, Par 70, SSS 70, Course record 63.
Club membership 800.
Visitors	with member only at weekends. Must contact in advance and have an introduction from own club.
Societies	must contact in advance.
Green Fees	£24 per day.
Facilities	⊗ ℳ by prior arrangement ㎏ ■ ♀ ⌂ 🖼(
Location	Braiswick (1.5m NW of town centre on B1508)
Hotel	★★★60% George Hotel, 116 High St, COLCHESTER ☎(0206) 578494 47⇨🖼

Stoke-by-Nayland ☎Nayland (0206) 262836
Two undulating courses (Gainsborough and Constable)
situated in Dedham Vale. Some water hazards and hedges.
On Gainsborough the 10th (par 4) takes 2 shots over a lake;
very testing par 3 at 11th.
Gainsborough Course: 18 holes, 6516yds, Par 72, SSS 71,
Course record 66.
Constable Course: 18 holes, 6544yds, Par 72, SSS 71, Course
record 67.
Club membership 1460.

Visitors	restricted at weekends. Must contact in advance.
Societies	weekdays only . Must contact in advance.
Green Fees	£25 per day (£28 weekends).
Facilities	⊗ ⊞ ⓛ ⬛ ♀ ⌂ 🏠 ⌐ ⌐ Kevin Lovelock.
Leisure	squash, sauna.
Location	Keepers Ln, Leavenheath (1.5m NW of Stoke-by-Nayland on B1068)
Hotel	★★★(red)⚐ Maison Talbooth, Stratford Rd, DEDHAM ☎(0206) 322367 10⇨🏠

EARLS COLNE
Map 05 TL82

Earls Colne Golf & Leisure Centre ☎(0787) 224466
Created on the site of a World War II airfield, this
challenging public course contains 14 lakes. Also 9-hole
course and 4-hole instruction course as well as a variety of
leisure facilities.
18 holes, 6900yds, Par 73, SSS 72, Course record 71.
Club membership 500.

Visitors	no restrictions.
Societies	must telephone in advance.
Green Fees	£15 per round (£18 weekends).
Facilities	⊗ ⊞ (Wed-Sat) ⓛ ⬛ ♀ ⌂ 🏠 ⌐ Owen Mckenna.
Leisure	hard tennis courts, heated indoor swimming pool, fishing, sauna, solarium, gymnasium.
Hotel	★★★67% White Hart Hotel, Market End, COGGESHALL ☎(0376) 561654 18⇨🏠

FRINTON-ON-SEA
Map 05 TM22

Frinton ☎(0255) 674618
Flat seaside links course, easy walking, windy. Also a short
course.
Long Course: 18 holes, 6259yds, Par 71, SSS 70, Course record
66.
Short Course: 18 holes, 2508yds, Par 66.
Club membership 800.

Visitors	must have a handicap certificate. Must contact in advance.
Societies	must contact in writing.
Green Fees	£23 per day Long Course; £8 per day Short Course.
Facilities	⊗ ⊞ ⓛ ⬛ ♀ ⌂ 🏠 ⌐ ⌐ Peter Taggart.
Leisure	snooker.
Location	1 The Esplanade (SW side of town centre)
Hotel	★★65% Maplin Hotel, Esplanade, FRINTON-ON-SEA ☎(0255) 673832 12rm(9⇨1🏠)

This guide is updated annually – make sure that
you use the up-to-date edition

GOSFIELD
Map 05 TL72

Gosfield Lake ☎Halstead (0787) 474747
Parkland course with bunkers, lake and water hazards.
Designed by Sir Henry Cotton/Mr Howard Swan and
opened in 1988. Also 9-hole course.
18 holes, 6512yds, Par 72, SSS 71, Course record 71.
Meadows: 9 holes, 4037yds, Par 66.
Club membership 850.

Visitors	a handicap certificate is required. With member only at weekends from noon.
Societies	apply in writing.
Green Fees	Lakes £20 per day (Meadows £8 per day).
Facilities	⊗ ⊞ ⓛ ⬛ ♀ ⌂ 🏠 ⌐ Richard Wheeler.
Location	The Manor House, Hall Dr
Hotel	★★68% White Hart Hotel, Bocking End, BRAINTREE ☎(0376) 21401 35⇨🏠

HARLOW
Map 05 TL40

Canon's Brook ☎(0279) 421482
Parkland course designed by Henry Cotton.
18 holes, 6728yds, Par 73, SSS 73.
Club membership 800.

Visitors	may not play at weekends.
Societies	must contact in advance.
Green Fees	£22.50 per day/per round.
Facilities	♀ ⌂ 🏠 ⌐ ⌐ R Yates.
Location	Elizabeth Way (3m S of M11)
Hotel	★★★70% Churchgate Manor Hotel, Churchgate St, Old Harlow, HARLOW ☎(0279) 420246 85⇨

HARWICH
Map 05 TM23

Harwich & Dovercourt ☎(0255) 503616
Flat moorland course with easy walking.
9 holes, 5742yds, SSS 68.
Club membership 420.

Visitors	with member only at weekends. Must contact in advance and have an introduction from own club.
Societies	must contact in writing.
Green Fees	not confirmed.
Facilities	⊗ ⊞ ⓛ & ⬛ by prior arrangement ♀ ⌂ 🏠
Location	Station Rd, Parkeston, Dovercourt (W side .25m from docks on A120)
Hotel	★★55% Cliff Hotel, Marine Pde, Dovercourt, HARWICH ☎(0255) 503345 & 507373 28⇨🏠

INGRAVE
Map 05 TQ69

Thorndon Park ☎Brentwood (0277) 811666
Among the best of the Essex courses with a fine new
purpose-built clubhouse and a lake. The springy turf is
easy on the feet. Many newly planted young trees now
replace the famous old oaks that were such a feature of
this course.
18 holes, 6455yds, Par 71, SSS 71.
Club membership 680.

Visitors	may not play at weekends. Must contact in advance.
Societies	must contact in advance.

Green Fees	£25 per round; £35 per day.
Facilities	⊗ ⛳ 🏌 ♀ ⚐ 🏠 ⛳ (Brian White.
Location	Ingrave Rd (W side of village on A128)
Hotel	★★★67% Forte Posthouse, Brook St, BRENTWOOD ☎(0277) 260260 120⇨

MALDON   Map 05 TL80

Forrester Park ☎(0621) 891406
Tight, undulating parkland course with tree-lined fairways and good views over the Blackwater estuary. Easy walking. Attractive 16th-century clubhouse.
18 holes, 60■yds, Par 71, SSS 69, Course record 68.
Club membership 1200.

Visitors	may not play on Tue mornings, Wed or weekends. Must contact in advance.
Societies	must telephone in advance.
Green Fees	£12 per round.
Facilities	⊗ ⛳ 🏌 ♀ ⚐ 🏠
Leisure	hard tennis courts.
Location	Beckingham Rd, Great Totham (3m SE of Witham on A12)
Hotel	★★61% Blue Boar Hotel, Silver St, MALDON ☎(0621) 852681 20⇨ Annexe8⇨

Maldon ☎(0621) 853212
Flat, parkland course in a triangle of land by the River Chelmer, the Blackwater Canal and an old railway embankment. Alternate tees on 2nd 9 holes.
9 holes, 6197yds, Par 71, SSS 69.
Club membership 480.

Visitors	may play after 2pm and at weekends only with member. Must have an introduction from own club.
Societies	may play Mon & Thu. Must contact in advance.
Green Fees	£20 per day; £15 per round (Mon-Fri).
Facilities	⊗ & ⫿ by prior arrangement ⛳ 🏌 ♀ ⚐ 🏠
Location	Beeleigh, Langford (1m NW off B1018)
Hotel	★★61% Blue Boar Hotel, Silver St, MALDON ☎(0621) 852681 20⇨ Annexe8⇨

ORSETT   Map 05 TQ68

Orsett ☎Grays Thurrock (0375) 891352
A very good test of golf - this heathland course with its sandy soil is quick drying and provides easy walking. Close to the Thames estuary it is seldom calm and the main hazards are the prevailing wind and thick gorse. Any slight deviation can be exaggerated by the wind and a lost ball in the gorse results. The clubhouse has been modernised.
18 holes, 6614yds, Par 72, SSS 72, Course record 68.
Club membership 900.
Visitors	restricted weekends & bank holidays. Must contact in advance and have an introduction from own club.
Societies	must contact in advance.
Green Fees	not confirmed.
Facilities	⊗ ⫿ ⛳ 🏌 ♀ ⚐ 🏠 ⛳ (Robert Newberry.
Leisure	snooker.
Location	Brentwood Rd (1.5m SE off A128)
Hotel	★★★67% Forte Crest Hotel, Cranes Farm Rd, BASILDON ☎(0268) 533955 110⇨

PURLEIGH   Map 05 TL80

Three Rivers ☎Maldon (0621) 828631
Parkland course.
Kings Course: 18 holes, 6348yds, Par 73, SSS 70, Course record 61.
Queens Course: 9 holes, 1071yds, Par 27.

Visitors	may not play at weekends & bank holidays. Must contact in advance and have an introduction from own club.
Societies	Tue & Thu only; must contact in advance.
Green Fees	£18 per day.
Facilities	⊗ ⫿ ⛳ 🏌 ♀ ⚐ 🏠 ⛴ (Lionel Platts.
Leisure	hard tennis courts, heated outdoor swimming pool, squash, snooker, sauna, solarium, gymnasium.
Location	Stow Rd (1m from Purleigh on B1012)
Hotel	★★61% Blue Boar Hotel, Silver St, MALDON ☎(0621) 852681 20⇨ Annexe8⇨

ROCHFORD   Map 05 H3

Rochford Hundred ☎(0702) 544302
Parkland course with ponds and ditches as natural hazards.
18 holes, 6292yds, Par 72, SSS 70.
Club membership 800.

Visitors	must contact in advance and have an introduction from own club.
Societies	must contact in writing.
Green Fees	not confirmed.
Facilities	♀ ⚐ 🏠 (
Location	Hall Rd (W on B1013)
Hotel	★69% Balmoral Hotel, 34 Valkyrie Rd, Westcliffe-on-Sea, SOUTHEND-ON-SEA ☎(0702) 342947 22⇨

SAFFRON WALDEN   Map 05 TL53

Saffron Walden ☎(0799) 22786
Undulating parkland course, beautiful views.
18 holes, 6617yds, Par 72, SSS 72, Course record 63 or 6419yds, Par 72, SSS 71, Course record 68.
Club membership 900.

Visitors	with member only at weekends. Must contact in advance and have an introduction from own club.
Societies	must contact in writing.
Green Fees	£25 per day/round.
Facilities	⊗ ⫿ ⛳ 🏌 ♀ ⚐ 🏠 (Philip Davis.
Location	Windmill Hill (NW side of town centre off B184)
Hotel	★★65% Saffron Hotel, 10-18 High St, SAFFRON WALDEN ☎(0799) 22676 21rm(8⇨8♠)

SOUTHEND-ON-SEA   Map 05 TQ88

Belfairs ☎(0702) 525345
Municipal parkland course run by the Borough Council. Tight second half through thick woods, easy walking.
18 holes, 5795yds, Par 70, SSS 68.
Club membership 300.

Visitors	restricted weekends & bank holidays.
Green Fees	not confirmed.

▶

Facilities	🏠 ⚑ (
Leisure	hard tennis courts.
Location	Eastwood Rd North, Leigh on Sea (3m W, N of A13)
Hotel	★69% Balmoral Hotel, 34 Valkyrie Rd, Westcliffe-on-Sea, SOUTHEND-ON-SEA ☎(0702) 342947 22⇔🏠

Thorpe Hall ☎(0702) 582205
Parkland course.
18 holes, 6286yds, Par 71, SSS 71.
Club membership 1000.

Visitors	with member only weekends & bank holidays. Must contact in advance and have an introduction from own club.
Societies	must contact one year in advance.
Green Fees	£25 per day/round.
Facilities	⊗ �🍴 🍺 & 🍺 (with member only) ♀ ⛱ 🏠 (Garry Harvey.
Leisure	squash, snooker, sauna.
Location	Thorpe Hall Av, Thorpe Bay (2m E off A13)
Hotel	★69% Balmoral Hotel, 34 Valkyrie Rd, Westcliffe-on-Sea, SOUTHEND-ON-SEA ☎(0702) 342947 22⇔🏠

SOUTH OCKENDON   Map 05 TQ58

Belhus Park Municipal ☎(0708) 854260
Flat parkland, easy going. Eleven-bay floodlit driving range.
18 holes, 5501yds, Par 68, SSS 68.

Visitors	not confirmed.
Green Fees	not confirmed.
Facilities	♀ ⛱ 🏠 ⚑ (
Location	Belhus Park (.5m N of M25 (junc 30) on B1335)
Hotel	★★★67% Forte Crest Hotel, Cranes Farm Rd, BASILDON ☎(0268) 533955 110⇔🏠

Thurrock Belhus Park ☎(0708) 354260
Municipal parkland type course with easy walking.
18 holes, 5450yds, Par 67.
Club membership 250.

Visitors	no restrictions.
Societies	must contact in writing.
Green Fees	not confirmed.
Facilities	⊗ 🍺 🍺 ♀ ⛱ 🏠 ⚑ (
Leisure	heated indoor swimming pool, squash, sauna, solarium, gymnasium, 11 bay floodlit driving range.
Location	Belhus Park (2m SW off B1335)
Hotel	★★★67% Forte Crest Hotel, Cranes Farm Rd, BASILDON ☎(0268) 533955 110⇔🏠

STAPLEFORD ABBOTTS   Map 05 TQ59

Stapleford Abbotts ☎(04023) 81108
Two championship 18-hole courses and a 9-hole par 3. Many lakes on each course.
Abbotts Course: 18 holes, 6431yds, Par 72, SSS 71.
Friars Course: 9 holes, 1140yds, Par 27.
Club membership 800.

Visitors	restricted at weekends. Must contact in advance.
Societies	by arrangement.
Green Fees	£15 per round (£30 weekends).

Facilities	⊗ 🍺 & 🍺 (during daylight hours) ♀ ⛱ 🏠 ⚑ (Scot Cranfield.
Leisure	sauna, gymnasium.
Location	Horsemanside, Tysea Hill (1m E off B175)
Hotel	★★59% Roebuck Hotel, North End, BUCKHURST HILL ☎081-505 4636 29⇔🏠

THEYDON BOIS   Map 05 TQ49

Theydon Bois ☎(037881) 3054
A new nine holes have been added to the old nine built into Epping Forest. They are well-planned and well-bunkered but are situated out in the open on the hillside. The old nine in the Forest are short and have three bunkers among them, but even so a wayward shot can be among the trees. The autumn colours here are truly magnificent.
18 holes, 5472yds, Par 68, SSS 68, Course record 66.
Club membership 625.

Visitors	must contact in advance and have an introduction from own club.
Societies	Mon & Tue only. Must contact in advance.
Green Fees	£23 per day (£15 after 5pm); £34.50 weekends & bank holidays (£20 after 5pm).
Facilities	⊗ (Mon-Thu only) 🍴 by prior arrangement 🍺 (Mon-Thu only) 🍺 ♀ ⛱ 🏠 ⚑ (
Location	Theydon Rd (1m N)
Hotel	★★★62% Forte Posthouse, High Rd, Bell Common, EPPING ☎(0378) 73137 Annexe79⇔🏠

TOLLESHUNT D'ARCY   Map 05 TL91

Quietwaters ☎Maldon (0621) 860410
Two 18-hole courses. The Links is a seaside course with a number of greenside ponds and strategically placed bunkers, while the Lakes is a championship course with large water features and mounding between fairways.
Links Course: 18 holes, 6194yds, Par 71, SSS 70.
Lakes Course: 18 holes, 6767yds, Par 72, SSS 72, Course record 67.
Club membership 600.

Visitors	restricted at weekends. Must contact in advance.
Societies	must contact in advance.
Green Fees	£25 per day; £18 per round (£30 per day; £22.50 per round weekends & bank holidays).
Facilities	⊗ 🍺 🍺 ♀ ⛱ 🏠 🏸 (Denis Pugh.
Leisure	hard tennis courts, heated indoor swimming pool, squash, fishing, snooker, sauna, solarium, gymnasium, 8 international bowling rinks.
Location	Colchester Rd (1.75m NE on B1026)
Hotel	★★65% Kings Ford Park Hotel, Layer Rd, Layer De La Haye, COLCHESTER ☎(0206) 34301 due to change to 734301 13⇔🏠

WOODHAM WALTER   Map 05 TL80

Bunsay Downs ☎Danbury (024541) 2648
Attractive 9-hole public course. Also Par 3.
Bunsay Downs: 9 holes, 5864yds, Par 70, SSS 68.
Badgers: 9 holes, 2638yds, Par 54.
Club membership 600.

Visitors	no restrictions.
Societies	Mon & Tue only. Must contact in advance.

Green Fees	£10 per round Bunsay Downs; £8 per round Badgers.
Facilities	⊗))∭ 🛏 🍺 ♀ ⚲ 🏠 ⛴ 𝄞 Miss Mickey Walker.
Location	Little Baddow Rd
Hotel	★★61% Blue Boar Hotel, Silver St, MALDON ☎(0621) 852681 20⇨🏠Annexe8⇨🏠

Warren ☎Danbury (024541) 3258
Attractive parkland course with natural hazards and good views.
18 holes, 6229yds, Par 70, SSS 70, Course record 66.
Club membership 840.

Visitors	must play with club member at weekends before 3pm. Must have an introduction from own club.
Societies	must contact in advance.
Green Fees	£28 per day; £22 per round.
Facilities	⊗))∭ 🛏 🍺 ♀ ⚲ 🏠 𝄞 Miss Mickey Walker.
Leisure	snooker.
Location	.5m SW
Hotel	★★61% Blue Boar Hotel, Silver St, MALDON ☎(0621) 852681 20⇨🏠Annexe8⇨🏠

GLOUCESTERSHIRE

CHELTENHAM   Map 03 SO92

Cotswold Hills ☎(0242) 515264
A gently undulating course with open aspects and views of the Cotswolds.
18 holes, 6345yds, Par 70, SSS 72.
Club membership 750.

Visitors	must have an introduction from own club.
Societies	must apply in writing.
Green Fees	£21 per round (£26 weekends).
Facilities	⊗))∭ 🛏 🍺 ♀ ⚲ 🏠 𝄞 Noel Boland.
Location	Ullenwood (3m S off A436)
Hotel	★★★68% Forte Crest Hotel, Crest Way, Barnwood, GLOUCESTER ☎(0452) 613311 123⇨🏠

Lilley Brook ☎(0242) 526785
Undulating parkland course. Magnificent views over Cheltenham and surrounding coutryside.
18 holes, 6226yds, Par 69, SSS 70, Course record 74.
Club membership 800.

Visitors	must have handicap certificate. With member only at weekends. Must contact in advance and have an introduction from own club.
Societies	Wed & Thu only, by prior arrangement.
Green Fees	£20 per day.
Facilities	⊗ &))∭ (ex Mon) 🛏 🍺 ♀ ⚲ 🏠 ⛴ 𝄞 Forbes Hadden.
Location	Cirencester Rd, Charlton Kings (3m S on A435)
Hotel	★★★★52% The Queen's, Promenade, CHELTENHAM ☎(0242) 514724 77⇨🏠
Additional hotel	★★★64% Prestbury House Hotel, The Burgage, Prestbury, CHELTENHAM ☎(0242) 529533 & 30106 9⇨🏠Annexe9⇨🏠

Entries highlighted in green identify courses which are considered to be particularly interesting

CIRENCESTER   Map 04 SP00

Cirencester ☎(0285) 652465
Undulating Cotswold course.
18 holes, 6002yds, Par 70, SSS 69, Course record 64.
Club membership 750.

Visitors	may not play on competition days. Must contact in advance and have an introduction from own club.
Societies	must contact in writing.
Green Fees	£20 per day (£25 weekends & bank holidays).
Facilities	⊗))∭ by prior arrangement 🛏 🍺 ♀ ⚲ 🏠 ⛴ 𝄞 Geoff Robbins.
Location	Cheltenham Rd, Bagendon (1.5m N on A435)
Hotel	★★★65% Stratton House Hotel, Gloucester Rd, CIRENCESTER ☎(0285) 651761 25⇨🏠

CLEEVE HILL   Map 03 SO92

Cleeve Hill ☎(024267) 2025
Undulating heathland course.
18 holes, 6217yds, Par 69, SSS 70.
Club membership 650.

Visitors	must contact in advance.
Societies	must contact in advance.
Green Fees	£6 (£7 weekends & bank holidays).
Facilities	⊗))∭ 🛏 🍺 ♀ ⚲ 🏠 ⛴ 𝄞 David Finch.
Leisure	skittle alley.
Location	nr Prestbury (1m NE on A46)
Hotel	★★★64% Hotel De La Bere, Southam, CHELTENHAM ☎(0242) 237771 32⇨🏠Annexe25⇨🏠

COLEFORD
Map 03 SO51

Royal Forest of Dean ☎Dean (0594) 32583
Established in 1973 and now matured into an extremely pleasant parkland course.
18 holes, 5535yds, Par 69, SSS 67.
Club membership 500.

Visitors	are required to give Tee-off times. Must contact in advance.
Societies	must telephone in advance.
Green Fees	£14 (£16 weekends & bank holidays).
Facilities	⊗ ⅲ ⓛ ⬛ ♀ ⚘ 🕋 ⚚ ⊨ ⎾ John Nicol.
Leisure	hard tennis courts, outdoor swimming pool, bowling green.
Location	Lords Hill (Off M5/M50 4m from Monmouth)
Hotel	★★63% The Speech House, Forest of Dean, COLEFORD ☎(0594) 822607 14⇥👂

DURSLEY
Map 03 ST79

Stinchcombe Hill
☎(0453) 542015
High on the hill with splendid views of the Cotswolds, the River Severn and the Welsh hills. A downland course with good turf, some trees and an interesting variety of greens.
18 holes, 5723yds, Par 68, SSS 68, Course record 64.
Club membership 500.

SCORECARD					
Hole	Yds	Par	Hole	Yds	Par
1	275	4	10	405	4
2	419	4	11	142	3
3	434	4	12	331	4
4	197	3	13	437	4
5	374	4	14	355	4
6	139	3	15	145	3
7	435	4	16	309	4
8	367	4	17	321	4
9	162	3	18	476	5
Out	2802	33	In	2921	35
			Totals	5723	68

Visitors	restricted at weekends. Must contact in advance.
Societies	must apply in writing.
Green Fees	£18 per day (£20 weekends & bank holidays).
Facilities	⊗ ⅲ ⓛ ⬛ ♀ ⚘ 🕋 ⎾ Tony Valentine.
Leisure	pool table.
Location	Stinchcombe Hill (1m W off A4135)
Hotel	★★63% The Old Schoolhouse Hotel, Canonbury St, BERKELEY ☎(0453) 811711 7⇥👂

GLOUCESTER
Map 03 SO81

Gloucester Hotel & Country Club ☎(0452) 411331
Undulating, wooded course, built around a hill with superb views over Gloucester and the Cotswolds. The 12th is a drive straight up a hill, nicknamed 'Coronary Hill'.
18 holes, 5613yds, Par 70, SSS 69.
Club membership 550.

Visitors	must book at weekends. Handicap certificate required.
Societies	weekends only, by arrangement.
Green Fees	£19.50 per day (£24 weekends & bank holidays).
Facilities	⊗ & ⅲ by prior arrangement ⓛ ⬛ ♀ ⚘ 🕋 ⚚ ⊨ ⎾
Leisure	hard tennis courts, heated indoor swimming pool, squash, snooker, sauna, solarium, gymnasium, table tennis, skittles, dry ski slope.
Location	Matson Ln, Robinswood Hill (2m SW off M5)
Hotel	★★★68% Gloucester Hotel & Country Club, Robinswood Hill, GLOUCESTER ☎(0452) 525653 97⇥👂 Annexe10⇥👂

LYDNEY
Map 03 SO60

Lydney ☎Dean (0594) 842614
Flat parkland/meadowland course with prevailing wind along fairways.
9 holes, 5329yds, Par 66, SSS 66, Course record 63.
Club membership 350.

Visitors	with member only at weekends & bank holidays.
Societies	must telephone in advance.
Green Fees	£12 per day.
Facilities	ⓛ ⬛ ♀ ⚘
Location	Lakeside Av (SE side of town centre)
Hotel	★★63% The Speech House, Forest of Dean, COLEFORD ☎(0594) 822607 14⇥👂

MINCHINHAMPTON
Map 03 SO80

Minchinhampton ☎Nailsworth (0453) 833866
Cotswold upland courses in rural surroundings.
Old Course: 18 holes, 6295yds, Par 72, SSS 70, Course record 65.
New Course: 18 holes, 6675yds, Par 72, SSS 72, Course record 66.
Club membership 1600.

Visitors	must have a handicap certificate. Must contact in advance.
Societies	must contact by telephone.
Green Fees	Old Course: £12 per day (£15 weekends & bank holidays) New Course: £22.50 per day (£28 weekends & bank holidays).
Facilities	⊗ ⅲ (ex Sun and Mon) ⓛ ⬛ ♀ ⚘ 🕋 ⚚ ⎾ Chris Steele.
Leisure	snooker.
Location	New Course (1.5m)
Hotel	★★★♨65% Burleigh Court, Minchinhampton, STROUD ☎(0453) 883804 11⇥👂 Annexe6⇥👂

PAINSWICK
Map 03 SO80

Painswick ☎(0452) 812180
Downland course set on Cotswold Hills at Painswick Beacon, with fine views. Short course more than compensated by natural hazards and tight fairways.
18 holes, 4895yds, Par 67, SSS 64, Course record 62.
Club membership 420.

Visitors	with member only on Sun.
Societies	must apply in writing.
Green Fees	£8 per round (£12 Sat).
Facilities	ⓛ (ex Mon) ⬛ (ex Sun & Mon) ♀ ⚘ 🕋
Location	1m N on A46
Hotel	★★★56% Bear of Rodborough Hotel, Rodborough Common, STROUD ☎(0453) 878522 47⇥👂

For a full list of golf courses included in the book, see the index at the end of the directory

TEWKESBURY   Map 03 SO83

Tewkesbury Park Hotel Golf & Country Club
☎(0684) 295405

A parkland course in a sheltered situation beside the River Severn. The par 3, 5th is an exacting hole calling for accurate distance judgement. The hotel and country club offer many sports facilities.
18 holes, 6197yds, Par 73, SSS 70, Course record 68.
Club membership 553.

SCORECARD: White Tees					
Hole	Yds	Par	Hole	Yds	Par
1	519	5	10	200	3
2	321	4	11	422	4
3	503	5	12	517	5
4	431	4	13	416	4
5	146	3	14	339	4
6	575	5	15	501	5
7	128	3	16	178	3
8	349	4	17	371	4
9	352	4	18	265	4
Out	3324	37	In	3209	36
			Totals	6533	73

Visitors	must contact in advance and have an introduction from own club.
Societies	apply in writing.
Green Fees	not confirmed.
Facilities	⊗ ℸ ⓛ 📭 ♀ ♠ 🝙 ㎡ ⊨ ℓ Peter Cane.
Leisure	hard tennis courts, heated indoor swimming pool, squash, snooker, sauna, solarium, gymnasium.
Location	Lincoln Green Ln (1m SW off A38)
Hotel	★★★66% Tewkesbury Park Hotel Golf & Country Club, Lincoln Green Ln, TEWKESBURY ☎(0684) 295405 78⇌🛏

WESTONBIRT   Map 03 ST88

Westonbirt ☎(066688) 242
A parkland course with good views.
9 holes, 4504yds, Par 64, SSS 64, Course record 62.
Club membership 150.

Visitors	no restrictions.
Societies	must apply in writing.
Green Fees	£6 per day (£6 per round weekends & bank holidays).
Facilities	♠
Location	Westonbirt School (E side of village off A433)
Hotel	★★★63% Hare & Hounds Hotel, Westonbirt, TETBURY ☎(066688) 233 22⇌🛏 Annexe8⇌🛏

WOTTON-UNDER-EDGE   Map 03 ST79

Cotswold Edge ☎Dursley (0453) 844167
Meadowland course situated in a quiet Cotswold valley. First half flat and open, second half more varied.
18 holes, 5816yds, Par 71, SSS 68, Course record 68.
Club membership 800.

Visitors	must play with member at weekends. Must contact in advance.
Societies	must contact in writing.
Green Fees	£15 per day.
Facilities	⊗ ⓛ 📭 ♀ ♠ 🝙 ㎡ ℓ David Gosling.
Location	Upper Rushmire (N of town on B4058 Wotton-Tetbury road)
Hotel	★★★(red)♨ Calcot Manor, Calcot, TETBURY ☎(0666) 890391 7⇌🛏 Annexe9⇌🛏

A golf-course name printed in ***bold italics*** means that we have been unable to verify information with the club's management for the current year

---

GREATER LONDON

Those courses which fall within the confines of the London Postal District area (ie have London postcodes—W1, SW1, etc) are listed under the county heading of **London** in the gazetteer (see page 151).

ADDINGTON   Map 05 TQ36

Addington Court ☎081-657 0281
Challenging, well-drained courses designed by F. Hawtree. Two 18-hole courses, 9-hole course and a pitch-and-putt course.
Old: 18 holes, 5577yds, Par 67, SSS 67, Course record 63.
New Falconwood: 18 holes, 5360yds, Par 66, SSS 66.
Club membership 350.

Visitors	no restrictions.
Societies	must telephone in advance.
Green Fees	£6-£11.
Facilities	⊗ ℸ by prior arrangement ⓛ 📭 ♀ ♠ 🝙 ㎡ ℓ Geoffrey A Cotton.
Location	Featherbed Ln (1m S off A2022)
Hotel	★★★★62% Selsdon Park Hotel, Sanderstead, CROYDON ☎081-657 8811 170⇌🛏

Addington Palace ☎081-654 3061
Hard-walking parkland course, with two (par 4) testing holes (2nd and 10th).
18 holes, 6262yds, Par 71, SSS 71.
Club membership 600.

Visitors	must play with member at weekends & bank holidays.
Societies	Tue, Wed & Fri only.
Green Fees	not confirmed.
Facilities	⊗ (Tue-Fri and Sun) ℸ by prior arrangement ⓛ 📭 ♀ ♠ 🝙 ℓ M Pilkington.
Location	Gravel Hill (.5m SW on A212)
Hotel	★★★★62% Selsdon Park Hotel, Sanderstead, CROYDON ☎081-657 8811 170⇌🛏

BARNEHURST   Map 05 TQ57

Barnehurst ☎(0322) 523746
Parkland course, easy walking.
9 holes, 5320yds, Par 66, SSS 66.
Club membership 300.

Visitors	restricted Tue, Thu, Sat (pm) & Sun.
Societies	by arrangement.
Green Fees	£5.10 per round (£8.20 weekends & bank holidays).
Facilities	⊗ ⓛ 📭 ♀ ♠ 🝙 ℓ B Finch.
Location	Mayplace Rd East (.75m NW of Crayford off A2000)
Hotel	★★★71% Forte Crest Hotel, Black Prince Interchange, Southwold Rd, BEXLEY ☎(0322) 526900 102⇌🛏

BARNET   Map 04 TQ29

Arkley ☎081-449 0394
Wooded parkland course situated on highest spot in Hertfordshire with fine views.
9 holes, 6045yds, Par 69, SSS 69.
Club membership 400.

▶

Visitors	with member only at weekends.
Societies	Wed, Thu, Fri, by arrangement.
Green Fees	£20 per day/round.
Facilities	⊗ 川 ㄴ ♨ 🍺 ♀ ♨ 🏠 ⚑ Mark Squire.
Location	Rowley Green Rd (2m W off A411)
Hotel	★★★63% Edgwarebury Hotel, Barnet Ln, ELSTREE ☎081-953 8227 50↹🐾

Dyrham Park Country Club ☎081-440 3361
Parkland course.
18 holes, 6369yds, Par 71, SSS 70, Course record 65.
Club membership 1200.

Visitors	must be accompanied by member.
Societies	Wed only.
Green Fees	not confirmed.
Facilities	⊗ 川 (Thu evening Club night) ㄴ ♨ ♀ (all day) ♨ 🏠 ⚑ Bill Large.
Leisure	hard tennis courts, heated outdoor swimming pool, fishing, snooker.
Location	Galley Ln (3m NW off A1081)
Hotel	★★★64% Forte Posthouse, Bignells Corner, SOUTH MIMMS ☎(0707) 43311 120↹🐾

Old Fold Manor ☎081-440 9185
Heathland course, good test of golf.
18 holes, 6449yds, Par 71, SSS 71, Course record 66.
Club membership 522.

Visitors	with member only weekends & bank holidays. Handicap certificate/letter of introduction required.
Societies	must apply in writing.
Green Fees	£27.75 per day; £22.50 per round.
Facilities	⊗ 川 by prior arrangement ㄴ ♨ (no catering Mon & Wed) ♀ (ex Mon & Wed) ♨ 🏠 ⚑ Peter Jones.
Leisure	snooker.
Location	Old Fold Ln, Hadley Green (N side of town centre on A1000)
Hotel	★★56% Holtwhites Hotel, 92 Chase Side, ENFIELD ☎081-363 0124 30rm(28↹🐾)

BECKENHAM   Map 05 TQ36

Beckenham Place ☎081-658 5374
Picturesque course in the grounds of a public park. The course is played over by the Braeside Golf Club.
18 holes, 5722yds, Par 68, SSS 68.
Club membership 200.

Visitors	no restrictions.
Societies	must contact in advance.
Green Fees	not confirmed.
Facilities	♀ ♨ 🏠 ⚑
Location	The Mansion (.5m N on B2015)
Hotel	★★★58% Bromley Court Hotel, Bromley Hill, BROMLEY ☎081-464 5011 122↹🐾

Langley Park ☎081-658 6849
This is a pleasant, but difficult, well-wooded, parkland course with natural hazards including a lake at the 18th hole.
18 holes, 6488yds, Par 69, SSS 71, Course record 65.
Club membership 650.

Visitors	may not play at weekends. Must contact in advance and have an introduction from own club.

Societies Wed & Thu only, must apply in writing.
Green Fees £30 per day/round.
Facilities ⊗ ㄴ ♨ ♀ ♨ 🏠 ⚑ George Ritchie.
Location Barnfield Wood Rd (.5 N on B2015)
Hotel ★★★58% Bromley Court Hotel, Bromley Hill, BROMLEY ☎081-464 5011 122↹🐾

BEXLEYHEATH   Map 05 TQ47

Bexleyheath ☎081-303 6951
Undulating course.
9 holes, 5239yds, Par 66, SSS 66, Course record 64.
Club membership 350.

Visitors	may not play weekends & bank holidays.
Societies	by arrangement.
Green Fees	not confirmed.
Facilities	⊗ 川 ㄴ ♨ (no catering on Mon & weekends) ♀ ♨
Location	Mount Dr, Mount Rd (1m SW)
Hotel	★★★71% Forte Crest Hotel, Black Prince Interchange, Southwold Rd, BEXLEY ☎(0322) 526900 102↹🐾

BIGGIN HILL   Map 05 TQ45

Cherry Lodge ☎(0959) 72250
Undulating parkland course with good views.
18 holes, 6652yds, Par 72, SSS 72.
Club membership 850.

Visitors	cannot play at weekends. Must contact in advance.
Societies	must telephone in advance.
Green Fees	£33 per day; £22 per round.
Facilities	⊗ 川 ㄴ ♨ ♀ ♨ 🏠 ⚑
Leisure	sauna.
Location	Jail Ln (1m E)
Hotel	★★★63% Kings Arms Hotel, Market Square, WESTERHAM ☎(0959) 62990 16↹🐾

BROMLEY   Map 05 TQ46

Magpie Hall Lane ☎081-462 7014
Flat course, ideal for beginners.
9 holes, 2745yds, Par 70, SSS 67.
Club membership 100.

Visitors	no restrictions.
Societies	must contact in advance.
Green Fees	not confirmed.
Facilities	♀ 🏠 ⚑
Location	Magpie Hall Ln (2m SE off A21)
Hotel	★★★58% Bromley Court Hotel, Bromley Hill, BROMLEY ☎081-464 5011 122↹🐾

Shortlands ☎081-460 2471
Easy walking parkland course with a brook as a natural hazard.
9 holes, 5261yds, Par 65, SSS 66.
Club membership 410.

Visitors	may not play on competition days. Must be accompanied by member and have an introduction from own club.
Green Fees	not confirmed.
Facilities	♨ 🏠 ⚑ J Bates.

Location	Meadow Rd, Shortlands (.75m W off A222)
Hotel	★★★58% Bromley Court Hotel, Bromley Hill, BROMLEY ☎081-464 5011 122⇾ ⁿ

Sundridge Park ☎081-460 0278
The East course is longer than the West but many think
the shorter of the two courses is the more difficult. The
East is surrounded by trees while the West is more hilly,
with good views. Both are certainly a good test of golf.
East Course: 18 holes, 6410yds, Par 70, SSS 71.
West Course: 18 holes, 6027yds, Par 68, SSS 69.
Club membership 1200.

Visitors	must contact in advance and have an introduction from own club.
Societies	must contact in advance.
Green Fees	not confirmed.
Facilities	⊗ ⊞ ⅃ ⬛ ♀ ☖ 🏠 ⚑ Bob Cameron.
Location	Garden Rd (N side of town centre off A2212)
Hotel	★★★58% Bromley Court Hotel, Bromley Hill, BROMLEY ☎081-464 5011 122⇾ ⁿ

CARSHALTON   Map 04 TQ26

Oaks Sports Centre ☎081-643 8363
Public parkland course with floodlit, covered driving range.
18 holes, 6033yds, Par 70, SSS 69 or 9 holes, 1443yds, Par 28,
SSS 28.
Club membership 750.

Visitors	no restrictions.
Societies	must apply in writing.
Green Fees	£8 per round (£10 weekends); £4 per round/9 holes (£4.90 weekends).
Facilities	⊗ ⊞ ⅃ ⬛ ♀ ☖ 🏠 ⚑ ⚑ G D Horley.
Leisure	squash, sauna, solarium.
Location	Woodmansterne Rd (.5m S on B278)
Hotel	★★★63% Forte Posthouse, Purley Way, CROYDON ☎081-688 5185 86⇾ ⁿ

CHESSINGTON   Map 04 TQ16

Chessington ☎081-391 0948
Tree-lined parkland course designed by Patrick Tallack.
9 holes, 1400yds, Par 27, SSS 28.
Club membership 200.

Visitors	must book 7.30am-noon weekends only.
Societies	must telephone 1 month in advance.
Green Fees	not confirmed.
Facilities	⊗ ⊞ ⬛ ♀ ☖ 🏠 ⚑ ⚑ B Cliff.
Location	Garrison Ln (Opp Chessington South Station nr Zoo)
Hotel	★★62% Heathside Hotel, Brighton Rd, BURGH HEATH ☎(0737) 353355 73⇾ ⁿ

CHISLEHURST   Map 05 TQ47

Chislehurst ☎081-467 2782
Pleasantly wooded undulating parkland/heathland course.
Magnificent clubhouse with historical associations.
18 holes, 5128yds, Par 66, SSS 65.
Club membership 800.

Visitors	must play with member at weekends. Must contact in advance and have an introduction from own club.
Societies	must contact in writing.
Green Fees	not confirmed.

Facilities	⊗ ⊞ by prior arrangement ⅃ ⬛ ♀ ☖ 🏠 ⚑ ⚑ Stuart Cortorphine.
Leisure	snooker.
Location	Camden, Park Rd
Hotel	★★★58% Bromley Court Hotel, Bromley Hill, BROMLEY ☎081-464 5011 122⇾ ⁿ

COULSDON   Map 04 TQ25

Coulsdon Court ☎081-660 0468
A public parkland course with good views. Clubhouse
formerly owned by the Byron family.
18 holes, 6037yds, Par 70, SSS 69, Course record 66.

Visitors	must book mid-week for weekends.
Societies	by arrangement.
Green Fees	£10.25 (£12.80 weekends).
Facilities	⊗ ⊞ ⅃ ⬛ ♀ ☖ 🏠 ⚑ ⚑ Colin Staff.
Leisure	hard tennis courts, squash, solarium, gymnasium.
Location	Coulsdon Rd (.75m E off A23 on B2030)
Hotel	★★★★62% Selsdon Park Hotel, Sanderstead, CROYDON ☎081-657 8811 170⇾ ⁿ

Woodcote Park ☎081-668 2788
Slightly undulating parkland course.
18 holes, 6600yds, Par 71, SSS 71.
Club membership 700.

Visitors	may not play at weekends. Must contact in advance and have an introduction from own club.
Societies	must contact in advance.
Green Fees	not confirmed.
Facilities	⊗ ⅃ ⬛ ♀ ☖ 🏠 ⚑ Ian Martin.
Leisure	snooker.
Location	Meadow Hill, Bridle Way (1m N of town centre off A237)
Hotel	★★★63% Forte Posthouse, Purley Way, CROYDON ☎081-688 5185 86⇾ ⁿ

CROYDON   Map 05 TQ36

Croham Hurst ☎081-657 5581
Parkland course with tree-lined fairways and bounded by
wooded hills. Easy walking.
18 holes, 6274yds, Par 70, SSS 70, Course record 64.
Club membership 800.

Visitors	with member only weekends & bank holidays. Must contact in advance and have an introduction from own club.
Societies	must book 1 year in advance.
Green Fees	£33 per day/round.
Facilities	⊗ ⊞ by prior arrangement ⅃ ⬛ ♀ ☖ 🏠 ⚑ ⚑ Eric Stillwell.
Location	Croham Rd (1.5m SE)
Hotel	★★★★62% Selsdon Park Hotel, Sanderstead, CROYDON ☎081-657 8811 170⇾ ⁿ

Selsdon Park ☎081-657 8811
Parkland course. Full use of hotel's sporting facilities by
residents.
18 holes, 6402yds, Par 71, SSS 69.

Visitors	restrictions at weekends for non-residents. Must contact in advance.
Societies	must contact in advance.
Green Fees	£20-£30 (18-36 holes).

▶

Facilities	⊗ 〗 ⅃ ⬛ ♀ ⌂ 🏠 ⅊ 🏌 ſ Tom O'Keefe & Iain Naylor.
Leisure	hard and grass tennis courts, outdoor and indoor heated swimming pools, squash, snooker, sauna, solarium, gymnasium, croquet, boule.
Location	Sanderstead (3m S on A2022)
Hotel	★★★★62% Selsdon Park Hotel, Sanderstead, CROYDON ☎081-657 8811 170⇨⊮

Shirley Park ☎081-654 1143
This parkland course lies amid fine woodland with good views of Shirley Hills. The more testing holes come in the middle section of the course. The remarkable 7th hole calls for a 187-yard iron or wood shot diagonally across a narrow valley to a shelved green set right-handed into a ridge.
18 holes, 6210yds, Par 71, SSS 70, Course record 65.
Club membership 1000.

SCORECARD: White Tees					
Hole	Yds	Par	Hole	Yds	Par
1	409	4	10	365	4
2	304	4	11	435	4
3	165	3	12	327	4
4	537	5	13	151	3
5	367	4	14	391	4
6	381	4	15	339	4
7	187	3	16	282	4
8	356	4	17	222	3
9	516	5	18	476	5
Out	3222	36	In	2988	35
			Totals	6210	71

Visitors	with member only at weekends. Must contact in advance and have an introduction from own club.
Societies	by arrangement.
Green Fees	£26 per day/round.
Facilities	⊗ 〗 by prior arrangement ⅃ ⬛ ♀ ⌂ 🏠 ⅊ ſ Hogan Stott.
Leisure	snooker.
Location	Addiscombe Rd (E side of town centre on A232)
Hotel	★★★★61% Croydon Park Hotel, 7 Altyre Rd, CROYDON ☎081-680 9200 214⇨⊮

DOWNE   Map 05 TQ46

High Elms ☎(0689) 58175
Municipal parkland course. Very tight 13th, 230 yds (par 3).
18 holes, 6340yds, Par 71, SSS 70.
Club membership 570.

Visitors	no restrictions.
Green Fees	not confirmed.
Facilities	⊗ 〗 ⅃ ⬛ ♀ ⌂ 🏠
Location	High Elms Rd (1.5m NE)
Hotel	★★★58% Bromley Court Hotel, Bromley Hill, BROMLEY ☎081-464 5011 122⇨⊮

West Kent ☎Orpington (0689) 851323
Partly hilly downland course.
18 holes, 6399yds, Par 70, SSS 70, Course record 62.
Club membership 750.

Visitors	with member only at weekends. Handicap certificate required. Must contact in advance and have an introduction from own club.
Societies	must telephone in advance.
Green Fees	£33 per day; £22 per round.
Facilities	⊗ by prior arrangement ⅃ ⬛ ♀ ⌂ 🏠 ſ Roger Fidler.
Location	West Hill (.75m SW)
Hotel	★★★58% Bromley Court Hotel, Bromley Hill, BROMLEY ☎081-464 5011 122⇨⊮

ENFIELD   Map 05 TQ39

Crews Hill ☎081-363 6674
Parkland course in country surroundings.
18 holes, 6230yds, Par 70, SSS 70.
Club membership 529.

Visitors	must contact in advance and have an introduction from own club.
Societies	must apply in writing.
Green Fees	on application.
Facilities	⊗ 〗 by prior arrangement ⅃ (no catering Mon) ⬛ ♀ ⌂ 🏠 ſ J Reynolds.
Location	Cattlegate Rd, Crews Hill (3m NW off A1005)
Hotel	★★56% Holtwhites Hotel, 92 Chase Side, ENFIELD ☎081-363 0124 30rm(28⇨⊮)

Enfield ☎081-363 3970
Public parkland course. Salmons Brook crosses 7 holes.
18 holes, 6137yds, Par 72, SSS 70, Course record 66 or 5924yds, Par 69, SSS 68.
Club membership 625.

Visitors	must play with member at weekends. Must contact in advance and have an introduction from own club.
Societies	must contact in advance.
Green Fees	not confirmed.
Facilities	⊗ ⬛ ♀ ⌂ 🏠 ſ Ian Martin.
Location	Old Park Rd South (W side of town centre off A110)
Hotel	★★56% Holtwhites Hotel, 92 Chase Side, ENFIELD ☎081-363 0124 30rm(28⇨⊮)

Enfield Municipal ☎081-363 4454
Flat wooded parkland course. 9th hole is a left-hand dog-leg with second shot over a brook.
18 holes, 5755yds, Par 68, SSS 68, Course record 62.
Club membership 350.

Visitors	must be accompanied by member.
Societies	must apply in writing to the secretary.
Green Fees	£5.60 (£7.60 weekends).
Facilities	🏠 ⅊ ſ David Lewis.
Location	Beggars Hollow, Clay Hill (N side of town centre)
Hotel	★★56% Holtwhites Hotel, 92 Chase Side, ENFIELD ☎081-363 0124 30rm(28⇨⊮)

GREENFORD   Map 04 TQ18

Ealing ☎081-997 0937
Flat, parkland course relying on natural hazards; trees, tight fairways, and the River Brent which affects 9 holes.
18 holes, 6216yds, Par 70, SSS 70, Course record 65.
Club membership 700.

Visitors	Mon-Fri only on application to pro shop. Must contact in advance.
Societies	Mon, Wed & Thu only by arrangement.
Green Fees	£30 per day.
Facilities	⊗ 〗 by prior arrangement ⅃ ⬛ ♀ ⌂ 🏠 ſ Arnold Stickley.
Location	Perivale Ln
Hotel	★★56% Osterley Hotel, 764 Great West Rd, OSTERLEY ☎081-568 9981 57⇨⊮Annexe5rm

Horsenden Hill ☎081-902 4555
A well-kept, tree-lined short course.
9 holes, 1618yds, Par 28, SSS 28.
Club membership 135.
Visitors   no restrictions.
Green Fees not confirmed.
Facilities ⚐ 🏠 ⚑
Location   Woodland Rise (3m NE on A4090)
Hotel   ★★★62% Master Brewer Hotel, Western Av,
                HILLINGDON ☎(0895) 51199 106⇌🛈

Perivale Park ☎081-578 1693
Parkland course.
9 holes, 2600yds, Par 68, SSS 65.
Club membership 180.
Visitors   no restrictions.
Green Fees not confirmed.
Facilities ⚐ 🏠 ⚑
Location   Ruislip Rd East (E side of town centre, off A40)
Hotel   ★★★70% Carnarvon Hotel, Ealing Common,
                LONDON ☎081-992 5399 145⇌🛈

Each golf-course entry has a recommended
AA-appointed hotel. For a wider choice of
places to stay, consult *AA Hotels and
Restaurants in Britain and Ireland* and
*AA Inspected Bed and Breakfast in
Britain and Ireland*

HADLEY WOOD   Map 04 TQ29

Hadley Wood ☎081-449 4328
A parkland course on the northwest edge of London. The
gently undulating fairways have a friendly width inviting
the player to open his shoulders, though the thick rough
can be very punishing to the unwary. The course is
pleasantly wooded and there are some admirable views.
18 holes, 6473yds, Par 72, SSS 71, Course record 67.
Club membership 600.
Visitors   with member only weekends. Must have
                letter of introduction from club or handicap
                certificate. Must contact in advance.
Societies   by arrangement.
Green Fees not confirmed.
Facilities ⊗ ⅃ ■ ♀ ⚐ 🏠 ⎰ Alan McGinn.
Leisure   snooker.
Location   Beech Hill (E side of village)
Hotel   ★★★★60% West Lodge Park Hotel,
                Cockfosters Rd, HADLEY WOOD ☎081-
                440 8311 48⇌🛈 Annexe2⇌🛈

HAMPTON WICK   Map 04 TQ16

Home Park ☎081-977 2658
Flat, parkland course with easy walking.
18 holes, 6218yds, Par 71, SSS 71.
Club membership 500.
Visitors   no restrictions.
Societies   must contact in advance.
Green Fees not confirmed.
Facilities ⊗ ⅲ ⅃ ■ ♀ ⚐ 🏠 ⎰ Len Roberts.
                                                        ►

Golf
On a 200 acre country estate

Our 6,402 yard Championship golf course is just the beginning.
The Selsdon Park Hotel offers guests enjoying a golfing holiday or
weekend an unparalleled opportunity to play – even after the round is completed.
The Tropical Leisure Complex, has a sauna, jacuzzi, gymnasium, steam
room, solarium and swimming pool.
Selsdon Park also offers fine cuisine in the surroundings you'd expect
of a 170 bedroom, four star hotel. Plus excellent facilities for tennis,
squash, croquet, putting, boules, jogging and snooker.
All of which helps make Selsdon Park Hotel the perfect place to play
golf. Reserve your break now. Selsdon Park is only 30 minutes from London
and just 10 minutes from junction 6 of the M25.

SELSDON PARK HOTEL

Sanderstead, South Croydon, Surrey CR2 8YA Tel: 081-657 8811 Fax: 081-651 6171 Telex: 945003

Location	Off A308 on W side of Kingston Bridge
Hotel	★★★64% Richmond Hill, 146-150 Richmond Hill, RICHMOND ☎081-940 2247 & 081-940 5466 123⇨🏾

HILLINGDON   Map 04 TQ08

Hillingdon ☎(0895) 233956
Parkland course west of London.
9 holes, 5490yds, Par 68, SSS 67.
Club membership 400.

Visitors	may not play Thu, weekends, or bank holidays. Must have an introduction from own club.
Societies	must apply in writing.
Green Fees	£20 per day; £15 per round.
Facilities	⊗ ▥ by prior arrangement ⊾ ▦ ♀ ♨ 🏠 ⊏
Location	Dorset Way, Vine Ln (W side of town off A4020)
Hotel	★★★62% Master Brewer Hotel, Western Av, HILLINGDON ☎(0895) 51199 106⇨🏾

HOUNSLOW   Map 04 TQ17

Airlinks ☎081-561 1418
Meadowland/parkland course designed by P. Alliss and D. Thomas.
18 holes, 5885yds, Par 71, SSS 69, Course record 65.
Club membership 500.

Visitors	may not play before noon at weekends.
Societies	must apply in writing.
Green Fees	£9.50 per round (£12 weekends).
Facilities	⊗ ⊾ ▦ ♀ ♨ 🏠 ⊏
Location	Southall Ln (W of Hounslow off M4 junc 3)
Hotel	★★★60% Master Robert Hotel, Great West Rd, HOUNSLOW ☎081-570 6261 100⇨🏾

Hounslow Heath Municipal ☎081-570 5271
Parkland course in a conservation area, planted with an attractive variety of trees. The 15th hole lies between the fork of two rivers.
18 holes, 5820yds, Par 69, SSS 68.
Club membership 300.

Visitors	may not play at weekends.
Societies	must telephone in advance.
Green Fees	not confirmed.
Facilities	♨ 🏠 ⚒ ⊏
Location	Staines Rd
Hotel	★★★65% Forte Crest, Sipson Road, West Drayton, WEST DRAYTON ☎081-759 2323 569⇨🏾

ILFORD   Map 05 TQ48

Ilford ☎081-554 2930
Fairly flat parkland course intersected five times by a river.
18 holes, 5702yds, Par 68, SSS 68.
Club membership 592.

Visitors	restricted on bank holidays. Must contact in advance.
Societies	must contact in advance.
Green Fees	not confirmed.
Facilities	⊗ ⊾ ▦ ♀ ♨ 🏠 ⊏

Location	Wanstead Park Rd (NW side of town centre off A12)
Hotel	★★★68% Woodford Moat House, Oak Hill, WOODFORD GREEN ☎081-505 4511 99⇨🏾

ISLEWORTH   Map 04 TQ17

Wyke Green ☎081-560 8777
Fairly flat parkland course.
18 holes, 6242yds, Par 69, SSS 70, Course record 64.
Club membership 700.

Visitors	restricted weekends & bank holidays. Handicap certificate required. Must contact in advance.
Societies	must apply in writing.
Green Fees	£25 per day/round.
Facilities	⊗ ▥ ⊾ ▦ ♀ ♨ 🏠 ⊏ Tony Fisher.
Leisure	snooker.
Location	Syon Ln (1.5m N on B454 off A4)
Hotel	★★★60% Master Robert Hotel, Great West Rd, HOUNSLOW ☎081-570 6261 100⇨🏾

KINGSTON UPON THAMES   Map 04 TQ16

Coombe Hill ☎081-942 2284
A splendid course in wooded terrain. The undulations and trees make it an especially interesting course of great charm. And there is a lovely display of rhododendrons in May and June.
18 holes, 6303yds, Par 71, SSS 71.
Club membership 550.

SCORECARD: Medal Tees					
Hole	Yds	Par	Hole	Yds	Par
1	320	4	10	440	4
2	368	4	11	408	4
3	407	4	12	186	3
4	510	5	13	314	4
5	452	5	14	341	4
6	180	3	15	494	5
7	346	4	16	400	4
8	418	4	17	145	3
9	184	3	18	390	4
Out	3185	36	In	3118	35
			Totals	6303	71

Visitors	with member only at weekends. Must contact in advance and have an introduction from own club.
Societies	must book one year in advance.
Green Fees	not confirmed.
Facilities	⊗ ⊾ ▦ ♀ ♨ 🏠 ⊏
Leisure	snooker, sauna.
Location	Golf Club Dr, Coombe Ln West (1.75m E on A238)
Hotel	★★★★73% Hyatt Carlton Tower Hotel, Cadogan Place, LONDON ☎071-235 5411 224⇨🏾

Coombe Wood ☎081-942 0388
Parkland course.
18 holes, 5210yds, Par 66, SSS 66, Course record 62.
Club membership 650.

Visitors	must play with member at weekends. Must contact in advance.
Societies	Wed, Thu & Fri; must contact in advance.
Green Fees	not confirmed.
Facilities	⊗ by prior arrangement ▥ ⊾ ▦ ♀ ♨ 🏠 ⚒ ⊏ David Butler.
Location	George Rd (1.25m NE on A308)
Hotel	★★62% Haven Hotel, Portsmouth Rd, ESHER ☎081-398 0023 16⇨🏾Annexe4⇨🏾

MITCHAM   Map 04 TQ26

Mitcham ☎081-648 4197
Heathland course (gravel base), wooded.
18 holes, 5935yds, Par 69, SSS 68, Course record 65.
Club membership 500.
Visitors   must contact in advance.
Societies   must contact in advance.
Green Fees   £10.
Facilities   ♀ ♨ 🍴 ⚑
Location   Carshalton Rd (1m S)
Hotel   ★★★63% Forte Posthouse, Purley Way,
               CROYDON ☎081-688 5185 86⇨☖

NEW MALDEN   Map 04 TQ26

Malden ☎081-942 0654
Parkland course with the hazard of the Beverley Brook
which affects 4 holes (3rd, 7th, 8th and 12th).
18 holes, 6201yds, Par 71, SSS 70, Course record 65.
Club membership 800.
Visitors   restricted weekends. Must contact in advance.
Societies   must apply in writing.
Green Fees   not confirmed.
Facilities   ⊗ ♨ ♣ ♀ ♨ 🍴 ⚑ Robert Hunter.
Location   Traps Ln (N side of town centre off B283)
Hotel   ★★★64% Kingston Lodge Hotel, Kingston
               Hill, KINGSTON UPON THAMES ☎081-541
               4481 62⇨☖

NORTHWOOD   Map 04 TQ09

Haste Hill ☎(09274) 22877
Parkland course with stream running through. Excellent
views.
18 holes, 5787yds, Par 68, SSS 68.
Club membership 350.
Visitors   no restrictions.
Green Fees   not confirmed.
Facilities   ♀ ♨ 🍴 ⚒
Location   The Drive (.5m S off A404)
Hotel   ★★66% Harrow Hotel, Roxborough Bridge,
               12-22 Pinner Rd, HARROW ☎081-427 3435
               76⇨☖

Northwood ☎(09274) 25329
A very old club to which, it is said, golfers used to drive
from London by horse-carriage. They would find their
golf interesting as present-day players do. The course is
relatively flat although there are some undulations, and
trees and whins add not only to the beauty of the course
but also to the test of golf.
18 holes, 6493yds, Par 71, SSS 71, Course record 66.
Club membership 800.
Visitors   with member only weekends.
Societies   Mon, Thu & Fri only, by arrangement.
Green Fees   £30 per day; £20 per round.
Facilities   ⊗ ⊪ ♨ ♣ ♀ ♨ 🍴 ⚑
Location   Rickmansworth Rd (SW side of village off
               A404)
Hotel   ★★66% Harrow Hotel, Roxborough
               Bridge, 12-22 Pinner Rd, HARROW ☎081-
               427 3435 76⇨☖

Sandy Lodge ☎(09274) 25429
Heathland course; links-type, very sandy.
18 holes, 6081yds, Par 70, SSS 69, Course record 64.
Club membership 750.
Visitors   restricted weekends & bank holidays. Must
               contact in advance and have an introduction
               from own club.
Societies   must apply in writing.
Green Fees   £27 per round.
Facilities   ⊗ ♨ ♣ ♀ ♨ 🍴 ⚑ Alex Fox.
Location   Sandy Lodge Ln (N side of town centre off
               A4125)
Hotel   ★★★66% Bedford Arms Thistle Hotel,
               CHENIES ☎(0923) 283301 10⇨☖

ORPINGTON   Map 05 TQ46

Cray Valley ☎(0689) 39677 & 31927
An open parkland course with two man-made lakes and open
ditches.
18 holes, 5400yds, Par 70, SSS 67.
Club membership 640.
Visitors   no restrictions.
Societies   by arrangement.
Green Fees   Weekends £15.50 per round.
Facilities   ⊗ ♨ ♣ ♀ ♨ 🍴 ⚑ John Gregory.
Location   Sandy Ln (1m off A20)
Hotel   ★★★58% Bromley Court Hotel, Bromley Hill,
               BROMLEY ☎081-464 5011 122⇨☖

Lullingstone Park ☎(0959) 34542
Popular 27-hole public course set in 690 acres of undulating
parkland. Championship length 18-holes, plus 9-hole course
and a further 9-hole pitch and putt.
18 holes, 6759yds, Par 72, SSS 72, Course record 71 or 9 holes,
2432yds, Par 33.
Club membership 400.
Visitors   welcome.
Societies   must telephone in advance.
Green Fees   not confirmed.
Facilities   ⊗ ♨ ♣ ♀ ♨ 🍴 ⚒ ⚑ David Cornford.
Location   Parkgate, Chelsfield (Leave M25 junct 4 and take
               Well Hill turn)
Hotel   ★★★58% Bromley Court Hotel, Bromley Hill,
               BROMLEY ☎081-464 5011 122⇨☖

Ruxley ☎(0689) 71490
Parkland course with public, floodlit driving range. Difficult
6th hole, par 4. Easy walking and good views.
18 holes, 4885yds, Par 65, SSS 65.
Club membership 250.
Visitors   may not play mornings on weekends & bank
               holidays. Must contact in advance.
Societies   must telephone two weeks in advance.
Green Fees   not confirmed.
Facilities   ⊗ ♨ ♣ ♀ ♨ 🍴 ⚑
Location   Sandy Ln, St Paul's Cray (2m NE on A223)
Hotel   ★★★58% Bromley Court Hotel, Bromley Hill,
               BROMLEY ☎081-464 5011 122⇨☖

We make every effort to ensure that our
information is accurate but details may change
after we go to print

PINNER
Map 04 TQ18

Grims Dyke ☎081-428 4539
Pleasant, undulating parkland course.
18 holes, 5600yds, Par 69, SSS 67, Course record 65.
Club membership 590.
Visitors	with member only at weekends. Must have an introduction from own club.
Societies	must apply in writing.
Green Fees	£35 per day.
Facilities	⊗ by prior arrangement ᴸ (summer only) ● (during bar hours) ♀ ♨ 🖼 ⟮
Location	Oxhey Ln, Hatch End (3m N on A4008)
Hotel	★★66% Harrow Hotel, Roxborough Bridge, 12-22 Pinner Rd, HARROW ☎081-427 3435 76⇨🏌

Pinner Hill ☎081-866 0963
A hilly, wooded parkland course.
18 holes, 6280yds, Par 72, SSS 70, Course record 63.
Club membership 750.
Visitors	are required to have handicap certificate on Mon, Tue & Fri, Wed & Thu are public days. Must contact in advance and have an introduction from own club.
Societies	Mon, Tue & Fri only, by arangement.
Green Fees	£25 (Wed & Thu £7.15).
Facilities	⊗ ⫚ by prior arrangement ᴸ ● (catering Mon, Tue & Fri only) ♀ (Mon, Tue & Fri) ♨ 🖼 ⟮ Mark Grieve.
Location	Southview Rd, Pinner Hill (2m NW off A404)
Hotel	★★66% Harrow Hotel, Roxborough Bridge, 12-22 Pinner Rd, HARROW ☎081-427 3435 76⇨🏌

PURLEY
Map 05 TQ36

Purley Downs ☎081-657 8347
Hilly downland course. Notable holes are 6th and 12th.
18 holes, 6020yds, Par 70, SSS 69, Course record 65.
Club membership 600.
Visitors	must have a handicap certificate, & play on weekdays only. Must contact in advance.
Societies	must contact in advance.
Green Fees	£25 per day.
Facilities	⊗ ⫚ by prior arrangement ᴸ ● ♀ ♨ 🖼 ⟮ Graham Wilson.
Leisure	snooker.
Location	106 Purley Downs Rd (E side of town centre off A235)
Hotel	★★★63% Forte Posthouse, Purley Way, CROYDON ☎081-688 5185 86⇨🏌

If you know of a golf course which welcomes
visitors and is not already in this guide,
we should be grateful for information

RICHMOND UPON THAMES
Map 04 TQ17

Richmond ☎081-940-4351
A beautiful and historic wooded, parkland course on the edge of Richmond Park, with six par-3 holes. The 4th is often described as the best short hole in the south of England. Low scores are uncommon because cunningly sited trees call for great accuracy. The clubhouse is one of the most distinguished small Georgian mansions in England.
18 holes, 5780yds, Par 70, SSS 69, Course record 61.
Club membership 700.
Visitors	may not play weekends.
Societies	must apply in writing.
Green Fees	£32 per day.
Facilities	⊗ ⫚ by prior arrangement ᴸ ● ♀ ♨ 🖼 ⫟ ⟮ Nick Job.
Location	Sudbrook Park, Petersham (1.5m S off A307)
Hotel	★★★64% Richmond Hill, 146-150 Richmond Hill, RICHMOND ☎081-940 2247 & 081-940 5466 123⇨🏌

Royal Mid-Surrey ☎081-940 1894
A long playing parkland course. The flat fairways are cleverly bunkered. The 18th provides an exceptionally good par 4 finish with a huge bunker before the green to catch the not quite perfect long second.
Outer Course: 18 holes, 6337yds, Par 69, SSS 70, Course record 64.
Inner Course: 18 holes, 5544yds, Par 68, SSS 67.
Club membership 1200.
Visitors	may not play at weekends. Must contact in advance.
Societies	must apply in writing.
Green Fees	not confirmed.
Facilities	⊗ ᴸ ● ♀ ♨ 🖼 ⫟ ⟮ David Talbot.
Leisure	snooker.
Location	Old Deer Park (.5m N of Richmond upon Thames off A316)
Hotel	★★★64% Richmond Hill, 146-150 Richmond Hill, RICHMOND ☎081-940 2247 & 081-940 5466 123⇨🏌

ROMFORD
Map 05 TQ58

Maylands Golf Club & Country Park
☎Ingrebourne (04023) 42055
Picturesque undulating parkland course.
18 holes, 6351yds, Par 71, SSS 70, Course record 67.
Club membership 700.
Visitors	with member only at weekends. Must have an introduction from own club.
Societies	Mon, Wed & Fri only, by arrangement.
Green Fees	£20 per round.
Facilities	⊗ ⫚ (Mon, Wed & Fri only, Apr-Oct) ᴸ ● ♀ ♨ 🖼 ⟮ John Hopkin.
Location	Colchester Rd, Harold Park
Hotel	★★★67% Forte Posthouse, Brook St, BRENTWOOD ☎(0277) 260260 120⇨

For a full list of golf courses included in the
book, see the index at the end of the directory

Romford ☎(0708) 40986
A many-bunkered parkland course with easy walking. It is said there are as many bunkers as there are days in the year. The ground is quick drying making a good course for winter play when other courses might be too wet.
18 holes, 6374yds, Par 72, SSS 70.
Club membership 693.

SCORECARD						
Hole	Yds	Par	Hole	Yds	Par	
1	359	4	10	448	4	
2	306	4	11	485	5	
3	190	3	12	391	4	
4	480	5	13	208	3	
5	503	5	14	448	4	
6	141	3	15	327	4	
7	336	4	16	335	4	
8	361	4	17	172	3	
9	386	4	18	498	5	
Out	3062	36	In	3312	36	
			Totals	6374	72	

Visitors	with member only weekends & bank holidays. Must contact in advance and have an introduction from own club.
Societies	must telephone in advance.
Green Fees	not confirmed.
Facilities	⊗ ⫴ ⅃ ♨ ♀ ⌂ 🛍 ʃ Harry Flatman.
Location	Heath Dr, Gidea Park (1m NE on A118)
Hotel	★★★67% Forte Posthouse, Brook St, BRENTWOOD ☎(0277) 260260 120⇥

RUISLIP   Map 04 TQ08

Ruislip ☎(08956) 32004
Municipal parkland course. Many trees.
18 holes, 5703yds, Par 69, SSS 68, Course record 65.
Club membership 450.

Visitors	no restrictions.
Societies	must telephone in advance.
Green Fees	£7.50 per day (£10 weekends).
Facilities	⊗ ⫴ ⅃ ♨ ♀ ⌂ 🛍 ⚑ ʃ Derek Nash.
Leisure	snooker, 40 booth driving range.
Location	Ickenham Rd (.5m SW on B466)
Hotel	★★★62% Master Brewer Hotel, Western Av, HILLINGDON ☎(0895) 51199 106⇥🐾

SIDCUP   Map 05 TQ47

Sidcup ☎081-300 2150
Easy walking parkland course with natural water hazards.
9 holes, 2861yds, Par 68, SSS 68, Course record 65.
Club membership 400.

Visitors	with member only weekends & bank holidays. Must contact in advance and have an introduction from own club.
Societies	must apply in writing.
Green Fees	£16 per round.
Facilities	⊗ ⫴ by prior arrangement ⅃ ♨ ♀ ⌂ 🛍 ʃ Ross V Taylor.
Leisure	snooker.
Location	7 Hurst Rd (N side of town centre off A222)
Hotel	★★★58% Bromley Court Hotel, Bromley Hill, BROMLEY ☎081-464 5011 122⇥🐾

SOUTHALL   Map 04 TQ17

West Middlesex ☎081-574 3450
Gently undulating parkland course.
18 holes, 6242yds, Par 69, SSS 70.
Club membership 500.

Visitors	restricted weekends & bank holidays.
Societies	apply in writing.

Green Fees	not confirmed.
Facilities	♀ ⌂ 🛍 ʃ
Location	Greenford Rd (W side of town centre on A4127 off A4020)
Hotel	★★★60% Master Robert Hotel, Great West Rd, HOUNSLOW ☎081-570 6261 100⇥🐾

STANMORE   Map 04 TQ19

Stanmore ☎081-954 2599
North London parkland course.
18 holes, 5884yds, Par 68, SSS 68, Course record 66.
Club membership 528.

Visitors	with member only at weekends & bank holidays. Must contact in advance and have an introduction from own club.
Societies	Wed & Thu only, by arrangement.
Green Fees	not confirmed.
Facilities	⌂ 🛍 ʃ V R Law.
Location	Gordon Av (S side of town centre)
Hotel	★★66% Harrow Hotel, Roxborough Bridge, 12-22 Pinner Rd, HARROW ☎081-427 3435 76⇥🐾

SURBITON   Map 04 TQ16

Surbiton ☎081-398 3101
Parkland course with easy walking.
18 holes, 6211yds, Par 70, SSS 70, Course record 64.
Club membership 750.

Visitors	with member only at weekends & bank holidays. Must contact in advance and have an introduction from own club.
Societies	must apply in writing.
Green Fees	£40.50 per day; £27 per round.
Facilities	⊗ & ⫴ by prior arrangement ⅃ ♨ ♀ ⌂ 🛍 ʃ Paul Milton.
Location	Woodstock Ln (2m S off A3)
Hotel	★★★64% Richmond Hill, 146-150 Richmond Hill, RICHMOND ☎081-940 2247 & 081-940 5466 123⇥🐾

TWICKENHAM   Map 04 TQ17

Fulwell ☎081-977 1833
Championship-length parkland course with easy walking. The 575-yd, 17th, is notable.
18 holes, 6490yds, Par 71, SSS 71, Course record 63.
Club membership 650.

Visitors	may not play weekends. Must contact in advance and have an introduction from own club.
Societies	must apply in writing.
Green Fees	£30 per day.
Facilities	⊗ (ex Mon) ⅃ ♨ ♀ ⌂ 🛍 ʃ David Haslam.
Location	Wellington Rd, Hampton Hill (1.5m S on A311)
Hotel	★★★64% Richmond Hill, 146-150 Richmond Hill, RICHMOND ☎081-940 2247 & 081-940 5466 123⇥🐾

Opening times of bar and catering facilities vary from place to place. Please remember to check in advance of your visit

Strawberry Hill ☎081-894 0165
Parkland course with easy walking.
9 holes, 2381yds, Par 64, SSS 62, Course record 61.
Club membership 350.
Visitors	with member only at weekends.
Societies	must apply in writing.
Green Fees	£25 per day; £18 per round.
Facilities	⊗ (ex Mon & Tue) ⅏ by prior arrangement 🍴 & 🍺 (bar hours only) ♀ ⛳ 🏠 ʈ Peter Buchan.
Location	Wellesley Rd (S side of town centre off A311)
Hotel	★★★64% Richmond Hill, 146-150 Richmond Hill, RICHMOND ☎081-940 2247 & 081-940 5466 123⇸🐾

Twickenham ☎081-941 0032
Municipal commonland course.
9 holes, 3180yds, Par 72, SSS 71.
Club membership 250.
Visitors	no restrictions.
Green Fees	not confirmed.
Facilities	♀ ⛳ 🏠 ⛳ ʈ
Location	Staines Rd (2m W on A305)
Hotel	★★★64% Richmond Hill, 146-150 Richmond Hill, RICHMOND ☎081-940 2247 & 081-940 5466 123⇸🐾

UPMINSTER   Map 05 TQ58

Upminster ☎(04022) 22788
Parkland course adjacent to river.
18 holes, 5951yds, Par 68, SSS 69.
Club membership 800.
Visitors	with member only at weekends. Must have an introduction from own club.
Societies	apply in writing.
Green Fees	not confirmed.
Facilities	♀ ⛳ 🏠 ʈ
Location	114 Hall Ln (N side of town centre)
Hotel	★★★67% Forte Posthouse, Brook St, BRENTWOOD ☎(0277) 260260 120⇸

UXBRIDGE   Map 04 TQ08

Uxbridge ☎(0895) 237287
Municipal parkland course, undulating and tricky.
18 holes, 5750yds, Par 68, SSS 68, Course record 64.
Club membership 700.
Visitors	no restrictions.
Societies	Thu by arrangment.
Green Fees	£8 per round (£10 weekends).
Facilities	⊗ ⅏ by prior arrangement 🍴 🍺 ♀ ⛳ 🏠 ⛳ ʈ Phil Howard.
Leisure	snooker.
Location	The Drive, Harefield Place (2m N off B467)
Hotel	★★★62% Master Brewer Hotel, Western Av, HILLINGDON ☎(0895) 51199 106⇸🐾

WEMBLEY   Map 04 TQ18

Sudbury ☎081-902 3713
Undulating parkland course very near centre of London.
18 holes, 6282yds, Par 69, SSS 70, Course record 63.
Club membership 650.

Visitors	must have handicap certificate. With member only at weekends.
Societies	must apply in writing.
Green Fees	£22.50 per round.
Facilities	⊗ 🍴 🍺 ♀ ⛳ 🏠 ʈ Neil Jordan.
Leisure	snooker.
Location	Bridgewater Rd (SW side of town centre on A4090)
Hotel	★★66% Harrow Hotel, Roxborough Bridge, 12-22 Pinner Rd, HARROW ☎081-427 3435 76⇸🐾

WEST DRAYTON   Map 04 TQ07

Holiday ☎(0895) 444232
Fairly large, testing, hilly par 3 course suitable both for beginners and scratch players.
9 holes, 1618yds, Par 28.
Club membership 120.
Visitors	restricted match days.
Societies	by arrangement.
Green Fees	£5 per round (£6 weekends & bank holidays).
Facilities	catering facilities available at hotel ♀ ⛳ 🏠 ⛳ 🍴
Leisure	heated indoor swimming pool, sauna, solarium, gymnasium.
Location	Stockley Rd (1m SE off A408)
Hotel	★★★59% Holiday Inn, Stockley Rd, West Drayton, WEST DRAYTON ☎(0895) 445555 380⇸

WOODFORD GREEN   Map 05 TQ49

Woodford ☎081-504 0553
Forest land course on the edge of Epping Forest. Views over the Lea Valley to the London skyline.
9 holes, 5806yds, Par 70, SSS 68, Course record 69.
Club membership 400.
Visitors	with member only Tue/Thu mornings, weekends & bank holidays. Must contact in advance.
Societies	must contact in advance.
Green Fees	£15 per round..
Facilities	⊗ (Tue-Fri) ⅏ by prior arrangement 🍴 🍺 (Mon-Fri) ♀ ⛳ 🏠 ʈ Ashley Johns.
Location	Sunset Av (NW side of town centre off A104)
Hotel	★★★68% Woodford Moat House, Oak Hill, WOODFORD GREEN ☎081-505 4511 99⇸🐾

GREATER MANCHESTER

ALTRINCHAM   Map 07 SJ78

Altrincham ☎061-928 0671
Municipal parkland course with easy walking, water on many holes, rolling contours and many trees. Driving range in grounds.
18 holes, 6162yds, Par 71, SSS 69, Course record 66.
Club membership 350.
Visitors	must contact in advance.
Societies	by prior arrangement.
Green Fees	£5 (£6 weekends & bank holidays).
Facilities	⛳ 🏠 ⛳

Location	Stockport Rd (.75 E of Altrincham on A560)
Hotel	★★★65% Cresta Court Hotel, Church St, ALTRINCHAM ☎061-927 7272 139⇔♠

Dunham Forest ☎061-928 2605
Attractive parkland course cut through magnificent beech woods.
18 holes, 6636yds, Par 72, SSS 72.
Club membership 600.

Visitors	may not play weekends & bank holidays.
Societies	telephone for availability.
Green Fees	£23 per round (£28 weekends).
Facilities	⊗ ⊪ by prior arrangement ▦ ■ ♀ ▲ 🏠 ⛳ (Ian Wrigley.
Leisure	hard tennis courts, squash, snooker.
Location	Oldfield Ln (1.5m W off A56)
Hotel	★★★66% Bowdon Hotel, Langham Rd, Bowdon, ALTRINCHAM ☎061-928 7121 82⇔

Ringway ☎061-980 2630
Parkland course, with interesting natural hazards. Easy walking, good views.
18 holes, 6307yds, Par 71, SSS 70.
Club membership 720.

Visitors	may not play before 9.30am or between 1-2pm. Must have an introduction from own club.
Societies	Thu only May-Sep.
Green Fees	not confirmed.
Facilities	⊗ ⊪ (Mon-Sat) ▦ ■ ♀ ▲ 🏠 (Nick Ryan.
Leisure	snooker.
Location	Hale Mount, Hale Barns (2.5m SE on A538)
Hotel	★★★65% Cresta Court Hotel, Church St, ALTRINCHAM ☎061-927 7272 139⇔♠

ASHTON-IN-MAKERFIELD   Map 07 SJ59

Ashton-in-Makerfield ☎(0942) 727267
Well-wooded parkland course. Easy walking.
18 holes, 6169yds, Par 70, SSS 69, Course record 66.
Club membership 800.

Visitors	restricted Sat & bank holidays. With member only on Sun.
Societies	apply in writing.
Green Fees	£18 per day.
Facilities	⊗ ⊪ ▦ ■ ♀ ▲ 🏠 ⛳ (Peter Allan.
Leisure	snooker.
Location	Garswood Park, Liverpool Rd (.5m W of M6 (Junc 24) on A58)
Hotel	★★★67% Forte Posthouse, Lodge Ln, Newton-Le-Willows, HAYDOCK ☎(0942) 717878 142⇔

ASHTON-UNDER-LYNE   Map 07 SJ99

Ashton-under-Lyne ☎061-330 1537
A testing, varied moorland course, with large greens. Easy walking. Three new holes have improved the course.
18 holes, 6300yds, Par 70, SSS 70, Course record 69.
Club membership 650.

Visitors	with member only weekends & bank holidays.
Societies	telephone in advance.
Green Fees	£18 per day/round.
Facilities	⊗ ⊪ ▦ ■ ♀ ▲ 🏠 (Colin Boyle.
Leisure	snooker.

Location	Gorsey Way, Higher Hurst (1.5m NE)
Hotel	★★70% York House Hotel, York Place, Richmond St, ASHTON-UNDER-LYNE ☎061-330 5899 24⇔♠ Annexe10⇔

Dukinfield ☎061-338 2340
Small but tricky hillside course with several difficult par 3s and a very long par 5. Being extended to 18 holes for summer 1992.
16 holes, 5586yds, Par 68, SSS 67, Course record 67.
Club membership 400.

Visitors	may not play on Wed afternoons & must play with member at weekends. Must contact in advance.
Societies	must contact in advance.
Green Fees	£14.50.
Facilities	⊗ ⊪ by prior arrangement ▦ ■ ♀ ▲ 🏠
Location	Lyne Edge, Yew Tree Ln (S off B6175)
Hotel	★★70% York House Hotel, York Place, Richmond St, ASHTON-UNDER-LYNE ☎061-330 5899 24⇔♠ Annexe10⇔

BOLTON   Map 07 SD70

Bolton ☎(0204) 43067
This well maintained heathland course is always a pleasure to visit. The 12th hole should be treated with respect and so too should the final four holes which have ruined many a card.
18 holes, 6300yds, Par 70, SSS 70, Course record 65.
Club membership 600.

Visitors	restricted at weekends.
Societies	welcome Mon, Thu & Fri, apply in writing.
Green Fees	£28-£32 per day; £24-£28 per round.
Facilities	⊗ ⊪ by prior arrangement ▦ ■ ♀ ▲ 🏠 (R Longworth.
Leisure	snooker.
Location	Lostock Park, Chorley New Rd (3m W on A673)
Hotel	★★★61% Pack Horse Hotel, Bradshawgate, Nelson Square, BOLTON ☎(0204) 27261 72⇔♠

Bolton Municipal ☎(0204) 42336
A parkland course.
18 holes, 6336yds, Par 71, SSS 69, Course record 68.
Club membership 300.

Visitors	no restrictions
Societies	telephone in advance.
Green Fees	£4 per round (£6 weekends & bank holidays).
Facilities	⊗ ⊪ by prior arrangement ▦ ■ ♀ ▲ 🏠 ⛳ (A K Holland.
Location	Links Rd (3m W on A673)
Hotel	★★★62% Forte Posthouse, Beaumont Rd, BOLTON ☎(0204) 651511 96⇔♠

Breightmet ☎(0204) 27381
Long parkland course.
9 holes, 6416yds, Par 72, SSS 71, Course record 67.
Club membership 350.

Visitors	may not play weekends. Must contact in advance.
Societies	welcome Tue & Thu only, apply in advance in writing.
Green Fees	£10 (£12 weekends).

▶

Facilities	⊗ ⏛ 🖺 💻 (no catering Mon) ♀ 🛆
Leisure	snooker.
Location	Red Bridge, Ainsworth (E side of town centre off A58)
Hotel	★★★61% Pack Horse Hotel, Bradshawgate, Nelson Square, BOLTON ☎(0204) 27261 72⇨🏠

Dunscar ☎(0204) 53321
A scenic moorland course with panoramic views. A warm friendly club.
18 holes, 5968yds, Par 71, SSS 69, Course record 64.
Club membership 600.

Visitors	may normally play after 9.30am; some restrictions at weekends. Must contact in advance and have an introduction from own club.
Societies	must telephone in advance.
Green Fees	not confirmed.
Facilities	⊗ ⏛ 🖺 💻 ♀ 🛆 🏠 ⚲ ℂ Gary Treadgold.
Leisure	snooker.
Location	Longworth Ln, Bromley Cross (3m N off A666)
Hotel	★★★64% Egerton House Hotel, Blackburn Rd, Egerton, BOLTON ☎(0204) 57171 32⇨🏠

Great Lever & Farnworth ☎(0204) 656137
Downland course with easy walking.
18 holes, 5859yds, Par 70, SSS 69.
Club membership 600.

Visitors	must contact in advance.
Societies	contact in advance.
Green Fees	£11 per day (£17 weekends & bank holidays).
Facilities	⊗ 🖺 💻 (no catering Mon) ♀ 🛆 🏠
Leisure	snooker.
Location	Lever Edge Ln (SW side of town centre off A575)
Hotel	★★★61% Pack Horse Hotel, Bradshawgate, Nelson Square, BOLTON ☎(0204) 27261 72⇨🏠

Harwood ☎(0204) 22878
Mainly flat parkland course.
9 holes, 5993yds, Par 71, SSS 69, Course record 67.
Club membership 410.

Visitors	with member only weekends.
Societies	contact in writing.
Green Fees	£12 per round.
Facilities	🖺 💻 ♀ 🛆
Leisure	snooker.
Location	Springfield, Roading Brook Rd, Harwood (2.5m NE off B6196)
Hotel	★★★64% Egerton House Hotel, Blackburn Rd, Egerton, BOLTON ☎(0204) 57171 32⇨🏠

Old Links ☎(0204) 42307
Championship moorland course.
18 holes, 6408yds, Par 72, SSS 72, Course record 64.
Club membership 750.

Visitors	welcome except championship days & Sat until 4pm. Must contact in advance.
Societies	apply by letter.
Green Fees	£25 per day (£30 weekends).
Facilities	⊗ (ex Mon) ⏛ by prior arrangement 🖺 💻 ♀ 🏠 ℂ Paul Horridge.
Leisure	snooker.

Location	Chorley Old Rd (NW of town centre on B6226)
Hotel	★★★61% Pack Horse Hotel, Bradshawgate, Nelson Square, BOLTON ☎(0204) 27261 72⇨🏠

Regent Park ☎(0204) 44170
Parkland course.
18 holes, 6069yds, Par 70, SSS 69.
Club membership 230.

Visitors	no restrictions.
Societies	must telephone in advance.
Green Fees	not confirmed.
Facilities	⊗ ⏛ by prior arrangement 🖺 💻 ♀ 🛆 🏠 ⚲ ℂ Keith Holland.
Location	Links Rd, Chorley New Rd (3.5m W off A673)
Hotel	★★★62% Forte Posthouse, Beaumont Rd, BOLTON ☎(0204) 651511 96⇨🏠

BRAMHALL   Map 07 SJ88

Bramall Park ☎061-485 3199
Well-wooded parkland course with splendid views of the Pennines.
18 holes, 6043yds, Par 70, SSS 69.
Club membership 600.

Visitors	must contact in advance.
Societies	apply in writing.
Green Fees	not confirmed.
Facilities	⊗ by prior arrangement ⏛ by prior arrangement 🖺 💻 ♀ 🛆 🏠 ℂ M Proffitt.
Leisure	snooker.
Location	20 Manor Rd (NW side of town centre off B5149)
Hotel	★★★68% Bramhall Moat House, Bramhall Ln South, BRAMHALL ☎061-439 8116 65⇨🏠

Bramhall ☎061-439 4057
Undulating parkland course, easy walking.
18 holes, 6293yds, Par 70, SSS 70, Course record 64.
Club membership 720.

Visitors	except Thu. Must contact in advance.
Societies	Wed only.
Green Fees	£25 per day (£35 weekends & bank holidays).
Facilities	⊗ ⏛ 🖺 💻 (all catering by arrangement) ♀ 🛆 🏠 ℂ Brian Nield.
Leisure	snooker.
Location	Ladythorn Rd (E side of town centre off A5102)
Hotel	★★★68% Bramhall Moat House, Bramhall Ln South, BRAMHALL ☎061-439 8116 65⇨🏠

BROMLEY CROSS   Map 07 SD71

Turton ☎Bolton (0204) 852235
Moorland course.
9 holes, 5584yds, Par 68, SSS 67, Course record 67.
Club membership 325.

Visitors	with member only at weekends & bank holidays.
Societies	must contact in writing.
Green Fees	£10 per day.
Facilities	⊗ ⏛ by prior arrangement 🖺 💻 ♀ 🛆
Location	Wood End Farm, Chapeltown Rd (3m N on A676)
Hotel	★★★64% Egerton House Hotel, Blackburn Rd, Egerton, BOLTON ☎(0204) 57171 32⇨🏠

BURY   Map 07 SD81

Bury ☎061-766 4897
Hard walking on hilly, moorland course.
18 holes, 5961yds, Par 69, SSS 69.
Club membership 650.
Visitors   may not play at weekends.
Societies   contact in advance.
Green Fees   not confirmed.
Facilities   ⊗ ⅷ by prior arrangement 🏌 ⬤ ♀ ᗑ 🏠 ſ
Leisure   snooker.
Location   Unsworth Hall, Blackford Bridge (2m S on A56)
Hotel   ★60% Woolfield House Hotel, Wash Ln, BURY ☎061-797 9775 16rm(3⇄7♠)

Lowes Park ☎061-764 1231
Moorland course, with easy walking. Usually windy.
9 holes, 6009yds, Par 70, SSS 69, Course record 67.
Club membership 250.
Visitors   may not play Wed & Sat and should book for Sun. Must contact in advance.
Societies   contact in advance.
Green Fees   not confirmed.
Facilities   ♀ (ex Mon)
Location   Hill Top, Walmersley (N side of town centre off A56)
Hotel   ★60% Woolfield House Hotel, Wash Ln, BURY ☎061-797 9775 16rm(3⇄7♠)

Walmersley ☎061-764 5057
Moorland hillside course, with wide fairways, large greens and extensive views. Testing holes: 2nd (484 yds) par 5; 4th (444 yds) par 4.
9 holes, 6114yds, Par 72, SSS 70, Course record 67.
Club membership 450.
Visitors   restricted at weekends. Must contact in advance and have an introduction from own club.
Societies   telephone one month in advance.
Green Fees   £10.
Facilities   ⊗ by prior arrangement ⅷ by prior arrangement 🏌 (ex Mon) ⬤ ♀ ᗑ
Location   Garretts Close, Walmersley (3m N off A56)
Hotel   ★★★62% Old Mill Hotel, Springwood, RAMSBOTTOM ☎(0706) 822991 36⇄

CHEADLE   Map 07 SJ88

Cheadle ☎061-491 4452
Parkland course with hazards on every hole; from sand bunkers and copses to a stream across six of the fairways.
9 holes, 5006yds, Par 64, SSS 65.
Club membership 446.
Visitors   may not play Tue & Sat. Must contact in advance and have an introduction from own club.
Societies   apply in writing.
Green Fees   £12 per round (£22.50 Sun & bank holidays).
Facilities   ⊗ ⅷ by prior arrangement 🏌 ⬤ ♀ ᗑ 🏠 ſ Martin Redrup.
Leisure   snooker.
Location   Cheadle Rd (S side of village off A5149)
Hotel   ★★62% Wycliffe Villa, 74 Edgeley Rd, Edgeley, STOCKPORT ☎061-477 5395 12⇄♠

DENTON   Map 07 SJ99

Denton ☎061-336 3218
Easy, flat parkland course with brook running through. Notable hole is one called 'Death and Glory'.
18 holes, 6290yds, Par 72, SSS 70.
Club membership 600.
Visitors   may not play at weekends. Must contact in advance.
Green Fees   not confirmed.
Facilities   ♀ ᗑ 🏠 ſ
Location   Manchester Rd (1.5m W on A57)
Hotel   ★★70% York House Hotel, York Place, Richmond St, ASHTON-UNDER-LYNE ☎061-330 5899 24⇄♠ Annexe10⇄

FAILSWORTH   Map 07 SD80

Brookdale ☎061-681 4534
Undulating parkland course, with river crossed 5 times in play. Hard walking.
18 holes, 6040yds, Par 68, SSS 68.
Club membership 500.
Visitors   restricted Sun. Must contact in advance and have an introduction from own club.
Societies   must contact in writing.
Green Fees   £18 per day (£21 weekends & bank holidays).
Facilities   ⊗ ⅷ 🏌 ⬤ ♀ ᗑ 🏠 ⛳ ſ B Connor.
Leisure   snooker.
Location   Ashbridge, Woodhouses (N side of Manchester)
Hotel   ★★61% Midway Hotel, Manchester Rd, Castleton, ROCHDALE ☎(0706) 32881 24⇄♠

FLIXTON   Map 07 SJ79

William Wroe Municipal ☎061-748 8680
Parkland course, with easy walking.
18 holes, 4395yds, Par 64, SSS 61, Course record 60.
Club membership 225.
Visitors   restricted weekends. Must contact in advance.
Green Fees   not confirmed.
Facilities   ᗑ 🏠 ⛳ ſ Roland West.
Location   Pennybridge Ln (E side of village off B5158)
Hotel   ★62% Beaucliffe Hotel, 254 Eccles Old Rd, Pendleton, SALFORD ☎061-789 5092 21rm(2⇄15♠)

GATLEY   Map 07 SJ88

Gatley ☎061-437 2091
Parkland course. Moderately testing.
9 holes, 5934yds, Par 68, SSS 68, Course record 65.
Club membership 400.
Visitors   may not play Tue & Sat. With member only weekends.
Societies   apply in writing.
Green Fees   £15 per day.
Facilities   ⊗ ⅷ & 🏌 by prior arrangement ♀ ᗑ 🏠 ſ Steve Clark.
Leisure   squash, snooker.

▶

Location	Waterfall Farm, Styal Rd, Heald Green (S side of village off B5166)
Hotel	★★★★60% Belfry Hotel, Stanley Rd, HANDFORTH ☎061-437 0511 81⇨

HALE   Map 07 SJ78

Hale ☎061-980 4225
Beautiful, undulating parkland course, with the River Bollin winding round fairways.
9 holes, 5780yds, Par 70, SSS 68.
Club membership 300.

Visitors	may not play before 4.30pm Thu; with member only weekends.
Societies	apply in writing.
Green Fees	£14 per day.
Facilities	⚐ 🏠
Location	Rappax Rd (1.25m SE)
Hotel	★★★66% Bowdon Hotel, Langham Rd, Bowdon, ALTRINCHAM ☎061-928 7121 82⇨

HINDLEY   Map 07 SD60

Hindley Hall ☎Wigan (0942) 55131
Parkland course with mostly easy walking.
18 holes, 5840yds, Par 69, SSS 68, Course record 63.
Club membership 500.

Visitors	restricted Wed and weekends. Must contact in advance and have an introduction from own club.
Societies	apply in writing.
Green Fees	£20 per day/round (£25 weekends & bank holidays).
Facilities	⊗ ⫫ by prior arrangement 🏌 ⚐ (no catering Mon) ⚐ ⚐ 🏠 ⎘ N Brazell.
Leisure	snooker.
Location	Hall Ln (1m N off A58)
Hotel	★★61% Brocket Arms Hotel, Mesnes Rd, WIGAN ☎(0942) 46283 27⇨🐾

HORWICH   Map 07 SD61

Horwich ☎(0204) 696980
Parkland course with natural hazards and generally windy. Hard walking.
9 holes, 5286yds, Par 67, SSS 67, Course record 64.
Club membership 300.

Visitors	must be accompanied by member.
Societies	must contact in writing.
Green Fees	£6 per day.
Facilities	⚐ ⚐
Location	Victoria Rd (SE side of village A673)
Hotel	★★★62% Forte Posthouse, Beaumont Rd, BOLTON ☎(0204) 651511 96⇨🐾

HYDE   Map 07 SJ99

Werneth Low ☎061-368 2503
Hard walking but good views from this moorland course. Exposed to wind.
9 holes, 5734yds, Par 70, SSS 68.
Club membership 350.

Visitors	may not play Tue mornings, weekends & bank holidays.

Societies	must contact in advance.
Green Fees	not confirmed.
Facilities	⊗ ⫫ by prior arrangement 🏌 ⚐ ⚐ ⎘ 🏠 ⎘ Tony Bacchus.
Location	Werneth Low (2m S of town centre)
Hotel	★★★56% Alma Lodge Hotel, 149 Buxton Rd, STOCKPORT ☎061-483 4431 56rm(52⇨)

LEIGH   Map 07 SD60

Pennington ☎(0942) 607278
Municipal parkland course, with natural hazards of brooks, ponds and trees, and easy walking.
9 holes, 2919yds, Par 35, SSS 34.
Club membership 150.

Visitors	no restrictions.
Societies	must contact in advance.
Green Fees	not confirmed.
Facilities	⚐ 🏠 ⎘ ⎘
Location	St Helen's Rd (SW side of town centre off A572)
Hotel	★★60% Kirkfield Hotel, 2/4 Church St, NEWTON LE WILLOWS ☎(0925) 228196 & 220489 17⇨🐾

MANCHESTER   Map 07 SJ89

Davyhulme Park ☎061-748 2260
Parkland course.
18 holes, 6237yds, Par 72, SSS 70, Course record 67.
Club membership 500.

Visitors	may not play on Wed & Sat; must play with member on Sun. Must have an introduction from own club.
Societies	must contact in advance.
Green Fees	not confirmed.
Facilities	⊗ ⫫ by prior arrangement 🏌 ⚐ ⚐ ⎘ 🏠 ⎘ ⎘ Hugh Lewis.
Leisure	snooker.
Location	Gleneagles Rd, Davyhulme (8m S adj to Park Hospital)
Hotel	★62% Beaucliffe Hotel, 254 Eccles Old Rd, Pendleton, SALFORD ☎061-789 5092 21rm(2⇨15🐾)

Didsbury ☎061-998 9278
Parkland course.
18 holes, 6273yds, Par 70, SSS 70, Course record 66.
Club membership 700.

Visitors	restricted Tue, Wed & weekends.
Societies	must contact in advance.
Green Fees	£18 per day (£22 weekends).
Facilities	⊗ ⫫ & 🏌 (Tue-Fri only, weekends by prior arrangement) ⚐ ⚐ ⎘ 🏠 ⎘ ⎘ Peter Barber.
Leisure	snooker.
Location	Ford Ln, Northenden (6m S of city centre off A5145)
Hotel	★★★62% Forte Posthouse, Palatine Rd, Northenden, MANCHESTER ☎061-998 7090 196⇨🐾

Fairfield ☎061-370 1641
Parkland course set around a reservoir. Course demands particularly accurate placing of shots.
18 holes, 5654yds, Par 70, SSS 68, Course record 65.
Club membership 400.

Visitors	may not play Wed, Thu & mornings at weekends.
Societies	apply in writing to Secretary.
Green Fees	£12 per day (£15 weekends & bank holidays).
Facilities	⊗ ⫿ ⌱ (catering by prior arrangement) ▬ ♀ △ 🏠 (D M Butler.
Leisure	snooker.
Location	Booth Rd, Audenshaw (1.5m W of Audenshaw off A635)
Hotel	★★70% York House Hotel, York Place, Richmond St, ASHTON-UNDER-LYNE ☎061-330 5899 24↩🛏Annexe10↩

Houldsworth ☎061-224 5055
Flat parkland course, tree-lined and with water hazards.
Testing holes 9th (par 5) and 13th (par 5).
18 holes, 5819yds, Par 70, SSS 68.
Club membership 520.

Visitors	may not play weekends & bank holidays. Must contact in advance.
Societies	by prior arrangement.
Green Fees	£12 per day; £11 per round.
Facilities	⊗ & ⫿ by prior arrangement ⌱ ▬ ♀ △ 🏠 (David Naylor.
Leisure	snooker.
Location	Wingate House, Higher Levenshulme (4m SE of city centre off A6)
Hotel	★★★58% Willow Bank Hotel, 340-342 Wilmslow Rd, Fallowfield, MANCHESTER ☎061-224 0461 116↩🛏

Northenden ☎061-998 4738
Parkland course surrounded by the River Mersey.
18 holes, 6469yds, Par 72, SSS 71, Course record 63.
Club membership 600.

Visitors	Tee reserved for members 8.30-9.15am & 12.30-1.15pm. Must contact in advance.
Societies	Tue & Fri only, telephone in advance.
Green Fees	not confirmed.
Facilities	⊗ ⫿ ⌱ ▬ ♀ △ 🏠 (W J McColl.
Leisure	snooker.
Location	Palatine Rd (6.5m S of city centre on B1567 off A5103)
Hotel	★★★62% Forte Posthouse, Palatine Rd, Northenden, MANCHESTER ☎061-998 7090 196↩🛏

Pike Fold ☎061-740 1136
Picturesque, hilly course. Good test of golf.
9 holes, 5785yds, Par 70, SSS 68, Course record 66.
Club membership 200.

Visitors	may not play Sun. Must be with member Sat & bank holidays.
Societies	apply in writing.
Green Fees	£12 per day.
Facilities	⊗ ⫿ ⌱ ▬ ♀ △
Leisure	snooker.
Location	Cooper Ln, Victoria Av, Blackley (4m N of city centre off Rochdale Rd)
Hotel	★★★62% The Bower Hotel, Hollinwood Av, Chadderton, OLDHAM ☎061-682 7254 66↩🛏

> Entries highlighted in green identify
> courses which are considered
> to be particularly interesting

Withington ☎061-445 9544
Flat parkland course.
18 holes, 6410yds, Par 71, SSS 71, Course record 65.
Club membership 550.

Visitors	welcome except Thu, restricted at weekends. Must contact in advance.
Societies	welcome except Thu, Sat & Sun.
Green Fees	£20 per day (£23 weekends).
Facilities	⊗ ⫿ by prior arrangement ⌱ ▬ ♀ △ 🏠 (R Line.
Leisure	snooker.
Location	243 Palatine Rd, West Didsbury (4m SW of city centre off B5167)
Hotel	★★★62% Forte Posthouse, Palatine Rd, Northenden, MANCHESTER ☎061-998 7090 196↩🛏

Worsley ☎061-789 4202
Well-wooded parkland course.
18 holes, 6220yds, Par 72, SSS 72, Course record 66.
Club membership 700.

Visitors	must have an introduction from own club.
Societies	Mon, Wed & Thu only.
Green Fees	£20 per day; £16 per round (£21 weekends & bank holidays).
Facilities	⊗ ⫿ ⌱ ▬ ♀ △ 🏠 🏌 (Ceri Cousins.
Leisure	snooker.
Location	Stableford Av, Monton Green, Eccles (6.5m NW of city centre off A572)
Hotel	★★★★61% Hotel Piccadilly, Piccadilly, MANCHESTER ☎061-236 8414 271↩🛏

MELLOR   Map 07 SJ98

Mellor & Townscliffe ☎061-427 2208
Scenic parkland and moorland course, undulating with some hard walking. Good views. Testing 200 yd, 9th hole, par 3.
18 holes, 5925yds, Par 70, SSS 69.
Club membership 550.

Visitors	with member only Sun.
Societies	apply by letter.
Green Fees	£16 per day (£25 weekends & bank holidays).
Facilities	⊗ ⫿ ⌱ ▬ (no catering Tue) ♀ (ex Tue) △ 🏠 (Michael J Williams.
Location	Gibb Ln, Tarden (.5m S)
Hotel	★74% Springfield Hotel, Station Rd, MARPLE ☎061-449 0721 6↩🛏

MIDDLETON   Map 07 SD80

Manchester ☎061-643 2718
Moorland golf of unique character over a spaciously laid out course with generous fairways sweeping along to large greens. A wide variety of holes will challenge the golfer's technique, particularly the testing last three holes. Driving range.
18 holes, 6464yds, Par 72, SSS 72, Course record 66.
Club membership 700.

SCORECARD: White Tees					
Hole	Yds	Par	Hole	Yds	Par
1	327	4	10	341	4
2	493	5	11	357	4
3	520	5	12	427	4
4	190	3	13	149	3
5	316	4	14	473	5
6	445	4	15	430	4
7	286	4	16	223	3
8	154	3	17	436	4
9	512	5	18	385	4
Out	3243	37	In	3221	35
			Totals	6464	72

Visitors	restricted weekends. Must contact in advance and have an introduction from own club.
Societies	apply in writing.
Green Fees	£25 per day/round (£30 weekends & bank holidays).
Facilities	⊗ ⊪ by prior arrangement ⬛ 💺 ♀ 👗 🏠 ℂ Brian Connor.
Leisure	snooker.
Location	Hopwood Cottage, Manchester (2.5m N off A664)
Hotel	★★61% Midway Hotel, Manchester Rd, Castleton, ROCHDALE ☎(0706) 32881 24⇨🐾

North Manchester ☎061-643 9033
A long, tight heathland course with natural water hazards. Excellent views of the Yorkshire Wolds.
18 holes, 6527yds, Par 72, SSS 72, Course record 66.
Club membership 800.

Visitors	no restrictions.
Societies	telephone in advance.
Green Fees	not confirmed.
Facilities	⊗ ⊪ ⬛ 💺 ♀ 👗 🏠 ⊪ ℂ Peter Lunt.
Leisure	snooker.
Location	Rhodes House, Manchester Old Rd (W side of town centre off A576)
Hotel	★★★62% The Bower Hotel, Hollinwood Av, Chadderton, OLDHAM ☎061-682 7254 66⇨🐾

MILNROW   Map 07 SD91

Tunshill ☎(0706) 342095
Testing moorland course, particularly 6th and 15th (par 5's).
9 holes, 5804yds, Par 70, SSS 68, Course record 66.
Club membership 275.

Visitors	restricted weekends & evenings. Must contact in advance.
Societies	apply in writing.
Green Fees	£8 per day.
Facilities	⬛ 💺 ♀ 👗
Leisure	snooker, pool table.
Location	Kiln Ln (1m NE M62 exit junc 21 off B6225)
Hotel	★★★68% Norton Grange Hotel, Manchester Rd, Castleton, ROCHDALE ☎(0706) 30788 50⇨🐾

OLDHAM   Map 07 SD90

Crompton & Royton ☎061-624 2154
Undulating moorland course.
18 holes, 6187yds, Par 70, SSS 69, Course record 65.
Club membership 721.

Visitors	may not play at weekends. Must contact in advance.
Societies	apply in writing or telephone.
Green Fees	£14.50-£18.50.
Facilities	⊗ & ⊪ (ex Mon) ⬛ 💺 ♀ 👗 🏠 ℂ David Melling.
Leisure	snooker.
Location	Highbarn (.5m NE of Royton)
Hotel	★★★62% The Bower Hotel, Hollinwood Av, Chadderton, OLDHAM ☎061-682 7254 66⇨🐾

Oldham ☎061-624 4986
Moorland course, with hard walking.
18 holes, 5045yds, Par 66, SSS 65.
Club membership 300.

Visitors	must contact in advance.
Societies	must contact in advance.
Green Fees	not confirmed.
Facilities	⊗ (ex Mon) ⊪ (ex Mon) ⬛ (ex Mon) 💺 (ex Mon) ♀ 👗 🏠 ⊪ ℂ Andrew Laverty.
Location	Lees New Rd (2.5m E off A669)
Hotel	★★70% York House Hotel, York Place, Richmond St, ASHTON-UNDER-LYNE ☎061-330 5899 24⇨🐾 Annexe10⇨

Werneth ☎061-624 1190
Semi-moorland course, with a deep gulley and stream crossing eight fairways. Testing hole: 3rd (par 3).
18 holes, 5363yds, Par 68, SSS 66, Course record 63.
Club membership 460.

Visitors	may not play on Tue or Thu. Must contact in advance.
Societies	must contact in advance.
Green Fees	£14.
Facilities	♀ 👗 🏠 ℂ John Richardson.
Leisure	snooker.
Location	Green Ln, Garden Suburb (S side of town centre off A627)
Hotel	★★70% York House Hotel, York Place, Richmond St, ASHTON-UNDER-LYNE ☎061-330 5899 24⇨🐾 Annexe10⇨

PRESTWICH   Map 07 SD80

Prestwich ☎061-773 2544
Parkland course, near to Manchester city centre.
18 holes, 4712yds, Par 64, SSS 63.
Club membership 450.

Visitors	restricted at weekends. Must have an introduction from own club.
Societies	apply in writing.
Green Fees	£15.
Facilities	⊗ ⊪ ⬛ 💺 ♀ 👗 🏠 ℂ G P Coope.
Leisure	snooker.
Location	Hilton Ln (N side of town centre on A6044)
Hotel	★62% Beaucliffe Hotel, 254 Eccles Old Rd, Pendleton, SALFORD ☎061-789 5092 21rm(2⇨15🐾)

ROCHDALE   Map 07 SD81

Rochdale ☎(0706) 43818
Parkland course with enjoyable golf and easy walking.
18 holes, 5780yds, Par 71, SSS 68.
Club membership 700.

Visitors	booking required Wed & Fri. Must contact in advance.
Societies	apply in writing.
Green Fees	not confirmed.
Facilities	⊗ ⊪ ⬛ 💺 (all catering by prior arrangement) ♀ 👗 🏠 ℂ Andrew Laverty.
Leisure	snooker.
Location	Edenfield Rd, Bagslate (1.75m W on A680)
Hotel	★★61% Midway Hotel, Manchester Rd, Castleton, ROCHDALE ☎(0706) 32881 24⇨🐾

Springfield Park ☎(0706) 56401 (weekend only)
Parkland/moorland course situated in a valley. The River
Roch adds an extra hazard to the course.
18 holes, 5237yds, Par 67, SSS 66, Course record 64.
Club membership 270.

Visitors	must book for weekends.
Societies	telephone in advance.
Green Fees	not confirmed.
Facilities	🏠 ⛳ (David Wills.
Location	Springfield Park, Bolton Rd (1.5m SW off A58)
Hotel	★★61% Midway Hotel, Manchester Rd, Castleton, ROCHDALE ☎(0706) 32881 24⇔🏌

ROMILEY   Map 07 SJ99

Romiley ☎061-430 2392
Parkland course, well-wooded.
18 holes, 6335yds, Par 70, SSS 70.
Club membership 700.

Visitors	must contact in advance.
Societies	apply in writing.
Green Fees	not confirmed.
Facilities	⊗ by prior arrangement ⫪ by prior arrangement 🍴 💺 ⛳ 🏠 (Garry Butler.
Leisure	snooker.
Location	Goose House Green (E side of town centre off B6104)
Hotel	★★★56% Alma Lodge Hotel, 149 Buxton Rd, STOCKPORT ☎061-483 4431 56rm(52⇔)

SALE   Map 07 SJ79

Ashton on Mersey ☎061-973 3220
Parkland course with easy walking.
9 holes, 6146yds, Par 72, SSS 69.
Club membership 360.

Visitors	with member only Sun & bank holidays, not Sat.
Green Fees	not confirmed.
Facilities	⊗ ⫪ 🍴 💺 ⛳ 🏠 (Paul Wagstaff.
Location	Church Ln (1m W of M63 junc 7)
Hotel	★★★65% Cresta Court Hotel, Church St, ALTRINCHAM ☎061-927 7272 139⇔🏌

Sale ☎061-973 1638
Parkland course.
18 holes, 6346yds, Par 71, SSS 70, Course record 67.
Club membership 600.

Visitors	dress regulations in club house.
Societies	apply by letter.
Green Fees	£17 per day (£25 weekends & bank holidays).
Facilities	⊗ ⫪ 🍴 💺 ⛳ 🏠 🍴 (Mike Stewart.
Leisure	snooker.
Location	Golf Rd (NW side of town centre off A6144)
Hotel	★★★65% Cresta Court Hotel, Church St, ALTRINCHAM ☎061-927 7272 139⇔🏌

SHEVINGTON   Map 07 SD50

Gathurst ☎Appley Bridge (02575) 2861
Testing parkland course, slightly hilly.
9 holes, 6282yds, Par 72, SSS 70.
Club membership 350.

Visitors	after 5pm, with member only Wed, weekends & bank holidays. Must have an introduction from own club.
Societies	apply in writing.
Green Fees	£20.
Facilities	⊗ 💺 ⛳ (catering Tue-Fri) ⛳ ⚐ 🏠 (D P Clarke.
Leisure	snooker.
Location	62 Miles Ln (W side of village B5375 off junc 27 of M6)
Hotel	★★★60% Bellingham Hotel, 149 Wigan Ln, WIGAN ☎(0942) 43893 30⇔🏌

STALYBRIDGE   Map 07 SJ99

Stamford ☎(0457) 832126
Undulating moorland course.
18 holes, 5687yds, Par 70, SSS 67, Course record 65.
Club membership 450.

Visitors	must telephone in advance.
Societies	must contact in writing 1 month in advance.
Green Fees	£20 (£30 weekends after 3pm).
Facilities	⊗ ⫪ 🍴 💺 (no catering Mon & Wed) ⛳ ⚐ 🏠 🍴
Leisure	snooker.
Location	Huddersfield Rd (2m NE off A635)
Hotel	★★70% York House Hotel, York Place, Richmond St, ASHTON-UNDER-LYNE ☎061-330 5899 24⇔🏌 Annexe10⇔

STOCKPORT   Map 07 SJ89

Heaton Moor ☎061-432 2134
Parkland course, easy walking.
18 holes, 5907yds, Par 70, SSS 69, Course record 66.
Club membership 400.

Visitors	restricted Tue & bank holidays.
Societies	apply in writing.
Green Fees	not confirmed.
Facilities	⊗ ⫪ by prior arrangement 🍴 💺 ⛳ ⚐ 🏠 🍴 (C Loydall.
Location	Heaton Mersey (N of town centre off B5169)
Hotel	★★★56% Alma Lodge Hotel, 149 Buxton Rd, STOCKPORT ☎061-483 4431 56rm(52⇔)

Marple ☎061-427 2311
Parkland course.
18 holes, 5475yds, Par 68, SSS 67, Course record 66.
Club membership 500.

Visitors	must have an introduction from own club.
Societies	must contact in advance.
Green Fees	not confirmed.
Facilities	⊗ ⫪ & by prior arrangement 💺 ⚐ 🏠 (Ian Scott.
Location	Barnsfold Rd, Hawk Green, Marple (S side of town centre)
Hotel	★★★56% Alma Lodge Hotel, 149 Buxton Rd, STOCKPORT ☎061-483 4431 56rm(52⇔)

Reddish Vale ☎061-480 2359
Undulating heathland course designed by Dr. A Mackenzie
and situated in the River Thame valley.
18 holes, 6100yds, Par 69, SSS 69, Course record 63.
Club membership 550.

Visitors	must play with member at weekends.

▶

Societies	must contact in writing.
Green Fees	£20.
Facilities	ⓑ ⬛ ♀ △ 🖿 ⸿ Richard Brown.
Leisure	snooker.
Location	Southcliffe Rd, Reddish (1.5m N off Reddish road)
Hotel	★★★56% Alma Lodge Hotel, 149 Buxton Rd, STOCKPORT ☎061-483 4431 56rm(52⇔)

Stockport ☎061-427 2001
A beautifully situated course in wide open countryside. It is not too long but requires that the player plays all the shots, to excellent greens.
18 holes, 6290yds, Par 71, SSS 71.
Club membership 500.

Visitors	no restrictions.
Societies	Wed & Thu only, apply in writing.
Green Fees	not confirmed.
Facilities	ⓧ ⫙ ⓑ (no catering Sun-Mon) ⬛ ♀ △ 🖿 ⸿ R G Tattersall.
Location	Offerton Rd (4m SE on A627)
Hotel	★★★56% Alma Lodge Hotel, 149 Buxton Rd, STOCKPORT ☎061-483 4431 56rm(52⇔)

SWINTON Map 07 SD70

Swinton Park ☎061-794 1785
One of Lancashire's longest inland courses. Clubhouse extensions have greatly improved the facilities.
18 holes, 6712yds, Par 73, SSS 72, Course record 66.
Club membership 600.

Visitors	restricted at weekends. Must contact in advance and have an introduction from own club.
Societies	by letter.
Green Fees	not confirmed.
Facilities	ⓧ ⫙ ⓑ ⬛ ♀ △ 🖿 ⸿ James Wilson.
Leisure	snooker.
Location	East Lancashire Rd (1m W off A580)
Hotel	★62% Beaucliffe Hotel, 254 Eccles Old Rd, Pendleton, SALFORD ☎061-789 5092 21rm(2⇔15�)

UPPERMILL Map 07 SD90

Saddleworth ☎Saddleworth (0457) 873653
Moorland course, with superb views of Pennines.
18 holes, 5976yds, Par 71, SSS 69, Course record 64.
Club membership 660.

Visitors	restricted at weekends. Must contact in advance.
Societies	apply in writing.
Green Fees	not confirmed.
Facilities	ⓧ by prior arrangement ⫙ by prior arrangement ⓑ ⬛ ♀ △ 🖿 ⸿ T Shard.
Leisure	snooker.
Location	Mountain Ash, Ladcastle Rd, Oldham (E side of town centre off A670)
Hotel	★★70% York House Hotel, York Place, Richmond St, ASHTON-UNDER-LYNE ☎061-330 5899 24⇔� Annexe10⇔

For an explanation of symbols and abbreviations, see page 32

URMSTON Map 07 SJ79

Flixton ☎061-748 2116
Meadowland course bounded by River Mersey.
9 holes, 6410yds, Par 71, SSS 71.
Club membership 450.

Visitors	with member only weekends & bank holidays.
Societies	apply by letter to Steward.
Green Fees	not confirmed.
Facilities	ⓧ & ⫙ by prior arrangement ⓑ ⬛ ♀ △ 🖿 ⸿ R Ling.
Leisure	snooker.
Location	Church Rd, Flixton (S side of town centre on B5213)
Hotel	★★★58% Ashley Hotel, Ashley Rd, Hale, ALTRINCHAM ☎061-928 3794 47⇔�

WALKDEN Map 07 SD70

Brackley Municipal ☎061-790 6076
Mostly flat course.
9 holes, 3003yds, Par 35, SSS 69.

Visitors	no restrictions.
Green Fees	not confirmed.
Facilities	🖿 ⸿
Location	2m NW on A6
Hotel	★62% Beaucliffe Hotel, 254 Eccles Old Rd, Pendleton, SALFORD ☎061-789 5092 21rm(2⇔15�)

WESTHOUGHTON Map 07 SD60

Westhoughton ☎(0942) 811085
Compact downland course.
9 holes, 5772yds, Par 70, SSS 68, Course record 64.
Club membership 300.

Visitors	with member only at weekends.
Societies	must contact in advance.
Green Fees	not confirmed.
Facilities	ⓧ by prior arrangement ⫙ by prior arrangement ⓑ ⬛ ♀ (8pm-11pm) △ 🖿 ⸿ Stephen Yates.
Leisure	snooker, pool table.
Location	Long Island (.5m NW off A58)
Hotel	★★★62% Forte Posthouse, Beaumont Rd, BOLTON ☎(0204) 651511 96⇔�

WHITEFIELD Map 07 SD80

Stand ☎061-766 2388
A semi-parkland course with five moorland holes. A fine test of golf with a very demanding finish.
18 holes, 6426yds, Par 72, SSS 71, Course record 67.
Club membership 680.

Visitors	may not play on Tue or weekends. Must contact in advance.
Societies	must contact in writing.
Green Fees	not confirmed.
Facilities	ⓧ ⫙ by prior arrangement ⓑ ⬛ ♀ △ 🖿 ⚲ ⸿ Mark Dance.
Leisure	snooker.
Location	The Dales, Ashbourne Grove (1m W off A667)
Hotel	★60% Woolfield House Hotel, Wash Ln, BURY ☎061-797 9775 16rm(3⇔7�)

Whitefield ☎061-766 3096
Fine sporting parkland course with well-watered greens.
18 holes, 6041yds, Par 69.
Club membership 500.

Visitors	must contact in advance and have an introduction from own club.
Societies	must contact in advance.
Green Fees	not confirmed.
Facilities	Catering on request ♀ ⌂ 🗋 ⚐ ⚑ Paul Reeves.
Leisure	hard tennis courts, snooker.
Location	Higher Ln (N side of town centre on A665)
Hotel	★★★★53% Portland Thistle Hotel, 3/5 Portland St, Piccadilly Gdns, MANCHESTER ☎061-228 3400 205⇨🏠

WIGAN   Map 07 SD50

Haigh Hall ☎(0942) 831107
Municipal parkland course, with hard walking, and a canal
forms the west boundary. Adjacent to 'Haigh Country Park'
with many facilities.
18 holes, 6423yds, Par 70, SSS 71, Course record 66.
Club membership 150.

Visitors	no restrictions.
Green Fees	not confirmed.
Facilities	⊗ ⊪ ⚑ ♀ (WE afternoons only) ⌂ 🗋 ⚐ ⚑ Ian Lee.
Location	Haigh Country Park, Haigh (2m NE off B5238)
Hotel	★★61% Brocket Arms Hotel, Mesnes Rd, WIGAN ☎(0942) 46283 27⇨🏠

Wigan ☎Standish (0257) 421360
Among the best of Lancashire's 9-hole courses. The fine old
clubhouse is the original Arley Hall, and is surrounded by a
moat.
9 holes, 6058yds, Par 70, SSS 69, Course record 64.
Club membership 320.

Visitors	welcome except Tue. Must contact in advance.
Societies	apply in writing.
Green Fees	£15 per day (£20 weekends & bank holidays).
Facilities	⊗ ⊪ ⚑ ⚐ ♀ ⌂
Leisure	snooker.
Location	Arley Hall, Haigh (3m NE off B5238)
Hotel	★★★60% Bellingham Hotel, 149 Wigan Ln, WIGAN ☎(0942) 43893 30⇨🏠

WOODFORD   Map 07 SJ88

Avro ☎061-439 2709
An attractive, tight and challenging 9-hole course.
9 holes, 5735yds, Par 69, SSS 68.
Club membership 400.

Visitors	must be accompanied by member.
Green Fees	not confirmed.
Facilities	⚑ ⌂
Location	Old Hall Ln (W side of village on A5102)
Hotel	★★★68% Bramhall Moat House, Bramhall Ln South, BRAMHALL ☎061-439 8116 65⇨🏠

A golf-course name printed in ***bold italics***
means that we have been unable to verify
information with the club's management
for the current year

WORSLEY   Map 07 SD70

Ellesmere ☎061-790 2122
Parkland course with natural hazards. Testing holes: 3rd
(par 5), 9th (par 3), 13th (par 4). Hard walking.
18 holes, 5954yds, Par 69, SSS 69, Course record 64.
Club membership 550.

Visitors	welcome except club competition days. Must contact in advance and have an introduction from own club.
Societies	Mon-Wed only contact in advance.
Green Fees	£13.50 (£17.50 weekends & bank holidays).
Facilities	⊗ ⊪ ⚑ ♟ ♀ ⌂ 🗋 ⚑ Terry Morley.
Leisure	snooker.
Location	Old Clough Ln (N side of village off A580)
Hotel	★62% Beaucliffe Hotel, 254 Eccles Old Rd, Pendleton, SALFORD ☎061-789 5092 21rm(2⇨15🏠)

HAMPSHIRE

ALDERSHOT   Map 04 SU85

Army ☎(0252) 540638
Picturesque heathland course with three par 3's, over 200
yds.
18 holes, 6550yds, Par 71, SSS 71.
Club membership 800.

Visitors	must be accompanied by member.
Societies	Mon & Thu only.
Green Fees	With member only: £10.50 per round; £12.50 per day.
Facilities	♀ ⌂ 🗋 ⚑ N Turner.
Location	Laffans Rd (1.5m N of town centre off A323/ A325)
Hotel	★★★64% Forte Crest, Lynchford Rd, FARNBOROUGH ☎(0252) 545051 110⇨🏠

ALRESFORD   Map 04 SU53

Alresford ☎(0962) 733746
Undulating parkland course with testing 4th and 10th holes
(par 4).
12 holes, 6038yds, Par 70, SSS 69, Course record 67.
Club membership 600.

Visitors	may not play before noon on weekends & bank holidays. Must contact in advance.
Societies	must telephone in advance.
Green Fees	£20 per day; £13 per round (£25 weekends & bank holidays).
Facilities	⊗ ⊪ ⚑ ♟ ♀ ⌂ 🗋 ⚐ ⚑ Malcolm Scott.
Location	Cheriton Rd, Tichborne Down (1m S on B3046)
Hotel	★★64% Grange Hotel, 17 London Rd, Holybourne, ALTON ☎(0420) 86565 27rm(23⇨🏠)Annexe6⇨🏠

ALTON   Map 04 SU73

Alton ☎(0420) 82042
Undulating meadowland course.
9 holes, 5744yds, Par 68, SSS 68, Course record 65.
Club membership 340.

▶

Visitors	must have a handicap of 18 or less to play at weekends & bank holidays, or be accompanied by a member.
Societies	weekdays only.
Green Fees	£16 per day; £11 per round (£20 per day; £16 per round weekends & bank holidays).
Facilities	♀ ⚘ 🏠 (Andy Lamb.
Location	Old Odiham Rd (2m N off A32)
Hotel	★★★61% Alton House Hotel, Normandy St, ALTON ☎(0420) 80033 38⇨🐾

AMPFIELD
Map 04 SU42

Ampfield Par Three ☎Braishfield (0794) 68480
Pretty parkland course designed by Henry Cotton in 1963. Well-bunkered greens.
18 holes, 2478yds, Par 54, SSS 53, Course record 49.
Club membership 510.

Visitors	must have a handicap certificate to play at weekends & bank holidays. Must contact in advance.
Societies	must contact in writing.
Green Fees	£15 per day; £8.80 per round (£15.50 per round weekends & bank holidays).
Facilities	⊗ 🏖 🛋 ♀ ⚘ 🏠 🐿 (Richard Benfield.
Location	Winchester Rd (4m NE of Romsey on A31)
Hotel	★★★64% Potters Heron Hotel, AMPFIELD ☎(0703) 266611 60⇨

ANDOVER
Map 04 SU34

Andover ☎(0264) 358040
Hilly downland course, fine views.
9 holes, 5933yds, Par 69, SSS 68, Course record 64.
Club membership 500.

Visitors	restricted mornings at weekends.
Societies	must contact in writing.
Green Fees	£11 per round; £16.50 per day (£22 weekends & bank holidays).
Facilities	⊗ 🎜 🏖 🛋 ♀ ⚘ 🏠 🐿 (Andrea Timms.
Location	51 Winchester Rd (1m S on A3057)
Hotel	★★54% Danebury Hotel, High St, ANDOVER ☎(0264) 323332 24⇨🐾

BARTON-ON-SEA
Map 04 SZ29

Barton-on-Sea
☎New Milton (0425) 615308
Though not strictly a links course, it is right on a cliff edge with views over the Isle of Wight and Christchurch Bay. On a still day there is nothing much to it - but when it blows the course undergoes a complete change in character. At present in process of reconstruction to 27 holes which should be in play during 1993.
18 holes, 5565yds, Par 67, SSS 67, Course record 62.
Club membership 700.

	SCORECARD: Medal Tees				
Hole	Yds	Par	Hole	Yds	Par
1	363	4	10	367	4
2	372	4	11	311	4
3	167	3	12	580	5
4	343	4	13	122	3
5	137	3	14	376	4
6	469	4	15	163	3
7	366	4	16	387	4
8	164	3	17	157	3
9	349	4	18	372	4
Out	2730	33	In	2835	34
			Totals	5565	67

Visitors	after 8.30am Mon-Fri & 11.15am weekends & bank holidays. Must contact in advance and have an introduction from own club.
Societies	Wed & Fri only. Must book well in advance.
Green Fees	£21 per day (£24 weekends & bank holidays).
Facilities	⊗ 🎜 (by prior arrangement for parties) 🏖 🔲 ♀ ⚘ 🏠 🐿 (P Coombs.
Location	Marine Dr East (E side of town)
Hotel	★★★★(red)🏨 Chewton Glen Hotel, Christchurch Rd, NEW MILTON ☎(0425) 275341 58⇨

BASINGSTOKE
Map 04 SU65

Basingstoke ☎(0256) 465990
A well-maintained parkland course with wide and inviting fairways. You are inclined to expect longer drives than are actually achieved - partly on account of the trees. There are many two-hundred-year-old beech trees, since the course was built on an old deer park.
18 holes, 6239yds, Par 70, SSS 70, Course record 65.
Club membership 700.

	SCORECARD: White Tees				
Hole	Yds	Par	Hole	Yds	Par
1	499	5	10	415	4
2	368	4	11	433	4
3	157	3	12	209	3
4	466	4	13	402	4
5	177	3	14	431	4
6	362	4	15	343	4
7	422	4	16	364	4
8	251	4	17	166	3
9	334	4	18	510	5
Out	3036	35	In	3273	35
			Totals	6309	70

Visitors	must play with member at weekends. Must have an introduction from own club.
Societies	Wed & Thu only.
Green Fees	£30 per day; £22 per round.
Facilities	⊗ 🎜 🏖 🔲 (all catering by prior arrangement) ♀ ⚘ 🏠 (Ian Hayes.
Location	Kempshott Park (3.5m SW on A30 M3 exit 7)
Hotel	★★★61% Forte Posthouse, Grove Rd, BASINGSTOKE ☎(0256) 468181 84⇨🐾

BORDON
Map 04 SU73

Blackmoor ☎(0420) 472775
A first-class moorland course with a great variety of holes. Fine greens and wide pine tree-lined fairways are a distinguishing feature. The ground is mainly flat and walking easy.
18 holes, 6200yds, Par 69, SSS 70, Course record 65.
Club membership 700.

Visitors	must have a letter of introduction from their club or a handicap certificate; must be accompanied by a member at weekends. Must contact in advance.
Societies	must telephone in advance.
Green Fees	£33.
Facilities	⊗ 🎜 🏖 🔲 ♀ ⚘ 🏠 🐿 (Andrew Hall.
Leisure	practice ground & nets.
Location	Whitehill
Hotel	★★★60% Bush Hotel, The Borough, FARNHAM ☎(0252) 715237 68⇨🐾

We make every effort to ensure that our information is accurate but details may change after we go to print

BOTLEY   Map 04 SU51

Botley Park Hotel & Country Club ☎(0489) 780888
Pleasantly undulating course with water hazards. Driving range and country club facilities.
18 holes, 6026yds, Par 70, SSS 70.
Club membership 750.

Visitors	must have handicap certificate. Must contact in advance.
Societies	contact in advance.
Green Fees	£23 per round (£30 weekends).
Facilities	⊗ ⍐ ⓺ 🍺 ♀ ⚐ 🏠 ⚑ 🖼 ⚑ 🛎 Tim Barter.
Leisure	hard tennis courts, heated indoor swimming pool, squash, snooker, sauna, solarium, gymnasium, croquet lawn, petanque.
Location	Winchester Rd, Boorley Green (1m NW of Botley on B3354)
Hotel	★★★★68% Botley Park Hotel & Country Club, Winchester Rd, Boorley Green, BOTLEY ☎(0489) 780888 100↝🛏

BROCKENHURST   Map 04 SU20

Brokenhurst Manor
☎Lymington (0590) 23332
An attractive woodland/heathland course set at the edge of the New Forest, with the unusual feature of three loops of six holes each to complete the round. Fascinating holes include the short 5th and 12th, and the 4th and 17th, both dog-legged. A stream also features on seven of the holes.

SCORECARD: White Tees					
Hole	Yds	Par	Hole	Yds	Par
1	316	4	10	208	3
2	495	5	11	404	4
3	174	3	12	168	3
4	374	4	13	412	4
5	167	3	14	297	4
6	327	4	15	322	4
7	384	4	16	520	5
8	449	4	17	414	4
9	459	4	18	332	4
Out	3145	35	In	3077	35
			Totals	6222	70

18 holes, 6222yds, Par 70, SSS 70, Course record 64.
Club membership 800.

Visitors	must have a handicap certificate. Must contact in advance and have an introduction from own club.
Societies	Thu only. Must telephone in advance.
Green Fees	£30 per day; £25 per round (£35 weekends & bank holidays).
Facilities	⊗ & ⍐ by prior arrangement 🍺 ♀ 🏠 ⚑ 🛎 Clive Bonner.
Location	Sway Rd (1m S on B3055)
Hotel	★★★62% Balmer Lawn Hotel, Lyndhurst Rd, BROCKENHURST ☎(0590) 23116 58↝🛏
Additional hotel	★★62% Watersplash Hotel, The Rise, BROCKENHURST ☎(0590) 22344 23↝🛏

BURLEY   Map 04 SU20

Burley ☎(04253) 2431
Undulating heather and gorseland. The 7th requires an accurately placed tee shot to obtain par 4. Played off different tees on second nine.
9 holes, 6149yds, Par 71, SSS 69, Course record 68.
Club membership 520.

Visitors	must have a handicap certificate. Must contact in advance.
Green Fees	£10 per day (£12.50 weekends & bank holidays).

Facilities	🍺 🍺 ♀ ⚐
Location	E side of village
Hotel	★★70% Struan Hotel & Restaurant, Horton Rd, Ashley Heath, RINGWOOD ☎(0425) 473553 & 473029 10↝🛏

CORHAMPTON   Map 04 SU62

Corhampton ☎Droxford (0489) 877279
Downland course.
18 holes, 6100yds, Par 69, SSS 69, Course record 64.
Club membership 650.

Visitors	must play with member at weekends & bank holidays. Must contact in advance.
Societies	Mon & Thu only. Must telephone in advance.
Green Fees	£32 per day; £20 per round (weekdays).
Facilities	⊗ & ⍐ (ex Tue) 🍺 (ex evenings) 🍺 ♀ ⚐ 🏠 ⚑ 🛎 Garry Stubbington.
Location	Sheep's Pond Ln (1m W off B3055)
Hotel	★★73% Old House Hotel, The Square, WICKHAM ☎(0329) 833049 9↝🛏 Annexe3↝🛏

CRONDALL   Map 04 SU74

Oak Park ☎Aldershot (0252) 850880
Gently undulating course overlooking pretty village. 16-bay floodlit driving range, practice green and practice bunker.
18 holes, 6437yds, Par 72, SSS 71.
Club membership 400.

Visitors	must contact in advance.
Societies	must telephone in advance.

▶

Green Fees	£15 per round (£22 weekends & bank holidays).
Facilities	⊗ (ex Sat) ∭ (ex Sun-Mon) ⤢ 🍺 ♀ ⌂ 🏠 ⛳
	🍴 Simon Coaker.
Location	Heath Ln (.5m E of village off A287)
Hotel	★★★60% Bush Hotel, The Borough,
	FARNHAM ☎(0252) 715237 68⇨🛏

DIBDEN   Map 04 SU40

Dibden ☎Southampton (0703) 207508
Municipal parkland course with views over Southampton
Water. A pond guards the green at the par 5, 3rd hole.
Twenty-bay driving range.
Course 1: 18 holes, 6206yds, Par 71, SSS 70, Course record 63.
Course 2: 9 holes, 1520yds, Par 29.
Club membership 600.

Visitors	no restrictions.
Societies	must contact in writing.
Green Fees	£5.20 for 18 holes.
Facilities	⊗ ∭ by prior arrangement ⤢ 🍺 ♀ ⌂ 🏠 ⛳
	🍴 Alan Bridge.
Location	Main Rd (2m NW of Dibden Purlieu)
Hotel	★★★60% Forest Lodge Hotel, Pikes Hill,
	Romsey Rd, LYNDHURST ☎(0703) 283677
	23⇨🛏

EASTLEIGH   Map 04 SU41

Fleming Park ☎(0703) 612797
Parkland course with stream-'Monks Brook'-running
through.
18 holes, 4436yds, Par 65, SSS 62.
Club membership 300.

Visitors	no restrictions.
Green Fees	not confirmed.
Facilities	♀ ⌂ 🏠 ⛳ 🍴
Location	Magpie Ln (E side of town centre)
Hotel	★★★62% Southampton Park Hotel,
	Cumberland Place, SOUTHAMPTON ☎(0703)
	223467 71⇨🛏

FARNBOROUGH   Map 04 SU85

Southwood ☎(0252) 548700
Municipal parkland course with stream running through.
18 holes, 5553yds, Par 69, SSS 67, Course record 64.
Club membership 560.

Visitors	must contact in advance.
Societies	must contact in advance.
Green Fees	£10 (£12 weekends).
Facilities	⊗ ∭ by prior arrangement ⤢ 🍺 ♀ ⌂ 🏠 ⛳
	🍴 Bob Hammond.
Location	Ively Rd (.5m W)
Hotel	★★★64% Forte Crest, Lynchford Rd,
	FARNBOROUGH ☎(0252) 545051 110⇨🛏

FLEET   Map 04 SU70

North Hants ☎(0252) 616443
Picturesque tree-lined course with much heather and
gorse close to the fairways. A comparatively easy par-4
first hole may lull the golfer into a false sense of security,
only to be rudely awakened at the testing holes which
follow. The ground is rather undulating and, though not
tiring, does offer some excellent 'blind' shots, and more
than a few surprises in judging distance.
18 holes, 6257yds, Par 69, SSS 70, Course record 66.
Club membership 700.

Visitors	must play with member at weekends. Must
	contact in advance and have an introduction
	from own club.
Societies	Tue & Wed only
Green Fees	£20-£25 per round.
Facilities	⊗ ∭ ⤢ 🍺 ♀ ⌂ 🏠 🍴 Steve Porter.
Location	Minley Rd (.25m N of Fleet station on
	B3013)
Hotel	★★★59% Lismoyne Hotel, Church Rd,
	FLEET ☎(0252) 628555 44⇨🛏

GOSPORT   Map 04 SZ69

Gosport & Stokes Bay ☎(0705) 527941
A testing links course overlooking the Solent, with plenty of
gorse and short rough. Changing winds.
9 holes, 5856yds, Par 72, SSS 69, Course record 65.
Club membership 500.

Visitors	may not play at weekends.
Societies	must telephone in advance.
Green Fees	£10 per day (£16 weekends).
Facilities	⊗ & ∭ by prior arrangement ⤢ 🍺 ♀ ⌂ 🏠
	⛳
Location	Off Fort Rd, Haslar (S side of town centre)
Hotel	★★57% Anglesey Hotel, Crescent Rd,
	Alverstoke, GOSPORT ☎(0705) 582157 &
	523932 18⇨🛏

HARTLEY WINTNEY   Map 04 SU75

Hartley Wintney ☎(025126) 2214
Easy walking, parkland course in pleasant countryside.
Played off different tees on back nine, with testing par 4s at
4th and 13th.
9 holes, 6096yds, Par 70, SSS 69, Course record 63.
Club membership 400.

Visitors	must contact in advance.
Societies	Tue & Thu only.
Green Fees	not confirmed.
Facilities	⊗ (ex Mon) ∭ by prior arrangement ⤢ 🍺 ♀
	⌂ 🏠 🍴 Martin Smith.
Location	London Rd (NE side of village on A30)
Hotel	★★★59% Lismoyne Hotel, Church Rd,
	FLEET ☎(0252) 628555 44⇨🛏

For an explanation of symbols and
abbreviations, see page 32

For a full range of AA guides and maps, visit
your local AA shop or any good bookshop

HAYLING ISLAND   Map 04 SU70

Hayling ☎(0705) 464446
A delightful links course among the dunes offering fine
sea-scapes and views across to the Isle of Wight. Varying
sea breezes and sometimes strong winds ensure that the
course seldom plays the same two days running. Testing
holes at the 12th and 13th, both par 4. Club selection is
important.
18 holes, 6489yds, Par 71, SSS 71, Course record 66.
Club membership 950.

Visitors	must have a handicap certificate. Must contact in advance and have an introduction from own club.
Societies	welcome Tue & Wed, apply in writing.
Green Fees	£24 (£30 weekends & bank holidays).
Facilities	⚐ 🏌 ✆ 🍴 R C A Gadd.
Location	Ferry Rd (SW side of island at West Town)
Hotel	★★★64% Forte Posthouse, Northney Rd, HAYLING ISLAND ☎(0705) 465011 96⇆

KINGSCLERE   Map 04 SU55

Sandford Springs ☎(0635) 297881
The course has unique variety in beautiful surroundings
and offers three distinctive loops of 9 holes. There are
water hazards, woodlands and gradients to negotiate,
providing a challenge for all playing categories. From its
highest point there are extensive views.
The Park : 9 holes, 2963yds, Par 35.
The Lakes : 9 holes, 3180yds, Par 35.
The Wood : 9 holes, 3042yds, Par 36.
Club membership 590.

Visitors	must play with member at weekends. Must contact in advance.
Societies	must contact in advance.
Green Fees	£20.20 per 18 holes, £30 for 36 holes.
Facilities	⊗ �𝄞 🏌 ⚐ ♀ ⚐ 🏌 ✆ 🍴 Kim Brake/ Anthony Dillon.
Location	Wolverton (on A339)
Hotel	★★★72% Millwaters, London Rd, NEWBURY ☎(0635) 528838 32⇆🐾

KINGSLEY   Map 04 SU73

Dean Farm ☎Bordon (0420) 2313
Undulating downland course.
9 holes, 1350yds, Par 27.

Visitors	no restrictions.
Green Fees	not confirmed.
Facilities	🏌 ⚐
Leisure	hard tennis courts.
Location	W side of village off B3004
Hotel	★★64% Grange Hotel, 17 London Rd, Holybourne, ALTON ☎(0420) 86565 27rm(23⇆🐾)Annexe6⇆🐾

This guide is updated annually – make sure that
you use the up-to-date edition

LECKFORD   Map 04 SU33

Leckford ☎(0264) 810710
A testing downland course with good views.
9 holes, 6444yds, Par 70, SSS 71.
Club membership 200.

Visitors	must be accompanied by member and contact in advance.
Green Fees	not confirmed.
Facilities	⚐
Location	1m SW off A3057
Hotel	★★★56% Grosvenor Hotel, High St, STOCKBRIDGE ☎(0264) 810606 25⇆

LEE-ON-SOLENT   Map 04 SU50

Lee-on-Solent ☎(0705) 551170
A modest parkland/heathland course, yet a testing one. The
five short holes always demand a high standard of play and
the 13th is rated one of the best in the country.
18 holes, 5959yds, Par 69, SSS 69, Course record 66.
Club membership 700.

Visitors	must play with member at weekends. Must contact in advance.
Societies	must contact in advance.
Green Fees	£20 per day/round.
Facilities	⊗ �𝄞 🏌 ⚐ ♀ ⚐ 🍴 John Richardson.
Location	Brune Ln (1m N off B3385)
Hotel	★★68% Red Lion Hotel, East St, FAREHAM ☎(0329) 822640 44⇆

LIPHOOK   Map 04 SU83

Liphook ☎(0428) 723271
Heathland course with easy walking and fine views.
18 holes, 6250yds, Par 70, SSS 70.
Club membership 800.

Visitors	may not play Sunday mornings, and must have a handicap certificate. Must contact in advance and have an introduction from own club.
Societies	must contact in advance.
Green Fees	£31 day (£41 weekends); £22.50 per round (£31 weekends).
Facilities	⊗ ⟁ by prior arrangement 🏌 ⚐ ♀ ⚐ 🍴 Ian Large.
Location	Wheatsheaf Enclosure (1.5m SW off A3)
Hotel	★★★72% Lythe Hill Hotel, Petworth Rd, HASLEMERE ☎(0428) 651251 40⇆

Old Thorns London Kosaido ☎(0428) 724555
A challenging 18-hole championship course designed around
magnificent oaks, beeches and Scots pine.
18 holes, 6041yds, Par 72, SSS 70.

Visitors	must contact in advance.
Societies	must telephone in advance.
Green Fees	not confirmed.
Facilities	⊗ ⟁ 🏌 ⚐ ♀ ⚐ 🍴 🏌 Philip Loxley.
Leisure	hard tennis courts, heated indoor swimming pool, sauna, solarium.
Location	Longmoor Rd (1m W on B2131)
Hotel	★★★72% Lythe Hill Hotel, Petworth Rd, HASLEMERE ☎(0428) 651251 40⇆

LYNDHURST   Map 04 SU20

Bramshaw ☎Southampton (0703) 813433
Two 18-hole courses. The Manor Course is landscaped parkland with excellent greens, and features mature trees and streams. The Forest Course is set amidst beautiful open forest. Easy walking. The Bell Inn Hotel, attached to the club, provides fine accommodation just a wedge shot from the first tee, and reserved tee times for its guests.
Manor Course: 18 holes, 6233yds, Par 71, SSS 70, Course record 66.
Forest Course: 18 holes, 5774yds, Par 69, SSS 68, Course record 66.
Club membership 1200.

Visitors	must be accompanied by member at weekends. Must contact in advance.
Societies	may not play at weekends. Must telephone in advance.
Green Fees	not confirmed.
Facilities	⊗ ⑪ ⌾ ⬤ ♀ ⚲ ⛬ ⛢ 𝄢 ᚛ Clive Bonner.
Location	Brook (On B3079 1m W of M27 junc 1)
Hotel	★★★68% Bell Inn, BROOK ☎(0703) 812214 22⊐

New Forest ☎(0703) 282450
This picturesque heathland course is laid out in a typical stretch of the New Forest on high ground a little above the village of Lynhurst. Natural hazards include the inevitable forest ponies. The first two holes are somewhat teasing, as is the 485-yard (par 5) 9th. Walking is easy.
18 holes, 5742yds, Par 69, SSS 68, Course record 65.
Club membership 900.

Visitors	must contact in advance.
Societies	must contact in advance.
Green Fees	£12 per day (£15 weekends & bank holidays).
Facilities	⊗ ⑪ by prior arrangement ⌾ ⬤ ♀ ⚲ 𝄢 ᚛ Ken Gilhespy.
Location	Southampton Rd (0.5m NE off A35)
Hotel	★★★68% Crown Hotel, High St, LYNDHURST ☎(0703) 282922 40⊐ᛰ

PETERSFIELD   Map 04 SU72

Petersfield ☎(0730) 62386
Part-heath, parkland course with a lake, and good views.
18 holes, 5649yds, Par 69, SSS 67, Course record 66.
Club membership 650.

Visitors	restricted weekends & bank holidays.
Societies	must contact in writing.
Green Fees	£14-£20 (£20-£25 weekends & bank holidays).
Facilities	⊗ & ⑪ by prior arrangement ⌾ ⬤ ♀ ⚲ 𝄢 ᚛ Stephen Clay.
Location	Heath Rd (E side of town centre off A3)
Hotel	★★★66% Spread Eagle Hotel, South St, MIDHURST ☎(0730) 816911 37⊐Annexe4ᛰ

Each golf-course entry has a recommended AA-appointed hotel. For a wider choice of places to stay, consult *AA Hotels and Restaurants in Britain and Ireland* and *AA Inspected Bed and Breakfast in Britain and Ireland*

PORTSMOUTH & SOUTHSEA   Map 04 SU60

Great Salterns Public Course ☎Portsmouth (0705) 664549 & 699519
Easy walking, seaside course with open fairways and testing shots onto well-guarded, small greens. Testing 13th hole, par 4, requiring 130yd shot across a lake.
18 holes, 5610yds, Par 69, SSS 66, Course record 63.
Club membership 700.

Visitors	no restrictions.
Societies	must contact in advance.
Green Fees	£8.20 per round (£6.15 winter).
Facilities	♀ 𝄢 ⛢ 𝄞 ᚛ Terry Healy.
Location	Eastern Rd (NE of town centre on A2030)
Hotel	★★★60% Hospitality Inn, St Helens Pde, SOUTHSEA ☎(0705) 731281 115⊐ᛰ

Southsea ☎Portsmouth (0705) 660945
Municipal, meadowland course.
18 holes, 5900yds, Par 72, SSS 68, Course record 64.
Club membership 650.

Visitors	no restrictions.
Societies	must contact in advance.
Green Fees	not confirmed.
Facilities	𝄢 ⛢ ᚛ Terry Healy.
Location	The Mansion, Great Salterns, Eastern Rd (.5m off M27)
Hotel	★★★60% Hospitality Inn, St Helens Pde, SOUTHSEA ☎(0705) 731281 115⊐ᛰ

ROMSEY   Map 04 SU32

Dunwood Manor Country Club ☎Lockerley (0794) 40549
Undulating parkland course with fine views. Testing 1st hole: Reynolds Leap (par 4).
18 holes, 5885yds, Par 69, SSS 69, Course record 61.
Club membership 700.

Visitors	restricted weekends. Must contact in advance and have an introduction from own club.
Societies	must contact in advance.
Green Fees	£25 per day; £20 per round (£30 weekends).
Facilities	⊗ ⑪ ⌾ ⬤ ♀ ⚲ 𝄢 ⛢ ᚛ Trevor Pearce.
Leisure	snooker.
Location	Shootash Hill (4m W off A27)
Hotel	★★★64% Potters Heron Hotel, AMPFIELD ☎(0703) 266611 60⊐

Romsey ☎Southampton (0703) 734637
Parkland/woodland course with narrow tree-lined fairways. Six holes are undulating, rest are sloping. There are superb views over the Test valley.
18 holes, 5851yds, Par 69, SSS 68, Course record 65.
Club membership 700.

Visitors	must play with member at weekends. Must have an introduction from own club.
Societies	must contact in advance.
Green Fees	£22.50 per day; £18.50 per round.
Facilities	⊗ ⑪ ⌾ ⬤ ♀ ⚲ 𝄢 ⛢ ᚛ Mark Desmond.
Location	Romsey Rd, Nursling (3m S on A3057)
Hotel	★★★60% Hospitality Inn, St Helens Pde, SOUTHSEA ☎(0705) 731281 115⊐ᛰ

For a full list of golf courses included in the book, see the index at the end of the directory

ROTHERWICK
Map 04 TQ89

Tylney Park ☎Hook (0256) 762079
Parkland course. Practice area.
18 holes, 6109yds, Par 70, SSS 69, Course record 65.
Club membership 700.

Visitors	must be with member at weekends or have a handicap certificate.
Societies	must telephone in advance.
Green Fees	not confirmed.
Facilities	⊗ by prior arrangement ⅷ by prior arrangement 🝙 🝙 ♀ ♨ 🏠 🝙 ⟨ C De Bruin/M Kimberley.
Location	.5m SW
Hotel	★★★★♨80% Tylney Hall Hotel, ROTHERWICK ☎(0256) 764881 35⇆Annexe56⇆

ROWLANDS CASTLE
Map 04 SU71

Rowlands Castle
☎Portsmouth (0705) 412784
Exceptionally dry in winter, this flat parkland course is a testing one with a number of tricky dog-legs and bunkers much in evidence. The 7th, at 522yds, is the longest hole on the course and leads to a well-guarded armchair green.
18 holes, 6381yds, Par 72, SSS 70, Course record 66.
Club membership 850.

SCORECARD: White Tees					
Hole	Yds	Par	Hole	Yds	Par
1	326	4	10	441	4
2	182	3	11	181	3
3	370	4	12	490	5
4	356	4	13	380	4
5	351	4	14	161	3
6	397	4	15	430	4
7	522	5	16	337	4
8	366	4	17	509	5
9	368	4	18	460	4
Out	3238	36	In	3389	36
			Totals	6627	72

Visitors	must play with member Sat; restricted Sun. Must contact in advance.
Societies	Tue & Thu only; must contact in writing.
Green Fees	£21 per day/round (£25 weekends & bank holidays).
Facilities	⊗ 🝙 🝙 ♀ ♨ 🏠 ⟨ Peter Klepacz.
Location	Links Ln (W side of village off B2149)
Hotel	★★★64% Forte Posthouse, Northney Rd, HAYLING ISLAND ☎(0705) 465011 96⇆

SHEDFIELD
Map 04 SU51

Meon Valley Hotel Golf & Country Club ☎Wickham (0329) 833455
It has been said that a golf course architect is as good as the ground on which he has to work. Here Hamilton Stutt had magnificent terrain at his disposal and a very good and lovely parkland course is the result. There are three holes over water. The hotel provides many sports facilities.
18 holes, 6009yds, Par 71, SSS 69.
Club membership 700.

SCORECARD: White Tees					
Hole	Yds	Par	Hole	Yds	Par
1	484	5	10	544	5
2	458	4	11	362	4
3	403	4	12	153	3
4	168	3	13	330	4
5	444	4	14	233	3
6	369	4	15	315	4
7	155	3	16	474	4
8	552	5	17	386	4
9	393	4	18	296	4
Out	3426	36	In	3093	35
			Totals	6519	71

Visitors	must contact in advance.
Societies	must contact in writing.
Green Fees	not confirmed.

Facilities	⊗ ⅷ 🝙 🝙 ♀ ♨ 🏠 🝙 🏊 ⟨ John Stirling.
Leisure	hard tennis courts, heated indoor swimming pool, squash, snooker, sauna, solarium, gymnasium.
Location	Sandy Ln (off A334 between Botley and Wickham)
Hotel	★★73% Old House Hotel, The Square, WICKHAM ☎(0329) 833049 9⇆🝙Annexe3⇆🝙

SOUTHAMPTON
Map 04 SU41

Southampton ☎(0703) 760472
This beautiful municipal parkland course always ensures a good game, fast in summer, slow in winter. Three par 4's over 450 yds.
18 holes, 6213yds, Par 69, SSS 70.
Club membership 500.

Visitors	no restrictions.
Societies	welcome.
Green Fees	not confirmed.
Facilities	♀ ♨ 🏠 🝙 ⟨
Location	Golf Course Rd, Bassett (4m N of city centre off A33)
Hotel	★★57% Star Hotel, High St, SOUTHAMPTON ☎(0703) 339939 45rm(38⇆🝙)

Stoneham ☎(0703) 769272
A hilly, heather course with sand or peat sub-soil; the fairways are separated by belts of woodland and gorse to present a varied terrain. The interesting 4th is a difficult par 4 and the fine 11th has cross-bunkers about 150 yards from the tee.
18 holes, 6310yds, Par 72, SSS 70, Course record 65.
Club membership 800.

SCORECARD: White Tees					
Hole	Yds	Par	Hole	Yds	Par
1	507	5	10	185	3
2	191	3	11	389	4
3	356	4	12	516	5
4	462	4	13	255	4
5	304	4	14	476	5
6	501	5	15	419	4
7	233	3	16	120	3
8	168	3	17	377	4
9	374	4	18	477	5
Out	3096	35	In	3214	37
			Totals	6310	72

Visitors	restricted at weekends. Must contact in advance.
Societies	must apply to secretary
Green Fees	£25 per day/round (£27.50 weekends).
Facilities	⊗ ⅷ by prior arrangement 🝙 🝙 ♀ (all day) ♨ 🏠 ⟨ Ian Young.
Location	Bassett Green Rd, Bassett (4m N of city centre off A27)
Hotel	★★★56% Polygon Hotel, Cumberland Place, SOUTHAMPTON ☎(0703) 330055 119⇆🝙

SOUTHWICK
Map 04 SU60

Southwick Park Naval Recreation Centre
☎Cosham (0705) 370683
Set in 100 acres of parkland.
18 holes, 5855yds, Par 69, SSS 68, Course record 64.
Club membership 700.

Visitors	weekday mornings only. Must contact in advance.
Societies	Tue only, telephone in advance.
Green Fees	not confirmed.

▶

Facilities	⊗ by prior arrangement ⅢҬ by prior arrangement 🏌 ♀ ⚲ 🏠 ☎ ͡ John Green.
Leisure	pitch & putt, skittle alley.
Location	Pinsley Dr (.5m SE off B2177)
Hotel	★★73% Old House Hotel, The Square, WICKHAM ☎(0329) 833049 9⇨🏠Annexe3⇨🏠

TADLEY   Map 04 SU66

Bishopswood ☎(0734) 815213
Wooded course, fairly tight, with stream and natural water hazards. Floodlit driving range.
9 holes, 6474yds, Par 72, SSS 71, Course record 68.
Club membership 500.

Visitors	Tue, Thu & Fri only. Mon & Wed with member. Must contact in advance.
Societies	must contact by telephone.
Green Fees	9 holes £7.15; 18 holes £12.25.
Facilities	⊗ ⅢҬ 🏌 ♠ ♀ ⚲ 🏠 ͡ Steve Ward.
Location	Bishopswood Ln (1m W off A340)
Hotel	★★★60% Romans Hotel, Little London Rd, SILCHESTER ☎(0734) 700421 11⇨Annexe13⇨🏠

TIDWORTH   Map 04 SU24

Tidworth Garrison
☎Stonehenge (0980) 42301
A breezy, dry downland course with lovely turf, fine trees and views over Salisbury Plain and the surrounding area. The 3rd and 12th holes are notable. The 564-yard 13th, going down towards the clubhouse, gives the big hitter a chance to let fly.
18 holes, 6075yds, Par 69, SSS 69, Course record 65.
Club membership 850.

SCORECARD: Medal Tees					
Hole	Yds	Par	Hole	Yds	Par
1	324	4	10	135	3
2	163	3	11	416	4
3	393	4	12	173	3
4	451	4	13	564	5
5	160	3	14	157	3
6	480	5	15	383	4
7	334	4	16	360	4
8	429	4	17	336	4
9	401	4	18	416	4
Out	3135	35	In	2940	34
			Totals	6075	69

Visitors	may not play after 3.30pm summer weekends & bank holidays. Must contact in advance.
Societies	must contact in writing.
Green Fees	£18 per day (£23 weekends).
Facilities	⊗ ⅢҬ 🏌 ♠ ♀ ⚲ 🏠 ☎ ͡ Terry Gosden.
Leisure	practice area putting & chipping greens.
Location	Bulford Rd (W side of village off A338)
Hotel	★★★61% Ashley Court, Micheldever Rd, ANDOVER ☎(0264) 357344 9⇨🏠Annexe26⇨🏠

WATERLOOVILLE   Map 04 SU60

Waterlooville ☎Portsmouth (0705) 263388
Parkland course, easy walking.
18 holes, 6647yds, Par 72, SSS 72, Course record 66.
Club membership 800.

Visitors	may only play on weekdays. Must contact in advance.
Societies	Thu only; apply by letter.
Green Fees	£25 per day; £20 per round.
Facilities	⊗ 🏌 ♠ ♀ ⚲ 🏠 ͡ John Hay.

| Location | Cherry Tree Av, Cowplain (NE side of town centre off A3) |
| Hotel | ★★★64% Forte Posthouse, Northney Rd, HAYLING ISLAND ☎(0705) 465011 96⇨ |

WINCHESTER   Map 04 SU42

Hockley ☎Twyford (0962) 713165
High downland course with good views.
18 holes, 6279yds, Par 71, SSS 70.
Club membership 700.

Visitors	must play with member at weekends.
Societies	must contact in writing.
Green Fees	£25.
Facilities	⊗ & ⅢҬ (ex Mon) 🏌 ♠ ♀ ⚲ 🏠 ☎ ͡
Location	Twyford (2m S on A333)
Hotel	★★★★62% Forte Crest, Paternoster Row, WINCHESTER ☎(0962) 861611 94⇨🏠

Royal Winchester
☎(0962) 852462
The Royal Winchester Club must be included in any list of notable clubs, because of its age (it dates from 1888) and also because the club was involved in one of the very first professional matches. To-day it still flourishes on its present sporting, downland course. Hilly in places.
18 holes, 5980yds, Par 71, SSS 69, Course record 68.
Club membership 700.

SCORECARD: White Tees					
Hole	Yds	Par	Hole	Yds	Par
1	284	4	10	490	5
2	348	4	11	188	3
3	204	3	12	382	4
4	374	4	13	456	4
5	357	4	14	263	4
6	465	4	15	414	4
7	158	3	16	501	5
8	360	4	17	148	3
9	482	5	18	338	4
Out	3032	35	In	3180	36
			Totals	6212	71

Visitors	must play with member at weekends. Must contact in advance and have an introduction from own club.
Societies	must contact in writing.
Green Fees	£25 per day weekdays.
Facilities	⊗ ⅢҬ 🏌 ♠ ♀ ⚲ 🏠 ☎ ͡ David Williams.
Location	Sarum Rd (1.5m W off A3090)
Hotel	★★★★≜71% Lainston House Hotel, Sparsholt, WINCHESTER ☎(0962) 863588 32rm(30⇨1🏠)

HEREFORD & WORCESTER

ALVECHURCH   Map 07 SP07

Kings Norton ☎Wythall (0564) 826706
An old club with three, 9-hole courses; the Blue, Red and Yellow. Parkland with some exacting water hazards, it has housed important events. There is also a 12-hole, par 3 course.
18 holes, 7064yds, Par 72, SSS 74, Course record 65.
Club membership 984.

Visitors	may not play at weekends.
Societies	must telephone in advance.
Green Fees	£27 per day; £24 per round.
Facilities	⊗ ⅢҬ 🏌 ♠ (no catering weekends) ♀ ⚲ 🏠 ͡ Clive Haycock.
Leisure	snooker.
Location	Brockhill Ln, Weatheroak (3m NE)

Hotel	★★★67% Forte Crest Leeds/Bradford, Otley Rd, BRAMHOPE ☎(0532) 842911 126⇄

BEWDLEY   Map 07 SO77

Little Lakes Golf and Country Club ☎(0299) 266385
A testing 9-hole undulating parkland course offering alternative tees for the second nine and some pleasing views.
9 holes, 6247yds, Par 73, SSS 72, Course record 70.
Club membership 500.

Visitors	may not play at weekends. Must contact in advance.
Societies	must telephone in advance.
Green Fees	£15 per day; £12 per round.
Facilities	⊗ ⅲ ⮾ ⬤ ♀ ⚲ 🖻 ℂ Mark Laing.
Leisure	hard tennis courts, outdoor swimming pool, fishing.
Location	Lye Head (2.25m W off A456)
Hotel	★★★63% Stourport Moat House, 35 Hartlebury Rd, STOURPORT-ON-SEVERN ☎(0299) 827733 68⇄🏵

BISHAMPTON   Map 03 SO95

Vale Golf & Country Club ☎(038682) 781
A new course offering an American-style layout, with large greens, trees and bunkers and several water hazards. Its rolling fairways provide a testing round, as well as superb views of the Malvern Hills. Picturesque and peaceful. Also 9-hole course and 20-bay driving range.
International: 18 holes, 7041yds, Par 73, SSS 73.
Lenches: 9 holes, 2980yds, Par 35, SSS 35.
Club membership 700.

Visitors	times may be restricted at peak times weekends. Booking preferred.
Societies	must apply in advance.
Green Fees	International Course £18 per round (£27 per day weekend).
Facilities	⊗ ⅲ ⮾ ⬤ ♀ (ex Sun) ⚲ 🖻 ℂ Russell Gardner.
Leisure	fishing.
Location	Hill Furze Rd
Hotel	★★62% Avonside Hotel, Main Rd, WYRE PIDDLE ☎(0386) 552654 7⇄🏵

BLAKEDOWN   Map 07 SO87

Churchill and Blakedown ☎(0562) 700200
Pleasant course on hilltop with extensive views.
9 holes, 6472yds, Par 72, SSS 71.
Club membership 365.

Visitors	with member only weekends & bank holidays.
Societies	Mon-Fri, by arrangement.
Green Fees	£15 per day/round.
Facilities	⊗ ⅲ ⮾ ⬤ ♀ ⚲ 🖻 ⅌ ℂ K M Wheeler.
Location	Churchill Ln (W side of village off A456)
Hotel	★★70% Gainsborough House Hotel, Bewdley Hill, KIDDERMINSTER ☎(0562) 820041 42⇄🏵

This guide is updated annually – make sure that you use the up-to-date edition

BROADWAY   Map 04 SP03

Broadway ☎(0386) 853683
At the edge of the Cotswolds this downland course lies at an altitude of 900 ft above sea level, with extensive views.
18 holes, 6216yds, Par 72, SSS 69.
Club membership 850.

Visitors	welcome except Sat unless with member. No ladies Sun (am). Must contact in advance.
Societies	must contact in advance.
Green Fees	£20.50 per round (£25.50 weekends & bank holidays).
Facilities	⊗ ⅲ ⮾ ⬤ (no catering Mon) ♀ ⚲ 🖻 ℂ Martyn Freeman.
Location	Willersey Hill (2m NE)
Hotel	★★★70% Dormy House Hotel, Willersey Hill, BROADWAY ☎(0386) 852711 26⇄🏵Annexe23⇄

DROITWICH   Map 03 SO86

Droitwich ☎(0905) 774344
Undulating parkland course.
18 holes, 6040yds, Par 70, SSS 69, Course record 63.
Club membership 785.

Visitors	with member only weekends & bank holidays.
Societies	must apply by telephone or letter.
Green Fees	£22 per day.
Facilities	⊗ ⅲ ⮾ ⬤ ♀ Tue-Sat ⚲ 🖻 ℂ C Thompson.
Leisure	snooker.
Location	Ford Ln (1.5m N off A38)
Hotel	★★★★70% Chateau Impney Hotel, DROITWICH ☎(0905) 774411 67⇄🏵

FLADBURY   Map 03 SO94

Evesham ☎Evesham (0386) 860395
Parkland, heavily wooded, with the River Avon running alongside 5th and 14th holes. Good views. Nine greens played from eighteen different tees.
18 holes, 6418yds, Par 72, SSS 71, Course record 70.
Club membership 360.

Visitors	except Tue & competition days. With members only at weekends. Handicap certificate required. Must be a member of a E.G.U. affiliated club. Must have an introduction from own club.
Societies	must apply by letter.
Green Fees	£25 per day; £15 per round.
Facilities	⊗ by prior arrangement ⅲ by prior arrangement ⮾ ⬤ ♀ ⚲ 🖻 ⅌ ℂ Charles Haynes.
Location	Craycombe Links, Old Worcester Rd (.75m N on B4084)
Hotel	★★★69% The Evesham Hotel, Coopers Ln, off Waterside, EVESHAM ☎(0386) 765566 40⇄🏵

HEREFORD   Map 03 SO53

Belmont Lodge Hotel & Golf Club ☎(0432) 352666
Partly wooded course, the seond half of which is on the banks of the River Wye.
18 holes, 6480yds, Par 71, SSS 71, Course record 70.
Club membership 500.

Visitors	must contact in advance.

▶

Societies	must contact in writing.
Green Fees	not confirmed.
Facilities	⊗ (Sun only) ⅲ 🖺 ♨ ♀ ⟂ 📷 🛏 𝄽 Mike Welsh.
Leisure	hard tennis courts, fishing, snooker.
Location	Belmont House, Belmont (2m S on A4654)
Hotel	★★★67% Hereford Moat House, Belmont Rd, HEREFORD ☎(0432) 354301 28⇨🏠Annexe32⇨🏠

HOLLYWOOD   Map 07 SP07

Gay Hill ☎021-474 6001
A meadowland course, some 7m from Birmingham.
18 holes, 6532yds, Par 72, SSS 71, Course record 66.
Club membership 715.

Visitors	must play with member at weekends. Must have an introduction from own club.
Societies	must contact in writing.
Green Fees	not confirmed.
Facilities	⊗ ⅲ 🖺 ♨ ♀ ⟂ 📷 ⊓ 𝄽 Andrew Hill.
Leisure	snooker.
Location	Alcester Rd (N side of village)
Hotel	★★★63% George Hotel, High St, SOLIHULL ☎021-711 2121 74⇨🏠

KIDDERMINSTER   Map 07 SO87

Habberley ☎(0562) 745756
Very hilly, wooded parkland course.
9 holes, 5400yds, Par 69, SSS 68, Course record 64.
Club membership 300.

Visitors	except competition days. Must contact in advance.
Societies	must apply in writing.
Green Fees	£12 weekdays.
Facilities	⊗ ⅲ 🖺 & ♨ by prior arrangement ♀ ⟂ 📷
Location	2m NW
Hotel	★★70% Gainsborough House Hotel, Bewdley Hill, KIDDERMINSTER ☎(0562) 820041 42⇨🏠

Kidderminster ☎(0562) 822303
Parkland course with natural hazards and some easy walking.
18 holes, 6223yds, Par 71, SSS 70, Course record 67.
Club membership 700.

Visitors	with member only weekends & bank holidays. Must have an introduction from own club.
Societies	must apply by letter
Green Fees	£20 per day.
Facilities	⊗ ⅲ 🖺 ♨ ♀ ⟂ 📷 𝄽 Nick Underwood.
Location	Russel Rd (.5m SE of town centre)
Hotel	★★70% Gainsborough House Hotel, Bewdley Hill, KIDDERMINSTER ☎(0562) 820041 42⇨🏠

If you know of a golf course which welcomes visitors and is not already in this guide, we should be grateful for information

KINGTON   Map 03 SO25

Kington ☎(0544) 230340
The highest 18-hole course in England, with magnificent views over seven counties. A natural heathland course with easy walking on mountain turf cropped by sheep. There is bracken to catch any really bad shots but no sand traps.
18 holes, 5840yds, Par 70, SSS 68, Course record 65.
Club membership 600.

Visitors	except weekends 10.15am-noon & 1.45-2.45pm & competition days.
Green Fees	£14 per day; £11 per round (£20/£16 weekends & bank holidays).
Facilities	⊗ ⅲ 🖺 ♨ ♀ ⟂
Location	Bradnor Hill (.5m N off B4355)
Hotel	★★★54% Talbot Hotel, West St, LEOMINSTER ☎(0568) 616347 20⇨🏠

LEOMINSTER   Map 03 SO45

Leominster ☎(0568) 612863
Sheltered parkland course alongside River Lugg with undulating land for nine holes.
18 holes, 5891yds, Par 68, SSS 68.
Club membership 600.

Visitors	except Sun (am). Must contact in advance and have an introduction from own club.
Societies	must apply in advance.
Green Fees	£14.50 per day (£17.50 WE).
Facilities	⊗ ⅲ 🖺 ♨ (no catering Mon) ♀ ⟂ 📷 ⊓ 𝄽 Russell Price.
Leisure	fishing.
Location	Ford Bridge (3m S on A49)
Hotel	★★56% Royal Oak Hotel, South St, LEOMINSTER ☎(0568) 612610 17⇨🏠Annexe1⇨
Additional hotel	★★★54% Talbot Hotel, West St, LEOMINSTER ☎(0568) 616347 20⇨🏠

MALVERN WELLS   Map 03 SO74

Worcestershire ☎Malvern (0684) 575992
Fairly easy walking on windy downland course with trees, ditches and other natural hazards. Outstanding views of Malvern Hills and Severn Valley. 17th hole (par 5) is approached over small lake.
18 holes, 6449yds, Par 71, SSS 71, Course record 67.
Club membership 800.

Visitors	only after 10am at weekends or with a member. Must contact in advance and have an introduction from own club.
Societies	must apply in writing.
Green Fees	not confirmed.
Facilities	⊗ ⅲ 🖺 ♨ ♀ ⟂ 📷 𝄽 Grahame Harris.
Leisure	snooker.
Location	Wood Farm, Hanley Rd (2m S of Gt Malvern on B4209)
Hotel	★★★58% Foley Arms Hotel, Worcester Rd, MALVERN ☎(0684) 573397 26⇨🏠Annexe2⇨🏠

For an explanation of symbols and abbreviations, see page 32

REDDITCH   Map 07 SP06

Abbey Park Golf & Country Club ☎(0527) 68006
Young parkland course opened in 1985, with rolling
fairways. A 'Site of Special Scientific Interest', the course
includes two fly-fishing lakes and is pleasant to play.
18 holes, 6411yds, Par 71, SSS 71, Course record 69.
Club membership 1400.

Visitors	with member only weekends (am).
Societies	must apply in writing.
Green Fees	£10 per day (£12.50 weekends).
Facilities	⊗ ∭ ⊑ ▆ ♀ ⌂ 🔔 ⁀ 🝞 ᘒ Kevin Bayliss.
Leisure	heated indoor swimming pool, snooker, sauna, solarium, gymnasium.
Location	Dagnell End Rd (1.25m N off A441 on B4101)
Hotel	★★★60% Southcrest Hotel, Pool Bank, Southcrest, REDDITCH ☎(0527) 541511 58⇝🝞

Pitcheroak ☎(0257) 541054
Woodland course, hilly in places.
9 holes, 4527yds, Par 66, SSS 62.
Club membership 350.

Visitors	no restrictions.
Societies	welcome.
Green Fees	not confirmed.
Facilities	⊗ ∭ ⊑ ▆ ♀ ⌂ 🔔 🝞 ᘒ David Stewart.
Location	Plymouth Rd (SW side of town centre off A448)
Hotel	★★★60% Southcrest Hotel, Pool Bank, Southcrest, REDDITCH ☎(0527) 541511 58⇝🝞

Redditch ☎(0527) 543309
Parkland course, the hazards including woods, ditches and
large ponds. The par 4, 14th is a testing hole.
18 holes, 6671yds, Par 72, SSS 72, Course record 68.
Club membership 873.

Visitors	with member only weekends & bank holidays.
Societies	must apply in writing.
Green Fees	£23 per day.
Facilities	⊗ ∭ ⊑ ▆ ♀ ⌂ 🔔 ᘒ F Powell.
Leisure	snooker.
Location	Lower Grinsty Ln, Callow Hill (2m SW)
Hotel	★★★62% Perry Hall Hotel, Kidderminster Rd, BROMSGROVE ☎(0527) 579976 55⇝🝞

ROSS-ON-WYE   Map 03 SO62

Ross-on-Wye ☎Gorsley (098982) 267
This undulating, parkland course has been cut out of a
silver birch forest; the fairways being well-screened from
each other. The fairways are tight, the greens good.
18 holes, 6500yds, Par 72, SSS 73.
Club membership 750.

Visitors	restricted at weekends. Must contact in advance.
Societies	must telephone in advance.
Green Fees	not confirmed.
Facilities	⊗ ∭ ⊑ ▆ ♀ ⌂ 🔔 ᘒ Adrian Clifford.
Leisure	snooker.
Location	Two Park, Gorsley (on B4221 N side of M50 junc 3)

Hotel	★★(red) Wharton Lodge Country House Hotel, Weston-under-Penyard, ROSS-ON-WYE ☎(0989) 81795 9⇝🝞

UPPER SAPEY   Map 07 SO66

Sapey ☎(08867) 288
Parkland course with views of the Malvern Hills. Trees,
lakes and water hazards. Not too strenuous a walk.
18 holes, 5900yds, Par 69, SSS 68, Course record 64.
Club membership 623.

Visitors	must contact in advance.
Societies	must contact in advance.
Green Fees	£12 (£19 per round weekends).
Facilities	⊗ ∭ & ⊑ (Wed-Sun) ▆ ♀ ⌂ 🔔 🝞 ᘒ Chris Knowles.
Hotel	★★★🏴77% Elms Hotel, ABBERLEY ☎(0299) 896666 16⇝🝞 Annexe9⇝🝞

WORCESTER   Map 03 SO85

Tolladine ☎(0905) 21074
Parkland course, hilly and very tight, but with excellent
views of the surrounding hills and Worcester city.
9 holes, 2813yds, Par 68, SSS 67.
Club membership 350.

Visitors	with member only weekend & bank holidays.
Societies	must apply in writing.
Green Fees	£12 per day.

▶

Facilities	🔲 ⛳ ⛴ 🏠
Location	Tolladine Rd (1.5m E)
Hotel	★★★57% Giffard Hotel, High St, WORCESTER ☎(0905) 726262 103⇔📞

Worcester Golf & Country Club ☎(0905) 422555
Fine parkland course with many trees, a lake, and views of the Malvern Hills.
18 holes, 4946yds, Par 68, SSS 68, Course record 67.
Club membership 1100.

Visitors	with member only weekends. Must contact in advance and have an introduction from own club.
Societies	must apply in advance.
Green Fees	not confirmed.
Facilities	⊗ �🎿 🛗 🔲 ⛳ ⛴ 🏠 🍴 C Colenso.
Leisure	hard and grass tennis courts, squash, snooker.
Location	Boughton Park (SW side of city centre off A4103)
Hotel	★★★57% Giffard Hotel, High St, WORCESTER ☎(0905) 726262 103⇔📞

WORMSLEY   Map 03 SO44

Herefordshire ☎Canon Pyon (0432) 71219
Undulating parkland course with expansive views.
18 holes, 6100yds, Par 70, SSS 69, Course record 64.
Club membership 800.

Visitors	must contact in advance.
Societies	must apply in advance.
Green Fees	£18 per day; £12 per round (£24/£16 weekends & bank holidays).
Facilities	⊗ �🎿 🛗 🔲 ⛳ ⛴ 🏠 🍴 C David Hemming.
Location	Ravens Causeway (E side of village)
Hotel	★★★59% The Green Dragon, Broad St, HEREFORD ☎(0432) 272506 88⇔

WYTHALL   Map 07 SP07

Fulford Heath ☎(0564) 822930
A mature parkland course encompassing two classic par threes. The 11th, a mere 149 yards, shoots from an elevated tee through a channel of trees to a well protected green. The 16th, a 166 yard par 3, elevated green, demands a 140 yard carry over an imposing lake.
18 holes, 5971yds, Par 70, SSS 69.
Club membership 700.

Visitors	with member only weekend & bank holidays. Must contact in advance and have an introduction from own club.
Societies	must apply in writing.
Green Fees	£25 weekdays.
Facilities	⊗ �🎿 🛗 🔲 ⛳ ⛴ 🏠 🍴
Leisure	snooker.
Location	Tanners Green Ln (1m SE off A435)
Hotel	★★★64% St John's Swallow Hotel, 651 Warwick Rd, SOLIHULL ☎021-711 3000 180⇔📞

For a full list of golf courses included in the book, see the index at the end of the directory

---

HERTFORDSHIRE

ALDENHAM   Map 04 TQ19

Aldenham Golf and Country Club ☎Watford (0923) 853929
Undulating parkland course.
Old Course: 18 holes, 6455yds, Par 70, SSS 71.
New Course: 9 holes, 2403yds, Par 33.
Club membership 500.

Visitors	restricted weekends before 1pm.
Societies	must contact in advance.
Green Fees	£20 per round (£28 weekends & bank holidays).
Facilities	⊗ �🎿 🛗 🔲 ⛳ ⛴ 🏠 🍴 C Alistair McKay.
Leisure	snooker.
Location	Church Ln (W side of village)
Hotel	★★★62% Dean Park Hotel, 30-40 St Albans Rd, WATFORD ☎(0923) 229212 90⇔📞

BERKHAMSTED   Map 04 SP90

Berkhamsted ☎(0442) 865832
There are no sand bunkers on this Championship heathland course but this does not make it any easier to play. The natural hazards will test the skill of the most able players, with a particularly testing hole at the 11th, 568 yards, par 5. Fine greens, long carries and heather and gorse. The clubhouse is very comfortable.
18 holes, 6605yds, Par 71, SSS 72, Course record 64.
Club membership 750.

Visitors	must have handicap certificate. Must contact in advance.
Societies	Wed & Fri only, by arrangement.
Green Fees	£32.50 per day (£39 weekends); £22.50 per round (£29 weekends).
Facilities	⊗ & ⚞ (ex Mon & Tue) 🛗 🔲 ⛳ ⛴ 🏠 🍴 C Basil Proudfoot.
Location	The Common (1.5m E)

BISHOP'S STORTFORD   Map 05 TL42

Bishop's Stortford ☎(0279) 654715
Parkland course, fairly flat.
18 holes, 6440yds, Par 71, SSS 71.
Club membership 700.

Visitors	may not play weekends & bank holidays. Must contact in advance and have an introduction from own club.
Societies	must contact in advance.
Green Fees	£21 per day/round.
Facilities	⊗ ⚞ by prior arrangement 🛗 🔲 ⛳ ⛴ 🏠 🍴 Vince Duncan.
Location	Dunmow Rd (1m W of M11 junc 8 on A1250)
Hotel	★★55% The Saracen's Head, High St, GREAT DUNMOW ☎(0371) 873901 24⇔

BRICKENDON   Map 04 TL30

Brickendon Grange ☎Bayford (099286) 258
Parkland course.
18 holes, 6349yds, Par 71, SSS 70, Course record 66.
Club membership 650.

Visitors	must have handicap certificate. With member only at weekends & bank holidays.

Societies   by arrangement.
Green Fees   £30 per day; £24 per round.
Facilities   🏌 🍴 ⚐ ⛳ 🏪 ⚑ J Hamilton.
Location   W side of village
Hotel   ★★★61% White Horse, Hertingfordbury,
               HERTFORD ☎(0992) 586791 42⇨

BROOKMANS PARK   Map 04 TL20

Brookmans Park
☎Potters Bar (0707) 52487

Brookmans Park is an undulating parkland course, with several cleverly constructed holes. But it is a fair course, although it can play long. The 11th, par 3, is a testing hole which plays across a lake.
18 holes, 6454yds, Par 71, SSS 71, Course record 66.
Club membership 750.

SCORECARD: White Tees					
Hole	Yds	Par	Hole	Yds	Par
1	434	4	10	395	4
2	384	4	11	168	3
3	484	5	12	426	4
4	200	3	13	499	5
5	479	5	14	329	4
6	141	3	15	182	3
7	503	5	16	405	4
8	411	4	17	428	4
9	151	3	18	435	4
Out	3187	36	In	3267	35
			Totals	6454	71

Visitors   must have a handicap certificate; must play with member at weekends & bank holidays. Must contact in advance.
Societies   Wed & Thu only; must contact in advance.
Green Fees   £28 per day; £22 per round.
Facilities   ⊗ 🏌 🍴 ⚐ ⛳ 🏪 ⚑ Ian Jelley.
Leisure   fishing, snooker.
Location   Golf Club Rd (N side of village off A1000)
Hotel   ★★★64% Forte Posthouse, Bignells Corner, SOUTH MIMMS ☎(0707) 43311 120⇨⚑

BUNTINGFORD   Map 05 TL32

East Herts ☎Ware (0920) 821978
An attractive undulating parkland course with magnificent specimen trees.
18 holes, 6185yds, Par 71, SSS 71, Course record 64.
Club membership 750.
Visitors   must have handicap certificate, but may not play on Wed & weekends. Must contact in advance and have an introduction from own club.
Societies   must contact in advance.
Green Fees   £30 per day; £23 per round.
Facilities   ⊗ & 🍴 by prior arrangement 🏌 🍴 ⚐ ⛳ 🏪 ⚑ Jim Hamilton.
Location   Hamels Park (1m N of Puckeridge off A10)
Hotel   ★★★63% Ware Moat House, Baldock St, WARE ☎(0920) 465011 50rm(43⇨6⚑)

BUSHEY   Map 04 TQ19

Bushey Hall ☎(0923) 225802
Parkland course.
18 holes, 6099yds, Par 70, SSS 69, Course record 66.
Club membership 650.
Visitors   must have handicap certificate. With member only at weekends. Must contact in advance.
Societies   must contact in writing.
Green Fees   £25 per day.
Facilities   ⊗ (Mon, Tue, Thu only) 🍴 (Wed & Fri) 🏌 (Sat & Sun) 🍴 ⚐ ⛳ 🏪 ⚑ D Fitzsimmons.

Location   Bushey Hall Dr (1.5m NW on A4008)
Hotel   ★★★62% Dean Park Hotel, 30-40 St Albans Rd, WATFORD ☎(0923) 229212 90⇨⚑

Hartsbourne Golf & Country Club ☎081-950 1133
Parkland course with good views.
18 holes, 6305yds, Par 71, SSS 70, Course record 62.
Club membership 750.
Visitors   must be guest of a member. Must be accompanied by member and have an introduction from own club.
Societies   must apply in writing.
Green Fees   not confirmed.
Facilities   ⊗ 🍴 by prior arrangement 🏌 🍴 ⚐ ⛳ 🏪 ⚑ Geoff Hunt.
Location   Hartsbourne Ave (S off A4140)
Hotel   ★★★62% Dean Park Hotel, 30-40 St Albans Rd, WATFORD ☎(0923) 229212 90⇨⚑

CHESHUNT   Map 05 F2

Cheshunt ☎(0992) 29777 & 24009
Municipal parkland course, well-bunkered with ponds, easy walking.
18 holes, 6613yds, Par 71, SSS 71, Course record 65.
Club membership 510.
Visitors   must book Tee-times through Pro shop. Must contact in advance.
Societies   must apply in writing.
Green Fees   £6.15 per round (£7.70 weekends & bank holidays).
Facilities   🍴 ⚐ ⛳ 🏪 ⚑ Chris Newton.
Location   Cheshunt Park, Park Ln (1.5m NW off B156)
Hotel   ★★★62% Forte Posthouse, High Rd, Bell Common, EPPING ☎(0378) 73137 Annexe79⇨⚑

CHORLEYWOOD   Map 04 TQ09

Chorleywood ☎(0923) 282009
Heathland course with natural hazards and good views.
9 holes, 5676yds, Par 68, SSS 67.
Club membership 300.
Visitors   restricted Tue & Thu mornings & weekends. Must contact in advance.
Societies   must apply in writing.
Green Fees   £12 per day/round.
Facilities   ⊗ 🍴 by prior arrangement 🏌 🍴 ⚐ ⛳ 🏪
Leisure   snooker.
Location   Common Rd (E side of village off A404)
Hotel   ★★★66% Bedford Arms Thistle Hotel, CHENIES ☎(0923) 283301 10⇨⚑

ESSENDON   Map 04 TL20

Hatfield London Country Club ☎Potters Bar (0707) 42624
Parkland course with many varied hazards, including ponds, a stream and a ditch. 19th-century manor clubhouse. 9-hole pitch and putt.
18 holes, 6854yds, Par 72, SSS 73.
Visitors   must contact in advance.
Societies   must apply in writing.
Green Fees   £13 per round, Sat £28 (£29 Sun & bank holidays).

►

Facilities	♿ & 💺 by prior arrangement ♀ (on request) ⛳ 🏠 🖳 ⚑ Norman Greer.
Leisure	hard tennis courts.
Location	Bedwell Park (1m S)
Hotel	★★★61% Hazel Grove Hotel, Roehyde Way, HATFIELD ☎(0707) 275701 76⇔🏠

GRAVELEY   Map 04 TL22

Family Golf Centre ☎Letchworth (0462) 482929
A revolutionary new golf course with the emphasis on facilities for the entire family. Its undulating, open downland course has an inland links feel. There is a 25-bay floodlit, covered driving range, a 9-hole Par 3 and many other facilities.
Chesfield Downs : 18 holes, 6630yds, Par 71, SSS 72, Course record 69.
Lannock Links : 9 holes, 975yds, Par 27, SSS 27.

Visitors	no restrictions.
Societies	apply giving one weeks notice.
Green Fees	£11 (£20 weekends).
Facilities	⊗ ⅲ ♿ 💺 ♀ ⛳ 🏠 🖳 ⚑
Location	Jack's Hill
Hotel	★★★60% Hertford Park Hotel, Danestrete, STEVENAGE ☎(0438) 350661 100⇔🏠

HARPENDEN   Map 04 TL11

Harpenden ☎(0582) 712580
Gently undulating parkland course, easy walking.
18 holes, 6037yds, Par 70, SSS 70.
Club membership 800.

Visitors	may not play Thu & weekends. Must contact in advance and have an introduction from own club.
Societies	must apply in writing.
Green Fees	£28 per day; £19 per round.
Facilities	⊗ ⅲ by prior arrangement ♿ 💺 ♀ ⛳ 🏠 ⚑ D Smith.
Location	Hammonds End, Redbourn Ln (1m S on B487)
Hotel	★★★67% Harpenden Moat House Hotel, 18 Southdown Rd, HARPENDEN ☎(0582) 764111 18⇔🏠 Annexe35⇔🏠

Harpenden Common ☎(0582) 715959
Flat, easy walking, good greens, typical common course.
18 holes, 5651yds, Par 68, SSS 67, Course record 66.
Club membership 864.

Visitors	must have handicap certificate. With member only at weekends. Must contact in advance.
Societies	Thu & Fri only, by arrangement.
Green Fees	£25 per day; £18 per round.
Facilities	⊗ ⅲ ♿ 💺 ♀ ⛳ 🏠 🖳 ⚑ Barney Putticks.
Location	Cravells Rd, East Common (1m S on A1081)
Hotel	★★★64% Glen Eagle Hotel, 1 Luton Rd, HARPENDEN ☎(0582) 760271 50⇔🏠

For an explanation of symbols and abbreviations, see page 32

HEMEL HEMPSTEAD   Map 04 TL00

Boxmoor ☎(0442) 242434
Challenging, very hilly, moorland course with sloping fairways divided by trees. Fine views. Testing holes: 3rd (par 3), 4th (par 4).
9 holes, 4302yds, Par 62, SSS 64, Course record 62.
Club membership 250.

Visitors	may not play on Sun.
Societies	must telephone in advance.
Green Fees	£10 per day (£15 weekends).
Facilities	♿ ♀ ⛳
Location	18 Box Ln, Boxmoor (2m SW on B4505)

Little Hay ☎(0442) 833798
Semi-parkland, inland links. Floodlit golf range. 9-hole pitch and putt.
Little Hay Golf Course : 18 holes, 6678yds, Par 72, SSS 72.

Visitors	no restrictions.
Societies	must contact in advance.
Green Fees	£5.90 per day (£8.75 weekends).
Facilities	⊗ ♿ 💺 ♀ ⛳ 🏠 🖳 ⚑ David Johnson & S J Proudfoot.
Location	Box Ln, Bovingdon (1.5m SW on B4505 off A41)

KNEBWORTH   Map 04 TL22

Knebworth ☎Stevenage (0438) 812752
Parkland course, easy walking.
18 holes, 6492yds, Par 71, SSS 71, Course record 69.
Club membership 900.

Visitors	must have handicap certificate , but may not play at weekends. Must have an introduction from own club.
Societies	by arrangement.
Green Fees	£25.50 per day/round.
Facilities	⊗ ⅲ ♿ 💺 ♀ ⛳ 🏠 ⚑ Bobby Mitchell.
Location	Deards End Ln (N side of village off B197)
Hotel	★★★54% Forte Posthouse, Old London Rd, Broadwater, STEVENAGE ☎(0438) 365444 54⇔🏠

LETCHWORTH   Map 04 TL23

Letchworth ☎(0462) 683203
Planned more than 50 years ago by Harry Vardon, this adventurous, parkland course is set in a peaceful corner of 'Norman' England. To its variety of natural and artificial hazards is added an unpredictable wind.
18 holes, 6181yds, Par 70, SSS 69, Course record 67.
Club membership 1000.

SCORECARD					
Hole	Yds	Par	Hole	Yds	Par
1	289	4	10	400	4
2	198	3	11	305	4
3	407	4	12	388	4
4	387	4	13	296	4
5	358	4	14	314	4
6	419	4	15	341	4
7	156	3	16	469	4
8	396	4	17	185	3
9	353	4	18	520	5
Out	2963	34	In	3218	36
			Totals	6181	70

Visitors	with member only at weekends. Must contact in advance and have an introduction from own club.
Societies	Wed, Thu & Fri only, must telephone in advance.

Green Fees	£22.25-£30.65 per day.
Facilities	⊗ &)Ⅲ (Tue-Fri only) ⊫ ■ ♀ ᐃ 🏠 (John Mutimer.
Location	Letchworth Ln (S side of town centre off A505)
Hotel	★★★59% Blakemore Thistle, Little Wymondley, HITCHIN ☎(0438) 355821 83⇉🏠

LITTLE GADDESDEN   Map 04 SP91

Ashridge ☎(0442) 842244
Good parkland course, challenging but fair. Good clubhouse facilities.
18 holes, 6217yds, Par 72, SSS 70, Course record 64.
Club membership 730.

Visitors	may not play Thu, weekends & bank holidays. Must contact in advance and have an introduction from own club.
Societies	weekdays except Thu (Mar-Oct), by arrangement.
Green Fees	£47 per day; £30 per round.
Facilities	⊗)Ⅲ ■ ♀ ᐃ 🏠 ↑ (Geoffrey Pook.
Hotel	★★★(red) Bell Inn, ASTON CLINTON ☎(0296) 630252 6⇉🏠 Annexe15⇉🏠

POTTERS BAR   Map 04 TL20

Potters Bar ☎(0707) 52020
Undulating parkland course with water in play on many holes.
18 holes, 6273yds, Par 71, SSS 70, Course record 65.
Club membership 520.

Visitors	must have handicap certificate. With member only at weekends. Must contact in advance and have an introduction from own club.
Societies	Mon-Fri only, by arrangement.
Green Fees	£29.37.
Facilities	⊗ ⊫ ■ ♀ ᐃ 🏠 (Kevin Hughes.
Location	Darkes Ln (N side of town centre)
Hotel	★★★64% Forte Posthouse, Bignells Corner, SOUTH MIMMS ☎(0707) 43311 120⇉🏠

RADLETT   Map 04 TL10

Porters Park ☎(0923) 854127
A splendid, undulating parkland course with fine trees and lush grass. The holes are all different and interesting - on many accuracy of shot to the green is of paramount importance.
18 holes, 6313yds, Par 70, SSS 70, Course record 65.
Club membership 800.

Visitors	must have handicap certificate. With member only on Fri afternoons & weekends. Must contact in advance.
Societies	Wed & Thu only, must telephone in advance.
Green Fees	£38.50 per day; £26 per round.
Facilities	⊗ ⊫ ■ ♀ ᐃ 🏠 ↑ (David Gleeson.
Location	Shenley Hill (NE side of village off A5183)
Hotel	★★★71% Noke Thistle Hotel, Watford Rd, ST ALBANS ☎(0727) 54252 111⇉🏠

REDBOURN   Map 04 TL11

Redbourn ☎(0582) 792150
Testing parkland course (five par 4's over 400 yds). Also 9-hole par 3 course. Driving range.
18 holes, 6407yds, Par 70, SSS 71 or 9 holes, 2722yds, Par 54.

Visitors	must play with member at weekends & bank holidays.
Societies	must telephone in advance.
Green Fees	£13.
Facilities	⊗)Ⅲ ⊫ ■ ♀ (1100-2300) ᐃ 🏠 (Steve Baldwin.
Leisure	snooker.
Location	Kinsbourne Green Ln (1m N off A5183)
Hotel	★★★67% Harpenden Moat House Hotel, 18 Southdown Rd, HARPENDEN ☎(0582) 764111 18⇉🏠 Annexe35⇉🏠

RICKMANSWORTH   Map 04 TQ09

Moor Park ☎(0923) 773146
Two parkland courses.
18 holes, 6713yds, Par 72, SSS 72, Course record 67.
West Golf Course: 18 holes, 5815yds, Par 69, SSS 68, Course record 63.
Club membership 1800.

Visitors	may not play at weekends, bank holidays or before 10am on Tue & Thu. Must contact in advance.
Societies	must apply in writing.
Green Fees	£45 per day; £25 per round.

F A M I L Y   G O L F

VISITORS WELCOME
Open Daily from 7.00 a.m. - 11.00 p.m.

- Superb 18 hole Chesfield Downs Course.
- 9 hole Lannock Links Course.
- 25 Bay floodlit, covered Driving Range, equipped with top grade two-piece range balls and superior quality practice mats.
- Well stocked Family Golf Superstore. Huge Choice - Competitive Prices - Expert Advice.
- The Family Golf Academy, featuring individual and group tuition from our team of Professionals.
- Hire Clubs available.
- "19th Hole" Bar & Bistro.
- 18 Hole Putting Green.
- Purpose built and well designed modern Clubhouse, including changing facilities and a fully equipped Function Room.
- Golf Societies and Corporate Golf Days available.
- Specialist Repair Centre.
- Creche and Adventure Playground.

☎ **0462 482929**
The Family Golf Centre
Jack's Hill, Graveley, Herts SG4 7EG
FAX: 0462 482930

Facilities	⊗ ⓛ ⬛ ♀ ⛖ 🏠 ⒧ Ross Whitehead.
Leisure	snooker.
Location	1.5m SE off A4145
Hotel	★★★62% Dean Park Hotel, 30-40 St Albans Rd, WATFORD ☏(0923) 229212 90⇨🛏

Rickmansworth ☏(0923) 775278
Undulating, municipal parkland course.
18 holes, 4238yds, Par 63, SSS 62, Course record 63.
Club membership 300.

Visitors	must contact the club in advance for weekend play.
Societies	must contact in advance.
Green Fees	£7.20 per round (£9.70 weekends).
Facilities	⊗ ⅲ ⓛ ⬛ ♀ ⛖ 🏠 ⒧ Iain Duncan.
Location	Moor Ln (2m S of town off A4145)
Hotel	★★★62% Dean Park Hotel, 30-40 St Albans Rd, WATFORD ☏(0923) 229212 90⇨🛏

ROYSTON   Map 05 TL34

Royston ☏(0763) 242696
Heathland course on undulating terrain and fine fairways.
18 holes, 6032yds, Par 70, SSS 67, Course record 65.
Club membership 650.

Visitors	with member only at weekends. Must contact in advance.
Societies	by arrangement.
Green Fees	£20 per day.
Facilities	⊗ ⅲ ⓛ ⬛ (no catering Sun) ♀ ⛖ 🏠 ⒧
Leisure	snooker.
Location	Baldock Rd (.5m W of town centre)
Hotel	★★★59% Blakemore Thistle, Little Wymondley, HITCHIN ☏(0438) 355821 83⇨🛏

ST ALBANS   Map 04 TL10

Batchwood Hall ☏(0727) 8333349
Municipal parkland course designed by J H Taylor and opened in 1935.
18 holes, 6465yds, Par 71, SSS 71, Course record 67.
Club membership 425.

Visitors	may not play on Sat & Sun mornings.
Green Fees	£10.50 per round.
Facilities	⬛ ♀ ⛖ 🏠 ⒧ Jimmy Thompson.
Leisure	hard tennis courts, squash, solarium.
Location	Batchwood Dr (1m NW off A5183)
Hotel	★★★60% St Michael's Manor Hotel, Fishpool St, ST ALBANS ☏(0727) 864444 22⇨

Verulam ☏(0727) 53327
Parkland course with fourteen holes having out-of-bounds.
Water affects the 5th, 6th and 7th holes. Samuel Ryder was
Captain here in 1927 when he began the now celebrated
Ryder Cup Competition.
18 holes, 8718yds, Par 72, SSS 71, Course record 65 or 64 holes.
Club membership 650.

Visitors	may not play at weekends. Must contact in advance.
Societies	must contact one year in advance.
Green Fees	Mon: £16 per day; £10.50 per round. Tue-Fri: £22 per day; £18 per round.
Facilities	⊗ ⓛ ⬛ ♀ (all day) ⛖ 🏠 ⒧ P Anderson.

| Location | London Rd (1m from junc 22 of M25 off A1081) |
| Hotel | ★★★★70% Sopwell House Hotel & Country Club, Cottonmill Ln, Sopwell, ST ALBANS ☏(0727) 864477 84⇨🛏 |

STEVENAGE   Map 04 TL22

Stevenage Golf Centre ☏(0438) 88424
Municipal course designed by John Jacobs, with natural
water hazards and some wooded areas.
18 holes, 6451yds, Par 72, SSS 71, Course record 65.

Visitors	no restrictions.
Societies	must contact 1 week in advance. Deposit required.
Green Fees	not confirmed.
Facilities	⊗ ⅲ ⓛ ⬛ ♀ (all day) ⛖ 🏠 ⒧ Keith Bond.
Location	Aston Ln (4m SE off B5169)
Hotel	★★★54% Forte Posthouse, Old London Rd, Broadwater, STEVENAGE ☏(0438) 365444 54⇨🛏

WARE   Map 05 TL31

Chadwell Springs ☏(0920) 461447
Quick drying moorland course on high plateau subject to
wind. The first two holes are par 5 and notable.
9 holes, 6042yds, Par 72, SSS 69.
Club membership 400.

Visitors	with member only at weekends.
Societies	apply in writing,
Green Fees	not confirmed.
Facilities	⊗ ⅲ by prior arrangement ⓛ ⬛ ♀ ⛖ 🏠 ⒧ A N Shearn.
Location	Hertford Rd (.75m W on A119)
Hotel	★★★63% Ware Moat House, Baldock St, WARE ☏(0920) 465011 50rm(43⇨🛏)

Hanbury Manor Golf & Country Club ☏(0920) 487722
Superb parkland course designed by Jack Nicklaus II. Large
oval tees, watered fairways and undulating greens make up
the first 9 holes. Attractive lakes and deep-faced bunkers are
strategically sited. Second 9 holes offer open panoramas and
challenging holes.
18 holes, 6922yds, Par 72, SSS 73.
Club membership 228.

Visitors	with handicap certificate, members guest and hotel residents welcome. Must contact in advance.
Green Fees	not confirmed.
Facilities	⊗ ⅲ ⓛ ⬛ ♀ (10am-11pm) ⛖ 🏠 ⒧ ⛡ ⒧ Peter Blaze.
Leisure	hard tennis courts, heated indoor swimming pool, squash, snooker, sauna, solarium, gymnasium.
Location	Thunderidge
Hotel	★★★★82% Hanbury Manor, Thundridge, WARE ☏(0920) 487722 71⇨🛏 Annexe27⇨🛏

For a full range of AA guides and maps, visit
your local AA shop or any good bookshop

WATFORD   Map 04 TQ19

West Herts ☎(0923) 36484
Another of the many clubs which were inaugurated in the 1890's when the game of golf was being given a tremendous boost by the performances of the first star professionals, Braid, Vardon and Taylor. The West Herts course is close to Watford but its tree-lined setting is beautiful and tranquil. Set out on a plateau the course is exceedingly dry. It also has a very severe finish with the 17th, a hole of 378 yards, the toughest on the course. The last hole measures over 480 yards.
18 holes, 6488yds, Par 72, SSS 71, Course record 67.
Club membership 705.
Visitors	may not play at weekends. Must contact in advance.
Societies	Wed & Fri only, must apply in writing.
Green Fees	£26 per day; £18.50 per round.
Facilities	⊗ ㄴ ☷ ☵ ♀ △ ☐ ⚐ ᚛ Charles Gough.
Location	Cassiobury Park (W side of town centre off A412)
Hotel	★★★62% Dean Park Hotel, 30-40 St Albans Rd, WATFORD ☎(0923) 229212 90➪⚐

WELWYN GARDEN CITY   Map 04 TL21

Panshanger Golf & Squash Complex ☎(0707) 333350
Municipal parkland course overlooking Mimram Valley.
18 holes, 6638yds, Par 72, SSS 70.
Visitors	no restrictions.
Societies	apply in writing.
Green Fees	not confirmed.
Facilities	⊗ ⚐ ㄴ ☷ (catering by prior arrangement) ♀ △ ☐ ⚐ ᚛
Leisure	squash.
Location	Herns Ln (N side of town centre off B1000)
Hotel	★★★61% Crest Hotel, Homestead Ln, WELWYN GARDEN CITY ☎(0707) 324336 58➪⚐

Welwyn Garden City ☎(0707) 325243
Undulating parkland course with a ravine. Course record holder is Nick Faldo.
18 holes, 6100yds, Par 70, SSS 69, Course record 63.
Club membership 650.
Visitors	may not play Sun. Must contact in advance and have an introduction from own club.
Societies	Wed & Thu only, by arrangement.
Green Fees	£25 per day; £21 per round..
Facilities	ㄴ ☷ ♀ △ ☐ ᚛ Simon Bishop.
Location	Mannicotts (W side of town centre off B197)
Hotel	★★★61% Crest Hotel, Homestead Ln, WELWYN GARDEN CITY ☎(0707) 324336 58➪⚐

For a full list of golf courses included in the book, see the index at the end of the directory

WHEATHAMPSTEAD   Map 04 TL11

Mid Herts ☎(058283) 2242
Commonland, wooded with heather and gorse-lined fairways.
18 holes, 6094yds, Par 69, SSS 69, Course record 66.
Club membership 600.
Visitors	may not play Tue, Wed afternoons & weekends. Must contact in advance and have an introduction from own club.
Societies	must contact in writing.
Green Fees	not confirmed.
Facilities	△ ☐ ᚛
Location	Gustard Wood (1m N on B651)
Hotel	★★★67% Harpenden Moat House Hotel, 18 Southdown Rd, HARPENDEN ☎(0582) 764111 18➪⚐Annexe35➪⚐

HUMBERSIDE

BEVERLEY   Map 08 TA03

Beverley & East Riding ☎ (0482) 867190
Picturesque parkland course with some hard walking and natural hazards - trees and gorse bushes. Also cattle and sheep (spring to autumn), horse-riders occasionally early morning.
18 holes, 5949yds, Par 68, SSS 68, Course record 62.
Club membership 460.
Visitors	restricted weekends & bank holidays.
Societies	telephone(0482) 868757 to arrange.
Green Fees	£10 per day (£12.50 weekends & bank holidays).
Facilities	⊗ ⚐ by prior arrangement ㄴ ☷ ♀ △ ☐ ᚛ Ian Mackie.
Location	The Westwood (1m SW on B1230)
Hotel	★★★67% Beverley Arms Hotel, North Bar Within, BEVERLEY ☎(0482) 869241 57➪⚐

BRANDESBURTON   Map 08 TA14

Hainsworth Park ☎Hornsea (0964) 542362
A parkland course with easy walking.
18 holes, 5930yds, Par 71, SSS 69.
Club membership 400.
Visitors	welcome except competition days. Must contact in advance.
Societies	apply in writing.
Green Fees	£8 per day (£10 weekends & bank holidays).
Facilities	⊗ 21ㄴ ☷ ♀ △ ☐ ⚐ ᚛
Leisure	squash.
Location	Burton Holme (SW side of village on A165)
Hotel	★★★63% Tickton Grange Hotel, Tickton, BEVERLEY ☎(0964) 543666 16➪⚐

BRIDLINGTON   Map 08 TA16

Bridlington ☎(0262) 674721
Clifftop, seaside course, windy at times, with hazards of bunkers, ponds, ditches and trees.
18 holes, 6491yds, Par 71, SSS 71, Course record 67.
Club membership 640.
Visitors	welcome except Sun until 11.15am and Wed 9-11.30am.

▶

Societies	telephone secretary (0262) 606367, one week in advance.
Green Fees	£12 per day/round (£18 weekends).
Facilities	⊗ ≡ by prior arrangement ᴸ ⬛ ♀ △ 🏠 ⛳ ⁌ David Rands.
Leisure	snooker.
Location	Belvedere Rd (1m S off A165)
Hotel	★★67% Monarch Hotel, South Marine Dr, BRIDLINGTON ☎(0262) 674447 40rm(36⇨🏠)

BROUGH   Map 08 SE92

Brough ☎Hull (0482) 667374
Parkland course.
18 holes, 6159yds, Par 68, SSS 69.
Club membership 700.

Visitors	with member only at weekends. Must have handicap certificate. Must contact in advance.
Societies	apply by letter.
Green Fees	£20 per day/round.
Facilities	⊗ ≡ ᴸ ⬛ ♀ △ 🏠 ⛳ ⁌ Gordon Townhill.
Leisure	snooker.
Location	Cave Rd (.5m N)
Hotel	★★★64% Forte Posthouse Hull, Ferriby High Rd, NORTH FERRIBY ☎(0482) 645212 97⇨🏠

CLEETHORPES   Map 08 TA30

Cleethorpes ☎(0472) 814060
Flat meadowland seaside course intersected by large dykes.
18 holes, 6018yds, Par 70, SSS 69, Course record 64.
Club membership 760.

Visitors	restricted Wed afternoons.
Societies	Tue, Thu or Fri only. Must contact in advance.
Green Fees	£15 per day (£20 weekends & bank holidays).
Facilities	⊗ & ≡ by prior arrangement ᴸ ⬛ ♀ △ 🏠 ⁌ Eric Sharp.
Location	Kings Rd (1.5m S off A1031)
Hotel	★★★70% Kingsway Hotel, Kingsway, CLEETHORPES ☎(0472) 601122 50⇨🏠

DRIFFIELD, GREAT   Map 08 TA05

Driffield ☎Driffield (0377) 43116
An easy walking, parkland course.
9 holes, 6202yds, Par 70, SSS 70.
Club membership 320.

Visitors	no restrictions.
Green Fees	not confirmed.
Facilities	♀ △ 🏠
Location	Sunderlandwick (2m S of off A164)
Hotel	★★⬛57% Wold House Country Hotel, Nafferton, DRIFFIELD ☎(0377) 44242 10rm(7⇨🏠)Annexe1🏠

ELSHAM   Map 08 TA01

Elsham ☎Barnetby (0652) 680291
Parkland course in country surroundings. Easy walking.
18 holes, 6411yds, Par 71, SSS 71.
Club membership 600.

Visitors	with member only weekends & bank holidays.
Societies	must contact in advance.
Green Fees	£20 per day/round.

Facilities	⊗ ≡ ᴸ ⬛ ♀ (1100-2230) △ 🏠 ⁌ Stuart Brewer.
Location	Barton Rd (2m SW on B1206)
Hotel	★★★64% Wortley House Hotel, Rowland Rd, SCUNTHORPE ☎(0724) 842223 38⇨🏠

FLAMBOROUGH   Map 08 TA27

Flamborough Head ☎Bridlington (0262) 850333
Undulating seaside course.
18 holes, 5438yds, Par 66, SSS 66, Course record 63.
Club membership 500.

Visitors	may not play before noon on Sun. Must contact in advance and have an introduction from own club.
Societies	must contact in advance.
Green Fees	£12 per day (£16 weekends & bank holidays).
Facilities	⊗ ≡ ᴸ ⬛ (no catering Mon) ♀ △
Leisure	snooker.
Location	Lighthouse Rd (2m E off B1259)
Hotel	★68% Flaneburg Hotel, North Marine Rd, FLAMBOROUGH ☎(0262) 850284 13rm(8🏠)

GRIMSBY   Map 08 TA21

Grimsby ☎(0472) 342630
Parkland course with easy walking.
18 holes, 6058yds, Par 70, SSS 69, Course record 66.
Club membership 725.

Visitors	restricted at weekends. Must contact in advance and have an introduction from own club.
Societies	welcome Mon-Fri only, telephone in advance.
Green Fees	£15 (£20 at weekends).
Facilities	⊗ & ≡ by prior arrangement ᴸ ⬛ ♀ △ 🏠 ⁌ Steve Houltby.
Leisure	bowling green.
Location	Littlecoates Rd (W side of town centre off A1136)
Hotel	★★★64% Forte Crest Hotel, Littlecoates Rd, GRIMSBY ☎(0472) 350295 52⇨🏠

HESSLE   Map 08 TA02

Hessle ☎Hull (0482) 650171
Well-wooded downland course, easy walking, windy.
18 holes, 6290yds, Par 72, SSS 70, Course record 68 or 6638yds, Par 72, SSS 72.
Club membership 650.

Visitors	must have a handicap certificate. Must contact in advance.
Societies	must telephone in advance.
Green Fees	not confirmed.
Facilities	⊗ ≡ ᴸ & ⬛ by prior arrangement ♀ △ 🏠 ⁌ Grahame Fieldsend.
Leisure	snooker.
Location	Westfield Rd, Raywell (4m NW off A164)
Hotel	★★★64% Forte Posthouse Hull, Ferriby High Rd, NORTH FERRIBY ☎(0482) 645212 97⇨🏠

We make every effort to ensure that our information is accurate but details may change after we go to print

HORNSEA
Map 08 TA14

Hornsea ☎(0964) 532020
Flat, parkland course with good greens.
18 holes, 6475yds, Par 71, SSS 71, Course record 66.
Club membership 600.

Visitors	with member only at weekends & after 3pm. Must contact in advance.
Societies	apply in writing.
Green Fees	£22.50 per day; £16.50 per round.
Facilities	⊗ ⏲ ▙ ☕ ♀ (all day) 🛄 ⛳ ♟ Brian Thompson.
Leisure	snooker, practice area.
Location	Rolston Rd (1m S of on B1242)
Hotel	★★★67% Beverley Arms Hotel, North Bar Within, BEVERLEY ☎(0482) 869241 57⇨♜

HOWDEN
Map 08 SE72

Boothferry ☎(0430) 30364
A heavily bunkered meadowland course with several dykes.
18 holes, 6600yds, Par 73.
Club membership 600.

Visitors	must contact in advance.
Societies	must contact in writing.
Green Fees	not confirmed.
Facilities	♀ ☖ 🛄 ⛳ ♟
Location	Spaldington Ln, Goole (2.5m N of Howden off B1228)
Hotel	★★59% Clifton Hotel, 1 Clifton Gardens, Boothferry Rd, GOOLE ☎(0405) 761336 10rm(5⇨3♜)

HULL
Map 08 TA02

Ganstead Park ☎(0482) 811121
Parkland course, easy walking.
18 holes, 6801yds, Par 72, SSS 73, Course record 67.
Club membership 700.

Visitors	welcome except Sun & Wed mornings.
Societies	must contact in advance.
Green Fees	£15 per day (£20 weekends).
Facilities	⊗ ⏲ ▙ ☕ (no catering Sun evenings or Mon) ♀ ☖ 🛄 ⛳ ♟ Michael J Smee.
Leisure	snooker.
Location	Longdales Ln, Coniston (6m NE off A165)
Hotel	★★62% Waterfront Hotel, Dagger Ln, HULL ☎(0482) 227222 30⇨♜

Hull ☎(0482) 658919
Parkland course.
18 holes, 6242yds, Par 70, SSS 70, Course record 64.
Club membership 750.

Visitors	with member only at weekends. Must contact in advance and have an introduction from own club.
Societies	apply in writing
Green Fees	£24 per day/round.
Facilities	⊗ ⏲ & ▙ by prior arrangement ☕ ♀ ☖ 🛄 ♟ David Jagger.
Leisure	snooker.
Location	The Hall, 27 Packman Ln (5m W of city centre off A164)
Hotel	★★★70% Willerby Manor Hotel, Well Ln, WILLERBY ☎(0482) 652616 36⇨♜

Springhead Park ☎(0482) 656309
Municipal parkland course with tight, tree-lined, undulating fairways.
18 holes, 6439yds, Par 71, SSS 71.
Club membership 667.

Green Fees	not confirmed.
Facilities	🛄 ⛳ ♟ Barry Herrington.
Location	Willerby Rd (5m W off A164)
Hotel	★★★70% Willerby Manor Hotel, Well Ln, WILLERBY ☎(0482) 652616 36⇨♜

Sutton Park ☎(0482) 74242
Municipal parkland course.
18 holes, 6251yds, Par 70, SSS 70.
Club membership 450.

Visitors	no restrictions.
Societies	apply to Hull Leisure Services, 79 Ferensway, Hull.
Green Fees	£3.25 per round (£4.50 weekends).
Facilities	⊗ & ⏲ by prior arrangement ▙ ☕ ♀ ☖ 🛄 ⛳ ♟ Paul Rushworth.
Leisure	snooker.
Location	Salthouse Rd (3m NE on B1237 off A165)
Hotel	★★62% Waterfront Hotel, Dagger Ln, HULL ☎(0482) 227222 30⇨♜

NORMANBY
Map 08 SE81

Normanby Hall ☎Scunthorpe (0724) 720226
Parkland course.
18 holes, 6548yds, Par 72, SSS 71, Course record 68.
Club membership 740.

Visitors	no restrictions.
Societies	may not play at weekends & bank holidays; must contact in advance.
Green Fees	not confirmed.
Facilities	⊗ ▙ ☕ ♀ ☖ 🛄 ⛳ ♟ C Mann.
Location	Normanby Park (5m N of Scunthorpe adj to Normanby Hall)
Hotel	★★63% Royal Hotel, Doncaster Rd, SCUNTHORPE ☎(0724) 282233 33⇨♜

SCUNTHORPE
Map 08 SE81

Holme Hall ☎(0724) 840909
Heathland course with sandy subsoil. Easy walking.
18 holes, 6475yds, Par 71, SSS 71.
Club membership 675.

Visitors	must play with member at weekends & bank holidays. Must contact in advance.
Societies	must contact in advance.
Green Fees	£15 per round/day.
Facilities	⊗ ⏲ by prior arrangement ▙ ☕ ♀ ☖ 🛄 ⛳ ♟ Richard McKiernan.
Leisure	snooker.
Location	Holme Ln, Bottesford (3m SE)
Hotel	★★63% Royal Hotel, Doncaster Rd, SCUNTHORPE ☎(0724) 282233 33⇨♜

Kingsway ☎(0724) 840945
Parkland course with many par 3's.
9 holes, 1915yds, Par 30, SSS 29.

Visitors	no restrictions.

▶

Green Fees	not confirmed.
Facilities	⛱ 🏠 ⛳
Location	Kingsway (W side of town centre off A18)
Hotel	★★63% Royal Hotel, Doncaster Rd, SCUNTHORPE ☎(0724) 282233 33⇨🏌

Scunthorpe ☎(0724) 866561
Very tight parkland course.
18 holes, 6028yds, Par 71, SSS 70.
Club membership 700.

Visitors	may not play Sun. Handicap certificate required. Must contact in advance.
Societies	apply in writing.
Green Fees	£16 per day.
Facilities	⊗ �🍴 🕍 ⬛ ⛳ ⛱ 🏠 🥂 Graham Bailey.
Leisure	snooker.
Location	Ashby Decoy, Burringham Rd (2.5m SW on B1450)
Hotel	★★63% Royal Hotel, Doncaster Rd, SCUNTHORPE ☎(0724) 282233 33⇨🏌

WITHERNSEA   Map 08 TA32

Withernsea ☎(0964) 612258
Exposed seaside links with narrow, undulating fairways, bunkers and small greens.
9 holes, 5112yds, Par 66, SSS 64, Course record 60.
Club membership 630.

Visitors	with member only at weekends.
Societies	apply in writing.
Green Fees	£8 per round.
Facilities	⊗ ⍾ 🕍 ⬛ (catering by prior arrangements weekdays) ⛳ ⛱ 🏠 🥂 Graham Harrison.
Location	Chesnut Av (S side of town centre off A1033)
Hotel	★★64% Pearson Park Hotel, Pearson Park, HULL ☎(0482) 43043 32⇨🏌

KENT

ADDINGTON   Map 05 TQ65

West Malling ☎(0732) 844785
Two 18-hole parkland courses.
Spitfire : 18 holes, 6142yds, Par 70, SSS 70.
Hurricane : 18 holes, 6011yds, Par 70, SSS 69.
Club membership 800.

Visitors	restricted weekends. Must have an introduction from own club.
Societies	must apply in writing.
Green Fees	not confirmed.
Facilities	⊗ ⍾ by prior arrangement 🕍 ⬛ ⛳ ⛱ 🏠 🥂 Paul Foston.
Leisure	squash, snooker, table tennis.
Location	London Rd (1m S off A20)
Hotel	★★★68% Great Danes Hotel, Ashford Rd, HOLLINGBOURNE ☎(0622) 30022 126⇨🏌

A golf-course name printed in *bold italics* means that we have been unable to verify information with the club's management for the current year

---

ASHFORD   Map 05 TR04

Ashford ☎(0233) 622655
Parkland course with good views and easy walking. Narrow fairways and tightly bunkered greens ensure a challenging game.
18 holes, 6246yds, Par 71, SSS 70, Course record 66.
Club membership 650.

Visitors	must have handicap certificate. Must contact in advance and have an introduction from own club.
Societies	Tue & Thu only, by arrangement.
Green Fees	not confirmed.
Facilities	⊗ ⍾ by prior arrangement 🕍 ⬛ ⛳ ⛱ 🏠 🥂 Hugh Sherman.
Location	Sandyhurst Ln (1.5m NW off A20)
Hotel	★★★57% Master Spearpoint Hotel, Canterbury Rd, Kennington, ASHFORD ☎(0233) 636863 36⇨🏌

BARHAM   Map 05 TR25

Broome Park ☎Canterbury (0227) 831701
Championship standard parkland course in a valley, with a 350-year-old mansion clubhouse.
18 holes, 6160yds, Par 72, SSS 72, Course record 66.
Club membership 340.

Visitors	must have handicap certificate, but may not play Sat/Sun mornings. Must contact in advance.
Societies	Mon-Fri only, by arrangement.
Green Fees	£28 per day (£30 weekends); £21 per round (£23 weekends).
Facilities	⊗ ⍾ 🕍 ⬛ ⛳ ⛱ 🏠 🥂 Tienie Britz.
Leisure	hard tennis courts, heated outdoor swimming pool, squash, riding, snooker, sauna, solarium, gymnasium, clay pigeon shooting croquet putting.
Location	1.5m SE on A260
Hotel	★★★57% Chaucer Hotel, Ivy Ln, CANTERBURY ☎(0227) 464427 43⇨🏌

BEARSTED   Map 05 TQ85

Bearsted ☎Maidstone (0622) 38198
Parkland course with fine views of the North Downs.
18 holes, 6278yds, Par 72, SSS 68.
Club membership 700.

Visitors	must be member of recognised golf club & have handicap certificate, but may not play at weekends. Must contact in advance and have an introduction from own club.
Societies	must apply in writing one year in advance.
Green Fees	£20 per round.
Facilities	⊗ 🕍 ⬛ ⛳ ⛱ 🏠 🥂 Tim Simpson.
Location	Ware St (2.5m E of Maidstone off A20)
Hotel	★★★68% Great Danes Hotel, Ashford Rd, HOLLINGBOURNE ☎(0622) 30022 126⇨🏌

For a full range of AA guides and maps, visit your local AA shop or any good bookshop

BOROUGH GREEN

Map 05 TQ65

Wrotham Heath ☎(0732) 884800
Parkland course, hilly, good views.
9 holes, 5918yds, Par 69, SSS 68, Course record 66.
Club membership 376.

Visitors	with member only at weekends. Must contact in advance and have an introduction from own club.
Societies	Fri only, by arrangement.
Green Fees	£20 per round.
Facilities	⊗ (ex Mon) ⅏ by prior arrangement 🏳 (ex Mon) 🍺 ♀ 🏌 🏧 🥢 Harry Dearden.
Location	Seven Mile Ln (2.25m E on B2016)
Hotel	★★61% Hotel Riviera, West Cliff Gardens, BOURNEMOUTH ☎(0202) 552845 34⇨🛏

BROADSTAIRS

Map 05 TR36

North Foreland ☎Thanet (0843) 62140
A picturesque course situated where the Thames Estuary widens towards the sea. North Foreland always seems to have a breath of tradition of golf's earlier days about it. Perhaps the ghost of one of its earlier professionals, the famous Abe Mitchell, still haunts the lovely turf of the fairways. Walking is easy and the wind is deceptive. The 8th and 17th, both par 4, are testing holes. There is also an approach and putting course.
18 holes, 6382yds, Par 71, SSS 71, Course record 65.
Short Course: 18 holes, 1760yds, Par 54, Course record 47.
Club membership 1000.

Visitors	for Main course are required to book in advance & have handicap certificate. Short course has no restrictions. Must contact in advance.
Societies	Wed & Fri only, by arrangement.
Green Fees	Main course £26 per day; £18 per round (£26 weekends). Short course £5 per day.
Facilities	⊗ ⅏ 🏳 🍺 ♀ 🏌 🏧 🥢 Mike Lee.
Leisure	hard tennis courts.
Location	Convent Rd, Kingsgate (1.5m N off B2052)
Hotel	★★67% Royal Albion Hotel, Albion St, BROADSTAIRS ☎(0843) 68071 19⇨🛏

CANTERBURY

Map 05 TR15

Canterbury ☎(0227) 453532
Undulating parkland course, densely wooded in places, with elevated tees and difficult drives on several holes.
18 holes, 6249yds, Par 70, SSS 70, Course record 66.
Club membership 700.

Visitors	may only play after 3pm weekends & bank holidays. Must have an introduction from own club.
Societies	by arrangement.
Green Fees	£29 per day; £21 per round (£29 weekends after 3pm).
Facilities	⊗ 🏳 🍺 ♀ 🏌 🏧 🥢 Paul Everard.
Location	Scotland Hills (1.5m E on A257)
Hotel	★★★57% Chaucer Hotel, Ivy Ln, CANTERBURY ☎(0227) 464427 43⇨🛏

This guide is updated annually – make sure that you use the up-to-date edition

CRANBROOK

Map 05 TQ73

Cranbrook ☎(0580) 712833
Scenic, parkland course with easy terrain, backed by Hemstead Forest and close to Sissinghurst Castle (1m) and Bodiam Castle (6m). Testing hole at 12th (530 yds par 5). Venue for the County Championships.
18 holes, 6351yds, Par 70, Course record 66.
Club membership 500.

Visitors	may not play at weekends before 11am.
Societies	must apply in writing.
Green Fees	£20 per round (£30 weekends).
Facilities	⊗ & ⅏ by prior arrangement 🏳 🍺 ♀ 🏌 🏧
Location	Benenden Rd (2m E)
Hotel	★★⁂69% Kennel Holt Country House Hotel, Goudhurst Rd, CRANBROOK ☎(0580) 712032 9⇨🛏 Annexe1🛏

DARTFORD

Map 05 TQ57

Dartford ☎(0322) 226455
Heathland course.
18 holes, 5914yds, Par 69, SSS 68, Course record 66.
Club membership 750.

Visitors	may not play at weekends. Must have an introduction from own club.
Societies	Mon & Fri only. Must telephone in advance.
Green Fees	£25.50.
Facilities	⊗ & ⅏ by prior arrangement 🏳 🍺 ♀ 🏌 🏧 🥢 Anthony Blackburn.
Location	Dartford Heath
Hotel	★★★71% Forte Crest Hotel, Black Prince Interchange, Southwold Rd, BEXLEY ☎(0322) 526900 102⇨🛏

DEAL

Map 05 TR35

Royal Cinque Ports
☎(0304) 374007
Famous championship seaside links, windy but with easy walking. Outward nine is generally considered the easier, inward nine is longer and includes the renowned 16th, perhaps the most difficult hole. On a fine day there are wonderful views across the Channel.
18 holes, 6741yds, Par 72, SSS 72.
Club membership 1200.

SCORECARD:
Championship Tees

Hole	Yds	Par	Hole	Yds	Par
1	361	4	10	362	4
2	399	4	11	398	4
3	492	5	12	437	4
4	153	3	13	420	4
5	502	5	14	222	3
6	315	4	15	455	4
7	366	4	16	506	5
8	170	3	17	372	4
9	404	4	18	407	4
Out	3162	36	In	3579	36
			Totals	6741	72

Visitors	restricted Wed mornings, weekends & bank holidays. Must contact in advance and have an introduction from own club.
Societies	must contact in advance.
Green Fees	£35 per round (£25 after 1pm) (£45 weekends & bank holidays).
Facilities	⊗ ⅏ by prior arrangement 🏳 🍺 ♀ 🏌 🏧 🥢 Andrew Reynolds.
Location	Golf Rd (Along seafront at N end of Deal)
Hotel	★★★62% Forte Posthouse, Singledge Ln, Whitfield, DOVER ☎(0304) 821222 67⇨

EDENBRIDGE   Map 05 TQ44

Edenbridge Golf & Country Club ☎(0732) 865097
Gently undulating course with a driving range.
18 holes, 6604yds, Par 73, SSS 72.
Club membership 820.

Visitors	restricted at weekends. Must contact in advance.
Societies	must contact in advance.
Green Fees	not confirmed.
Facilities	⊗ ⊪ ♭ ☕ ♀ ☖ 🏌 ♪ ⟨
Leisure	fishing.
Location	Crouch House Rd (1m W of town centre)
Hotel	★★★(red)♨ Gravetye Manor Hotel, EAST GRINSTEAD ☎(0342) 810567 18⇨

FAVERSHAM   Map 05 TR06

Faversham ☎(079589) 561
A beautiful inland course laid
out over part of a large estate
with pheasants walking the
fairways quite tamely. Play
follows two heavily wooded
valleys but the trees affect
only the loose shots going out
of bounds. Fine views.
*18 holes, 6030yds, Par 70, SSS
69, Course record 65.*
Club membership 800.

SCORECARD					
Hole	Yds	Par	Hole	Yds	Par
1	476	5	10	370	4
2	299	4	11	398	4
3	156	3	12	445	4
4	421	4	13	182	3
5	336	4	14	397	4
6	358	4	15	330	4
7	544	5	16	140	3
8	355	4	17	302	4
9	139	3	18	373	4
Out	3084	36	In	2937	34
			Totals	6021	70

Visitors	must have handicap certificate. With member only at weekends. Contacting the club in advance is advisable.
Societies	must contact in advance.
Green Fees	£28 per day; £21 per round.
Facilities	⊗ ⊪ ♭ ☕ ♀ ☖ ☖ ⟨ Gordon Nixon.
Location	Belmont Park (3.5m S)
Hotel	★★★★(red)♨ Eastwell Manor Hotel, Eastwell Park, Boughton Lees, ASHFORD ☎(0233) 635751 23⇨🏌

GILLINGHAM   Map 05 TQ76

Gillingham ☎Medway (0634) 53017
Parkland course.
18 holes, 5879yds, Par 70, SSS 68, Course record 65.
Club membership 830.

Visitors	must be member of recognised golf club. With member only weekends & bank holidays. Must contact in advance and have an introduction from own club.
Societies	must apply in writing.
Green Fees	£18 per day.
Facilities	⊗ & ⊪ (ex Mon & Tue) ♭ ☕ ♀ ☖ ☖ ⟨ Brian Impett.
Location	Woodlands Rd (1.5m SE on A2)
Hotel	★★★68% Forte Crest Hotel, Maidstone Rd, ROCHESTER ☎(0634) 687111 105⇨🏌

A golf-course name printed in ***bold italics***
means that we have been unable to verify
information with the club's management
for the current year

GRAVESEND   Map 05 TQ67

Mid Kent ☎(0474) 568035
A well-maintained downland course with some easy
walking and some excellent greens. The first hole is short,
but nonetheless a real challenge. The slightest hook and
the ball is out of bounds or lost.
18 holes, 6206yds, Par 70, SSS 70, Course record 64.
Club membership 1200.

Visitors	must play with member at weekends. Must contact in advance and have an introduction from own club.
Societies	Tue only; must contact in advance.
Green Fees	not confirmed.
Facilities	⊗ ⊪ by prior arrangement ♭ ☕ ♀ ☖ ☖ 🏌 ⟨ Robert Lee.
Location	Singlewell Rd (S side of town centre off A227)
Hotel	★★★★66% Bridgewood Manor Hotel, Bridgewood Roundabout, Maidstone Rd, ROCHESTER ☎(0634) 201333 100⇨

HAWKHURST   Map 05 TQ73

Hawkhurst ☎(0580) 752396
Undulating parkland course.
9 holes, 5774yds, Par 72, SSS 68, Course record 68.
Club membership 350.

Visitors	with member only at weekends. Must contact in advance.
Societies	must apply in writing.
Green Fees	£18.
Facilities	♭ ☕ ♀ ☖ ☖ 🏌 ⟨ Tony Collins.
Leisure	squash.
Location	High St (W side of village off A268)
Hotel	★★65% Tudor Court Hotel, Rye Rd, HAWKHURST ☎(0580) 752312 18⇨🏌

HERNE BAY   Map 05 TR16

Herne Bay ☎(0227) 373964
Parkland course with bracing air.
18 holes, 5466yds, Par 68, SSS 67.
Club membership 350.

Visitors	may not play mornings at weekends.
Green Fees	not confirmed.
Facilities	♀ ☖ ☖ ⟨
Location	Thanet Way (1m S on A291)
Hotel	★★★62% Falstaff Hotel, St Dunstans St, CANTERBURY ☎(0227) 462138 24⇨🏌

HOLTYE   Map 05 TQ43

Holtye ☎Cowden (0342) 850635
Undulating forest/heathland course with tree-lined fairways
providing testing golf. Difficult tees on back nine.
9 holes, 5289yds, Par 66, SSS 66, Course record 65.
Club membership 500.

Visitors	may not play weekend & Thu mornings. Must contact in advance.
Societies	Tue & Fri only, by arrangement.
Green Fees	£17 per day.
Facilities	⊗ ⊪ ♭ ☕ ♀ ☖ ☖ ⟨ Kevin Hinton.

Location	N side of village on A264
Hotel	★★★(red)🏨 Gravetye Manor Hotel, EAST GRINSTEAD ☎(0342) 810567 18⇨

HOO   Map 05 TQ77

Deangate Ridge ☎Medway (0634) 251180
Parkland, municipal course designed by Fred Hawtree. 18-hole pitch and putt.
18 holes, 6300yds, Par 71, SSS 70, Course record 65.
Club membership 950.

Visitors	no restrictions.
Societies	must apply in writing.
Green Fees	£8.50 per day (£10.50 weekends & bank holidays).
Facilities	⊗ ⅷ ㄴ 里 ♀ △ 🏠 ᛉ ⌊ Barry Aram.
Leisure	hard tennis courts.
Location	4m NE of Rochester off A228
Hotel	★★★68% Forte Crest Hotel, Maidstone Rd, ROCHESTER ☎(0634) 687111 105⇨🐾

HYTHE   Map 05 TR13

Hythe Imperial ☎(0303) 267554
A 9-hole links course played off alternative tees on the second nine. Flat but interesting and testing. Hotel provides many leisure and sports facilities.
9 holes, 5533yds, Par 68, SSS 67, Course record 65.
Club membership 440.

Visitors	must have handicap certificate, but may not play at weekends. Must contact in advance.
Societies	must apply in writing.
Green Fees	£20 per day.
Facilities	⊗ ⅷ ㄴ 里 ♀ △ 🏠 ᛉ ⇝ ⌊ Gordon Ritchie.
Leisure	hard and grass tennis courts, heated indoor swimming pool, squash, snooker, sauna, solarium, gymnasium, bowling croquet putting.
Location	Princes Pde (SE side of town)
Hotel	★★★★67% The Hythe Imperial Hotel, Princes Pde, HYTHE ☎(0303) 267441 100⇨🐾

Sene Valley ☎(0303) 268513
A two-level downland course which provides interesting golf over an undulating landscape with sea views.
18 holes, 6276yds, Par 71, SSS 70, Course record 61.
Club membership 650.

Visitors	must be member of recognised golf club or have handicap certificate. Must contact in advance and have an introduction from own club.
Societies	must contact in advance.
Green Fees	not confirmed.
Facilities	⊗ ⅷ ♀ △ 🏠 ⌊ Trevor Dungate.
Leisure	snooker.
Location	Sene (1m NE off B2065)
Hotel	★★★★67% The Hythe Imperial Hotel, Princes Pde, HYTHE ☎(0303) 267441 100⇨🐾

Each golf-course entry has a recommended AA-appointed hotel. For a wider choice of places to stay, consult *AA Hotels and Restaurants in Britain and Ireland* and *AA Inspected Bed and Breakfast in Britain and Ireland*

KINGSDOWN   Map 05 TR34

Walmer & Kingsdown ☎(0304) 373256
This course near Deal has through the years been overshadowed by its neighbours at Deal and Sandwich, yet it is a testing circuit with many undulations. The course is famous as being the one on which, in 1964, Assistant Professional, Roger Game became the first golfer in Britain to hole out in one at two successive holes; the 7th and 8th. The course is situated on top of the cliffs, with fine views.
18 holes, 6451yds, Par 72, SSS 71, Course record 69.
Club membership 600.

Visitors	may not play before noon on weekends & bank holidays. Must contact in advance and have an introduction from own club.
Societies	must contact in advance & give one month's notice.
Green Fees	£20 per day/round (£22 weekends & bank holidays).
Facilities	⊗ ⅷ ㄴ 里 ♀ △ 🏠 ⌊ Tim Hunt.
Location	The Leas (.5m S off B2057)
Hotel	★★★62% Forte Posthouse, Singledge Ln, Whitfield, DOVER ☎(0304) 821222 67⇨

LAMBERHURST   Map 05 TQ63

Lamberhurst ☎(0892) 890591
Parkland course crossing river twice. Fine views.
18 holes, 6232yds, Par 72, SSS 69, Course record 65.
Club membership 700.

Visitors	restricted weekend & bank holiday mornings.
Societies	Tue, Wed & Thu only, by arrangement.
Green Fees	£25 per day/round (£30 weekends & bank holidays).
Facilities	⊗ ⅷ by prior arrangement ㄴ 里 ♀ △ 🏠 ⌊ Mike Travers.
Location	Church Rd (N side of village on A21)
Hotel	★★67% Star & Eagle Hotel, High St, GOUDHURST ☎(0580) 211512 & 211338 11rm(9⇨🐾)

LITTLESTONE   Map 05 TR02

Littlestone ☎New Romney (0679) 63355
Located in the Romney Marshes, this flattish seaside links course calls for every variety of shot. The 8th, 15th, 16th and 17th are regarded as classics by international golfers. Allowance for wind must always be made. Extensive practice area.
18 holes, 6424yds, Par 71, SSS 71, Course record 66.
Shore Course : 9 holes, 1998yds, Par 32, SSS 63.
Club membership 500.

Visitors	restricted all week. Must contact in advance and have an introduction from own club.
Societies	must contact one year in advance.
Green Fees	not confirmed.
Facilities	⊗ ㄴ 里 ♀ △ 🏠 ᛉ ⌊ Stephen Watkins.
Location	St Andrew's Rd (N side of village)
Hotel	★★★★67% The Hythe Imperial Hotel, Princes Pde, HYTHE ☎(0303) 267441 100⇨🐾

MAIDSTONE

Map 05 TQ75

Cobtree Manor Park ☎(0622) 681560
An undulating parkland course with some water hazards.
18 holes, 5716yds, Par 69, SSS 68, Course record 67.
Club membership 550.

Visitors	no restrictions.
Societies	Mon-Fri only, by arrangement.
Green Fees	£7.50 (£11.25 weekends & bank holidays) £2 supplement for players without booking card..
Facilities	⊗ ⍰ ⮋ ⬛ ♀ ⌂ 🖛 ⌐ 🏌 ℂ Martin Drew.
Location	Chatham Rd, Sandling (on A229 .25m N of M20 junc 6)
Hotel	★★57% Boxley House Hotel, Boxley Rd, Boxley, MAIDSTONE ☎(0622) 692269 11⇆🏱Annexe7⇆🏱

RAMSGATE

Map 05 TR36

St Augustine's ☎Thanet (0843) 590333
A comfortably flat course in this famous bracing Championship area of Kent. Neither as long nor as difficult as its lordly neighbours, St Augustine's will nonetheless extend most golfers. Dykes run across the course.
18 holes, 5138yds, Par 69, SSS 65, Course record 59.
Club membership 600.

Visitors	must have a handicap certificate. Must contact in advance and have an introduction from own club.
Societies	must contact in advance.
Green Fees	not confirmed.
Facilities	⊗ (ex Mon) ⍰ (ex Mon) ⮋ ⬛ ♀ ⌂ 🖛 ℂ Derek Scott.
Location	Cottington Rd, Cliffsend
Hotel	★★★59% Marina Resort Hotel, Harbour Pde, RAMSGATE ☎(0843) 588276 59⇆🏱

ROCHESTER

Map 05 TQ76

Rochester & Cobham Park
☎Shorne (047 482) 3411
A first-rate course of challenging dimensions in undulating parkland. All holes differ and each requires accurate drive placing to derive the best advantage. The clubhouse and course are situated a quarter of a mile from the western end of the M2. The club was formed in 1891.
18 holes, 6440yds, Par 72, SSS 71, Course record 66.
Club membership 700.

SCORECARD: White Tees					
Hole	Yds	Par	Hole	Yds	Par
1	303	4	10	350	4
2	358	4	11	181	3
3	434	4	12	339	4
4	190	3	13	479	5
5	476	5	14	311	4
6	382	4	15	492	5
7	402	4	16	159	3
8	204	3	17	503	5
9	432	4	18	445	4
Out	3181	35	In	3259	37
			Totals	6440	72

Visitors	with member only weekends & bank holidays. Must contact in advance and have an introduction from own club.
Societies	Tue & Thu only, by arrangement.
Green Fees	£36 per day; £26 per round.
Facilities	⊗ ⍰ ⮋ ⬛ ♀ ⌂ 🖛 ℂ Matt Henderson.
Location	Park Pale (2.5m W on A2)
Hotel	★★★★66% Bridgewood Manor Hotel, Bridgewood Roundabout, Maidstone Rd, ROCHESTER ☎(0634) 201333 100⇆

SANDWICH

Map 05 TR35

Prince's ☎(0304) 611118
Championship links of the highest calibre and comparable to its near neighbours, Royal Cinque Ports. Typical flat duneland running along the shore of Sandwich Bay. The ball must be struck well to attain a good score. 27 holes in three loops of nine.
Dunes: 9 holes, 3343yds, Par 36, SSS 71.
Himalayas: 9 holes, 3163yds, Par 35, SSS 71.
Shore: 9 holes, 3347yds, Par 36, SSS 72.
Club membership 450.

Visitors	handicap certificate required. Must contact in advance.
Societies	must contact in advance.
Green Fees	£29 per day; £26 per round (£34-£39 per day weekends, £31 per round,) apply for bank holiday prices.
Facilities	⊗ ⍰ ⮋ ⬛ ♀ ⌂ 🖛 ⌐ ℂ Philip Sparks.
Leisure	snooker.
Location	Prince's Dr, Sandwich Bay (2m E via toll road)
Hotel	★★62% The Bow Window Inn, High St, LITTLEBOURNE ☎(0227) 721264 8⇆🏱

Royal St George's See page 135

SEVENOAKS

Map 05 TQ55

Knole Park ☎(0732) 452150
The course is set in a majestic park with many fine trees and deer running loose. It has a wiry turf seemingly impervious to rain. Certainly a pleasure to play on. Excellent views of Knole House and the North Downs. Outstanding greens.
18 holes, 6249yds, Par 70, SSS 70, Course record 63.
Club membership 850.

SCORECARD					
Hole	Yds	Par	Hole	Yds	Par
1	197	3	10	163	3
2	345	4	11	426	4
3	403	4	12	200	3
4	413	4	13	319	4
5	174	3	14	438	4
6	415	4	15	483	5
7	480	5	16	199	3
8	177	3	17	502	5
9	512	5	18	400	4
Out	3119	35	In	3130	35
			Totals	6249	70

Visitors	must have handicap certificate, but may not play at weekends. Must contact in advance.
Societies	must apply in writing one year in advance.
Green Fees	£25.50 per round.
Facilities	⊗ ⮋ ⬛ ♀ ⌂ 🖛 ℂ P E Gill.
Leisure	squash, snooker.
Location	Seal Hollow Rd (SE side of town centre off B2019)
Hotel	★★59% Sevenoaks Park Hotel, Seal Hollow Rd, SEVENOAKS ☎(0732) 454245 16rm(3⇆3🏱)Annexe10⇆🏱

SHEERNESS

Map 05 TQ97

Sheerness ☎(0795) 662585
Marshland/meadowland course, few bunkers, but many ditches and water hazards. Often windy.
18 holes, 6460yds, Par 72, SSS 71, Course record 68.
Club membership 600.

Visitors	with member only at weekends. Must have an introduction from own club.
Societies	must apply in writing.
Green Fees	£20 per day; £15 per round.

▶

SCORE CARD: Old Course					
Hole	Yds	Par	Hole	Yds	Par
1	370	4	10	318	4
2	411	4	11	172	3
3	352	4	12	316	4
4	419	4	13	398	4
5	514	5	14	523	5
6	374	4	15	401	4
7	359	4	16	351	4
8	166	3	17	461	4
9	307	4	18	354	4
Out	3272	36	In	3294	36
			Totals	6566	72

SANDWICH   Map05TR35

Royal St George's ☎ (0304) 613090

John Ingham writes: Sandwich is one of the most beautiful and unspoiled towns in southern England. Driving to this part of Kent is much like stepping back into history. The big golf course here, Royal St Goerge's, is where Sandy Lyle won the Open Championship in 1985, by one shot from that colourful American, Payne Stewart.

Close to the sea, overlooking Pegwell Bay, any kind of wind can make this man-size test even tougher. The sweeping rough at the first can be daunting, so can the bunkers and the huge sandhills. But there are classic shots here; it is the truest links you will find in all England and the R&A, in its wisdom, choose it for major championships knowing it will find the pedigree player at the end of a week.

The clubhouse is old-fashioned and the seats near the window, in the bar, seem to have been there forever. The bar staff may know as much about fishing or lifeboats as they know about beer, and make a visit there a delight, providing you are not looking for modern sophistication.

Off-sea breezes can turn to incredible gales, and it is possible to find the course virtually unplayable. A smooth swing can be blown inside out and stories of three good woods to reach certain greens, into wind, are commonplace. Often the problem in high winds is simply to stand up, and address the ball. Putting, too, can be almost impossible with the ball blown off the surface, and maybe into the sand! Christy O'Connor Jnr put together a 64 here, and no wonder it's the record.

18 holes, 6903, Par 70, SSS74. Membership 675

Visitors	must contact in advance and have a letter of introduction from their own club. Restricted weekends.
Societies	must apply in writing.
Green fees	£33 (18 holes); £47 (36 holes)
Facilities	⊗ 坒 ⬛ ⚲ 🛆 🖃 ⛾ ↾ (Niall Cameron).
Location	1.5m E of town

WHERE TO STAY AND EAT NEARBY

HOTELS:

CANTERBURY ★★★ 62% Flagstaff, St Dunstans St ☎ (0227) 462138.
24 ⟨⋅⋆↾ . ⊴ English & Continental cuisine.

DOVER ★★★ 62% Forte Posthouse, Singledge Ln, Whitfield (3m NW jct A2/A256) ☎ (0304) 821222.
67 ⟨⋅⋆ .

LITTLEBOURNE ★★ 62% The Bow Window Inn, High St. ☎ Canterbury (0227) 721264.
8 ⟨⋅⋆↾ . ⊴ English & French cuisine.

RAMSGATE ★★★ 59% Marina Resort, Harbour Pde. ☎ Thanet (0843) 588276.
59 ⟨⋅⋆↾ . ⊴ English & continental cuisine.

RESTAURANTS:

CANTERBURY ✕ Ristorante Tuo e Mio, 16 The Borough. ☎ (0227) 761471. ⊴ Italian cuisine.

ST MARGARET'S AT CLIFFE
✕✕ Wallets Court, West Cliffe. ☎ Dover (0304) 852424. ⊴ English & French cuisine.

Facilities	⊗ (ex Mon) ⅷ by prior arrangement 🏓 ⬛ ♀ 🔺 🏠 ſ Alan Gillard.
Location	Power Station Rd (1.5m E off A249)
Hotel	★★★68% Great Danes Hotel, Ashford Rd, HOLLINGBOURNE ☎(0622) 30022 126⇨🐾

SHOREHAM   Map 05 TQ56

Darenth Valley ☎Otford (09592) 2944
Easy walking parkland course in beautiful valley. Testing 12th hole, par 4.
18 holes, 6356yds, Par 72, SSS 71, Course record 68.

Visitors	may not play at weekends & bank holidays.
Societies	must contact in advance.
Green Fees	not confirmed.
Facilities	⊗ & ⅷ by prior arrangement 🏓 ⬛ ♀ 🔺 🏠 ⛶ ſ Scott Fotheringham.
Location	Station Rd (1m E on A225)
Hotel	★★★67% Royal Oak Hotel, Upper High St, SEVENOAKS ☎(0732) 451109 23rm(19⇨32🐾)Annexe16⇨🐾

SITTINGBOURNE   Map 05 TQ96

Sittingbourne & Milton Regis ☎Newington (0795) 842261
A downland course with pleasant vistas. There are a few uphill climbs, but the course is far from difficult. The 166-yard, 2nd hole is a testing par 3.
18 holes, 6121yds, Par 70, SSS 69, Course record 66.
Club membership 714.

Visitors	may not play at weekends & are restricted Wed. Must contact in advance and have an introduction from own club.
Societies	must apply in writing.
Green Fees	£18.50 per round.
Facilities	⊗ ⅷ 🏓 ⬛ ♀ 🔺 🏠 ⛶ ſ John Hearn.
Location	Wormdale, Newington (3m W off A249)
Hotel	★★★68% Great Danes Hotel, Ashford Rd, HOLLINGBOURNE ☎(0622) 30022 126⇨🐾

TENTERDEN   Map 05 TQ83

Tenterden ☎(05806) 3987
Attractive parkland course, last 3 holes are hilly.
9 holes, 6030yds, Par 70, SSS 69, Course record 65.
Club membership 650.

Visitors	restricted weekends & bank holidays. Must contact in advance.
Societies	must apply in writing.
Green Fees	£18 per day.
Facilities	⊗ ⅷ by prior arrangement 🏓 ⬛ ♀ 🔺 🏠 ſ Gary Potter.
Location	Woodchurch Rd (.75m E on B2067)
Hotel	★★⬛69% Kennel Holt Country House Hotel, Goudhurst Rd, CRANBROOK ☎(0580) 712032 9⇨🐾Annexe1🐾

This guide is updated annually – make sure that you use the up-to-date edition

TONBRIDGE   Map 05 TQ54

Poultwood ☎(0732) 364039
Public 'pay and play' woodland/parkland course. Easy but varied walking, water hazards.
18 holes, 5569yds, Par 68, SSS 67.

Visitors	no restrictions.
Societies	must apply in writing.
Green Fees	£7 per round (£10.50 weekends).
Facilities	⊗ ⅷ 🏓 ⬛ ♀ 🔺 🏠 ⛶ ſ Ken Adwick.
Leisure	squash.
Location	Higham Ln
Hotel	★★67% Rose & Crown Hotel, High St, TONBRIDGE ☎(0732) 357966 50rm(49⇨🐾)

TUNBRIDGE WELLS (ROYAL)   Map 05 TQ53

Nevill ☎(0892) 525818
Just within Sussex, the county boundary with Kent runs along the northern perimeter of the course. Open undulating ground, well-wooded with much heather and gorse for the first half. The second nine holes slope away from the clubhouse to a valley where a narrow stream hazards two holes.
18 holes, 6336yds, Par 71, SSS 70, Course record 66.
Club membership 950.

Visitors	must contact in advance.
Societies	must apply in writing.
Green Fees	£28 per day.
Facilities	⊗ ⅷ by prior arrangement 🏓 ⬛ ♀ 🔺 🏠 ſ Paul Huggett.
Location	Benhall Mill Rd
Hotel	★★★76% Spa Hotel, Mount Ephraim, TUNBRIDGE WELLS ☎(0892) 20331 76⇨🐾

Tunbridge Wells ☎(0892) 523034
Somewhat hilly, well-bunkered parkland course with lake; trees form natural hazards.
9 holes, 4560yds, Par 65, SSS 62, Course record 59.
Club membership 600.

Visitors	must be members of an affiliated club and possess handicap certificate. Must contact in advance.
Societies	apply in writing.
Green Fees	£26.50 per day; £20 per round.
Facilities	⊗ ⅷ by prior arrangement 🏓 ⬛ ♀ 🔺 🏠 ſ Keith Smithson.
Location	Langton Rd (1m W on A264)
Hotel	★★★76% Spa Hotel, Mount Ephraim, TUNBRIDGE WELLS ☎(0892) 20331 76⇨🐾

WESTGATE ON SEA   Map 05 TR37

Westgate and Birchington ☎Thanet (0843) 31115
Seaside course.
18 holes, 4926yds, Par 64, SSS 64.
Club membership 310.

Visitors	restricted at weekends. Must contact in advance and have an introduction from own club.
Societies	must contact three months in advance.
Green Fees	£13 per day (£16 weekends & bank holidays).
Facilities	🏓 ⬛ ♀ 🔺 🏠 ſ

Location	176 Canterbury Rd (E side of town centre off A28)
Hotel	★★54% Ivyside Hotel, 25 Sea Rd, WESTGATE ON SEA ☎(0843) 31082 due to change to 831082 67rm(65⇨🏠)

WEST KINGSDOWN   Map 05 TQ56

Woodlands Manor ☎(09592) 3806
Interesting, undulating parkland course with testing 1st, 9th and 15th holes.
18 holes, 5858yds, Par 69, SSS 68.
Club membership 550.

Visitors	with member only weekend afternoons.
Societies	apply in writing.
Green Fees	not confirmed.
Facilities	♀ 🛆 🏠 ⛳ ℓ
Location	Woodlands (2m S off A20)
Hotel	★★59% Sevenoaks Park Hotel, Seal Hollow Rd, SEVENOAKS ☎(0732) 454245 16rm(3⇨3🏠)Annexe10⇨🏠

WHITSTABLE   Map 05 TR16

Chestfield (Whitstable) ☎Chestfield (022779) 4411
Parkland course with sea views.
18 holes, 6181yds, Par 70, SSS 70, Course record 66.
Club membership 730.

Visitors	may not play at weekends. Must contact in advance and have an introduction from own club.
Societies	must apply in writing.
Green Fees	£24 per day; £16 per round.
Facilities	⊗ ⅲ ⅃ ♀ 🛆 🏠 ℓ John J Brotherton.
Location	103 Chestfield Rd (2m SE off A299)
Hotel	★★★57% Chaucer Hotel, Ivy Ln, CANTERBURY ☎(0227) 464427 43⇨🏠

Whitstable & Seasalter ☎(0227) 272020
Links course.
9 holes, 5276yds, Par 65, SSS 63.
Club membership 300.

Visitors	must play with member at weekends.
Green Fees	£15 per round.
Facilities	♀ 🛆 🏠
Location	Collingwood Rd (W side of town centre off B2205)
Hotel	★★★57% Chaucer Hotel, Ivy Ln, CANTERBURY ☎(0227) 464427 43⇨🏠

LANCASHIRE

ACCRINGTON   Map 07 SD72

Baxenden & District ☎(0254) 34555
Moorland course.
18 holes, 5740yds, SSS 68.

Visitors	no restrictions.
Societies	must contact in advance.
Green Fees	not confirmed.
Facilities	♀ 🛆

Location	Top o' th' Meadow, Baxenden (1.5m SE off A680)
Hotel	★★★64% Dunkenhalgh Hotel, Blackburn Rd, Clayton le Moors, ACCRINGTON ☎(0254) 398021 29⇨🏠Annexe51⇨🏠

Green Haworth ☎(0254) 237580
Moorland course dominated by quarries and difficult in windy conditions.
9 holes, 5556yds, Par 68, SSS 67, Course record 69.
Club membership 300.

Visitors	must play with member on Sun.
Societies	apply in writing.
Green Fees	not confirmed.
Facilities	⊗ ⅃ ■ ♀ 🛆 🏠 ℓ Gerry Bond.
Location	Green Haworth (2m S off A680)
Hotel	★★★60% Blackburn Moat House, Preston New Rd, BLACKBURN ☎(0254) 264441 98⇨🏠

BACUP   Map 07 SD82

Bacup ☎(0706) 873170
Moorland course, predominantly flat except climbs to 1st and 10th holes.
9 holes, 5652yds, Par 68, SSS 67.
Club membership 350.

Visitors	must contact in advance.
Societies	must contact in writing.
Green Fees	not confirmed.
Facilities	⊗ ⅲ ⅃ ■ ♀ 🛆
Location	Bankside Ln (W side of town off A671)
Hotel	★★★63% Keirby Hotel, Keirby Walk, BURNLEY ☎(0282) 27611 49⇨🏠

BARNOLDSWICK   Map 07 SD84

Ghyll ☎Earby (0282) 842466
Excellent, parkland course with outstanding views, especially from the 8th tee where you can see the Three Peaks. Testing 3rd hole is an uphill par 4.
9 holes, 5422yds, Par 68, SSS 66, Course record 62.
Club membership 310.

Visitors	may not play Tue mornings, Fri after 4.30pm & Sun.
Societies	must contact in writing.
Green Fees	£10.50 (£15.50 weekends & bank holidays).
Facilities	♀ (from 7.30pm) 🛆
Location	Ghyll Brow (1m NE on B6252)
Hotel	★★★65% Stirk House Hotel, GISBURN ☎(0200) 445581 36⇨🏠Annexe12⇨

BLACKBURN   Map 07 SD62

Blackburn ☎(0254) 51122
Parkland course on a high plateau with stream and hills. Superb views of Lancashire coast and the Pennines.
18 holes, 6140yds, Par 71, SSS 70, Course record 63.
Club membership 800.

Visitors	restricted Tue & weekends.
Societies	must contact in advance.
Green Fees	£15 per day (£18 weekends & bank holidays).
Facilities	⊗ ⅲ ⅃ ■ (no catering Mon) ♀ 🛆 🏠 ℓ Alan Rodwell.

▶

Leisure	pool & snooker table.
Location	Beardwood Brow (1.25m NW of town centre off A677)
Hotel	★★★60% Blackburn Moat House, Preston New Rd, BLACKBURN ☎(0254) 264441 98⇨🛏

BLACKPOOL   Map 07 SD33

Blackpool North Shore ☎(0253) 52054
Undulating parkland course.
18 holes, 6400yds, Par 71, SSS 71, Course record 67.
Club membership 900.

Visitors	may not play Thu & Sat. Advisable to contact in advance.
Societies	must contact in advance.
Green Fees	£21 per day (£23 weekends).
Facilities	⊗ ⅲ by prior arrangement � ■ ♀ △ 🏠 ᛐ ᚨ
Leisure	snooker.
Location	Devonshire Rd (On A587 N of town centre)
Hotel	★★68% Brabyns Hotel, Shaftesbury Av, North Shore, BLACKPOOL ☎(0253) 54263 22⇨🛏 Annexe3⇨🛏

BURNLEY   Map 07 SD83

Burnley ☎(0282) 21045
Moorland course with hilly surrounds.
18 holes, 5800yds, Par 69, SSS 69, Course record 65.
Club membership 600.

Visitors	may not play at weekends. Must contact in advance.
Societies	must contact in advance.
Green Fees	£15 (£20 weekends).
Facilities	⊗ ⅲ ㄴ ■ (no catering Mon) ♀ △ 🏠 ᚨ William Tye.
Leisure	snooker.
Location	Glen View (1.5m S off A646)
Hotel	★★★63% Keirby Hotel, Keirby Walk, BURNLEY ☎(0282) 27611 49⇨🛏

Towneley ☎(0282) 38473
Parkland course, with other sporting facilities.
18 holes, 5812yds, Par 70, SSS 68, Course record 65.
Club membership 300.

Visitors	must contact in advance at weekends.
Societies	must contact in advance.
Green Fees	not confirmed.
Facilities	⊗ (ex Mon) ⅲ by prior arrangement ㄴ (ex Mon) ■ ♀ △ 🏠 ᛐ ᚨ
Location	Towneley Park, Todmorden Rd (1m SE of town centre on A671)
Hotel	★★★71% Oaks Hotel, Colne Rd, Reedley, BURNLEY ☎(0282) 414141 58⇨🛏

CHORLEY   Map 07 SD51

Chorley ☎(0257) 480263
A splendid moorland course with plenty of fresh air. The
well-sited clubhouse affords some good views of the
Lancashire coast and of Angelzarke, a local beauty spot.
Beware of the short 3rd hole with its menacing out-of-
bounds.
18 holes, 6277yds, Par 71, SSS 70, Course record 64.
Club membership 500.

Visitors	restricted Sat-Mon. Must contact in advance and have an introduction from own club.
Societies	must contact in advance.
Green Fees	£20 per day (£30 weekends & bank holidays).
Facilities	⊗ ⅲ by prior arrangement ㄴ ■ ♀ △ 🏠 ᚨ Paul Wesselingh.
Leisure	snooker, pool table, TV.
Location	Hall o' th' Hill, Heath Charnock (2.5m SE on A673)
Hotel	★★★67% Pines Hotel, Clayton-le-Woods, CHORLEY ☎(0772) 38551 39⇨🛏

Duxbury Jubilee Park ☎(02572) 65380
Municipal parkland course.
18 holes, 6390yds, Par 71, SSS 70.
Club membership 225.

Visitors	must book 6 days in advance.
Societies	weekdays only. Must contact in advance.
Green Fees	£4.20 per round (£5.80 weekends & bank holi-days).
Facilities	⊗ ㄴ ■ △ 🏠 ᛐ ᚨ David Clarke.
Location	Duxbury Park (2.5m S off A6)
Hotel	★★58% Welcome Lodge, Mill Ln, CHARNOCK RICHARD ☎(0257) 791746 100⇨

Shaw Hill Hotel Golf & Country Club ☎(02572) 69221
A fine course designed by one of Europe's most prominent
golf architects and offering a considerable challenge as
well as tranquillity and scenic charm. Seven lakes guard
par 5 and long par 4 holes.
18 holes, 6467yds, Par 72, SSS 71, Course record 68.

Visitors	no restrictions.
Societies	must telephone in advance.
Green Fees	not confirmed.
Facilities	⊗ ⅲ ㄴ ■ ♀ △ 🏠 ᛐ ⊨ ᚨ Ian Evans.
Leisure	snooker, sauna, solarium.
Location	Preston Rd, Whittle-Le-Woods (On A6 1.5m N)
Hotel	★★★64% Shaw Hill Hotel Golf & Country Club, Preston Rd, Whittle-le-Woods, CHORLEY ☎(0257) 269221 22⇨🛏

A golf-course name printed in **_bold italics_**
means that we have been unable to verify
information with the club's management
for the current year

For an explanation of symbols and
abbreviations, see page 32

CLITHEROE   Map 07 SD74

Clitheroe ☎(0200) 22292
One of the best inland courses in the country. Clitheroe is a parkland-type course with water hazards and good scenic views, particularly on towards Longridge, and Pendle Hill. The Club has been the venue for the Lancashire Amateur Championships, and for the 1991 County Championships Tournament.
18 holes, 6322yds, Par 71, SSS 71, Course record 67.
Club membership 720.

SCORECARD: White Tees					
Hole	Yds	Par	Hole	Yds	Par
1	464	5	10	372	4
2	346	4	11	406	4
3	447	4	12	445	4
4	298	4	13	518	5
5	144	3	14	187	3
6	345	4	15	379	4
7	434	4	16	317	4
8	168	3	17	151	3
9	379	4	18	522	5
Out	3025	35	In	3297	36
			Totals	6322	71

Visitors may not play on Thu or at weekends. Must contact in advance.
Societies must contact in writing.
Green Fees £19 per day/round (£24 weekends & bank holidays).
Facilities ⊗ ℳ ㄥ ⬛ ♀ ♘ 🏠 ⚐ ⚑ 《 John Twissell.
Location Whalley Rd, Pendleton (2m S on A671)
Hotel ★★70% Shireburn Arms Hotel, HURST GREEN ☎(025486) 518 15⇨☜

COLNE   Map 07 SD84

Colne ☎(0282) 863391
Moorland course.
9 holes, 5961yds, Par 70, SSS 69, Course record 67.
Club membership 300.
Visitors restricted Thu. Must contact in advance.
Societies must contact in advance.
Green Fees £11 per day (£13 weekends & bank holidays).
Facilities ♀ ♘
Leisure snooker.
Location Law Farm, Skipton Old Rd (1m E off A56)
Hotel ★★★65% Stirk House Hotel, GISBURN ☎(0200) 445581 36⇨☜ Annexe12⇨

DARWEN   Map 07 SD62

Darwen ☎(0254) 701287
Moorland course.
18 holes, 5752yds, Par 68, SSS 68, Course record 64.
Club membership 600.
Visitors may not play on Sat.
Societies must telephone in advance.
Green Fees not confirmed.
Facilities ⊗ ℳ ㄥ ⬛ (no catering Mon) ♀ (ex Mon) ♘ 🏠 《 W Lennon.
Location Winter Hill (1m NW)
Hotel ★★★57% Whitehall Hotel, Springbank, Whitehall, DARWEN ☎(0254) 701595 18rm(14⇨☜)

For a full range of AA guides and maps, visit your local AA shop or any good bookshop

FLEETWOOD   Map 07 SD34

Fleetwood ☎(0253) 873661
Championship length, flat seaside links where the player must always be alert to changes of direction or strengh of the wind.
18 holes, 6723yds, Par 72, SSS 72.
Club membership 600.
Visitors may not play on competition days.
Societies must contact in advance. A deposit of £2 per player is required.
Green Fees £20 per day (£25 weekends & bank holidays).
Facilities ⊗ ℳ by prior arrangement ㄥ ⬛ ♀ ♘ 🏠 《 Clive Thomas Burgess.
Leisure snooker.
Location Princes Way (W side of town centre)
Hotel ★★★65% North Euston Hotel, The Esplanade, FLEETWOOD ☎(0253) 876525 56⇨☜

HARWOOD, GREAT   Map 07 SD73

Great Harwood ☎Blackburn (0254) 884391
Flat parkland course with fine views of the Pendle region.
9 holes, 6411yds, Par 73, SSS 71, Course record 68.
Club membership 325.
Visitors may not play on competition days. Must contact in advance.
Societies must contact in writing.
Green Fees £10 per day (£12 weekends & bank holidays).
Facilities ⊗ ℳ ㄥ & ⬛ (ex Mon) ♀ ♘
Leisure snooker.
Location Harwood Bar, Whallwy Rd (E side of town centre on A680)
Hotel ★★70% Shireburn Arms Hotel, HURST GREEN ☎(025486) 518 15⇨☜

HASLINGDEN   Map 07 SD72

Rossendale ☎Rossendale (0706) 831339
Testing, and usually windy meadowland course.
18 holes, 6267yds, Par 72, SSS 70, Course record 67.
Club membership 700.
Visitors restricted Sun. Must contact in advance.
Societies must telephone in advance & confirm in writing.
Green Fees £12 per day; £18 per round (£25 per round weekends & bank holidays).
Facilities ⊗ ℳ ㄥ ⬛ ♀ ♘ 🏠 《 S J Nicholls.
Leisure snooker.
Location Ewood Ln Head (1.5m S off A56)
Hotel ★★★60% Blackburn Moat House, Preston New Rd, BLACKBURN ☎(0254) 264441 98⇨☜

HEYSHAM   Map 07 SD46

Heysham ☎Lancaster (0524) 51011
Seaside parkland course.
18 holes, 6400yds, Par 69, SSS 70, Course record 65.
Club membership 900.
Visitors no restrictions.
Societies must contact in writing.
Green Fees £20 per day; £16 per round (£25 per day/round weekends & bank holidays).

▶

Facilities	⊗ 🍴 🏌 💺 ♀ ⛳ 🏠 ⚐ ⎛ R Williamson.
Leisure	snooker.
Location	Trumcar Park, Middleton Rd (.75m S off A589)
Hotel	★★60% Clarendon Hotel, Promenade, West End, MORECAMBE ☎(0524) 410180 33rm(20⇔7↑)

KNOTT END-ON-SEA   Map 07 SD34

Knott End ☎Blackpool (0253) 810576
Pleasant, undulating parkland course on banks of River
Wyre. Open to sea breezes.
18 holes, 5789yds, Par 68, SSS 68, Course record 63.
Club membership 700.

Visitors	must contact in advance.
Societies	must contact in writing.
Green Fees	£18 (£22 weekends).
Facilities	⊗ 🍴 🏌 💺 ♀ ⛳ 🏠 ⎛ Kevin Short.
Leisure	snooker.
Location	Wyre-Side (W side of village off B5377)
Hotel	★★★65% North Euston Hotel, The Esplanade, FLEETWOOD ☎(0253) 876525 56⇔↑

LANCASTER   Map 07 SD46

Lancaster Golf & Country Club ☎(0524) 751247
This course is unusual for parkland golf as it is exposed to
the winds coming off the Irish Sea. It is situated on the
Lune estuary and has some natural hazards and easy
walking. There are however several fine holes among
woods near the old clubhouse.
18 holes, 6282yds, Par 71, SSS 71.
Club membership 925.

Visitors	restricted at weekends. Must contact in advance and have an introduction from own club.
Societies	Mon-Fri only . Must contact in advance. Handicap certificate and letters of introduction required.
Green Fees	£22 per day/round.
Facilities	⊗ 🍴 🏌 & 💺 (Mon-Fri) ♀ ⛳ 🏠 🛏 ⎛ David Sutcliffe.
Leisure	snooker.
Location	Ashton Hall, Ashton-with-Stodday (3m S on A588)
Hotel	★★★66% Strathmore Hotel, East Promenade, MORECAMBE ☎(0524) 421234 51⇔↑

Lansil ☎(0532) 685180
Parkland course.
9 holes, 5608yds, Par 70, SSS 67.
Club membership 375.

Visitors	may not play before 1pm at weekends.
Societies	weekdays only; must contact in writing.
Green Fees	not confirmed.
Facilities	⛳
Location	Caton Rd (N side of town centre on A683)
Hotel	★★★62% Forte Posthouse, Waterside Park, Caton Rd, LANCASTER ☎(0524) 65999 110⇔↑

LEYLAND   Map 07 SD52

Leyland ☎(0772) 436457
Parkland course, fairly flat and usually breezy.
18 holes, 6123yds, Par 70, SSS 69.
Club membership 860.

Visitors	restricted weekends & bank holidays. Must contact in advance.
Societies	must contact in advance.
Green Fees	£20 per day/round.
Facilities	⊗ 🏌 💺 ♀ ⛳ 🏠 ⎛ Colin Burgess.
Location	Wigan Rd (E side of town centre on A49)
Hotel	★★★67% Pines Hotel, Clayton-le-Woods, CHORLEY ☎(0772) 38551 39⇔↑

LONGRIDGE   Map 07 SD63

Longridge ☎(0772) 783291
Moorland course 850 ft high with views of the Ribble Valley,
Trough of Bowland, The Fylde and Welsh Mountains.
18 holes, 5970yds, Par 70, SSS 68, Course record 66.
Club membership 600.

Visitors	may not play 8-9.30am, noon-1pm, Sun 11am-12.15pm (winter) & weekends in summer.
Societies	must contact in writing.
Green Fees	£14 Mon-Thu; £17 Fri-Sun.
Facilities	⊗ 🍴 🏌 💺 ♀ ⛳ 🏠 ⎛ N S James.
Leisure	snooker.
Location	Fell Barn, Jeffrey Hill
Hotel	★★70% Shireburn Arms Hotel, HURST GREEN ☎(025486) 518 15⇔↑

LYTHAM ST ANNES   Map 07 SD32

Fairhaven ☎(0253) 736741
A flat, but interesting parkland/links course of good
standard. There are natural hazards as well as numerous
bunkers and players need to produce particularly accurate
second shots.
18 holes, 6884yds, Par 74, SSS 73, Course record 65.
Club membership 950.

Visitors	must contact in advance and have an introduction from own club.
Societies	must contact in advance.
Green Fees	£30 per day; £25 per round (£30 per round weekends).
Facilities	⊗ 🍴 🏌 💺 ♀ ⛳ 🏠 ⚐ ⎛ I Howieson.
Leisure	snooker.
Location	Lytham Hall Park, Ansdell (E side of town centre off B5261)
Hotel	★★★68% Bedford Hotel, 307-311 Clifton Dr South, LYTHAM ST ANNES ☎(0253) 724636 36⇔↑

Lytham Green Drive ☎(0253) 737390
Pleasant parkland course, ideal for holidaymakers.
18 holes, 6175yds, Par 70, SSS 69, Course record 64.
Club membership 760.

Visitors	may not play at weekends. Must have a handicap certificate. Must contact in advance.
Societies	must contact in advance.
Green Fees	£22 per day/round.
Facilities	⊗ 🍴 by prior arrangement 🏌 💺 ♀ ⛳ 🏠 ⎛ F W Accleton.

Leisure snooker.
Location Ballam Rd (E side of town centre off B5259)
Hotel ★★★★50% Clifton Arms, West Beach, Lytham, LYTHAM ST ANNES ☎(0253) 739898 41⇥📞

Royal Lytham & St Annes See page 143

St Annes Old Links ☎(0253) 723597
Seaside links, qualifying course for Open Championship; compact and of very high standard, particularly greens. Windy, very long 5th, 17th and 18th holes. Famous hole: 9th (171 yds), par 3. Exceptional club facilities.
18 holes, 6616yds, Par 72, SSS 72, Course record 66.
Club membership 950.
Visitors may not play on Sat or before 9.15am & between noon-2pm. Sundays by prior arrangement only. Must have an introduction from own club.
Societies must contact in advance.
Green Fees £25 per day (£30 weekends & bank holidays).
Facilities ⊗ 🍴 🏌 🍺 ♀ 🛄 🏡 ⁅ G G Hardiman.
Leisure snooker.
Location Highbury Rd (N side of town centre)
Hotel ★★★68% Bedford Hotel, 307-311 Clifton Dr South, LYTHAM ST ANNES ☎(0253) 724636 36⇥📞

MORECAMBE   Map 07 SD46

Morecambe ☎(0524) 412841
Holiday golf at its most enjoyable. The well-maintained, wind-affected seaside parkland course is not long but full of character. Even so the panoramic views across Morecambe Bay and to the Lake District and Pennines make concentration difficult. The 4th is a testing hole.
18 holes, 5770yds, Par 67, SSS 68, Course record 64.
Club membership 1200.

SCORECARD					
Hole	Yds	Par	Hole	Yds	Par
1	338	4	10	194	3
2	451	4	11	326	4
3	143	3	12	183	3
4	439	4	13	366	4
5	194	3	14	412	4
6	372	4	15	419	4
7	387	4	16	174	3
8	351	4	17	336	4
9	386	4	18	295	4
Out	3061	34	In	2705	33
			Totals	5766	67

Visitors may not play before 9.30am, noon-1.30pm Mon-Sat or before 11.15am Sun. Must have an introduction from own club.
Societies must contact in advance.
Green Fees £16 per day; £14 per round (£20 per day; £18 per round weekends & bank holidays).
Facilities ⊗ 🍴 🏌 🍺 (no catering Mon) ♀ 🛄 🏡 ⁅ P De Valle.
Leisure snooker.
Location Bare (N side of town centre on A5105)
Hotel ★★★52% Elms Hotel, Bare, MORECAMBE ☎(0524) 411501 40⇥📞

NELSON   Map 07 SD83

Marsden Park ☎(0282) 67525
Hilly, parkland course open to the wind.
18 holes, 5806yds, Par 70, SSS 68, Course record 66.
Club membership 320.
Visitors must telephone in advance at weekends.
Societies may not play on Sat. Must contact in writing.
Green Fees £6.20 per day (£7.35 weekends & bank holidays).

Facilities 🏌 & 🍺 (weekends or by prior arrangement) ♀ (weekends or by prior arrangement) 🛄 🏡 ⁅ Nick Brown.
Location Nelson Municipal Golf Course, Townhouse Rd (E side of town centre off A56)
Hotel ★★★71% Oaks Hotel, Colne Rd, Reedley, BURNLEY ☎(0282) 414141 58⇥📞

Nelson ☎(0282) 614583
Hilly moorland course, usually windy, with good views. Testing 8th hole, par 4.
18 holes, 5967yds, Par 70, SSS 69, Course record 65.
Club membership 600.
Visitors may not play Thu afternoons & Sat Apr-Oct. Must contact in advance and have an introduction from own club.
Societies must contact in writing.
Green Fees £14 per day (£16 weekends & bank holidays).
Facilities ⊗ (ex Mon) 🍴 🏌 & 🍺 (ex Mon & Fri) ♀ 🛄 🏡 ⁅ Michael J Herbert.
Location King's Causeway, Brierfield (1.5m SE)
Hotel ★★★71% Oaks Hotel, Colne Rd, Reedley, BURNLEY ☎(0282) 414141 58⇥📞

ORMSKIRK   Map 07 SD40

Ormskirk ☎(0695) 72112
A pleasantly secluded, fairly flat, parkland course with much heath and silver birch. Accuracy from the tees will provide an interesting variety of second shots.
18 holes, 6358yds, Par 70, SSS 70.
Club membership 300.
Visitors restricted Sat. Must contact in advance and have an introduction from own club.
Societies must contact in writing.
Green Fees £30 per day; £25 per round (£35 per day; £30 per round Wed, Sat, Sun & bank holidays).
Facilities ⊗ 🍴 🏌 🍺 (no catering Mon) ♀ 🛄 🏡 ⁅ Jack Hammond.
Location Cranes Ln, Lathom (1.5m NE)
Hotel ★★65% Bold Hotel, Lord St, SOUTHPORT ☎(0704) 532578 22rm(15⇥6📞)

PLEASINGTON   Map 07 SD62

Pleasington ☎Blackburn (0254) 202177
Plunging and rising across lovely moorland turf this course tests judgement of distance through the air to greens of widely differing levels. The 11th and 17th are testing holes.
18 holes, 6417yds, Par 71, SSS 71, Course record 64.
Club membership 605.
Visitors may play Mon & Wed-Fri only. Must contact in advance and have an introduction from own club.
Societies must contact in advance.
Green Fees £22.50 (£27.50 weekends & bank holidays).
Facilities ⊗ 🍴 by prior arrangement 🏌 🍺 ♀ 🛄 🏡 ⁅ G J Furey.
Location W side of village
Hotel ★★★60% Blackburn Moat House, Preston New Rd, BLACKBURN ☎(0254) 264441 98⇥📞

POULTON-LE-FYLDE   Map 07 SD33

Poulton-le-Fylde ☎(0253) 892444
Municipal parkland course, with easy walking.
9 holes, 5958yds, Par 70, SSS 69.
Club membership 200.

Visitors	no restrictions.
Societies	must contact in advance.
Green Fees	£4 (£5.50 weekends & bank holidays).
Facilities	⊗ ⓑ ☕ ♀ 🏠 ⚐ ⚑
Leisure	heated indoor swimming pool, snooker.
Location	Breck Rd (N side of town)
Hotel	★★★64% Savoy Hotel, Queens Promenade, North Shore, BLACKPOOL ☎(0253) 52561 147⇨🛏

PRESTON   Map 07 SD52

Ashton & Lea ☎(0772) 726480
Heathland/parkland course with pond and streams, offering
pleasant walks and some testing holes.
18 holes, 6289yds, Par 71, SSS 70, Course record 65.
Club membership 825.

Visitors	must contact in advance.
Societies	Mon, Tue & weekends only. Must contact in writing.
Green Fees	£18 (Mon-Thu); £20 Fri; £24 weekends & bank holidays.
Facilities	⊗ ⓑ ☕ ♀ 🏠 ⚐ ⚑
Leisure	snooker.
Location	Tudor Av, Lea (3m W on A5085)
Hotel	★★★60% Forte Crest Hotel, The Ringway, PRESTON ☎(0772) 59411 126⇨🛏

Fishwick Hall ☎(0772) 798300
Meadowland course overlooking River Ribble. Natural
hazards.
18 holes, 6092yds, Par 70, SSS 69, Course record 66.
Club membership 650.

Visitors	must contact in advance.
Societies	must contact in advance.
Green Fees	£20 per day (£25 weekends & bank holidays).
Facilities	⊗ ⓑ ☕ ♀ 🏠 ⚑ Stuart Bence.
Leisure	snooker.
Location	Glenluce Dr, Farringdon Park
Hotel	★★★60% Forte Crest Hotel, The Ringway, PRESTON ☎(0772) 59411 126⇨🛏

Ingol ☎(0772) 734556
Long, high course with natural water hazards.
18 holes, 6225yds, Par 72, SSS 70, Course record 67.
Club membership 800.

Visitors	may not play on competition days. Must contact in advance.
Societies	must contact in writing.
Green Fees	£16 per day (£22 weekends & bank holidays).
Facilities	⊗ ⓑ (summer) ☕ ♀ 🏠 ⚑ Mark Cartwright.
Leisure	squash, snooker.
Location	Tanterton Hall Rd, Ingol (2m NW junc 32 of M55 off B5411)
Hotel	★★★60% Forte Crest Hotel, The Ringway, PRESTON ☎(0772) 59411 126⇨🛏

Penwortham ☎(0772) 744630
A progressive golf club set
close to the banks of the River
Ribble. The course has tree-
lined fairways, excellent
greens, and provides easy
walking. Testing holes include the 178-yd, par 3 third,
the 480-yd, par 5 sixth, and
the 398-yd par 4 sixteenth.
*18 holes, 5915yds, Par 69, SSS
68, Course record 62.*
Club membership 870.

SCORECARD: White Tees					
Hole	Yds	Par	Hole	Yds	Par
1	389	4	10	443	4
2	328	4	11	350	4
3	178	3	12	135	3
4	398	4	13	307	4
5	361	4	14	524	5
6	480	5	15	148	3
7	315	4	16	398	4
8	396	4	17	437	4
9	157	3	18	171	3
Out	3002	35	In	2913	34
			Totals	5915	69

Visitors	restricted daily after 10am. Must contact in advance.
Societies	Mon & Wed-Fri only. Must contact in advance.
Green Fees	£20 per day (£25 weekends & bank holidays).
Facilities	⊗ ⓑ ⓑ ☕ ♀ 🏠 ⚑ John Wright.
Leisure	snooker.
Location	Blundell Ln, Penwortham (W side of town centre off A59)
Hotel	★★★66% Tickled Trout, Preston New Rd, Samlesbury, PRESTON ☎(0772) 877671 72⇨🛏

Preston ☎(0772) 794234
Pleasant inland golf at this course set in very agreeable
parkland. There is a well-balanced selection of holes,
undulating amongst groups of trees, and not requiring great
length.
18 holes, 6233yds, Par 71, SSS 70, Course record 65.
Club membership 600.

Visitors	may play midweek only. Must contact in advance and have an introduction from own club.
Societies	must contact in writing.
Green Fees	£20.50 per day; £17.50 per round.
Facilities	⊗ & ⓑ by prior arrangement ⓑ ☕ ♀ 🏠 ⚑ P A Wells.
Leisure	snooker.
Location	Fulwood Hall Ln, Fulwood (N side of town centre)
Hotel	★★★68% Broughton Park Hotel & Country Club, Garstang Rd, Broughton, PRESTON ☎(0772) 864087 98⇨🛏

RISHTON   Map 07 SD73

Rishton ☎Great Harwood (0254) 884442
Undulating moorland course.
*Rishton Golf Club: 9 holes, 6199yds, Par 70, SSS 69, Course
record 65.*
Club membership 250.

Visitors	must play with member on weekends and bank holidays.
Societies	must contact in advance.
Green Fees	£10 per round.
Facilities	⊗ & ⓑ by prior arrangement ⓑ (evenings only) ☕ ♀ 🏠
Location	Eachill Links, Hawthorn Dr (S side of town off A678)
Hotel	★★★64% Dunkenhalgh Hotel, Blackburn Rd, Clayton le Moors, ACCRINGTON ☎(0254) 398021 29⇨🛏 Annexe51⇨🛏

SCORE CARD: Old Course					
Hole	Yds	Par	Hole	Yds	Par
1	370	4	10	318	4
2	411	4	11	172	3
3	352	4	12	316	4
4	419	4	13	398	4
5	514	5	14	523	5
6	374	4	15	401	4
7	359	4	16	351	4
8	166	3	17	461	4
9	307	4	18	354	4
Out	3272	36	In	3294	36
			Totals	6566	72

LYTHAM ST ANNES   Map07SD32

Royal Lytham & St Annes ☎ (0253) 724206

John Ingham writes: Venue for many Open Championships, the most famous winner here was amateur Bobby Jones who, in 1926, put together a four-round total of 291 using wooden clubs and the old-fashioned ball. In the last round, when level with Al Watrous with two to play, Jones bunkered his teeshot at the 17th while Watrous hit a perfect drive and then a fine second onto the green. Jones climbed into the bunker, decided a 175-yard shot was needed if he had any chance, and hit a club similar to today's 4-iron. The shot was brilliant and finished, not only on the green, but nearer than his rival. Shaken, Watrous 3-putted, Jones got his four and finished with a perfect par while Watrous, rattled, had taken six. The club placed a plaque by the famous bunker and it's there, to this day.

Since that time the course, which runs close to the railway but slightly inland from the sea, has staged other historic Opens. Bob Charles of New Zealand, became the only left-hander to win the title while Tony Jacklin, in 1969, signalled the re-awakening of British golf by winning.

This huge links, not far from Blackpool, is not easy. When the wind gets up it can be a nightmare. And not everyone approves a championship course that starts with a par 3 hole and it is, in fact, a rare thing in Britain. Some object to the close proximity of red-bricked houses, and aren't keen on trains that rattle passed. But it's a test full of history and must be played.

18 holes, 6673 yds, Par 71, SSS 73, Course record 65 (Seve Ballesteros).

Visitors	weekdays only. Must contact in advance, and have a letter of introduction from their own club along with a handicap certificate
Societies	must apply to Secretary
Green fees	£55 per day; £40 per round
Facilities	⊗ ☷ (by arrangement) ⚑ ⬤ ♀ 🍴 △ ⛿ ┌ (E.Birchenough).
Leisure	snooker
Location	Links Gate (0.5m E of St Annes town)

SILVERDALE   Map 07 SD47

Silverdale ☎(0524) 701300
Difficult heathland course with rock outcrops. Excellent views.
9 holes, 5288yds, Par 70, SSS 67, Course record 66.
Club membership 500.

Visitors	may only play on Sun in summer if accompanied by a member.
Societies	must contact in writing.
Green Fees	£10 per day (£15 weekends).
Facilities	♀ (weekends) △
Location	Red Bridge Ln (opposite Silverdale Station)
Hotel	★62% Wheatsheaf Hotel, BEETHAM ☎(05395) 62123 6⇨🐾

UPHOLLAND   Map 07 SD50

Beacon Park ☎(0695) 622700
Undulating/hilly parkland course, designed by Donald Steel, with magnificent views of the Welsh hills and Blackpool Tower. Twenty-four-bay floodlit driving range.
18 holes, 5997yds, Par 72, SSS 69, Course record 68.
Club membership 300.

Visitors	must contact in advance.
Societies	must contact by phone at least 6 days in advance.
Green Fees	£3.90 per day (£5.50 weekends).
Facilities	⊗ ∭ ⅃ 🍺 ♀ △ 🏠 🐾 (Ray Peters.
Leisure	orienteering park.
Location	Beacon Ln (S of Ashurst Beacon Hill)
Hotel	★★66% Holland Hall Hotel, 6 Lafford Ln, UPHOLLAND ☎(0695) 624426 29⇨🐾 Annexe5⇨🐾

Dean Wood ☎(0695) 622219
This parkland course has a varied terrain - flat front nine, undulating back nine. Beware the par 4, 11th and 17th holes, which has ruined many a card. If there were a prize for the best maintained course in Lancashire, Dean Wood would be a strong contender.
18 holes, 6137yds, Par 71, SSS 70, Course record 66.
Club membership 850.

SCORECARD: White Tees					
Hole	Yds	Par	Hole	Yds	Par
1	367	4	10	157	3
2	389	4	11	398	4
3	335	4	12	343	4
4	157	3	13	358	4
5	368	4	14	371	4
6	338	4	15	206	3
7	514	5	16	192	3
8	522	5	17	279	4
9	337	4	18	506	5
Out	3327	37	In	2810	34
			Totals	6137	71

Visitors	restricted weekends, bank holidays & competition days. Must contact in advance.
Societies	must contact in writing.
Green Fees	£21 per day (£25 weekends & bank holidays).
Facilities	⊗ ∭ ⅃ 🍺 ♀ △ 🏠 (Tony Coop.
Leisure	snooker.
Location	Lafford Ln (.5m NE off A577)
Hotel	★★66% Holland Hall Hotel, 6 Lafford Ln, UPHOLLAND ☎(0695) 624426 29⇨🐾 Annexe5⇨🐾

For a full list of golf courses included in the book, see the index at the end of the directory

WHALLEY   Map 07 SD73

Whalley ☎(0254) 822236
Parkland course on Pendle Hill, overlooking the Ribble Valley. Superb views. Ninth hole over pond.
9 holes, 5444mtrs, Par 70, SSS 69, Course record 67.
Club membership 325.

Visitors	restricted Thu 12.30-4pm & Sat Apr-Sep
Societies	must give 4 weeks notice Apr-Sep.
Green Fees	£12 per day (£20 weekends).
Facilities	⊗ ∭ ⅃ 🍺 ♀ △ 🏠 🐾 (H Smith.
Location	Long Leese Barn, Portfield Ln (1m SE off A671)
Hotel	★★★60% Blackburn Moat House, Preston New Rd, BLACKBURN ☎(0254) 264441 98⇨🐾

WHITWORTH   Map 07 SD81

Lobden ☎Rochdale (0706) 343228
Moorland course, with hard walking. Windy.
9 holes, 5750yds, Par 70, SSS 68, Course record 63.
Club membership 200.

Visitors	may not play Tue 3pm-7pm, Wed after 4pm or Sat.
Societies	must contact in writing.
Green Fees	£5 per day (£9 weekends & bank holidays).
Facilities	🍺 (ex Fri) ♀ (ex Fri) △
Leisure	snooker.
Location	Lobden Moor (E side of town centre off A671)
Hotel	★★61% Midway Hotel, Manchester Rd, Castleton, ROCHDALE ☎(0706) 32881 24⇨🐾

WILPSHIRE   Map 07 SD63

Wilpshire ☎Blackburn (0254) 248260
Semi-moorland course. Testing 17th hole (229 yds) par 3. Extensive views of Ribble Valley, the coast and the Yorkshire Dales.
18 holes, 5921yds, Par 69, SSS 68, Course record 64.
Club membership 794.

Visitors	may not play on competition days. Must contact in advance and have an introduction from own club.
Societies	must contact in writing.
Green Fees	not confirmed.
Facilities	⊗ ∭ ⅃ 🍺 ♀ △ 🏠 (W Slaven.
Leisure	snooker.
Location	72 Whalley Rd (E side of village off A666)
Hotel	★★★60% Blackburn Moat House, Preston New Rd, BLACKBURN ☎(0254) 264441 98⇨🐾

LEICESTERSHIRE

ASHBY-DE-LA-ZOUCH   Map 08 SK31

Willesley Park ☎(0530) 414596
Undulating heathland and parkland course with quick draining sandy subsoil.
18 holes, 6304yds, Par 70, SSS 70.
Club membership 600.

Visitors	may not play before 9.30am on weekends & bank holidays. Must contact in advance and have an introduction from own club.
Societies	telephone to book, up to a year in advance.
Green Fees	£25 per day (£30 weekends & bank holidays).
Facilities	⊗ (ex Mon) 🍴 🏌 🛒 ♀ ⚒ 🏠 (C J Hancock.
Leisure	snooker.
Location	Measham Rd (SW side of town centre on A453)
Hotel	★★★57% Royal Osprey Hotel, Station Rd, ASHBY-DE-LA-ZOUCH ☎(0530) 412833 31⇆🐾

BIRSTALL
Map 04 SK40

Birstall ☎Leicester (0533) 674322
Parkland course with trees, shrubs, ponds and ditches.
18 holes, 6203yds, Par 70, SSS 70.
Club membership 500.

Visitors	with member only Tue & weekends.
Societies	apply in writing.
Green Fees	£20 per day.
Facilities	⚒ 🏠 (D R Clarke.
Leisure	snooker, practise ground.
Location	Station Rd (SW side of town centre off A6)
Hotel	★★★60% Hotel Saint James, Abbey St, LEICESTER ☎(0533) 510666 72⇆🐾

BOTCHESTON
Map 04 SK40

Leicestershire Forest Golf Centre ☎Hinckley (0455) 824800
Parkland course with many trees, four par 4s, but no steep gradients.
18 holes, 6111yds, Par 72, SSS 69, Course record 76.
Club membership 450.

Visitors	must contact in advance for weekends.
Societies	must telephone in advance.
Green Fees	£8 (£12 weekends).
Facilities	⊗ 🍴 🏌 🛒 ♀ ⚒ 🏠 ⛳ (Martin Wing.
Location	Markfield Ln
Hotel	★★★71% Field Head Hotel, Markfield Ln, MARKFIELD ☎(0530) 245454 28⇆🐾

COSBY
Map 04 SP59

Cosby ☎Leicester (0533) 864759
Undulating parkland course.
18 holes, 6277yds, Par 71, SSS 70, Course record 65.
Club membership 680.

Visitors	before 4pm & with member only weekends & bank holidays. Must contact in advance and have an introduction from own club.
Societies	book with secretary.
Green Fees	£20 per day; £18 per round.
Facilities	⊗ 🍴 🏌 🛒 by prior arrangement (no catering Mon) ♀ ⚒ 🏠 (David Bowring.
Leisure	snooker.
Location	Chapel Ln, Broughton Rd (S side of village off)
Hotel	★★★56% Forte Posthouse, Braunstone Ln East, LEICESTER ☎(0533) 630500 172⇆

If you know of a golf course which welcomes visitors and is not already in this guide, we should be grateful for information

GREETHAM
Map 08 SK91

Greetham Valley ☎Empingham (078086) 666
Set in 200 acres, including mature woodland and water hazards, Greetham Valley comprises an 18-hole course and clubhouse (both opening April 1992), a 9-hole Par 3 and a 16-bay floodlit driving range.
18 holes, 6656yds, Par 72.
Club membership 650.

Visitors	must contact in advance.
Societies	apply in writing.
Green Fees	£15 per round (£20 weekends).
Facilities	⊗ 🍴 🏌 🛒 ♀ ⚒ 🏠 ⛳ (Mark Cunningham.
Location	Off B668 in Greetham
Hotel	★★68% Ram Jam Inn, Great North Rd, STRETTON ☎(0780) 410776 Annexe8⇆

HINCKLEY
Map 04 SP49

Hinckley ☎(0455) 615124
Rolling parkland with lake features, and lined fairways.
18 holes, 6592yds, Par 71, SSS 71.
Club membership 1000.

Visitors	with member only weekends. Must contact in advance and have an introduction from own club.
Societies	apply by letter.
Green Fees	£23.50 per day; £18.50 per round.
Facilities	⊗ 🍴 🏌 (ex Sun) 🛒 ♀ ⚒ 🏠 (Richard Jones.
Leisure	snooker.
Location	Leicester Rd (1.5m NE on A47)
Hotel	Longshoot Toby Hotel, Watling St, NUNEATON ☎(0203) 329711 Annexe47⇆🐾

KETTON
Map 04 SK90

Luffenham Heath ☎Stamford (0780) 720205
This undulating heathland course with low bushes, much gorse and many trees, lies in a conservation area for flora and fauna. From the higher part of the course there is a magnificent view across the Chater Valley.
18 holes, 6250yds, Par 70, SSS 70, Course record 64.
Club membership 555.

Visitors	handicap certificate required. Must contact in advance and have an introduction from own club.
Societies	must telephone in advance
Green Fees	£30 per day (£34 weekend & bank holiday).
Facilities	⊗ by prior arrangement 🍴 by prior arrangement 🏌 🛒 ♀ ⚒ 🏠 (J A Lawrence.
Location	Stamford (1.5m SW on A6121)
Hotel	★★★75% George of Stamford Hotel, St Martins, STAMFORD ☎(0780) 55171 47⇆🐾

KIBWORTH
Map 04 SP69

Kibworth ☎(0533) 792301
Parkland course with easy walking. A brook affects a number of fairways
18 holes, 6282yds, Par 71, SSS 70, Course record 64.
Club membership 700.

Visitors	a handicap certificate is required. With member only weekends.

▶

Societies	must contact in advance.
Green Fees	£20 per day.
Facilities	⊗ ⅲ ᕍ 🍴 ♀ 🏔 🏠 ⚐ ⚒ Alan Strange.
Leisure	snooker.
Location	Weir Rd, Beauchamp (S side of village)
Hotel	★★★61% Three Swans Hotel, 21 High St, MARKET HARBOROUGH ☎(0858) 466644 21⇨🐾 Annexe16⇨🐾

KIRBY MUXLOE — Map 04 SK 50

Kirby Muxloe ☎Leicester (0533) 393457
Parkland course.
18 holes, 6303yds, Par 71, SSS 70.
Club membership 700.

Visitors	restricted at weekends. Must contact in advance and have an introduction from own club.
Societies	must telephone in advance.
Green Fees	not confirmed.
Facilities	⊗ (Mon-Fri) ⅲ ᕍ 🍴 ♀ 🏔 🏠 ⚒ R T Stephenson.
Leisure	snooker.
Location	Station Rd (S side of village off B5380)
Hotel	★★★★60% Holiday Inn, St Nicholas Circle, LEICESTER ☎(0533) 531161 188⇨🐾

LEICESTER — Map 04 SK 50

Humberstone Heights ☎(0533) 764674
Municipal parkland course with 9 hole pitch and putt.
18 holes, 6300yds, Par 70, SSS 71, Course record 67.
Club membership 500.

Visitors	no restrictions.
Societies	must telephone in advance.
Green Fees	not confirmed.
Facilities	⊗ by prior arrangement ⅲ by prior arrangement ᕍ 🍴 ♀ (ex Mon) 🏔 🏠 ⚐ ⚒ Philip Highfield.
Location	Gypsy Ln (2.5m NE of city centre)
Hotel	★★★60% Park International Hotel, Humberstone Rd, LEICESTER ☎(0533) 620471 220⇨🐾

Leicestershire ☎(0533) 738825
Pleasantly undulating parkland course.
18 holes, 6312yds, Par 68, SSS 70, Course record 63.
Club membership 750.

Visitors	must contact in advance and have an introduction from own club.
Societies	must telephone in advance.
Green Fees	£25 per day (£30 weekends).
Facilities	⊗ & ⅲ by prior arrangement ᕍ 🍴 ♀ 🏔 🏠 ⚒ John R Turnbull.
Location	Evington Ln (2m E of city off A6030)
Hotel	★★★65% Leicestershire Moat House, Wigston Rd, Oadby, LEICESTER ☎(0533) 719441 57⇨🐾

Western ☎(0533) 872339
Pleasant, undulating parkland course with open aspect fairways in two loops of nine holes. Driving range planned for June 1992.
18 holes, 6561yds, Par 72, SSS 71, Course record 68.
Club membership 400.

Visitors	must book for weekends.
Societies	must contact in advance.

Green Fees	£5.30 per round (£6.50 weekends).
Facilities	⊗ ⅲ ᕍ 🍴 ♀ 🏔 🏠 ⚐ ⚒ Bruce Nicholas Whipham.
Location	Scudamore Rd, Braunstone Frith (1.5m W of city centre off A47)
Hotel	★★★56% Forte Posthouse, Braunstone Ln East, LEICESTER ☎(0533) 630500 172⇨🐾

LOUGHBOROUGH — Map 08 SK 51

Longcliffe ☎(0509) 239129
A re-designed course of natural heathland with outcrops of granite forming natural hazards especially on the 1st and 15th. The course is heavily wooded and has much bracken and gorse. There are a number of tight fairways and one blind hole.
18 holes, 6551yds, Par 71, SSS 72, Course record 68.
Club membership 600.

SCORECARD: White Tees					
Hole	Yds	Par	Hole	Yds	Par
1	179	3	10	367	4
2	390	4	11	331	4
3	381	4	12	487	4
4	461	5	13	405	4
5	139	3	14	315	4
6	273	4	15	167	3
7	463	4	16	378	4
8	565	5	17	495	5
9	417	4	18	338	4
Out	3268	36	In	3283	36
			Totals	6551	72

Visitors	with member only at weekends. Must contact in advance and have an introduction from own club.
Societies	by prior arrangement.
Green Fees	£25 per day; £20 per round.
Facilities	⊗ ⅲ ᕍ 🍴 ♀ 🏔 🏠 ⚒ Ian Bailey.
Location	Snell's Nook Ln, Nanpantan (3m SW off B5350)
Hotel	★★★60% King's Head Hotel, High St, LOUGHBOROUGH ☎(0509) 233222 78⇨🐾

LUTTERWORTH — Map 04 SP 58

Lutterworth ☎(0455) 552532
Hilly course with River Swift running through.
18 holes, 5570yds, Par 67, SSS 67.
Club membership 600.

Visitors	may not play at weekends.
Societies	Mon-Fri; must contact in advance.
Green Fees	not confirmed.
Facilities	⊗ ⅲ ᕍ 🍴 ♀ 🏔 🏠 ⚒ Nick Melvin.
Location	Rugby Rd (.5m S on A426)
Hotel	★★★69% Denbigh Arms Hotel, High St, LUTTERWORTH ☎(0455) 553537 34⇨🐾

MARKET HARBOROUGH — Map 04 SP 78

Market Harborough ☎(0858) 463684
A parkland course situated close to the town. There are wide-ranging views over the surrounding countryside.
9 holes, 6080yds, Par 71, SSS 69, Course record 67.
Club membership 330.

Visitors	must play with member at weekends.
Societies	must telephone (0536) 771771 in advance.
Green Fees	not confirmed.
Facilities	⊗ ⅲ ᕍ 🍴 (no catering Mon) ♀ 🏔 🏠 ⚐ ⚒ Frazer Baxter.
Location	Oxendon Rd (1m S on A508)
Hotel	★★★61% Three Swans Hotel, 21 High St, MARKET HARBOROUGH ☎(0858) 466644 21⇨🐾 Annexe16⇨🐾

MELTON MOWBRAY   Map 08 SK71

Melton Mowbray ☎(0664) 62118
Downland but flat course providing easy walking. Open to
the wind.
18 holes, 5792yds, Par 70, SSS 70.
Club membership 447.
Visitors	no restrictions.
Societies	must contact in advance.
Green Fees	not confirmed.
Facilities	⬤ ♀ ⌂
Location	Thorpe Arnold (2m NE on A607)
Hotel	★★62% Sysonby Knoll Hotel, Asfordby Rd, MELTON MOWBRAY ☎(0664) 63563 24rm(19⇨3🐾)Annexe1⇨

OADBY   Map 04 SK60

Oadby ☎(0533) 700326
Municipal parkland course.
18 holes, 6228yds, Par 71, SSS 69.
Club membership 400.
Visitors	no restrictions.
Societies	must contact in advance.
Green Fees	not confirmed.
Facilities	♀ ⌂ 🏠 ⛽ (
Location	Leicester Rd (West side of town centre off A6)
Hotel	★★★65% Leicestershire Moat House, Wigston Rd, Oadby, LEICESTER ☎(0533) 719441 57⇨🐾

ROTHLEY   Map 08 SK51

Rothley Park ☎Leicester (0533) 302809
Parkland course in picturesque situation.
18 holes, 6167yds, Par 70, SSS 69, Course record 67.
Club membership 600.
Visitors	restricted Tue, weekends & competitions. Handicap certificate required. Must contact in advance.
Societies	apply in writing.
Green Fees	£37.50 per day; £25 per round.
Facilities	⊗ �🍴 🏠 ⬤ ♀ ⌂ 🏠 (Peter Dolan.
Location	Westfield Ln (.75m W on B5328)
Hotel	★★★71% Rothley Court Hotel, Westfield Ln, ROTHLEY ☎(0533) 374141 15⇨🐾Annexe21⇨🐾

SCRAPTOFT   Map 04 SK60

Scraptoft ☎(0533) 418863
Pleasant, inland country course.
18 holes, 6166yds, Par 69, SSS 69, Course record 66.
Club membership 550.
Visitors	with member only weekends. Must have an introduction from own club.
Societies	apply in writing.
Green Fees	£20.50 per day.
Facilities	⌂ 🏠 (Simon Sherratt.
Location	Beeby Rd (1m NE)
Hotel	★★★65% Leicestershire Moat House, Wigston Rd, Oadby, LEICESTER ☎(0533) 719441 57⇨🐾

ULLESTHORPE   Map 04 SP58

Ullesthorpe ☎Leire (0455) 209023
Parkland course. Many leisure facilities.
18 holes, 6650yds, Par 72, SSS 72.
Club membership 640.
Visitors	may not play weekends. Must contact in advance.
Societies	contact in advance.
Green Fees	£17.50.
Facilities	⊗ ⍨ 🍴 ⬤ ♀ ⌂ 🏠 🏄 (Ian Sadler.
Leisure	hard tennis courts, heated indoor swimming pool, snooker, sauna, solarium, gymnasium.
Location	Frolesworth Rd (.5m N off B577)
Hotel	★★★69% Denbigh Arms Hotel, High St, LUTTERWORTH ☎(0455) 553537 34⇨🐾

WHETSTONE   Map 04 SP59

Whetstone ☎(0533) 861424
Small and very flat parkland course adjacent to motorway.
9 holes, 6212yds, Par 72, SSS 69.
Club membership 70.
Visitors	no restrictions.
Societies	must contact in writing.
Green Fees	not confirmed.
Facilities	♀ ⌂ 🏠 ⛽ (
Location	Cambridge Rd, Cosby (1m S of village)
Hotel	★★★56% Forte Posthouse, Braunstone Ln East, Leicester ☎(0533) 630500 172⇨

WOODHOUSE EAVES   Map 08 SK51

Charnwood Forest ☎Loughborough (0509) 890259
Hilly heathland course with hard walking, but no bunkers.
9 holes, 5960yds, Par 69, SSS 69, Course record 66.
Club membership 325.
Visitors	may be restricted Tue. Must contact in advance and have an introduction from own club.
Societies	apply in writing.
Green Fees	£17.50 for 18 holes; £20.50 for 36 holes.
Facilities	⊗ & ⍨ by prior arrangement 🏠 ⬤ ⌂ 🏠 (Mark Lawrence.
Location	Breakback Ln (.75m NW off B591)
Hotel	★★★60% King's Head Hotel, High St, LOUGHBOROUGH ☎(0509) 233222 78⇨🐾

Lingdale ☎(0509) 890703
Parkland course located in Charnwood Forest with some
hard walking at some holes. The par 3, (3rd) and par 5, (8th)
are testing holes. The 4th and 5th have water hazards.
18 holes, 6556yds, Par 71, SSS 71.
Club membership 550.
Visitors	restricted weekends & competition days. Must contact in advance.
Societies	must contact in writing.
Green Fees	£15 per day (£20 per day weekends).
Facilities	⊗ ⍨ 🏠 ⬤ ♀ ⌂ 🏠 (Peter Sellears.
Leisure	practice ground, pool table.
Location	Joe Moore's Ln (1.5m S off B5330)
Hotel	★★★60% King's Head Hotel, High St, LOUGHBOROUGH ☎(0509) 233222 78⇨🐾

LINCOLNSHIRE

BELTON   Map 08 SK 93

Belton Woods Hotel & Country Club
☎Grantham (0476) 593200
Two challenging 18-hole courses, a 9-hole Par 3 and a driving
range. The Lancaster Course has 13 lakes, while the
Wellington boasts the third longest hole in Europe at 613
yards. Many leisure facilities.
*Lancaster: 18 holes, 7021yds, Par 73, SSS 74, Course record
69.*
Wellington: 18 holes, 6875yds, Par 72, SSS 73.
Spitfire: 9 holes, 1184yds, Par 27.
Club membership 900.

Visitors	no advanced booking permitted.
Societies	advance booking required.
Green Fees	£18 per day; £12 per 18 holes; £5 per 9 holes (£22/ £16/£5 weekends & bank holidays).
Facilities	⊗ ℳ ㎐ ⬤ ♀ ⚎ 🏠 ⛳ 🍴 ⛽ Dean Vannet.
Leisure	hard tennis courts, heated indoor swimming pool, squash, snooker, sauna, solarium, gymnasium.
Location	On A607, 2m N of Grantham
Hotel	★★★★65% Belton Woods Hotel & Country Club, BELTON ☎(0476) 593200 96⇄🛏

BLANKNEY   Map 08 TF06

Blankney ☎Metheringham (0526) 20263
Open parkland course with mature trees; fairly flat.
18 holes, 6378yds, Par 71, SSS 71, Course record 69.
Club membership 689.

Visitors	may not play Sun & winter weekends, restricted Sat. Must contact in advance.
Societies	contact in advance.
Green Fees	£20 per day; £15 per round.
Facilities	⊗ by prior arrangement ℳ by prior arrangement ㎐ ⬤ ♀ ⚎ 🏠 ⛽ Graham Bradley.
Leisure	snooker.
Location	1m SW on B1188
Hotel	★★★54% Moor Lodge Hotel, BRANSTON ☎(0522) 791366 25⇄🛏

BOSTON   Map 08 TF34

Boston ☎(0205) 350589
Parkland course with water hazards in play on ten holes.
18 holes, 5825yds, Par 69, SSS 68, Course record 66.
Club membership 650.

Visitors	welcome except weekend & bank holidays. Must contact in advance.
Societies	apply two weeks in advance.
Green Fees	not confirmed.
Facilities	⊗ ℳ ㎐ ⬤ ♀ ⚎ 🏠 ⛽ Terry Squires.
Location	Cowbridge, Horncastle Rd (2m N off B1183)
Hotel	★★61% New England, 49 Wide Bargate, BOSTON ☎(0205) 365255 25⇄

A golf-course name printed in *bold italics*
means that we have been unable to verify
information with the club's management
for the current year

GAINSBOROUGH   Map 08 SK 88

Gainsborough ☎(0427) 613088
Scenic parkland course. Floodlit driving range.
18 holes, 6620yds, Par 73, SSS 72.
Club membership 600.

Visitors	welcome weekdays. Must contact in advance.
Societies	must telephone in advance.
Green Fees	£24 per day; £18 per round.
Facilities	⊗ ℳ ㎐ ⬤ ♀ ⚎ 🏠 ⛽ Steven Cooper.
Leisure	snooker.
Location	Thonock (1m N off A159)
Hotel	★★65% Hickman-Hill Hotel, Cox's Hill, GAINSBOROUGH ☎(0427) 613639 8rm(3⇄3🛏)

GRANTHAM   Map 08 SK 93

Belton Park ☎(0476) 67399
Parkland course, wooded, with water features, deer park and
Canadian Geese Reserve. Famous holes: 5th, 12th, 16th and
18th. 27-holes, with three 9-hole combinations.
18 holes, 6420yds, Par 71, SSS 71, Course record 65.
Ancaster: 18 holes, 6252yds, Par 70, SSS 70.
Belmont: 18 holes, 6016yds, Par 69, SSS 69.
Club membership 850.

Visitors	no restrictions.
Societies	apply in writing.
Green Fees	£20.50 per day; £15 per round (£30/£25 weekends & bank holidays).
Facilities	⊗ ℳ ㎐ ⬤ ♀ ⚎ 🏠 ⛽ B McKee.
Location	Belton Ln, Londonthorpe Rd (1.5m NE off A607)
Hotel	★★★65% Angel & Royal Hotel, High St, GRANTHAM ☎(0476) 65816 30⇄🛏

HORNCASTLE   Map 08 TF26

Horncastle ☎(0507) 526800
Heathland course with many water hazards and bunkers;
very challenging. There is a 25-bay floodlit driving range.
18 holes, 5782yds, Par 70, SSS 70, Course record 75.
Club membership 300.

Visitors	no restrictions.
Societies	apply in writing.
Green Fees	£15 per day; £10 per round.
Facilities	⊗ ℳ ㎐ ⬤ ♀ ⚎ 🏠 ⛽ E C Wright.
Leisure	fishing.
Location	West Ashby (1.5m N Horncastle)
Hotel	★★★66% Petwood House Hotel, Stixwould Rd, WOODHALL SPA ☎(0526) 52411 46⇄🛏

LINCOLN   Map 08 SK 97

Canwick Park ☎(0522) 522166
Parkland course. Testing 14th hole (par 3).
18 holes, 6237yds, Par 70, SSS 70.
Club membership 576.

Visitors	restricted at weekends. Must contact in advance.
Societies	must contact 1 month in advance.
Green Fees	£8 per day (£12 weekends & bank holidays).
Facilities	⊗ ℳ by prior arrangement (ex Mon) ㎐ ⬤ ♀ ⚎ 🏠 ⛽

| Location | Canwick Park, Washingborough Rd (2m SE on B1190) |
| Hotel | ★★★62% Forte Crest, Eastgate, LINCOLN ☎(0522) 520341 70⇱ |

Carholme ☎(0522) 23725
Parkland course where prevailing west winds can add interest. Good views.
18 holes, 6114yds, Par 71, SSS 69, Course record 63.
Club membership 700.

Visitors	may not play Sat, Sun & bank holidays. Must contact in advance.
Societies	apply in writing.
Green Fees	£20 per say; £14 per round.
Facilities	⊗ ℳ ᒪ ▆ ♀ ⌂ 🏠 ⊤⊦ ⱡ Gary Leslie.
Location	Carholme Rd (1m W of city centre on A57)
Hotel	★★★★62% The White Hart, Bailgate, LINCOLN ☎(0522) 26222 50⇱

LOUTH   Map 08 TF38

Louth ☎(0507) 603681
Undulating parkland course, fine views.
18 holes, 6502yds, Par 71, SSS 71.
Club membership 900.

Visitors	must contact in advance and have an introduction from own club.
Societies	must contact 1 month in advance.
Green Fees	not confirmed.
Facilities	⊗ by prior arrangement ℳ by prior arrangement ᒪ ▆ ♀ ⌂ 🏠 ⊤⊦ ⱡ A Blundell.
Leisure	squash.
Location	Crowtree Ln (SE side of town centre off A157)
Hotel	★★65% Priory Hotel, Eastgate, LOUTH ☎(0507) 602930 12rm(6⇱3♠)

MARKET RASEN   Map 08 TF18

Market Rasen & District ☎(0673) 842416
Picturesque, well-wooded heathland course, easy walking, breezy with becks forming natural hazards. Good views of Lincolnshire Wolds.
18 holes, 6043yds, Par 70, SSS 69, Course record 65.
Club membership 550.

Visitors	must play with member at weekends. Must contact in advance.
Societies	Tue & Fri only; must contact in advance.
Green Fees	not confirmed.
Facilities	⌂ 🏠 ⱡ
Location	Legsby Rd (2m SE)
Hotel	★★★62% Forte Crest, Eastgate, LINCOLN ☎(0522) 520341 70⇱

SKEGNESS   Map 09 TF56

North Shore Hotel & Golf Club ☎(0754) 763298
A half-links, half-parkland course designed by James Braid in 1910. Easy walking and good sea views.
18 holes, 6134yds, Par 71, SSS 69, Course record 71.
Club membership 400.

Visitors	must observe dress rules & must be competent golfers.
Societies	telephone in advance.
Green Fees	£17 per day; £12 per round (£22/£16 weekends).

Facilities	⊗ ℳ ᒪ ▆ ♀ ⌂ 🏠 ⇄ ⱡ John Cornelius.
Leisure	hard tennis courts, snooker.
Location	North Shore Rd (1m N of town centre off A52)
Hotel	★★★58% Crown Hotel, Drummond Rd, Seacroft, SKEGNESS ☎(0754) 610760 27⇱♠

Seacroft ☎(0754) 3020
A typical seaside links with flattish fairways separated by low ridges and good greens. Easy to walk round. To the east are sandhills leading to the shore. Southward lies 'Gibraltar Point Nature Reserve'.
18 holes, 6501yds, Par 71, SSS 71, Course record 67.
Club membership 620.

Visitors	must contact in advance and have an introduction from own club.
Societies	contact in advance.
Green Fees	£25.50 per day; £18.50 per round (£30.50/£25.50 weekends).
Facilities	⊗ ℳ ᒪ ▆ ♀ ⌂
Location	Drummond Rd, Seacroft (S side of town centre)
Hotel	★★★58% Crown Hotel, Drummond Rd, Seacroft, SKEGNESS ☎(0754) 610760 27⇱♠

SLEAFORD   Map 08 TF04

Sleaford ☎South Rauceby (05298) 273
Inland links-type course, moderately wooded and fairly flat.
18 holes, 6443yds, Par 72, SSS 71, Course record 65.
Club membership 650.

Visitors	may not play Sun in winter. Must have an introduction from own club.
Societies	apply in writing.
Green Fees	£16.50 per day (£24.50 weekends & bank holidays).
Facilities	⊗ ℳ by prior arrangement ᒪ ▆ (no catering Mon) ♀ ⌂ 🏠 ⱡ Steve Harrison.
Location	South Rauceby (1m W off A153)
Hotel	★★★65% Angel & Royal Hotel, High St, GRANTHAM ☎(0476) 65816 30⇱♠

SPALDING   Map 08 TF22

Spalding ☎(077585) 386 & 474
A pretty, well-laid-out course in a fenland area. The River Glen runs beside the 1st and 2nd holes, and streams, ponds and new tree plantings add to the variety of this well-maintained course.
18 holes, 5807yds, Par 68, SSS 67, Course record 64.
Club membership 500.

Visitors	must contact in advance and have an introduction from own club.
Societies	must contact in advance.
Green Fees	£20 per day; £14 per round (£22.50/£17.50 weekends).
Facilities	⊗ ℳ ᒪ ▆ ♀ ⌂ 🏠 ⱡ John Spencer.
Location	Surfleet (5m N off A16)
Hotel	★★66% Woodlands Hotel, 80 Pinchbeck Rd, SPALDING ☎(0775) 769933 18⇱♠

We make every effort to ensure that our information is accurate but details may change after we go to print

STAMFORD Map 04 TF00

Burghley Park ☎(0780) 53789
Open parkland course with superb greens, many new trees, ponds and bunkers. Situated in the grounds of Burghley House.
18 holes, 6200yds, Par 70, SSS 70, Course record 64.
Club membership 950.

Visitors	with member only weekends. Handicap certificate required. Must contact in advance and have an introduction from own club.
Societies	apply in writing.
Green Fees	£20 per day.
Facilities	⊗ ⍿ (ex Tue & Sun) ⅃ ♥ ♀ ⌂ 🖻 ⌀ Glenn Davies.
Location	St Martins (1m S of town on B1081)
Hotel	★★★75% George of Stamford Hotel, St Martins, STAMFORD ☎(0780) 55171 47⇨🏠

STOKE ROCHFORD Map 08 SK92

Stoke Rochford ☎Great Ponton (047683) 275
Parkland course designed by C. Turner.
18 holes, 6251yds, Par 70, SSS 70, Course record 65.
Club membership 525.

Visitors	restricted to 9am weekdays, 10.30am weekends & bank holidays. Must contact in advance and have an introduction from own club.
Societies	contact one year in advance.
Green Fees	£20 per day; £14 per round (£30/£23 weekends & bank holidays).
Facilities	⊗ & ⍿ by prior arrangement ⅃ ♥ ♀ ⌂ 🖻 ⌀ Angus Dow.
Leisure	snooker.
Location	Off A1 5m S of Grantham
Hotel	★★63% Kings Hotel, North Pde, GRANTHAM ☎(0476) 590800 22rm(21⇨🏠)

SUTTON BRIDGE Map 09 TF42

Sutton Bridge ☎Holbeach (0406) 350323
Parkland course.
9 holes, 5850yds, Par 70, SSS 68, Course record 62.
Club membership 350.

Visitors	may not play competition days, weekends & bank holidays. Must contact in advance and have an introduction from own club.
Societies	telephone in advance
Green Fees	£15 per day/round.
Facilities	⊗ ⍿ ⅃ ♥ (no catering Mon) ♀ (ex Mon) ⌂ 🖻 ⌀ R Wood.
Location	New Rd (E side of village off A17)
Hotel	★★★64% The Duke's Head, Tuesday Market Pl, KING'S LYNN ☎(0553) 774996 71⇨

SUTTON ON SEA Map 09 TF58

Sandilands ☎(0521) 41432
Flat links course on the sea shore.
18 holes, 5995yds, Par 70, SSS 69, Course record 66.
Club membership 300.

Visitors	no restrictions.
Societies	welcome weekdays only, telephone in advance.

Green Fees	£16 per day; £11 per round (£16 per round weekends & bank holidays).
Facilities	⊗ ⅃ ♥ ♀ ⌂ 🖻 ⌀ ⌀ David Vernon.
Location	1.5m S off A52
Hotel	★★65% Grange & Links Hotel, Sea Ln, Sandilands, MABLETHORPE ☎(0507) 441334 23⇨🏠

TORKSEY Map 08 SK87

Lincoln ☎(042771) 210
A testing inland course with quick-drying sandy subsoil and easy walking.
18 holes, 6438yds, Par 71, SSS 71.
Club membership 700.

Visitors	may not play between 1230-1400 or on weekends & bank holidays. Must contact in advance and have an introduction from own club.
Societies	apply by letter.
Green Fees	£20 per day; £17 per round.
Facilities	⊗ ⍿ ⅃ ♥ (catering by arrangement) ♀ ⌂ 🖻 ⌀ A Carter.
Location	SW side of village
Hotel	★★★★62% The White Hart, Bailgate, LINCOLN ☎(0522) 26222 50⇨

WOODHALL SPA Map 08 TF16

Woodhall Spa
☎(0526) 52511
One of the country's greatest and most beautiful heathland courses, founded in 1905, and originally laid out by Harry Vardon. It provides flat, easy walking amongst heather and tree-lined fairways, and is renowned for its vast bunkers and clubhouse atmosphere.
18 holes, 6907yds, Par 73, SSS 73, Course record 68.
Club membership 500.

SCORECARD					
Hole	Yds	Par	Hole	Yds	Par
1	363	4	10	338	4
2	408	4	11	442	4
3	417	4	12	157	3
4	415	4	13	437	4
5	155	3	14	489	5
6	506	5	15	325	4
7	438	4	16	398	4
8	193	3	17	322	4
9	560	5	18	544	5
Out	3455	36	In	3452	37
			Totals	6907	73

Visitors	must be a member of a golf club affiliated to the appropriate Golf Union, maximum handicap gentlemen 20-ladies 30, handicap certificate must be produced. Must contact in advance and have an introduction from own club.
Societies	must book in advance.
Green Fees	£28 per day; £21 per round (£31/£23 weekends & bank holidays).
Facilities	⊗ ⍿ ⅃ ♥ ♀ ⌂ 🖻 ⌀ P D Fixter.
Location	The Broadway (NE side of village off B1191)
Hotel	★★★70% Fownes Hotel, City Walls Rd, WORCESTER ☎(0905) 613151 61⇨🏠

For an explanation of symbols and abbreviations, see page 32

LONDON

Courses within the London Postal District area (ie those that have London Postcodes - W1, SW1 etc) are listed here in postal district order commencing East then North, South and West. Courses outside the London Postal area, but within Greater London are to be found listed under the county of **Greater London** in the gazetteer (see page 93).

E4 CHINGFORD

Royal Epping Forest ☎081-529 2195
Woodland course. 'Red' garments must be worn.
18 holes, 6620yds, Par 72, SSS 70, Course record 65.
Club membership 495.

Visitors	no restrictions.
Green Fees	not confirmed.
Facilities	⏃ 🏠 ⸾ R Gowers.
Location	Forest Approach, Chingford (300 yds S of Chingford Station)
Hotel	★★★68% Woodford Moat House, Oak Hill, WOODFORD GREEN ☎081-505 4511 99⇨🟆

West Essex ☎081-529 7558
Testing parkland course within Epping Forest. Notable holes are 8th (par 4), 16th (par 4), 18th (par 5).
18 holes, 6289yds, Par 71, SSS 70, Course record 65.
Club membership 645.

Visitors	may not play on Tue morning, Thu afternoon & weekends. Must contact in advance and have an introduction from own club.
Societies	must contact in advance.
Green Fees	£35 per day; £28 per round.
Facilities	⊗ ⅷ ⺊ ⬤ ⵛ ⏃ 🏠 ⸾ Charles Cox.
Leisure	snooker.
Location	Bury Rd, Sewardstonebury (off N Circular Rd at Chingford on M25)
Hotel	★★59% Roebuck Hotel, North End, BUCKHURST HILL ☎081-505 4636 29⇨🟆

E11 LEYTONSTONE

Wanstead ☎081-989 3938
A flat, picturesque parkland course with many trees and shrubs and providing easy walking. The par 3, 16th, involves driving across a lake.
18 holes, 6109yds, Par 69, SSS 69, Course record 61.
Club membership 500.

Visitors	may only play Mon, Tue & Fri. Must contact in advance.
Societies	by arrangement.
Green Fees	£25 per day.
Facilities	⊗ ⅷ ⬤ ⵛ ⏃ 🏠 ⸾ Gary Jacom.
Leisure	fishing.
Location	Overton Dr, Wanstead (from central London A11 NE to Wanstead)
Hotel	★★★68% Woodford Moat House, Oak Hill, WOODFORD GREEN ☎081-505 4511 99⇨🟆

N2 EAST FINCHLEY

Hampstead ☎081-455 0203
Undulating parkland course.
9 holes, 5812yds, Par 68, SSS 68, Course record 65.
Club membership 500.

Visitors	a handicap certificate is required. Must contact in advance.
Societies	apply in writing.
Green Fees	£23 per 18 holes; £28 per day (£30 per 18 holes at weekends).
Facilities	⊗ by prior arrangement ⺊ ⬤ ⵛ ⏃ 🏠 ⸾ Peter Brown.
Location	Winnington Rd
Hotel	★★★64% Forte Posthouse, Haverstock Hill, LONDON ☎071-794 8121 138⇨🟆

N6 HIGHGATE

Highgate ☎081-340 1906
Parkland course.
18 holes, 5985yds, Par 69, SSS 69, Course record 66.
Club membership 705.

Visitors	may not play Wed & weekends.
Societies	by arrangement.
Green Fees	not confirmed.
Facilities	⊗ by prior arrangement ⺊ ⬤ ⵛ ⏃ 🏠 ⸾ Robin Turner.
Location	Denewood Rd
Hotel	★★★★65% Holiday Inn Swiss Cottage, 128 King Henry's Rd, Swiss Cottage, LONDON ☎071-722 7711 303⇨🟆

N9 LOWER EDMONTON

Picketts Lock ☎081-803 3611
Tricky municipal parkland course with some narrow fairways and the River Lea providing a natural hazard.
9 holes, 2400yds, Par 32, SSS 32.

Visitors	no restrictions.
Green Fees	not confirmed.
Facilities	⺊ ⬤ (lunchtime) ⵛ (lunchtime) ⏃ 🏠 ⅷ ⸾ R Gerken.
Leisure	heated indoor swimming pool, squash, snooker, sauna, solarium, gymnasium.
Location	Picketts Lock Sports Centre, Edmonton
Hotel	★★56% Holtwhites Hotel, 92 Chase Side, ENFIELD ☎081-363 0124 30rm(28⇨🟆)

N14 SOUTHGATE

Trent Park ☎081-366 7432
Parkland course set in 150 acres of green belt area. Seven holes played across Merryhills brook. Testing holes are 2nd (423 yds) over brook, 190 yds from the tee, and up to plateau green; 7th (463 yds) dog-leg, over brook, par 4.
18 holes, 6008yds, Par 69, SSS 69, Course record 64.
Club membership 950.

Visitors	restricted at weekends. Must contact in advance.
Societies	must contact in advance.
Green Fees	not confirmed.
Facilities	⺊ ⬤ ⵛ ⏃ 🏠 ⸾ Craig Easton.
Location	Bramley Rd, Southgate
Hotel	★★★★60% West Lodge Park Hotel, Cockfosters Rd, HADLEY WOOD ☎081-440 8311 48⇨🟆 Annexe2⇨🟆

N20 WHETSTONE

North Middlesex ☎081-445 1604
Short parkland course renowned for its tricky greens.
18 holes, 5625yds, Par 69, SSS 66, Course record 65.
Club membership 600.

Visitors	are advised to have handicap certificate. Must contact in advance.
Societies	must telephone in advance.
Green Fees	£27.50 per day; £22 per round.
Facilities	⊗ ⅲ ⅖ ⬛ ♀ 🛆 🏠 (Steve Roberts.
Location	The Manor House, Friern Barnet Ln, Whetstone
Hotel	★★★63% Edgwarebury Hotel, Barnet Ln, ELSTREE ☎081-953 8227 50➪ 🐾

South Herts ☎081-445 2035
An open undulating parkland course officially in Hertfordshire, but now in a London postal area. It is, perhaps, most famous for the fact that two of the greatest of all British professionals, Harry Vardon and Dai Rees, CBE were professionals at the club. The course is testing, over rolling fairways, especially in the prevailing south-west wind.
18 holes, 6432yds, Par 72, SSS 71, Course record 66.
Club membership 830.

Visitors	must have handicap certificate. Must contact in advance.
Societies	Wed-Fri only, must apply in writing.
Green Fees	£30 per day; £25 per round.
Facilities	⊗ ⅖ ⬛ ♀ 🛆 🏠 🟟 (Richard Livingston.
Location	Links Dr, Totteridge
Hotel	★★★64% Forte Posthouse, Bignells Corner, SOUTH MIMMS ☎(0707) 43311 120➪ 🐾

N21 WINCHMORE

Bush Hill Park ☎081-360 5738
Pleasant parkland course surrounded by trees.
18 holes, 5809yds, Par 70, SSS 68.
Club membership 700.

Visitors	may not play at weekends & bank holidays. Must contact in advance and have an introduction from own club.
Societies	by arrangement.
Green Fees	£30 per day; £25 per round.
Facilities	⊗ & ⅲ by prior arrangement ⅖ ⬛ ♀ (ex Sun) 🛆 🏠 (George Low.
Location	Bush Hill, Winchmore Hill
Hotel	★★56% Holtwhites Hotel, 92 Chase Side, ENFIELD ☎081-363 0124 30rm(28➪ 🐾)

N22 WOOD GREEN

Muswell Hill ☎081-888 1764
Narrow parkland course.
18 holes, 6474yds, Par 71, SSS 71, Course record 67.
Club membership 500.

Visitors	restricted Tue morning, weekends & bank holidays. Must contact in advance.
Societies	by arrangement.

Green Fees £33 per day; £23 per round (£35 weekends & bank holidays.

Facilities	⊗ ⅲ ⅖ ⬛ ♀ 🛆 🏠
Location	Rhodes Av, Wood Green (off N Circular Rd at Bounds Green)
Hotel	★★56% Holtwhites Hotel, 92 Chase Side, ENFIELD ☎081-363 0124 30rm(28➪ 🐾)

NW7 MILL HILL

Finchley ☎081-346 2436
Easy walking on wooded parkland course.
18 holes, 6411yds, Par 72, SSS 71, Course record 65.
Club membership 500.

Visitors	can play most weekdays and after mid-day at weekends. Must contact in advance.
Societies	must apply by telephone.
Green Fees	£31 per day (£35 weekends); £26 per round.
Facilities	⊗ ⅲ ⅖ ⬛ by prior arrangement ♀ 🛆 🏠 🟟 (David Brown.
Location	Nether Court, Frith Ln, Mill Hill (Near Mill Hill East Tube Station)
Hotel	★★★63% Edgwarebury Hotel, Barnet Ln, ELSTREE ☎081-953 8227 50➪ 🐾

Hendon ☎081-346 6023
Easy walking, parkland course with a good variety of trees, and providing testing golf.
18 holes, 6266yds, Par 70, SSS 70.
Club membership 525.

Visitors	restricted weekends & bank holidays. Must contact in advance.
Societies	must contact in advance.
Green Fees	On application.
Facilities	⊗ ⬛ (pm) ♀ 🛆 🏠 🟟 (Stuart Murray.
Location	Sanders Ln, Mill Hill
Hotel	★★★63% Edgwarebury Hotel, Barnet Ln, ELSTREE ☎081-953 8227 50➪ 🐾

Mill Hill ☎081-959 2339
Undulating parkland course with all holes separated by good tree and shrub cover.
18 holes, 6247yds, Par 69, SSS 70, Course record 65.
Club membership 550.

Visitors	restricted weekends & bank holidays. Must contact in advance.
Societies	must contact in advance.
Green Fees	£30 per day; £23 per round (£40 weekends & bank holidays.
Facilities	⊗ ⅲ by prior arrangement ⅖ ⬛ ♀ 🛆 🏠 🟟 (Alex Daniel.
Leisure	snooker.
Location	100 Barnet Way, Mill Hill (On A1 S bound carriageway)
Hotel	★★★63% Edgwarebury Hotel, Barnet Ln, ELSTREE ☎081-953 8227 50➪ 🐾

SE9 ELTHAM

Eltham Warren ☎081-850 1166
Parkland course running alongside the A210 on one side and Eltham Park on the other.
9 holes, 5840yds, Par 69, SSS 68, Course record 66.
Club membership 450.

Visitors	may not play at weekends. Must contact in advance and have an introduction from own club.
Societies	must telephone in advance.
Green Fees	£25 per day.
Facilities	⊗ ⅷ 🏌 💺 ♀ 🍴 🏠 ſ Ian Coleman.
Leisure	snooker.
Location	Bexley Rd, Eltham
Hotel	★★★58% Bromley Court Hotel, Bromley Hill, BROMLEY ☎081-464 5011 122⇨🛏

Royal Blackheath ☎081-850 1795

A pleasant, parkland course of great character as befits the antiquity of the Club; the clubhouse dates from the 17th century. Many great trees survive and there are two ponds. The 18th requires a pitch to the green over a thick clipped hedge, which also crosses the front of the 1st tee.

18 holes, 6209yds, Par 70, SSS 70, Course record 66.

Club membership 750.

	SCORECARD				
Hole	Yds	Par	Hole	Yds	Par
1	472	4	10	347	4
2	391	4	11	377	4
3	428	4	12	173	3
4	197	3	13	518	5
5	360	4	14	382	4
6	476	5	15	349	4
7	379	4	16	164	3
8	158	3	17	397	4
9	365	4	18	276	4
Out	3226	35	In	2983	35
			Totals	6209	70

Visitors	may play mid-week only, handicap certificate is required. Must contact in advance and have an introduction from own club.
Societies	mid-week only, must apply in writing.
Green Fees	£36 per day; £26 per round.
Facilities	⊗ (ex Mon) 🏌 💺 ♀ 🍴 🏠 ſ I McGregor.
Location	Court Rd
Hotel	★★★58% Bromley Court Hotel, Bromley Hill, BROMLEY ☎081-464 5011 122⇨🛏

SE18 WOOLWICH

Shooters Hill ☎081-854 6368

Hilly and wooded parkland course with good views and natural hazards.

18 holes, 5736 yds, Par 69, SSS 68, Course record 62.

Club membership 960.

Visitors	must have handicap certificate. Must have an introduction from own club.
Societies	Tue & Thu only, by arrangement.
Green Fees	£27 per day; £22 per round.
Facilities	⊗ ⅷ 🏌 💺 ♀ 🍴 🏠 ſ Michael Ridge.
Location	Eaglesfield Rd, Shooters Hill (Shooters Hill Rd from Blackheath)
Hotel	★★★71% Forte Crest Hotel, Black Prince Interchange, Southwold Rd, BEXLEY ☎(0322) 526900 102⇨🛏

SE21 DULWICH

Dulwich & Sydenham Hill ☎081-693 3961

Parkland course overlooking London. Hilly with narrow fairways.

18 holes, 6192yds, Par 69, SSS 69.

Club membership 850.

Visitors	with member only weekends. Must have an introduction from own club.
Societies	must telephone in advance.
Green Fees	not confirmed.

Facilities	⊗ (ex WE) ⅷ by prior arrangement 🏌 💺 ♀ 🍴 🏠 ſ David Baillie.
Location	Grange Ln, College Rd
Hotel	★★★58% Bromley Court Hotel, Bromley Hill, BROMLEY ☎081-464 5011 122⇨🛏

SE22 EAST DULWICH

Aquarius ☎081-693 1626

Course laid-out on two levels around and over covered reservoir; hazards include vents and bollards.

9 holes, 5213yds, Par 66, SSS 65, Course record 62.

Club membership 440.

Visitors	must be accompanied by member and have an introduction from own club.
Green Fees	£10 per day.
Facilities	⊗ ⅷ 🏌 💺 ♀ 🍴 🏠 ſ Frederick Private.
Location	Marmora Rd, Honor Oak, Off Forest Hill Rd
Hotel	★★★58% Bromley Court Hotel, Bromley Hill, BROMLEY ☎081-464 5011 122⇨🛏

SW15 PUTNEY

Richmond Park ☎081-876 1795

Two public parkland courses.

Richmond Park: 36 holes, 5909yds, Par 68, SSS 68, Course record 62.

Dukes: 18 holes, 5486yds, Par 72.

Visitors	welcome but not spectators or caddies.
Societies	must contact in advance.
Green Fees	not confirmed.
Facilities	⊗ ⅷ 💺 ♀ 🍴 🏠 ſ
Location	Roehampton Gate
Hotel	★★★64% Richmond Hill, 146-150 Richmond Hill, RICHMOND ☎081-940 2247 & 081-940 5466 123⇨🛏

SW19 WIMBLEDON

Royal Wimbledon ☎081-946 2125

A club steeped in the history of the game, it is also of great age, dating back to 1865. Of sand and heather like so many of the Surrey courses its 12th hole (par 4) is rated as the best on the course.

18 holes, 6300yds, Par 70, SSS 70, Course record 64.

Club membership 1050.

	SCORECARD				
Hole	Yds	Par	Hole	Yds	Par
1	405	4	10	476	5
2	426	4	11	421	4
3	382	4	12	455	4
4	401	4	13	161	3
5	164	3	14	455	4
6	261	4	15	421	4
7	500	5	16	390	4
8	221	3	17	138	3
9	282	4	18	341	3
Out	3042	35	In	3258	34
			Totals	6300	69

Visitors	restricted weekends & bank holidays. Must be accompanied by member, contact in advance and have an introduction from own club.
Societies	welcome Wed-Fri.
Green Fees	not confirmed.
Facilities	⊗ 🏌 💺 ♀ 🍴 🏠 ſ Hugh Boyle.
Location	29 Camp Rd
Hotel	★★★64% Richmond Hill, 146-150 Richmond Hill, RICHMOND ☎081-940 2247 & 081-940 5466 123⇨🛏

Wimbledon Common ☎081-946 0294
Quick-drying course on Wimbledon Common. Well wooded, with long challenging short holes but no bunkers. All players must wear plain red upper garments.
18 holes, 5438yds, Par 68, SSS 66, Course record 63.
Club membership 250.

Visitors	with member only at weekends.
Societies	must telephone in advance.
Green Fees	£20 per day; £13.50 per round.
Facilities	⊗ ⊾ 🍴 ⚲ △ 🏠 (J S Jukes.
Leisure	snooker.
Location	Camp Rd
Hotel	★★★63% Cannizaro House Hotel, West Side, Wimbledon Common, LONDON ☎081-879 1464 48⇨🐾

Wimbledon Park ☎081-946 1002
Easy walking on parkland course. Sheltered lake provides hazard on 3 holes.
18 holes, 5465yds, Par 66, SSS 66, Course record 62.
Club membership 700.

Visitors	restricted weekends & bank holidays. Must contact in advance and have an introduction from own club.
Societies	must apply in writing.
Green Fees	£25 per day (£25 per round weekends after 1500).
Facilities	⊗ ⊾ 🍴 ⚲ △ 🏠 (D Wingrove.
Location	Home Park Rd, Wimbledon (400 yds from Wimbledon Park Station)
Hotel	★★★64% Richmond Hill, 146-150 Richmond Hill, RICHMOND ☎081-940 2247 & 081-940 5466 123⇨🐾

W7 HANWELL

Brent Valley ☎081-567 1287
Municipal parkland course with easy walking. The River Brent winds through the course.
18 holes, 5426yds, Par 67, SSS 66.
Club membership 350.

Visitors	no restrictions.
Societies	one month's notice required.
Green Fees	not confirmed.
Facilities	⊗ (vary with season) 🍴 by prior arrangement ⊾ 🍴 ⚲ △ 🏠 🏌 (Peter Byrne.
Location	138 Church Rd, Hanwell
Hotel	★★★60% Master Robert Hotel, Great West Rd, HOUNSLOW ☎081-570 6261 100⇨🐾

MERSEYSIDE

BEBINGTON   Map 07 SJ38

Brackenwood ☎051-608 3093
Municipal parkland course with easy walking.
18 holes, 6285yds, Par 70, SSS 70.
Club membership 320.

Societies	must apply in advance.
Green Fees	not confirmed.
Facilities	⊾ 🍴 🏠 🏌 (
Location	Brackenwood Park (.75m N of M53 junc 4 on B5151)
Hotel	★★★62% Bowler Hat Hotel, 2 Talbot Rd, Oxton, BIRKENHEAD ☎051-652 4931 29⇨🐾

BIRKENHEAD   Map 07 SJ38

Arrowe Park ☎051-677 1527
Pleasant municipal parkland course.
18 holes, 6435yds, Par 72, SSS 71.
Club membership 210.

Visitors	no restrictions.
Societies	must telephone in advance.
Green Fees	not confirmed.
Facilities	⊾ △ 🏠 (Clive Scanlon.
Location	Woodchurch (1m from M53 junc 3 on A551)
Hotel	★★★62% Bowler Hat Hotel, 2 Talbot Rd, Oxton, BIRKENHEAD ☎051-652 4931 29⇨🐾

Prenton ☎051-608 1461
Parkland course with easy walking and views of the Welsh hills.
18 holes, 5966yds, Par 70, SSS 69.
Club membership 760.

Visitors	restricted to yellow course.
Societies	welcome Wed & Fri, contact in advance.
Green Fees	£23 per day (£25 weekends & bank holidays).
Facilities	⊗ 🍴 by prior arrangement ⊾ 🍴 ⚲ △ 🏠 (Robin Thompson.
Leisure	snooker.
Location	Golf Links Rd, Prenton (S side of town centre off B5151)
Hotel	★★64% Riverhill Hotel, Talbot Rd, Oxton, BIRKENHEAD ☎051-653 3773 16⇨🐾

Wirral Ladies ☎051-652 1255
Heathland course with heather and birch.
18 holes, 4966yds, SSS 70.
Club membership 450.

Visitors	must contact in advance and have an introduction from own club.
Societies	must telephone in advance.
Green Fees	not confirmed.
Facilities	⊗ 🍴 by prior arrangement ⊾ 🍴 ⚲ △ 🏠 (Philip Chandler.
Location	93 Bidston Rd, Oxton (W side of town centre on B5151)
Hotel	★★★62% Bowler Hat Hotel, 2 Talbot Rd, Oxton, BIRKENHEAD ☎051-652 4931 29⇨🐾

BLUNDELLSANDS   Map 07 SJ39

West Lancashire ☎051-924 1076
Challenging, traditional links with sandy subsoil overlooking the Mersey Estuary. There are many fine holes, particularly the four short ones.
18 holes, 6763yds, Par 72, SSS 73.
Club membership 650.

Visitors	may not play on competition days; must have a handicap certificate. Must contact in advance.
Societies	must contact in advance.
Green Fees	£30 per day; £20 per round (£35 per round weekends & bank holidays).
Facilities	⊗ 🍴 by prior arrangement ⊾ 🍴 ⚲ △ 🏠 (
Location	Hall Rd West (N side of village)

Hotel	★★★62% Blundellsands Hotel, Serpentine, BLUNDELLSANDS ☎051-924 6515 41⟜🏠

BOOTLE   Map 07 SJ39

Bootle ☎051-928 1371
Municipal seaside course, with NW wind. Testing holes: 5th (200 yds) par 3; 7th (415 yds) par 4.
18 holes, 6362yds, Par 70, SSS 70.

Visitors	no restrictions.
Societies	must contact in advance.
Green Fees	not confirmed.
Facilities	♀ ⚓ 🏠 ⛳ 🍷
Location	Dunnings Bridge Rd (2m NE on A5036)
Hotel	★★★62% Blundellsands Hotel, Serpentine, BLUNDELLSANDS ☎051-924 6515 41⟜🏠

BROMBOROUGH   Map 07 SJ38

Bromborough ☎051-334 2155
Parkland course.
18 holes, 6650yds, Par 72, SSS 73.
Club membership 700.

Visitors	may not play on Sun, Tue mornings & Sat before 2.30pm.
Societies	normal society day Wed ; must telephone in advance.
Green Fees	not confirmed.
Facilities	�🍴 by prior arrangement ⛳ 🍷 ♀ ⚓ 🏠 🍷
Location	Raby Hall Rd (.5m W of Station)
Hotel	★★★62% Bowler Hat Hotel, 2 Talbot Rd, Oxton, BIRKENHEAD ☎051-652 4931 29⟜🏠

CALDY   Map 07 SJ28

Caldy ☎051-625 5660
A parkland course situated on the estuary of the River Dee with many of the fairways running parallel to the river. Of Championship length, the course is subject to variable winds that noticeably alter the day to day playing of each hole. There are excellent views of North Wales and Snowdonia.
18 holes, 6675yds, Par 72, SSS 73, Course record 68.
Club membership 800.

Visitors	may play on weekdays only. Must contact in advance and have an introduction from own club.
Societies	must telephone in advance.
Green Fees	not confirmed.
Facilities	⊗ ⍫ ⛳ 🍷 ♀ ⚓ 🏠 🍷 K Jones.
Leisure	snooker.
Location	Links Hey Rd (SE side of village)
Hotel	★★62% Parkgate Hotel, Boathouse Ln, PARKGATE ☎051-336 5001 27⟜🏠

EASTHAM   Map 07 SJ38

Eastham Lodge ☎051-327 3008
A 15-hole parkland course with many trees. Three holes played twice to make 18, but restricted to 15 holes in winter.
15 holes, 5813yds, Par 69, SSS 68, Course record 67.
Club membership 500.

Visitors	with member only at weekends.
Societies	welcome Tues only, must apply in advance.
Green Fees	£18 weekdays.
Facilities	⊗ ⍫ by prior arrangement ⛳ 🍷 ♀ (1200-2300) ⚓ 🏠 ⛳ 🍷 Ivor Jones.
Location	117 Ferry Rd (1.5m N)
Hotel	★★★67% Cromwell Hotel, High St, BROMBOROUGH ☎051-334 2917 31⟜🏠

FORMBY   Map 07 SD30

Formby ☎(07048) 72164
Championship seaside links through sandhills and partly through pine trees.
18 holes, 6490yds, Par 72, SSS 72.
Club membership 600.

Visitors	may not play Wed, weekends or bank holidays. Must contact in advance and have an introduction from own club.
Societies	Tues & Thu only. Must contact in advance.
Green Fees	£40 per day.
Facilities	⊗ (ex Mon) ⛳ 🍷 ♀ ⚓ 🏠 🍷
Location	Golf Rd (N side of town)
Hotel	★★★62% Blundellsands Hotel, Serpentine, BLUNDELLSANDS ☎051-924 6515 41⟜🏠

If you know of a golf course which welcomes visitors and is not already in this guide, we should be grateful for information

Formby Ladies ☎(07048) 73493
Seaside links - one of the few independent ladies clubs in the country. Course has contrasting hard-hitting holes in flat country and tricky holes in sandhills and woods.
18 holes, 5374yds, Par 71, SSS 71, Course record 63.
Club membership 423.

Visitors	except Thu. Must contact in advance.
Societies	must apply in advance.
Green Fees	£22.50 per day (£28 weekends & bank holidays).
Facilities	ⓑ ◻ ♀ ◻ (
Location	Golf Rd (N side of town)
Hotel	★★★62% Blundellsands Hotel, Serpentine, BLUNDELLSANDS ☎051-924 6515 41⇨♠

HESWALL   Map 07 SJ28

Heswall ☎(051342) 1237
A pleasant parkland course in soft undulating country overlooking the estuary of the River Dee. There are excellent views of the Welsh hills and coastline, and a good test of golf. The clubhouse is modern and well-appointed with good facilities.
18 holes, 6472yds, Par 72, SSS 72, Course record 63.
Club membership 900.

SCORECARD: White Tees					
Hole	Yds	Par	Hole	Yds	Par
1	421	4	10	435	4
2	393	4	11	148	3
3	337	4	12	490	5
4	209	3	13	330	4
5	494	5	14	431	4
6	396	4	15	327	4
7	434	4	16	151	3
8	160	3	17	520	5
9	509	5	18	287	4
Out	3353	36	In	3119	36
			Totals	6472	72

Visitors	handicap certificate required. Must contact in advance.
Societies	welcome Wed & Fri only, must apply in advance.
Green Fees	£24 per day (£30 WE & BH).
Facilities	⊗ ⊞ by prior arrangement ⓑ ◻ ♀ △ ◻ ♈ (Alan Thompson.
Leisure	snooker.
Location	Cottage Ln (1m S off A540)
Hotel	★★62% Parkgate Hotel, Boathouse Ln, PARKGATE ☎051-336 5001 27⇨♠

HOYLAKE   Map 07 SJ28

Hoylake Municipal ☎051-632 2956
Flat, generally windy semi-links course. Tricky fairways.
18 holes, 3613yds, Par 70, SSS 70, Course record 67.
Club membership 286.

Visitors	must contact in advance.
Societies	must telephone 051-632 4883 (M E Down)
Green Fees	£4 per round.
Facilities	⊗ ⊞ ⓑ ◻ ♀ (ex Fri) △ ◻ ♈ (R Boobyer.
Location	Carr Ln (SW side of town off A540)
Hotel	★★★62% Bowler Hat Hotel, 2 Talbot Rd, Oxton, BIRKENHEAD ☎051-652 4931 29⇨♠

Royal Liverpool ☎051-632 3101
A world famous seaside links course, windswept.
18 holes, 6840yds, Par 72, SSS 74, Course record 64.
Club membership 800.

Visitors	must have a handicap certificate. Must play with member at weekends. Must contact in advance and have an introduction from own club.
Societies	must contact in writing.

Green Fees	£45 per day; £32 per round (£75 per day;£45 per round weekends).
Facilities	⊗ ⓑ ◻ ♀ (all day in summer) △ ◻ ♈ (John Heggarty.
Leisure	snooker.
Location	Meols Dr (SW side of town on A540)
Hotel	★★★62% Bowler Hat Hotel, 2 Talbot Rd, Oxton, BIRKENHEAD ☎051-652 4931 29⇨♠

HUYTON   Map 07 SJ49

Bowring ☎051-489 1901
Flat parkland course.
9 holes, 2009yds, Par 34.
Club membership 80.

Visitors	no restrictions.
Green Fees	not confirmed.
Facilities	△ ◻ (
Location	Bowring Park, Roby Rd (On A5080 adjacent M62 junc 5)

Huyton & Prescot ☎051-489 3948
Parkland course, easy walking, excellent golf.
18 holes, 5738yds, Par 68, SSS 68.
Club membership 700.

Visitors	restricted at weekends. Must contact in advance and have an introduction from own club.
Societies	must telephone in advance.
Green Fees	not confirmed.
Facilities	⊗ ⊞ by prior arrangement ⓑ ◻ ♀ △ ◻ ♈ (Ronald Pottage.
Leisure	snooker.
Location	Hurst Park, Huyton Ln (1.5m NE off B5199)
Hotel	★58% Rockland Hotel, View Rd, RAINHILL ☎051-426 4603 10rm(9⇨)

LIVERPOOL   Map 07 SJ39

Allerton Park ☎051-428 8510
Parkland course.
18 holes, 5459yds, Par 67, SSS 67, Course record 62.
Club membership 300.

Visitors	no restrictions.
Green Fees	not confirmed.
Facilities	ⓑ ◻ ♀ ◻ ♈ (
Location	Allerton Manor Golf Estate, Allerton Rd (5.5m SE of city centre off A562 and B5180)
Hotel	★★63% Grange Hotel, Holmfield Rd, Aigburth, LIVERPOOL ☎051-427 2950 25⇨♠

Childwall ☎051-487 0654
Parkland golf is played here over a testing course, where accuracy from the tee is well-rewarded. The course is very popular with visiting societies for the clubhouse has many amenities. Course designed by James Braid.
18 holes, 6425yds, Par 69, SSS 69, Course record 65.
Club membership 600.

Visitors	must use yellow tees only. Must have an introduction from own club.
Societies	must telephone in advance.
Green Fees	not confirmed.
Facilities	⊗ ⊞ ⓑ ◻ ♀ △ ◻ ♈ (Nigel M Parr.
Leisure	snooker.

Location Naylors Rd, Gateacre (7m E of city centre off B5178)
Hotel ★58% Rockland Hotel, View Rd, RAINHILL ☎051-426 4603 10rm(9🛁)

Lee Park ☎051-487 9861
Flat course with ponds in places.
18 holes, 5508mtrs, Par 71, SSS 69.
Club membership 500.
Visitors must contact in advance and have an introduction from own club.
Societies must contact in advance.
Green Fees not confirmed.
Facilities ⊗)Ⅲ by prior arrangement 🍺 ☕ 🍷 🧥
Leisure snooker.
Location Childwall Valley Rd (7m E of city centre off B5178)
Hotel ★★★★59% Liverpool Moat House Hotel, Paradise St, LIVERPOOL ☎051-709 0181 251🛁⛳

Liverpool Municipal ☎051-546 5435
Flat, easy course.
18 holes, 6588yds, Par 72, SSS 71, Course record 70.
Club membership 150.
Visitors must contact in advance.
Societies must contact 1 week in advance.
Green Fees not confirmed.
Facilities ⊗ by prior arrangement)Ⅲ by prior arrangement 🍺 ☕ 🍷 🧥 🏠 ⚑ 🏌 Dave Weston.
Location Ingoe Ln, Kirkby (7.5m NE of city centre on A506)
Hotel ★★★★59% Liverpool Moat House Hotel, Paradise St, LIVERPOOL ☎051-709 0181 251🛁⛳

West Derby ☎051-228 1540
A parkland course always in first-class condition, and so giving easy walking. The fairways are well-wooded. Care must be taken on the first nine holes to avoid the brook which guards many of the greens. A modern well-designed clubhouse with many amenities, overlooks the course.
18 holes, 6333yds, Par 72, SSS 70.
Club membership 550.
Visitors may not play before 9.30am.
Societies may not play on Sat, Sun & bank holidays; must contact in advance.
Green Fees not confirmed.
Facilities ⊗)Ⅲ 🍺 ☕ 🍷 🧥 🏠 🏌 Nicholas Brace.
Leisure snooker.
Location Yew Tree Ln, West Derby (4.5m E of city centre off A57)

Woolton ☎051-486 1298
Parkland course providing a good round of golf for all standards.
18 holes, 5706yds, Par 69, SSS 68.
Club membership 650.
Visitors must contact in advance.
Societies must apply in writing.
Green Fees not confirmed.
Facilities ⊗)Ⅲ 🍺 ☕ 🍷 🧥 🏠 🏌
Leisure snooker.

Location Speke Rd (7m SE of city centre off A562)
Hotel ★★63% Grange Hotel, Holmfield Rd, Aigburth, LIVERPOOL ☎051-427 2950 25🛁⛳

NEWTON-LE-WILLOWS Map 07 SJ59

Haydock Park
☎(0925) 228525
A well-wooded parkland course, close to the well-known racecourse, and always in excellent condition. The pleasant undulating fairways offer some very interesting golf and the 6th, 9th, 11th and 13th holes are particularly testing. The clubhouse is very comfortable.
18 holes, 6043yds, Par 70, SSS 69, Course record 65.
Club membership 550.

SCORECARD

Hole	Yds	Par	Hole	Yds	Par
1	408	4	10	363	4
2	182	3	11	375	4
3	490	5	12	151	3
4	119	3	13	449	4
5	523	5	14	283	4
6	362	4	15	495	5
7	310	4	16	328	4
8	191	3	17	380	4
9	438	4	18	196	3
Out	3023	35	In	3020	35
			Totals	6043	70

Visitors must be member of a recognised club. With member only weekends & bank holidays. Must contact in advance and have an introduction from own club.
Societies must apply in writing.
Green Fees £18.50 per day.
Facilities ⊗)Ⅲ 🍺 ☕ 🍷 🧥 🏠 🏌 Peter Kenwright.
Leisure snooker.
Location Golborne Park, Rob Ln (.75m NE off A49)
Hotel ★★★67% Forte Posthouse, Lodge Ln, Newton-Le-Willows, HAYDOCK ☎(0942) 717878 142🛁

ST HELENS Map 07 SJ59

Grange Park ☎(0744) 26318
A course of Championship length set in plesant country surroundings - playing the course it is hard to believe that industrial St Helens lies so close at hand. The course is a fine test of golf and there are many attractive holes liable to challenge all grades.
18 holes, 6429yds, Par 72, SSS 71, Course record 65.
Club membership 700.
Visitors weekdays only. Must contact in advance and have an introduction from own club.
Societies must apply in writing.
Green Fees £21 (27 holes).
Facilities ⊗)Ⅲ 🍺 ☕ 🍷 🧥 🏠 ⚑ 🏌 Paul G Evans.
Leisure snooker.
Location Prescot Rd (1.5m W on A58)
Hotel ★★★67% Forte Posthouse, Lodge Ln, Newton-Le-Willows, HAYDOCK ☎(0942) 717878 142🛁

Sherdley Park ☎(0744) 813149
Fairly hilly course with ponds in places.
18 holes, 5941yds, Par 70, SSS 69.
Club membership 160.
Visitors no restrictions.
Green Fees not confirmed.
Facilities 🧥 🏠 ⚑ 🏌
Location Sherdley Rd (2m S off A570)
Hotel ★★★67% Forte Posthouse, Lodge Ln, Newton-Le-Willows, HAYDOCK ☎(0942) 717878 142🛁

SOUTHPORT   Map 07 SD31

The Hesketh ☎(0704) 36897
Hesketh is the senior club in Southport, founded in 1885.
The Championship course comprises much of the original
territory plus a large area of reclaimed land on the seaward
side - essentially 'Links' in character.
18 holes, 6478yds, Par 71, SSS 72, Course record 66.
Club membership 580.
Visitors	must have an introduction from own club.
Societies	welcome.
Green Fees	not confirmed.
Facilities	⊗ 〼 ﾑ ➋ ♀ ⚘ 🏠 ⚐ ⚑ John Donoghue.
Leisure	snooker.
Location	Cockle Dick's Ln, off Cambridge Rd (1m NE of town centre off A565)
Hotel	★★65% Bold Hotel, Lord St, SOUTHPORT ☎(0704) 532578 22rm(15⇔6↑)

Hillside ☎(0704) 67169
Championship links course with natural hazards open to
strong wind.
18 holes, 6850yds, Par 72, SSS 72, Course record 66.
Club membership 750.
Visitors	restricted Tue (am), weekends & bank holidays. Must contact in advance.
Societies	must apply in advance.
Green Fees	not confirmed.
Facilities	⊗ 〼 ﾑ ➋ ♀ ⚘ 🏠 ⚑ B Seddon.
Leisure	snooker.
Location	Hastings Rd, Hillside (2m SW of town centre on A565)
Hotel	★★★62% Royal Clifton Hotel, Promenade, SOUTHPORT ☎(0704) 533771 107⇔↑

Park ☎(0704) 30133
Very flat municipal parkland course.
18 holes, 6200yds, Par 70, SSS 70.
Club membership 400.
Visitors	restricted weekends, telephone for details.
Green Fees	not confirmed.
Facilities	♀ (members only) 🏠 ⚑
Location	Park Rd (N side of town centre off A565)
Hotel	★★★62% Royal Clifton Hotel, Promenade, SOUTHPORT ☎(0704) 533771 107⇔↑

Royal Birkdale See page 159

Southport & Ainsdale
☎(0704) 78000
'S and A', as it is known in
the North is another of the
fine Championship courses
for which this part of the
country is famed. This Club
has staged many important
events and offers golf of the
highest order.
*18 holes, 6603yds, Par 72,
SSS 73.*
Club membership 815.
Visitors	except Wed, Thu, weekends & bank holidays. Must contact in advance and have an introduction from own club.

SCORECARD: White Tees					
Hole	Yds	Par	Hole	Yds	Par
1	200	3	10	160	3
2	520	5	11	447	4
3	418	4	12	401	4
4	316	4	13	145	3
5	447	4	14	383	4
6	386	4	15	353	4
7	480	5	16	510	5
8	157	3	17	443	4
9	482	5	18	355	4
Out	3406	37	In	3197	35
			Totals	6603	72

Societies	must apply in advance.
Green Fees	£35 per day; £25 per round.
Facilities	⊗ 〼 ﾑ & ➋ by prior arrangement ♀ 🏠 ⚑ Michael Houghton.
Leisure	snooker.
Location	Bradshaws Ln, Ainsdale (3m S off A565)
Hotel	★★★62% Royal Clifton Hotel, Promenade, SOUTHPORT ☎(0704) 533771 107⇔↑

Southport Municipal ☎(0704) 535286
Municipal seaside links course. Played over by Alt Golf
Club.
18 holes, 6400yds, Par 70, SSS 69.
Club membership 750.
Visitors	must contact in advance.
Societies	must telephone 6 days in advance.
Green Fees	not confirmed.
Facilities	⊗ ﾑ ➋ ♀ ⚘ 🏠 ⚑ Bill Fletcher.
Leisure	snooker.
Location	Park Rd West (N side of town centre off A565)
Hotel	★★★62% Royal Clifton Hotel, Promenade, SOUTHPORT ☎(0704) 533771 107⇔↑

Southport Old Links ☎(0704) 28207
Seaside course with tree-lined fairways and easy walking.
One of the oldest courses in Southport, Henry Vardon won
the 'Leeds Cup' here in 1922.
9 holes, 6378yds, Par 72, SSS 71, Course record 68.
Club membership 400.
Visitors	except Wed, Sun & bank holidays. Must contact in advance and have an introduction from own club.
Societies	welcome except Wed & Sun, must apply in advance.
Green Fees	£15 per day (£20 weekends & bank holidays).
Facilities	⊗ 〼 ﾑ ➋ ♀ ⚘
Location	Moss Ln, Churchtown (NW side of town centre off A5267)
Hotel	★★65% Bold Hotel, Lord St, SOUTHPORT ☎(0704) 532578 22rm(15⇔6↑)

WALLASEY   Map 07 SJ29

Bidston ☎051-638 3412
Parkland course, with westerly winds.
18 holes, 5827yds, Par 70, SSS 71.
Club membership 550.
Visitors	restricted weekends. Must contact in advance.
Societies	must apply in writing.
Green Fees	not confirmed.
Facilities	⊗ 〼 ﾑ ➋ ♀ ⚘ 🏠 ⚑ R J Law.
Leisure	snooker.
Location	Scoresby Rd, Leasowe, Moreton (.5m W of M53 junc 1 entrance off A551)
Hotel	★★★62% Bowler Hat Hotel, 2 Talbot Rd, Oxton, BIRKENHEAD ☎051-652 4931 29⇔↑

Leasowe ☎051-677 5852
Rather flat, semi-links, seaside course.
18 holes, 6204yds, Par 71, SSS 71, Course record 63.
Club membership 500.
Visitors	may not play 1-2pm.
Societies	must contact 14 days in advance.

▶

SCORE CARD: White Tees					
Hole	Yds	Par	Hole	Yds	Par
1	447	4	10	372	4
2	416	4	11	374	4
3	407	4	12	181	3
4	202	3	13	436	4
5	341	4	14	198	3
6	488	5	15	542	5
7	150	3	16	344	4
8	414	4	17	502	5
9	413	4	18	476	5
Out	3278	35	In	3425	37
			Totals	6703	72

SOUTHPORT   Map07SD31

Royal Birkdale ☎ (0704) 67920

John Ingham writes: There are a few seaside links in the world that can be described as 'great'. And Royal Birkdale, with its expanse of sandhills and willow scrub, is one of them. Founded in 1889, there have been some changes, even since Arnold Palmer hit that wondrous recovery shot which helped him win an Open in the early 'sixties, and led to a plaque being erected at the spot from which the divot was taken.

Well bunkered, the sandhills run along the edges of the fairways and make ideal platforms from which to view the Open Championship, played frequently here because the examination is supreme in the United Kingdom. Maybe the links, in a wind, is too difficult for the weekender.

Certainly it found out Dai Rees in 1961 when he was chasing Palmer for the title. In the last round the course struck at the very first hole. Rees had hit his teeshot a might to the left, and then had to wait for the players to hole out on the green ahead, before attempting a powerful shot with a lofted wood from the fairway. The ball smacked into the back of a bunker, and fell back into sand. Rees took an awful seven and Palmer beat him for the trophy - by one shot. The Welshman had stormed back in 31 but his chance to win an Open had gone forever. But Rees still touched his hat to the links, and held it in great respect as, indeed, does Arnold Palmer.

But for the amateur, another problem is simply hitting the ball far enough because, if you play it from the Open Championship back tees, it measures 7080 yards and par 73 takes some getting, even with your handicap allowance.

They have hosted everything that matters here, including the Ryder Cup and will probably get the match again, soon.

18 holes, 6703 yds, Par 72, SSS73, Course record 63 (C.Pavin). Membership 800

Visitors	must contact in advance, and have a letter of introduction from their own club along with a handicap certificate.
Societies	must apply in writing or by telephone in advance.
Green fees	weekdays: £67 per day; £46 per round
Facilities	⊗ &)☰ (only for parties over 20) ⌕ ⬛ ♀ ⛄ ▣ ⛳ ↑ (Richard Bradbeer).
Leisure	snooker
Location	Waterloo Road, Birkdale (1.5m S of town on A580).

WHERE TO STAY AND EAT NEARBY

HOTELS:

SOUTHPORT   ★★★ 62% Royal Clifton, Promenade. ☎ (0704) 533771. 107 ↩ ↑. ♤ English & French cuisine.

★★★ 61% Scarisbrick, Lord St. ☎ (0704) 543000. 66 ↩ ↑. ♤ English & French cuisine.

★★ 68% Balmoral Lodge, 41 Queens Rd. ☎ (0704) 544298. 15 ↩ ↑

★★ 67% Stutelea Hotel & Leisure Club, Alexandra Rd. ☎ (0704) 544220. 20 ↩ ↑

RESTAURANT:

WRIGHTINGTON   ×××High Moor, Highmoor Ln (jct 27 off M6, take B5239). ☎ Appleby Bridge (02575) 2364. ♤ English & French cuisine.

Green Fees	£16 per day (£20 weekends).
Facilities	⊗ 〗 ⊾ ⬛ ♀ ⛲ 🏠 ⚷ 𝄢 Mike Adams.
Location	Moreton (2m W on A551)
Hotel	★★★62% Bowler Hat Hotel, 2 Talbot Rd, Oxton, BIRKENHEAD ☎051-652 4931 29⊖🏠

Wallasey ☎051-691 1024

A well-established sporting links, adjacent to the Irish Sea, with huge sandhills and many classic holes where the player's skills are often combined with good fortune. Large, firm greens and fine views.

18 holes, 6605yds, Par 72, SSS 73, Course record 68.

Club membership 700.

Visitors	must be member of a recognised club & have handicap certificate. Must contact in advance.
Societies	must apply in writing.
Green Fees	£25.50 per day (£30.50 weekends).
Facilities	⊗ 〗 by prior arrangement ⊾ ⬛ ♀ ⛲ 🏠 𝄢 ⚷ Mike Adams.
Location	Bayswater Rd (N side of town centre off A554)
Hotel	★★★62% Bowler Hat Hotel, 2 Talbot Rd, Oxton, BIRKENHEAD ☎051-652 4931 29⊖🏠

Warren ☎051-639 8323

Short, undulating links course with first-class greens and prevailing winds off the sea.

9 holes, 5854yds, Par 72, SSS 68, Course record 69.

Club membership 150.

Visitors	except Sun until 10.30.am.
Green Fees	£3.60 per round.
Facilities	♀ 🏠 𝄢 ⚷ Ken Lamb.
Location	Grove Rd (N side of town centre off A554)
Hotel	★★★62% Bowler Hat Hotel, 2 Talbot Rd, Oxton, BIRKENHEAD ☎051-652 4931 29⊖🏠

NORFOLK

BARNHAM BROOM   Map 05 TG00

Barnham Broom Golf and Country Club ☎(060545) 393

Attractive river valley courses with modern hotel and leisure complex.

Hill Course: 18 holes, 6628yds, Par 72, SSS 72.

Valley Course: 18 holes, 6470yds, Par 71, SSS 71.

Visitors	must have handicap certificate. With member only at weekends. Must contact in advance.
Societies	must apply in writing.
Green Fees	£30 per day; £25 per round.
Facilities	⊗ 〗 ⊾ ⬛ ♀ ⛲ 🏠 𝄢 🏊 ⚷ Stephen Beckham.
Leisure	hard tennis courts, heated indoor swimming pool, squash, snooker, sauna, solarium, gymnasium, hairdressing salon beautician jacuzzi.
Location	Honingham Rd (1m N, S of A47)
Hotel	★★★65% Barnham Broom Hotel Conference & Leisure, Centre, BARNHAM BROOM ☎(060545) 393 52⊖🏠 **See advertisement on page 163**

BAWBURGH   Map 05 TG10

Bawburgh ☎(0603) 746390

An open-links. Driving range available.

9 holes, 2639yds, Par 33, SSS 66, Course record 66.

Club membership 300.

Visitors	must contact in advance.
Societies	must contact in advance.
Green Fees	not confirmed.
Facilities	⛲ 🏠 ⚷ Robert Waugh.
Location	Norwich Golf Centre, Long Ln
Hotel	★★★70% Park Farm Hotel, HETHERSETT ☎(0603) 810264 6⊖🏠 Annexe32⊖🏠

BRANCASTER   Map 09 TF74

Royal West Norfolk

☎(0485) 210087

If you want to see what golf courses were like years ago, then go to the Royal West Norfolk where tradition exudes from both clubhouse and course. Close by the sea, the links are laid out in the grand manner and are characterised by sleepered greens, superb cross-bunkering and salt marshes.

18 holes, 6428yds, Par 71, SSS 71, Course record 69.

Club membership 767.

	SCORECARD					
Hole	Yds	Par	Hole	Yds	Par	
1	410	4	10	151	3	
2	449	4	11	478	5	
3	407	4	12	386	4	
4	128	3	13	317	4	
5	421	4	14	432	4	
6	186	3	15	188	3	
7	486	5	16	346	4	
8	478	5	17	377	4	
9	404	4	18	384	4	
Out	3369	36	In	3059	35	
			Totals	6428	71	

Visitors	may only play after 10am at weekends with permission. Must contact in advance.
Societies	must contact in advance.
Green Fees	£30 per day (£40 weekends).
Facilities	⊗ ⊾ ⬛ ♀ ⛲ 🏠 𝄢 ⚷
Leisure	practice ground.
Hotel	★★72% Titchwell Manor Hotel, TITCHWELL ☎(0485) 210221 & 210284 11rm(7⊖🏠)Annexe4⊖🏠

CROMER   Map 09 TG24

Royal Cromer ☎(0263) 512884

Seaside course set out on cliff edge, hilly and subject to wind.

18 holes, 6508yds, Par 72, SSS 71, Course record 68.

Club membership 700.

Visitors	must have handicap certificate. Must contact in advance.
Societies	by arrangement.
Green Fees	£25 per day (£30 weekends & bank holidays).
Facilities	⊗ 〗 by prior arrangement ⊾ ⬛ ♀ 🏠 ⚷
Location	145 Overstrand Rd (1m E on B1159)
Hotel	★★★65% Links Country Park Hotel & Golf Club, Sandy Ln, WEST RUNTON ☎(026375) 691 30⊖🏠 Annexe10⊖

A golf-course name printed in ***bold italics*** means that we have been unable to verify information with the club's management for the current year

DENVER   Map 05 TF60

Ryston Park ☏Downham Market (0366) 383834
Parkland course.
9 holes, 3146yds, Par 35, SSS 70, Course record 66.
Club membership 320.
Visitors   may not play weekends or bank holidays.
Societies   Mon-Fri only, must telephone in advance.
Green Fees   £20 per day.
Facilities   ⊗ ∭ ⒧ ◨ ♀ ♨ ◸
Location   .5m S on A10
Hotel   ★61% Crown Hotel, Bridge St, DOWNHAM
                MARKET ☏(0366) 382322 10rm(5⇦2♠)

DISS   Map 05 TM18

Diss ☏(0379) 642847
Commonland course with natural hazards.
18 holes, 6238yds, Par 73, SSS 70.
Club membership 650.
Visitors   may not play weekends & bank holidays. Must
              contact in advance.
Societies   by arrangement.
Green Fees   £16 per day/round.
Facilities   ⊗ ∭ ⒧ ◨ ♀ ♨ ◸ ❴ Nigel Taylor.
Location   Stuston (1.5m SE on B1118)
Hotel   ★★55% Scole Inn, SCOLE ☏(0379) 740481
                12⇦♠Annexe11⇦♠

EAST DEREHAM   Map 09 TF91

Dereham ☏Dereham (0362) 695900
Parkland course.
9 holes, 6225yds, Par 71, SSS 70, Course record 67.
Club membership 520.
Visitors   must have a handicap certificate; must play
              with member at weekends. Must contact in
              advance and have an introduction from own
              club.
Societies   must contact in advance.
Green Fees   not confirmed.
Facilities   ⊗ ∭ ⒧ ◨ ♀ ♨ ◸ ♟ ❴ S Fox.
Location   Quebec Rd (N side of town centre off B1110)
Hotel   ★★64% King's Head Hotel, Norwich St,
                DEREHAM ☏(0362) 693842 & 693283
                10rm(4⇦2♠)Annexe5⇦♠

GORLESTON-ON-SEA   Map 05 TG50

Gorleston ☏Great Yarmouth (0493) 661911
Seaside course.
18 holes, 6400yds, Par 71, SSS 71, Course record 66.
Club membership 900.
Visitors   must have handicap certificate. Must have an
              introduction from own club.
Societies   must apply in writing.
Green Fees   £15 per day/round (£20 weekends).
Facilities   ⊗ ∭ ⒧ ◨ ♀ ♨ ◸ ❴ Ralph Moffitt.
Leisure   snooker.
Location   Warren Rd (S side of town centre)
Hotel   ★★★71% Cliff Hotel, Gorleston, GREAT
                YARMOUTH ☏(0493) 662179 30⇦♠

HUNSTANTON   Map 09 TF64

Hunstanton ☏(0485) 532811
Links course.
18 holes, 6670yds, Par 72, SSS 72, Course record 65.
Club membership 670.
Visitors   must be a club member with handicap
              certificate, but may play at weekends & bank
              holidays. Must contact in advance.
Societies   must apply in writing.
Green Fees   £28 per day (£34 weekends).
Facilities   ⊗ (ex Mon) ∭ by prior arrangement ⒧ ◨
              ♀ ♨ ◸ ♟ ❴ John Carter.
Location   1.5m N off A149
Hotel   ★★67% Caley Hall Motel, Old Hunstanton
                Rd, HUNSTANTON ☏(0485) 533486
                Annexe29rm(27⇦)
Additional   ★★61% The Lodge Hotel, Old Hunstanton
hotel   Rd, HUNSTANTON ☏(0485) 532896
                16⇦♠

KING'S LYNN   Map 09 TF62

King's Lynn ☏Castle Rising (0553) 631654
Challenging, wooded parkland course.
18 holes, 6646yds, Par 72, SSS 72, Course record 64.
Club membership 945.
Visitors   must have handicap certificate. Must contact in
              advance.
Societies   by arrangement.
Green Fees   £26 per day/round (£33 weekends).   ▶

Facilities	⊗ ⅢI by prior arrangement ⸠ ⬤ ⅋ ⌂ ⌘ ⸠ Chris Hanlon.
Leisure	snooker.
Location	Castle Rising (4m NE off A148)
Hotel	★★★64% The Duke's Head, Tuesday Market Pl, KING'S LYNN ☎(0553) 774996 71⇔

MIDDLETON   Map 09 F4

Middleton Hall ☎King's Lynn (0553) 841800
The 9-hole King's course (played off 18 tees) is a pleasant parkland course constructed with conservation in mind around numerous mature trees, pond and reservoir. Additional par 3 pitch and putt course.
9 holes, 5570yds, Par 68, SSS 67.
Club membership 300.

Visitors	no restrictions.
Societies	must contact in advance.
Green Fees	not confirmed.
Facilities	⊗ ⅢI by prior arrangement ⸠ ⬤ ⅋ ⌂ ⌘ ⸠ John Laing.
Location	4m from King's Lynn off A47
Hotel	★★★65% Butterfly Hotel, Beveridge Way, Hardwick Narrows, KING'S LYNN ☎(0553) 771707 50⇔

MUNDESLEY   Map 09 TG33

Mundesley ☎(0263) 720279
Seaside course, good views, windy.
9 holes, 5410yds, Par 68, SSS 66.
Club membership 400.

Visitors	restricted Wed & weekends. Must contact in advance.
Societies	must contact one month in advance.
Green Fees	not confirmed.
Facilities	⊗ ⅢI & ⸠ (ex Thu) ⬤ ⅋ ⌂ ⌘ ⸠ T G Symmons.
Location	Links Rd (W side of village off B1159)
Hotel	★★⬤72% Felmingham Hall Country House Hotel, FELMINGHAM ☎(069269) 631 12⇔⬤Annexe6⇔⬤

NORWICH   Map 05 TG20

Eaton ☎(0603) 51686
An undulating, tree-lined parkland course with excellent trees.
18 holes, 6135yds, Par 70, SSS 69, Course record 59.
Club membership 1000.

Visitors	restricted before 1130 weekends, must have handicap certificate. Must contact in advance.
Societies	by arrangement.
Green Fees	£25 per day (£30 weekends).
Facilities	⊗ ⅢI ⸠ ⬤ ⅋ ⌂ ⌘ ⸠ R Hill.
Location	Newmarket Rd (2.5m SW of city centre off A11)
Hotel	★★61% Arlington Hotel, 10 Arlington Ln, Newmarket Rd, NORWICH ☎(0603) 617841 44⇔

Royal Norwich ☎(0603) 429928
Undulating heathland course.
18 holes, 6603yds, Par 72, SSS 72, Course record 66.
Club membership 650.

Visitors	may not play at weekends & bank holidays. Must contact in advance and have an introduction from own club.
Societies	must contact in advance.
Green Fees	£25 per day.
Facilities	⊗ ⸠ ⬤ ⅋ ⌂ ⌘ ⅂ ⸠ Alan Hemsley.
Location	Drayton High Rd, Hellesdon (2.5m NW of city centre on A1067)
Hotel	★★★65% Hotel Norwich, 121-131 Boundary Rd, NORWICH ☎(0603) 787260 108⇔⬤

SHERINGHAM   Map 09 TG14

Sheringham ☎(0263) 823488
Splendid cliff-top links with gorse, good 'seaside turf' and plenty of space. Straight driving is essential for a low score. The course is close to the shore and can be very windswept, but offers magnificent views.
18 holes, 6464yds, Par 70, SSS 71, Course record 66.
Club membership 730.

SCORECARD: White Tees					
Hole	Yds	Par	Hole	Yds	Par
1	335	4	10	444	4
2	543	5	11	163	3
3	424	4	12	425	4
4	327	4	13	351	4
5	452	4	14	354	4
6	217	3	15	195	3
7	490	5	16	349	4
8	157	3	17	405	4
9	410	4	18	423	4
Out	3355	36	In	3109	34
			Totals	6464	70

Visitors	must have handicap certificate. Must contact in advance and have an introduction from own club.
Societies	must apply in writing.
Green Fees	£25 per day (£30 weekends & bank holidays).
Facilities	⊗ ⅢI ⸠ ⬤ ⅋ ⌂ ⌘ ⮂ ⸠ R H Emery.
Location	Weybourne Rd (W side of town centre on A149)
Hotel	★★65% Beaumaris Hotel, South St, SHERINGHAM ☎(0263) 822370 24rm(17⇔5⬤)

SWAFFHAM   Map 05 TF80

Swaffham ☎(0706) 721611
Heathland course.
9 holes, 6252yds, Par 72, SSS 70.
Club membership 510.

Visitors	with member only at weekends. Must contact in advance.
Societies	must contact one month in advance.
Green Fees	£20 per day; £15 per round.
Facilities	⊗ & ⅢI (ex Mon-Tue) ⸠ ⬤ ⅋ ⌂ ⸠ Chris Norton.
Location	Cley Rd (1.5m SW)
Hotel	★★★61% George Hotel, Station Rd, SWAFFHAM ☎(0760) 721238 27rm(24⇔1⬤)

Opening times of bar and catering facilities vary from place to place. Please remember to check in advance of your visit

For a full range of AA guides and maps, visit your local AA shop or any good bookshop

THETFORD   Map 05 TL88

Thetford ☎(0842) 752169

This is a course with a good pedigree. It was laid-out by a fine golfer, C H Mayo, later altered by James Braid and then again altered by another famous course designer, Mackenzie Ross. It is a testing heathland course with a particularly stiff finish.

18 holes, 6879yds, Par 72, SSS 73, Course record 66.
Club membership 700.

SCORECARD: White Tees					
Hole	Yds	Par	Hole	Yds	Par
1	195	3	10	546	5
2	365	4	11	205	3
3	157	3	12	369	4
4	407	4	13	522	5
5	380	4	14	429	4
6	495	5	15	375	4
7	417	4	16	157	3
8	451	4	17	521	5
9	421	4	18	467	4
Out	3288	35	In	3591	37
			Totals	6879	72

Visitors   must have handicap certificate. With member only at weekends. Must contact in advance and have an introduction from own club.
Societies   must contact in advance.
Green Fees £28.
Facilities ⊗ ⊪ ⮐ 🍺 ♀ 👥 🏠 ℭ
Location   Brandon Rd (.75m W on B1107)
Hotel   ★★★61% Bell Hotel, King St, THETFORD ☎(0842) 754455 47⇾🛏

WATTON   Map 05 TF90

Richmond Park ☎(0953) 881803
Meadowland course dotted with newly planted trees and set on either side of the Little Wissey River.
18 holes, 6300yds, Par 72, SSS 71.
Club membership 500.
Visitors   handicap certificates are required for Sat & Sun mornings.
Societies   apply in writing.
Green Fees £14 (£18 weekends & bank holidays).
Facilities ⊗ ⊪ (Tue-Sat) 🍺 🍺 ♀ 👥 🏠 ⮐ ℭ Alison Sheard.
Leisure   gymnasium.
Location   Saham Rd
Hotel   ★★67% Clarence House Hotel, 78 High St, WATTON ☎(0953) 884252 & 884487 6⇾🛏

WEST RUNTON   Map 09 TG14

Links Country Park Hotel & Golf Club ☎(026 375) 691
Parkland course 500 yds from the sea, with superb views overlooking West Runton. The hotel offers extensive leisure facilities.
9 holes, 4814yds, Par 66, SSS 64.
Club membership 250.
Visitors   must have a handicap certificate.
Societies   must telephone in advance.
Green Fees not confirmed.
Facilities ⊗ ⊪ 🍺 🍺 ♀ 👥 🏠 ⮐ ⮐ ℭ Mike Jubb.
Leisure   hard tennis courts, heated indoor swimming pool, riding, sauna, solarium.
Location   S side of village off A149
Hotel   ★★★65% Links Country Park Hotel & Golf Club, Sandy Ln, WEST RUNTON ☎(026375) 691 30⇾🛏 Annexe10⇾

YARMOUTH, GREAT   Map 05 TG50

Great Yarmouth & Caister ☎(0493) 728699
This great old club, which celebrated its centenary in 1982, has played its part in the development of the game. It is a fine old-fashioned links where not many golfers have bettered the SSS in competitions. The 468-yard 8th (par 4), is a testing hole.
18 holes, 6284yds, Par 70, SSS 70, Course record 63.
Club membership 775.
Visitors   restricted Sun until 11.30am. Must have an introduction from own club.
Societies   must apply in writing.
Green Fees £20 (£24 weekends).
Facilities ⊗ ⊪ by prior arrangement 🍺 ♀ 👥 🏠 ⮐ ℭ Nick Catchpole.
Location   Beach House, Caister on Sea (.5m N off A149)
Hotel   ★★★62% Imperial Hotel, North Dr, GREAT YARMOUTH ☎(0493) 851113 39⇾🛏

A golf-course name printed in ***bold italics*** means that we have been unable to verify information with the club's management for the current year

NORTH YORKSHIRE

ALDWARK   Map 08 SE46

Aldwark Manor Hotel & Golf Club ☎Tollerton (03473) 353
Nine-hole, scenic parkland course with two holes beside the
River Ure. Easy walking. The course surrounds the
Victorian Aldwark Manor Hotel and will be extended to 18
holes (6, 075 yards, par 71), opening in June 1992.
9 holes, 5120yds, Par 68, SSS 66, Course record 67.
Club membership 270.

Visitors	may not play until after 1pm on Sun. Must contact in advance.
Societies	must telephone in advance.
Green Fees	£12 (£17 weekends & bank holidays).
Facilities	⊗ ⟨ 🍴 ⬛ ♀ ⌂ 🏠 🏌 ⛵
Leisure	fishing.
Hotel	★★★★🏊78% Aldwark Manor Hotel, ALDWARK ☎(03473) 8146 17⇆🐾Annexe3⇆🐾

BEDALE   Map 08 SE28

Bedale ☎(0677) 422451
Secluded parkland course with many trees.
18 holes, 5737yds, Par 69, SSS 68, Course record 65.
Club membership 800.

Visitors	must contact in advance.
Societies	must apply in advance.
Green Fees	£16 per day (£24 weekends).
Facilities	⊗ ⟨ 🍴 ⬛ ♀ ⌂ 🏠 🏌 A D Johnson.
Location	Leyburn Rd (N side of town on A684)
Hotel	★★62% Motel Leeming, Great North Rd, BEDALE ☎(0677) 423611 40⇆🐾

BENTHAM   Map 07 SD66

Bentham ☎(05242) 62455
Moorland course with glorious views.
9 holes, 5760yds, Par 70, SSS 69, Course record 69.
Club membership 480.

Societies	must apply in advance.
Green Fees	£10 per day (£13 weekends & bank holidays).
Facilities	♀ ⌂
Location	Robin Ln (N side of High Bentham)
Hotel	★★★55% Royal Hotel, Main St, KIRKBY LONSDALE ☎(05242) 71217 20rm(15⇆1🐾)

CATTERICK GARRISON   Map 08 SE19

Catterick Garrison ☎Richmond (0748) 833268
Scenic parkland/moorland course of Championship
standard, with good views of the Pennines and Cleveland
hills. Testing 1st and 3rd holes.
18 holes, 6331yds, Par 71, SSS 70.
Club membership 750.

Visitors	may need a handicap certificate. Must contact in advance.
Societies	must contact in writing.
Green Fees	£14 per day (£20 weekends & bank holidays).
Facilities	⊗ ⟨ 🍴 ⬛ ♀ ⌂ 🏠 🏌 (Andy Marshall.
Location	Leyburn Rd (1m W)
Hotel	★★55% Bridge House Hotel, CATTERICK BRIDGE ☎(0748) 818331 15rm(4⇆9🐾)

COPMANTHORPE   Map 08 SE54

Pike Hills ☎York (0904) 706566
Parkland course surrounding nature reserve. Level terrain.
18 holes, 6121yds, Par 71, SSS 69, Course record 65.
Club membership 820.

Visitors	with member only weekends & bank holidays. Must contact in advance.
Societies	must apply in advance.
Green Fees	£18 per day/round summer (£14 winter).
Facilities	⊗ (ex Mon) ⟨ by prior arrangement 🍴 ⬛ ♀ ⌂ 🏠 (Ian Gradwell.
Location	Tadcaster Rd (3m N of York on A64)
Hotel	★★★72% Swallow Chase Hotel, Tadcaster Rd, YORK ☎(0904) 701000 112⇆🐾

EASINGWOLD   Map 08 SE56

Easingwold ☎(0347) 21964
Parkland course easy walking. Trees are a major feature
and on six holes water hazards come into play.
18 holes, 6045yds, Par 72, SSS 70, Course record 65.
Club membership 575.

Visitors	with member only weekends & bank holidays (winter). Must contact in advance.
Societies	welcome except Wed, must apply in advance.
Green Fees	£19 per day (£25 weekends & bank holidays).
Facilities	⊗ ⟨ 🍴 ⬛ ♀ (summer weekdays) ⌂ 🏠 (John Hughes.
Location	Stillington Rd (1m S)
Hotel	★★69% Beechwood Close Hotel, 19 Shipton Rd, Clifton, YORK ☎(0904) 658378 14⇆🐾

FILEY   Map 08 TA18

Filey ☎Scarborough (0723) 513293
Parkland course with good views, windy. Stream runs
through course. Testing 9th and 13th holes.
18 holes, 6080yds, Par 70, SSS 69, Course record 64.
Club membership 950.

Visitors	except bank holidays & special competition days. Must contact in advance.
Societies	must apply in advance.
Green Fees	£16.50 per day (£20.50 weekends).
Facilities	⊗ ⟨ 🍴 ⬛ ♀ ⌂ 🏠 (D England.
Leisure	snooker.
Location	West Av (.5m S)
Hotel	★★ Wrangham House Hotel, 10 Stonegate, Hunmanby, FILEY ☎(0723) 891333 9⇆🐾Annexe4⇆🐾

GANTON   Map 08 SE97

Ganton ☎Sherburn (0944) 70329
Championship course, heathland, gorse-lined fairways
and heavily bunkered; variable winds.
18 holes, 6720yds, Par 72, SSS 73, Course record 65.
Club membership 580.

Visitors	except weekends. Must contact in advance.
Societies	must apply in advance.
Green Fees	not confirmed.
Facilities	⊗ by prior arrangement ≋ by prior arrangement 🝔 ⬛ ♀ △ 🏠 (Gary Brown.
Location	.25m NW off A64
Hotel	★★65% Downe Arms Hotel, WYKEHAM ☎(0723) 862471 10⇥ ♞

HARROGATE   Map 08 SE35

Harrogate ☎(0423) 862999
One of Yorkshire's oldest and best courses was designed in 1897 by 'Sandy' Herd. A perfect example of golf architecture, its greens and fairways offer an interesting but fair challenge. The undulating parkland course once formed part of the ancient Forest of Knaresborough. Excellent clubhouse.
18 holes, 6241yds, Par 70, SSS 70.
Club membership 650.

SCORECARD: White Tees					
Hole	Yds	Par	Hole	Yds	Par
1	315	4	10	343	4
2	429	4	11	509	5
3	171	3	12	179	3
4	274	4	13	467	4
5	219	3	14	175	3
6	382	4	15	406	4
7	514	5	16	455	4
8	373	4	17	392	4
9	227	3	18	411	4
Out	2904	34	In	3337	35
			Totals	6241	69

Visitors	must have a handicap certificate. Must contact in advance.
Societies	must contact in writing.
Green Fees	£25 per day (£35 weekends & bank holidays).
Facilities	⊗ ≋ 🝔 ⬛ ♀ △ 🏠 (
Leisure	snooker.
Location	Forest Ln Head, Starbeck (2.25m on A59)
Hotel	★★★69% Balmoral Hotel & Restaurant, Franklin Mount, HARROGATE ☎(0423) 508208 20⇥ ♞

Oakdale ☎(0423) 567162
A pleasant, undulating parkland course which provides a good test of golf for the low handicap player without intimidating the less proficient. A special feature is an attractive stream which comes in to play on four holes. Excellent views from the clubhouse which has good facilities.
18 holes, 6456yds, Par 71, SSS 71, Course record 66.
Club membership 850.

Visitors	except 8-9.30am & 12.30-1.30pm. Must contact in advance.
Societies	must apply at least one month in advance.
Green Fees	not confirmed.
Facilities	⊗ ≋ by prior arrangement 🝔 ⬛ ♀ 🏠 🝙 (Richard Jessop.
Leisure	snooker.
Location	Oakdale (N side of town centre off A61)
Hotel	★★★68% Grants Hotel, 3-13 Swan Rd, HARROGATE ☎(0423) 560666 41⇥ ♞

KIRKBYMOORSIDE   Map 08 SE68

Kirkbymoorside ☎(0751) 31525
Hilly parkland course with narrow fairways, gorse and hawthorn bushes. Beautiful views.
18 holes, 6000yds, Par 69, SSS 69.
Club membership 600.

Visitors	must contact in advance.
Societies	must apply in advance.
Green Fees	£15 daily (£20 weekends & bank holidays).
Facilities	⊗ ≋ 🝔 ⬛ ♀ △
Location	Manor Vale (N side of village)
Hotel	★★68% George & Dragon Hotel, 17 Market Place, KIRKBYMOORSIDE ☎(0751) 31637 14⇥ ♞ Annexe8⇥ ♞

KNARESBOROUGH   Map 08 SE35

Knaresborough ☎Harrogate (0423) 862690
Undulating parkland course with mature trees.
18 holes, 6232yds, Par 70, SSS 70, Course record 65.
Club membership 750.

Visitors	must contact in advance.
Societies	must contact at least 2 weeks in advance.
Green Fees	not confirmed.
Facilities	⊗ ≋ 🝔 ⬛ ♀ △ 🏠 (K I Johnstone.
Location	Boroughbridge Rd (1.25 N on A6055)
Hotel	★★★69% Dower House Hotel, Bond End, KNARESBOROUGH ☎(0423) 863302 28⇥ ♞ Annexe4⇥ ♞

MALTON   Map 08 SE77

Malton & Norton ☎(0653) 693882
Parkland course with panoramic views of the moors. Very testing 1st hole (564 yds dog-leg, left).
18 holes, 6426yds, Par 72, SSS 71.
Club membership 700.

Visitors	must contact in advance.

▶

Societies	must apply in writing.
Green Fees	£17 (£22 weekends & bank holidays).
Facilities	⊗ ⅢⅢ ⅃ ◖ ♀ ♙ 🎒 ⊢ ⸀ S Robinson.
Location	Welham Park, Norton (1m S)
Hotel	★★63% Talbot Hotel, Yorkersgate, MALTON
	☎(0653) 694031 29⇥▐

MASHAM   Map 08 SE28

Masham ☎Ripon (0765) 689379
Flat parkland course crossed by River Burn, which comes into play on two holes.
9 holes, 5244yds, Par 66, SSS 66, Course record 69.
Club membership 302.

Visitors	must play with member at weekends & bank holidays.
Societies	must contact the secretary in advance.
Green Fees	£15 per day.
Facilities	⊗ by prior arrangement ⅃ ◖ ♀ ♙
Location	Burnholme, Swinton Rd (1m SW off A6108)
Hotel	★★⚑74% Jervaulx Hall Hotel, MASHAM
	☎(0677) 60235 10⇥▐

PANNAL   Map 08 SE35

Pannal ☎Harrogate (0423) 872628
Fine championship course. Moorland turf but well-wooded with trees closely involved with play.
18 holes, 6659yds, Par 72, SSS 72.
Club membership 782.

Visitors	restricted 8-9.30am & 12-1.30pm weekdays, after 2.30pm weekends. Must contact in advance.
Societies	must apply several months in advance.
Green Fees	£28 per day (£31 weekends & bank holidays).
Facilities	⊗ ⅢⅢ by prior arrangement ⅃ ◖ ♀ ♙ 🎒 ⊢ ⸀ Murray Burgess.
Location	Follifoot Rd (E side of village off A61)
Hotel	★★★★63% The Majestic, Ripon Rd, HARROGATE ☎(0423) 568972 156⇥▐

RICHMOND   Map 07 NZ10

Richmond ☎(0748) 825319
Parkland course.
18 holes, 5704yds, Par 70, SSS 68, Course record 64.
Club membership 600.

Visitors	may not play before 11.30am on Sun.
Societies	must contact in writing.
Green Fees	£13 per day; £11 per round (£22 per day; £17 per round weekends & bank holidays).
Facilities	⊗ ⅢⅢ ⅃ ◖ (no catering Mon) ♀ ♙ 🎒 ⊢ ⸀ Paul Jackson.
Location	Bend Hagg (.75m N)
Hotel	★★67% King's Head Hotel, Market Place, RICHMOND ☎(0748) 850220 24⇥▐ Annexe4⇥▐

Entries highlighted in green identify
courses which are considered
to be particularly interesting

RIPON   Map 08 SE37

Ripon City ☎(0765) 603640
Hard-walking on undulating parkland course; two testing par 3's at 5th and 7th.
9 holes, 5285yds, Par 70, SSS 68, Course record 65.
Club membership 600.

Visitors	must contact in advance.
Green Fees	£10 (£15 weekends & bank holidays).
Facilities	◖ ♀ (times vary) 🎒 ⸀ T M Davis.
Location	Palace Rd (1m N on A6108)
Hotel	★★★67% Ripon Spa Hotel, Park St, RIPON ☎(0765) 602172 40⇥▐

SCARBOROUGH   Map 08 TA08

Scarborough North Cliff ☎(0723) 360786
Seaside parkland course begining on cliff top overlooking bay and castle. Good views.
18 holes, 6425yds, Par 71, SSS 71, Course record 66.
Club membership 860.

Visitors	must be member of a club with handicap certificate.
Societies	must apply in writing.
Green Fees	£18 per round (£24 weekends & bank holidays).
Facilities	⊗ ⅢⅢ ⅃ ◖ ♀ ♙ 🎒 ⊢ ⸀ S N Deller.
Location	North Cliff Av (2m N of town centre off A165)
Hotel	★★★63% Esplanade Hotel, Belmont Rd, SCARBOROUGH ☎(0723) 360382 73⇥▐

Scarborough South Cliff ☎(0723) 374737
Parkland/seaside course designed by Dr Mackenzie.
18 holes, 6085yds, Par 70, SSS 69.
Club membership 650.

Visitors	must contact in advance and have an introduction from own club.
Societies	must apply in advance.
Green Fees	£19 per day (£25 weekends & bank holidays).
Facilities	⊗ ⅢⅢ (ex Mon) ⅃ ◖ ♀ ♙ 🎒 ⸀ David Edwards.
Location	Deepdale Av (1m S on A165)
Hotel	★★66% Bradley Court, 7-9 Filey Rd, South Cliff, SCARBOROUGH ☎(0723) 360476 40rm(22⇥17▐)

SELBY   Map 08 SE63

Selby ☎(0757) 228622
Mainly flat, links-type course; prevailing SW wind. Testing holes including the 3rd, 7th and 16th.
18 holes, 6246yds, Par 70, SSS 70, Course record 65.
Club membership 780.

Visitors	restricted 11am-1pm (Nov-Mar). With member only weekends. Must contact in advance and have an introduction from own club.
Societies	welcome Wed-Fri, must apply in advance.
Green Fees	£18 per round.
Facilities	⊗ ⅢⅢ ⅃ ◖ ♀ ♙ 🎒 ⊢ ⸀ Andrew Smith.
Leisure	snooker.
Location	Brayton Barff
Hotel	★★★⚑68% Monk Fryston Hall, MONK FRYSTON ☎(0977) 682369 29⇥▐

SETTLE
Map 07 SD86

Settle ☎(07292) 3912
Picturesque parkland course.
9 holes, 4596yds, Par 64, SSS 62.
Club membership 170.

Visitors	restricted on Sun.
Societies	apply in writing.
Green Fees	not confirmed.
Facilities	♀
Location	Buckhaw Brow, Giggleswick (1m N on A65)
Hotel	★★★62% Falcon Manor Hotel, Skipton Rd, SETTLE ☎(0729) 823814 15⇨🐾 Annexe5⇨🐾

SKIPTON
Map 07 SD95

Skipton ☎(0756) 793922
Undulating parkland course with some water hazards and panoramic views.
18 holes, 5771yds, Par 70, SSS 69.
Club membership 650.

Visitors	except competition days. Must contact in advance.
Societies	must apply in writing.
Green Fees	£17 per day summer £12 winter (£22 weekends & bank holidays summer £20 winter).
Facilities	⊗ ◢ 🏠 ♀ 🏌 (no catering Mon) ♀ △ 🏠 ⛳ (J Hammond.
Location	Off North West By-Pass (1m N on A65)
Hotel	★★★78% Devonshire Arms Country House Hotel, BOLTON ABBEY ☎(0756) 710441 40⇨

STOCKTON-ON-THE-FOREST
Map 08 SE65

Forest Park ☎York (0904) 400425
New parkland/meadowland course, opened in Spring 1991, with natural features including a stream and mature and new trees. Driving range.
18 holes, 6211yds, Par 70, SSS 70.
Club membership 650.

Visitors	welcome, subject to tee availability. Advisable to contact club in advance.
Societies	by prior arrangement.
Green Fees	£12 (£17 weekends & bank holidays).
Facilities	⊗ & ◢ by prior arrangement 🏠 🏌 ♀ △ 🏠
Hotel	★★★68% York Pavilion Hotel, 45 Main St, Fulford, YORK ☎(0904) 622099 11⇨Annexe10⇨🐾

THIRSK
Map 08 SE48

Thirsk & Northallerton ☎(0845) 522170
The course has good views of the nearby Hambleton Hills. Testing course, mainly flat land.
9 holes, 6257yds, Par 72, SSS 70, Course record 69.
Club membership 389.

Visitors	must be a member of recognised golf club & cannot play before 9.30am. With member only Sun. Must contact in advance and have an introduction from own club.
Societies	must apply in writing.
Green Fees	not confirmed.
Facilities	⊗ by prior arrangement ◢ by prior arrangement 🏠 ◢ ♀ △ 🏠 ⛳ (Andrew Wright.
Location	Thornton-le-Street (2m N on A168)
Hotel	★★★66% Golden Fleece Hotel, Market Place, THIRSK ☎(0845) 523108 22rm(6⇨)

WHITBY
Map 08 NZ81

Whitby ☎(0947) 602768
Seaside course on cliff top. Good views and fresh sea breeze.
18 holes, 5706yds, Par 69, SSS 67, Course record 66.
Club membership 800.

Visitors	may not play on competition days.
Societies	must contact in writing.
Green Fees	not confirmed.
Facilities	⊗ ◢ 🏠 ◢ ♀ △ 🏠 ⛳ (Andrew Brook.
Location	Low Straggleton, Sandsend Rd (1.5m NW on A174)
Hotel	★★★65% White House Hotel, Upgang Lane, West Cliff, WHITBY ☎(0947) 600469 12rm(7⇨4🐾)

YORK
Map 08 SE65

Fulford ☎(0904) 413579
A flat, parkland/moorland course well-known for the superb quality of its turf, particularly the greens, and now famous as the venue for some of the best golf tournaments in the British Isles.
18 holes, 6775yds, Par 72, SSS 72, Course record 62.
Club membership 600.

SCORECARD: White Tees					
Hole	Yds	Par	Hole	Yds	Par
1	412	4	10	165	3
2	438	4	11	504	5
3	189	3	12	321	4
4	458	4	13	473	4
5	167	3	14	175	3
6	561	5	15	443	4
7	415	4	16	361	4
8	371	4	17	356	4
9	486	5	18	480	5
Out	3497	36	In	3278	36
			Totals	6775	72

Visitors	must contact in advance and have an introduction from own club.
Societies	must contact in writing.
Green Fees	not confirmed.
Facilities	⊗ ◢ 🏠 ◢ ♀ △ 🏠 ⛳ (Bryan Hessay.
Location	Heslington Ln (2m SE)
Hotel	★★★★63% Viking Hotel, North St, YORK ☎(0904) 659822 188⇨🐾

Heworth ☎(0904) 424618
Eleven-hole parkland course, easy walking. Holes 3 to 9 played twice from different tees.
11 holes, 6141yds, Par 70, SSS 69.
Club membership 460.

Visitors	may not play on Sun mornings in winter. Must contact in advance.
Societies	must contact the secretary in writing.
Green Fees	£14 per day (£17 weekends & bank holidays).
Facilities	⊗ (ex Mon) ◢ by prior arrangement 🏠 (ex Mon) ◢ ♀ △ 🏠 ⛳ (Neil Cheetham.
Location	Muncaster House, Muncaster Gate (1.5m NE of city centre on A1036)
Hotel	★★★72% Dean Court Hotel, Duncombe Place, YORK ☎(0904) 625082 40⇨🐾

York ☎(0904) 491840
A pleasant, well-designed, heathland course with easy
walking. The course is of good length but being flat the going
does not tire. There are two testing pond holes.
18 holes, 6285yds, Par 70, SSS 70, Course record 65.
Club membership 700.

Visitors	after 9am & not between 12-1.30pm. With member only weekends. Must contact in advance.
Societies	must apply in advance.
Green Fees	£20 per day (£24 weekends & bank holidays).
Facilities	⊗ ℿ ℊ ♏ ♀ ⏃ 🏠 ℂ A B Mason.
Location	Lords Moor Ln, Strensall (6m NE, E of Strensall village)
Hotel	★★★72% Dean Court Hotel, Duncombe Place, YORK ☎(0904) 625082 40⊰🐾

NORTHAMPTONSHIRE

CHACOMBE   Map 04 SP44

Cherwell Edge ☎(0295) 711591
Parkland course open since 1980.
18 holes, 5800yds, Par 70, SSS 68, Course record 67.
Club membership 500.

Visitors	no restrictions.
Societies	must apply in writing.
Green Fees	not confirmed.
Facilities	⊗ ℿ ℊ ♏ ♀ ⏃ 🏠 ℸ ℂ
Location	.5m S off B4525
Hotel	★★★67% Whately Hall Hotel, Banbury Cross, BANBURY ☎(0295) 263451 74⊰🐾

COLD ASHBY   Map 04 SP67

Cold Ashby ☎Northampton (0604) 740099
Undulating parkland course, nicely matured, with superb
views.
18 holes, 6020yds, Par 70, SSS 69, Course record 63.
Club membership 600.

Visitors	restricted weekends.
Societies	by arrangement.
Green Fees	Weekdays £18 per day; £12 per round.
Facilities	⊗ ℿ ℊ ♏ ♀ ⏃ 🏠 ℸ ℂ Tony Skingle.
Location	Stanford Rd (1m W)
Hotel	★★★66% Forte Posthouse Northampton/ Rugby, CRICK ☎(0788) 822101 88⊰🐾

Each golf-course entry has a recommended
AA-appointed hotel. For a wider choice of
places to stay, consult *AA Hotels and
Restaurants in Britain and Ireland* and
*AA Inspected Bed and Breakfast in
Britain and Ireland*

COLLINGTREE   Map 04 B7

Collingtree Park
☎(0604) 700000
Superb 18-hole resort course
designed by former U.S. and
British Open champion
Johnny Miller. Stunning island green at the 18th hole.
Green fee includes buggy cart
and range balls. The Golf
Academy includes a driving
range, practice holes, indoor
video teaching room, golf cus-
tom-fit centre.

SCORECARD: White Tees					
Hole	Yds	Par	Hole	Yds	Par
1	348	4	10	348	4
2	386	4	11	387	4
3	431	4	12	192	3
4	533	5	13	423	4
5	179	3	14	542	5
6	367	4	15	170	3
7	388	4	16	392	4
8	166	3	17	401	4
9	498	5	18	541	5
Out	3296	36	In	3396	36
			Totals	6692	72

*18 holes, 6692yds, Par 72, SSS
72.*
Club membership 600.

Visitors	must have a handicap certificate. Must contact in advance.
Societies	contact Irene Kilbane.
Green Fees	£40-£60 per day; £25-£35 per round (£50/£90 weekends).
Facilities	⊗ ℿ ℊ ♏ ♀ ⏃ 🏠 ℸ
Location	Windingbrook Ln (M1-junc 15 on A508 to Northampton)
Hotel	★★★★59% Swallow Hotel, Eagle Dr, NORTHAMPTON ☎(0604) 768700 122⊰🐾

CORBY   Map 04 SP88

Priors Hall ☎(0536) 60756
Municipal course laid out on made-up quarry ground and
open to prevailing wind. Wet in winter.
18 holes, 6677yds, Par 72, SSS 72.
Club membership 650.

Visitors	no restrictions.
Societies	must apply in writing.
Green Fees	£4 (£5.50 weekends & bank holidays).
Facilities	⊗ ℊ ♏ ♀ ⏃ 🏠 ℸ ℂ Malcolm Summers.
Location	Stamford Rd, Weldon (4m NE on A43)
Hotel	★★★66% The Talbot, New St, OUNDLE ☎(0832) 273621 40⊰

DAVENTRY   Map 04 SP56

Daventry & District ☎(0327) 702829
A hilly course with hard walking.
18 holes, 5555yds, Par 69, SSS 67.
Club membership 300.

Visitors	restricted Sun mornings & weekends (Oct-Mar). Must contact in advance.
Facilities	♀ ⏃ 🏠 ℸ ℂ
Location	Norton Rd (1m NE)
Hotel	★★★66% Northampton Moat House, Silver Street, Town Centre, NORTHAMPTON ☎(0604) 22441 142⊰🐾

For a full list of golf courses included in the
book, see the index at the end of the directory

FARTHINGSTONE   Map 04 SP65

Woodlands ☎(032736) 291
Pleasant rambling course with open aspect and widespread views.
18 holes, 6248yds, Par 71, SSS 71, Course record 66.
Club membership 600.

Visitors   must contact in advance.
Societies   must contact in writing.
Green Fees   not confirmed.
Facilities   ⊗ ⊪ ⅃ ☞ ♀ ⅄ 🏠 ⅂ 🏌 (Mike Gallagher.
Leisure   squash, snooker, table tennis.
Location   1m W
Hotel   ★★★69% Crossroads Hotel, WEEDON ☎(0327) 40354 10⊰Annexe40⊰

HELLIDON   Map 04 SP55

Hellidon Lakes Hotel & Country Club ☎Byfield (0327) 62550
Spectacular parkland course designed by David Snell.
18 holes, 6691yds, Par 72, SSS 72, Course record 73.
Club membership 500.

Visitors   must have handicap certificate at weekends. Must contact in advance.
Societies   must telephone in advance.
Green Fees   £28.50 per day; £19 per round (£26 per round weekends & bank holidays).
Facilities   ⊗ ⊪ ⅃ ☞ ♀ ⅄ 🏠 ⅂ 🏌 (Neil Dainton.
Leisure   hard tennis courts, riding, sauna, solarium, gymnasium.
Hotel   ★★★★65% Hellidon Lakes Hotel & Country Club, HELLIDON ☎(0327) 62550 25⊰🏠

KETTERING   Map 04 SP87

Kettering ☎(0536) 512074
A very pleasant, mainly flat parkland course with easy walking.
18 holes, 6035yds, Par 69, SSS 69, Course record 64.
Club membership 500.

Visitors   with member only weekends & bank holidays. Must have an introduction from own club.
Societies   by arrangement.
Green Fees   £18 per day/round.
Facilities   ⊗ by prior arrangement ⊪ (ex Mon) ⅃ ☞ ♀ ⅄ 🏠 (Kevin Theobald.
Location   Headlands (S side of town centre)
Hotel   ★★59% High View Hotel, 156 Midland Rd, WELLINGBOROUGH ☎(0933) 278733 14⊰🏠Annexe3rm

NORTHAMPTON   Map 04 SP76

Delapre Golf Complex ☎(0604) 764036
Rolling parkland course, part of municipal golf complex, which includes two 9-hole, par 3 courses, pitch-and-putt and 33 bay driving-range.
18 holes, 6356yds, Par 70, SSS 70, Course record 66.
Club membership 1000.

Visitors   must pre-book and pay in advance.

Societies   must book and pay full green fees 2 weeks in advance.
Green Fees   not confirmed.
Facilities   ⊗ ⊪ ⅃ ☞ ♀ ⅄ 🏠 ⅂ (John Corby.
Location   Eagle Dr, Nene Valley Way (2m SE)
Hotel   ★★★63% Westone Moat House, Ashley Way, Weston Favell, NORTHAMPTON ☎(0604) 406262 30⊰Annexe36⊰

Kingsthorpe ☎(0604) 710610
Undulating parkland, town course.
18 holes, 6006yds, Par 69, SSS 69, Course record 63.
Club membership 650.

Visitors   must have handicap certificate. With member only weekends & bank holidays. Must contact in advance and have an introduction from own club.
Societies   by arrangement.
Green Fees   £16 per day/round.
Facilities   ⊗ ⊪ by prior arrangement ⅃ ☞ ♀ ⅄ 🏠 (Paul Smith.
Location   Kingsley Rd (N side of town centre on A5095)
Hotel   ★★★63% Westone Moat House, Ashley Way, Weston Favell, NORTHAMPTON ☎(0604) 406262 30⊰Annexe36⊰

Northampton ☎(0604) 845155
New parkland course with water in play on three holes.
18 holes, 6534yds, Par 72, SSS 71.
Club membership 910.

Visitors   must have handicap certificate. With member only at weekends. Must contact in advance and have an introduction from own club.
Societies   by arrangement.
Green Fees   £25 per day.
Facilities   ⊗ ⊪ ⅃ ☞ ♀ ⅄ 🏠 (Mark Chamberlain.
Location   Harlestone (NW of town centre on A428)
Hotel   ★★★66% Northampton Moat House, Silver Street, Town Centre, NORTHAMPTON ☎(0604) 22441 142⊰🏠

Northamptonshire County ☎(0604) 843025
Undulating heathland/woodland course with gorse, heather and fine pine woods.
18 holes, 6503yds, Par 70, SSS 71.
Club membership 900.

Visitors   restricted weekends. Must contact in advance and have an introduction from own club.
Societies   Wed & Thu only, must contact in advance.
Green Fees   £30 day/round.
Facilities   ⊗ ⊪ ⅃ ☞ ♀ ⅄ 🏠 (Tim Rouse.
Location   Church Brampton (4m NW of town centre off A50)
Hotel   ★★★63% Westone Moat House, Ashley Way, Weston Favell, NORTHAMPTON ☎(0604) 406262 30⊰Annexe36⊰

OUNDLE   Map 04 TL08

Oundle ☎(0832) 273267
Undulating parkland course, shortish but difficult. A small brook affects some of the approaches to the greens.
18 holes, 5549yds, Par 70, SSS 67, Course record 64.
Club membership 630.

▶

Visitors	may not play before 10.30am weekends unless with member.
Societies	must apply in writing.
Green Fees	£18 per day (£25 weekends).
Facilities	⊗ ℿ ╚ ■ ♀ ⚐ (M Cunningham.
Location	Benefield Rd (1m W on A427)
Hotel	★★★66% The Talbot, New St, OUNDLE ☎(0832) 273621 40⇌

STAVERTON   Map 04 SP56

Staverton Park ☎Daventry (0327) 705911
Open course, fairly testing with good views.
18 holes, 6204yds, Par 71, SSS 71, Course record 67.
Club membership 478.

Visitors	restricted weekends. Must contact in advance.
Societies	by arrangement.
Green Fees	£19 per round (£21 weekends).
Facilities	⊗ ℿ ╚ ■ ♀ ⚐ ⇤ (Brian & Richard Mudge.
Leisure	snooker, sauna, solarium, trimnasium.
Location	.75m NE of Staverton on A425
Hotel	★★★69% Crossroads Hotel, WEEDON ☎(0327) 40354 10⇌Annexe40⇌

WELLINGBOROUGH   Map 04 SP86

Rushden ☎Rushden (0933) 312581
Parkland course with brook running through the middle.
10 holes, 6335yds, Par 71, SSS 70.
Club membership 400.

Visitors	may not play Wed afternoon. With member only weekends.
Societies	must apply in writing.
Green Fees	£12 per round.
Facilities	⊗ & ℿ (summer only) ╚ ■ (no catering Mon) ♀ (ex Mon) △
Location	Kimbolton Rd, Chelveston (2m E of Higham Ferrers on A45)
Hotel	★★★57% Hind Hotel, Sheep St, WELLINGBOROUGH ☎(0933) 222827 34⇌ⁿ

Wellingborough ☎(0933) 677234
An undulating parkland course with many trees. The 514-yd, 14th is a testing hole. The clubhouse is a stately home.
18 holes, 6620yds, Par 72, SSS 72, Course record 69.
Club membership 850.

Visitors	must have handicap certificate, but may not play at weekends & bank holidays. Must contact in advance.
Societies	must apply in writing.
Green Fees	£27.50 per day; £22 per round.
Facilities	⊗ ℿ ╚ ■ ♀ △ ⚐ (David Clifford.
Leisure	outdoor swimming pool, fishing, snooker.
Location	Gt Harrowden Hall (2m N on A509)
Hotel	★★★57% Hind Hotel, Sheep St, WELLINGBOROUGH ☎(0933) 222827 34⇌ⁿ

A golf-course name printed in ***bold italics***
means that we have been unable to verify
information with the club's management
for the current year

NORTHUMBERLAND

ALLENDALE   Map 12 NY85

Allendale ☎091-267 5875
Slightly hilly, rural course with fine views. Club moving to new course in early May '92, one and a half miles south of Allendale on B6295 Allenheads road.
9 holes, 4488yds, Par 66, SSS 63, Course record 65.
Club membership 120.

Visitors	restricted Sun mornings & Aug bank holiday till 4pm.
Societies	contact 2-3 weeks in advance.
Green Fees	£4 (£5 weekends).
Facilities	■ △ ⚐
Leisure	riding.
Location	Thornley Gate (.75m W)
Hotel	★★64% County Hotel, Priestpopple, HEXHAM ☎(0434) 602030 9⇌ⁿ

ALNMOUTH   Map 12 NU21

Alnmouth ☎(0665) 830231
Coastal course with pleasant views.
18 holes, 6500yds, Par 71, SSS 71, Course record 65.
Club membership 850.

Visitors	may not play Wed, Fri, weekends & bank holidays. Must contact in advance.
Societies	by arrangement.
Green Fees	£20 per day.
Facilities	⊗ ℿ ╚ ■ ♀ △ ⚐ ⇤
Location	Foxton Hall (1m NE)
Hotel	★★★63% White Swan Hotel, Bondgate Within, ALNWICK ☎(0665) 602109 43⇌ⁿ

Alnmouth Village ☎(0665) 830370
Seaside course with part coastal view.
9 holes, 6078yds, Par 70, SSS 70.
Club membership 480.

Visitors	no restrictions.
Societies	must contact in advance.
Facilities	♀ △
Location	Marine Rd (E side of village)
Hotel	★★★63% White Swan Hotel, Bondgate Within, ALNWICK ☎(0665) 602109 43⇌ⁿ

ALNWICK   Map 12 NU11

Alnwick ☎(0665) 602632
Parkland course offering a fair test of golfing skills.
9 holes, 5387yds, Par 66, SSS 66, Course record 62.
Club membership 402.

Visitors	may not play on competition days.
Societies	must contact in advance.
Green Fees	£15 per day; £10 per round (£20 per day; £15 per round weekends & bank holidays).
Facilities	⊗ ╚ ■ ♀ △
Location	Swansfield Park (S side of town)
Hotel	★★★63% White Swan Hotel, Bondgate Within, ALNWICK ☎(0665) 602109 43⇌ⁿ

BAMBURGH   Map 12 NU13

Bamburgh Castle
☎(06684) 378
This is not a long, links course, but there are those who have played golf all over the world who say that for sheer breath-taking beauty this northern seaside gem cannot be bettered. And the course itself is the greatest fun to play. Magnificent views of Farne Island, Lindisfarne and Holy Island.
18 holes, 5465yds, Par 68, SSS 67, Course record 63.
Club membership 650.

SCORECARD					
Hole	Yds	Par	Hole	Yds	Par
1	182	3	10	196	3
2	213	3	11	334	4
3	510	5	12	413	4
4	476	5	13	406	4
5	314	4	14	149	3
6	224	3	15	404	4
7	279	4	16	268	4
8	162	3	17	260	4
9	361	4	18	314	4
Out	2721	34	In	2744	34
			Totals	5465	68

Visitors   with member only bank holidays & competition days. Handicap certificate required. Must contact in advance.
Societies   apply in writing.
Green Fees £15 per day/round (£25 per day; £20 per round weekend & bank holidays).
Facilities ⊗ Ⅷ ⌱ ⬤ ♀ △ 🏠
Location 6m E of A1 via B1341 or B1342
Hotel ★★69% Lord Crewe Arms, Front St, BAMBURGH ☎(06684) 243 25rm(14⇨6🏾)

BEDLINGTON   Map 12 NZ28

Bedlingtonshire ☎(0670) 822087
Meadowland/parkland course with easy walking. Under certain conditions the wind can be a distinct hazard.
18 holes, 6813yds, Par 73, SSS 73, Course record 65.
Club membership 850.
Visitors   restricted in summer. Must contact in advance.
Societies   apply in advance to: Wansbeck DC, Ashington.
Green Fees not confirmed.
Facilities ⊗ Ⅷ ⌱ ⬤ ♀ △ 🏠 ⫞ 𝄃 Marcus Webb.
Location Acorn Bank (1m SW on A1068)
Hotel ★★★★54% Holiday Inn Newcastle, Great North Rd, SEATON BURN ☎091-236 5432 150⇨🏾

BELLINGHAM   Map 12 NY88

Bellingham ☎(0434) 220530
Nine-hole downland course with natural hazards and 18 tees.
9 holes, 5245yds, Par 67, SSS 66, Course record 63.
Club membership 250.
Visitors   by appointment only on Sun.
Societies   must contact in advance.
Green Fees £8 (£10 weekends & bank holidays).
Facilities ⊗ Ⅷ ⌱ ⬤ (catering by prior arrangement) ♀ △
Location Boggle Hole (N side of village on B6320)
Hotel ★★66% Riverdale Hall Hotel, BELLINGHAM ☎(0434) 220254 20⇨🏾

We make every effort to ensure that our information is accurate but details may change after we go to print

BERWICK-UPON-TWEED   Map 12 NT95

Berwick-upon-Tweed (Goswick) ☎(0289) 87256
Natural seaside links course, with undulating fairways, elevated tees and good greens.
18 holes, 6425yds, Par 72, SSS 71, Course record 64.
Club membership 450.
Visitors   may not play between 10am-noon weekdays & after 2pm weekends. Must contact in advance.
Societies   party of 8 or more by arrangement.
Green Fees £18 per day; £15 per round (£24/£18 weekends).
Facilities Ⅷ by prior arrangement ⌱ ⬤ ♀ △ 🏠 𝄃 Paul Terras.
Location Goswick (6m S off A1)
Hotel ★★★63% Turret House Hotel, Etal Rd, Tweedmouth, BERWICK-UPON-TWEED ☎(0289) 330808 13⇨🏾

Magdalene Fields ☎(0289) 306384
Seaside course with natural hazards formed by sea bays. Last 9 holes open to winds. Testing 18th hole over bay (par 3).
18 holes, 6551yds, Par 72, SSS 71, Course record 69.
Club membership 200.
Visitors   must possess individual sets of clubs. Must contact in advance and have an introduction from own club.
Societies   must contact in advance.
Green Fees not confirmed.
Facilities ⊗ by prior arrangement ⌱ ⬤ ♀ △ ⫞
Location Magdalene Fields (E side of town centre)

▶

Hotel   ★★★63% Turret House Hotel, Etal Rd,
Tweedmouth, BERWICK-UPON-TWEED
☎(0289) 330808 13➪🏌

BLYTH   Map 12 NZ38

Blyth ☎(0670) 367728
Course built over old colliery. Parkland with water hazards.
18 holes, 6300yds, Par 72, SSS 71, Course record 64.
Club membership 815.
Visitors   with member only after 3pm & at weekends.
Societies   apply in writing.
Green Fees   £14 per day.
Facilities   ⊗ ⅢⅬ 🍺 ♀ 🛆 🛎 🌱
Leisure   pool table.
Location   New Delaval (6m N of Whitley Bay)
Hotel   ★★66% Windsor Hotel, South Pde, WHITLEY
BAY ☎091-252 3317 45➪🏌

CRAMLINGTON   Map 12 NZ27

Arcot Hall ☎091-236 2794
A wooded parkland course, reasonably flat.
18 holes, 6389yds, Par 70, SSS 70, Course record 65.
Club membership 700.
Visitors   with member only weekends & bank holidays.
Must be member of a Golf Club. Must contact
in advance.
Societies   welcome midweek only, contact in advance.
Green Fees   £20.
Facilities   ⊗ Ⅲ Ⅼ 🍺 ♀ 🛆 🛎 🌱 ℂ Graham Cant.
Leisure   snooker.
Location   2m SW off A1
Hotel   ★★★★54% Holiday Inn Newcastle, Great
North Rd, SEATON BURN ☎091-236 5432
150➪🏌

EMBLETON   Map 12 NU22

Dunstanburgh Castle ☎(0665) 576562
Rolling links designed by James Braid, with castle and bird
sanctuary either side. Superb views.
18 holes, 6039yds, Par 70, SSS 69.
Club membership 410.
Visitors   no restrictions.
Societies   contact in advance.
Green Fees   £10.50 per day (£16.50 per day;£12.50 per round
weekends & bank holidays).
Facilities   ⊗ Ⅲ Ⅼ 🍺 ♀ 🛆 🛎 🌱
Location   .5m E
Hotel   ★★74% Beach House Hotel, Sea Front,
SEAHOUSES ☎(0665) 720337 14➪🏌

HEXHAM   Map 12 NY96

Hexham ☎(0434) 603072
A very pretty undulating parkland course with interesting
natural contours. From parts of the course, particularly
the elevated 6th tee, there are the most exquisite views of
the valley below. As good a parkland course as any in the
North of England.
18 holes, 6000yds, Par 70, SSS 68.
Club membership 700.

Visitors   must contact in advance.
Societies   welcome weekdays, contact in advance.
Green Fees   not confirmed.
Facilities   ⊗ by prior arrangement Ⅲ by prior arrange-
ment Ⅼ 🍺 ♀ 🛆 🛎 ℂ Ian Waugh.
Leisure   squash, snooker.
Location   Spital Park (1m NW on B6531)
Hotel   ★★★70% Beaumont Hotel, Beaumont St,
HEXHAM ☎(0434) 602331 23➪🏌

Tynedale ☎No telephone
Flat, easy moorland course. Bounded by river and railway.
9 holes, 5643yds, Par 69, SSS 67.
Club membership 275.
Visitors   may not play Sun.
Green Fees   not confirmed.
Location   Tyne Green (N side of town)
Hotel   ★★★70% Beaumont Hotel, Beaumont St,
HEXHAM ☎(0434) 602331 23➪🏌

MORPETH   Map 12 NZ28

Morpeth ☎(0670) 519980
Parkland course with views of the Cheviots.
18 holes, 5956yds, Par 72, SSS 70, Course record 67.
Club membership 700.
Visitors   restricted weekends & bank holidays. Must
contact in advance and have an introduction
from own club.
Societies   apply in writing.
Green Fees   £19.75 per day; £13 per round (£25.75/£19.75
weekends & bank holidays..
Facilities   ⊗ Ⅲ Ⅼ 🍺 ♀ 🛆 🛎 ℂ Martin Jackson.
Leisure   snooker.
Location   The Common (S side of town centre on A197)
Hotel   ★★★★75% Linden Hall Hotel,
LONGHORSLEY ☎(0670) 516611 45➪🏌

NEWBIGGIN-BY-THE-SEA   Map 12 NY96

Newbiggin-by-the-Sea ☎(0670) 817344
Seaside-links course.
18 holes, 6452yds, Par 72, SSS 71, Course record 67.
Club membership 500.
Visitors   may not play before 10am or on competition
days. Must contact in advance.
Societies   apply in writing.
Green Fees   not confirmed.
Facilities   ⊗ Ⅲ Ⅼ 🍺 ♀ 🛆 🛎 🌱
Leisure   snooker.
Location   N side of town
Hotel   ★★★★75% Linden Hall Hotel,
LONGHORSLEY ☎(0670) 516611 45➪🏌

PONTELAND   Map 12 NZ17

Ponteland ☎(0661) 22689
Open parkland course, good views and testing golf.
18 holes, 6524yds, Par 72, SSS 71, Course record 63.
Club membership 720.

Visitors	with member only weekends & bank holidays. Must have an introduction from own club.
Societies	welcome Tue & Thu only.
Green Fees	£18.50 per day.
Facilities	⊗ ⅷ by prior arrangement ⅊ ⬤ ♀ ⌂ ⊞ 𝄢 Alan Crosby.
Location	53 Bell Villas (.5m E on A696)
Hotel	★★★64% Airport Moat House Hotel, Woolsington, NEWCASTLE UPON TYNE AIRPORT ☎(0661) 24911 100⇆𝄢

PRUDHOE   Map 12 NZ06

Prudhoe ☎(0661) 32466
Parkland course with natural hazards, easy walking.
18 holes, 5812yds, Par 69, SSS 68.
Club membership 390.

Visitors	must contact in writing.
Societies	must contact in writing.
Green Fees	not confirmed.
Facilities	♀ ⌂ ⊞
Location	Eastwood Park (E side of town centre off A695)
Hotel	★★64% County Hotel, Priestpopple, HEXHAM ☎(0434) 602030 9⇆𝄢

ROTHBURY   Map 12 NU00

Rothbury ☎(0669) 20718
Very flat parkland course alongside the River Coquet.
9 holes, 2788yds, Par 68, SSS 67, Course record 64.
Club membership 400.

Visitors	may not play at weekends.
Societies	may not play at weekends.
Green Fees	£9 per day (£14 weekends).
Facilities	♀ (evenings/weekends) ⌂
Location	Old Race Course (S side of town off B6342)
Hotel	★★★63% White Swan Hotel, Bondgate Within, ALNWICK ☎(0665) 602109 43⇆𝄢

SEAHOUSES   Map 12 NU23

Seahouses ☎Alnwick (0665) 720794
Typical links course with many hazards, including the famous 10th, 'Logans Loch', water hole.
18 holes, 5399yds, Par 66, SSS 66, Course record 65.
Club membership 450.

Visitors	must contact in advance for weekends.
Societies	apply in writing.
Green Fees	£11.50 per day (£14.50 per day; £12/50 per round weekends & bank holidays).
Facilities	⊗ ⅷ ⅊ ⬤ (no catering Mon pm) ♀ ⌂ ⊞
Location	Beadnell Rd (S side of village on B1340)
Hotel	★★70% Olde Ship Hotel, SEAHOUSES ☎(0665) 720200 12⇆𝄢 Annexe4⇆𝄢

STOCKSFIELD   Map 12 NZ06

Stocksfield ☎(0661) 843041
Challenging course: parkland (9 holes), woodland (9 holes).
18 holes, 5594yds, Par 68, SSS 68, Course record 65.
Club membership 700.

Visitors	welcome except weekends until 4pm. Must contact in advance.
Societies	must contact in advance.

Green Fees	not confirmed.
Facilities	⅊ ⬤ ♀ ⌂ ⊞
Location	New Ridley Rd (2.5m SE off A695)
Hotel	★★★70% Beaumont Hotel, Beaumont St, HEXHAM ☎(0434) 602331 23⇆𝄢

WARKWORTH   Map 12 NU20

Warkworth ☎(0665) 711596
Seaside links course, with good views and alternative tees for the back nine.
9 holes, 6000yds, Par 70, SSS 68, Course record 66.
Club membership 440.

Visitors	welcome except Tue & Sat.
Societies	apply in writing.
Green Fees	£12 per day (£18 weekends & bank holidays).
Facilities	⊗ ⅊ ⬤ ♀ ⌂
Location	The Links (.5m E of village off A1068)
Hotel	★★★63% White Swan Hotel, Bondgate Within, ALNWICK ☎(0665) 602109 43⇆𝄢

NOTTINGHAMSHIRE

EAST LEAKE   Map 08 SK52

Rushcliffe ☎(0509) 852959
Hilly, tree-lined and picturesque parkland course.
18 holes, 6020yds, Par 70, SSS 68, Course record 63.
Club membership 800.

Visitors	restricted weekends & bank holidays 9.30-11am & 3-4.30pm.
Societies	must apply in advance.
Green Fees	£20 per day (£23 weekends).
Facilities	⊗ ⅷ ⅊ ⬤ ♀ ⌂ ⊞ 𝄢 Tim Smart.
Leisure	snooker.
Location	Stocking Ln (1m N)
Hotel	★★★62% Novotel Nottingham Derby, Bostock Ln, LONG EATON ☎(0602) 720106 110⇆𝄢

KEYWORTH   Map 08 SK63

Stanton on the Wolds ☎Plumtree (06077) 2006
Parkland course, fairly flat with stream running through four holes.
18 holes, 6437yds, Par 73, SSS 71, Course record 65.
Club membership 900.

Visitors	restricted Tue & competition days. Must contact in advance and have an introduction from own club.
Societies	must apply in Oct
Green Fees	£22 per day; £20 per round.
Facilities	⊗ ⅷ ⅊ ⬤ ♀ ⌂ ⊞ 𝄢 Nick Hernon.
Location	E side of village
Hotel	★★65% Rufford Hotel, 53 Melton Road, West Bridgford, NOTTINGHAM ☎(0602) 814202 35𝄢

If you know of a golf course which welcomes
visitors and is not already in this guide,
we should be grateful for information

KIRKBY IN ASHFIELD Map 08 SK 55

Notts ☎ Mansfield (0623) 753225
Undulating heathland Championship course. Driving range.
18 holes, 7020yds, Par 73, SSS 74, Course record 67.
Club membership 500.

Visitors	except weekends & bank holidays unless with member. Must contact in advance and have an introduction from own club.
Societies	must apply in advance.
Green Fees	£38 per day; £30 per round.
Facilities	⊗ by prior arrangement ﬞﬞ by prior arrangement ⅃ 🎭 ⬛ ♀ ⌂ 🏌 Brian Waites.
Location	Hollinwell (1.5m SE off A611)
Hotel	★★★69% Swallow Hotel, Carter Ln East, SOUTH NORMANTON ☎(0773) 812000 161⇨🏠

MANSFIELD Map 08 SK 56

Sherwood Forest ☎(0623) 26689
As the names suggests, the Forest is the main feature of this natural heathland course with its heather, silver birch and pine trees. The homeward nine holes are particularly testing. The 11th and 14th are notable par 4 holes on this well-bunkered course designed by the great James Braid.
18 holes, 6714yds, Par 71, SSS 73, Course record 65.
Club membership 775.

Visitors	allowed Mon, Thu & Fri only. Must contact in advance and have an introduction from own club.
Societies	welcome Mon, Thu & Fri, must apply in advance.
Green Fees	£25 per round; £30 per day.
Facilities	⊗ ﬞﬞ ⅃ 🎭 ⬛ ♀ ⌂ 🏌 Kenneth Hall.
Location	Eakring Rd (2.5m E)
Hotel	★★★58% Forte Posthouse Nottingham/ Derby, Bostocks Ln, SANDIACRE ☎(0602) 397800 97⇨🏠

MANSFIELD WOODHOUSE Map 08 SK 56

Mansfield Woodhouse ☎ Mansfield (0623) 23521
Easy walking on heathland.
9 holes, 2150yds, Par 62, SSS 60 or 2411yds, Par 68, SSS 65.
Club membership 100.

Visitors	no restrictions.
Societies	must contact in writing.
Green Fees	not confirmed.
Facilities	⊗ ﬞﬞ ⅃ 🎭 ⬛ ♀ ⌂ 🏌 Leslie Highfield.
Location	Leeming Ln North (N side of town centre off A60)
Hotel	★★64% Pine Lodge Hotel, 281-283 Nottingham Rd, MANSFIELD ☎(0623) 22308 21rm(19⇨🏠)

NEWARK-ON-TRENT Map 08 SK 75

Newark ☎(0636) 626282
Wooded, parkland course in secluded situation with easy walking.
18 holes, 6421yds, Par 71, SSS 71, Course record 70.
Club membership 650.

Visitors	must have handicap certificate. Must contact in advance.
Societies	must apply in writing.
Green Fees	£22 per day; £17 per round.
Facilities	⊗ ﬞﬞ ⅃ 🎭 ⬛ ♀ ⌂ 🏌 H A Bennett.
Leisure	snooker.
Location	Coddington (4m E on A17)
Hotel	★★66% Grange Hotel, 73 London Rd, NEWARK ☎(0636) 703399 10⇨🏠 Annexe5⇨🏠

NOTTINGHAM Map 08 SK 53

Beeston Fields ☎(0602) 257062
Parkland course with sandy subsoil and wide, tree-lined fairways. The par 3, 14th has elevated tee and small bunker-guarded green.
18 holes, 6414yds, Par 71, SSS 71, Course record 68.
Club membership 750.

Visitors	must contact in advance.
Societies	must apply in advance.
Green Fees	not confirmed.
Facilities	⊗ ﬞﬞ ⅃ 🎭 ⬛ ♀ ⌂ 🏌 Alun Wardle.
Leisure	snooker.
Location	Beeston (4m SW off A52)
Hotel	★★★58% Forte Posthouse Nottingham/ Derby, Bostocks Ln, SANDIACRE ☎(0602) 397800 97⇨🏠

Bulwell Forest ☎(0602) 278008
Municipal heathland course with many natural hazards. Very tight fairways and subject to wind.
18 holes, 5606yds, Par 68, SSS 67.
Club membership 450.

Visitors	restricted weekends. Must contact in advance and have an introduction from own club.
Societies	must apply in writing.
Green Fees	£6.65-£8.50.
Facilities	⊗ 🎭 ⬛ ♀ ⌂ 🏠 🏌 C D Hall.
Location	Hucknall Rd, Bulwell (4m NW of city centre on A611)
Hotel	★★★66% Nottingham Moat House, Mansfield Rd, NOTTINGHAM ☎(0602) 602621 172⇨🏠

Chilwell Manor ☎(0602) 258958
Flat parkland course.
18 holes, 6379yds, Par 70, SSS 69.
Club membership 750.

Visitors	with member only weekends. Must contact in advance and have an introduction from own club.
Societies	welcome Mon, must apply in advance.
Green Fees	£20 per day/round.
Facilities	⊗ ﬞﬞ ⅃ 🎭 ⬛ ♀ ⌂ 🏌 E McCausland.
Location	Meadow Ln, Chilwell (4m SW on A6005)
Hotel	★★60% Europa Hotel, 20 Derby Rd, LONG EATON ☎(0602) 728481 19rm(14⇨🏠)

Mapperley ☎(0602) 265611
Hilly meadowland course but with easy walking.
18 holes, 6283yds, Par 71, SSS 70.
Club membership 450.

Visitors	must be member of recognised club.
Green Fees	not confirmed.

Facilities ⊗ ☽ ⛳ & ☕ by prior arrangement 🍷 ⌂ ▣ ⚲ Richard Daibell.
Leisure pool table.
Location Central Av, Mapperley Plains (3m NE of city centre off B684)
Hotel ★★★★60% Forte Crest, Saint James's St, NOTTINGHAM ☎(0602) 470131 139⇨

Nottingham City ☎(0602) 278021
A pleasant municipal parkland course on the city outskirts.
18 holes, 6218yds, Par 69, SSS 70, Course record 66.
Club membership 425.
Visitors restricted Sat 7am-3pm.
Societies welcome except weekends.
Green Fees £6.50 (£8.20 weekends).
Facilities ⊗ ☽ by prior arrangement ⛳ ☕ 🍷 ⌂ ▣ ⚲ Cyril Jepson.
Location Bulwell Hall Park (4m NW of city centre off A6002)
Hotel ★★★66% Nottingham Moat House, Mansfield Rd, NOTTINGHAM ☎(0602) 602621 172⇨♠

Wollaton Park ☎(0602) 787574
A pleasant, fairly level course set in a park close to the centre of Nottingham, with red and fallow deer herds. The fairways are tree-lined. The 502-yd dog-leg 15th is a notable hole. The stately home - Wollaton Hall - is situated in the park.
18 holes, 6494yds, Par 71, SSS 71, Course record 66.
Club membership 770.
Visitors must contact in advance.
Societies welcome Tue & Fri, must apply in advance.
Green Fees £23.50 per day (£28 weekends & bank holidays); £15.50 per round (£19 weekends & bank holidays).
Facilities ⊗ by prior arrangement ☽ by prior arrangement ⛳ ☕ 🍷 ▣ ⚲ John Lower.
Leisure snooker.
Location Wollaton Park (2.5m W of city centre off A52)
Hotel ★★★59% Waltons Hotel, 2 North Road, The Park, NOTTINGHAM ☎(0602) 475215 13⇨♠

Oxton — Map 08 SK65

Oakmere Park ☎Nottingham (0602) 653545
Set in rolling parkland in the heart of picturesque Robin Hood country. The par 4 (16th) and par 5 (1st) are notable. Thirty-bay floodlit driving range.
North Course: 18 holes, 6617mtrs, Par 72, SSS 72, Course record 65.
South Course: 9 holes, 3193mtrs, Par 37.
Club membership 450.
Visitors must contact in advance.
Societies must apply in writing.
Green Fees North £20 per day £15 per round; South £6 per round.
Facilities ⊗ ☽ ⛳ ☕ 🍷 ⌂ ▣ ⚲ Geoff Norton.
Location Oaks Ln (1m NW off A6097)
Hotel ★★★65% Saracen's Head Hotel, Market Place, SOUTHWELL ☎(0636) 812701 27⇨♠

Radcliffe-on-Trent — Map 08 SK63

Radcliffe-on-Trent ☎(0602) 333000
Fairly flat, parkland course with three good finishing holes: 16th (427 yds) par 4; 17th (180 yds) through spinney, par 3; 18th (331 yds) dog-leg par 4. Excellent views.
18 holes, 6381yds, Par 70, SSS 71.
Club membership 650.
Visitors restricted Tue. Must have an introduction from own club.
Societies welcome Wed.
Green Fees £20.50 per day (£26 weekends & bank holidays).
Facilities ⊗ ☽ by prior arrangement ⛳ ☕ 🍷 ⌂ ▣ ⚲ Philip Hinton.
Location Drewberry Ln, Cropwell Rd (1m SE off A52)
Hotel ★★★59% Waltons Hotel, 2 North Road, The Park, NOTTINGHAM ☎(0602) 475215 13⇨♠

Ruddington — Map 08 SK53

Ruddington Grange ☎Nottingham (0602) 846141
Undulating parkland course with water hazards on 12 holes.
18 holes, 6490yds, Par 71, SSS 71, Course record 71.
Club membership 650.
Visitors a handicap certificate is required, contact in advance if possible. Play may be restricted Sat & Wed mornings.
Societies must contact in advance.
Green Fees £20-£22 (£24-£26 weekends).
Facilities ⊗ ☽ ⛳ ☕ 🍷 ⌂ ▣ ⚲ Robert Ellis.
Location Wilford Rd (5m S of Nottingham, A60 to Ruddington)
Hotel ★★★69% Swans Hotel & Restaurant, 84-90 Radcliffe Rd, West Bridgford, NOTTINGHAM ☎(0602) 814042 31⇨♠

Serlby — Map 08 SK68

Serlby Park ☎(0777) 818268
Parkland course.
9 holes, 5325yds, Par 66, SSS 66.
Club membership 300.
Visitors must be accompanied by member.
Green Fees not confirmed.
Facilities 🍷 (weekends & special occasions) ⌂ ▣
Location E side of village off A638
Hotel ★★★63% Charnwood Hotel, Sheffield Rd, BLYTH ☎(0909) 591610 20⇨♠

Each golf-course entry has a recommended AA-appointed hotel. For a wider choice of places to stay, consult *AA Hotels and Restaurants in Britain and Ireland* and *AA Inspected Bed and Breakfast in Britain and Ireland*

SUTTON IN ASHFIELD
Map 08 SK45

Coxmoor ☎Mansfield (0623) 557359

Undulating moorland/heathland course with easy walking and excellent views. The clubhouse is modern with a well-equipped games room. The course lies adjacent to Forestry Commission land over which there are several footpaths and extensive views.
18 holes, 6251yds, Par 73, SSS 70, Course record 65.
Club membership 600.

SCORECARD: Medal Tees					
Hole	Yds	Par	Hole	Yds	Par
1	423	4	10	152	3
2	167	3	11	354	4
3	477	5	12	371	4
4	295	4	13	520	5
5	395	4	14	300	4
6	476	5	15	289	4
7	136	3	16	519	5
8	371	4	17	174	3
9	333	4	18	499	5
Out	3073	36	In	3178	37
			Totals	6251	73

Visitors restricted weekends & bank holidays. Must contact in advance.
Societies must apply in advance.
Green Fees £22 per day.
Facilities ⊗ ℳ ⅃ ♨ ♀ ⅄ 🏠 ⅃ David Ridley.
Leisure snooker.
Location Coxmoor Rd (2m SE off A611)
Hotel ★★★69% Swallow Hotel, Carter Ln East, SOUTH NORMANTON ☎(0773) 812000 161⇨🐾

WORKSOP
Map 08 SK57

Kilton Forest ☎(0909) 472488
Slightly undulating, parkland course on the north edge of Sherwood Forest. Includes three ponds.
18 holes, 6569yds, Par 72, SSS 72, Course record 69.
Club membership 450.
Visitors may not play on Sun & competition days. Must contact in advance.
Societies must contact in writing.
Green Fees £5.50 per round (£7.50 weekends).
Facilities ⊗ ℳ by prior arrangement ⅃ ♨ ♀ ⅄ 🏠 ⅂ ⅃ Peter W Foster.
Location Blyth Rd (1m NE of town centre on B6045)
Hotel ★★★63% Ye Olde Bell Hotel, BARNBY MOOR ☎(0777) 705121 55⇨🐾

Lindrick ☎(0909) 475282
Heathland course with some trees and masses of gorse.
18 holes, 6377yds, Par 69, SSS 70, Course record 65.
Club membership 500.
Visitors restricted Tue & weekends. Must contact in advance.
Societies welcome except Tue (am) & weekends.
Green Fees £35 per day/round.
Facilities ⊗ ℳ ♨ ♀ ⅄ 🏠 ⅃ Peter Cowen.
Leisure snooker.
Location Lindrick Common (3m NW on A57)
Hotel ★★★63% Ye Olde Bell Hotel, BARNBY MOOR ☎(0777) 705121 55⇨🐾

Worksop ☎(0909) 472696
Adjacent to Clumber Park this course has a heathland-type terrain, with gorse, broom, oak and birch trees. Fast, true greens, dry all year round.
18 holes, 6651yds, Par 72, SSS 72, Course record 67.
Club membership 500.
Visitors must contact in advance.

Societies must apply in advance.
Green Fees £25 weekday; £18 round (£25 weekends & bank holidays).
Facilities ⊗ ℳ by prior arrangement ⅃ ♨ ♀ ⅄ 🏠 ⅃
Leisure snooker.
Location Windmill Ln (1.75m S off A620)
Hotel ★★★63% Ye Olde Bell Hotel, BARNBY MOOR ☎(0777) 705121 55⇨🐾

OXFORDSHIRE

BURFORD
Map 04 SP21

Burford ☎(099382) 2583
Created out of open-farmland, this parkland course has high quality fairways and greens.
18 holes, 6405yds, Par 71, SSS 71.
Club membership 800.
Visitors must contact in advance.
Societies by contact in advance.
Green Fees not confirmed.
Facilities ⊗ ℳ ⅃ ♨ ♀ 🏠 ⅂ ⅃
Location Swindon Rd (.5m S off A361)
Hotel ★★64% Golden Pheasant Hotel, High St, BURFORD ☎(099382) 3223 & 3417 12⇨🐾

CHESTERTON
Map 04 SP52

Chesterton Country ☎Bicester (0869) 241204
Laid out over one-time farmland. Well-bunkered, and water hazards increase the difficulty of the course.
18 holes, 6230yds, Par 71, SSS 70, Course record 68.
Club membership 750.
Visitors must pre-book for weekends & bank holidays.
Societies must contact in advance.
Green Fees £12 per day (£18 weekends & bank holidays).
Facilities ⊗ ℳ by prior arrangement ⅃ ♨ ♀ ⅄ 🏠 ⅃ J W Wilkshire.
Leisure snooker.
Location .5m W on A4095
Hotel ★★65% Jersey Arms Hotel, MIDDLETON STONEY ☎(086989) 234 & 505 6⇨Annexe10⇨
Additional hotel ★★70% Holcombe Hotel & Restaurant, High St, DEDDINGTON ☎(0869) 38274 17⇨🐾

CHIPPING NORTON
Map 04 SP32

Chipping Norton ☎(0608) 642383
Pleasant downland course open to winds.
18 holes, 6280yds, Par 71, SSS 70, Course record 67.
Club membership 930.
Visitors with member only at weekends. Must contact in advance.
Societies must apply in writing.
Green Fees £20 per day.
Facilities ⊗ ℳ ⅃ ♨ ♀ ⅄ 🏠 ⅂ ⅃ Bob Gould.
Location Southcombe (1.5m E on A44)
Hotel ★★66% Chadlington House Hotel, CHADLINGTON ☎(060876) 437 11rm(5⇨5🐾)

For a full list of golf courses included in the book, see the index at the end of the directory

FRILFORD   Map 04 SU49

Frilford Heath ☎(0865) 390864
Two 18-hole heathland courses. Both the Red and the
Green courses are of outstanding interest and beauty.
Heather, pine, birch and, in particular, a mass of flowering
gorse enhance the terrain. The greens are extensive.
18 holes, 6768yds, Par 73, SSS 73, Course record 65.
Club membership 900.

Visitors	restricted weekends & bank holidays. Must contact in advance and have an introduction from own club.
Societies	Mon, Wed & Fri only.
Green Fees	not confirmed.
Facilities	⊗ ⅏ ☒ ♀ ⌂ 🏠 ⊣ ⋌ Derek Craik.
Location	Abingdon (1m N off A338)
Hotel	★★★62% Abingdon Lodge Hotel, Marcham Rd, ABINGDON ☎(0235) 553456 63⇨♠

HENLEY-ON-THAMES   Map 04 SU78

Badgemore Park ☎(0491) 572206
Parkland course with many trees and easy walking. The 13th
is a very difficult par 3 hole played over a valley to a narrow
green.
18 holes, 6112yds, Par 69, SSS 69, Course record 66.
Club membership 880.

Visitors	must have handicap certificate. Must contact in advance.
Societies	must apply in writing.
Green Fees	£26 per day (£29 weekends & bank holidays).
Facilities	⊗ ☒ ☒ ♀ ⌂ 🏠 ⋌ Mark Wright.
Leisure	squash.
Location	1m W
Hotel	★★★62% Red Lion Hotel, Hart St, HENLEY-ON-THAMES ☎(0491) 572161 26rm(23⇨♠)

Henley ☎(0491) 575742
Undulating parkland course. 6th hole, blind (par 4), with
steep hill.
18 holes, 6130yds, Par 69, SSS 69, Course record 65.
Club membership 830.

Visitors	must have handicap certificate & can play Mon-Fri, except bank holiday Mons. Must contact in advance.
Societies	must contact in advance.
Green Fees	£30 per round.
Facilities	⊗ by prior arrangement ☒ ☒ ♀ 🏠 ⊣ ⋌ Mark Howell.
Location	Harpsden (1.25m S off A4155)
Hotel	★★★62% Red Lion Hotel, Hart St, HENLEY-ON-THAMES ☎(0491) 572161 26rm(23⇨♠)

A golf-course name printed in ***bold italics***
means that we have been unable to verify
information with the club's management
for the current year

NUFFIELD   Map 04 SU68

Huntercombe
☎(0491) 641207
This heathland/woodland
course overlooks the Oxford-
shire plain and has many
attractive and interesting fairways and greens. Walking is
easy after the 3rd which is a
notable hole. The course is
subject to wind and grass pot
bunkers are interesting hazards.
*18 holes, 6301yds, Par 70, SSS
70.*
Club membership 600.

SCORECARD: White Tees					
Hole	Yds	Par	Hole	Yds	Par
1	150	3	10	184	3
2	394	4	11	336	4
3	366	4	12	409	4
4	335	4	13	408	4
5	396	4	14	432	4
6	525	5	15	175	3
7	214	3	16	492	5
8	436	4	17	279	4
9	369	4	18	401	4
Out	3185	35	In	3116	35
			Totals	6301	70

Visitors	may not play weekends & are restricted before 1000 weekdays. Must contact in advance and have an introduction from own club.
Societies	must apply in writing.
Green Fees	£30 per round.
Facilities	⊗ ⅏ by prior arrangement ☒ ☒ ♀ ⌂ 🏠 ⋌ John B Draycott.
Location	N off A423
Hotel	★★★62% Shillingford Bridge Hotel, Shillingford, WALLINGFORD ☎(086732) 8567 23⇨♠ Annexe10⇨♠

OXFORD Map 04 SP50

North Oxford ☎(0865) 54415
Gently undulating parkland course.
18 holes, 5807yds, Par 67, SSS 67, Course record 64.
Club membership 650.

Visitors	with member only at weekends. Must contact in advance.
Societies	must contact in advance.
Green Fees	£27 per day.
Facilities	⊗ ╫ ⊾ ⬛ ♀ △ 🏠 (R Harris.
Location	Banbury Rd (3m N of city centre on A423)
Hotel	★★★64% Oxford Moat House, Godstow Rd, Wolvercote Rbt, OXFORD ☎(0865) 59933 155⇨

Southfield ☎(0865) 242158
Home of the City, University and Ladies Clubs, and well-known to graduates throughout the world. A challenging course, in varied parkland setting, providing a real test for players.
18 holes, 5973yds, Par 69, SSS 69.
Club membership 850.

Visitors	with member only at weekends.
Societies	must apply in writing.
Green Fees	not confirmed.
Facilities	⊗ ╫ ⊾ ⬛ ♀ △ 🏠 (Tony Rees.
Location	Hill Top Rd (1.5m SE of city centre off B480)
Hotel	★★★62% Eastgate Hotel, The High, Merton St, OXFORD ☎(0865) 248244 43⇨

SHRIVENHAM Map 04 SU28

Shrivenham Park ☎(0793) 783853
Parkland course with easy walking. The par 4, 17th is a difficult dog-leg.
18 holes, 5527yds, Par 68.

Visitors	must contact in advance.
Societies	must apply in writing.
Green Fees	£15.50 per day (£18.50 weekends); £9 per round (£12 weekends).
Facilities	⊗ ╫ ⊾ ⬛ ♀ △ 🏠 ⌐ (Sean Harrison & Paul Joesph.
Location	Pennyhooks (.5m NE of town centre)
Hotel	★★★60% Forte Crest Hotel, Oxford Rd, Stratton St Margaret, SWINDON ☎(0793) 831333 94⇨🐾

TADMARTON Map 04 SP33

Tadmarton Heath ☎Hook Norton (0608) 737278
A mixture of heath and sandy land, the course, which is open to strong winds, incorporates the site of an old Roman encampment. The clubhouse is an old farm building with a 'holy well' from which the greens are watered. The 7th is a testing hole over water.
18 holes, 5682yds, Par 69, SSS 68, Course record 63.
Club membership 600.

Visitors	with member only at weekends. Must contact in advance and have an introduction from own club.
Societies	by arrangement.
Green Fees	£25 per day.
Facilities	⊗ ╫ ⊾ ⬛ ♀ △ 🏠 ⌐ (Les Bond.
Leisure	fishing.
Location	1m SW of Lower Tadmarton off B4035
Hotel	★★61% Olde School Hotel, Church St, BLOXHAM ☎(0295) 720369 11⇨🐾Annexe27⇨🐾

SHROPSHIRE

BRIDGNORTH Map 07 SO79

Bridgnorth ☎(0746) 763315
A pleasant course laid-out on parkland on the bank of the River Severn.
18 holes, 6673yds, Par 73, SSS 72, Course record 65.
Club membership 560.

Visitors	may not play on Wed. Must contact in advance.
Societies	must contact in writing.
Green Fees	£16.50 day (£22.50 weekends & bank holidays).
Facilities	⊗ ╫ ⊾ ⬛ (no catering Mon) ♀ (ex Mon) △ 🏠 (P Hinton.
Leisure	fishing.
Location	Stanley Ln (1m N off B4373)
Hotel	★★61% Falcon Hotel, Saint John St, Lowtown, BRIDGNORTH ☎(0746) 763134 15rm(5⇨37🐾)

CHURCH STRETTON Map 07 SO49

Church Stretton ☎(0694) 722281
Hillside course constructed by James Braid on the lower slopes of the Long Mynd.
18 holes, 5008yds, Par 66, SSS 65, Course record 63.
Club membership 500.

Visitors	may not play before 10.30am at weekends & bank holidays. Must contact in advance and have an introduction from own club.
Societies	must contact in advance.
Green Fees	not confirmed.
Facilities	⊗ ╫ by prior arrangement ⊾ ⬛ (catering Apr-Oct) ♀ △ 🏠
Location	Trevor Hill (NW side of village off B4370)
Hotel	★★★55% Stretton Hall Hotel, All Stretton, CHURCH STRETTON ☎(0694) 723224 13⇨🐾

LILLESHALL Map 07 SJ71

Lilleshall Hall ☎Telford (0952) 603840
Heavily-wooded parkland course. Easy walking.
18 holes, 5906yds, Par 68, SSS 68, Course record 65.
Club membership 650.

Visitors	must play with member at weekends. Must contact in advance.
Societies	must apply in writing by Dec for the following year.
Green Fees	£18 (£30 bank holidays & following day).
Facilities	⊗ ╫ & ⊾ by prior arrangement ⬛ ♀ △ 🏠 (N Bramall.
Location	Newport (3m SE)
Hotel	★★64% Royal Victoria Hotel, St Mary's St, NEWPORT ☎(0952) 820331 24rm(16⇨7🐾)

LUDLOW
Map 07 SP57

Ludlow ☎Bromfield (058477) 285
A long-established parkland course in the middle of the
racecourse. Very flat, quick drying, with broom and gorse-
lined fairways.
18 holes, 6239yds, Par 70, SSS 70.
Club membership 650.

Visitors	must play with member at weekends. Must contact in advance and have an introduction from own club.
Societies	must contact in writing.
Green Fees	£15 per day (£20 weekends).
Facilities	⊗ & ⊞ by prior arrangement ⊾ 🍺 ⍾ ⌂ 🏠 ℂ Graham J Farr.
Location	Bromfield (2m N off A49)
Hotel	★★★68% The Feathers at Ludlow, Bull Ring, LUDLOW ☎(0584) 875261 40⇨�）

MARKET DRAYTON
Map 07 SJ63

Market Drayton ☎(0630) 652266
Parkland course in quiet, picturesque surroundings
providing a good test of golf. Bungalow on course is made
available for golfing holidays.
18 holes, 6400yds, Par 71, SSS 70, Course record 69.
Club membership 450.

Visitors	may not play on Sun; must play with member on Sat. Must contact in advance.
Societies	must contact in advance.
Green Fees	not confirmed.
Facilities	⊗ ⊞ ⊾ 🍺 ⍾ ⌂ 🏠 ℂ Russel Clewes.
Location	Sutton (1m SW)
Hotel	★★70% Corbet Arms Hotel, High St, MARKET DRAYTON ☎(0630) 652037 11⇨�

MEOLE BRACE
Map 07 SJ41

Meole Brace ☎(0743) 64050
Pleasant municipal course.
12 holes, 3066yds, Par 43, SSS 42.

Visitors	no restrictions.
Green Fees	not confirmed.
Facilities	⍾ ⌂ ⍾ ℂ
Location	NE side of village off A49
Hotel	★★★62% Lion Hotel, Wyle Cop, SHREWSBURY ☎(0743) 353107 59⇨�

OSWESTRY
Map 07 SJ22

Oswestry ☎Queens Head (069188) 535
Parkland course laid-out on undulating ground.
18 holes, 6024yds, Par 70, SSS 69, Course record 62.
Club membership 700.

Visitors	must be a member of a recognised Golf Club. Must contact in advance and have an introduction from own club.
Societies	Wed & Fri only. Must contact in advance.
Green Fees	£15 per day (£20 weekends).
Facilities	⊗ ⊞ ⊾ 🍺 ⍾ ⌂ 🏠 ℂ David Skelton.
Leisure	snooker.
Location	Aston Park (2m SE on A5)
Hotel	★★★67% Wynnstay Hotel, Church St, OSWESTRY ☎(0691) 655261 27⇨�

PANT
Map 07 SJ22

Llanymynech ☎Llanymynech (0691) 830983
Upland course on the site of an early Iron Age/Roman
hillfort with far- reaching views. The 4th fairway crosses the
Welsh border.
18 holes, 6114yds, Par 70, SSS 69, Course record 65.
Club membership 805.

Visitors	must play with member after 4.30pm. Must contact in advance.
Societies	must contact in writing.
Green Fees	£15 per day; £11 per round (£18 per day; £16.50 per round weekends).
Facilities	⊗ ⊞ 🍺 (no catering Mon) ⍾ (ex Mon) ⌂ 🏠 ⍾ ℂ Andrew Griffiths.
Location	.5m SW off A483
Hotel	★★★67% Wynnstay Hotel, Church St, OSWESTRY ☎(0691) 655261 27⇨�

SHIFNAL
Map 07 SJ70

Shifnal ☎Telford (0952) 460330
Well-wooded parkland course. Walking is easy and an
attractive country mansion serves as the clubhouse.
18 holes, 6468yds, Par 71, SSS 71, Course record 64.
Club membership 560.

Visitors	must play with member on weekends & bank holidays. Must contact in advance and have an introduction from own club.
Societies	must contact in advance.
Green Fees	£22 per day; £18.50 per round.
Facilities	⊗ ⊞ ⊾ 🍺 (no catering Mon) ⍾ ⌂ 🏠 ℂ Justin Flanagan.
Leisure	snooker.
Location	Decker Hill (1m N off B4379)
Hotel	★★★★62% Park House Hotel, Silvermere Park, Park St, SHIFNAL ☎(0952) 460128 54⇨�

SHREWSBURY
Map 07 SJ41

Shrewsbury ☎Bayston Hill (074372) 2976
Parkland course. First nine flat, second undulating with good
views.
18 holes, 6300yds, Par 70, SSS 70, Course record 61.
Club membership 872.

Visitors	may only play between 10am-noon and after 2.15pm at weekends. Must contact in advance and have an introduction from own club.
Societies	must contact in writing.
Green Fees	£16 per day; £11 per round (£20 weekends).
Facilities	⊗ ⊞ ⊾ 🍺 ⍾ ⌂ 🏠 ℂ Peter Seal.
Leisure	snooker.
Location	Condover (4m S off A49)
Hotel	★★★56% Radbrook Hall Hotel, Radbrook Rd, SHREWSBURY ☎(0743) 236676 28⇨�

Entries highlighted in green identify
courses which are considered
to be particularly interesting

TELFORD
Map 07 SJ60

Telford Hotel Golf & Country Club ☎(0952) 585642
Rolling parkland course with easy walking. Three lakes and large sand traps are hazards to the fine greens.
18 holes, 6766yds, Par 72, SSS 72, Course record 62.
Club membership 625.

Visitors	must have a handicap certificate Must contact in advance and have an introduction from own club.
Societies	must contact in writing.
Green Fees	£20 per day (£25 weekends & bank holidays).
Facilities	⊗ ⏇ ⮾ ⬛ ♀ ⬠ 🛆 ⏳ ⤹ 𝄢 Steve Marr.
Leisure	heated indoor swimming pool, squash, snooker, sauna, solarium, gymnasium, whirlpool bath steam room.
Location	Sutton Hill (4m S of town centre off A442)
Hotel	★★★65% Telford Hotel Golf & Country Club, Great Hay Dr, Sutton Hill, TELFORD ☎(0952) 585642 86⇦🛏

WELLINGTON
Map 07 SJ61

Wrekin ☎Telford (0952) 244032
Downland course with some hard walking but rewarding views.
18 holes, 5699yds, Par 66, SSS 67, Course record 65.
Club membership 700.

Visitors	must contact in advance.
Societies	must telephone in advance.
Green Fees	not confirmed.
Facilities	⊗ ⏇ ⮾ ⬛ (no catering on Mon) ♀ 🛆 🏠 ⤹ K Housden.
Location	Ercall Woods (1.25m S off B5061)
Hotel	★★★66% Buckatree Hall Hotel, Wellington, TELFORD ☎(0952) 641821 64⇦🛏

WESTON-UNDER-REDCASTLE
Map 07 SJ52

Hawkstone Park Hotel ☎(093924) 611
Two courses in a beautiful setting, both with natural hazards and good views. Hawkstone Course has been established for over 50 years and enjoys a superb setting whilst the newer Weston Course has developed well.
18 holes, 6203yds, Par 72, SSS 70.
Club membership 450.

Visitors	must contact in advance.
Green Fees	not confirmed.
Facilities	🛆 🏠 ⤹ 𝄢
Location	N side of village .75m E of A49
Hotel	★★65% Bear Hotel, HODNET ☎(063084) 214 & 788 6⇦🛏

Each golf-course entry has a recommended AA-appointed hotel. For a wider choice of places to stay, consult *AA Hotels and Restaurants in Britain and Ireland* and *AA Inspected Bed and Breakfast in Britain and Ireland*

WHITCHURCH
Map 07 SJ54

Hill Valley ☎(0948) 3584
This parkland course opened in 1975, and its Main Course was designed to championship standard by Peter Alliss and Dave Thomas. The hilly terrain is enhanced by many glorious views. There are natural water hazards on seven holes. Also 9-hole Northern Course and par 3 course.

SCORECARD: White Tees					
Hole	Yds	Par	Hole	Yds	Par
1	490	5	10	380	4
2	404	4	11	388	4
3	403	4	12	339	4
4	181	3	13	449	4
5	518	5	14	346	4
6	183	3	15	157	3
7	491	5	16	489	5
8	403	4	17	169	3
9	349	4	18	378	4
Out	3422	37	In	3095	35
			Totals	6517	72

Championship: 18 holes, 6517yds, Par 72, SSS 71.
Northern: 18 holes, 6050yds, Par 72, SSS 69.
Par 3: 9 holes, 793yds, Par 27.
Club membership 600.

Visitors	must contact in advance.
Societies	must contact in advance; a deposit will be required.
Green Fees	£18 (£24 weekends).
Facilities	⊗ ⏇ ⮾ ⬛ ♀ 🛆 🏠 ⤹ 𝄢 𝄢 A R Minshall.
Leisure	hard tennis courts, squash, snooker.
Location	Terrick Rd (1m N)
Hotel	★★★63% Terrick Hall Country Hotel, Hill Valley, WHITCHURCH ☎(0948) 3031 10⇦🛏Annexe7⇦🛏

SOMERSET

BURNHAM-ON-SEA
Map 03 ST34

Brean ☎Brean Down (0278) 751570
Level and open moorland course with water hazards. Facilities of 'Brean Leisure Park' adjoining.
18 holes, 5714yds, Par 69, SSS 68.
Club membership 550.

Visitors	may not play on Sat & Sun. Must have an introduction from own club.
Societies	weekdays only. Must contact in advance.
Green Fees	£10 per round (£15 weekends).
Facilities	⮾ ⬛ ♀ 🛆 🏠 ⤹ 𝄢 Graham Coombe.
Leisure	heated indoor swimming pool.
Location	Coast Rd, Brean (6m N on coast rd)
Hotel	★★64% Battleborough Grange Country Hotel, Bristol Rd, BRENT KNOLL ☎(0278) 760208 18rm(8⇦6🛏)

Burnham & Berrow ☎Burham-on-Sea (0278) 783137
Links championship course with large sandhills.
Championship: 18 holes, 6327yds, Par 71, SSS 72, Course record 66.
9 Hole: 9 holes, 6332yds, Par 72, SSS 70.
Club membership 940.

Visitors	must have handicap certificate. Must contact in advance.
Societies	must apply in advance.
Green Fees	£26 per day (£36 weekends & bank holidays); 9 hole £8.

Facilities	⊗ ⎢⎢⎢ ⏚ ◖ (catering 11am-6pm or by prior arrangement) ♀ 📧 ⤟ ⏃ Mark Crowther-Smith.
Location	St Christopher's Way (N side of town off B3140)
Hotel	★★64% Battleborough Grange Country Hotel, Bristol Rd, BRENT KNOLL ☎(0278) 760208 18rm(8⇨6🛏)

CHARD Map 03 ST30

Windmill Golf, Squash & Country Club ☎(046030) 231
Parkland course at 735 ft above sea level with outstanding views over the Somerset Levels to the Bristol Channel and South Wales.
East/West Course: 18 holes, 6500yds, Par 73, SSS 71.
North Course: 9 holes, 3200yds.
Club membership 600.

Visitors	must contact in advance.
Societies	must apply in advance.
Green Fees	not confirmed.
Facilities	⊗ ⎢⎢⎢ by prior arrangement ⏚ ◖ ♀ ⏃ 📧
Leisure	squash.
Location	Cricket St Thomas (3m E on A30)
Hotel	★★62% Shrubbery Hotel, ILMINSTER ☎(0460) 52108 12⇨🛏

ENMORE Map 03 ST23

Enmore Park ☎Spaxton (0278) 671481
Hilly, parkland course with water features on foothills of Quantocks. Wooded countryside and views of Quantocks and Mendips. 1st and 10th are testing holes.
18 holes, 6241yds, Par 71, SSS 71, Course record 66.
Club membership 730.

Visitors	restricted competition days & weekends.
Societies	must apply in writing.
Green Fees	£25 per day (£30 weekends & bank holidays); £18 per round (£25 weekends & bank holidays).
Facilities	⊗ ⎢⎢⎢ by prior arrangement ⏚ ◖ ♀ 📧 ⏃ N Wixon.
Location	1m E
Hotel	★★★68% Walnut Tree Inn, North Petherton, BRIDGWATER ☎(0278) 662255 28⇨

GURNEY SLADE Map 03 ST64

Mendip ☎Oakhill (0749) 840570
Undulating downland course offering an interesting test of golf on superb fairways.
18 holes, 6330yds, Par 71, SSS 70.
Club membership 780.

Visitors	must have handicap certificate weekends. Must contact in advance.
Societies	must apply in advance.
Green Fees	£25 per day (£30 weekends & bank holidays); £17 per round.
Facilities	⊗ ⎢⎢⎢ ⏚ ◖ ♀ ⏃ 📧 ⏏ ⏃ R F Lee.
Location	1.5m S off A37
Hotel	★★66% Crown Hotel, Market Place, WELLS ☎(0749) 73457 15⇨🛏

For an explanation of symbols and abbreviations, see page 32

MINEHEAD Map 03 SS94

Minehead & West Somerset
☎(0643) 702057
Flat seaside links, very exposed to wind, with good turf set on a shingle bank. The last five holes adjacent to the beach are testing. The 215-yard 18th is wedged between the beach and the club buildings and provides a good finish.
18 holes, 6228yds, Par 71, SSS 71, Course record 68.
Club membership 543.

SCORECARD: White Tees					
Hole	Yds	Par	Hole	Yds	Par
1	276	4	10	133	3
2	379	4	11	493	5
3	384	4	12	424	4
4	218	3	13	354	4
5	476	5	14	149	3
6	310	4	15	310	4
7	541	5	16	425	4
8	392	4	17	332	4
9	417	4	18	215	3
Out	3393	37	In	2835	34
			Totals	6228	71

Visitors	no restrictions.
Societies	must contact in writing.
Green Fees	not confirmed.
Facilities	⊗ ⎢⎢⎢ by prior arrangement ⏚ ◖ ♀ ⏃ 📧 ⏃
Location	The Warren (E side of town centre)
Hotel	★★★67% Northfield Hotel, Northfield Rd, MINEHEAD ☎(0643) 705155 24⇨🛏

TAUNTON Map 03 ST22

Taunton & Pickeridge ☎(082342) 537
Downland course with extensive views.
18 holes, 5927yds, Par 69, SSS 68, Course record 66.
Club membership 600.

Visitors	must contact in advance and have an introduction from own club.
Societies	must telephone in advance.
Green Fees	not confirmed.
Facilities	⊗ ⎢⎢⎢ ⏚ ◖ ♀ ⏃ 📧 ⏃ Graham Glew.
Leisure	snooker.
Location	Corfe (4m S off B3170)
Hotel	★★★59% County Hotel, East St, TAUNTON ☎(0823) 337651 66⇨🛏

Vivary Park Municipal ☎(0823) 333875
A parkland course, tight and narrow with ponds.
18 holes, 4620yds, Par 63, SSS 63.

Visitors	must contact in advance.
Societies	apply in writing.
Green Fees	not confirmed.
Facilities	⏃ 📧 ⏃ ⏃
Leisure	snooker.
Location	Fons George (S side of town centre off A38)
Hotel	★★64% Falcon Hotel, Henlade, TAUNTON ☎(0823) 442502 11⇨🛏

WELLS Map 03 ST54

Wells (Somerset) ☎(0749) 675005
Beautiful wooded course with wonderful views. The prevailing SW wind complicates the 448-yd, 3rd.
18 holes, 5354yds, Par 67, SSS 66, Course record 64.
Club membership 800.

Visitors	must have handicap certificate weekends. Tee times restricted. Must contact in advance.
Societies	must apply in writing.

▶

Green Fees £18 per day (£23 weekends & bank holidays); £15 per round (£18 weekends & bank holidays).
Facilities ⊗ 〗 🛏 💺 ♀ ⤳ 🛍 ⸯ ⸢ Andrew England.
Location East Horrington Rd (1.5m E off B3139)
Hotel ★★★61% Swan Hotel, Sadler St, WELLS ☎(0749) 78877 due to change to 678877 32⇔🛏

YEOVIL Map 03 ST51

Yeovil ☎(0935) 22965
The opener lies by the River Yeo before the gentle climb to high downs with good views. The outstanding 14th and 15th holes present a challenge, being below the player with a deep railway cutting on the left of the green.
18 holes, 6144yds, Par 72, SSS 69, Course record 66.
Club membership 720.

SCORECARD: White Tees					
Hole	Yds	Par	Hole	Yds	Par
1	324	4	10	159	3
2	158	3	11	523	5
3	405	4	12	288	4
4	333	4	13	136	3
5	518	5	14	469	5
6	382	4	15	232	3
7	347	4	16	497	5
8	388	4	17	310	4
9	316	4	18	359	4
Out	3171	36	In	2973	36
			Totals	6144	72

Visitors must contact in advance and have an introduction from own club.
Societies may play on weekdays only.
Green Fees not confirmed.
Facilities ⊗ 〗 🛏 💺 ♀ ⤳ 🛍 ⸯ ⸢ Geoff Kite.
Leisure snooker.
Location Sherborne Rd (1m E on A30)
Hotel ★★★64% The Manor Hotel, Hendford, YEOVIL ☎(0935) 23116 20⇔🛏 Annexe21⇔🛏

SOUTH YORKSHIRE

BARNSLEY Map 08 SE30

Barnsley ☎(0226) 382856
Undulating, municipal parkland course with easy walking apart from last 4 holes. Testing 8th and 18th holes.
18 holes, 6042yds, Par 69, SSS 69, Course record 64.
Club membership 450.
Visitors no restrictions.
Societies by arrangement.
Green Fees £6 per day (£7 weekends).
Facilities ⊗ by prior arrangement 🛏 💺 ♀ ⤳ 🛍 ⸯ ⸢ Mike Melling.
Location Wakefield Rd, Staincross (3m N on A61)
Hotel ★★★66% Ardsley Moat House, Doncaster Rd, Ardsley, BARNSLEY ☎(0226) 289401 73⇔🛏

BAWTRY Map 08 SK69

Austerfield Park ☎Doncaster (0302) 710841
Long moorland course with postage stamp 8th and testing 618 yd-7th. Driving range attached.
18 holes, 6854yds, Par 73, SSS 73, Course record 72.
Club membership 600.
Visitors no restrictions.
Societies must apply in writing.
Green Fees £13 per day (£17 weekends).
Facilities ⊗ 〗 🛏 💺 ♀ ⤳ 🛍 ⸯ ⸢
Leisure bowling green.

Location Cross Ln (2m NE on A640)
Hotel ★★64% Falcon Hotel, Henlade, TAUNTON ☎(0823) 442502 11⇔🛏

CONISBROUGH Map 08 SK59

Crookhill Park Municipal ☎Rotherham (0709) 862979
A rolling parkland course.
18 holes, 5839yds, Par 70, SSS 68, Course record 66.
Club membership 500.
Visitors restricted weekends before 9am. Must contact in advance.
Societies by arrangement.
Green Fees £7.
Facilities ⊗ 〗 🛏 💺 ♀ ⤳ 🛍 ⸯ ⸢ Richard Swaine.
Leisure pool table.
Location 1.5m SE on B6094
Hotel ★★★62% Danum Swallow Hotel, High St, DONCASTER ☎(0302) 342261 66⇔🛏

DONCASTER Map 08 SE50

Doncaster ☎(0302) 868316
Pleasant undulating heathland course with wooded surroundings. Quick drying, ideal autumn, winter and spring.
18 holes, 6230yds, Par 69, SSS 70, Course record 66.
Club membership 600.
Visitors may not play before 11am weekends & bank holidays.
Societies must contact in advance.
Green Fees not confirmed.
Facilities ⊗ 〗 🛏 💺 ♀ ⤳ 🛍 ⸯ ⸢
Location 278 Bawtry Rd, Bessacarr (5m SE on A638)
Hotel ★★★64% Mount Pleasant Hotel, Great North Rd, ROSSINGTON ☎(0302) 868696 & 868219 33⇔🛏

Doncaster Town Moor ☎(0302) 535286
Easy walking, but testing, heathland course with good true greens. Friendly club. Notable hole is 11th (par 4), 464 yds. Situated in centre of racecourse.
18 holes, 6094yds, Par 69, SSS 69, Course record 65.
Club membership 520.
Visitors may not play on Sun morning.
Societies must contact in advance.
Green Fees £14 per day (£16 weekends & bank holidays); £12 per round (£14 weekends & bank holidays).
Facilities 🛏 & 💺 by prior arrangement ♀ (contact steward) ⤳ 🛍 ⸢ Steve Poole.
Location The Bell Vue Club, Belle Vue (1.5m E, at racecourse, on A638)
Hotel ★★★62% Danum Swallow Hotel, High St, DONCASTER ☎(0302) 342261 66⇔🛏

Wheatley ☎(0302) 831655
Fairly flat well-bunkered, lake-holed, parkland course.
18 holes, 6169yds, Par 70, SSS 69.
Club membership 600.
Visitors must contact in advance and have an introduction from own club.
Societies must contact in advance.
Green Fees not confirmed.
Facilities ⊗ 〗 🛏 💺 ♀ ⤳ 🛍 ⸢ T C Parkinson.
Location Armthorpe Rd (NE side of town centre off A18)

Hotel ★★★64% Mount Pleasant Hotel, Great North Rd, ROSSINGTON ☎(0302) 868696 & 868219 33⇨🛏🏵

HICKLETON   Map 08 SE40

Hickleton ☎Rotherham (0709) 896081
Undulating parkland course with stream running through; designed by Neil Coles and Brian Huggett.
18 holes, 6403yds, Par 71, SSS 71, Course record 68.
Club membership 600.
Visitors   restricted weekends. Must contact in advance.
Societies   must contact in advance on (0709) 895170.
Green Fees   £17 per day (£25 weekends).
Facilities   ⊗ ⫴ 🛁 & 🍺 by prior arrangement ♀ 🛆 🖃 🏌 ⌘ Paul Shepherd.
Location   .5m W on B6411
Hotel   ★★★62% Danum Swallow Hotel, High St, DONCASTER ☎(0302) 342261 66⇨🛏🏵

HIGH GREEN   Map 08 SK39

Tankersley Park ☎Sheffield (0742) 468247
Akin to an inland links, this parkland course is hilly, windy and has good views.
18 holes, 6212yds, Par 69, SSS 71, Course record 64.
Club membership 500.
Visitors   may not play Tue. With member only at weekends. Must contact in advance and have an introduction from own club.
Societies   must apply in writing.
Green Fees   £17.50 per day; £14.50 per round.
Facilities   ⊗ ⫴ by prior arrangement 🛁 🍺 ♀ 🛆 🖃 🏌 ⌘ Ian Kirk.
Location   1m NE
Hotel   ★★69% Rutland Hotel, 452 Glossop Rd, Broomhill, SHEFFIELD ☎(0742) 664411 73rm(68⇨1🏵)Annexe17⇨🛏🏵

RAWMARSH   Map 08 SK49

Wath ☎(0709) 872149
Parkland course, not easy in spite of its length; 17th hole (par 3) is a difficult 244yds with narrow driving area.
18 holes, 5857yds, Par 68, SSS 68, Course record 67.
Club membership 550.
Visitors   must play with member at weekends; must have a handicap certificate. Must contact in advance.
Societies   must be in writing.
Green Fees   £14 per day.
Facilities   ⊗ ⫴ 🛁 🍺 ♀ 🛆 🖃 ⌘ Chris Bassett.
Location   Abdy Ln (2.5m N off A633)
Hotel   ★★69% Brentwood Hotel, Moorgate Rd, ROTHERHAM ☎(0709) 382772 33⇨🛏🏵Annexe10⇨🛏🏵

A golf-course name printed in **bold italics** means that we have been unable to verify information with the club's management for the current year

ROTHERHAM   Map 08 SK49

Grange Park ☎(0709) 558884
Parkland/meadowland course, with panoramic views especially from the back nine. The golf is testing, particularly at the 1st, 4th and 18th holes (par 4), and 8th, 12th and 15th (par 5).
18 holes, 6461yds, Par 71, SSS 70.
Club membership 325.
Visitors   no restrictions.
Green Fees   not confirmed.
Facilities   ⊗ (ex Mon) 🛁 (ex Mon) 🍺 ♀ 🛆 🖃 🏌 ⌘ Eric Clark.
Location   Upper Wortley Rd (3m NW off A629)
Hotel   ★★69% Brentwood Hotel, Moorgate Rd, ROTHERHAM ☎(0709) 382772 33⇨🛏🏵Annexe10⇨🛏🏵

Phoenix ☎(0709) 363864
Undulating meadowland course with variable wind.
18 holes, 6145yds, Par 71, SSS 69, Course record 65.
Club membership 750.
Visitors   no restrictions.
Societies   must apply in writing.
Green Fees   not confirmed.
Facilities   ⊗ ⫴ by prior arrangement 🛁 🍺 ♀ 🛆 🖃 🏌 ⌘ Andrew Limb.
Leisure   hard tennis courts, squash, fishing, snooker, gymnasium.
Location   Pavilion Ln, Brinsworth (SW side of town centre off A630)

▶

Hotel ★★69% Brentwood Hotel, Moorgate Rd,
ROTHERHAM ☎(0709) 382772
33⌐ᵈ Annexe10⌐ᵈ

Rotherham Golf Club Ltd ☎(0709) 850812
Parkland course with easy walking along tree-lined fairways.
18 holes, 6324yds, Par 70, SSS 70, Course record 66.
Club membership 440.
Visitors must contact in advance.
Societies must contact in advance.
Green Fees not confirmed.
Facilities ⊗ ⅏ ⅃ ⬛ ⅄ ⌂ (Simon Thornhill.
Leisure snooker.
Location Thrybergh Park, Thrybergh (3.5m E on A630)
Hotel ★★69% Brentwood Hotel, Moorgate Rd,
ROTHERHAM ☎(0709) 382772
33⌐ᵈ Annexe10⌐ᵈ

Sitwell Park ☎(0709) 541046
Parkland course with easy walking.
18 holes, 6203yds, Par 71, SSS 70, Course record 67.
Club membership 500.
Visitors restricted weekends. Must contact in advance.
Societies must contact in advance.
Green Fees £21 per day (£24 weekends & bank holidays);
£17 per round (£20 weekends & bank holidays).
Facilities ⊗ ⅏ by prior arrangement ⅃ ⬛ ⅄ ⌂ (
Nic Taylor.
Leisure snooker.
Location Shrogs Wood Rd
Hotel ★★69% Brentwood Hotel, Moorgate Rd,
ROTHERHAM ☎(0709) 382772
33⌐ᵈ Annexe10⌐ᵈ

SHEFFIELD Map 08 SK 38

Abbeydale ☎(0742) 360743
Parkland course, well-kept and wooded. Testing hole: 12th,
par 3.
18 holes, 6419yds, Par 72, SSS 71.
Club membership 750.
Visitors restricted Wed 1000-1330. Must contact in advance.
Societies must apply in writing.
Green Fees £25 per day (£30 weekends & bank holidays).
Facilities ⊗ ⅏ ⅃ ⬛ ⅄ ⌂ (Nigel Perry.
Leisure snooker.
Location Twentywell Ln, Dore (4m SW of city centre off A621)
Hotel ★★★64% Forte Crest, Manchester Rd,
Broomhill, SHEFFIELD ☎(0742) 670067
135⌐ᵈ

Beauchief Municipal ☎(0742) 367274
Municipal course with natural water hazards. The rolling
land looks west to the Pennines and a 12th-century abbey
adorns the course.
18 holes, 5452yds, Par 67, SSS 66, Course record 65.
Club membership 450.
Visitors no restrictions.
Societies weekdays only, must apply in writing.
Green Fees £6.50 per round.
Facilities ⊗ ⅃ & ⬛ (ex Tue) ⅄ (ex Tue) ⌂ ⌂ ⊣⌐ (
Brian English.

Location Abbey Ln (4m SW of city centre off A621)
Hotel ★★53% Manor Hotel, 10 High St,
DRONFIELD ☎(0246) 413971 10⌐ᵈ

Birley Wood ☎(0742) 647262
Undulating meadowland course with well-varied features,
easy walking and good views. Practice range and green.
18 holes, 5452yds, Par 68, SSS 67, Course record 61.
Club membership 100.
Visitors no restrictions.
Societies apply in writing.
Green Fees not confirmed.
Facilities ⌂ ⌂ ⊣⌐ (Peter Ball.
Location Birley Ln (4.5m SE of city centre off A621)
Hotel ★★★65% Mosborough Hall Hotel, High St,
Mosborough, SHEFFIELD ☎(0742) 484353
23⌐ᵈ

Concord Park ☎(0742) 456806
Hilly municipal parkland course with some fairways wood-
flanked, good views, often windy. Eight par 3 holes.
18 holes, 4321yds, Par 65, SSS 62, Course record 58.
Club membership 170.
Visitors no restrictions.
Green Fees £3.60 (£5.20 weekends).
Facilities ⌂
Location Shiregreen Ln (3.5m N of city centre on B6086 off A6135)
Hotel ★★★64% Forte Crest, Manchester Rd,
Broomhill, SHEFFIELD ☎(0742) 670067
135⌐ᵈ

Dore & Totley ☎(0742) 360492
Flat parkland course.
18 holes, 6265yds, Par 70, SSS 70.
Club membership 580.
Visitors may not play 9.30am-noon & after 2.30pm.
Must contact in advance and have an
introduction from own club.
Societies must apply in writing.
Green Fees £20.
Facilities ⊗ ⅏ ⅃ ⬛ (no catering on Mon) ⅄ ⌂ ⌂ (
Mark Pearson.
Leisure snooker.
Location Bradway Rd, Bradway (7m S of city centre on B6054 off A61)
Hotel ★★★64% Forte Crest, Manchester Rd,
Broomhill, SHEFFIELD ☎(0742) 670067
135⌐ᵈ

Hallamshire ☎(0742) 302153
Situated on a shelf of land at a height of 850 ft. Magnificent
view to the west. Moorland turf, long carries over ravine.
Good natural drainage.
18 holes, 6396yds, Par 71, SSS 71, Course record 63.
Club membership 550.
Visitors no restrictions.
Societies by arrangement.
Green Fees not confirmed.
Facilities ⊗ ⅏ ⅃ ⬛ ⅄ ⌂ ⌂ (G Tickell & M Higgenbottom.
Leisure snooker.
Location Redmires Rd, Sandygate (3m W of city centre off A57)

Hotel	★★★64% Forte Crest, Manchester Rd, Broomhill, SHEFFIELD ☎(0742) 670067 135⇨📶

Hillsborough ☎(0742) 343608
Beautiful moorland/woodland course 500 ft above sea-level, reasonable walking.
18 holes, 6204yards, Par 71, SSS 70, Course record 65.
Club membership 700.
Visitors	restricted weekends. Must contact in advance and have an introduction from own club.
Societies	must apply in writing.
Green Fees	£24 (£30 weekends & bank holidays).
Facilities	⊗ ⏝ ⏝ & ⏝ by prior arrangement ♀ △ 📦 ⊂ G Walker.
Leisure	snooker.
Location	Worrall Rd (3m NW of city centre off A616)
Hotel	★★69% Rutland Hotel, 452 Glossop Rd, Broomhill, SHEFFIELD ☎(0742) 664411 73rm(68⇨1📶)Annexe17⇨📶

Lees Hall ☎(0742) 554402
Parkland/meadowland course with panoramic view of city.
18 holes, 6137yds, Par 71, SSS 69, Course record 63.
Club membership 725.
Visitors	restricted Wed.
Societies	must apply in writing.
Green Fees	£20 per day; £16 per round (£25 weekends & bank holidays).
Facilities	⊗ & ⏝ (ex Tue) ⏝ by prior arrangement (ex Tue) ⏝ ♀ △ 📦 ⊂ J R Wilkinson.
Leisure	snooker.
Location	Hemsworth Rd, Norton (3.5m S of city centre off A6102)
Hotel	★★★64% Forte Crest, Manchester Rd, Broomhill, SHEFFIELD ☎(0742) 670067 135⇨📶

Tinsley Park Municipal Golf ☎(0742) 42237
Undulating meadowland course with plenty of trees and rough.
18 holes, 6064yds, Par 71, SSS 69.
Club membership 420.
Visitors	no restrictions.
Green Fees	£6.60 weekends. Reduced weekdays.
Facilities	⊗ & ⏝ by prior arrangement ⏝ & ⏝ (ex Mon) ♀ (ex Mon) △ 📦 ⊓⊏ ⊂ A P Highfield.
Location	High Hazels Park (4m E of city centre off A630)
Hotel	★★★65% Mosborough Hall Hotel, High St, Mosborough, SHEFFIELD ☎(0742) 484353 23⇨📶

SILKSTONE   Map 08 SE20

Silkstone ☎Barnsley (0226) 790328
Parkland/downland course, fine views over the Pennines. Testing golf.
18 holes, 6078yds, Par 70, SSS 70.
Club membership 450.
Visitors	with member only at weekends.
Societies	apply in writing.
Green Fees	not confirmed.
Facilities	⊗ ⏝ ⏝ ⏝ ♀ △ 📦 ⊂ Kevin Guy.
Leisure	snooker.

| Location | Field Head, Elmhurst Ln (1m E off A628) |
| Hotel | ★★★66% Ardsley Moat House, Doncaster Rd, Ardsley, BARNSLEY ☎(0226) 289401 73⇨📶 |

STOCKSBRIDGE   Map 08 SK29

Stocksbridge & District ☎Sheffield (0742) 882003
Hilly moorland course.
18 holes, 5200yds, Par 66, SSS 65, Course record 61.
Club membership 450.
Visitors	no restrictions.
Societies	apply to secretary.
Green Fees	not confirmed.
Facilities	⊗ ⏝ (lunch time) ⏝ ♀ △
Location	30 Royd Ln, Townend (S side of town centre)
Hotel	★★★64% Forte Crest, Manchester Rd, Broomhill, SHEFFIELD ☎(0742) 670067 135⇨📶

WORTLEY   Map 08 SK39

Wortley ☎Sheffield (0742) 885294
Well-wooded, undulating parkland course sheltered from prevailing wind.
18 holes, 5983yds, Par 68, SSS 69, Course record 65.
Club membership 300.
Visitors	may not play Wed & Fri. Must contact in advance and have an introduction from own club.
Societies	Wed & Fri only, by arrangement.
Green Fees	£16.50 per day/round (£24 weekends & bank holidays).
Facilities	⊗ ⏝ ⏝ & ⏝ by prior arrangement (no catering Mon) ♀ △ 📦 ⊂ J Tilson.
Location	Hermit Hill Ln (.5m NE of village off A629)
Hotel	★★★64% Forte Crest, Manchester Rd, Broomhill, SHEFFIELD ☎(0742) 670067 135⇨📶

STAFFORDSHIRE

BARLASTON   Map 07 SJ83

Barlaston ☎(078139) 2795
Picturesque meadowland course designed by Peter Alliss.
18 holes, 5800yds, Par 69, SSS 68, Course record 68.
Club membership 600.
Visitors	no restrictions.
Societies	apply in writing.
Green Fees	not confirmed.
Facilities	⊗ by prior arrangement ⏝ by prior arrangement ⏝ ⏝ ♀ △ 📦 ⊂ Ian Rogers.
Leisure	fishing.
Location	Meaford Rd
Hotel	★★★67% Stone House Hotel, STONE ☎(0785) 815531 50⇨📶

For a full range of AA guides and maps, visit your local AA shop or any good bookshop

BROCTON   Map 07 SJ91

Brocton Hall ☎(0785) 661901
Parkland course undulating in places, easy walking.
18 holes, 6095yds, Par 69, SSS 69.
Club membership 750.
Visitors   restricted competition days. Must contact in
                    advance.
Societies   must apply in advance.
Green Fees   £25 per day (£30 weekends & bank holidays).
Facilities   ⊗ ⫼ ⬙ & ⬛ by prior arrangement ♀ ♙ 🏠
                    (R G Johnson.
Leisure   snooker.
Location   NW side of village off A34
Hotel   ★★65% Garth Hotel, Wolverhampton Rd,
                    Moss Pit, STAFFORD ☎(0785) 56124 60⇨🛏

BURTON-UPON-TRENT   Map 08 SK22

Branston ☎(0283) 43207
Parkland course, adjacent to River Trent, on undulating
ground with natural water hazards.
18 holes, 6480yds, Par 72, SSS 71, Course record 69.
Club membership 700.
Visitors   with member only weekends. Must contact in
                    advance.
Societies   must apply in writing.
Green Fees   £16 & £20.
Facilities   ⊗ ⫼ by prior arrangement ⬙ ⬛ ♀ ♙ 🏠 ⍦
                    (S D Warner.
Location   Burton Rd, Branston (1.5m SW on A5121)
Hotel   ★★★61% Riverside Inn, Riverside Dr,
                    Branston, BURTON UPON TRENT ☎(0283)
                    511234 22⇨

Burton-upon-Trent ☎(0283) 44551
Undulating parkland course with trees a major feature.
There are testing par 3s at 10th and 12th. The 18th has a lake
around its green.
18 holes, 6555yds, Par 71, SSS 71.
Club membership 600.
Visitors   must have a handicap certificate or play with
                    member. Must contact in advance and have an
                    introduction from own club.
Societies   must contact in writing for parties of 16 & over.
Green Fees   £25 per day; £20 per round (£30 per day; £25 per
                    round weekends & bank holidays).
Facilities   ⊗ ⫼ by prior arrangement & ⬙ (ex Mon) ⬛
                    ♀ ♙ 🏠 ⍦ (
Leisure   snooker.
Location   43 Ashby Rd East (2m E on A50)
Hotel   ★★★56% Newton Park Hotel, NEWTON
                    SOLNEY ☎(0283) 703568 51⇨🛏

ENVILLE   Map 07 SO88

Enville ☎Kinver (0384) 872074
Easy walking on two fairly flat parkland/moorland courses -
the 'Highgate' and the 'Lodge'.
Highgate : 18 holes, 6541yds, Par 72, SSS 72, Course record 68.
Lodge : 18 holes, 6207yds, Par 72, SSS 72, Course record 68.
Club membership 900.

Visitors   must play with member at weekends. Must
                    contact in advance and have an introduction
                    from own club.
Societies   must contact in writing.
Green Fees   not confirmed.
Facilities   ⊗ ⫼ ⬙ ⬛ by prior arrangement ♀ ♙ 🏠 (
                    Sean Power.
Location   Highgate Common (2m NE)
Hotel   ★★63% Talbot Hotel, High St,
                    STOURBRIDGE ☎(0384) 394350
                    25rm(13⇨7🛏)

GOLDENHILL   Map 07 SJ85

Goldenhill ☎Stoke-on-Trent (0782) 784715
Rolling parkland course with water features on six of the
back nine holes.
Goldenhill Golf Course : 18 holes, 5957yds, Par 71, SSS 68,
Course record 71.
Club membership 400.
Visitors   contact in advance for weekend play.
Societies   must apply in writing.
Green Fees   £4.50 (£5.50 weekends).
Facilities   ⊗ ⬙ ♀ ♙ 🏠 ⍦ (Tony Clingan.
Location   Mobberley Rd (on A50, 4m N of Stoke)
Hotel   ★★★66% Manor House Hotel, Audley Rd,
                    ALSAGER ☎(0270) 884000 57⇨🛏

HAZELSLADE   Map 07 SK01

Beau Desert ☎Hednesford (0543) 422626
Woodland course.
18 holes, 6300yds, Par 70, SSS 71.
Club membership 500.
Visitors   restricted weekends. Must contact in advance
                    and have an introduction from own club.
Societies   must apply in writing.
Green Fees   not confirmed.
Facilities   ⊗ ⫼ ⬙ ⬛ ♀ ♙ 🏠 (Barrie Stevens.
Location   .5m NE of village
Hotel   ★★★64% Roman Way Hotel, Watling St,
                    Hatherton, CANNOCK ☎(0543) 572121 56⇨🛏

HIMLEY   Map 07 SO89

Himley Hall Golf Centre ☎Wolverhampton (0902) 895207
Parkland course set in grounds of Himley Hall Park, with
lovely views. Large practice area including a pitch-and-putt.
9 holes, 3125yds, Par 36, SSS 36.
Club membership 200.
Visitors   restricted weekends. Must contact in advance.
Green Fees   £4.50 per round (£5 weekends) (18 holes).
Facilities   ⊗ ⬙ ⬛ 🏠
Location   Log Cabin, Himley Hall Park (.5m E on B4176)
Hotel   ★★★68% Himley Country Club & Hotel,
                    School Rd, HIMLEY ☎(0902) 896716 76⇨🛏

For a full list of golf courses included in the
book, see the index at the end of the directory

LEEK

Map 07 SJ95

Leek ☎(0538) 384779
Undulating, challenging moorland course.
18 holes, 6240yds, Par 70, SSS 70, Course record 63.
Club membership 750.

Visitors	restricted before 3pm. Must contact in advance and have an introduction from own club.
Societies	must apply in advance.
Green Fees	£22 per day (£30 weekends & bank holidays).
Facilities	⊗ ☶ (ex Sun & Mon) ☶ ☷ ♀ ⌁ ☎ ℓ Peter Stubbs.
Leisure	snooker.
Location	Birchall (.75m S on A520)
Hotel	★★★70% Stakis Grand Hotel, 66 Trinity St, Hanley, STOKE-ON-TRENT ☎(0782) 202361 128⇨🏾

LICHFIELD

Map 07 SK10

Seedy Mill ☎(0543) 417333
New, gently-undulating parkland course in picturesque rural setting. Lakes and streams are abundant, and there are four challenging par 3s. Well-contoured greens, good bunkering. Superb 9-hole Par 3 course expected to be ready for play towards the end of 1992.
18 holes, 6247yds, Par 72, SSS 70.
Club membership 1100.

Visitors	must play to max. offical handicap standard (28 men, 36 ladies). Must contact in advance.
Societies	must contact in advance.
Green Fees	not confirmed.
Facilities	⊗ ☶ ☶ ☷ ♀ (restricted on Sun) ⌁ ☎ ☂
Location	Elmhurst (at Elmhurst, 1.5m N of Lichfield, off A515)
Hotel	★★★61% Little Barrow Hotel, Beacon St, LICHFIELD ☎(0543) 414500 24⇨

Whittington Barracks ☎(0543) 432317
18 magnificent holes winding their way through heathland and trees, presenting a good test for the serious golfer. Leaving the fairway can be severely punished. The dog-legs are most tempting, inviting the golfer to chance his arm. Local knowledge is a definite advantage. Clear views of the famous three spires of Lichfield Cathedral.
18 holes, 6547yds, Par 70, SSS 70.
Club membership 600.

Visitors	must have handicap certificate, restricted weekends. Must contact in advance and have an introduction from own club.
Societies	welcome Wed & Thu, must apply in writing.
Green Fees	£28.
Facilities	⊗ ☶ ☶ ☷ ♀ ⌁ ☎ ☂ ℓ Adrian Sadler.
Leisure	snooker.
Location	Tamworth Rd (2.5m SE on A51)
Hotel	★★★ George Hotel, Bird St, LICHFIELD ☎(0543) 414822 38⇨🏾

NEWCASTLE-UNDER-LYME

Map 07 SJ84

Newcastle Municipal ☎(0782) 627596
Open course on the side of a hill without mature trees.
18 holes, 6367yds, Par 72, SSS 70, Course record 63.
Club membership 316.

Visitors	must contact in advance.
Green Fees	£4.50 weekday (£5.50 WE).
Facilities	⊗ ☶ ☷ ♀ ☎ ℓ Colin Smith.
Location	Keele Rd (2m W on A525)
Hotel	★★★62% Clayton Lodge, Clayton Rd, NEWCASTLE ☎(0782) 613093 50⇨🏾

Newcastle-Under-Lyme ☎(0782) 618526
Parkland course.
18 holes, 6229yds, Par 72, SSS 71.

Visitors	must have handicap certificate. With member only weekends. Must contact in advance.
Societies	welcome Wed & Thu (pm). Phone (0782) 617006 in advance.
Green Fees	not confirmed.
Facilities	⊗ ☶ ☶ ☷ ♀ ⌁ ☎ ℓ Paul Symonds.
Location	Whitmore Rd (1m SW on A53)
Hotel	★★★62% Clayton Lodge, Clayton Rd, NEWCASTLE ☎(0782) 613093 50⇨🏾

Wolstanton ☎(0782) 622413
Meadowland/parkland course in an urban area.
18 holes, 5807yds, Par 68, SSS 68, Course record 65.
Club membership 677.

Visitors	with member only at weekends & bank holidays.
Societies	must apply in advance.
Green Fees	£15.
Facilities	⊗ (ex Fri & Sun) ☶ (ex Fri & Sun) ☶ ☷ ♀ ⌁ ☎
Leisure	snooker.
Location	Dimsdale Old Hall, Hassam Pde, Wolstanton (1.5m NW of Newcastle, off A34)
Hotel	★★★62% Clayton Lodge, Clayton Rd, NEWCASTLE ☎(0782) 613093 50⇨🏾

ONNELEY

Map 07 SJ74

Onneley ☎Stoke-on-Trent (0782) 750577
A tight, picturesque, hillside parkland course.
9 holes, 5584yds, Par 70, SSS 67, Course record 67.
Club membership 400.

Visitors	restricted weekends & bank holidays.
Societies	must apply in writing.
Green Fees	£12.50.
Facilities	☶ ☷ (Tue-Thu lunchtime only) ♀ (Tue-Thu lunch only) ⌁
Location	2m from Woore on A525
Hotel	★★★57% Crewe Arms Hotel, Nantwich Rd, CREWE ☎(0270) 213204 53⇨🏾

PATTINGHAM

Map 07 SO89

Patshull Park Hotel Golf & Country Club
☎Wolverhampton (0902) 700100
Picturesque course set in 280 acres of glorious Capability Brown landscaped parkland. Designed by John Jacobs, the course meanders alongside trout fishing lakes. Many leisure facilities.
Patshull Park Golf Club: 18 holes, 6412yds, Par 72, SSS 71, Course record 65.
Club membership 500.

Visitors	must have handicap certificate. Must contact in advance.

▶

Societies	must apply in advance.
Green Fees	£20.50 per round (£27.50 weekends).
Facilities	⊗ ⦀ ⮸ 🍺 ♀ ⌣ 🏠 ⛳ 🛏 ↿ Duncan MacDowall.
Leisure	hard tennis courts, heated indoor swimming pool, fishing, snooker, sauna, solarium, gymnasium.
Location	Off A464
Hotel	★★★↟68% Old Vicarage Hotel, WORFIELD ☎(07464) 497 10↩🐾Annexe4↩🐾

PERTON   Map 07 SO89

Perton Park Golf Centre ☎Wolverhampton (0902) 380103
Flat meadowland course set in open countryside.
18 holes, 7036yds, Par 74, SSS 72.
Club membership 400.

Visitors	no wide wheel trolleys, no jeans & shirt must have collars.
Societies	welcome anytime, phone for further information.
Green Fees	£5 per round (£6 Sat, Sun & bank holidays).
Facilities	⊗ ⦀ by prior arrangement ⮸ 🍺 ♀ ⌣ 🏠 ⛳ ↿ Robert Franklin.
Leisure	snooker.
Location	Wrottesley Park Rd (3m W of Wolverhampton, off A454 or A41)
Hotel	★★★59% Mount Hotel, Mount Road, Tettenhall Wood, WOLVERHAMPTON ☎(0902) 752055 49↩🐾

STAFFORD   Map 07 SJ92

Stafford Castle ☎(0785) 223821
Parkland type course.
9 holes, 6073yds, Par 71, SSS 69.
Club membership 400.

Visitors	restricted weekends (am).
Societies	welcome Mon-Fri, must apply in advance.
Green Fees	£12.50 per day (£15.50 weekends & bank holidays).
Facilities	⊗ ⦀ ⮸ 🍺 ♀ ⌣ 🏠 ⛳
Location	Newport Rd (SW side of town centre off A518)
Hotel	★★60% Swan Hotel, Greengate St, STAFFORD ☎(0785) 58142 32↩🐾

STOKE-ON-TRENT   Map 07 SJ84

Burslem ☎(0782) 837006
A moorland course on the outskirts of Tunstall with hard walking.
9 holes, 5354yds, Par 66, SSS 66, Course record 64.
Club membership 250.

Visitors	except Sun & with member only Sat & bank holidays.
Societies	must telephone in advance.
Green Fees	not confirmed.
Facilities	⦀ by prior arrangement ⮸ by prior arrangement 🍺 ♀ ⌣
Location	Wood Farm, High Ln, Tunstall (4m N of city centre on B5049)
Hotel	★★★70% Stakis Grand Hotel, 66 Trinity St, Hanley, STOKE-ON-TRENT ☎(0782) 202361 128↩🐾

Greenway Hall ☎(0782) 503158
Moorland course with fine views of the Pennines.
18 holes, 5678yds, Par 67, SSS 67, Course record 64.
Club membership 400.

Visitors	may not play Sat & Sun mornings.
Societies	must telephone in advance.
Green Fees	not confirmed.
Facilities	♀ ⌣
Location	Stanley Rd, Stockton Brook (5m NE off A53)
Hotel	★★★70% Stakis Grand Hotel, 66 Trinity St, Hanley, STOKE-ON-TRENT ☎(0782) 202361 128↩🐾

Trentham ☎(0782) 658109
Parkland course. The par 3, 4th is a testing hole reached over a copse of trees.
18 holes, 6644yds, Par 72, SSS 72, Course record 66.
Club membership 680.

Visitors	must have handicap certificate, restricted Sat.
Societies	must apply in writing a year in advance.
Green Fees	£25 per day (£30 weekends).
Facilities	⊗ ⦀ by prior arrangement ⮸ 🍺 ♀ ⌣ 🏠 ⛳ ↿ Nigel Blake.
Leisure	squash, snooker.
Location	14 Barlaston Old Rd, Trentham (3m S off A5035)
Hotel	★★★78% Hanchurch Manor Hotel, Hanchurch, STOKE-ON-TRENT ☎(0782) 643030 7↩Annexe5↩🐾

Trentham Park ☎(0782) 658800
Fine woodland course.
18 holes, 6403yds, Par 71, SSS 71, Course record 63.
Club membership 640.

Visitors	restricted competition days.
Societies	welcome Wed & Fri, must apply in advance.
Green Fees	£22 per day (£27 weekends & bank holidays).
Facilities	⊗ ⦀ ⮸ 🍺 ♀ ⌣ 🏠 ↿ R Clarke.
Leisure	snooker.
Location	Trentham Park (3m SW off A34)
Hotel	★★★61% Forte Posthouse, Clayton Rd, NEWCASTLE ☎(0782) 717171 122↩🐾

STONE   Map 07 SJ93

Stone ☎(0785) 813103
Nine-hole parkland course with easy walking and 18 different tees.
9 holes, 6299yds, Par 71, SSS 70, Course record 68.
Club membership 350.

Visitors	with member only weekends & bank holidays.
Societies	must apply in writing.
Green Fees	£15 per day/round.
Facilities	⊗ ⦀ ⮸ 🍺 ♀ ⌣
Leisure	snooker.
Location	Filleybrooks (.5m W on A34)
Hotel	★★★67% Stone House Hotel, STONE ☎(0785) 815531 50↩🐾

A golf-course name printed in ***bold italics*** means that we have been unable to verify information with the club's management for the current year

TAMWORTH   Map 07 SK 20

Drayton Park ☎(0827) 251139
Parkland course designed by James Braid. Club established since 1897.
18 holes, 6214yds, Par 71, SSS 71.
Club membership 450.

Visitors	restricted weekends. Must contact in advance.
Societies	must apply in writing.
Green Fees	£22 per day/round.
Facilities	⊗ ⅲ ⅬⅬ ● ♀ ⌂ 🏠 ℂ M W Passmore.
Leisure	snooker.
Location	Drayton Park (2m S on A4091)
Hotel	★★★★68% The Belfry, Lichfield Rd, WISHAW ☎(0675) 470301 219⇨ᵈ

Tamworth Municipal ☎(0827) 53850
First-class, municipal parkland course and a good test of golf.
18 holes, 6083mtrs, Par 73, SSS 72, Course record 65.
Club membership 700.

Visitors	must contact in advance.
Societies	must contact in writing.
Green Fees	£7 per 18 holes.
Facilities	ⅬⅬ ● ♀ ⌂ 🏠 ⅇ ℂ Barry Jones.
Leisure	snooker.
Location	Eagle Dr (2.5m E off B5000)
Hotel	★★72% Angel Croft Hotel, Beacon St, LICHFIELD ☎(0543) 258737 11rm(3⇨6🔦)Annexe8⇨🔦

UTTOXETER   Map 07 SK 03

Uttoxeter ☎(0889) 564884
Downland course with open aspect.
18 holes, 5456yds, Par 69, SSS 67, Course record 66.
Club membership 600.

Visitors	restricted weekends.
Societies	must apply in advance.
Green Fees	£13 per day (£17 weekends & bank holidays).
Facilities	⊗ ⅲ ⅬⅬ & ● (Tue-Sun only) ♀ ⌂ 🏠 ℂ John Pearsall.
Location	Wood Ln (1m SE off B5017)
Hotel	★★★58% Ye Olde Dog & Partridge Hotel, High St, TUTBURY ☎(0283) 813030 3⇨Annexe14⇨🔦

WESTON   Map 07 SJ 92

Ingestre Park ☎(0889) 270304
Parkland course set in the grounds of Ingestre Hall, former home of the Earl of Shrewsbury, with mature trees and pleasant views.
18 holes, 6334yds, Par 70, SSS 70.
Club membership 750.

Visitors	with member only weekends & bank holidays.
Societies	must apply in advance.
Green Fees	£22.50 per day.
Facilities	⊗ ⅲ ⅬⅬ ● ♀ ⌂ 🏠 ℂ Danny Scullion.
Leisure	snooker.
Location	2m SE off A51
Hotel	★★★64% Tillington Hall, Eccleshall Rd, STAFFORD ☎(0785) 53531 90⇨🔦

SUFFOLK

ALDEBURGH   Map 05 TM 45

Aldeburgh ☎(0728) 452890
A most enjoyable and not unduly difficult seaside course; ideal for golfing holidaymakers. A bracing and fairly open terrain with some trees and heathland.
18 holes, 6330yds, Par 68, SSS 71, Course record 65.
River Course: 9 holes, 2114yds, Par 32, SSS 32.
Club membership 750.

Visitors	must have handicap certificate for 18 hole course. Must contact in advance and have an introduction from own club.
Societies	must contact in advance.
Green Fees	not confirmed.
Facilities	⊗ ● ♀ ⌂ 🏠 ⅇ ℂ K R Preston.
Location	Saxmundham Rd (1m W on A1094)
Hotel	★★★67% Wentworth Hotel, Wentworth Rd, ALDEBURGH ☎(0728) 452312 31rm(24⇨4🔦)

BECCLES   Map 05 TM 49

Beccles ☎(0502) 712244
Heathland course with natural hazards and particularly exposed to wind.
9 holes, 2781yds, Par 68, SSS 67.
Club membership 200.

Visitors	must play with member on Sun.
Societies	must contact in advance.
Green Fees	not confirmed.
Facilities	♀ ⌂ 🏠 ℂ
Location	The Common (NE side of town)
Hotel	★★61% Waveney House Hotel, Puddingmoor, BECCLES ☎(0502) 712270 13⇨🔦

BUNGAY   Map 05 TM 38

Bungay & Waveney Valley ☎(0986) 892337
Heathland course partly comprising Neolithic stone workings, easy walking.
18 holes, 5950yds, Par 69, SSS 68.
Club membership 756.

Visitors	with member only weekends & bank holidays. Must contact in advance.
Societies	must contact in advance.
Green Fees	£18 per day/round.
Facilities	⊗ & ⅲ by prior arrangement ⅬⅬ ● ♀ ⌂ 🏠 ⅇ ℂ Nigel Whyte.
Leisure	large practice area.
Location	Outney Common (.5m NW on A143)
Hotel	★★55% Scole Inn, SCOLE ☎(0379) 740481 12⇨🔦Annexe11⇨🔦

BURY ST EDMUNDS   Map 05 TL 86

Bury St Edmunds ☎(0284) 755979
Undulating parkland course with easy walking and attractive short holes.
18 holes, 6615yds, Par 72, SSS 72, Course record 67 or 9 holes, 2332yds, Par 31, SSS 31.
Club membership 830.

▶

Visitors	with member only at weekends.
Societies	must apply in writing.
Green Fees	£22 per day/round.
Facilities	⊗ ∭ by prior arrangement ⌐ ◫ ♀ △ 🖻 ⊓ ⌐ Mark Jillings.
Leisure	snooker.
Location	Tuthill (2m NW on B1106 off A45)
Hotel	★★★76% Angel Hotel, Angel Hill, BURY ST EDMUNDS ☎(0284) 753926 41⇨🏳

Fornham Park ☎(0284) 706777
Flat parkland course with many water hazards. Also country club facilities.
18 holes, 6229yds, Par 71, SSS 70, Course record 67.
Club membership 600.

Visitors	may not play Tue afternoon or weekends before 1pm. Must contact in advance.
Societies	by arrangement.
Green Fees	£25 per day; £20 per round (£25 weekends).
Facilities	⊗ ∭ ⌐ ◫ ♀ △ 🖻 ⊓ ⌐ Sean Clark.
Location	St John's Hill Plantation, The Street, Fornham All Saints (2m N off A134)
Hotel	★★★⚑75% Ravenwood Hall Hotel, Rougham, BURY ST EDMUNDS ☎(0359) 70345 14⇨Annexe6rm

CRETINGHAM   Map 05 TM26

Cretingham ☎Earl Soham (0728) 685275
Parkland course.
9 holes, 1995yds, Par 30, Course record 28.
Club membership 360.

Visitors	no restrictions.
Societies	must telephone in advance.
Green Fees	not confirmed.
Facilities	◫ △ 🖻 ⊓
Leisure	hard tennis courts, outdoor swimming pool, snooker, table tennis.
Location	Grove Farm (2m from A1120 at Earl Soham)
Hotel	★★67% Crown Hotel, Market Hill, FRAMLINGHAM ☎(0728) 723521 14⇨

FELIXSTOWE   Map 05 TM33

Felixstowe Ferry ☎(0394) 286834
Seaside links course, pleasant views, easy walking. Testing 491-yd, 7th hole.
18 holes, 6324yds, Par 72, SSS 70, Course record 66.
Club membership 800.

Visitors	may not play before 9am. Must be accompanied by member and have an introduction from own club.
Societies	must contact in advance.
Green Fees	£21 (£24 weekends).
Facilities	⊗ ∭ by prior arrangement ⌐ ◫ ♀ △ 🖻 ⋈ ⌐ Ian MacPherson.
Location	Ferry Rd (NE side of town centre)
Hotel	★★★69% Orwell Moat House Hotel, Hamilton Rd, FELIXSTOWE ☎(0394) 285511 58⇨🏳

This guide is updated annually – make sure that you use the up-to-date edition

FLEMPTON   Map 05 TL86

Flempton ☎Bury St Edmunds (0284) 728291
Breckland course.
9 holes, 6080yds, Par 70, SSS 69, Course record 64.
Club membership 300.

Visitors	must have handicap certificate. With member only weekends & bank holidays. Must contact in advance.
Green Fees	£22.50 per day; £17.50 per round.
Facilities	△ 🖻 ⌐ Gary Kitley.
Location	.5m W on A1101
Hotel	★★64% Suffolk Hotel, 38 The Buttermarket, BURY ST EDMUNDS ☎(0284) 753995 33⇨🏳

HAVERHILL   Map 05 TL64

Haverhill ☎(0440) 61951
Parkland course with small river running through three fairways.
9 holes, 5707yds, Par 68, SSS 67, Course record 67.
Club membership 445.

Visitors	may not play on bank holidays before 1300.
Societies	must contact in advance.
Green Fees	£15 per day (£21 weekends & bank holidays).
Facilities	⌐ ◫ ♀ △ 🖻 ⊓ ⌐ Simon Mayfield.
Location	Coupals Rd (1m SE off A604)
Hotel	★★65% Bell Hotel, Market Hill, CLARE ☎(0787) 277741 10rm(3⇨4🏳)Annexe11⇨

HINTLESHAM   Map 05 H7

Hintlesham Hall ☎(047387) 334
Magnificent new championship length course blending harmoniously with the ancient parkland surrounding this exclusive hotel. The 6630yd parkland course was designed by Hawtree and Son, one of the oldest established firms of golf course architects in the world. The course is fair but challenging for low and high handicappers alike. Hotel offers beautiful accommodation, excellent cuisine and many facilities.
18 holes, 6630yds, Par 72, SSS 72.
Club membership 971.

Visitors	must be hotel residents or member's guest. Must contact in advance.
Societies	must telephone in advance.
Green Fees	£39 per round £45 weekends & bank holidays).
Facilities	⊗ ∭ ⌐ ◫ ♀ △ 🖻 ⊓ ⋈ ⌐ Alastair Spink.
Leisure	hard tennis courts, fishing, sauna, croquet.
Location	In village on A1071
Hotel	★★★(red)⚑ Hintlesham Hall Hotel, HINTLESHAM ☎(047387) 334 & 268 33⇨🏳

We make every effort to ensure that our information is accurate but details may change after we go to print

IPSWICH   Map 05 TM14

Ipswich ☎(0473) 728941
Many golfers are suprised when they hear that Ipswich has, at Purdis Heath, a first-class golf course. In some ways it resembles some of Surrey's better courses; a beautiful heathland/parkland course with two lakes and easy walking.

SCORECARD					
Hole	Yds	Par	Hole	Yds	Par
1	330	4	10	153	3
2	512	5	11	531	5
3	163	3	12	363	4
4	425	4	13	406	4
5	433	4	14	440	4
6	182	3	15	141	3
7	437	4	16	298	4
8	373	4	17	497	5
9	308	4	18	413	4
Out	3163	35	In	3242	36
			Totals	6405	71

18 holes, 6405yds, Par 71, SSS 71, Course record 64 or 9 holes, 1930yds, Par 31, SSS 31.
Club membership 850.
Visitors   must have a handicap certificate for 18 hole coures. Must contact in advance and have an introduction from own club.
Societies   must contact in advance.
Green Fees   not confirmed.
Facilities   ⊗ ℳ ⅃ ▰ ♀ (all day) ⌂ ⌂ ℓ Stephen Whymark.
Location   Purdis Heath (E side of town centre off A1156)
Hotel   ★★★71% Marlborough Hotel, Henley Rd, IPSWICH ☎(0473) 257677 22⇔♠

Rushmere ☎(0473) 725648
Heathland course with gorse and prevailing winds. Testing 5th hole - dog leg, 419 yards (par 4).
18 holes, 6287yds, Par 70, SSS 70, Course record 64.
Club membership 800.
Visitors   restricted weekends & bank holidays.
Societies   by arrangement.
Green Fees   £18 per day/round.
Facilities   ⊗ ℳ by prior arrangement ⅃ ▰ ♀ ⌂ ⌂ ℓ
Location   Rushmere Heath (2m E off A12)
Hotel   ★★★71% Marlborough Hotel, Henley Rd, IPSWICH ☎(0473) 257677 22⇔♠

LOWESTOFT   Map 05 TM59

Rookery Park ☎(0502) 560380
Parkland course. 9-hole , par 3 adjacent.
18 holes, 6385yds, Par 72, SSS 72.
Club membership 600.
Visitors   must have handicap certificate. Must have an introduction from own club.
Societies   by arrangement.
Green Fees   £20 per day (£25 weekends & bank holidays).
Facilities   ⊗ ℳ ⅃ ▰ ♀ ⌂ ⌂ ℓ
Leisure   snooker.
Location   Carlton Colville (3.5m SW on A146)
Hotel   ★★63% Broadlands Hotel, Bridge Rd, Oulton Broad, LOWESTOFT ☎(0502) 516031 52⇔

NEWMARKET   Map 05 TL66

Links ☎(0638) 663000
Gently undulating parkland.
18 holes, 6424yds, Par 72, SSS 71, Course record 67.
Club membership 700.

Visitors   must have handicap certificate, restricted Sun after 11.30am. Must have an introduction from own club.
Societies   must contact in advance.
Green Fees   not confirmed.
Facilities   ⊗ ℳ ⅃ ▰ ♀ ⌂ ⌂ ℓ John Sharkey.
Location   Cambridge Rd (1m SW on A1034)
Hotel   ★★★65% Newmarket Moat House, Moulton Rd, NEWMARKET ☎(0638) 667171 49⇔♠

NEWTON   Map 05 TL94

Newton Green ☎Newton Green (0787) 77217
Flat, commonland course.
9 holes, 5488yds, Par 68, SSS 67, Course record 60.
Club membership 360.
Visitors   may not play on Tue, weekends & bank holidays. Must be accompanied by member and contact in advance.
Green Fees   not confirmed.
Facilities   ⊗ ℳ by prior arrangement ⅃ ▰ ♀ ⌂ ⌂ ℓ Kevin Lovelock.
Location   Sudbury Rd (W side of village on A134)
Hotel   ★★★66% Bull Hotel, Hall St, LONG MELFORD ☎(0787) 78494 25⇔♠

SOUTHWOLD   Map 05 TM57

Southwold ☎(0502) 723234
Commonland course with 4-acre practice ground and panoramic views of the sea.
9 holes, 3004yds, Par 70, SSS 69.
Club membership 450.
Visitors   restricted Sun, bank holidays & competition days. Must contact in advance.
Societies   must apply in writing.
Green Fees   £13 (£16 weekends).
Facilities   ⊗ (ex Mon) ℳ by prior arrangement ⅃ ▰ ♀ ⌂ ⌂ ℓ Brian Allen.
Location   The Common (.5m W off A1095)
Hotel   ★★★70% Swan Hotel, Market Place, SOUTHWOLD ☎(0502) 722186 27⇔♠Annexe18⇔

STOWMARKET   Map 05 TM05

Stowmarket ☎Rattlesden (0449) 736473
Parkland course.
18 holes, 6101yds, Par 69, SSS 69, Course record 66.
Club membership 600.
Visitors   restricted except Wed morning. Must contact in advance and have an introduction from own club.
Societies   Thu & Fri only, by arrangement.
Green Fees   £20 per day (£35 weekends & bank holidays).
Facilities   ⊗ ℳ by prior arrangement (ex Mon & Tue) ⅃ ▰ ♀ ⌂ ⌂ ℓ C Aldred.
Location   Lower Rd, Onehouse (2.5m SW off B115)
Hotel   ★★57% Cedars Hotel, Needham Rd, STOWMARKET ☎(0449) 612668 24⇔♠

If you know of a golf course which welcomes visitors and is not already in this guide, we should be grateful for information

THORPENESS   Map 05 TM45

Thorpeness 🏨Aldeburgh
(0728) 452176
The holes of this moorland
course are pleasantly varied
with several quite difficult par
4's. Natural hazards abound.
The 15th, with its sharp left
dog-leg, is one of the best
holes. Designed by James
Braid.
*18 holes, 6241yds, Par 69, SSS
71, Course record 63.*
Club membership 390.

SCORECARD: White Tees					
Hole	Yds	Par	Hole	Yds	Par
1	324	4	10	179	3
2	186	3	11	312	4
3	394	4	12	370	4
4	449	4	13	424	4
5	420	4	14	499	5
6	377	4	15	416	4
7	145	3	16	191	3
8	402	4	17	280	4
9	439	4	18	434	4
Out	3136	34	In	3105	35
			Totals	6241	69

Visitors must contact in advance.
Societies by arrangement.
Green Fees not confirmed.
Facilities ⊗ ⊼ ⅃ ⬛ ♀ ⌂ 🛇 ⇄ ⟨ T Pennock.
Location W side of village off B1353
Hotel ★64% White Horse Hotel, Station Rd,
LEISTON ☎(0728) 830694
10rm(1⇌7♠)Annexe3♠

UFFORD   Map 05 TM25

Ufford Park Hotel Golf & Leisure
🏨Woodbridge (0394) 383555
Challenging new course set in ancient parkland adjacent to
hotel and leisure complex (due to open April 1992).
18 holes, 6224yds, Par 70.
Visitors no restrictions.
Societies must telephone in advance.
Green Fees £15 per round (£18 weekends).
Facilities ⊗ ⊼ ⅃ ⬛ ♀ ⌂ 🛇 ⇄
Leisure heated indoor swimming pool, sauna, solarium,
gymnasium.
Location Yarmouth Rd
Hotel ★★★♨73% Seckford Hall Hotel,
WOODBRIDGE ☎(0394) 385678
24⇌♠Annexe10⇌♠

WOODBRIDGE   Map 05 TM24

Woodbridge ☎(03943) 2038
A beautiful course, one of the
best in East Anglia. It is
situated on high ground and
in different seasons present
golfers with a great variety of
colour. Some say that of the
many good holes the 14th is
the best.
*18 holes, 6314yds, Par 70, SSS
70, Course record 64 or 9 holes,
2243yds, Par 31, SSS 31.*
Club membership 900.

SCORECARD: White Tees					
Hole	Yds	Par	Hole	Yds	Par
1	346	4	10	431	4
2	329	4	11	392	4
3	529	5	12	184	3
4	330	4	13	310	4
5	371	4	14	425	4
6	401	4	15	188	3
7	149	3	16	460	4
8	514	5	17	400	4
9	198	3	18	357	4
Out	3167	36	In	3147	34
			Totals	6314	70

Visitors must play with member at weekends & bank
holidays. Must contact in advance and have
an introduction from own club.
Societies must contact in writing up to 1 year in
advance.
Green Fees not confirmed.

Facilities ⊗ ⊼ ⅃ ⬛ ♀ ⌂ 🛇 ⟨ Leslie Jones.
Location Bromeswell Heath (2.5m NE off A1152)
Hotel ★★★♨73% Seckford Hall Hotel,
WOODBRIDGE ☎(0394) 385678
24⇌♠Annexe10⇌♠

WORLINGTON   Map 05 TL67

Royal Worlington & Newmarket ☎(0638) 712216
Inland 'links' course. Favourite 9-hole course of many
golf writers.
9 holes, 3105yds, Par 35, SSS 70, Course record 28.
Club membership 325.
Visitors with member only at weekends. Must contact
in advance and have an introduction from
own club.
Societies must apply in writing.
Green Fees £25 per day.
Facilities ⊗ by prior arrangement ⅃ ⬛ ♀ ⌂ 🛇
⊓⟨ Malcolm Hawkins.
Location .5m SE
Hotel ★★★64% Riverside Hotel, Mill St,
MILDENHALL ☎(0638) 717274
21rm(12⇌5♠)

SURREY

ASHFORD   Map 04 TQ07

Ashford Manor ☎(0784) 252049
Parkland course, looks easy but is difficult.
18 holes, 6343yds, Par 70, SSS 70.
Club membership 600.
Visitors must contact in advance and have an
introduction from own club.
Societies must contact in advance.
Green Fees not confirmed.
Facilities 🛇 ⌂ ⊓⟨
Location Fordbridge Rd (2m E of Staines via A308 Staines
by-pass)
Hotel ★★★59% Thames Lodge Hotel, Thames St,
STAINES ☎(0784) 464433 44⇌♠

BANSTEAD   Map 04 TQ25

Banstead Downs ☎081-642 2284
Downland course with narrow fairways and hawthorns.
18 holes, 6169yds, Par 69, SSS 69, Course record 63.
Club membership 542.
Visitors must have handicap certificate. With member
only weekends. Must have an introduction from
own club.
Green Fees not confirmed.
Facilities ⊗ ⅃ & ⬛ (ex Mon) ♀ (1200-1500) 🛇 ⟨
Location Burdon Ln, Belmont, Sutton (1.5m N on A217)
Hotel ★★62% Heathside Hotel, Brighton Rd,
BURGH HEATH ☎(0737) 353355 73⇌♠

Opening times of bar and catering facilities
vary from place to place. Please remember
to check in advance of your visit

Cuddington ☎081-393 0952
Parkland course with easy walking and good views.
18 holes, 6352yds, Par 70, SSS 70, Course record 69.
Club membership 790.
Visitors	must contact in advance and have an introduction from own club.
Societies	welcome Thu, must apply in advance.
Green Fees	£30 per day; (£35 per round weekends).
Facilities	⊗ ╚ ▙ ♀ △ 🖻 ⎰ James Morgan.
Location	Banstead Rd (N of Banstead station on A2022)
Hotel	★★62% Heathside Hotel, Brighton Rd, BURGH HEATH ☎(0737) 353355 73⇨🏨

BRAMLEY   Map 04 TQ04

Bramley ☎Guildford (0483) 892696
Downland course, fine views from top.
18 holes, 5966yds, Par 69, SSS 69.
Club membership 780.
Visitors	must play with member at weekends & bank holidays. Must contact in advance.
Societies	must telephone in advance.
Green Fees	£25.50 per day, £20.50 per round.
Facilities	⊗ ⫙ ╚ ▙ ♀ 🖻 ⎰ G Peddie.
Location	.5 m N on A281
Hotel	★★★★62% Forte Crest, Egerton Rd, GUILDFORD ☎(0483) 574444 111⇨🏨

BROOKWOOD   Map 04 SU95

West Hill ☎(04867) 4365
Worplesdon's next-door neighbour and a comparably great heath-and-heather course. Slightly tighter than Worplesdon with more opportunities for getting into trouble - but a most interesting and challenging course with wonderful greens. Water also provides natural hazards. The 15th is a testing par 3.
18 holes, 6368yds, Par 69, SSS 70, Course record 65.
Club membership 568.

SCORECARD: White Tees					
Hole	Yds	Par	Hole	Yds	Par
1	395	4	10	422	4
2	377	4	11	392	4
3	454	4	12	297	4
4	193	3	13	149	3
5	532	5	14	462	4
6	419	4	15	212	3
7	170	3	16	384	4
8	387	4	17	512	5
9	171	3	18	440	4
Out	3098	34	In	3270	35
			Totals	6368	69

Visitors	restricted weekends & bank holidays. Must contact in advance and have an introduction from own club.
Societies	must apply in writing.
Green Fees	£39 per day; £29 per round.
Facilities	⊗ ⫙ ╚ ▙ ♀ △ 🖻 ⎰ John Clements.
Leisure	practice golf range, putting green nets.
Location	Bagshot Rd (E side of village on A332)
Hotel	★★★★♨72% Pennyhill Park Hotel, London Rd, BAGSHOT ☎(0276) 71774 22⇨🏨 Annexe54⇨🏨

A golf-course name printed in ***bold italics*** means that we have been unable to verify information with the club's management for the current year

CAMBERLEY   Map 04 SU86

Camberley Heath ☎(0276) 23258
One of the great 'heath and heather' courses so frequently associated with Surrey. Several very good short holes - especially the 8th. The 10th is a difficult and interesting par 4, as also is the 17th, where the drive must be held well to the left as perdition lurks on the right. Course architect Harry Colt.
18 holes, 6337yds, Par 72, SSS 70.
Visitors	with member only weekends. Must contact in advance and have an introduction from own club.
Societies	must apply in advance.
Green Fees	£25 per round (£35 weekends).
Facilities	⊗ ╚ ▙ ♀ △ 🖻 ⎰⎰ Gary Smith.
Location	Golf Dr (1.25m SE of town centre off A325)
Hotel	★★★★♨72% Pennyhill Park Hotel, London Rd, BAGSHOT ☎(0276) 71774 22⇨🏨 Annexe54⇨🏨

CHERTSEY   Map 04 TQ06

Barrow Hills ☎(0256) 72037
Parkland course with natural hazards.
18 holes, 3090yds, Par 56, SSS 53, Course record 58.
Club membership 235.
Visitors	restricted at weekends & bank holidays in the afternoons. Must be accompanied by member.
Green Fees	not confirmed.
Facilities	▙
Location	Longcross (3m W on B386)
Hotel	★★★59% Thames Lodge Hotel, Thames St, STAINES ☎(0784) 464433 44⇨🏨

Laleham ☎(0932) 564211
Well-bunkered parkland/meadowland course.
18 holes, 6210yds, Par 70, SSS 70.
Club membership 600.
Visitors	restricted after 9.30am Tue & Thu. Must contact in advance and have an introduction from own club.
Societies	must contact in writing.
Green Fees	not confirmed.
Facilities	⊗ ⫙ by prior arrangement ╚ ▙ ♀ △ 🖻 ⎰ T Whitton.
Leisure	snooker.
Location	Laleham Reach (1.5m N)
Hotel	★★★59% Thames Lodge Hotel, Thames St, STAINES ☎(0784) 464433 44⇨🏨

CHIPSTEAD   Map 04 TQ25

Chipstead ☎Downland (0737) 555781
Hilly parkland course, hard walking, good views. Testing 18th hole.
18 holes, 5454yds, Par 67, SSS 67, Course record 64.
Club membership 650.
Visitors	restricted weekends.
Societies	must apply in advance.
Green Fees	£25 per day (£20 after 2pm).
Facilities	⊗ ╚ ▙ ♀ △ 🖻 ⎰ Gary Torbett.
Location	How Ln (.5m N of village)
Hotel	★★★★62% Selsdon Park Hotel, Sanderstead, CROYDON ☎081-657 8811 170⇨🏨

COBHAM
Map 04 TQ16

Silvermere ☎(0932) 866007
Parkland course with many very tight holes through
woodland, 17th has 170 yds carry-over lake. Driving range.
18 holes, 6333yds, Par 71, SSS 71.
Club membership 850.

Visitors	may not play at weekends until 1pm. Must contact in advance.
Societies	must contact by telephone.
Green Fees	£14 per day (£18.50 weekends).
Facilities	⊗ ⅢⅢ ﮮ 🍺 ♀ ᐃ 🏠 ⚲ ᵴ
Leisure	fishing.
Location	Redhill Rd (2.25m NW off A245)
Hotel	★★★59% Thatchers Resort Hotel, Epsom Rd, EAST HORSLEY ☎(04865) 4291 36⇨🏠Annexe23⇨🏠

CRANLEIGH
Map 04 TQ03

Fernfell Golf & Country Club ☎(0483) 268855
Scenic woodland/parkland course at the base of the Surrey
hills, easy walking. Clubhouse in 400-year-old barn.
18 holes, 5071yds, Par 68, SSS 67, Course record 68.
Club membership 1000.

Visitors	may not play at weekends. Must contact in advance.
Societies	must contact in advance.
Green Fees	not confirmed.
Facilities	⊗ ⅢⅢ ﮮ 🍺 ♀ ᐃ 🏠 ⚲ ᵴ Trevor Longmuir.
Leisure	hard tennis courts, heated outdoor swimming pool, snooker, sauna.
Location	Barhatch Ln (1m N)
Hotel	★★★★62% Forte Crest, Egerton Rd, GUILDFORD ☎(0483) 574444 111⇨🏠

DORKING
Map 04 TQ14

Betchworth Park ☎(0306) 882052
Parkland course, with hard walking on southern ridge of
Boxhill.
18 holes, 6266yds, Par 69, SSS 70.
Club membership 750.

Visitors	restricted Tue & Wed (am), Fri & weekends. Must contact in advance.
Societies	welcome Mon-Thu, must apply in advance.
Green Fees	£28 per day.
Facilities	⊗ ﮮ 🍺 ♀ ᐃ 🏠 ᵴ R Blackie.
Location	Reigate Rd (1m E on A25)
Hotel	★★★53% The White Horse, High St, DORKING ☎(0306) 881138 36⇨🏠Annexe32⇨🏠

Dorking ☎(0306) 889786
Undulating parkland course, easy slopes, wind-sheltered.
Testing holes: 5th 'Tom's Puddle' (par 4); 7th 'Rest and Be
Thankful' (par 4); 9th 'Double Decker' (par 4).
9 holes, 5163yds, Par 66, SSS 65, Course record 64.
Club membership 425.

Visitors	with member only weekends & bank holidays. Must contact in advance.
Societies	must apply in writing.
Green Fees	£16 weekdays.

Facilities	⊗ & ⅢⅢ (ex Mon) ﮮ 🍺 ♀ ᐃ 🏠 ⚲ ᵴ Paul Napier.
Location	Chart Park (1m S on A24)
Hotel	★★★★57% The Burford Bridge, Burford Bridge, Box Hill, DORKING ☎(0306) 884561 48⇨🏠

EAST HORSLEY
Map 04 TQ05

Drift ☎(04865) 4641
Woodland course with sheltered fairways and many ponds.
18 holes, 5957yds, Par 71, SSS 68.

Visitors	with member only weekends & bank holidays. Must contact in advance.
Societies	must apply in writing.
Green Fees	£26 per day (£17 after 1pm).
Facilities	⊗ ⅢⅢ by prior arrangement ﮮ 🍺 ♀ ᐃ 🏠 ᵴ
Location	1.5m N off B2039
Hotel	★★★59% Thatchers Resort Hotel, Epsom Rd, EAST HORSLEY ☎(04865) 4291 36⇨🏠Annexe23⇨🏠

EFFINGHAM
Map 04 TQ15

Effingham ☎Bookham (0372) 452203
Easy-walking downland course laid out on 27- acres with
tree-lined fairways. It is one of the longest of the Surrey
courses with wide subtle greens that provide a provocative
but by no means exhausting challenge. Fine views.
18 holes, 6488yds, Par 71, SSS 71.
Club membership 1200.

Visitors	with member only weekends & bank holidays. Must contact in advance.
Societies	must apply in advance.
Green Fees	£37.50 per day.
Facilities	⊗ ⅢⅢ ﮮ 🍺 ♀ 🏠 ⚲ ᵴ S Hoatson.
Leisure	hard and grass tennis courts, squash, snooker.
Location	Guildford Rd (W side of village on A246)
Hotel	★★★59% Thatchers Resort Hotel, Epsom Rd, EAST HORSLEY ☎(04865) 4291 36⇨🏠Annexe23⇨🏠

ENTON GREEN
Map 04 SU94

West Surrey ☎Godalming (04868) 21275
A good parkland-type course in rolling, well-wooded
setting. Some fairways are tight with straight driving at a
premium. The 17th is a testing hole with a long hill walk.
18 holes, 6300yds, Par 71, SSS 70.
Club membership 600.

Visitors	must be member of recognised club with handicap certificate. Must contact in advance and have an introduction from own club.
Societies	must apply in writing.
Green Fees	£32 per day (£39.50 weekends); £22.50 per round.
Facilities	⊗ ⅢⅢ by prior arrangement ﮮ 🍺 ♀ ᐃ 🏠 ᵴ
Leisure	snooker.
Location	S side of village
Hotel	★★★59% Hog's Back Hotel, Hog's Back, SEALE ☎(02518) 2345 75⇨🏠

EPSOM   Map 04 TQ26

Epsom ☎(03727) 21666
Downland course.
18 holes, 5118yds, Par 67, SSS 65.
Club membership 660.

Visitors	restricted weekends & bank holidays.
Societies	must apply in writing.
Green Fees	£12 per round (£16.50 weekends & bank holidays).
Facilities	⊗ by prior arrangement ⫞ by prior arrangement ⤢ ☛ ♀ ⌂ ⌂ ℂ Robert Wynn.
Location	Longdown Ln South, Epsom Downs (SE side of town centre on B288)
Hotel	★★62% Heathside Hotel, Brighton Rd, BURGH HEATH ☎(0737) 353355 73⇦╢

Horton Park Country Club ☎081-394 2626
Parkland course.
18 holes, 5208yds, Par 69, SSS 65.
Club membership 560.

Visitors	must book for weekends.
Societies	must telephone in advance.
Green Fees	£10.25 per 18 holes, £6 per 9 holes (£13 weekends).
Facilities	⊗ ⫞ (Thu-Sat evenings) ⤢ ☛ ♀ ⌂ ⌂ ᛟ ℂ G Clements, M Hirst.
Location	Hook Rd
Hotel	★★62% Heathside Hotel, Brighton Rd, BURGH HEATH ☎(0737) 353355 73⇦╢

ESHER   Map 04 TQ16

Moore Place ☎(0372) 463533
Public course on attractive, undulating parkland laid out some 60 years ago by Harry Vardon. Examples of most of the trees that will survive in the UK are to be found on the course. Testing short holes at 4th, 5th and 7th.
9 holes, 2062yds, Par 32, SSS 30, Course record 25.
Club membership 150.

Green Fees	£4.50 (£6 weekends & bank holidays).
Facilities	⊗ ⫞ ⤢ ☛ ♀ ⌂ ⌂ ᛟ ℂ David Allen.
Location	Portsmouth Rd (SW side of town centre on A244)
Hotel	★★★61% Ship Thistle Hotel, Monument Green, WEYBRIDGE ☎(0932) 848364 39⇦╢

Sandown Golf Centre ☎(0372) 463340
Flat parkland course in middle of racecourse. Additional facilities include a driving range, and a pitch-and-putt course.
New Course: 9 holes, 2828yds, Par 35, SSS 34, Course record 62.
Par 3: 9 holes, 1193yds, Par 27.
Club membership 600.

Visitors	restricted weekends & bank holidays.
Societies	must apply in writing.
Green Fees	New course £4.95 (£6 weekends); Par 3 course £3.20 (£3.95 weekends).
Facilities	⌂ ⌂ ℂ Neal Bedward.
Location	Sandown Park, More Ln (1m NW off A307)
Hotel	★★62% Haven Hotel, Portsmouth Rd, ESHER ☎081-398 0023 16⇦╢Annexe4⇦╢

We make every effort to ensure that our information is accurate but details may change after we go to print

Thames Ditton & Esher ☎081-398 1551
Commonland course, public right of way.
18 holes, 5190yds, Par 66, SSS 65, Course record 61.
Club membership 400.

Visitors	may not play on Sun mornings.
Societies	must contact in advance.
Green Fees	not confirmed.
Facilities	⤢ (ex Thu and Sun) ☛ (ex Thu and Sun) ♀ ⌂ ⌂ ℂ Rodney Hutton.
Location	Marquis of Granby, Portsmouth Rd (1m NE on A307)
Hotel	★★62% Haven Hotel, Portsmouth Rd, ESHER ☎081-398 0023 16⇦╢Annexe4⇦╢

FARNHAM   Map 04 SU84

Farnham ☎Runfold (02518) 2109
A mixture of meadowland and heath with quick drying sandy subsoil. Several of the earlier holes have interesting features, the finishing holes rather less.
18 holes, 6325yds, Par 72, SSS 70.
Club membership 705.

Visitors	must be member of recognised club & have handicap certificate. With member only weekends. Must contact in advance.
Societies	must apply one year in advance.
Green Fees	£25.50 per round.
Facilities	⊗ ⫞ ⤢ ☛ ♀ ⌂ ⌂ ℂ Grahame Cowlishaw.
Location	The Sands (3m E off A31)
Hotel	★★★60% Bush Hotel, The Borough, FARNHAM ☎(0252) 715237 68⇦╢

Farnham Park ☎(0252) 715216
Municipal parkland course in Farnham Park.
9 holes, 1163yds, Par 27.

Visitors	must contact in advance.
Societies	must apply in advance.
Green Fees	£2.90 per day (£3.70 weekends).
Facilities	⊗ ☛ ⌂ ᛟ ℂ Peter Chapman.
Location	Folly Hill, Farnham Park (N side of town centre on A287)
Hotel	★★★60% Bush Hotel, The Borough, FARNHAM ☎(0252) 715237 68⇦╢

GUILDFORD   Map 04 SU94

Guildford ☎(0483) 66765
A downland course but with some trees and much scrub. The holes provide an interesting variety of play, an invigorating experience.
18 holes, 6080yds, Par 69, SSS 70, Course record 64.
Club membership 700.

Visitors	with member only weekends & bank holidays. Must contact in advance.
Societies	must apply in advance.
Green Fees	£32 per day; £24 per round.
Facilities	⤢ ☛ ♀ ⌂ ⌂ ℂ Peter Hollington.
Leisure	snooker.
Location	High Path Rd, Merrow (E side of town centre off A246)
Hotel	★★★★62% Forte Crest, Egerton Rd, GUILDFORD ☎(0483) 574444 111⇦╢

HINDHEAD   Map 04 SU83

Hindhead ☎(0428) 604614
A good example of a Surrey heath-and-heather course, and most picturesque. Players must be prepared for some hard walking. The first nine fairways follow narrow valleys requiring straight hitting; the second nine are much less restricted.
18 holes, 6349yds, Par 70, SSS 70, Course record 65.
Club membership 820.

SCORECARD					
Hole	Yds	Par	Hole	Yds	Par
1	410	4	10	177	3
2	478	5	11	431	4
3	182	3	12	415	4
4	526	5	13	274	4
5	389	4	14	387	4
6	142	3	15	130	3
7	384	4	16	513	5
8	238	3	17	411	4
9	420	4	18	442	4
Out	3169	35	In	3180	35
			Totals	6349	70

Visitors	must contact in advance.
Societies	Wed & Thu only.
Green Fees	not confirmed.
Facilities	⊗ ⓑ ▆ ♀ ⚐ 🏠 ⚑ (
Leisure	snooker.
Location	Churt Rd (1.5m NW on A287)
Hotel	★★★67% Frensham Pond Hotel, CHURT ☎(025125) 3175 7⇌🏵Annexe12⇌🏵

KINGSWOOD   Map 04 TQ25

Kingswood ☎Mogador (0737) 832188
Flat parkland course, easy walking.
18 holes, 6855yds, Par 72, SSS 73, Course record 67.
Club membership 630.

Visitors	restricted before noon weekends.
Societies	must apply in advance.
Green Fees	£40 per day; £28 per round (£40 weekends).
Facilities	⊗ by prior arrangement ⅷ by prior arrangement ⓑ ▆ ♀ ⚐ 🏠 ⚑ (Martin Platts.
Leisure	squash, snooker.
Location	Sandy Ln (5m S of village off A217)
Hotel	★★62% Heathside Hotel, Brighton Rd, BURGH HEATH ☎(0737) 353355 73⇌🏵

LEATHERHEAD   Map 04 TQ15

Leatherhead ☎Oxshott (037284) 3966
Parkland course with numerous ditches and only two hills, so walking is easy.
18 holes, 6107yds, Par 71, SSS 69, Course record 67.
Club membership 650.

Visitors	restricted Thu, Sat & Sun (am). Must contact in advance.
Societies	must apply in advance.
Green Fees	£30 per round (£42.50 weekends & bank holidays).
Facilities	⊗ ⓑ ▆ ♀ ⚐ 🏠 ⚑ (Richard Hurst.
Leisure	sauna.
Location	Kingston Rd (1.25m N on A244)
Hotel	★★★59% Thatchers Resort Hotel, Epsom Rd, EAST HORSLEY ☎(04865) 4291 36⇌🏵Annexe23⇌🏵

Tyrrells Wood ☎(0372) 376025
Undulating parkland course with magnificent views and mature trees.
18 holes, 6234yds, Par 71, SSS 70, Course record 65.
Club membership 800.

Visitors	play Yellow tee markers only. Handicap certificate required. Restricted weekends. Must contact in advance and have an introduction from own club.
Societies	must apply in writing.
Green Fees	£42 per day; £27 per round.
Facilities	⊗ ⅷ by arrangement ⓑ ▆ ♀ ⚐ 🏠 ⚑ (Philip & Max Taylor.
Leisure	snooker.
Location	1.25m N on A244
Hotel	★★★★57% The Burford Bridge, Burford Bridge, Box Hill, DORKING ☎(0306) 884561 48⇌🏵

LIMPSFIELD   Map 05 TQ45

Limpsfield Chart ☎(0883) 722106
Tight heathland course set in National Trust land.
9 holes, 5718yds, Par 70, SSS 68, Course record 62.
Club membership 350.

Visitors	with member only weekends & not before 3.30 Thu.
Societies	must apply in advance.
Green Fees	£17 per day/round (£20 weekends).
Facilities	⊗ by prior arrangement ⅷ by prior arrangement ⓑ ▆ ♀ ⚐ 🏠
Location	Westerham Rd (1m E on A25)
Hotel	★★★65% Reigate Manor Hotel, Reigate Hill, REIGATE ☎(0737) 240125 51⇌🏵

LINGFIELD   Map 05 TQ34

Lingfield Park Golf Club ☎(0342) 834602
Difficult and challenging, tree-lined parkland course set in 210 acres of beautiful Surrey countryside. Driving range.
18 holes, 6473yds, Par 71, SSS 72, Course record 67.
Club membership 700.

Visitors	welcome, but only after 1pm on Sat & Sun.
Societies	must telephone in advance.
Green Fees	£30 per day; £20 per round (£30 per round weekends).
Facilities	⊗ ⅷ ⓑ ▆ ♀ ⚐ 🏠 ⚑ (Trevor Collingwood.
Location	Racecourse Rd (entrance next to Lingfield race course)
Hotel	★★★66% Woodbury House Hotel, Lewes Rd, EAST GRINSTEAD ☎(0342) 313657 13⇌🏵Annexe1🏵

OCKLEY   Map 04 TQ14

Gatton Manor Hotel Golf & Country Club ☎(030679) 555
Undulating course through woods and over many challenging water holes.
18 holes, 6145yds, Par 72, SSS 69, Course record 68.
Club membership 300.

Visitors	must give 2 weeks prior notice. Restricted Sun (am). Must contact in advance.
Societies	must apply in advance.
Green Fees	£24 per day (£40 weekends); £14 per round (£20 weekends).
Facilities	⊗ ⅷ ⓑ ▆ ♀ ⚐ 🏠 ⚕ (
Leisure	grass tennis courts, fishing, bowls.
Location	1.5m SW off A29

Hotel   ★★★53% The White Horse, High St,
                 DORKING ☎(0306) 881138
                 36⇔🌂 Annexe32⇔🌂

OTTERSHAW   Map 04 TQ06

Foxhills ☎(093287) 2050
A pair of parkland courses designed in the grand manner
and with American course-design in mind. One course is
tree-lined, the other, as well as trees, has massive bunkers
and artificial lakes which contribute to the interest. Both
courses offer testing golf and they finish on the same long
'double green'. Par 3 'Manor' course also available.
*Chertsey: 18 holes, 6658yds, Par 73, SSS 72, Course record
65.*
Longcross: 18 holes, 6406yds, Par 72, SSS 71.
Club membership 1100.

Visitors   restricted before noon weekends. Must con-
                 tact in advance.
Societies   welcome Mon-Fri, must apply in advance.
Green Fees   £40 per round (£50 weekends & bank
                 holidays).
Facilities   ⊗ ⫯ 🍴 ♨ ♀ ⛳ 📷 🏴 🛄 ƒ Bernard
                 Hunt MBE.
Leisure   hard tennis courts, outdoor and indoor heated
                 swimming pools, squash, snooker, sauna,
                 solarium, gymnasium, clay shoot, croquet
                 lawn, archery, boule.
Location   Stonehill Rd (1m NW)
Hotel   ★★★59% Thames Lodge Hotel, Thames
                 St, STAINES ☎(0784) 464433 44⇔🌂

PIRBRIGHT   Map 04 SU95

Goal Farm ☎(04867) 3183 & 3205
Beautiful lanscaped parkland 'Pay and Play' course with
excellent greens.
9 holes, 1273yds, Par 54, SSS 54.
Club membership 400.

Visitors   may not play on Sat mornings. Must be
                 accompanied by member.
Facilities   📷 🏴
Location   Gole Rd (1.5m NW on B3012)
Hotel   ★★★64% Forte Crest, Lynchford Rd,
                 FARNBOROUGH ☎(0252) 545051 110⇔🌂

PUTTENHAM   Map 04 SU94

Puttenham ☎Guildford (0483) 810498
Picturesque tree-lined heathland course offering testing golf,
easy walking.
18 holes, 6214yds, Par 71, SSS 70, Course record 71.
Club membership 650.

Visitors   with member only weekends. Must contact in
                 advance.
Societies   must apply in advance.
Green Fees   £25.50 per day; £20.50 per round.
Facilities   ⊗ ⫯ 🍴 ♨ ♀ ⛳ 📷 ƒ Gary Simmons.
Location   1m SE on B3000
Hotel   ★★★59% Hog's Back Hotel, Hog's Back,
                 SEALE ☎(02518) 2345 75⇔🌂

REDHILL   Map 04 TQ25

Redhill & Reigate ☎Reigate (0737) 240777
Parkland course.
18 holes, 5238yds, Par 67, SSS 66.
Club membership 600.

Visitors   restricted after 11am weekends except Sun (Jun-
                 Sep). Must contact in advance.
Societies   must apply in writing.
Green Fees   £12 per day (£18 weekends).
Facilities   ⊗ & ⫯ 🍴 by prior arrangement ⛳ & 💺 (Tue-Fri)
                 ♀ ⛺ 📷 🏴 ƒ Barry Davies.
Location   Clarence Rd, Pendelton Rd (1m S on A23)
Hotel   ★★★65% Reigate Manor Hotel, Reigate Hill,
                 REIGATE ☎(0737) 240125 51⇔🌂

REIGATE   Map 04 TQ25

Reigate Heath ☎(0737) 242610
Heathland course.
9 holes, 5554yds, Par 67, SSS 67, Course record 64.
Club membership 400.

Visitors   with member only weekends & bank holidays.
                 Must contact in advance.
Societies   must apply in writing.
Green Fees   £25 per day; £18 per round.
Facilities   ⊗ (ex Mon) ⫯ 🍴 by prior arrangement ⛳ (ex
                 Mon) 💺 ♀ ⛺ 📷 ƒ Harry Carter.
Location   1.5m W off A25
Hotel   ★★★65% Reigate Manor Hotel, Reigate Hill,
                 REIGATE ☎(0737) 240125 51⇔🌂

RIPLEY   Map 04 TQ05

Wisley ☎(0483) 211022
A 27-hole course designed by Robert Trent Jones Jnr,
and the first that this well-known American golf architect
has designed in the UK. Penncross Bent grasses have
been used to provide a superb playing surface.
The Church: 9 holes, 3355yds, Par 36, SSS 73.
The Mill: 9 holes, 3473yds, Par 36, SSS 73.
The Garden: 9 holes, 3385yds, Par 36, SSS 73.
Club membership 400.

Visitors   must be accompanied by member.
Green Fees   £35.
Facilities   ⊗ (Tue-Sun) ⫯ 🍴 (Tue-Sat) ⛳ 💺 ♀ ⛺ 📷
                 ƒ Bill Reid.
Leisure   fishing, snooker, sauna.
Hotel   ★★★59% Thatchers Resort Hotel, Epsom
                 Rd, EAST HORSLEY ☎(04865) 4291
                 36⇔🌂 Annexe23⇔🌂

TANDRIDGE   Map 05 TQ35

Tandridge ☎Oxted (0883) 712274
Rolling parkland, Colt designed course; good views.
18 holes, 6250yds, Par 70, SSS 70, Course record 68.
Club membership 750.

Visitors   restricted Fri-Sun & Tue. Must contact in
                 advance and have an introduction from own
                 club.
                                                          ▶

Societies must apply in advance.
Green Fees not confirmed.
Facilities ⊗ 🍺 ♀ ⚐ 🏠 ⛵ ℓ Allan Farquhar.
Location 1m NE off A25
Hotel ★★★70%, Nutfield Priory, NUTFIELD
🕿(0737) 822066 52⇨📶

TILFORD   Map 04 SU84

Hankley Common 🕿Frensham (025125) 2493
A natural heathland course subject to wind. Greens are
first rate. The 18th, a long par 4, is most challenging, the
green being beyond a deep chasm which traps any but the
perfect second shot. The 7th is a spectacular one-shotter.
18 holes, 6418yds, Par 71, SSS 71, Course record 62.
Club membership 700.
Visitors handicap certificate required, restricted Wed
& alternate weekends. Must contact in
advance and have an introduction from own
club.
Societies apply in writing.
Green Fees not confirmed.
Facilities ⊗ 🍺 ♀ ⚐ 🏠 ℓ Peter Stow.
Location .75m SE
Hotel ★★★67% Frensham Pond Hotel, CHURT
🕿(025125) 3175 7⇨📶Annexe12⇨📶

VIRGINIA WATER   Map 04 TQ00

Wentworth See page 199

WALTON-ON-THAMES   Map 04 TQ16

Burhill 🕿(0932) 227345
A relatively short and easy
parkland course with some
truly magnificent trees. The
18th is a splendid par 4
requiring a well-placed drive
and a long firm second. This
course is always in
immaculate condition.
18 holes, 6224yds, Par 69,
SSS 70, Course record 65.
Club membership 1100.

SCORECARD					
Hole	Yds	Par	Hole	Yds	Par
1	433	4	10	209	3
2	376	4	11	382	4
3	382	4	12	325	4
4	284	4	13	153	3
5	406	4	14	530	5
6	128	3	15	441	4
7	374	4	16	152	3
8	410	4	17	440	4
9	370	4	18	429	4
Out	3163	35	In	3061	34
			Totals	6224	69

Visitors may not play at weekends. Must contact in
advance and have an introduction from own
club.
Societies apply in writing.
Green Fees not confirmed.
Facilities ⊗ 🍺 by prior arrangement 🍺 🍺 (no
catering Mon) ♀ 🏠 ℓ Lee Johnson.
Leisure squash, badminton.
Location Burwood Rd (2m S)
Hotel ★★★61% Ship Thistle Hotel, Monument
Green, WEYBRIDGE 🕿(0932) 848364
39⇨📶

WALTON-ON-THE-HILL   Map 04 TQ25

Walton Heath See page 201

WEST BYFLEET   Map 04 TQ06

West Byfleet
🕿Byfleet (0932) 343433
An attractive course set
against a background of
woodland and gorse. The
13th is the famous 'pond'
shot with a water hazard and
two bunkers fronting the
green. No less than six holes
of 420 yards or more.
18 holes, 6211yds, Par 70,
SSS 70, Course record 64.
Club membership 650.

SCORECARD					
Hole	Yds	Par	Hole	Yds	Par
1	405	4	10	452	4
2	378	4	11	159	3
3	425	4	12	392	4
4	123	3	13	160	3
5	307	4	14	365	4
6	430	4	15	421	4
7	499	5	16	425	4
8	276	4	17	173	3
9	322	4	18	499	5
Out	3165	36	In	3046	34
			Totals	6211	70

Visitors with member only weekends. Restricted
Thu (Ladies Day). Must contact in advance.
Societies must apply in writing.
Green Fees £33 per day; £27 per round.
Facilities ⊗ 🍺 🍺 🍺 ♀ 🏠 ℓ David Regan.
Leisure snooker.
Location Sheerwater Rd (W side of village on A245)
Hotel ★★★59% Thatchers Resort Hotel, Epsom
Rd, EAST HORSLEY 🕿(04865) 4291
36⇨📶Annexe23⇨📶

WEST END   Map 04 SU96

Windlemere 🕿(0276) 858727
A parkland course, undulating in parts with natural water
hazards. There is also a floodlit driving range.
9 holes, 2673yds, Par 34.
Visitors no restrictions.
Societies must contact in advance.
Green Fees not confirmed.
Facilities 🍺 🍺 ♀ 🏠 🏠 ⛵ ℓ David Thomas & Alistair
Kelso.
Leisure 12 bay driving range.
Location Windlesham Rd (N side of village off A319)
Hotel ★★★★♨72% Pennyhill Park Hotel, London
Rd, BAGSHOT 🕿(0276) 71774
22⇨📶Annexe54⇨📶

WEYBRIDGE   Map 04 TQ06

St George's Hill 🕿(0932) 842406
Comparable and similar to Wentworth, a feature of this
course is the number of long and difficult par 4s. To score
well it is necessary to place the drive - and long driving
pays handsomely. Walking is hard on this undulating,
heavily wooded course with plentiful heather and rhodod-
endrons.
*A + B Course: 18 holes, 6569yds, Par 70, SSS 71, Course
record 65.*
A + C Course: 18 holes, 6097yds, Par 70, SSS 69.
B + C Course: 18 holes, 6210yds, Par 70, SSS 70.
Club membership 600.
Visitors must contact in advance and have an
introduction from own club.
Societies must contact in advance.
Green Fees £40 per day; £30 per round.
Facilities ⊗ 🍺 ♀ 🏠 🏠 ℓ A C Rattue.
Location 2m S off B374

▶

SCORE CARD: West Course					
Hole	Yds	Par	Hole	Yds	Par
1	471	4	10	186	3
2	155	3	11	376	4
3	452	4	12	483	5
4	501	5	13	441	4
5	191	3	14	179	3
6	344	4	15	466	4
7	399	4	16	380	4
8	398	4	17	571	5
9	450	4	18	502	5
Out	3361	36	In	3584	37
			Totals	6945	73

VIRGINIA WATER   MapO4TQO6

Wentworth Club ☎ (0344) 842201

John Ingham writes: Among the famous inland courses in England you have to name Woodhall Spa, Sunningdale, Swinley Forest - and Wentworth. The attraction at Wentworth is that the great players, including Ben Hogan and Sam Snead, have played here. The challenge, in terms of sheer yards, is enormous. But the qualities go beyond this, and include the atmosphere, the silver birch and fairway-side homes.

The West Course is the one every visitor wishes to play. You can't possibly name the best hole. Bernard Gallacher the local pro has his view, but you may select the seventh where the drive rolls downhill, and the second shot has to be played high up to a stepped green. The closing holes really sort out the best of them too.

The clubhouse offers Country Club facilities not typical of British golf courses. The pro shop resembles a plush city store; evening hospitality events are frequent and society meetings here are catered for as at few other centres for sport, and it's all done in five-star style.

Probably it is during the World Match-Play championship when Wentworth can be seen at its best. The tents are up, the superstars pile in and out of huge cars and the air is one of luxury and opulence.

Gary Player has won marvellously at Wentworth, beating Tony Lema after being seven down in the 36-hole match! Great competitors from the past have stamped their mark here. Arnold Palmer, back in the 1960s, beat Neil Coles in the Match-Play final but then, a generation later, faced young Seve Ballesteros. The Spaniard saved his bacon by pitching in for an eagle three at the last against Palmer, to take the clash into extra holes, where he won.

63 holes. West Course 18 holes, 6945 yds, Par 73, SSS 74, Course record 63 (Wayne Riley). East Course 18 holes, 6176 yds, Par 68, SSS 70, Course record 62. Edinburgh 18 holes, 6979 yds, Par 72, SSS 73, Course record 68

Visitors	weekdays only. Must contact in advance, and have a letter of introduction from their own club along with a current handicap certificate.
Societies	apply in advance (handicap restrictions).
Green fees	West Course £80; East Course £55; Edinburgh Course £65
Facilities	⊗ ⅃ ♏ ♀ (all day) private rooms ⌂ ⌂↑♈ ℓ (Bernard Gallacher).
Leisure	tennis (hardcourt & grass), outdoor-heated swimming pool, gymnasium
Location	Wentworth Drive (W side of Virginia Water, off B389 and A30)

WHERE TO STAY AND EAT NEARBY

HOTELS:

ASCOT   ★★★★ 57% Berystede, Bagshot Rd, Sunninghill ☎ (0344) 23311. 91 ⌂♈ . ⌕ European cuisine.

★★ 65% Highclere, 19 Kings Road, Sunninghill. ☎ (0344) 25220. 12 ⌂♈ . ⌕ European cuisine.

BAGSHOT   ★★★★ ⌸ 72% Pennyhill Park, London Rd ☎ (0276) 71774. 22 ⌂♈ , Annexe 54 ⌂♈ . ⌕ English & French cuisine.

RESTAURANTS:

BRAY   ××× The Waterside, River Cottage, Ferry Rd ☎ Maidenhead (0628) 20691 & 22941. ⌕ French cuisine.

EGHAM   ×× La Bonne Franquette, 5 High Street ☎ (0784) 439494. ⌕ French cuisine.

Hotel	★★★61% Ship Thistle Hotel, Monument Green, WEYBRIDGE ☎(0932) 848364 39⇨🌂

WOKING
Map 04 TQ05

Hoebridge Golf Centre ☎(0483) 722611
Public courses set in parkland. Also 25-bay floodlit driving range.
Main Course : 18 holes, 6536yds, Par 72, SSS 71.
Shey Course : 9 holes, 2294yds, Par 33.
Maybury : 18 holes, 2230yds, Par 54.
Club membership 400.

Visitors	must contact in advance.
Societies	Mon–Fri only; must contact in advance.
Green Fees	Main : £12; Shey : £6.75; Maybury : £6.
Facilities	⊗ ⅏ ㎚ ♨ ♀ ⚲ 🏠 ⛴ 𝄃 Tim Powell.
Leisure	snooker.
Location	Old Woking Rd, Old Woking (1m SE of Woking Rd)
Hotel	★★★★⚑72% Pennyhill Park Hotel, London Rd, BAGSHOT ☎(0276) 71774 22⇨🌂Annexe54⇨🌂

Worplesdon
☎(04867) 2277 due to change to (0483) 472277
The scene of the celebrated mixed-foursomes competition. Accurate driving is essential on this heathland course. The short 10th across a lake from tee to green is a notable hole, and the 18th provides a wonderfully challenging par-4 finish.
18 holes, 6440yds, Par 71, SSS 71, Course record 64.
Club membership 590.

Visitors	must play with member at weekends & bank holidays. Must contact in advance and have an introduction from own club.
Societies	must contact in writing.
Green Fees	£35 per round.
Facilities	♀ ⚲ 🏠 ⛴ 𝄃 J Christine.
Location	Heath House Rd (3.5m SW off B380)
Hotel	★★★★⚑72% Pennyhill Park Hotel, London Rd, BAGSHOT ☎(0276) 71774 22⇨🌂Annexe54⇨🌂

WOLDINGHAM
Map 05 TQ35

North Downs ☎(0883) 652057
Downland course, 850 ft above sea-level, with several testing holes.
18 holes, 5787yds, Par 69, SSS 68, Course record 66.
Club membership 700.

Visitors	must play with member at weekends and bank holidays. Must contact in advance and have an introduction from own club.
Societies	must contact in writing.
Green Fees	not confirmed.
Facilities	⊗ ⅏ ㎚ ♨ ♀ ⚲ 🏠 𝄃 Peter Ellis.
Location	Northdown Rd (.75m S)
Hotel	★★59% Sevenoaks Park Hotel, Seal Hollow Rd, SEVENOAKS ☎(0732) 454245 16rm(3⇨3🌂)Annexe10⇨🌂

This guide is updated annually – make sure that you use the up-to-date edition

TYNE & WEAR

BACKWORTH
Map 12 NZ37

Backworth ☎091-268 1048
Parkland course with easy walking, natural hazards and good scenery.
9 holes, 5930yds, Par 71, SSS 69, Course record 66.
Club membership 500.

Visitors	may not play on Tue & Thu after 5pm & Sun mornings. Must have an introduction from own club.
Societies	must contact in writing.
Green Fees	£10 per round (£12 weekends & bank holidays).
Facilities	⊗ ⅏ ㎚ & ♨ by prior arrangement ♀ ⚲
Leisure	archery, bowls, cricket, football.
Location	The Hall (W side of town on B1322)
Hotel	★★★61% Ship Thistle Hotel, Monument Green, WEYBRIDGE ☎(0932) 848364 39⇨🌂

BIRTLEY
Map 12 NZ25

Birtley ☎091-410 2207
Parkland course.
9 holes, 5660, Par 66, SSS 67, Course record 64.
Club membership 270.

Visitors	must play with member at weekends.
Societies	must contact 1 month in advance in summer.
Green Fees	not confirmed.
Facilities	⚲
Location	Portobello Rd
Hotel	★★★61% Forte Posthouse, Emerson District 5, WASHINGTON ☎091-416 2264 138⇨🌂

BOLDON
Map 12 NZ36

Boldon ☎091-536 5360 & 091-536 4182
Parkland links course, easy walking, distant sea views, windy.
18 holes, 6362yds, Par 72, SSS 70, Course record 67.
Club membership 700.

Visitors	may not play after 3.30pm at weekends & bank holidays. Must contact in advance.
Societies	must contact in advance.
Green Fees	£16 (£20 weekends & bank holidays).
Facilities	⊗ ⅏ ㎚ ♨ ♀ ⚲ 🏠 ⛴ 𝄃
Leisure	snooker.
Location	Dipe Ln, East Boldon (S side of village off A184)
Hotel	★★★72% Swallow Hotel, Queen's Pde, Seaburn, SUNDERLAND ☎091-529 2041 66⇨🌂

CHOPWELL
Map 12 NZ15

Garesfield ☎(0207) 561278
Undulating parkland course with good views and picturesque woodland surroundings.
18 holes, 6603yds, Par 72, SSS 72.
Club membership 720.

Visitors	weekends after 1630 only, unless with member. Must contact in advance.
Societies	must contact in advance.

▶

SCORE CARD: Old Course					
Hole	Yds	Par	Hole	Yds	Par
1	370	4	10	318	4
2	411	4	11	172	3
3	352	4	12	316	4
4	419	4	13	398	4
5	514	5	14	523	5
6	374	4	15	401	4
7	359	4	16	351	4
8	166	3	17	461	4
9	307	4	18	354	4
Out	3272	36	In	3294	36
			Totals	6566	72

WALTON-ON-THE-HILL   MapO4TQ25

Walton Heath ☎ (0737) 812380

John Ingham writes: Several historic names are etched on the Honours Board at Walton Heath, almost 700 feet above sea level. The rare atmosphere here is justified because this Surrey course can claim to be the toughest inland examination in Britain. Based on sand, the fairways equal the best on any seaside links and quickly dry out, even after a severe storm.

Weekend players are tormented in awful fashion. Erratic shots, wide of the prepared surface, are wickedly punished. Nobody escapes undamaged from the gorse and bracken but it is the heather, with those tough stems, that really snarl up any attempt at an over-ambitious recovery shot. So be advised - if you're caught off the fairway, don't attempt anything fancy. Play back on the shortest route to comparative security.

The course is famous for staging the Ryder Cup, but older players will remember it best for the Match-Play Championship battles that involved Sir Henry Cotton and Dai Rees as well as huge money matches that brought names such as Bobby Locke and Fred Daly to public prominence. Once owned by the News of the World newspaper, MP's, Lords and significant members of the press would be invited down to Walton Heath by Sir Emsley Carr one of the first to employ a lady as secretary and manager of a well-known championship venue.

While the Old Course is most frequently played by visitors, the New Course also offers classic silver birch trees, and all the subtle shots required if you are to get the ball near the hole. And, in the clubhouse, they serve a spectacular lunch.

36 holes. Old Course 18 holes, 6459 yds, Par 73, SSS 71. New Course 18 holes, 6360 yds, Par 72, SSS 70.

Visitors	weekdays only. Must contact in advance, and have a letter of introduction from their own club or a handicap certificate.
Societies	apply in writing.
Green fees	£55 per day: before 11.30, £45 after 11.30. am.
Facilities	⊗ ☕ (3.30-6.30pm) ♀ (closes 7pm winter, 9pm summer) ⌂ 🏠 ☏ (Ken McPherson).
Location	Deans Lane (SE side of village, off B2032)

WHERE TO STAY AND EAT NEARBY

HOTELS:

BURGH HEATH ★★ 62% Heathside, Brighton Rd. ☎ (0737) 353355. 73 ⊸🛏 . ♀ English & French cuisine.

DORKING ★★★★ 57% The Burford Bridge, Burford Bridge, Box Hill (2m NE A24). ☎ (0306) 884561. 48 ⊸🛏 .

REIGATE ★★★ 65% Reigate Manor, Reigate Hill. ☎ (0737) 240125. 51 ⊸🛏 . ♀ English & French cuisine.

STOKE D'ABERNON ★★★ 71% Woodlands Park, Woodlands Ln. ☎ Oxshott (037284) 3933. 59rm (58 ⊸🛏) . ♀ English & French cuisine.

RESTAURANTS:

DORKING ✗✗ Partners West Street, 2-4 West St. ☎ (0306) 882826. ♀ French cuisine.

SUTTON ✗ Partners Brasserie, 23 Stonecot Hill. ☎ 081-644 7743. ♀ English & French cuisine.

Green Fees £11 per day; £9 per day (£10 weekends & bank
holidays).
Facilities ⊗ & ⅷ by prior arrangement 🏌 ⬤ ♀ △ 🗋
Location .5m N
Hotel ★★★63% Swallow Hotel, Newgate Arcade,
NEWCASTLE UPON TYNE ☎091-232 5025
93⇨🐾

FELLING   Map 12 NZ26

Heworth ☎(0632) 692137
Fairly flat, parkland course.
18 holes, 6437yds, Par 71, SSS 71, Course record 69.
Club membership 500.
Visitors may not play Sat & before 10am Sun.
Societies must apply in writing.
Green Fees £13 (£16 weekends & bank holidays).
Facilities ⊗ ⅷ 🏌 ⬤ ♀ △
Location Gingling Gate, Heworth (On A195, .5m NW of
junc with A1(M))
Hotel ★★★61% Forte Posthouse, Emerson District
5, WASHINGTON ☎091-416 2264 138⇨🐾

GATESHEAD   Map 12 NZ26

Ravensworth ☎091-487 6014
Moorland/parkland course 600 ft above sea-level with fine
views. Testing 13th hole (par 3).
18 holes, 5872yds, Par 68, SSS 68, Course record 63.
Club membership 600.
Visitors no restrictions.
Societies must contact in advance.
Green Fees £13 per round (£21 weekends & bank holidays).
Facilities ⊗ ⅷ 🏌 ⬤ ♀ △ 🗋
Location Moss Heaps, Wrekenton (3m SE off A6127)
Hotel ★★★66% Swallow Hotel-Gateshead, High
West St, GATESHEAD ☎091-477 1105 103⇨🐾

GOSFORTH   Map 12 NZ26

Gosforth ☎091-285 3495
Parkland course with natural water hazards, easy walking.
18 holes, 6043yds, Par 69, SSS 69.
Club membership 480.
Visitors may not play on Tue & competition days. Must
contact in advance.
Societies must contact in advance.
Green Fees not confirmed.
Facilities ⅷ (ex Mon) ⅷ (ex Mon, Tue and Fri) 🏌 ⬤ ♀
△ 🗋 🍴 (David Race.
Location Broadway East (N side of town centre off A6125)
Hotel ★★★65% Swallow Gosforth Park Hotel,
High Gosforth Park, Gosforth, NEWCASTLE
UPON TYNE ☎091-236 4111 178⇨🐾

Gosforth Park ☎091-236 4480
A flat, tree-lined parkland course with a burn running
through many holes. There is also a 30-bay covered floodlit
driving range and a 9-hole pitch-putt.
18 holes, 6100yds, Par 71, SSS 70, Course record 66.
Club membership 650.
Visitors must contact in advance.
Societies must apply in writing.

Green Fees £10 per round (£12 weekends).
Facilities ⊗ ⅷ 🏌 ⬤ ♀ △ 🗋 (Grahame Garland.
Location Parklands Golf Club, High Gosforth Park (2m
N on B1318 off A6125)
Hotel ★★★★65% Swallow Gosforth Park Hotel,
High Gosforth Park, Gosforth, NEWCASTLE
UPON TYNE ☎091-236 4111 178⇨🐾

HOUGHTON-LE-SPRING   Map 12 NZ35

Houghton-le-Spring ☎091-845 1198
Hilly, downland course with natural slope hazards.
18 holes, 6416yds, Par 72, SSS 71.
Club membership 600.
Visitors may not play at weekends & bank holidays.
Societies must contact in advance.
Green Fees not confirmed.
Facilities 🏌 ⬤ ♀ △ 🗋 🍴 (
Location Copt Hill (.5m E on B1404)
Hotel ★★★69% Ramside Hall Hotel, Carrville,
DURHAM ☎091-386 5282 82⇨🐾

NEWCASTLE UPON TYNE   Map 12 NZ26

City of Newcastle ☎091-285 1775
A well-manicured parkland course in the Newcastle suburbs,
subject to wind.
18 holes, 6508yds, Par 72, SSS 71, Course record 67.
Club membership 570.
Visitors may not play competition days.
Societies by arrangement.
Green Fees £14.50 per day (£18.50 weekends & bank holi-
days).
Facilities ⊗ ⅷ 🏌 (ex Mon) ⬤ ♀ (all day) △ 🗋 (
Anthony Matthew.
Leisure snooker.
Location Three Mile Bridge (3m N on A1)
Hotel ★★★64% Airport Moat House Hotel,
Woolsington, NEWCASTLE UPON TYNE
AIRPORT ☎(0661) 24911 100⇨🐾

Newcastle United ☎091-286 4693
Moorland course with natural hazards.
18 holes, 6484yds, Par 72, SSS 71, Course record 64.
Club membership 500.
Visitors must play with member at weekends.
Societies must contact in writing.
Green Fees not confirmed.
Facilities ⊗ 🏌 ⬤ ♀ △ 🗋
Location Ponteland Rd, Cowgate (1.25m NW of city
centre off A6127)
Hotel ★★★57% Imperial Hotel, Jesmond Rd,
NEWCASTLE UPON TYNE ☎091-281 5511
129⇨

Northumberland ☎091-236 2498
Many golf courses have been sited inside racecourses,
although not so many survive today. One which does is
the Northumberland Club's course at High Gosforth
Park. Naturally the course is flat but there are plenty of
mounds and other hazards to make it a fine test of golf. It
should be said that not all the holes are within the confines
of the racecourse, but both inside and out there are some

good holes. This is a Championship course.
18 holes, 6629yds, Par 72, SSS 72.
Club membership 550.

Visitors	may not play at weekends or competition days. Must contact in advance and have an introduction from own club.
Societies	must apply in writing.
Green Fees	£30 per round.
Facilities	⊗ ⚐ ⚑ ♀
Location	High Gosforth Park (4m N of city centre off A1)
Hotel	★★★★65% Swallow Gosforth Park Hotel, High Gosforth Park, Gosforth, NEWCASTLE UPON TYNE ☎091-236 4111 178⇔♠

Westerhope ☎091-286 9125
Attractive parkland course with tree-lined fairways, and easy walking. Good open views towards the airport.
18 holes, 6468yds, Par 72, SSS 71, Course record 65.
Club membership 778.

Visitors	with member only at weekends.
Societies	must apply in writing.
Green Fees	£17 per day; £12 per round.
Facilities	⊗ ⍀ ⚐ ⚑ ♀ ⚲ ☖ ♦ Nigel Brown.
Location	Bowerbank, Whorlton Grange, Westerhope (4.5m NW of city centre off B6324)
Hotel	★★★★65% Swallow Gosforth Park Hotel, High Gosforth Park, Gosforth, NEWCASTLE UPON TYNE ☎091-236 4111 178⇔♠

RYTON   Map 12 NZ16

Ryton ☎091-413 3737
Parkland course.
18 holes, 5968yds, Par 70, SSS 68.
Club membership 400.

Visitors	with member only at weekends.
Green Fees	not confirmed.
Facilities	♀ ⚲
Location	Clara Vale (NW side of town off A695)
Hotel	★★64% County Hotel, Priestpopple, HEXHAM ☎(0434) 602030 9⇔♠

Tyneside ☎091-413 2177
Open parkland course, not heavily bunkered. Water hazard, hilly, practice area.
18 holes, 6042yds, Par 70, SSS 69, Course record 65.
Club membership 660.

Visitors	no restriction.
Societies	must apply in writing.
Green Fees	not confirmed.
Facilities	⊗ ⍀ ⚐ ⚑ ♀ ⚲ ☖ ♦ Malcolm Gunn.
Location	Westfield Ln (NW side of town off A695)
Hotel	★★64% County Hotel, Priestpopple, HEXHAM ☎(0434) 602030 9⇔♠

A golf-course name printed in ***bold italics***
means that we have been unable to verify
information with the club's management
for the current year

SOUTH SHIELDS   Map 12 NZ36

South Shields ☎091-456 8942
A slightly undulating downland course on a limestone base ensuring good conditions underfoot. Open to strong winds, the course is testing but fair. There are fine views of the coastline.
18 holes, 6264yds, Par 71, SSS 70.
Club membership 800.

Visitors	must contact in advance and have an introduction from own club.
Societies	by arrangement.
Green Fees	£18 per day (£24 weekends & bank holidays).
Facilities	⊗ ⍀ ⚐ ⚑ ♀ ⚲ ☖ ♦ Gary Parsons.
Location	Cleadon Hills (SE side of town centre off A1300)
Hotel	★★★60% Sea Hotel, Sea Rd, SOUTH SHIELDS ☎091-427 0999 33⇔♠

Whitburn ☎091-529 2144
Parkland course.
18 holes, 6046yds, Par 70, SSS 69, Course record 65.
Club membership 600.

Visitors	restricted Sun, Tue & competition days.
Societies	must apply in writing.
Green Fees	£15 per day (£20 weekends & bank holidays).
Facilities	⊗ ⍀ ⚐ ⚑ ♀ ⚲ ☖ ♦ D Stephenson.
Leisure	snooker.
Location	Lizard Ln (2.5m SE off A183)
Hotel	★★★72% Swallow Hotel, Queen's Pde, Seaburn, SUNDERLAND ☎091-529 2041 66⇔♠

SUNDERLAND   Map 12 NZ35

Wearside ☎091-534 2518
Open, undulating parkland course rolling down to the River Wear and beneath the shadow of the famous Penshaw Monument built on the lines of an Athenian temple it is a well-known landmark. Two ravines cross the course presenting a variety of challenging holes.
18 holes, 6373yds, Par 71, SSS 74, Course record 64.
Club membership 729.

Visitors	may not play before 9.30am & after 4pm. Must have an introduction from own club.
Societies	must apply in writing.
Green Fees	£12 per day (£18 weekends & bank holidays).
Facilities	⊗ ⍀ by prior arrangement ⚐ ⚑ ♀ ⚲ ☖ ♦ Steven Wynn.
Location	Coxgreen (3.5m W off A183)
Hotel	★★★72% Swallow Hotel, Queen's Pde, Seaburn, SUNDERLAND ☎091-529 2041 66⇔♠

TYNEMOUTH   Map 12 NZ36

Tynemouth ☎091-257 4578
Well-drained parkland/downland course, easy walking.
18 holes, 6082yds, Par 70, SSS 69, Course record 65.
Club membership 824.

Visitors	must play with member weekends & bank holidays.
Societies	must contact in writing.
Green Fees	£15 per day.

▶

Facilities	⊗ ⫟ ⏚ ⬛ ♀ ⏃ 🕋 ⟨ J P McKenna.
Location	Spital Dene (.5m W)
Hotel	★★★58% Park Hotel, Grand Pde, TYNEMOUTH ☎091-257 1406 49rm(43⇥🏠)

WALLSEND   Map 12 NZ26

Wallsend ☎091-262 1973
Parkland course.
18 holes, 6608yds, Par 72, SSS 72, Course record 68.
Club membership 750.

Visitors	may not play before 1230 weekends. Must contact in advance.
Societies	must apply in writing.
Green Fees	£10 per round (£12 weekends & bank holidays).
Facilities	⊗ ⫟ & ⏚ (summer only) ⬛ ♀ ⏃ 🕋 ⟨ Ken Phillips.
Location	Rheydt Av, Bigges Main (NW side of town centre off A193)
Hotel	★★★60% Newcastle Moat House, Coast Rd, WALLSEND ☎091-262 8989 & 091-262 7044 150⇥🏠

WASHINGTON   Map 12 NZ25

Washington Moat House ☎(091) 4172626
Championship course. Also a 9-hole (par 3) course, putting green and 21-bay floodlit driving range. 'Bunkers Bar' at the 10th tee is one of the few 'spike' bars in the country.
18 holes, 6267yds, Par 73, SSS 71, Course record 64.
Club membership 650.

Visitors	must contact in advance.
Societies	must apply in writing.
Green Fees	£13 (£19 weekends & bank holidays).
Facilities	⊗ ⫟ ⏚ ⬛ ♀ ⏃ 🕋 ⫠ 🐎 ⟨ Lynne Chesterton.
Leisure	heated indoor swimming pool, squash, snooker, sauna, solarium, gymnasium.
Location	Stone Cellar Rd, High Usworth
Hotel	★★★68% Washington Moat House, Stone Cellar Rd, District 12, High Usworth, WASHINGTON ☎091-417 2626 106⇥🏠

WHICKHAM   Map 12 NZ26

Whickham ☎091-488 7309
Parkland course, some uphill walking, fine views.
18 holes, 6129yds, Par 68, SSS 69, Course record 61.
Club membership 600.

Visitors	must have an introduction from own club.
Societies	by arrangement.
Green Fees	not confirmed.
Facilities	⊗ & ⫟ by prior arrangement ⏚ ⬛ ♀ ⏃ 🕋
Leisure	snooker.
Location	Hollinside Park (1.5m S)
Hotel	★★★66% Swallow Hotel-Gateshead, High West St, GATESHEAD ☎091-477 1105 103⇥🏠

We make every effort to ensure that our information is accurate but details may change after we go to print

---

WHITLEY BAY   Map 12 NZ37

Whitley Bay ☎091-252 0180
Downland course close to the sea. A stream runs through the undulating terrain.
18 holes, 6617yds, Par 71, SSS 72, Course record 66.
Club membership 700.

Visitors	with member only at weekends & bank holidays.
Societies	Mon-Fri, by arrangement.
Green Fees	£24 per day; £17 per round.
Facilities	⊗ ⫟ ⏚ ⬛ (no catering Mon) ♀ ⏃ 🕋 ⟨ W J Light.
Location	Claremont Rd (NW side of town centre off A1148)
Hotel	★★63% Holmedale Hotel, 106 Park Av, WHITLEY BAY ☎091-251 3903 & 091-253 1162 18rm(7⇥9🏠)

WARWICKSHIRE

ATHERSTONE   Map 04 SP39

Atherstone ☎(0827) 713110
Parkland course, established in 1894 and laid out on hilly ground.
18 holes, 6235yds, Par 73, SSS 70, Course record 65.
Club membership 350.

Visitors	handicap certificate required. With member only weekends & bank holidays.
Societies	weekdays only, by prior arrangement with secretary, handicap certificates are required.
Green Fees	£15 per day (£25 bank holidays).
Facilities	⊗ ⫟ ⏚ ⬛ ♀ ⏃ 🕋
Location	The Outwoods, Coleshill Rd (.5m S on B4116)
Hotel	★★58% Chase Hotel, Higham Ln, NUNEATON ☎(0203) 383406 28⇥🏠

BRANDON   Map 04 SP47

City of Coventry-Brandon Wood ☎Coventry (0203) 543141
Municipal parkland course surrounded by fields and bounded by River Avon on east side. Floodlit driving range.
18 holes, 6530yds, Par 72, SSS 71, Course record 68.
Club membership 1000.

Visitors	no restrictions.
Societies	apply in writing.
Green Fees	£6.65 Tue-Thu; £8.30 Fri-Sun.
Facilities	⊗ & ⫟ by prior arrangement ⏚ ⬛ ♀ ⏃ 🕋 ⫠ ⟨ Chris Gledhill.
Location	Brandon Ln (1m W)
Hotel	★★★61% The Chace Hotel, London Rd, Willenhall, COVENTRY ☎(0203) 303398 67⇥🏠

COLESHILL   Map 04 SP28

Maxstoke Park ☎(0675) 464915
Parkland course with easy walking. Numerous trees and a lake form natural hazards.
18 holes, 6478yds, Par 71, SSS 71, Course record 65.
Club membership 600.

Visitors	with member only at weekends & bank holidays.
Societies	must telephone in advance.
Green Fees	£30 per day; £20 per round.
Facilities	⊗ ⅏ ⅃ ♟ ♀ ⌂ 🏠 ♺ R A Young.
Location	Castle Ln (2m E)
Hotel	★★63% Swan Hotel, High St, COLESHILL ☎(0675) 462212 32⇥♠

KENILWORTH   Map 04 SP27

Kenilworth ☎(0926) 58517
Parkland course in open hilly situation. Club founded in 1887.
18 holes, 6263yds, Par 72, SSS 71.
Club membership 700.

Visitors	welcome except competition days. Must contact in advance.
Societies	apply in writing.
Green Fees	£22.50 per day (£33.75 weekends).
Facilities	⊗ ⅏ ⅃ ♟ ♀ ⌂ 🏠 ♺ ♺ Steven Yates.
Leisure	snooker.
Location	Crew Ln (.5m NE)
Hotel	★★64% Clarendon House Hotel, Old High St, KENILWORTH ☎(0926) 57668 31⇥♠

LEA MARSTON   Map 07 SP29

Lea Marston Hotel & Leisure Complex
☎Curdworth (0675) 470707
Par 3, 'pay-and-play' course, with water hazards, out of bounds, and large bunkers. The venue for the past two years of the Midlands Professional Par 3 Competition. Golf driving range.
9 holes, 783yds, Par 27.

Visitors	no restrictions.
Societies	must telephone in advance.
Green Fees	£4.25 for 18 holes; £3 for 9 holes. Prices due to be increased.
Facilities	⊗ ⅏ ⅃ ♟ ♀ ⌂ 🏠 ♺ 🐎 ♺ Andrew Jinks & Neil McEwan.
Leisure	hard tennis courts, sauna, solarium, gymnasium.
Location	Haunch Ln
Hotel	★★★64% Lea Marston Hotel & Leisure Complex, Haunch Ln, LEA MARSTON ☎(0675) 470468 19⇥♠

LEAMINGTON SPA   Map 04 SP36

Leamington & County ☎(0926) 425961
Undulating parkland course with extensive views.
18 holes, 6424yds, Par 71, SSS 71, Course record 65.
Club membership 700.

Societies	telephone in advance.
Green Fees	£23.50 per day; £20.50 per round (£30.50 per round weekends).
Facilities	⊗ ⅏ ⅃ ♟ ♀ ⌂ 🏠 ♺ I A Grant.
Leisure	snooker.
Location	Golf Ln, Whitnash (S side of town centre)
Hotel	★★★58% Manor House Hotel, Avenue Rd, LEAMINGTON SPA ☎(0926) 423251 53⇥♠

Newbold Comyn ☎(0926) 421157
Municipal parkland course with hilly front nine. The par 4, 9th is a 467-yd testing hole.
18 holes, 6315yds, Par 70, SSS 70.
Club membership 420.

Visitors	must contact in advance.
Societies	apply to professional.
Green Fees	£5.20 for 18 holes; £3.40 for 9 holes (£6.70/£4.80 weekends).
Facilities	♀ ⌂ 🏠 ♺ ♺ D Knight.
Location	Newbold Ter East (.75m E of town centre off B4099)
Hotel	★★★58% Manor House Hotel, Avenue Rd, LEAMINGTON SPA ☎(0926) 423251 53⇥♠

NUNEATON   Map 04 SP39

Nuneaton ☎(0203) 347810
Undulating moorland and woodland course.
18 holes, 6429yds, Par 71, SSS 71.
Club membership 675.

Visitors	with member only at weekends.
Societies	apply in writing.
Green Fees	not confirmed.
Facilities	⊗ ⅏ ⅃ ♟ (no catering Mon) ♀ ⌂ 🏠 ♺ Graham Davison.
Leisure	snooker.
Location	Golf Dr, Whitestone (2m SE off B4114)
Hotel	★★58% Chase Hotel, Higham Ln, NUNEATON ☎(0203) 383406 28⇥♠

Purley Chase ☏Chapel End (0203) 393118
Meadowland course with tricky water hazards on eight holes
and undulating greens. 13-bay driving range.
18 holes, 6800yds, Par 71, SSS 71, Course record 64.
Club membership 700.
Visitors	welcome except mornings at weekend & competition days.
Societies	by prior arrangement at least 3 weeks in advance.
Green Fees	£15 per round (£18 weekends & bank holidays).
Facilities	⊗ ℳ (Fri & Sat) ⓛ ⬤ ♀ ⌂ 🏠 (David Llewelyn.
Leisure	fishing.
Location	Ridge Ln (2m NW off B4114)
Hotel	Longshoot Toby Hotel, Watling St, NUNEATON ☏(0203) 329711 Annexe47⇨▮

RUGBY   Map 04 SP57

Rugby ☏(0788) 542306
Parkland course with brook running through the middle and
crossed by a viaduct.
18 holes, 5457yds, Par 68, SSS 67.
Club membership 550.
Visitors	weekends & bank holidays with member only. Must contact in advance and have an introduction from own club.
Societies	apply in writing.
Green Fees	not confirmed.
Facilities	⊗ by prior arrangement (ex Tue) ℳ by prior arrangement (ex Tue) ⓛ ⬤ ♀ ⌂ 🏠 ⊤ (D Sutherland.
Leisure	snooker.
Location	Clifton Rd (1m NE on B5414)
Hotel	★★★60% Grosvenor Hotel, Clifton Rd, RUGBY ☏(0788) 535686 21⇨▮

STRATFORD-UPON-AVON   Map 04 SP25

Stratford-upon-Avon ☏(0789) 205749
Beautiful parkland course. The par 3, 16th is tricky and the
par 5, 17th and 18th, provide a tough end.
18 holes, 6309yds, Par 72, SSS 70, Course record 64.
Club membership 750.
Visitors	restricted on Wed. Must contact in advance.
Societies	must telephone in advance.
Green Fees	not confirmed.
Facilities	⊗ ℳ ⓛ ⬤ ♀ ⌂ 🏠 ⊤ (N D Powell.
Location	Tiddington Rd (0.75m E on B4086)
Hotel	★★★59% Alveston Manor Hotel, Clopton Bridge, STRATFORD-UPON-AVON ☏(0789) 204581 108⇨▮

Welcombe Hotel ☏(0789) 295252
Wooded parkland course of great character and boasting
superb views of the River Avon, Stratford and the
Cotswolds. Set within the hotel's 157-acre estate, it has two
lakes and water features.
18 holes, 6202yds, Par 70, SSS 70.
Club membership 400.
Visitors	welcome except before 11am weekends. Must contact in advance.
Societies	booking via Hotel.
Green Fees	£30 (£35 weekends & bank holidays) Golf buggies £17.50.

Facilities	⊗ ℳ (at hotel) ⓛ ⬤ ♀ ⌂ 🏠 ⊤ ⇥
Leisure	hard tennis courts, fishing, snooker, putting green.
Location	Warwick Rd (1.5m NE off A46)
Hotel	★★★★64% Welcombe Hotel and Golf Course, Warwick Rd, STRATFORD-UPON-AVON ☏(0789) 295252 76⇨▮

TANWORTH-IN-ARDEN   Map 07 SP17

Ladbrook Park ☏(05644) 2264
Parkland course lined with trees.
18 holes, 6418yds, Par 71, SSS 71, Course record 67.
Club membership 750.
Visitors	with member only weekends. Handicap certificate required. Must contact in advance and have an introduction from own club.
Societies	telephone in advance.
Green Fees	not confirmed.
Facilities	⊗ ℳ ⓛ ⬤ (no catering Mon) ♀ ⌂ 🏠 (G R Taylor.
Leisure	snooker.
Location	Poolhead Ln (1m NW on A4023)
Hotel	★★★★64% St John's Swallow Hotel, 651 Warwick Rd, SOLIHULL ☏021-711 3000 180⇨▮

WARWICK   Map 04 SP26

Warwick ☏(0926) 494316
Parkland course with easy walking. Driving range with
floodlit bays.
9 holes, 2682yds, Par 34, SSS 66.
Club membership 150.
Visitors	welcome except Sun mornings.
Green Fees	not confirmed.
Facilities	⬤ ♀ ⌂ 🏠 ⊤ (Steve Hutchinson.
Leisure	snooker.
Location	The Racecourse (W side of town centre)
Hotel	★★57% Lord Leycester Hotel, Jury St, WARWICK ☏(0926) 491481 52⇨▮

◦ WEST MIDLANDS ◦

ALDRIDGE   Map 07 SK00

Druids Heath ☏(0922) 55595
Testing, undulating heathland course.
18 holes, 6914yds, Par 72, SSS 73, Course record 66.
Club membership 621.
Visitors	with member only at weekends. Must contact in advance and have an introduction from own club.
Societies	must contact in advance.
Green Fees	£18.50 (£24.50 weekends).
Facilities	⊗ ⓛ ⬤ ♀ ⌂ 🏠 ⊤ (Mark P Daubney.
Location	Stonnall Rd (NE side of town centre off A454)
Hotel	★★★66% Fairlawns Hotel, 178 Little Aston Road, Aldridge, WALSALL ☏(0922) 55122 36⇨▮

For a full list of golf courses included in the
book, see the index at the end of the directory

BIRMINGHAM   Map 07 SP08

Brandhall ☎021-552 2195
Private golf club on municipal parkland course, easy walking, good hazards. Testing holes: 1st-502 yds (par 5); 10th-455 yds dog-leg (par 5).
18 holes, 5734yds, Par 70.
Club membership 300.

Visitors	restricted weekends. Must contact in advance.
Societies	by arrangement.
Green Fees	£5 per round (£6.50 weekends).
Facilities	⊗ (ex Tue) ⊪ by prior arrangement ⬛ (ex Tue) ♀ (guests only) 📇 ⚒ ⎈ G Mercer.
Location	Heron Rd, Oldbury, Warley (5.5m W of city centre off A4123)
Hotel	★★★62% Forte Posthouse Birmingham, Chapel Ln, GREAT BARR ☎021-357 7444 204⇨⟟

Cocks Moors Woods Municipal ☎021-444 3584
Tree-lined, parkland course.
18 holes, 5888yds, Par 69, SSS 68.
Club membership 250.

Visitors	no restrictions.
Societies	must contact in advance.
Green Fees	not confirmed.
Facilities	⚲ 📇 ⚒
Location	Alcester Rd South, Kings Heath (5m S of city centre on A435)
Hotel	★★★★51% Forte Crest, Smallbrook Queensway, BIRMINGHAM ☎021-643 8171 254⇨⟟

Edgbaston ☎021-454 1736
Parkland course in lovely country.
18 holes, 6118yds, Par 69, SSS 69, Course record 65.
Club membership 858.

Visitors	must have handicap certificate. Must contact in advance.
Societies	must apply in writing.
Green Fees	£27.50 per day (£35 weekends & bank holidays).
Facilities	⊗ ⊪ by prior arrangement ⬛ ♀ ⚲ 📇 ⎈ Andrew H Bownes.
Leisure	snooker.
Location	Church Rd, Edgbaston (1m S of city centre on B4217 off A38)
Hotel	★★★★62% Plough & Harrow, Hagley Rd, Edgbaston, BIRMINGHAM ☎021-454 4111 44⇨⟟

Great Barr ☎021-358 4376
Parkland course with easy walking. Pleasant views of Barr Beacon National Park.
18 holes, 6545yds, Par 73, SSS 72.
Club membership 600.

Visitors	restricted at weekends. Must have an introduction from own club.
Societies	must contact in writing.
Green Fees	not confirmed.
Facilities	⊗ by prior arrangement ⊪ by prior arrangement ⬛♀ ⚲ 📇 ⚒ ⎈ S Doe.
Leisure	snooker.
Location	Chapel Ln, Great Barr (6m N of city centre off A34)

▶

Hotel	★★★62% Forte Posthouse Birmingham, Chapel Ln, GREAT BARR ☎021-357 7444 204⇨🛏🏌

Handsworth ☎021-554 0599
Undulating parkland course with some tight fairways but subject to wind.
18 holes, 6057yds, Par 70, SSS 70.
Club membership 920.

Visitors	restricted weekends, bank holidays & Xmas. Must contact in advance and have an introduction from own club.
Societies	Mon-Fri only, must apply in writing.
Green Fees	£25 per day/round.
Facilities	⊗ ⅲ 🍴 (no catering Mon) 🍺 ♀ 🏌 🏠 ⌂ L Bashford.
Leisure	squash, snooker.
Location	Sunningdale Close, Handsworth Wood (3.5m NW of city centre off A4040)
Hotel	★★★62% West Bromwich Moat House, Birmingham Rd, WEST BROMWICH ☎021-553 6111 180⇨🛏🏌

Harborne ☎021-427 3058
Parkland course in hilly situation, with brook running through.
18 holes, 6240yds, Par 70, SSS 70, Course record 65.
Club membership 550.

Visitors	must have a handicap certificate; may not play weekends, bank holidays or 27 Dec-1 Jan. Must contact in advance.
Societies	must telephone in advance.
Green Fees	£25 per weekday.
Facilities	⊗ ⅲ 🍴 🍺 (no catering Sun & Mon) ♀ 🏌 🏠 ⌂ ⌂ Alan Quarterman.
Leisure	snooker.
Location	40 Tennal Rd, Harborne (3.5 m SW of city centre off A4040)
Hotel	★★★★62% Plough & Harrow, Hagley Rd, Edgbaston, BIRMINGHAM ☎021-454 4111 44⇨🏌

Harborne Church Farm ☎021-427 1204
Parkland course with water hazards and easy walking. Some holes might prove difficult.
9 holes, 2366yds, Par 66, SSS 64, Course record 63.
Club membership 250.

Visitors	no restrictions.
Green Fees	£5 per round (18 holes); £2.50 (9 holes).
Facilities	⊗ ⅲ 🍺 🏌 🏠 ⌂ ⌂ Mark J Hampton.
Location	Vicarage Rd, Harborne (3.5m SW of city centre off A4040)
Hotel	★★★55% Apollo Hotel, 243-247 Hagley Rd, Edgbaston, BIRMINGHAM ☎021-455 0271 128⇨🏌

Hatchford Brook ☎021-743 9821
Fairly flat, municipal parkland course.
18 holes, 6200yds, Par 69, SSS 69.
Club membership 400.

Visitors	no restrictions.
Green Fees	£5.60 per round.
Facilities	🏌 🏠 ⌂ P Smith.
Location	Coventry Rd, Sheldon (6m E of city centre on A45)

Hotel	★★★61% Forte Posthouse, Coventry Rd, Elmdon, BIRMINGHAM AIRPORT ☎021-782 8141 136⇨🛏🏌

Hilltop ☎021-554 4463
Testing and hilly municipal parkland course.
18 holes, 6114yds, Par 71, SSS 69, Course record 65.
Club membership 300.

Visitors	no restrictions.
Societies	welcome.
Green Fees	£5.10 per round (£5.60 weekends).
Facilities	⊗ ⅲ 🍺 🏌 🏠 ⌂ ⌂ Kevin Highfield.
Location	Park Ln, Handsworth (3.5m N of city centre off A4040)
Hotel	★★★62% West Bromwich Moat House, Birmingham Rd, WEST BROMWICH ☎021-553 6111 180⇨🏌

Lickey Hills ☎021-453 3159
Hilly municipal course overlooking the city.
18 holes, 6610yds, Par 69, SSS 69.
Club membership 300.

Visitors	no restrictions.
Societies	must contact in advance.
Green Fees	not confirmed.
Facilities	♀ 🏌 🏠 ⌂ ⌂
Location	Rednal (10m SW of city centre on B4096)
Hotel	★★★62% Perry Hall Hotel, Kidderminster Rd, BROMSGROVE ☎(0527) 579976 55⇨🏌

Moseley ☎021-444 2115
Parkland course with a lake, pond and stream to provide natural hazards. The par-3, 5th goes through a cutting in woodland to a tree and garden-lined amphitheatre, and the par-4, 6th entails a drive over a lake to a dog-leg fairway.
18 holes, 6285yds, Par 70, SSS 70, Course record 64.
Club membership 560.

Visitors	may not play at weekends. Must contact in advance and have an introduction from own club.
Societies	welcome.
Green Fees	not confirmed.
Facilities	⊗ (ex Mon) ⅲ by prior arrangement 🍴 🍺 ♀ 🏌 🏠 ⌂ G Edge.
Location	Springfield Rd, Kings Heath (4m S of city centre on B4146 off A435)
Hotel	★★64% Norwood Hotel, 87-89 Bunbury Rd, Northfield, BIRMINGHAM ☎021-411 2202 15⇨🏌

Warley ☎021-429 2440
Municipal parkland course in Warley Woods.
9 holes, 2606yds, Par 33, SSS 64, Course record 62.
Club membership 150.

Visitors	no restrictions.
Green Fees	not confirmed.
Facilities	⊗ 🍴 🍺 🏌 🏠 ⌂ ⌂ David Owen.
Location	Lightswood Hill, Bearwood (4m W of city centre off A456)
Hotel	★★★55% Apollo Hotel, 243-247 Hagley Rd, Edgbaston, BIRMINGHAM ☎021-455 0271 128⇨🏌

For an explanation of symbols and abbreviations, see page 32

COVENTRY   Map 04 SP37

Coventry ☎(0203) 414152
The scene of several major professional events, this
undulating parkland course has a great deal of quality.
More than that, it usually plays its length, and thus scoring
is never easy, as many professionals have found to their
cost.
18 holes, 6613yds, Par 73, SSS 72, Course record 66.
Club membership 760.

Visitors	must have handicap certificate, but may not play at weekends. Must contact in advance.
Societies	by arrangement.
Green Fees	£30 per day.
Facilities	🏠 ℄ P J Weaver.
Leisure	snooker.
Location	Finham Park (3m S of city centre on A444)
Hotel	★★★61% Hylands Hotel, Warwick Rd, COVENTRY ☎(0203) 501600 55rm(54➪)

The Grange ☎(0203) 451465
Flat parkland course with very tight out of bounds on a
number of holes, and a river which affects play on five of
them. Well-bunkered, with plenty of trees.
9 holes, 6002yds, Par 72, SSS 69.
Club membership 300.

Visitors	may not play before 2pm weekdays or after noon on Sun.
Societies	must contact in advance.
Green Fees	not confirmed.
Facilities	♀ ⛲
Location	Copsewood, Binley Rd (2m E of city centre on A428)
Hotel	★★★61% The Chace Hotel, London Rd, Willenhall, COVENTRY ☎(0203) 303398 67➪🐾

Hearsall ☎(0203) 713470
Parkland course with fairly easy walking. A brook provides
an interesting hazard.
18 holes, 5603yds, Par 70, SSS 67, Course record 63.
Club membership 600.

Visitors	with member only at weekends.
Societies	by arrangement.
Green Fees	£23.
Facilities	⛲ 🏠 ℄
Location	Beechwood Av (1.5m SW of city centre off A429)
Hotel	★★★61% Hylands Hotel, Warwick Rd, COVENTRY ☎(0203) 501600 55rm(54➪)

DUDLEY   Map 07 SO99

Dudley ☎(0384) 233877
Exposed and very hilly parkland course.
18 holes, 5832yds, Par 69, SSS 68.
Club membership 300.

Visitors	may not play at weekends.
Societies	must contact in advance.
Green Fees	not confirmed.
Facilities	⊗ 🍴 by prior arrangement 🍺 ♬ ♀ ⛲ 🏠 ℄ David Down.
Leisure	snooker.

Location	Turner's Hill (2m S of town centre off B4171)
Hotel	★★60% Station Hotel, Birmingham Rd, DUDLEY ☎(0384) 253418 38➪🐾

Swindon ☎Wombourne (0902) 897031
Attractive undulating woodland/parkland course, with
spectacular views.
Old Course: 18 holes, 6042yds, Par 71, SSS 69, Course record 68.
New Course: 9 holes, 1135yds, Par 27.
Club membership 700.

Visitors	cannot bring wide wheel trolleys.
Societies	Mon-Fri only, telephone in advance.
Green Fees	£20 per day (£30 weekends & bank holidays); £13 per round (£20 weekends & bank holidays).
Facilities	⊗ 🍴 by prior arrangement 🍺 ♬ ♀ ⛲ 🏠
Leisure	fishing, snooker.
Location	Bridgnorth Rd, Swindon
Hotel	★★60% Station Hotel, Birmingham Rd, DUDLEY ☎(0384) 253418 38➪🐾

HALESOWEN   Map 07 SO98

Halesowen ☎021-501 3606
Parkland course in convenient position.
18 holes, 5754yds, Par 69, SSS 68, Course record 65.
Club membership 600.

Visitors	may not play weekends.
Societies	must apply in writing.
Green Fees	£16 per round.
Facilities	⊗ 🍴 🍺 ♬ ♀ ⛲ 🏠 🐾 ℄ David Down.
Leisure	snooker.
Location	The Leasowes (1m E)
Hotel	★★★55% Apollo Hotel, 243-247 Hagley Rd, Edgbaston, BIRMINGHAM ☎021-455 0271 128➪🐾

KNOWLE   Map 07 SP17

Copt Heath ☎(0564) 772650
Parkland course designed by H. Vardon.
18 holes, 6500yds, Par 71, SSS 71, Course record 68.
Club membership 700.

Visitors	must use yellow tees only. Must contact in advance.
Societies	by arrangement.
Green Fees	£30 per day/round.
Facilities	⊗ 🍴 🍺 ♬ ♀ ⛲ 🏠 ℄ B J Barton.
Location	1220 Warwick Rd (On A41 .25m S of junc 5 of M42)
Hotel	★★★64% St John's Swallow Hotel, 651 Warwick Rd, SOLIHULL ☎021-711 3000 180➪🐾

MERIDEN   Map 04 SP28

Forest of Arden Hotel Golf and Country Club
☎Meridan (0676) 22335
Two parkland courses, set within the grounds of Packington
Park, with extensive water hazards and offering a fine test of
golf. On-site hotel with many leisure facilities.
Arden Course: 18 holes, 6472yds, Par 72, SSS 71.
Aylesford Course: 18 holes, 6258yds, Par 72, SSS 69.
Club membership 800.

▶

Visitors must have handicap certificate, but may not play weekends (unless hotel resident). Must contact in advance and have an introduction from own club.
Societies by arrangement.
Green Fees not confirmed.
Facilities ⊗ ⅷ ㏇ ▣ ♀ ⚎ 🏠 ⛿ 🏌 ℂ Mike Tarn.
Leisure hard tennis courts, heated indoor swimming pool, squash, fishing, snooker, sauna, solarium, gymnasium, steam room beauty salon.
Location Maxstoke Ln (1m SW on B4102)
Hotel ★★★68% Manor Hotel, MERIDEN ☎(0676) 22735 74⇨🛏

North Warwickshire ☎(0676) 22259
Parkland course with easy walking.
9 holes, 3186yds, Par 72, SSS 70, Course record 67.
Club membership 350.
Visitors restricted Thu, weekends & bank holidays. Must contact in advance.
Societies must apply in writing.
Green Fees £20 per day.
Facilities ⊗ ㏇ (ex Mon) ▣ ♀ ⚎ 🏠 ℂ Simon Edwin.
Location Hampton Ln (1m SW on B4102)
Hotel ★★★68% Manor Hotel, MERIDEN ☎(0676) 22735 74⇨🛏

SOLIHULL Map 07 SP17

Olton ☎021-705 1083
Parkland course with prevailing southwest wind.
18 holes, 6229yds, Par 69, SSS 71, Course record 63.
Club membership 600.
Visitors may not play Wed & with member only at weekends. Must have an introduction from own club.
Societies by arrangement.
Green Fees £30 per round.
Facilities ⚎ 🏠 ℂ D Playdon.
Leisure snooker.
Location Mirfield Rd (1m NW off A41)
Hotel ★★★64% St John's Swallow Hotel, 651 Warwick Rd, SOLIHULL ☎021-711 3000 180⇨🛏

Robin Hood ☎021-706 0061
Pleasant parkland course with easy walking and open to good views. Modern clubhouse.
18 holes, 6609yds, Par 72, SSS 72, Course record 68.
Club membership 700.
Visitors with member only at weekends. Must contact in advance.
Societies must contact in advance.
Green Fees £31 per day; £26 per round.
Facilities ㏇ (Tue-Fri only) ▣ ♀ ⚎ 🏠 ℂ R S Thompson.
Location St Bernards Rd (2m W off B4025)
Hotel ★★★64% St John's Swallow Hotel, 651 Warwick Rd, SOLIHULL ☎021-711 3000 180⇨🛏

Shirley ☎021-744 6001
Fairly flat parkland course.
18 holes, 6510yds, Par 72, SSS 71, Course record 68.
Club membership 500.

Visitors may not play bank holidays & with member only at weekends. Handicap certificate is required.
Societies must contact in advance.
Green Fees £30 per day; £25 per round.
Facilities ⊗ ⅷ ㏇ ▣ ♀ ⚎ 🏠 ℂ C J Wicketts.
Leisure snooker.
Location Stratford Rd, Monkpath (3m SW off A34)
Hotel ★★★63% George Hotel, High St, SOLIHULL ☎021-711 2121 74⇨🛏

STOURBRIDGE Map 07 SO98

Hagley Golf & Country Golf ☎Hagley (0562) 883701
Undulating parkland course set beneath the Clent Hills; there are superb views. Testing 15th, par 5, 557 yards.
18 holes, 6353yds, Par 72, SSS 72, Course record 71.
Club membership 640.
Visitors restricted Wed & with member only at weekends.
Societies Mon-Fri only, must apply in writing.
Green Fees £25 per day; £20 per round.
Facilities ⊗ ⅷ ㏇ ▣ ♀ ⚎ 🏠 ℂ Iain Clark.
Leisure squash.
Location Wassell Grove, Hagley (1m E of Hagley off A456)
Hotel ★★63% Talbot Hotel, High St, STOURBRIDGE ☎(0384) 394350 25rm(13⇨7🛏)

Stourbridge ☎(0384) 395566
Parkland course.
18 holes, 6178yds, Par 69, SSS 69, Course record 63.
Club membership 720.
Visitors may not play Wed afternoon & weekends. Must have an introduction from own club.
Societies must apply in writing.
Green Fees £22 per day/round.
Facilities ⊗ ⅷ & ㏇ (ex Sun & Mon) ▣ ♀ ⚎ 🏠 ⛿ ℂ W H Firkins.
Leisure snooker.
Location Worcester Ln, Pedmore (2m from town centre)
Hotel ★★63% Talbot Hotel, High St, STOURBRIDGE ☎(0384) 394350 25rm(13⇨7🛏)

SUTTON COLDFIELD Map 07 SP19

Belfry ☎Curdworth (0675) 70301
Famed for hosting recent Ryder Cup matches. The two 18-hole courses here, the Brabazon and Derby have been designed by Peter Alliss and Dave Thomas. The Brabazon, a demanding championship course, has eleven holes on which one has to negotiate water.
Brabazon: 18 holes, 6975yds, Par 73, SSS 73, Course record 63.
Derby: 18 holes, 5953yds, Par 69, SSS 69.

SCORECARD: Brabazon Course					
Hole	Yds	Par	Hole	Yds	Par
1	408	4	10	301	4
2	340	4	11	365	4
3	455	4	12	225	3
4	569	5	13	364	4
5	389	4	14	184	3
6	386	4	15	540	5
7	173	3	16	400	4
8	476	5	17	555	5
9	390	4	18	455	4
Out	3586	37	In	3389	36
			Totals	6975	73

Visitors	a handicap certificate is required for Brabazon course. Must contact in advance.
Societies	must telephone in advance.
Green Fees	not confirmed.
Facilities	 ⊗ ⅲ ⅼ ⅬⅬ ♀ ⌂ ⌐ ☂ ⊨ ⌊ G Laidlow & P McGovern.
Leisure	hard tennis courts, heated indoor swimming pool, squash, snooker, sauna, solarium, Nightclub in grounds of Belfry.
Location	Lichfield Rd, Wishaw (exit junc 9 M42 4m E)
Hotel	★★★★68% The Belfry, Lichfield Rd, WISHAW ☎(0675) 470301 219⇨
Additional hotel	★★★59% Sutton Court Hotel, 60-66 Lichfield Rd, SUTTON COLDFIELD ☎021-355 6071 56⇨☝ Annexe8⇨☝

Little Aston ☎021-353 2066
Parkland course.
18 holes, 6724yds, Par 72, SSS 73, Course record 67.
Club membership 250.

Visitors	may not play at weekends. Must contact in advance and have an introduction from own club.
Societies	must apply in writing.
Green Fees	£35 per day/round.
Facilities	⊗ ⅲ by prior arrangement ⅼ ⌐ ♀ ⌂ ⌐ ⌊ J Anderson.
Location	Streetly (3.5m NW off A454)
Hotel	★★61% Parson & Clerk Motel, Chester Rd, STREETLY ☎021-353 1747 30⇨☝

Moor Hall ☎021-308 6130
Parkland course. The 14th is a notable hole.
18 holes, 6249yds, Par 70, SSS 70.
Club membership 600.

Visitors	with member only weekends & bank holidays. Must contact in advance.
Societies	must apply in writing.
Green Fees	£30 per day; £18 per round.
Facilities	⊗ ⅲ ⅼ & ⌐ by prior arrangement ♀ (ring steward) ⌂ ⌐ ⌊ Alan Partridge.
Location	Moor Hall Dr (2.5 m N of town centre off A453)
Hotel	★★★67% Moor Hall Hotel, Moor Hall Dr, Four Oaks, SUTTON COLDFIELD ☎021-308 3751 75⇨☝

Pype Hayes ☎021-351 1014
Attractive, fairly flat course with excellent greens.
18 holes, 5811yds, Par 70.
Club membership 300.

Green Fees	not confirmed.
Facilities	⊗ ⌐ ⌂ ⌐ ☂ ⌊ James Bayliss.
Location	Eachelhurst Rd, Walmley (2.5m S off B4148)
Hotel	★★★★58% Penns Hall Hotel, Penns Ln, Walmley, SUTTON COLDFIELD ☎021-351 3111 114⇨☝

Sutton Coldfield ☎021-353 9633
A fine natural, heathland course, with tight fairways, gorse, heather and trees; which is surprising as the high-rise buildings of Birmingham are not far away.

18 holes, 6541yds, Par 72, SSS 71.
Club membership 500.

Visitors	must have handicap certificate. Must contact in advance.
Societies	must give at least 3 months notice.
Green Fees	£26 per day/round.
Facilities	⊗ ⅲ by prior arrangement ⅼ ⌐ by prior arrangement ♀ ⌂ ⌐ ⌊ J K Hayes.
Leisure	snooker.
Location	Thornhill Rd, Streetly (3m NW on B4138)
Hotel	★★61% Parson & Clerk Motel, Chester Rd, STREETLY ☎021-353 1747 30⇨☝

Walmley ☎021-373 0029
Pleasant parkland course with many trees. The hazards are not difficult.
18 holes, 6537yds, Par 72, SSS 72, Course record 69.
Club membership 700.

Visitors	with member only at weekends. Must contact in advance and have an introduction from own club.
Societies	must contact in advance.
Green Fees	£25 per day; £20 per round.
Facilities	⊗ & ⅲ (ex Mon) ⅼ (ex weekends) ⌐ ♀ (Mon-Fri) ⌂ ⌐ ⌊ M J Skerritt.
Leisure	snooker.
Location	Brooks Rd, Wylde Green (2m S off A5127)
Hotel	★★★★58% Penns Hall Hotel, Penns Ln, Walmley, SUTTON COLDFIELD ☎021-351 3111 114⇨☝

WALSALL   Map 07 SP09

Bloxwich ☎Bloxwich (0922) 405724
Undulating parkland course with natural hazards and
subject to strong north wind.
18 holes, 6258yds, Par 71, SSS 70, Course record 65.
Club membership 550.
Visitors	may not play at weekends. Must have an introduction from own club.
Societies	must apply in writing.
Green Fees	£25 per day; £20 per round.
Facilities	⊗ ⑪ ⓛ ⬤ ♀ △ ➔ ⑪ ℓ Brian Janes.
Leisure	snooker.
Location	Stafford Rd, Bloxwich (3m N of town centre on A34)
Hotel	★★★58% Baron's Court Hotel, Walsall Rd, Walsall Wood, WALSALL ☎(0543) 452020 100⇨

Walsall ☎(0922) 613512
Well wooded parkland course with easy walking. The greens
are very extensive.
18 holes, 6243yds, Par 70, SSS 70.
Club membership 700.
Visitors	may not play weekends & bank holidays.
Societies	must apply in writing.
Green Fees	£40 per day; £30 per round.
Facilities	⊗ ⑪ ⓛ ⬤ ♀ ➔ ℓ
Leisure	snooker.
Location	The Broadway (1m S of town centre off A34)
Hotel	★★★62% Forte Posthouse, Birmingham Rd, WALSALL ☎(0922) 33555 98⇨

WEST BROMWICH   Map 07 SP09

Dartmouth ☎021-588 2131
Meadowland course with undulating but easy walking. The
617 yd (par 5) first hole is something of a challenge.
9 holes, 6060yds, Par 71, SSS 70, Course record 66.
Club membership 350.
Visitors	with member only at weekends.
Societies	must apply in writing.
Green Fees	£16.50 per day.
Facilities	⊗ & ⑪ by prior arrangement ⓛ ⬤ ♀ △ ➔ ℓ Nigel Wylie.
Leisure	snooker.
Location	Vale St (E side of town centre off A4041)
Hotel	★★★62% West Bromwich Moat House, Birmingham Rd, WEST BROMWICH ☎021-553 6111 180⇨

Sandwell Park ☎021-553 4637
Undulating parkland course situated in the Sandwell Valley.
18 holes, 6470yds, Par 71, SSS 72, Course record 68.
Club membership 600.
Visitors	must contact in advance.
Societies	must apply in writing.
Green Fees	not confirmed.
Facilities	⊗ ⑪ ⓛ ⬤ ♀ ➔ ℓ A W Mutton.
Leisure	snooker.
Location	Birmingham Rd (SE side of town centre off A4040)
Hotel	★★★62% West Bromwich Moat House, Birmingham Rd, WEST BROMWICH ☎021-553 6111 180⇨

WOLVERHAMPTON   Map 07 SO99

Oxley Park ☎(0902) 20506
Parkland course with easy walking on the flat.
18 holes, 6028yds, Par 71, SSS 69.
Club membership 615.
Visitors	must contact in advance.
Societies	must apply in writing.
Green Fees	£20.50 per day (£22.50 weekends); £16.50 per round (£18.50 weekends).
Facilities	⊗ ⑪ by prior arrangement ⓛ ⬤ ♀ △ ➔ ℓ Les Burlison.
Leisure	snooker.
Location	Stafford Rd, Bushbury (N of town centre off A449)
Hotel	★★★59% Mount Hotel, Mount Road, Tettenhall Wood, WOLVERHAMPTON ☎(0902) 752055 49⇨

Penn ☎(0902) 341142
Heathland course just outside the town.
18 holes, 6465yds, Par 70, SSS 71, Course record 67.
Club membership 620.
Visitors	must be member of recognised club, can only play weekdays & must use yellow tees.
Societies	must apply in writing.
Green Fees	£17-£25 per day.
Facilities	⊗ (ex Sun & Mon) ⑪ (ex Sun, Mon, Wed) ⓛ ⬤ (ex Mon & Wed) ♀ △ ➔ ⑪ ℓ Alistair Briscoe.
Leisure	snooker.
Location	Penn Common, Penn (SW side of town centre off A449)
Hotel	★★★60% Park Hall Hotel, Park Drive, Goldthorn Park, WOLVERHAMPTON ☎(0902) 331121 57⇨

South Staffordshire ☎(0902) 751065
A parkland course.
18 holes, 6653yds, Par 72, SSS 72, Course record 67.
Club membership 570.
Visitors	may not play weekends & before 2pm Tue. Must contact in advance.
Societies	must contact in advance.
Green Fees	£25 per day/round (£30 Sun).
Facilities	⊗ ⑪ ⓛ ⬤ ♀ △ ➔ ℓ Jim Rhodes.
Leisure	snooker.
Location	Danescourt Rd, Tettenhall (3m NW off A41)
Hotel	★★★59% Mount Hotel, Mount Road, Tettenhall Wood, WOLVERHAMPTON ☎(0902) 752055 49⇨

WEST SUSSEX

ANGMERING   Map 04 TQ00

Ham Manor ☎(0903) 783288
Two miles from the sea, this parkland course has fine
springy turf and provides an interesting test in two loops
of nine holes each.
18 holes, 6243yds, Par 70, SSS 70, Course record 62.
Club membership 850.

Visitors	must have a handicap certificate. Must contact in advance and have an introduction from own club.
Societies	must contact in writing.
Green Fees	£25 (£35 weekends).
Facilities	⊗ �𝄢 by prior arrangement ⮾ 🍺 ♀ ⌂ 🏠 ✆ Simon Buckley.
Leisure	snooker, bowling green, table tennis.
Location	.75m SW
Hotel	★★★58% Chatsworth Hotel, Steyne, WORTHING ☎(0903) 36103 due to change to 236103 107⇾🏠

BOGNOR REGIS   Map 04 SZ99

Bognor Regis ☎(0243) 865867

This flattish, parkland course has more variety than is to be found on some of the South Coast courses. The club is also known far and wide for its enterprise in creating a social atmosphere. The course is open to the prevailing wind.

18 holes, 6238yds, Par 70, SSS 70, Course record 65.
Club membership 650.

Visitors	restricted Tue; must play with member at weekends Apr-Oct. Must contact in advance and have an introduction from own club.
Societies	must contact in writing.
Green Fees	not confirmed.
Facilities	⮾ 🍺 ♀ ⌂ 🏠 ✆ Robin P Day.
Location	Downview Rd, Felpham (1.5m NE off A259)
Hotel	★★★♨67% Bailiffscourt Hotel, CLIMPING ☎(0903) 723511 18⇾Annexe2⇾

CHICHESTER   Map 04 SU80

Chichester Golf Centre ☎(0243) 533833

Set amongst lush farmland, this challenging course has four lakes which bring water into play on seven holes. The 2nd, 8th and 15th are particularly challenging holes. Floodlit driving range.

18 holes, 6177yds, Par 72, SSS 69, Course record 68.
Club membership 100.

Visitors	a strict dress code is in operation. It is advisable to contact in advance.
Societies	must contact in advance.
Green Fees	£12 (£16.50 weekends & public holidays).
Facilities	⊗ ⮾ 🍺 ⌂ 🏠 🍴 ♨ ✆ Adrian Wratting.
Leisure	grass tennis courts.
Location	Hoe Farm, Hunston (3m S of Chichester, on B2145 at Hunston)
Hotel	★★★61% The Dolphin & Anchor, West St, CHICHESTER ☎(0243) 785121 49⇾🏠

Goodwood ☎(0243) 774968

Downland course designed by the master architect, James Braid. Many notable holes, particularly the finishing ones: 17 down an avenue of beech trees and 18 along in front of the terrace. Superb views of the downs and the coast.

18 holes, 6383yds, Par 72, SSS 70, Course record 68.
Club membership 900.

Visitors	must have a handicap certificate. Must contact in advance.
Societies	must contact in writing.
Green Fees	not confirmed.
Facilities	⊗ ⯭ ⮾ 🍺 ♀ ⌂ 🏠 ✆ Kieth MacDonald.
Leisure	snooker.
Location	4.5m NE off A27
Hotel	★★★66% Goodwood Park Hotel, Golf & Country Club, GOODWOOD ☎(0243) 775537 89⇾

COPTHORNE   Map 04 TQ33

Copthorne ☎(0342) 712033 & 712508

Despite it having been in existence since 1892, this club remains one of the lesser known Sussex courses. It is hard to know why because it is most attractive with plenty of trees and much variety

18 holes, 6505yds, Par 71, SSS 71, Course record 68.
Club membership 600.

SCORECARD: White Tees					
Hole	Yds	Par	Hole	Yds	Par
1	370	4	10	354	4
2	396	4	11	395	4
3	199	3	12	156	3
4	332	4	13	485	5
5	400	4	14	399	4
6	485	5	15	185	3
7	186	3	16	471	4
8	488	5	17	370	4
9	440	4	18	394	4
Out	3296	36	In	3209	35
			Totals	6505	71

Visitors	restricted at weekends after 1pm. Must contact in advance.
Societies	Thu & Fri only; must contact well in advance.
Green Fees	£32 per day (£40 weekends & bank holidays after 1pm); £25 per round.
Facilities	⊗ ⯭ (Wed evening) ⮾ 🍺 ♀ ⌂ 🏠 ✆ Joe Burrell.
Location	Borers Arms Rd (E side of village junc 10 of M23 off A264)
Hotel	★★★★67% Copthorne Hotel, Copthorne Rd, COPTHORNE ☎(0342) 714971 227⇾🏠

Effingham Park ☎(0342) 716528

Parkland course.

9 holes, 1749yds, Par 30, Course record 26.
Club membership 430.

Visitors	restricted at weekends after 1pm.
Green Fees	not confirmed.
Facilities	⊗ ⮾ 🍺 ♀ ⌂ 🏠 🍴 🛏 ✆ Ian Dryden.
Leisure	heated indoor swimming pool, sauna, solarium, gymnasium, dance studio, jacuzzi steam room.
Location	2m E on B2028
Hotel	★★★★67% Copthorne Hotel, Copthorne Rd, COPTHORNE ☎(0342) 714971 227⇾🏠

CRAWLEY   Map 04 TQ23

Cottesmore ☎(0293) 528256

The old North Course is undulating with four holes over water. The new South Course is shorter and less testing. But both are lined with silver birch, pine and oak, with rhododendrons ablaze in June.

Old Course: 18 holes, 6113yds, Par 72, SSS 70, Course record 66.
New South Course: 18 holes, 5469yds, Par 69, SSS 68.
Club membership 1300.

Visitors	may only play after noon on Old Course at weekends. Must contact in advance.

▶

Societies	Mon, Wed & Fri Apr-1 Nov. Must contact in advance.
Green Fees	Old Course: £24 per day (£30 weekends); New Course: £16 per day (£22 weekends).
Facilities	⊗ ⅃ ⅃ ⅃ ⅃ ⅃ ⅃ ⅃
Leisure	hard tennis courts, heated indoor swimming pool, squash, sauna, solarium, gymnasium.
Location	Buchan Hill, Pease Pottage (3m SW 1m W of M23 junc 11)
Hotel	★★★63% Goffs Park Hotel, 45 Goffs Park Road, Crawley, CRAWLEY ☎(0293) 535447 37⇌⁐Annexe28⇌⁐

Gatwick Manor ☎(0293) 538587
Interesting, pay and play short course.
9 holes, 2492yds, Par 56, SSS 50, Course record 50.
Club membership 63.

Visitors	no restrictions.
Societies	must telephone in advance.
Green Fees	£3 per round.
Facilities	⊗ ⅃ ⅃ ⅃ ⅃ ⅃ ⅃ ⅃ ⅃ Colin Jenkins.
Location	Lowfield Heath (2m N on A23)
Hotel	★★61% Gatwick Manor Hotel, London Rd, Lowfield Heath, Crawley, CRAWLEY ☎(0293) 526301 & 535251 30⇌⁐

Ifield Golf & Country Club ☎(0293) 520222
Parkland course.
18 holes, 6314yds, Par 70, SSS 70, Course record 67.
Club membership 800.

Visitors	may not play after 3pm Fri; must play with member at weekends. Must contact in advance and have an introduction from own club.
Societies	Mon-Wed afternoons & Thu.
Green Fees	£25 per round/day.
Facilities	⊗ ⅃ by prior arrangement ⅃ ⅃ ⅃ ⅃ ⅃ ⅃ Jon Earl.
Leisure	squash, snooker.
Location	Rusper Rd, Ifield (1m W side of town centre off A23)
Hotel	★★★56% George Hotel, High St, CRAWLEY ☎(0293) 524215 86⇌⁐

HAYWARDS HEATH   Map 05 TQ32

Haywards Heath ☎(0444) 414866
Pleasant parkland with several challenging par 4s and 3s.
18 holes, 6204yds, Par 71, SSS 70.
Club membership 750.

Visitors	must be a member of a recognised golf club and have a handicap certificate. Must contact in advance.
Societies	Wed & Thu only.
Green Fees	£20 per round; £25 per day (£25 per round; £30 per day weekends & bank holidays).
Facilities	⊗ ⅃ by prior arrangement ⅃ ⅃ ⅃ ⅃ ⅃ ⅃ Michael Henning.
Location	High Beech Ln (1.25m N off B2028)
Hotel	★★★73% Ockenden Manor, Ockenden Ln, CUCKFIELD ☎(0444) 416111 22⇌⁐

For a full range of AA guides and maps, visit your local AA shop or any good bookshop

LITTLEHAMPTON   Map 04 TQ00

Littlehampton ☎(0903) 717170
A delightful seaside links in an equally delightful setting - and the only links course in the area.
18 holes, 6202yds, Par 70, SSS 70.
Club membership 650.

Visitors	no restrictions.
Societies	Mon, Tue & Fri.
Green Fees	not confirmed.
Facilities	⅃ ⅃ ⅃ ⅃
Location	Rope Walk, West Beach (1m W off A259)
Hotel	★★★ Norfolk Arms Hotel, High St, ARUNDEL ☎(0903) 882101 21⇌⁐Annexe13⇌

MANNINGS HEATH   Map 04 TQ22

Mannings Heath ☎Horsham (0403) 210228
The course meanders up hill and down dale over heathland with streams affecting 11 of the holes. Wooded valleys protect the course from strong winds. Famous holes at 12th (the 'Waterfall', par 3), 13th (the 'Valley', par 4).
18 holes, 6402yds, Par 73, SSS 71, Course record 66.
Club membership 710.

Visitors	must have a handicap certificate. Must contact in advance.
Societies	must contact in advance.
Green Fees	£18 per round (£25 weekends).
Facilities	⊗ ⅃ ⅃ ⅃ ⅃ ⅃ ⅃ ⅃ Mike Denny.
Location	Goldings Ln (N side of village)
Hotel	★★★★⅃70% South Lodge Hotel, Brighton Rd, LOWER BEEDING ☎(0403) 891711 39⇌

MIDHURST   Map 04 SU82

Cowdray Park ☎(0730) 813599
Parkland course, hard walking up to 4th green.
18 holes, 6212yds, Par 70, SSS 70, Course record 69.
Club membership 700.

Visitors	may play after 9am on weekdays, 11am Sat & 3pm Sun. Must contact in advance and have an introduction from own club.
Societies	must contact in writing.
Green Fees	£20 per day (£25 weekends & bank holidays).
Facilities	⊗ ⅃ by prior arrangement ⅃ ⅃ ⅃ ⅃ ⅃ ⅃ Stephen Hall.
Location	1m E on A272
Hotel	★★★66% Spread Eagle Hotel, South St, MIDHURST ☎(0730) 816911 37⇌Annexe4⁐

PULBOROUGH   Map 04 TQ01

West Sussex ☎(0798) 872563
Heathland course.
18 holes, 6221yds, Par 68, SSS 70, Course record 61.
Club membership 800.

Visitors	must have a handicap certificate. Must contact in advance and have an introduction from own club.
Societies	Wed & Thu only. Must contact in advance.
Green Fees	On application.
Facilities	⊗ ⅃ ⅃ ⅃ ⅃ ⅃ ⅃ Tim Packham.
Location	Hurston Warren (1.5m E off A283)

| Hotel | ★★★63% Roundabout Hotel, Monkmead Ln, WEST CHILTINGTON ☎(0798) 813838 23⇥♠ |

PYECOMBE   Map 04 TQ21

Pyecombe ☎(0273) 845372
Typical downland course on the inland side of the South Downs. Hilly, but magnificent views.
18 holes, 6124yds, Par 70, SSS 70, Course record 67.
Club membership 624.

Visitors	may not play after 9.15 weekdays, 2pm Sat & 3pm Sun.
Societies	must telephone in advance.
Green Fees	£18 per day; £16 per round (£25 weekends).
Facilities	⊗ ⅢL ⛳ ▆ ♀ ⛏ 🛆 ➡ ⬦ ╏ C White.
Location	Clayton Hill (E side of village on A273)
Hotel	★★★56% Courtlands Hotel, 19-27 The Drive, HOVE ☎(0273) 731055 53⇥♠Annexe5⇥

SELSEY   Map 04 SZ89

Selsey ☎(0243) 602203
Fairly difficult seaside course, exposed to wind and has natural ditches.
9 holes, 5932yds, Par 68, SSS 68, Course record 66.
Club membership 433.

Visitors	may not play at weekends & bank holidays. Must have an introduction from own club.
Societies	must contact in writing.
Green Fees	not confirmed.
Facilities	⊗ Ⅲ ⛳ ▆ ♀ 🛆 ➡ ╏ Peter Grindley.
Leisure	hard tennis courts, bowling green.
Location	Golf Links Ln (1m N off B2145)
Hotel	★★★61% The Dolphin & Anchor, West St, CHICHESTER ☎(0243) 785121 49⇥♠

WEST CHILTINGTON   Map 04 TQ01

West Chiltington ☎(0798) 813574
The Main Course is situated on gently undulating, well-drained greensand and offers panoramic views of the Sussex Downs. Three large double greens provide an interesting feature to this new course. Also 9-hole short course and 13-bay driving range.
18 holes, 6000yds, Par 70, SSS 69, Course record 69.
Club membership 600.

Visitors	it is advisable to contact the club in advance for weekends.
Societies	telephone for booking form.
Green Fees	£13 per round (£18 weekends).
Facilities	⊗ ⛳ ▆ ♀ 🛆 ➡ ⬦ ╏ B Barnes, R Tisdall.
Location	Broadford bridge Rd (on N side of village)
Hotel	★★★63% Roundabout Hotel, Monkmead Ln, WEST CHILTINGTON ☎(0798) 813838 23⇥♠

WORTHING   Map 04 TQ10

Hill Barn Municipal ☎(0903) 37301
Downland course with views of both Isle of Wight and Brighton.
18 holes, 6224yds, Par 70, SSS 70.
Club membership 1000.

Visitors	no restrictions.
Societies	must telephone in advance.
Green Fees	£9.50 (£11 weekends & bank holidays).
Facilities	⊗ Ⅲ ⛳ ▆ ♀ 🛆 ➡ ⬦ ╏ A Higgins.
Location	Hill Barn Ln (N side of town at junction of A24/A27)
Hotel	★★★58% Chatsworth Hotel, Steyne, WORTHING ☎(0903) 36103 due to change to 236103 107⇥♠

Worthing ☎(0903) 60801
The Upper Course, short and tricky with entrancing views, will provide good entertainment. 'Lower Course' is considered to be one of the best downland courses in the country.
Lower Course: 18 holes, 6519yds, Par 71, SSS 72, Course record 66.
Upper Course: 18 holes, 5243yds, Par 66, SSS 66.
Club membership 1146.

Visitors	must contact in advance and have an introduction from own club.
Societies	must contact in writing 6 months in advance.
Green Fees	not confirmed.
Facilities	⊗ Ⅲ (Fri) ⛳ ▆ ♀ 🛆 ➡ ╏ S Rolley.
Leisure	snooker.
Location	Links Rd (N side of town centre off A27)
Hotel	★★59% Ardington Hotel, Steyne Gardens, WORTHING ☎(0903) 30451 55rm(22⇥22♠)

❋ WEST YORKSHIRE ❋

ALWOODLEY   Map 08 SE24

| **Alwoodley** ☎Leeds (0532) 681680 A fine heathland course with length, trees and abundant heather. Many attractive situations - together a severe test of golf. *18 holes, 6686yds, Par 72, SSS 72.* *Club membership 250.* |
Visitors	restricted weekends & bank holidays. Must contact in advance.
Societies	must apply in advance.
Green Fees	not confirmed.
Facilities	⊗ by prior arrangement Ⅲ by prior arrangement ⛳ by prior arrangement ♀ 🛆 ➡ ╏ John Green.
Location	Wigton Ln (5m N off A61)
Hotel	★★★65% Parkway Hotel, Otley Rd, LEEDS ☎(0532) 672551 103⇥♠

BAILDON   Map 07 SE13

Baildon ☎(0274) 595162
Moorland course with much bracken rough. The 5th is a hard climb.
18 holes, 6225yds, Par 70, SSS 70, Course record 64.
Club membership 600.

Visitors	restricted Tue & weekends.
Societies	may not play Tue & weekends; must contact in advance.
Green Fees	not confirmed.
Facilities	⊗ Ⅲ by prior arrangement ⛳ ▆ (no catering Mon) ♀ (ex Mon) 🛆 ➡ ⬦ ╏ R Masters.
Leisure	snooker.

►

Location	Moorgate (N off A6038)
Hotel	★★★64% Bankfield Hotel, Bradford Rd, BINGLEY ☎(0274) 567123 103⇨🏠

BINGLEY   Map 07 SE13

Bingley St Ives ☎Bradford (0274) 562506
Parkland/moorland course.
18 holes, 6312yds, Par 71, SSS 71, Course record 62.
Club membership 650.

Visitors	restricted Mon-Fri after 4.30pm & Sat.
Societies	must apply in advance.
Green Fees	£20 per day; £15 per round (£20 Sun & bank holidays).
Facilities	⊗ ⅏ ┗ 💺 ♀ ⚓ 🏠 ℂ Ray Firth.
Leisure	snooker.
Location	The Mansion, St Ives Estate, Harden (.75m W off B6429)
Hotel	★★★64% Bankfield Hotel, Bradford Rd, BINGLEY ☎(0274) 567123 103⇨🏠

BRADFORD   Map 07 SE13

Bradford Moor ☎(0274) 638313
Parkland course, hard walking.
9 holes, 5854yds, Par 70, SSS 68.
Club membership 376.

Visitors	no restrictions.
Societies	must contact in advance.
Green Fees	not confirmed.
Facilities	♀ ⚓ 🏠 ⚐℩ ℂ
Location	Scarr Hall, Pollard Ln (2m NE of city centre off A658)
Hotel	★★62% Park Drive Hotel, 12 Park Dr, BRADFORD ☎(0274) 480194 11⇨🏠

Clayton ☎(0274) 880047
Moorland course, difficult in windy conditions.
9 holes, 5407yds, Par 68, SSS 67, Course record 63.
Club membership 350.

Visitors	may not play after 4pm on Sun.
Societies	must contact in advance.
Green Fees	£8 per round (£10 weekdays).
Facilities	⊗ ⅏ ┗ 💺 (no catering Mon) ♀ (not Mon) ⚓
Leisure	snooker.
Location	Thornton View Rd, Clayton (2.5m W of city centre on A647)
Hotel	★★★57% Novotel Bradford, Merrydale Rd, BRADFORD ☎(0274) 683683 132⇨🏠

East Bierley ☎(0274) 681023
Hilly moorland course with narrow fairways. Two par 3 holes over 200 yds.
9 holes, 4700yds, Par 64, SSS 63.
Club membership 200.

Visitors	restricted Sat (am), Sun & Mon evening. Must contact in advance.
Societies	must apply in writing.
Green Fees	not confirmed.
Facilities	⊗ ⅏ ┗ 💺 ♀ ⚓
Leisure	snooker.

Location	South View Rd, East Bierley (4m SE of city centre off A650)
Hotel	★★★57% Novotel Bradford, Merrydale Rd, BRADFORD ☎(0274) 683683 132⇨🏠

Headley ☎(0274) 833481
Hilly moorland course, short but very testing, windy, fine views.
9 holes, 4914yds, Par 64, SSS 64, Course record 61.
Club membership 200.

Visitors	must play with member on Sun. Must contact in advance.
Societies	must telephone in advance.
Green Fees	not confirmed.
Facilities	⊗ by prior arrangement ⅏ by prior arrangement ┗ 💺 ♀
Location	Headley Ln, Thornton (4m W of city centre off B6145 at Thornton)
Hotel	★★62% Park Drive Hotel, 12 Park Dr, BRADFORD ☎(0274) 480194 11⇨🏠

Phoenix Park ☎(0274) 667573
Very short, tight, moorland course, rather testing.
9 holes, 2491yds, Par 66, SSS 64, Course record 66.
Club membership 260.

Visitors	restricted weekends.
Societies	must apply in advance.
Green Fees	not confirmed.
Facilities	♀ ⚓ 🏠
Location	Phoenix Park, Thornbury (E side of city centre on A647)
Hotel	★★62% Park Drive Hotel, 12 Park Dr, BRADFORD ☎(0274) 480194 11⇨🏠

Queensbury ☎(0274) 882155
Undulating woodland/parkland course.
18 holes, 5400yds, Par 66, SSS 65, Course record 63.
Club membership 350.

Visitors	restricted weekends. Must have an introduction from own club.
Societies	must apply in advance.
Green Fees	£10 per day (£17 weekends).
Facilities	⊗ ⅏ ┗ 💺 ♀ ⚓ 🏠 ⚐℩ ℂ Geoff Howard.
Leisure	snooker.
Location	Brighouse Rd, Queensbury (4m from Bradford on A647)
Hotel	★★62% Park Drive Hotel, 12 Park Dr, BRADFORD ☎(0274) 480194 11⇨🏠

South Bradford ☎(0274) 679195
Hilly course with good greens, trees and ditches. Interesting short 2nd hole (par 3) 200 yds, well-bunkered and played from an elevated tee.
9 holes, 6028yds, Par 70, SSS 69, Course record 65.
Club membership 305.

Visitors	restricted competition days.
Societies	must apply in writing.
Green Fees	£10 per day (£15 weekends & bank holidays).
Facilities	⊗ ┗ & 💺 (ex Mon) ⅏ by prior arrangement ♀ ⚓ 🏠 ℂ Michael Hillas.
Leisure	snooker.
Location	Pearson Rd, Odsal (2m S of city centre off A638)
Hotel	★★★57% Novotel Bradford, Merrydale Rd, BRADFORD ☎(0274) 683683 132⇨🏠

West Bowling ☏(0274) 724449
Undulating, tree-lined parkland course. Testing hole: 'the coffin' short par 3, very narrow.
18 holes, 5657yds, Par 69, SSS 67, Course record 66.
Club membership 400.

Visitors	restricted before 9.30am, 12-1.30pm & weekends. Must contact in advance and have an introduction from own club.
Societies	must apply in writing.
Green Fees	£20 day/round (£25 weekends).
Facilities	⊗ ⫫ by prior arrangement ⬚ by prior arrangement ▣ ♀ ♨ ⛬ ⅋ ₵ Allan Swaine.
Leisure	snooker.
Location	Newall Hall, Rooley Ln (S side of city centre off A638)
Hotel	★★★57% Novotel Bradford, Merrydale Rd, BRADFORD ☏(0274) 683683 132⇨₦

West Bradford ☏West Bradford (0274) 542767
Parkland course, windy, especially 3rd, 4th, 5th and 6th holes. Hilly but not hard.
18 holes, 5752yds, Par 69, SSS 68.
Club membership 440.

Visitors	restricted Sat.
Societies	must apply in writing.
Green Fees	£14.50 per day (£20.50 weekends).
Facilities	⊗ ⫫ ⬚ & ▣ (ex Mon) ♀ (ex Mon) ⛬ ♨ ₵ Nigel Barber.
Leisure	snooker.
Location	Chellow Grange Rd (W side of city centre off B6269)
Hotel	★★★64% Bankfield Hotel, Bradford Rd, BINGLEY ☏(0274) 567123 103⇨₦

CLECKHEATON   Map 08 SE12

Cleckheaton & District ☏(0274) 851266
Parkland course with gentle hills.
18 holes, 5847yds, Par 71, SSS 69.
Club membership 500.

Visitors	must contact in advance and have an introduction from own club.
Societies	weekdays only; must contact in advance.
Green Fees	not confirmed.
Facilities	⊗ (ex Mon) ⫫ by prior arrangement ⬚ (ex 2pm-4pm) ▣ (ex 2pm-4pm) ♀ ⛬ ♨ ⅋ ₵ Mike Ingham.
Leisure	snooker.
Location	Bradford Rd (1.5m NW on A638 junc 26 M62)
Hotel	★★★57% Novotel Bradford, Merrydale Rd, BRADFORD ☏(0274) 683683 132⇨₦

DEWSBURY   Map 08 SE22

Hanging Heaton ☏(0924) 461606
Arable land course, easy walking, fine views. Testing 4th hole (par 3).
9 holes, 5400mtrs, Par 69, SSS 67.
Club membership 550.

Visitors	must play with member at weekends & bank holidays. Must contact in advance.
Societies	must telephone in advance.
Green Fees	not confirmed.
Facilities	⊗ ⬚ ▣ ♀ ⛬ ♨ ₵ G Hutchinson.

Leisure	snooker.
Location	White Cross Rd (.75m NE off A653)
Hotel	★★★60% Forte Posthouse, Queen's Dr, Ossett, WAKEFIELD ☏(0924) 276388 99⇨₦

ELLAND   Map 07 SE12

Elland ☏(0422) 72505
Parkland course.
9 holes, 2815yds, Par 66, SSS 66.
Club membership 250.

Visitors	no restrictions.
Green Fees	not confirmed.
Facilities	⊗ ⫫ ⬚ ▣ ♀ ⛬ ♨ ₵ Jeremy Tindall.
Location	Hammerstones, Leach Ln (1m SW)
Hotel	★★★★64% Forte Crest, Clifton Village, BRIGHOUSE ☏(0484) 400400 94⇨₦

FENAY BRIDGE   Map 08 SE11

Woodsome Hall ☏Huddersfield (0484) 602971
Historic clubhouse; parkland course with views.
18 holes, 6080yds, Par 70, SSS 69, Course record 65.
Club membership 900.

Visitors	must have handicap certificate. Restricted weekends & competitions. Must contact in advance.
Societies	must apply in writing.
Green Fees	£25 per day/round (£30 weekends & bank holidays).
Facilities	⊗ by prior arrangement ⫫ by prior arrangement ⬚ ▣ ♀ ⛬ ♨ ₵ M Grantham.
Leisure	snooker.
Location	1.5m SW off A629
Hotel	★★★67% The George Hotel, St George's Square, HUDDERSFIELD ☏(0484) 515444 59rm(47⇨)

GARFORTH   Map 08 SE43

Garforth ☏Leeds (0532) 862021
Parkland course with fine views, easy walking.
18 holes, 6005yds, Par 69, SSS 69, Course record 65.
Club membership 500.

Visitors	must have handicap certificate. With member only weekends & bank holidays. Must contact in advance.
Societies	must apply in advance.
Green Fees	£25 per day; £20 per round.
Facilities	⊗ ⫫ ⬚ ▣ ♀ ⛬ ♨ ⅋ ₵ K Findlater.
Leisure	snooker.
Location	1m N
Hotel	★★★64% Stakis Windmill Hotel, Mill Green View, Seacroft, LEEDS ☏(0532) 732323 100⇨₦

GUISELEY   Map 08 SE14

Bradford ☏(0943) 875570
Moorland course with eight par 4 holes of 360 yds or more.
18 holes, 6259yds, Par 71, SSS 71, Course record 67.
Club membership 600.

Visitors	restricted weekends. Must have an introduction from own club.

▶

Societies	welcome Mon-Fri, must apply in advance.
Green Fees	£22 per day/ round (£30 weekends).
Facilities	⊗ by prior arrangement 🍴 by prior arrangement 🏠 💻 ♀ (restricted Sun) ⌂ 🏠 (Sydney Weldon.
Leisure	snooker.
Location	Hawksworth Ln (SW side of town centre off A6038)
Hotel	★★★52% Cow & Calf Hotel, Moor Top, ILKLEY ☎(0943) 607335 20⇨🏠

HALIFAX   Map 07 SE02

Halifax ☎(0422) 244171
Hilly moorland course crossed by streams, natural hazards, and offering fine views. Testing 172-yd 17th (par3).
18 holes, 6037yds, Par 70, SSS 70, Course record 66.
Club membership 500.

Visitors	restricted competition days. Must contact in advance.
Societies	must apply in advance.
Green Fees	£20 per day (£30 weekends); with handicap certificate £15 per day (£25 weekends).
Facilities	⊗ 🍴 🏠 💻 ♀ ⌂ 🏠 (Steven Foster.
Leisure	snooker.
Location	Bob Hall, Union Ln, Ogden (4m NW off A629)
Hotel	★★★73% Holdsworth House Hotel, Holmfield, HALIFAX ☎(0422) 240024 40⇨🏠

Lightcliffe ☎(0422) 202459
Heathland course.
9 holes, 5388yds, Par 68, SSS 68, Course record 62.
Club membership 545.

Visitors	must be a member of a recognised Golf Club.
Societies	must contact 21 days in advance.
Green Fees	£16 per round.
Facilities	⊗ 🍴 by prior arrangement 🏠 💻 ♀ ⌂ 🏠 (Matthew Cassidy.
Location	Knowle Top Rd, Lightcliffe (3.5m E on A58)
Hotel	★★★73% Holdsworth House Hotel, Holmfield, HALIFAX ☎(0422) 240024 40⇨🏠

West End ☎(0422) 353608
Semi-moorland course.
18 holes, 6003yds, Par 68, SSS 69, Course record 65.
Club membership 530.

Visitors	may play between 10am-2pm. Must contact in advance and have an introduction from own club.
Societies	must apply in writing.
Green Fees	£15.50 per day (£20.50 weekends & bank holidays); £12.50 per round (£15.50 weekends & bank holidays).
Facilities	⊗ 🍴 🏠 💻 ♀ ⌂ 🏠 (David Rishworth.
Leisure	snooker.
Location	Paddock Ln, Highroad Well (W side of town centre off A646)
Hotel	★★★73% Holdsworth House Hotel, Holmfield, HALIFAX ☎(0422) 240024 40⇨🏠

A golf-course name printed in ***bold italics*** means that we have been unable to verify information with the club's management for the current year

HEBDEN BRIDGE   Map 07 SD92

Hebden Bridge ☎(0422) 842896
Moorland course with splendid views.
9 holes, 5107yds, Par 68, SSS 65, Course record 63.
Club membership 400.

Visitors	restricted competition days.
Societies	by arrangment with directors.
Green Fees	£7.50 per round (£10 weekends).
Facilities	⊗ by prior arrangement 🍴 by prior arrangement 🏠 💻 (no catering Mon) ♀ ⌂ 🏠
Location	Mount Skip, Wadsworth (1.5m E off A6033)
Hotel	★★68% Hebden Lodge Hotel, New Rd, HEBDEN BRIDGE ☎(0422) 845272 12⇨🏠

HOLYWELL GREEN   Map 07 SE01

Halifax Bradley Hall ☎Halifax (0422) 374108
Moorland/parkland course, tightened by recent tree planting, easy walking.
18 holes, 6213yds, Par 70, SSS 70, Course record 65.
Club membership 608.

Societies	must apply in writing.
Green Fees	£15 per day (£20 weekends & bank holidays).
Facilities	⊗ 🍴 🏠 💻 (catering by prior arrangement Mon-Tue) ♀ ⌂ 🏠 (Peter Wood.
Leisure	snooker.
Location	S on A6112
Hotel	★★68% Rock Inn Hotel & Churchills Restaurant, HOLYWELL GREEN ☎(0422) 379721 18⇨🏠

HUDDERSFIELD   Map 07 SE11

Bradley Park ☎(0484) 539988
Parkland course, challenging with good mix of long and short holes. Also 14-bay floodlit driving range and 9-hole par 3 course, ideal for beginners. Superb views.
18 holes, 6220yds, Par 70, SSS 70, Course record 68.
Par 3 : 9 holes, 1019yds, Par 27.
Club membership 300.

Visitors	must contact for weekend play.
Societies	welcome midweek only, must apply by letter.
Green Fees	£7 per round (£9 weekends).
Facilities	⊗ 🍴 🏠 💻 ♀ ⌂ 🏠 ⭐ (Parnell E Reilly.
Location	Off Bradley Rd (3m N on A6107)
Hotel	★★★67% The George Hotel, St George's Square, HUDDERSFIELD ☎(0484) 515444 59rm(47⇨)

Crosland Heath ☎(0484) 653216
Moorland course with fine views over valley.
18 holes, 5972yds, Par 70, SSS 70.
Club membership 350.

Visitors	must contact in advance and have an introduction from own club.
Societies	must telephone in advance.
Green Fees	not confirmed.
Facilities	⊗ 🍴 🏠 💻 ♀ ⌂ 🏠 (Richard Jessop.
Location	Felk Stile Rd, Crosland Heath (SW off A62)
Hotel	★★★67% The George Hotel, St George's Square, HUDDERSFIELD ☎(0484) 515444 59rm(47⇨)

Huddersfield ☎(0484) 426203
A testing heathland course of championship standard laid out in 1891.
18 holes, 6364yds, Par 71, SSS 71.
Club membership 730.

Visitors	restricted Tue (ladies day). Must contact in advance.
Societies	welcome Mon-Fri, must apply in writing.
Green Fees	£35 per day (£45 weekends); £25 per round (£35 weekends).
Facilities	⊗ ⅲ ┗ ➠ by prior arrangement ♀ (by prior arrangement) ⌂ 🖻 (Paul Carman.
Leisure	snooker.
Location	Fixby Hall, Lightridge Rd, Fixby (2m N off A641)
Hotel	★★★67% The George Hotel, St George's Square, HUDDERSFIELD ☎(0484) 515444 59rm(47⇨)

Longley Park ☎(0484) 422304
Lowland course.
9 holes, 5269yds, Par 66, SSS 66.
Club membership 400.

Visitors	restricted Thu & weekends. Must contact in advance and have an introduction from own club.
Societies	welcome except Thu, Sat & Sun, must apply in writing.
Green Fees	£11 per round.
Facilities	⊗ ⅲ by prior arrangement ┗ ➠ ♀ ⌂ 🖻 ⚑ (Neil Suckling.
Location	Maple St, Off Somerset Rd (.5m SE of town centre off A629)
Hotel	★★★67% The George Hotel, St George's Square, HUDDERSFIELD ☎(0484) 515444 59rm(47⇨)

ILKLEY　　　　　　　　　　　　　　　　Map 07 SE14

Ben Rhydding ☎(0943) 608759
Moorland/parkland course with splendid views over the Wharfe valley.
9 holes, 4711yds, Par 65, SSS 64, Course record 64.
Club membership 300.

Visitors	restricted Sat & Sun.
Green Fees	£7.50 per day/round.
Location	High Wood, Ben Rhydding (SE side of town)
Hotel	★★76% Rombalds Hotel & Restaurant, 11 West View, Wells Rd, ILKLEY ☎(0943) 603201 15⇨⚑

Each golf-course entry has a recommended AA-appointed hotel. For a wider choice of places to stay, consult *AA Hotels and Restaurants in Britain and Ireland* and *AA Inspected Bed and Breakfast in Britain and Ireland*

Ilkley ☎(0943) 600214
This beautiful parkland course is situated in Wharfedale and the Wharfe is a hazard on each of the first seven holes. In fact, the 3rd is laid out entirely on an island in the middle of the river.
18 holes, 6262yds, Par 69, SSS 70, Course record 66.
Club membership 500.

SCORECARD: Medal Tees					
Hole	Yds	Par	Hole	Yds	Par
1	410	4	10	316	4
2	166	3	11	443	4
3	206	3	12	400	4
4	504	5	13	153	3
5	200	3	14	433	4
6	497	5	15	146	3
7	423	4	16	426	4
8	351	4	17	416	4
9	395	4	18	377	4
Out	3152	35	In	3110	34
			Totals	6262	69

Visitors	must contact in advance and have an introduction from own club.
Societies	welcome except Tue, Fri & weekends.
Green Fees	£25 per day/round.
Facilities	⊗ ⅲ ┗ ➠ ♀ 🖻 (
Leisure	fishing, snooker.
Location	Middleton (W side of town centre off A65)
Hotel	★★76% Rombalds Hotel & Restaurant, 11 West View, Wells Rd, ILKLEY ☎(0943) 603201 15⇨⚑

KEIGHLEY　　　　　　　　　　　　　　　Map 07 SE04

Branshaw ☎Haworth (0535) 643235
Picturesque moorland course with fairly narrow fairways and good greens. Extensive views.
18 holes, 5858yds, Par 69, SSS 69, Course record 65.
Club membership 500.

Visitors	may not play on competition days (Sun).
Societies	must contact in writing, or telephone secretary on (0535) 605003.
Green Fees	£12 per day (£17 weekdays).
Facilities	⊗ & ⅲ by prior arrangement ┗ (ex Mon) ➠ by prior arrangement ♀ (ex Mon) ⌂
Location	Branshaw Moor (2m SW on B6143)
Hotel	★★68% Dalesgate Hotel, 406 Skipton Rd, Utley, KEIGHLEY ☎(0535) 664930 21⇨⚑

Keighley ☎(0535) 604778
Parkland course with good views down the Aire Valley.
18 holes, 6149yds, Par 69, SSS 70, Course record 65.
Club membership 600.

Visitors	restricted Sat & Sun. Must contact in advance.
Societies	must apply in advance.
Green Fees	£24 per day; £20 per round.
Facilities	⊗ ⅲ ┗ ➠ ♀ ⌂ 🖻 (S A Dixon.
Location	Howden Park, Utley (1m NW of town centre off B6143)
Hotel	★★68% Dalesgate Hotel, 406 Skipton Rd, Utley, KEIGHLEY ☎(0535) 664930 21⇨⚑

LEEDS　　　　　　　　　　　　　　　　　Map 08 SE33

Gotts Park ☎(0532) 638232
Municipal parkland course; very hilly in part.
18 holes, 4960yds, Par 65, SSS 64.
Club membership 250.

Green Fees	not confirmed.
Facilities	➠ ♀ (ex Thu) 🖻 ⚑ (John F Simpson.

▶

Location   Armley Ridge Rd (3m E of city centre off A647)
Hotel   ★★★65% Parkway Hotel, Otley Rd, LEEDS
                 ☎(0532) 672551 103⇔↑

Headingley ☎(0532) 679573
An undulating course with a wealth of natural features
offering fine views from higher ground. Its most striking
hazard is the famous ravine at the 18th. Leeds's oldest
course, founded in 1892.
18 holes, 6298yds, Par 69, SSS 70, Course record 64.
Club membership 630.
Visitors   restricted before 9.30 & 12-1.30pm. Must
                 contact in advance.
Societies   must apply in writing.
Green Fees   £27.50 per day; £22 per round (£36 per day/round
                 weekends & bank holidays).
Facilities   ⊗ by prior arrangement ⅏ by prior arrangement
                 ⅃ ⬛ ♀ △ 🏠 ʕ Andrew Dyson.
Leisure   snooker.
Location   Back Church Ln, Adel (5.5m N of city centre off
                 A660)
Hotel   ★★★67% Forte Crest Leeds/Bradford, Otley
                 Rd, BRAMHOPE ☎(0532) 842911 126⇔

Horsforth ☎(0532) 586819
Moorland course overlooking airport.
18 holes, 6243yds, Par 71, SSS 70, Course record 66.
Club membership 750.
Visitors   restricted Sat & with member only Sun.
Societies   must apply in writing.
Green Fees   £20 per day; £18 per round.
Facilities   ⊗ ⅏ ⅃ ⬛ ♀ △ 🏠 ʕ Laurie Turner.
Leisure   snooker.
Location   Layton Rise, Layton Rd, Horsforth (6.5m NW
                 of city centre off A65)
Hotel   ★★★67% Forte Crest Leeds/Bradford, Otley
                 Rd, BRAMHOPE ☎(0532) 842911 126⇔

Leeds ☎(0532) 658775
Parkland course with pleasant views.
18 holes, 6097yds, Par 69, SSS 69, Course record 63.
Club membership 600.
Visitors   with member only weekends, yellow tees only.
                 Must contact in advance.
Societies   must apply in writing.
Green Fees   £24 per day; £18 per round.
Facilities   ⊗ ⅏ by prior arrangement ⅃ ⬛ ♀ 🏠 ʕ
Leisure   snooker.
Location   Elmete Ln (5m NE of city centre on A6120 off
                 A58)
Hotel   ★★★64% Stakis Windmill Hotel, Mill Green
                 View, Seacroft, LEEDS ☎(0532) 732323
                 100⇔↑

Middleton Park Municipal ☎(0532) 700449
Parkland course.
18 holes, 5263yds, Par 68, SSS 66.
Club membership 300.
Visitors   no restrictions.
Green Fees   not confirmed.
Facilities   △ 🏠 ⅌ ʕ David Bulmer.
Location   Middleton Park, Middleton (3m S off A653)
Hotel   ★★★64% Stakis Windmill Hotel, Mill Green
                 View, Seacroft, LEEDS ☎(0532) 732323
                 100⇔↑

Moor Allerton
☎(0532) 661154
The Moor Allerton Club has
27 holes set in 220 acres of
undulating parkland, with
magnificent views extending
across the Vale of York. The
Championship Course was
designed by Robert Trent
Jones, the famous American
course architect, and is the
only course of his design in
the British Isles.

SCORECARD: The Lakes (Championship Tees)					
Hole	Yds	Par	Hole	Yds	Par
1	436	4	10	436	4
2	394	4	11	340	4
3	348	4	12	388	4
4	143	3	13	166	3
5	483	5	14	489	5
6	296	4	15	345	4
7	180	3	16	388	4
8	562	5	17	147	3
9	400	4	18	373	4
Out	3242	36	In	3072	35
			Totals	6314	71

*Lakes: 18 holes, 6314yds, Par
71, SSS 72.*
Blackmoor: 18 holes, 6502yds, Par 71, SSS 72.
High Course: 18 holes, 6672yds, Par 72, SSS 73.
Club membership 500.
Visitors   restricted Sun.
Societies   must apply in advance.
Green Fees   £35 per day; £32 per round.
Facilities   ⊗ ⅏ ⅃ ⬛ ♀ △ 🏠 ⅌ ʕ Richard Lane.
Leisure   snooker, sauna, bowling green.
Location   Coal Rd, Wike (5.5m N of city centre on
                 A61)
Hotel   ★★★66% Harewood Arms Hotel,
                 Harrogate Rd, HAREWOOD ☎(0532)
                 886566 24⇔↑

Moortown ☎(0532) 686521
Championship course, tough but fair. Springy moorland
turf, natural hazards of heather, gorse and streams,
cunningly placed bunkers and immaculate greens.
18 holes, 6544yds, Par 71, SSS 72.
Club membership 550.
Visitors   weekend by prior arrangement. Must contact
                 in advance.
Societies   must apply in advance.
Green Fees   not confirmed.
Facilities   ⊗ by prior arrangement ⅏ by prior arrange-
                 ment ⅃ ⬛ ♀ △ 🏠 ʕ B Hutchinson.
Location   Harrogate Rd, Alwoodley (6m N of city
                 centre on A61)
Hotel   ★★★66% Harewood Arms Hotel,
                 Harrogate Rd, HAREWOOD ☎(0532)
                 886566 24⇔↑

Roundhay ☎(0532) 662695
Attractive municipal parkland course, natural hazards, easy
walking.
9 holes, 5166yds, Par 65, SSS 68.
Club membership 350.
Societies   must apply in advance to Leeds City Council.
Green Fees   £5.35.
Facilities   ⊗ ⅏ ⅃ ⬛ ♀ △ 🏠 ʕ Jim Pape.
Location   Park Ln (4m NE of city centre off A58)
Hotel   ★★★64% Stakis Windmill Hotel, Mill Green
                 View, Seacroft, LEEDS ☎(0532) 732323
                 100⇔↑

We make every effort to ensure that our
information is accurate but details may change
after we go to print

Sand Moor ☎(0532) 685180
A beautiful, undulating course overlooking Lord Harewood's estate and the Eccup Reservoir. The course is wooded with some holes adjacent to water. The 12th is perhaps the most difficult where the fairway falls away towards the reservoir.
18 holes, 6429yds, Par 71, SSS 71, Course record 62.
Club membership 553.

SCORECARD: White Tees					
Hole	Yds	Par	Hole	Yds	Par
1	491	5	10	173	3
2	258	4	11	381	4
3	413	4	12	522	5
4	379	4	13	339	4
5	358	4	14	464	4
6	472	4	15	160	3
7	383	4	16	548	5
8	186	3	17	156	3
9	364	4	18	382	4
Out	3304	36	In	3125	35
			Totals	6429	71

Visitors restricted weekends & bank holidays. Must contact in advance and have an introduction from own club.
Societies must apply in advance.
Green Fees £30 per day; £25 per round.
Facilities ⊗ ⅲ (Mon-Fri) 💻 ♀ 👟 🍴 ℓ Mr J R Foss.
Leisure snooker.
Location Alwoodley Ln (5m N of city centre off A61)
Hotel ★★★67% Forte Crest Leeds/Bradford, Otley Rd, BRAMHOPE ☎(0532) 842911 126⇨

South Leeds ☎(0532) 700479
Parkland couse, windy, hard walking, good views.
18 holes, 5769yds, Par 69, SSS 68, Course record 66.
Club membership 632.
Visitors must contact in advance and have an introduction from own club.
Societies must apply in advance.
Green Fees not confirmed.
Facilities ⊗ ⅲ ⅃ & 💻 (ex Mon) ♀ (ex Mon) 👟 🍴 ℓ Mike Lewis.
Location Gipsy Ln, Beeston (3m S of city centre off A653)
Hotel ★★★★66% The Queen's, City Square, LEEDS ☎(0532) 431323 188⇨🌑

Temple Newsam ☎(0532) 645624
Two parkland courses. Testing long 13th (563 yds) on second course.
Lord Irwin: 18 holes, 6460yds, Par 69, SSS 71.
Lady Dorothy: 18 holes, 6276yds, Par 70, SSS 70.
Club membership 520.
Societies must apply in advance.
Green Fees £4.90 per day (£5.20 weekends & bank holidays).
Facilities ⊗ (weekends only) ⅃ 💻 (weekends only) ♀ 👟 🍴 ℓ David Bulmer.
Leisure snooker.
Location Temple-Newsam Rd (3.5m E of city centre off A63)
Hotel ★★★64% Stakis Windmill Hotel, Mill Green View, Seacroft, LEEDS ☎(0532) 732323 100⇨🌑

If you know of a golf course which welcomes visitors and is not already in this guide, we should be grateful for information

MARSDEN Map 07 SE01

Marsden ☎(0484) 844253
Moorland course with good views, natural hazards, windy.
9 holes, 5702yds, Par 68, SSS 68.
Club membership 185.
Visitors must play with member at weekends.
Societies Mon-Fri; must contact in advance.
Green Fees not confirmed.
Facilities ⊗ ⅃ 💻 ♀ 👟
Leisure hard tennis courts.
Location Mount Rd, Hemplow (S side off A62)
Hotel ★★★62% Briar Court Hotel, Halifax Road, Birchencliffe, HUDDERSFIELD ☎(0484) 519902 48⇨🌑

MELTHAM Map 07 SE01

Meltham ☎Huddersfield (0484) 850227
Parkland course with good views. Testing 548 yd, 13th hole (par 5).
18 holes, 6145yds, Par 70, SSS 70, Course record 65.
Club membership 455.
Visitors restricted Sat & Wed (ladies day).
Societies must apply in advance.
Green Fees £16.50 per day (£20 weekends & bank holidays).
Facilities ⊗ by prior arrangement ⅲ by prior arrangement ⅃ 💻 ♀ 👟 🍴 🍴 ℓ Paul Davies.
Leisure snooker.
Location Thick Hollins Hall (SE side of village off B6107)
Hotel ★★★67% The George Hotel, St George's Square, HUDDERSFIELD ☎(0484) 515444 59rm(47⇨)

MIRFIELD Map 08 SE21

Dewsbury District ☎(0924) 492399
Heathland/parkland course with panoramic view from top, hard walking. Ponds in middle of 3rd fairway, left of 5th green and 17th green.
18 holes, 6248yds, Par 71, SSS 71, Course record 64.
Club membership 650.
Visitors restricted weekends before 4pm & bank holidays. Must contact in advance.
Societies must apply in advance.
Green Fees £18 per day.
Facilities ⊗ by prior arrangement ⅲ by prior arrangement ⅃ 💻 (catering ex Mon) ♀ 👟 🍴 🍴 ℓ
Leisure snooker.
Location Sands Ln (1m S off A644)
Hotel ★★★67% The George Hotel, St George's Square, HUDDERSFIELD ☎(0484) 515444 59rm(47⇨)

MORLEY Map 08 SE22

Howley Hall ☎Batley (0924) 478417
Parkland course with easy walking and good views.
18 holes, 6029yds, Par 71, SSS 69.
Club membership 500.
Visitors standard course only. Must contact in advance.
Societies must apply in writing.
Green Fees £21.50 per day; £18.50 per round (£25 day/round weekends).

▶

Facilities	⊗ 🏌 💷 (no catering Mon) ♀ 🏠 ⚑ Stephen A Spinks.
Location	Scotchman Ln (1.5m S on B6123)
Hotel	★★66% Alder House Hotel, Towngate Rd, off Healey Ln, BATLEY ☎(0924) 444777 22rm(21⇨♠)

NORMANTON   Map 08 SE32

Normanton ☎Wakefield (0924) 892943
A pleasant, flat course with tight fairways in places and an internal out of bounds requiring accuracy.
9 holes, 5288yds, Par 66, SSS 66.
Club membership 250.

Visitors	may not play on Sun.
Societies	mid-week only.
Green Fees	not confirmed.
Facilities	⊗ �𝄂 🏌 💷 ♀ 🏌 🏠 ⚑ ⚑ Martin Evans.
Location	Snydale Rd (.5m SE on B6133)
Hotel	★★★63% Swallow Hotel, Queens St, WAKEFIELD ☎(0924) 372111 64⇨♠

OSSETT   Map 08 SE22

Low Laithes ☎(0924) 273275
Testing parkland course.
18 holes, 6463yds, Par 72, SSS 71, Course record 67.
Club membership 450.

Visitors	restricted weekends 10am-2pm. Must contact in advance.
Societies	welcome Mon-Fri, must apply in advance.
Green Fees	£15 per day/round (£18 weekends).
Facilities	🏌 🏠 ⚑ ⚑ P Browning.
Location	Parkmill Ln, Flushdyke (1.5m SE off A128)
Hotel	★★★66% Forte Posthouse Northampton/Rugby, CRICK ☎(0788) 822101 88⇨♠

OTLEY   Map 08 SE24

Otley ☎(0943) 461015
An expansive course with magnificent views across Wharfedale. It is well-wooded with streams crossing the fairway. The 4th is a fine hole which generally needs two woods to reach the plateau green. The 17th is a good short hole.
18 holes, 6235yds, Par 70, SSS 70, Course record 62.
Club membership 650.

SCORECARD: White Tees					
Hole	Yds	Par	Hole	Yds	Par
1	423	4	10	276	4
2	169	3	11	402	4
3	398	4	12	392	4
4	444	4	13	420	4
5	208	3	14	264	4
6	490	5	15	131	3
7	387	4	16	368	4
8	480	5	17	180	3
9	361	4	18	432	4
Out	3360	36	In	2865	34
			Totals	6225	70

Visitors	restricted Sat.
Societies	must apply in writing.
Green Fees	£22 per day (£27 weekends).
Facilities	⊗ �𝄂 by prior arrangement 🏌 💷 ♀ 🏌 🏠 ⚑ Stephen McNally.
Leisure	snooker.
Location	Off West Busk Ln (1.5m SW off A6038)
Hotel	★★★67% Forte Crest Leeds/Bradford, Otley Rd, BRAMHOPE ☎(0532) 842911 126⇨

OUTLANE   Map 07 SE01

Outlane ☎Halifax (0422) 374762
Moorland course.
18 holes, 5735yds, Par 71, SSS 68.
Club membership 500.

Visitors	restricted Thu. Must contact in advance and have an introduction from own club.
Societies	must contact 14 days in advance.
Green Fees	not confirmed.
Facilities	⊗ (ex Mon) �𝄂 (ex Mon & Sun) 🏌 (ex Mon & Sun) 💷 (ex Mon) ♀ (ex Mon) 🏌 🏠 ⚑ ⚑ David Chapman.
Location	Slack Ln (S side of village off A640)
Hotel	★★★64% Old Golf House Hotel, New Hey Rd, OUTLANE ☎(0422) 379311 50⇨♠

PONTEFRACT   Map 08 SE42

Pontefract & District ☎(0977) 792241
Parkland course.
18 holes, 6227yds, Par 72, SSS 70, Course record 63.
Club membership 800.

Visitors	welcome except Wed & weekends. Must contact in advance and have an introduction from own club.
Societies	welcome except Wed & weekends.
Green Fees	£20 per day (£25 weekends & bank holidays).
Facilities	⊗ ⟨ 🏌 💷 ♀ 🏌 🏠 ⚑ J Coleman.
Location	Park Ln (1.5m W on B6134)
Hotel	★★★⬩65% Wentbridge House Hotel, WENTBRIDGE ☎(0977) 620444 12⇨♠

PUDSEY   Map 08 SE23

Fulneck ☎(0532) 565191
Picturesque, hilly parkland course. Compact but strenuous.
9 holes, 5432yds, Par 67, SSS 65, Course record 64.
Club membership 300.

Visitors	must contact in advance.
Societies	must apply in writing.
Green Fees	£12 per round.
Facilities	🏌
Leisure	pool table.
Location	S side of town centre
Hotel	★★★57% Novotel Bradford, Merrydale Rd, BRADFORD ☎(0274) 683683 132⇨♠

Woodhall Hills ☎(0532) 564771
Meadowland course, prevailing SW winds, fairly hard walking. Testing holes: 8th, 377 yd (par 4); 14th, 206 yd (par 3).
18 holes, 6102yds, Par 71, SSS 69, Course record 66.
Club membership 612.

Visitors	restricted Mon-Fri until 9.30am.
Societies	must apply in writing.
Green Fees	£20.50 per day/round (£25.50 weekends & bank holidays).
Facilities	⊗ ⟨ 🏌 💷 by prior arrangement ♀ 🏌 🏠 ⚑ Darren Tear.
Leisure	snooker.
Location	Calverley (2.5m NW off A647)
Hotel	★★62% Park Drive Hotel, 12 Park Dr, BRADFORD ☎(0274) 480194 11⇨♠

RAWDON
Map 08 SE23

Rawdon Golf & Lawn Tennis Club ☎(0532) 506040
Undulating parkland course.
9 holes, 5980yds, Par 72, SSS 69, Course record 64.
Club membership 700.

Visitors	must play with member at weekends. Must contact in advance and have an introduction from own club.
Societies	must contact in advance.
Green Fees	not confirmed.
Facilities	⊗ ⫫ ♨ ⬤ ♀ (ex Mon) ⌁ 🖴 ⌁ John Clapham.
Leisure	hard and grass tennis courts, snooker.
Location	Buckstone Dr (S side of town off A65)
Hotel	★★★67% Forte Crest Leeds/Bradford, Otley Rd, BRAMHOPE ☎(0532) 842911 126⇨

RIDDLESDEN
Map 07 SE04

Riddlesden ☎Keighley (0535) 602148
Undulating moorland course with two quarry hazards, prevailing west winds, some hard walking and beautiful views.
18 holes, 4247yds, Par 63, SSS 61.
Club membership 250.

Visitors	restricted before 2pm weekends.
Societies	must apply in writing.
Green Fees	£8 per day (£12 weekends).
Facilities	⊗ ⫫ ♨ ⬤ (no catering Mon) ♀ ⌁
Location	Howden Rough (1m NW)
Hotel	★★68% Dalesgate Hotel, 406 Skipton Rd, Utley, KEIGHLEY ☎(0535) 664930 21⇨🖴

SCARCROFT
Map 08 SE34

Scarcroft ☎Leeds (0532) 892311
Undulating parkland course with prevailing west wind and easy walking.
18 holes, 6426yds, Par 71, SSS 71.
Club membership 667.

Visitors	must contact in advance.
Societies	must contact in advance.
Green Fees	£30 per day; £25 per round (£35 weekends & bank holidays).
Facilities	⊗ & ⫫ (ex Mon) ♨ ⬤ ♀ (ex Sun) ⌁ 🖴 ⌁ ⌁ Martin Ross.
Leisure	snooker.
Location	Syke Ln (.5m N of village off A58)
Hotel	★★★64% Stakis Windmill Hotel, Mill Green View, Seacroft, LEEDS ☎(0532) 732323 100⇨🖴

SHIPLEY
Map 07 SE13

Northcliffe ☎Bradford (0274) 584085
Parkland course with magnificent views of moors. Testing 1st hole (18th green 100 feet below tee).
18 holes, 6104yds, Par 71, SSS 69, Course record 65.
Club membership 657.

Visitors	no restrictions.
Societies	must apply in writing.
Green Fees	£16 per day/round (£24 weekends & bank holidays).

Facilities	⊗ ⫫ ♨ ⬤ ♀ 🖴 ⌁ ⌁ Simon Poot.
Leisure	snooker.
Location	High Bank Ln (1.25m SW off A650)
Hotel	★★★64% Bankfield Hotel, Bradford Rd, BINGLEY ☎(0274) 567123 103⇨🖴

SILSDEN
Map 07 SE04

Silsden ☎Steeton (0535) 52998
Tight downland course which can be windy. Good views of the Aire Valley.
14 holes, 4870yds, Par 65, SSS 64.
Club membership 300.

Visitors	no restrictions.
Societies	welcome.
Green Fees	not confirmed.
Facilities	♀ ⌁
Location	High Brunthwaite (1m E)
Hotel	★★68% Dalesgate Hotel, 406 Skipton Rd, Utley, KEIGHLEY ☎(0535) 664930 21⇨🖴

SOWERBY
Map 07 SE02

Ryburn ☎Halifax (0422) 831355
Moorland course, easy walking.
9 holes, 4996yds, Par 66, SSS 64.
Club membership 200.

Visitors	must contact in advance.
Societies	welcome.
Green Fees	not confirmed.
Facilities	♀ ⌁
Location	The Shaw, Norland (1m S of Sowerby Bridge off A58)
Hotel	★★72% The Hobbit Hotel, Hob Ln, Norlands, SOWERBY BRIDGE ☎(0422) 832202 17⇨🖴Annexe5⇨🖴

TODMORDEN
Map 07 SD92

Todmorden ☎(070681) 298681
Pleasant moorland course.
9 holes, 5818yds, Par 68, SSS 68, Course record 67.
Club membership 140.

Visitors	restricted Sat (pm) & competition days.
Green Fees	£10 per day (£15 weekends).
Facilities	🖴
Location	Rive Rocks, Cross Stone Rd (NE off A646)
Hotel	★★★♨70% Scaitcliffe Hall, Burnley Rd, TODMORDEN ☎(0706) 818888 13⇨🖴

WAKEFIELD
Map 08 SE32

City of Wakefield ☎(0924) 374316
Parkland course.
18 holes, 6299yds, Par 72, SSS 70, Course record 66.
Club membership 850.

Visitors	restricted weekends.
Societies	must apply in advance.
Green Fees	£4.75 weekdays (£7.20 weekends & bank holidays).
Facilities	⊗ ⫫ by prior arrangement ♨ ⬤ ♀ ⌁ 🖴 ⌁ ⌁ Roger Holland.

▶

Location	Lupset Park, Horbury Rd (1.5m W of city centre on A642)
Hotel	★★★60% Forte Posthouse, Queen's Dr, Ossett, WAKEFIELD ☎(0924) 276388 99⇨🏌

Painthorpe House ☎(0924) 255083
Undulating meadowland course, easy walking.
9 holes, 4520yds, Par 62, SSS 62, Course record 68.
Club membership 150.

Visitors	restricted weekends.
Societies	must apply in advacne.
Green Fees	£3 per round (£5 weekends).
Facilities	⊗ ⅲ ᄕ & ■ by prior arrangement ♀ by prior arrangement 🏠
Leisure	bowling green.
Location	Painthorpe Ln, Painthorpe, Crigglestone (2m S off A636)
Hotel	★★★60% Forte Posthouse, Queen's Dr, Ossett, WAKEFIELD ☎(0924) 276388 99⇨🏌

Wakefield ☎(0924) 255104
A well-sheltered meadowland/heath course with easy walking and good views.
18 holes, 6611yds, Par 72, SSS 72, Course record 67.
Club membership 550.

Societies	must apply in writing.
Green Fees	£22 per day/round (£25 weekends & bank holidays).
Facilities	⊗ ⅲ ᄕ ■ ♀ 🏌 🏠 ⨍ I M Wright.
Leisure	snooker.
Location	Woodthorpe Ln, Sandal (3m S off A61)
Hotel	★★★60% Forte Posthouse, Queen's Dr, Ossett, WAKEFIELD ☎(0924) 276388 99⇨🏌

WETHERBY Map 08 SE44

Wetherby ☎(0937) 582527
Parkland course with fine views.
18 holes, 5888yds, Par 69, SSS 68, Course record 66.
Club membership 750.

Societies	welcome Wed-Fri, must apply in writing.
Green Fees	£25 per day; £20 per round (£30 day/round weekends).
Facilities	⊗ ⅲ by prior arrangement ᄕ ■ ♀ 🏌 🏠 ⨍ David Padgett.
Location	Linton Ln (1m W off A661)
Hotel	★★★57% Wetherby Resort Hotel, Leeds Rd, WETHERBY ☎(0937) 583881 72⇨🏌

WIGHT, ISLE OF

COWES Map 04 SZ49

Cowes ☎(0983) 292303
Fairly level, tight parkland course with difficult par 3s and Solent views.
9 holes, 5934yds, Par 70, SSS 68, Course record 67.
Club membership 300.

Visitors	restricted Thu, Fri & Sun mornings.
Societies	must contact in writing.
Green Fees	£16 (£19 weekends).
Facilities	⊗ ᄕ & ■ (Apr-Oct ex Sun) ♀ 🏌 🏌

Location	Crossfield Av (NW side of town)
Hotel	★★55% Fountain Hotel, High St, COWES ☎(0983) 292397 20⇨

EAST COWES Map 04 SZ59

Osborne ☎(0983) 295421
Undulating parkland course in the grounds of Osborne House. Quiet and peaceful situation.
9 holes, 6276yds, Par 70, SSS 70, Course record 66.
Club membership 350.

Visitors	restricted Tue 9am-1pm & weekends before noon. Must have an introduction from own club.
Societies	must contact in advance.
Green Fees	£15 per day (£18 weekends).
Facilities	⊗ ⅲ by prior arrangement ᄕ ■ ♀ 🏌 🏠 🏌 ⨍ Ian Taylor.
Location	Osborne (E side of town centre off A3021)
Hotel	★★62% Cowes Hotel, 260 Artic Rd, COWES ☎(0983) 291541 15⇨🏌

FRESHWATER Map 04 SZ38

Freshwater Bay ☎(0983) 752955
A downland/seaside links with wide fairways and spectacular coastal views of the Solent and Channel.
18 holes, 5662yds, Par 68, SSS 68, Course record 64.
Club membership 600.

Visitors	may not play before 9.30am weekdays & 10am Sun.
Societies	must confirm in writing.
Green Fees	£16 per day (£20 weekends & bank holidays).
Facilities	⊗ ⅲ ᄕ ■ ♀ 🏌 🏌
Location	Afton Down (.5m E of village off A3055)
Hotel	★★★57% Albion Hotel, FRESHWATER ☎(0983) 753631 42rm(39⇨🏌)

NEWPORT Map 04 SZ48

Newport ☎(0983) 525076
Downland course, fine views.
9 holes, 5704yds, Par 68, SSS 67, Course record 64.
Club membership 300.

Visitors	may not play after 3pm Sat & noon Sun.
Societies	must telephone in advance.
Green Fees	£10 per day (£12 weekends & bank holidays).
Facilities	ᄕ ■ ♀ 🏌 🏠 🏌
Location	St George's Down (1.5m S off A3020)
Hotel	★★★57% Melville Hall Hotel, Melville St, SANDOWN ☎(0983) 406526 33⇨🏌

RYDE Map 04 SZ59

Ryde ☎(0983) 614809
Downland course with wide views over the Solent.
9 holes, 5287yds, Par 66, SSS 66.
Club membership 375.

Visitors	may not play Wed afternoons & Sun mornings. Must have an introduction from own club.
Societies	must contact in writing.
Green Fees	£15 per day (£20 weekends).
Facilities	⊗ ⅲ by prior arrangement ᄕ ■ ♀ 🏌 🏠

Location	Binstead Rd (1m W on A3054)
Hotel	★★67% Biskra House Beach Hotel, 17 Saint Thomas's St, RYDE ☎(0983) 67913 9⇨🐾

SANDOWN   Map 04 SZ58

Shanklin & Sandown ☎(0983) 403217
Heathland course.
18 holes, 6000yds, Par 70, SSS 69, Course record 65.
Club membership 720.

Visitors	must be member of a recognised club with a handicap certificate. Must contact in advance and have an introduction from own club.
Societies	limited bookings; telephone in advance.
Green Fees	£21 per round (£25 weekends & bank holidays).
Facilities	⊗ & ⅏ by prior arrangement ⅃ ⬛ ♀ △ 🖻 🖘 ⌇ Peter Hammond.
Location	Fairway, Lake (1m NW)
Hotel	★★★61% Cliff Tops Hotel, Park Rd, SHANKLIN ☎(0983) 863262 88⇨🐾

VENTNOR   Map 04 SZ57

Ventnor ☎(0983) 853326
Downland course subject to wind. Fine seascapes.
9 holes, 5752yds, Par 70, SSS 68, Course record 73.
Club membership 200.

Visitors	may not play Fri noon-3.30pm or Sun mornings.
Societies	must contact in advance.
Green Fees	£12 per day (£15 weekends & bank holidays).
Facilities	⅃ ⬛ △ 🖘 🖻
Leisure	pool table.
Location	Steep Hill Down Rd, Upper Ventnor (1m NW off B3327)
Hotel	★★★62% Ventnor Towers Hotel, Madeira Rd, VENTNOR ☎(0983) 852277 27rm(26⇨🐾)

✼ WILTSHIRE ✼

BISHOPS CANNINGS   Map 04 SU06

North Wilts ☎(038086) 627
High, downland course with fine views.
18 holes, 6484yds, Par 72, SSS 71, Course record 67.
Club membership 800.

Visitors	welcome a handicap certificate is required at weekends. Must contact in advance.
Societies	must book in advance.
Green Fees	£25 per day; £18 per round (£30 weekends).
Facilities	⊗ ⅏ ⅃ ⬛ ♀ △ 🖻 ⌇ Graham Laing.
Location	2m NW
Hotel	★★★62% Bear Hotel, Market Place, DEVIZES ☎(0380) 722444 24⇨

CHIPPENHAM   Map 03 ST97

Chippenham ☎(0249) 652040
Easy walking on downland course. Testing holes at 1st and 15th.
18 holes, 5559yds, Par 69, SSS 67.
Club membership 650.

Visitors	must have a handicap certificate. Must contact in advance and have an introduction from own club.
Societies	must contact in writing; handicap certificates required.
Green Fees	not confirmed.
Facilities	⊗ (ex Mon) ⅏ (ex Sun and Mon) ⅃ ⬛ ♀ △ 🖻 🖘 ⌇ Bill Creamer.
Location	Malmesbury Rd (1.5m N on A429)
Hotel	★★★★⅏76% Manor House Hotel, CASTLE COMBE ☎(0249) 782206 12⇨🐾Annexe24⇨🐾

DURNFORD, GREAT   Map 04 SU13

High Post ☎Middle Woodford (072273) 356
An interesting downland course on Wiltshire chalk with good turf and splendid views over the southern area of Salisbury Plain. The par 3, 17th and the two-shot 18th require good judgement.
18 holes, 6297yds, Par 70, SSS 70, Course record 64.
Club membership 600.

Visitors	a handicap certificate is equired at weekends. Must contact in advance.
Societies	welcome except weekends.
Green Fees	£23 per day; £18 per round (£30/£23 week-ends).
Facilities	⊗ ⅏ ⅃ ⬛ ♀ △ 🖻 ⌇ Anthony John Harman.
Location	1.75m SE on A345
Hotel	★★★60% Rose & Crown Hotel, Harnham Rd, Harnham, SALISBURY ☎(0722) 327908 28⇨🐾

HIGHWORTH   Map 04 SU29

Highworth Community Golf Centre ☎Swindon (0793) 766014
Public downland course, situated in a high position affording good views.
9 holes, 3120yds, Par 35, SSS 35.

Visitors	no restrictions.
Societies	must telephone in advance.
Green Fees	£4.30 (£4.60 weekends).
Facilities	⬛ △ 🖻 🖘 ⌇ Kevin Pickett.
Location	Swindon Rd
Hotel	★★★60% Forte Crest Hotel, Oxford Rd, Stratton St Margaret, SWINDON ☎(0793) 831333 94⇨🐾

KINGSDOWN   Map 03 SU18

Kingsdown ☎Box (0225) 742530
Fairly flat heathland course with surrounding wood.
18 holes, 6445yds, Par 72, SSS 71, Course record 66.
Club membership 620.

Visitors	welcome except at weekends. Handicap certificate required. Must contact in advance and have an introduction from own club.
Societies	apply by letter.
Green Fees	£22 per day.
Facilities	⊗ (ex Mon) ⅏ ⅃ ⬛ ♀ △ 🖻 ⌇ Peter Evans.
Location	W side of village
Hotel	★★65% Methuen Arms Hotel, High St, CORSHAM ☎(0249) 714867 19⇨🐾Annexe6⇨🐾

MARLBOROUGH
Map 04 SU16

Marlborough ☎(0672) 512147
Downland course open to prevailing wind. Extensive views.
18 holes, 6526yds, Par 72, SSS 71.
Club membership 920.

Visitors	restricted at certain times; must have a handicap certificate at weekends. Must contact in advance.
Societies	must telephone in advance.
Green Fees	not confirmed.
Facilities	⊗ ⦚ ♿ ➡ ♀ ⛳ ⛳ (L Ross, B McAdams, G Clough.
Location	The Common (N side of town centre on A345)
Hotel	★★★59% Castle & Ball Hotel, High St, MARLBOROUGH ☎(0672) 515201 36⇨

OGBOURNE ST GEORGE
Map 04 SU27

Swindon ☎(067284) 327
Downland turf and magnificent greens.
18 holes, 6226yds, Par 71, SSS 70, Course record 66.
Club membership 800.

Visitors	welcome weekdays only, handicap certificate required. Must contact in advance.
Societies	apply by letter.
Green Fees	£23 per day; £17 per round.
Facilities	⊗ ♿ ➡ ♀ ⛳ ⛳ (Colin Harraway.
Leisure	practice ground.
Location	N side of village on A3459
Hotel	★★★60% Forte Crest Hotel, Oxford Rd, Stratton St Margaret, SWINDON ☎(0793) 831333 94⇨♠

SALISBURY
Map 04 SU12

Salisbury & South Wilts ☎(0722) 742645
Gently undulating parkland course in country setting with panoramic views of the Cathedral and surrounding country.
Main Course: 18 holes, 6528yds, Par 70, SSS 71.
Old Course: 18 holes, 6177yds, Par 70, SSS 70.
Club membership 980.

Visitors	welcome except for competitions days. Must contact in advance.
Societies	apply in writing.
Green Fees	£20.50 per day (£29 per day wekends & bank holidays).
Facilities	⊗ ⦚ ♿ ➡ ♀ ⛳ ⛳ ⛳ (Gary Emerson.
Location	Netherhampton (2m W on A3094)
Hotel	★★★60% Rose & Crown Hotel, Harnham Rd, Harnham, SALISBURY ☎(0722) 327908 28⇨♠

SWINDON
Map 04 SU18

Broome Manor Golf Complex ☎(0793) 532403
Two courses and a 20-bay floodlit driving range. Parkland with water hazards, open fairways and short cut rough. Walking is easy on gentle slopes.
18 holes, 6359yds, Par 71, SSS 70, Course record 67 or 9 holes, 2745yds, Par 66, SSS 67.
Club membership 1300.

Visitors	tee booking advised for 18 holes. Must contact in advance.
Societies	welcome Mon-Thu only.

Green Fees	£7.15/£4.60 per round (£7.65/£4.60 weekends & bank holidays).
Facilities	⊗ ⦚ ♿ ➡ ♀ ⛳ ⛳ ⛳ (Barry Sandry.
Leisure	clay pigeon shooting.
Location	Pipers Way (1.75m SE of town centre off B4006)
Hotel	★★★60% Forte Crest Hotel, Oxford Rd, Stratton St Margaret, SWINDON ☎(0793) 831333 94⇨♠

UPAVON
Map 04 SU15

RAF Upavon ☎Stonehenge (0980) 630787
Downland course set on sides of valley, with some wind affecting play. The 2nd, 9th, 11th and 18th are all par 3 to small greens.
18 holes, 5116mtrs, Par 69, SSS 67, Course record 66.
Club membership 350.

Visitors	may not play before noon on Sun. Must contact in advance.
Societies	apply by letter.
Green Fees	£12 per day (£15 weekends).
Facilities	catering for societies by prior arrangement. ⛳ 🏠
Location	York Rd (2m E on A342)
Hotel	★★★62% Bear Hotel, Market Place, DEVIZES ☎(0380) 722444 24⇨

WARMINSTER
Map 03 ST84

West Wilts ☎(0985) 212702
A hilltop course among the Wiltshire downs without trees and somewhat windswept. First-class springy turf with many interesting holes.
18 holes, 5709yds, Par 70, SSS 68, Course record 62.
Club membership 600.

Visitors	with member only weekends, handicap certificate required. Must contact in advance.
Societies	apply by letter.
Green Fees	£20 per day (£30 weekends).
Facilities	⊗ ⦚ ♿ ➡ ♀ ⛳ 🏠 (John G Jacobs.
Location	Elm Hill (N side of town centre off A350)
Hotel	★★★★67% Bishopstrow House Hotel, WARMINSTER ☎(0985) 212312 32⇨♠

CHANNEL ISLANDS

ALDERNEY

ALDERNEY
Map 16

Alderney ☎(0481) 822835
Undulating seaside course with sea on all sides and offering magnificent views from its high tees and greens. Course designed by Frank Pennink.
9 holes, 2528yds, Par 32, SSS 65, Course record 29.
Club membership 560.

Visitors	may not play before 10am at weekends.
Societies	must contact in advance.
Green Fees	£10 per day (£16 weekends & bank holidays).

Facilities	⊗ ⽊ by prior arrangement ⊨ ⬛ ♀ 占 🏠 ⵀ
Leisure	bowling green & boules pitch.
Location	Route des Carrières (1m E of St Annes)
Hotel	★★57% Inchalla Hotel, St Anne, ALDERNEY ☎(048182) 3220 11rm(8⇌)

GUERNSEY

L'ANCRESSE VALE   Map 16

Royal Guernsey ☎(0481) 47022

Not quite as old as its neighbour Royal Jersey, Royal Guernsey is a sporting course which was re-designed after World War II by Mackenzie Ross, who has many fine courses to his credit. It is a pleasant links, well-maintained, and administered by the States of Guernsey in the form of the States Tourist Committee. The 8th hole, a good par 4, requires an accurate second shot to the green set amongst the gorse and thick rough. The 18th, with lively views, needs a strong shot to reach the green well down below. The course is windy, with hard walking. There is a junior section.

18 holes, 6206yds, Par 70, SSS 70.
Club membership 1500.

Visitors	must have a handicap certificate; may not play on Thu & Sat afternoons & Sun. Must have an introduction from own club.
Societies	Oct-Apr; must telephone in advance.
Green Fees	not confirmed.
Facilities	⊗ ⽊ (ex Sun and Mon) ⊨ ⬛ ♀ 占 🏠 ⵀ ℄ Norman Wood.
Leisure	snooker.
Location	3m N of St Peter Port
Hotel	★★★★67% St Pierre Park Hotel, Rohais, ST PETER PORT ☎(0481) 28282 135⇌🌂

ST PETER PORT   Map 16

St Pierre Park Golf Club ☎(0481) 727039 & 728282

Par 3 parkland course with delightful setting, with lakes, streams and many tricky holes.

9 holes, 2511yds, Par 54, SSS 48.
Club membership 290.

Visitors	no restrictions.
Societies	must contact in advance.
Green Fees	not confirmed.
Facilities	⊗ ⽊ ⊨ ⬛ ♀ 占 🏠 ⵀ ▱
Leisure	hard tennis courts, heated indoor swimming pool, snooker, sauna, solarium, gymnasium, croquet petanque.
Location	Rohais (1m W off Rohais Rd)
Hotel	★★★★67% St Pierre Park Hotel, Rohais, ST PETER PORT ☎(0481) 28282 135⇌🌂

A golf-course name printed in ***bold italics*** means that we have been unable to verify information with the club's management for the current year

JERSEY

GROUVILLE   Map 16

Royal Jersey ☎Jersey (0534) 54416

A seaside links, historic because of its age: its centenary was celebrated in 1978. It is also famous for the fact that Britian's greatest golfer, Harry Vardon, was born in a little cottage on the edge of the course and learned his golf here.

18 holes, 6059yds, Par 70, SSS 70, Course record 62.
Club membership 1364.

Visitors	restricted to 10am-noon & 2pm-4pm.
Societies	Mon-Fri afternoons only.
Green Fees	£30 per round (£35 weekends & bank holidays).
Facilities	⊗ ⽊ ⊨ ⬛ ♀ 占 🏠 ⵀ ℄ T A Horton.
Leisure	snooker.
Location	4m E of St Helier off coast rd
Hotel	★★★★(red)⚑ Longueville Manor Hotel, ST SAVIOUR ☎(0534) 25501 32⇌🌂

LA MOYE   Map 16

La Moye ☎Jersey (0534) 43401

Seaside championship links course (venue for the Jersey Open) situated in an exposed position on the south western corner of the island overlooking St Ouens Bay. Offers spectacular views, two start points, full course all year - no temporary greens.

18 holes, 6698yds, Par 72, SSS 72, Course record 62.
Club membership 1300.

SCORECARD: White Tees					
Hole	Yds	Par	Hole	Yds	Par
1	158	3	10	370	4
2	522	5	11	502	5
3	185	3	12	163	3
4	437	4	13	396	4
5	449	4	14	190	3
6	482	5	15	345	4
7	379	4	16	482	5
8	415	4	17	419	4
9	407	4	18	397	4
Out	3434	36	In	3264	36
			Totals	6698	72

Visitors	must contact in advance and have an introduction from own club.
Societies	must contact in advance.
Green Fees	£50 per day (lunch incl); £30 per round.
Facilities	⊗ ⽊ ⊨ ⬛ ♀ 占 🏠 ⵀ ℄ David Melville.
Leisure	snooker.
Location	W side of village off A13
Hotel	★★67% Les Arches Hotel, Archirondel Bay, ARCHIRONDEL ☎(0534) 53839 54⇌🌂

ST CLEMENT   Map 16

St Clement ☎Jersey (0534) 21938

Very tight moorland course. Holes cross over fairways, impossible to play to scratch. Suitable for middle to high handicaps.

9 holes, 2244yds, Par 30.
Club membership 500.

Visitors	must contact in advance.
Green Fees	not confirmed.
Facilities	占
Leisure	hard tennis courts.

▶

Location	Jersey Recreation Grounds (E side of St Helier on A5)
Hotel	★★★★(red)🏨 Longueville Manor Hotel, ST SAVIOUR ☎(0534) 25501 32⇨🐾

ISLE OF MAN

CASTLETOWN   Map 06 SC26

Castletown Golf Links ☎(0624) 822201
Set on the Langness Peninsula, this superb Championship course is surrounded on three sides by the sea, and holds many surprises from its Championship tees. The hotel offers many leisure facilities.
18 holes, 6713yds, Par 72, SSS 73, Course record 65.
Club membership 350.

Visitors	must book tee one month in advance unless a hotel resident.
Societies	must telephone in advance.
Green Fees	£18.50 per day Mon-Thu (£24.50 Fri-Sun & bank holidays).
Facilities	⊗ ⅲ ⅳ ⅼ ⅰ ♀ ⌂ 🏠 ♟ 🏌 ⚐ Murray Crowe.
Leisure	heated indoor swimming pool, fishing, riding, snooker, sauna, solarium, putting green, croquet.
Location	Fort Island, Derbyhaven
Hotel	★★★66% Castletown Golf Links Hotel, Fort Island, CASTLETOWN ☎(0624) 822201 58rm(44⇨12🐾)

DOUGLAS   Map 06 SC37

Pulrose ☎(0624) 75952
Hilly, mainly moorland course under the control of Douglas Corporation.
18 holes, 6080yds, Par 70, SSS 69.
Club membership 430.

Visitors	no restrictions.
Green Fees	not confirmed.
Facilities	♀ ⌂ 🏠 ♟ ⚐
Location	1m W off A1
Hotel	★★★68% The Empress Hotel, Central Promenade, DOUGLAS ☎(0624) 661155 102⇨🐾

ONCHAN   Map 06 SC47

King Edward Bay Golf & Country Club
☎Douglas (0624) 620430
Club plays over King Edward Bay course. Hilly seaside links course with natural hazards and good views.
18 holes, 5457yds, Par 67, SSS 66.
Club membership 200.

Visitors	must have a handicap certificate.
Societies	must contact in advance.
Green Fees	£6 per day (£8 weekends & bank holidays).
Facilities	⊗ ⅲ ⅳ ⅼ ⅰ ♀ ⌂ ♟
Leisure	snooker, sauna, solarium.
Location	Howstrake, Groudle Rd (E side of town off A11)
Hotel	★★★64% Sefton Hotel, Harris Promenade, DOUGLAS ☎(0624) 626011 80⇨🐾

PEEL   Map 06 SC28

Peel ☎(062484) 2227 or 3456
Moorland course, with natural hazards and easy walking. Good views. 11th hole is a par 4, dog-leg.
18 holes, 5914yds, Par 69, SSS 68, Course record 64.
Club membership 600.

Visitors	not before 10.30am weekends & bank holidays. Must have an introduction from own club.
Societies	must contact in advance.
Green Fees	£14 per day; £7 per round (£18 per day; £10 per round weekends & bank holidays).
Facilities	⊗ ⅲ by prior arrangement ⅼ ♀ ⌂ 🏠
Location	Rheast Ln (SE side of town centre on A1)
Hotel	★★★68% The Empress Hotel, Central Promenade, DOUGLAS ☎(0624) 661155 102⇨🐾

PORT ERIN   Map 06 SC16

Rowany ☎Isle of Man (0624) 834108 or 837072
Undulating seaside course with testing later holes.
18 holes, 5840yds, Par 70, SSS 69, Course record 69.
Club membership 600.

Visitors	must contact in advance and have an introduction from own club.
Societies	weekends only; must contact in advance.
Green Fees	£10 per day (£15 weekends & bank holidays).
Facilities	⊗ ⅲ by prior arrangement ⅼ ♀ ⌂ 🏠
Leisure	pool table, darts, putting green.
Location	Rowany Dr (N side of village off A32)
Hotel	★★★66% Castletown Golf Links Hotel, Fort Island, CASTLETOWN ☎(0624) 822201 58rm(44⇨12🐾)

RAMSEY   Map 06 SC49

Ramsey ☎(0624) 812244
Parkland course, with easy walking. Windy. Good views. Testing holes: 1st, par 5; 18th, par 3.
18 holes, 5657yds, Par 69, SSS 67.
Club membership 1000.

Visitors	restricted Tue mornings, Sat & Sun.
Societies	not Sat & Sun; must contact in writing.
Green Fees	Winter: £10 per day (£12 weekends); summer: £15 per day (£18 weekends).
Facilities	⊗ ⅲ (Thu-Sat only) ⅼ ♀ ⌂ 🏠 ♟ ⚐ Peter Lowrey.
Leisure	snooker.
Location	Brookfield (SW side of town)
Hotel	★★★★56% Grand Island Hotel, Bride Rd, RAMSEY ☎(0624) 812455 54⇨🐾

Each golf-course entry has a recommended AA-appointed hotel. For a wider choice of places to stay, consult *AA Hotels and Restaurants in Britain and Ireland* and *AA Inspected Bed and Breakfast in Britain and Ireland*

WALES

CLWYD

ABERGELE   Map 06 SH97

Abergele & Pensarn ☎(0745) 824034
A beautiful parkland course with views of the Irish Sea and
Gwyrch Castle. There are splendid finishing holes, a testing
par 5, 16th; a 185 yd, 17th to an elevated green, and a superb
par 5 18th with out of bounds just behind the green.
18 holes, 6520yds, Par 72, SSS 71, Course record 70.
Club membership 1200.

Visitors	restricted Tue.
Societies	must contact in writing.
Green Fees	not confirmed.
Facilities	⊗ ⋔ ⅃ ⬤ ♀ △ 🖼 (Iain R Runcie.
Location	Tan-y-Goppa Rd (.5m W off A547/A55)
Hotel	★★63% Kinmel Manor Hotel, St Georges Rd, ABERGELE ☎(0745) 832014 42⇥ ♠

BRYNFORD   Map 07 SJ17

Holywell ☎Holywell (0352) 710040
Exposed moorland course, with bracken and gorse flanking
undulating fairways. 720 ft above sea level.
18 holes, 6005yds, Par 70, SSS 70, Course record 70.
Club membership 450.

Visitors	with member only weekend & bank holidays.
Societies	must have handicaps, telephone in advance.
Green Fees	£8 per day (£12 weekends & bank holidays).
Facilities	⊗ & ⋔ by prior arrangement ⅃ ⬤ ♀ △ 🖼 (Martin Carty.
Leisure	snooker.
Location	Brynford (1.25m SW off B5121)
Hotel	★★67% Stamford Gate Hotel, Halkyn Rd, HOLYWELL ☎(0352) 712942 & 712968 12⇥ ♠

COLWYN BAY   Map 06 SH87

Old Colwyn ☎(0492) 515581
Hilly, meadowland course with sheep and cattle grazing on it
in parts.
9 holes, 5000yds, Par 68, SSS 66.
Club membership 300.

Visitors	no restrictions.
Societies	must contact in advance.
Facilities	♀ (WE) △
Location	Woodland Av, Old Colwyn (E side of town centre on B5383)
Hotel	★★69% Hopeside Hotel, Princes Dr, West End, COLWYN BAY ☎(0492) 533244 19⇥ ♠

DENBIGH   Map 06 SJ06

Denbigh ☎(0745) 814159
Parkland course, giving a testing and varied game. Good
views.
18 holes, 5581yds, Par 68, SSS 67, Course record 64.
Club membership 750.

Visitors	may not play before 9.30am weekdays or 10.30am weekends. Must contact in advance.
Societies	must telephone in advance.
Green Fees	£15 per day/round (£20 weekends).
Facilities	⊗ ⋔ ⅃ ⬤ ♀ △ 🖼 ⅂ (M D Jones.
Leisure	snooker.
Location	Henllan Rd (1.5m NW on B5382)
Hotel	★★63% Kinmel Manor Hotel, St Georges Rd, ABERGELE ☎(0745) 832014 42⇥ ♠

FLINT   Map 07 SJ27

Flint ☎(0352) 732327
Parkland course incorporating woods and streams. Excellent
views of Dee estuary.
9 holes, 5953yds, Par 69, SSS 69, Course record 65.
Club membership 430.

Visitors	with member only at weekends.
Societies	apply in advance.
Green Fees	£8 per day/round.
Facilities	⊗ & ⋔ by prior arrangement ⅃ ⬤ ♀ △ 🖼
Leisure	hard tennis courts, snooker.
Location	Cornist Park (1m W)
Hotel	★★★64% The Chequers Country House Hotel, Chester Rd, NORTHOP HALL ☎(0244) 816181 27⇥ ♠

HAWARDEN   Map 07 SJ36

Hawarden ☎(0244) 531447
Parkland course with comfortable walking and good views.
9 holes, 5630yds, Par 68, SSS 67, Course record 64.
Club membership 430.

Visitors	with member or by appointment. Must contact in advance and have an introduction from own club.
Societies	apply in writing.
Green Fees	£10 per round.
Facilities	⊗ ⋔ ⅃ ⬤ ♀ △ 🖼
Location	Groomsdale Ln (W side of town off B5125)
Hotel	★★★64% The Chequers Country House Hotel, Chester Rd, NORTHOP HALL ☎(0244) 816181 27⇥ ♠

LLANGOLLEN   Map 07 SJ24

Vale of Llangollen ☎(0978) 860040
Parkland course, set in superb scenery by the River Dee.
18 holes, 6661yds, Par 72, SSS 72, Course record 67.
Club membership 660.

Visitors	must contact in advance.
Societies	apply in writing.
Green Fees	£18 per day (£22 weekends & bank holidays).
Facilities	⊗ ⋔ ⅃ ⬤ ♀ △ 🖼 ⅂ (David Vaughan.
Location	Holyhead Rd (1.5m E on A5)
Hotel	★★★60% Bryn Howel Hotel & Restaurant, LLANGOLLEN ☎(0978) 860331 38⇥ ♠

This guide is updated annually – make sure that
you use the up-to-date edition

MOLD
Map 07 SJ26

Old Padeswood ☎Buckley (0244) 547401
Meadowland course, undulating in parts. Driving range.
18 holes, 6639yds, Par 72, SSS 72, Course record 69 or
6138yds, Par 72, SSS 70 or 5596yds, Par 73, SSS 73.
Club membership 600.

Visitors	must contact in advance and have an introduction from own club.
Societies	must contact in advance.
Green Fees	not confirmed.
Facilities	⊗ ⑪ by prior arrangement ⅃ ⬤ ♀ △ 🏠 🥢 Tony Davies.
Leisure	fishing, riding.
Location	Station Rd, Padeswood (3m SE off A5118)
Hotel	★★★64% The Chequers Country House Hotel, Chester Rd, NORTHOP HALL ☎(0244) 816181 27➪🐾

Padeswood & Buckley ☎(0244) 550537
Gently undulating parkland course, with natural hazards and good views of the Welsh hills.
18 holes, 5823yds, Par 68, SSS 68, Course record 66.
Club membership 600.

Visitors	Sat & Sun by arrangement.
Societies	must contact in advance.
Green Fees	£16 per round.
Facilities	⊗ ⑪ ⅃ ⬤ ♀ △ 🏠 🥢 🥢 David Ashton.
Location	The Caia, Station Ln (3m SE off A5118)
Hotel	★★★64% The Chequers Country House Hotel, Chester Rd, NORTHOP HALL ☎(0244) 816181 27➪🐾

PANTYMWYN
Map 07 SJ16

Mold ☎(0352) 740318
Meadowland course with some hard walking and natural hazards. Fine views.
18 holes, 5548yds, Par 67, SSS 67.
Club membership 600.

Visitors	may not play on captains day, or when county matches are held.
Societies	apply in writing.
Green Fees	£10 (£14 weekends).
Facilities	⊗ by prior arrangement ⑪ by prior arrangement ⅃ ⬤ ♀ △ 🏠 🥢 🥢 Martin Carty.
Location	E side of village
Hotel	★★★64% The Chequers Country House Hotel, Chester Rd, NORTHOP HALL ☎(0244) 816181 27➪🐾

PRESTATYN
Map 06 SJ08

Prestatyn ☎(0745) 854320
Very flat seaside links exposed to stiff breeze. Testing holes: 9th, par 4, bounded on 3 sides by water; 10th, par 4; 16th, par 4.
18 holes, 6792yds, Par 72, SSS 73, Course record 68.
Club membership 650.

Visitors	welcome except Sat & Tue mornings. Must contact in advance and have an introduction from own club.
Societies	must contact in advance.
Green Fees	£16 per day (£20 weekends & bank holidays).

Facilities	⊗ ⑪ ⅃ ⬤ ♀ △ 🏠 🥢 🥢 Malcolm Staton.
Leisure	snooker.
Location	Marine Rd East (.5m N off A548)
Hotel	★★63% Kinmel Manor Hotel, St Georges Rd, ABERGELE ☎(0745) 832014 42➪🐾

St Melyd ☎(0745) 854914
Parkland course with good views of mountains and Irish Sea. Testing 1st hole (423 yds) par 4. 18 tees.
9 holes, 5829yds, Par 68, SSS 68.
Club membership 400.

Visitors	welcome except for competitions days. Must have an introduction from own club.
Societies	must telephone in advance.
Green Fees	£16 (£20 weekends).
Facilities	⊗ & ⑪ (ex Tue) ⅃ ⬤ ♀ △ 🏠 🥢 Nigel H Lloyd.
Leisure	snooker.
Location	The Paddock, Meliden Rd (.5m S on A547)
Hotel	★★★62% Oriel House Hotel, Upper Denbigh Rd, ST ASAPH ☎(0745) 582716 19➪🐾

RHUDDLAN
Map 06 SJ07

Rhuddlan ☎(0745) 590217
Attractive, gently undulating parkland course with good views. Well bunkered with trees and water hazards.
18 holes, 6487yds, Par 71, SSS 71, Course record 67.
Club membership 953.

Visitors	must play with member on Sun. Must contact in advance and have an introduction from own club.
Societies	must contact in advance.
Green Fees	£18 per day (£25 Sat & bank holidays).
Facilities	⊗ ⑪ ⅃ ⬤ ♀ △ 🏠 🥢 🥢 Ian Worsley.
Leisure	snooker.
Location	Meliden Rd (E side of town on A547)
Hotel	★★★62% Oriel House Hotel, Upper Denbigh Rd, ST ASAPH ☎(0745) 582716 19➪🐾

RHYL
Map 06 SJ08

Rhyl ☎(0745) 353171
Seaside course.
9 holes, 3109yds, Par 35, SSS 35.
Club membership 350.

Visitors	restricted Sun in summer. Must contact in advance.
Societies	must contact in advance.
Green Fees	not confirmed.
Facilities	⊗ ⑪ ⅃ ⬤ (no catering Mon) ♀ (ex Mon) △ 🏠 🥢
Leisure	snooker.
Location	Coast Rd (1m E on A548)
Hotel	★★★62% Oriel House Hotel, Upper Denbigh Rd, ST ASAPH ☎(0745) 582716 19➪🐾

RUTHIN
Map 06 SJ15

Ruthin-Pwllglas ☎(08242) 4658
Hilly parkland course in elevated position with panoramic views. Stiff climb to 3rd and 9th holes.
10 holes, 5362yds, Par 66, SSS 66, Course record 64.
Club membership 380.

Visitors welcome except for competition days.
Societies contact in advance.
Green Fees not confirmed.
Facilities ☖
Location Pwllglas (2.5m S off A494)
Hotel ★★★63% Ruthin Castle, RUTHIN ☎(08242) 2664 58⇨♄

WREXHAM   Map 07 SJ35

Wrexham ☎(0978) 261033
Inland, sandy course with easy walking. Testing dog-legged 7th hole (par 4), and short 14th hole (par 3) with full carry to green.
18 holes, 6078yds, Par 70, SSS 69, Course record 66.
Club membership 650.
Visitors may not play competition days. Must contact in advance and have an introduction from own club.
Societies welcome except for Tue, Wed & weekends.
Green Fees not confirmed.
Facilities ⊗ ⦀ ⓛ ▨ ♀ ☖ 🖼 ⱡ David Larvin.
Leisure snooker.
Location Holt Rd (1.75m NE on A534)
Hotel ★★★63% Wynnstay Arms, High Street/Yorke St, WREXHAM ☎(0978) 291010 75⇨♄

DYFED

ABERYSTWYTH   Map 06 SN58

Aberystwyth ☎(0970) 615104
Undulating meadowland course. Testing holes: 16th (The Loop) par 3; 17th, par 4; 18th, par 3. Good views over Cardigan Bay.
18 holes, 5835yds, Par 68, SSS 68, Course record 63.
Club membership 400.
Visitors must contact in advance at weekends & bank holidays. Must have an introduction from own club.
Societies must contact in advance.
Green Fees not confirmed.
Facilities ⊗ ⦀ ⓛ ▨ ♀ ☖ 🖼 ⱡ Graeme Brownlie.
Location Brynymor Rd (N side of town)
Hotel ★★64% Belle Vue Royal Hotel, Marine Ter, ABERYSTWYTH ☎(0970) 617558 37rm(30⇨♄)

BORTH   Map 06 SN69

Borth & Ynslas ☎(0970) 871202
Seaside links, over 100 years old, with strong winds at times. Some narrow fairways.
18 holes, 6116yds, Par 69, SSS 70, Course record 65.
Club membership 200.
Visitors may not play before 10am or between 1-2.30pm at weekends. Must have an introduction from own club.
Societies apply in writing or telephone (0970) 871325.
Green Fees £12 per day (£15 weekends).
Facilities ⊗ ⦀ ⓛ ▨ ♀ ☖ 🖼 ⱡ J G Lewis.
Location .5m N on B4353

Hotel ★★63% Four Seasons Hotel, 50-54 Portland St, ABERYSTWYTH ☎(0970) 612120 14rm(11⇨♄)

BURRY PORT   Map 02 SN40

Ashburnham ☎(05546) 2269
This course has a lot of variety. In the main it is of the seaside type although the holes in front of the clubhouse are of an inland character. They are, however, good holes which make a very interesting finish. Course record holder, Sam Torrance.
18 holes, 6916yds, Par 72, SSS 73, Course record 67.
Club membership 750.

SCORECARD: Championship Tees					
Hole	Yds	Par	Hole	Yds	Par
1	188	3	10	553	5
2	447	4	11	434	4
3	325	4	12	372	4
4	401	4	13	140	3
5	496	5	14	556	5
6	189	3	15	471	4
7	389	4	16	169	3
8	536	5	17	435	4
9	438	4	18	377	4
Out	3409	36	In	3507	36
			Totals	6916	72

Visitors special times available. Must contact in advance and have an introduction from own club.
Societies apply in writing.
Green Fees £22 per day; £17 per round (£28/£22 weekends).
Facilities ⊗ ⦀ ⓛ ▨ ♀ ☖ 🖼 ⱡ Robert Ryder.
Leisure pool table.
Location Cliffe Ter (W side of town on B4311)
Hotel ★★★61% Diplomat Hotel, Felinfoel, LLANELLI ☎(0554) 756156 23⇨♄ Annexe8⇨♄

CARDIGAN   Map 02 SN14

Cardigan ☎(0239) 612035
A links course, very dry in winter, with wide fairways, light rough and gorse. Every hole overlooks the sea.
18 holes, 6641yds, Par 72, SSS 72, Course record 67.
Club membership 500.
Visitors may not play between 1-2pm. Must have an introduction from own club.
Societies must telephone in advance.
Green Fees £15 per day (£18 weekends).
Facilities ⊗ ⦀ ⓛ ▨ ♀ ☖ 🖼 ⱡ Colin Parsons.
Leisure squash.
Location Gwbert-on Sea (3m N off B4548)
Hotel ★★★55% Cliff Hotel, GWBERT ☎(0239) 613241 75⇨♄

CARMARTHEN   Map 02 SN42

Carmarthen ☎(026787) 493
Hilltop course with good views.
18 holes, 6210yds, Par 71, SSS 71.
Club membership 750.
Visitors no restrictions.
Societies must contact in advance.
Green Fees £15 per day (£20 weekends).
Facilities ⊗ & ⦀ (ex Wed, order before play) ⓛ ▨ ♀ ☖ ⱡ P Gillis.
Location Blaenycoed Rd (4m NW)
Hotel ★★★63% The Ivy Bush Royal, Spilman St, CARMARTHEN ☎(0267) 235111 78⇨♄

HAVERFORDWEST — Map 02 SM91

Haverfordwest ☎(0437) 764523
Parkland course in attractive surroundings.
18 holes, 6005yds, Par 70, SSS 69.
Club membership 720.

Visitors	must contact in advance.
Societies	must telephone in advance.
Green Fees	£15 per day (£20 weekends).
Facilities	⊗ ⅢⅢ by prior arrangement ⤦ 🍺 ♀ ⚲ 🏠 ♛ ✆ Alex Pile.
Location	Arnolds Down (1m E on A40)
Hotel	★★55% Mariners Inn, NOLTON HAVEN ☎(0437) 710469 14⇨♙

LLANDYBIE — Map 02 SN61

Glynhir ☎(0269) 850472
Parkland course with good views, latter holes close to Upper Loughor River. The 14th is a 394-yd dog leg.
18 holes, 6090yds, Par 69, SSS 69, Course record 67.
Club membership 450.

Visitors	with member only weekends. Must contact in advance and have an introduction from own club.
Societies	welcome weekdays only, must telephone in advance.
Green Fees	£12 per day (£16 weekends & bank holidays).
Facilities	⊗ (ex Mon) ⅢⅢ by prior arrangement ⤦ 🍺 ♀ 🏠 ♛ ⤧ ✆ Ian Roberts.
Location	Glynhir Rd (2m NE)
Hotel	★★67% Mill at Glynhir, Glyn-Hir, Llandybie, AMMANFORD ☎(0269) 850672 9⇨Annexe2⇨♙

LLANGYBI — Map 02 SN65

Cilgwyn ☎(0570) 45286
Picturesque parkland course in secluded valley, with natural hazards of ponds, stream and woodland.
9 holes, 5327yds, Par 68, SSS 67, Course record 67.
Club membership 150.

Societies	must telephone in advance.
Green Fees	£12 per day; £8 per round (£10 per round weekends).
Facilities	Catering by arrangement ♀ ♛
Location	.5m NW off A485
Hotel	★★★66% Falcondale Country House Hotel, LAMPETER ☎(0570) 422910 19⇨♙

LLANRHYSTUD — Map 06 SN56

Penrhos Golf & Country Club ☎Llanon (0974) 202999
Beautifully scenic course incorporating five lakes and spectacular coastal and inland views. Many leisure facilities.
18 holes, 6578yds, Par 72, SSS 71.
Club membership 300.

Visitors	must contact in advance and have an introduction from own club.
Societies	apply in writing.
Green Fees	£15 per day; £11 per round (£20/£16 weekends & bank holidays).
Facilities	⊗ ⅢⅢ ⤦ 🍺 ♀ ⚲ 🏠 ⤧ ✆ Paul Diamond.
Leisure	hard tennis courts, heated indoor swimming pool, fishing, sauna, solarium, gymnasium, bowls, shooting.
Location	.5m SE on B4337
Hotel	★★★66% Conrah Hotel, Ffosrhydygaled, Chancery, ABERYSTWYTH ☎(0970) 617941 11rm(9⇨)Annexe9⇨♙

MILFORD HAVEN — Map 02 SM90

Milford Haven ☎(0646) 692368
Parkland course with excellent greens and views of the Milford Haven waterway.
18 holes, 6030yds, Par 71, SSS 70.
Club membership 400.

Visitors	no restrictions.
Societies	telephone to book.
Green Fees	not confirmed.
Facilities	⊗ & ⅢⅢ (tel (0646) 690600 to book) ⤦ 🍺 ♀ ⚲ 🏠 ♛
Location	Woodbine House, Hubberstone (1.5m W)
Hotel	★★60% Lord Nelson Hotel, Hamilton Ter, MILFORD HAVEN ☎(0646) 695341 32⇨♙

NEWPORT — Map 02 SN03

Newport (Pemb) ☎(0239) 820244
Seaside links course, with easy walking and good views of the Prescelly Hills and Newport Bay.
9 holes, 5815yds, Par 70, SSS 69, Course record 68.
Club membership 220.

Visitors	no restrictions.
Societies	must telephone in advance.
Green Fees	£8 per day.
Facilities	⊗ ⅢⅢ ⤦ 🍺 ♀ ⚲ 🏠 ♛ ⤧ ✆ Colin Parsons.
Location	The Golf Club (1.25m N)
Hotel	★★63% Cartref Hotel, 15-19 High St, FISHGUARD ☎(0348) 872430 12rm(10⇨♙)

PEMBROKE DOCK — Map 02 SM90

South Pembrokeshire ☎(0646) 683817
Parkland course overlooking the Cleddau River.
9 holes, 5804yds, Par 70, SSS 69.
Club membership 350.

Visitors	must contact in advance.
Societies	apply in writing.
Green Fees	£8 per day.
Facilities	⊗ ⅢⅢ ⤦ 🍺 (catering by arrangement) ♀ ⚲
Location	Defensible Barracks (SW side of town centre off B4322)
Hotel	★★58% Old Kings Arms, Main St, PEMBROKE ☎(0646) 683611 21⇨

ST DAVID'S — Map 02 SM72

St David's City ☎Croesgoch (0437) 831607
Links course with alternative tees for 18 holes. Panoramic views of St David's Head and Ramsey Island.
9 holes, 5961yds, Par 70, SSS 70, Course record 67.
Club membership 200.

Visitors	welcome. No sharing of golf bags.
Societies	must telephone in advance.
Green Fees	£10 per round.

Facilities	🏌 ⛳
Hotel	★★★⚑64% Warpool Court Hotel, ST DAVID'S ☎(0437) 720300 25🛏🐾

TENBY   Map 02 SN10

Tenby ☎(0834) 2978
A fine old seaside links, with sea views and natural
hazards providing good golf.
18 holes, 6232yds, Par 69, SSS 71.
Club membership 650.

Visitors	subject to competition & tee reservation. Must produce handicap certificate.
Societies	must telephone in advance.
Green Fees	£18 per day (£22.50 weekends & bank holidays).
Facilities	⛳
Leisure	snooker.
Location	The Burrows
Hotel	★★71% Atlantic Hotel, Esplanade, TENBY ☎(0834) 2881 & 4176 36🛏🐾

GWENT

ABERGAVENNY   Map 03 SO21

Monmouthshire ☎(0873) 853171
This parkland course is very picturesque, with the
beautifully wooded River Usk running alongside. There
are a number of par 3 holes and a testing par 4 at the 15th.
18 holes, 5961yds, Par 72, SSS 69.
Club membership 700.

Visitors	must play with member at weekends. Must contact in advance and have an introduction from own club.
Societies	must contact in writing.
Green Fees	£20 per day (£25 weekends & bank holidays).
Facilities	⊗ ⊪ 🏌 ⛳ ⚑ ⛳ 🛒 ↑ ⛳ P Worthing.
Leisure	fishing.
Location	Gypsy Ln, LLanfoist (2m S off B4269)
Hotel	★★★★68% Craigendarroch Hotel & Country Club, Braemar Rd, BALLATER ☎(03397) 55858 50🛏🐾

BETTWS NEWYDD   Map 03 SO30

Alice Springs ☎Nantyderry (0873) 880772
Undulating parkland course with magnificent views of the
Usk Valley. Testing 7th and 15th holes. The 6,500-yard
King's Course is due to open in the summer of 1992.
18 holes, 6041yds, Par 67, SSS 69.

Visitors	no restriction, but telephone for weekends.
Societies	telephone in advance.
Green Fees	£12.50 per 18 holes.
Facilities	⊗ & ⊪ by arrangement 🏌 ⚑ ⛳ (all day) ⛳ 🛒 ⛳ T Morgan
Hotel	★★72% Glen-yr-Afon, Pontypool Rd, USK ☎(02913) 2302 10🛏 5🐾

This guide is updated annually – make sure that
you use the up-to-date edition

BLACKWOOD   Map 03 ST19

Blackwood ☎(0495) 223152
Heathland course with sand bunkers. Undulating, with hard
walking. Testing 2nd hole par 4. Good views.
9 holes, 5304yds, Par 66, SSS 66.
Club membership 250.

Visitors	must play with member at weekends & bank holidays. Must contact in advance and have an introduction from own club.
Societies	may not play weekends & bank holidays.
Green Fees	not confirmed.
Facilities	🏌 ⛳ ⛳
Location	Cwmgelli (.75m N off A4048)
Hotel	★★★56% Maes Manor Hotel, BLACKWOOD ☎(0495) 224551 & 220011 8🛏Annexe14🛏

CAERWENT   Map 03 ST49

Dewstow ☎Caldicot (0291) 430444
A newly-established, picturesque parkland course with
spectacular views over the Severn estuary towards Bristol.
Testing holes include the par 3 7th, which is approached over
water, some 50 feet lower than the tee. There is also a 26-bay
floodlit driving range.
18 holes, 6100yds, Par 72, SSS 70, Course record 74.
Club membership 500.

Visitors	may book two days in advance.
Societies	apply in writing or telephone secretary.
Green Fees	£10 per round (£12-£13 weekends & bank holidays).
Facilities	⊗ ⊪ 🏌 ⚑ ⛳ ⛳ 🛒 ↑ ⛳ Mark Kedward.

►

Location	.5m S of A48 at Caerwent
Hotel	★★★69% St Pierre Hotel, Golf & Country Club, St Pierre Park, CHEPSTOW ☎(0291) 625261 106⇔📺♪Annexe41⇔📺♪

CHEPSTOW

Map 03 ST59

St Pierre Hotel Golf and Country Club ☎(0291) 625261

Parkland/meadowland championship course. The Old is home to the Epson Grand Prix of Europe, and is one of Britain's major courses. Its long par 5, 12th hole of 545 yds, tests even the finest golfers. Accommodation and a wide range of sports and leisure facilities.

	SCORECARD: Old Course (White Tees)				
Hole	Yds	Par	Hole	Yds	Par
1	576	5	10	362	4
2	388	4	11	393	4
3	135	3	12	545	5
4	379	4	13	219	3
5	420	4	14	521	5
6	165	3	15	375	4
7	442	4	16	426	4
8	309	4	17	412	4
9	444	4	18	237	3
Out	3258	35	In	3490	36
			Totals	6748	71

Old Course: 18 holes, 6700yds, Par 71, SSS 73, Course record 63.
Mathern Course: 18 holes, 5762yds, Par 68, SSS 68, Course record 65.
Club membership 900.

Visitors	must have a handicap certificate. Must contact in advance.
Societies	must make an advance reservation.
Green Fees	Old: from £35 per round; Mathern: from £20 per round.
Facilities	⊗ ⅏ 🛒 (weekends only) 💺 ♀ ⛳ 📷 ⚑ ♨ ⚑ ✆ Renton Doig.
Leisure	hard tennis courts, heated indoor swimming pool, squash, snooker, sauna, gymnasium, badminton, jacuzzi, crown bowling, croquet.
Location	St Pierre Park (3m SW off A48)
Hotel	★★★69% St Pierre Hotel, Golf & Country Club, St Pierre Park, CHEPSTOW ☎(0291) 625261 106⇔📺♪Annexe41⇔📺♪

CWMBRAN

Map 03 ST29

Pontnewydd ☎(06333) 2170
Mountainside course, with hard walking. Good views across the Severn Estuary.
10 holes, 5353yds, Par 68, SSS 67, Course record 63.
Club membership 250.

Visitors	must play with member weekends & bank holidays.
Green Fees	not confirmed.
Facilities	♀ ⛳
Location	Maesgwyn Farm, West Pontnewydd (N side of town centre)
Hotel	★★58% Priory Hotel, High St, Caerleon, NEWPORT ☎(0633) 421241 16⇔📺♪Annexe5⇔📺♪

LLANWERN

Map 03 ST38

Llanwern ☎(0633) 412029
Two parkland courses.
New Course: 18 holes, 6115yds, Par 70, SSS 69, Course record 65.
Old Course: 9 holes, 5237yds, Par 67, SSS 67, Course record 66.
Club membership 850.

Visitors	must be a member of a recognised golf club. Must have an introduction from own club.
Societies	must contact in writing.
Green Fees	£25 per 18 holes; £20 per 9 holes (£30 for 18 holes weekends).
Facilities	⊗ ⅏ 🛒 💺 ♀ ⛳ 📷 ✆ Stephen Price.
Leisure	snooker.
Location	Tennyson Av (.5m S off A455)
Hotel	★★64% New Inn Hotel, LANGSTONE ☎(0633) 412426 34⇔📺♪

MONMOUTH

Map 03 SO51

Monmouth ☎(0600) 712212
Parkland course in scenic setting. High, undulating land with good views. Testing 1st and 4th holes.
9 holes, 5523yds, Par 68, SSS 66, Course record 62.
Club membership 425.

Visitors	may only play with member at weekends, but not before 11.15am on Sun.
Societies	Mon-Fri only. Must telephone (0594) 33394 in advance.
Green Fees	£10 per day.
Facilities	⊗ ⅏ 🛒 💺 (catering Mon-Fri only) ♀ (Mon-Fri only) ⛳ 📷
Location	Leasebrook Ln (1.5m NE off A40)
Hotel	★★★61% Kings Head Hotel, Agincourt Square, MONMOUTH ☎(0600) 712177 29rm(27⇔📺♪)

Rolls of Monmouth ☎(0600) 715353
A hilly and challenging parkland course encompassing several lakes and ponds and surrounded by woodland. Set within a beautiful private estate complete with listed mansion.
18 holes, 6723yds, Par 72, SSS 72, Course record 68.
Club membership 220.

Visitors	may not play on open days. Must contact in advance.
Societies	must contact in advance.
Green Fees	£25 per day (£30 weekends & bank holidays).
Facilities	⊗ ⅏ 🛒 💺 ♀ ⛳ 📷 ♨
Location	The Hendre (4m W on B4233)
Hotel	★★★61% Kings Head Hotel, Agincourt Square, MONMOUTH ☎(0600) 712177 29rm(27⇔📺♪)

NANTYGLO

Map 03 SO11

West Monmouthshire ☎(0495) 310233
Mountain and heathland course with picturesque views, hard walking and natural hazards. Testing 3rd hole, par 5, and 7th hole, par 4.
18 holes, 6118yds, Par 71, SSS 69, Course record 65.
Club membership 700.

Visitors	no restrictions.
Societies	must telephone 1 week in advance.
Green Fees	£8 weekdays & bank holidays (£10-£15 weekends).
Facilities	⊗ ⅏ 🛒 💺 ♀ ⛳
Location	Pond Rd (.25m W off A467)
Hotel	★★★58% Angel Hotel, Cross St, ABERGAVENNY ☎(0873) 7121 due to change to 857121 29⇔📺♪

NEWPORT
Map 03 ST38

Newport ☎(0633) 896794 & 892643
An undulating parkland course, part-wooded. The 2nd hole is surrounded by bunkers - a difficult hole. The 11th hole is a bogey 4 and the fairway runs through an avenue of trees, making a straight drive preferable. Set 300ft above sea level, it offers fine views.
18 holes, 6431yds, Par 72, SSS 71, Course record 64.
Club membership 700.

SCORECARD: White Tees					
Hole	Yds	Par	Hole	Yds	Par
1	328	4	10	397	4
2	144	3	11	377	4
3	463	4	12	486	5
4	479	5	13	429	4
5	513	5	14	170	3
6	178	3	15	364	4
7	482	5	16	179	3
8	229	3	17	392	4
9	344	4	18	477	5
Out	3160	36	In	3271	36
			Totals	6431	72

Visitors   must contact in advance and have an introduction from own club.
Societies   must contact in writing.
Green Fees   £25 per round; £40 per day.
Facilities   ⊗ ⽊ ⽢ ⬛ ♀ △ 🖾 ⟨ R F Skuse.
Location   Great Oak, Rogerstone (3m NW of city centre off B4591)
Hotel   ★★★★63% Celtic Manor Hotel, Coldra Woods, NEWPORT ☎(0633) 413000 73⇥🌂

Tredegar Park ☎(0633) 895219
A parkland course with River Ebbw and streams as natural hazards. The ground is very flat with narrow fairways and small greens. The 17th hole (par 3) is played on to a plateau where many players spoil their medal round.
18 holes, 6095ydss, Par 71, SSS 70, Course record 67.
Club membership 800.
Visitors   must be a member of a recognised golf club. Must contact in advance and have an introduction from own club.
Societies   must contact in advance.
Green Fees   £16 per day (£22 weekends & bank holidays).
Facilities   ⊗ ⽊ ⽢ ⬛ ♀ △ 🖾 ⍦ ⟨ Mervyn Morgan.
Leisure   snooker.
Location   Bassaleg Rd (2m SW off A467 exit 276 of M4)
Hotel   ★★★67% Kings Hotel, High St, NEWPORT ☎(0633) 842020 47⇥🌂

PONTYPOOL
Map 03 SO20

Pontypool ☎(0495) 763655
Undulating, mountain course with magnificent views.
18 holes, 6046yds, Par 69, SSS 69.
Club membership 600.
Visitors   must have a handicap certificate. Must contact in advance and have an introduction from own club.
Societies   must contact secretary in advance.
Green Fees   £13.50 per day (£18 weekends & bank holidays).
Facilities   ⊗ ⽊ ⽢ ⬛ ♀ △ 🖾 ⍦ ⟨ Jim Howard.
Leisure   snooker, pratice area.
Location   Trevethin (1.5m N off A4043)
Hotel   ★★72% Glen-yr-Afon Hotel, Pontypool Rd, USK ☎(02913) 2302 & 3202 16rm(10⇥5🌂)

TREDEGAR
Map 03 SO10

Tredegar and Rhymney ☎Rhymney (0685) 840743
Mountain course with lovely views.
9 holes, 5504yds, Par 68.
Club membership 194.
Visitors   no restrictions.
Societies   must contact in writing.
Green Fees   £10 per day (£12.50 weekends).
Facilities   ⽊ by prior arrangement ⽢ ♀ △
Location   Cwmtysswg, Rhymney (1.75m SW on B4256)
Hotel   ★★67% Tregenna Hotel, Park Ter, MERTHYR TYDFIL ☎(0685) 723627 & 82055 14⇥🌂Annexe7⇥🌂

GWYNEDD

ABERDOVEY
Map 06 SN69

Aberdovey ☎(0654) 767210
A beautiful championship course at the mouth of the Dovey estuary, Aberdovey has all the true characteristics of a seaside links. It has some fine holes among them the 3rd, the 12th, an especially good short hole, and the 15th. There are some striking views to be had from the course.
18 holes, 6445yds, Par 71, SSS 71, Course record 67.
Club membership 750.
Visitors   members have priority between 8-10pm & 12.30-2pm. Must have an introduction from own club.
Societies   apply in writing to the secretary.
Green Fees   £30 per day; £18 per round.
Facilities   ⊗ ⽊ by prior arrangement ⽢ ⬛ ♀ △ 🖾 ⟨ John Davies.
Leisure   snooker.
Location   .5m W on A493
Hotel   ★★★65% Trefeddian Hotel, ABERDOVEY ☎(0654) 767213 46rm(37⇥5🌂)

ABERSOCH
Map 06 SH32

Abersoch ☎(075881) 2622
Seaside links, with five parkland holes.
18 holes, 5994yds, Par 69, SSS 69.
Club membership 500.
Visitors   no restrictions.
Societies   must apply in writing.
Green Fees   not confirmed.
Facilities   ⊗ ⽊ ⽢ ⬛ ♀ △ 🖾
Location   S side of village
Hotel   ★★★63% Abersoch Harbour Hotel, ABERSOCH ☎(075881) 2406 & 3632 9⇥🌂Annexe5⇥🌂

AMLWCH
Map 06 SH49

Bull Bay ☎(0407) 830960
Pleasant seaside course with natural meadow, rock, gorse and wind hazards. Views from all tees across Irish Sea to Isle of Man.
18 holes, 6132yds, Par 70, SSS 70.
Club membership 800.

▶

Visitors	must have handicap certificate at weekends.
Societies	apply in writing.
Green Fees	£12 per day (£18 weekends & bank holidays).
Facilities	⊗ ⅲ by prior arrangement 🏌 ⚑ ♀ ⛳ 🏠 (Neil Dunroe.
Location	1m NW on A5025
Hotel	★★59% Trecastell Hotel, Bull Bay, AMLWCH ☎(0407) 830651 12rm(8⇨3🐾)

BALA   Map 06 SH93

Bala ☎(0678) 520359
Mountainous course with natural hazards.
10 holes, 5980yds, Par 66, SSS 64, Course record 64.
Club membership 250.

Visitors	must telephone for bank holidays.
Societies	must telephone in advance.
Green Fees	£10 per day.
Facilities	♀ ⛳ 🏠
Leisure	snooker.
Location	Penlan (.5m SW off A494)
Hotel	★★57% Plas Coch Hotel, High St, BALA ☎(0678) 520309 10⇨🐾

BANGOR   Map 06 SH57

St Deiniol ☎(0248) 353098
Elevated parkland course with panoramic views of
Snowdonia, Menai Straits and Anglesey.
18 holes, 5068mtrs, Par 68, SSS 67, Course record 63.
Club membership 500.

Visitors	restricted weekends.
Societies	must contact in writing.
Green Fees	not confirmed.
Facilities	⊗ ⅲ 🏌 ⚑ (no catering Mon) ♀ ⛳ 🏠 (Paul Lovell.
Leisure	snooker.
Location	Penybryn (E side of town centre off A5122)
Hotel	★★73% Menai Court Hotel, Craig y Don Rd, BANGOR ☎(0248) 354200 12⇨🐾

BEAUMARIS   Map 06 SH67

Baron Hill ☎(0286) 810231
Undulating course with natural hazards of rock and gorse.
Testing 3rd and 4th holes (par 4's).
9 holes, 5062mtrs, Par 68, SSS 67, Course record 65.
Club membership 400.

Visitors	no restrictions.
Societies	apply in writing.
Green Fees	£10 per day.
Facilities	⛳
Location	1m SW off A545
Hotel	★★66% Bishopsgate House Hotel, 54 Castle St, BEAUMARIS ☎(0248) 810302 10⇨🐾

BETWS-Y-COED   Map 06 SH75

Betws-y-Coed ☎(06902) 556
Attractive parkland course set between two rivers in
Snowdonia National Park.
9 holes, 4996yds, Par 64, SSS 64, Course record 63.
Club membership 350.

Visitors	no restrictions.

Societies	welcome.
Green Fees	£10 (£15 weekends).
Facilities	⊗ ⅲ 🏌 ⚑ ♀
Location	NE side of village off A5
Hotel	★★★66% Royal Oak, Holyhead Rd, BETWS-Y-COED ☎(0690) 710219 27⇨🐾

CAERNARFON   Map 06 SH46

Caernarfon ☎(0286) 3783
Parkland course with gentle gradients.
18 holes, 5870yds, Par 69, SSS 69.
Club membership 700.

Visitors	may not play competition days.
Societies	must apply in advance.
Green Fees	£17 per day; £15 per round.
Facilities	⊗ ⅲ 🏌 ⚑ ♀
Location	Llanfaglan (1.75m SW)
Hotel	★★65% Stables Hotel, LLANWNDA ☎(0286) 830711 & 830935 Annexe14⇨🐾
Additional hotel	★★★77% Seiont Manor Hotel, Llanrug, CAERNARFON ☎(0286) 673366 28⇨🐾

CONWY   Map 06 SH77

Conwy (Caernarvonshire) ☎Aberconwy (0492) 593400
This course close by the old town of Conwy is a real
seaside links with gorse, rushes, sandhills and fine old
turf. There are plenty of natural hazards, the gorse
providing more than its share. The course has a
spectacular setting between sea and mountains.
18 holes, 6901yds, Par 72, SSS 73, Course record 70.
Club membership 960.

Visitors	must have a certified club handicap. Restricted weekends & competitions.
Societies	must contact in advance.
Green Fees	£18 per day (£23 weekends & bank holidays).
Facilities	⊗ (ex Tue) ⅲ (ex Mon and Tue) 🏌 (ex Tue) ⚑ ♀ ⛳ 🏠 (Peter Lees.
Location	The Morfa (1m W of town centre on A55)
Hotel	★★66% Bryn Cregin Garden Hotel, Ty Mawr Rd, DEGANWY ☎(0492) 585266 16⇨🐾

CRICCIETH   Map 06 SH43

Criccieth ☎(0766) 522154
Hilly course on Lleyn Peninsula. Good views.
18 holes, 5787yds, Par 69, SSS 68, Course record 65.
Club membership 234.

Visitors	no restrictions.
Societies	no restrictions.
Green Fees	£8 (£10 weekends).
Facilities	⊗ ⅲ 🏌 ⚑ ♀ ⛳ 🏠
Location	Ednyfed Hill (1m NE)
Hotel	★★57% George IV Hotel, CRICCIETH ☎(0766) 522168 & 522603 34⇨🐾

Opening times of bar and catering facilities
vary from place to place. Please remember
to check in advance of your visit

DOLGELLAU   Map 06 SH71

Dolgellau ☎(0341) 422603
Undulating parkland course. Good views of mountains and Mawddach estuary.
9 holes, 4671yds, Par 66, SSS 63.
Club membership 280.

Visitors	may not play on Sat.
Societies	must contact in advance.
Green Fees	not confirmed.
Facilities	⊗ ℿ ⅃ (ex Tue) ⅃ ♣ ♀ △ ☎ ♈
Location	Pencefn Rd (.5m N)
Hotel	★★63% Royal Ship Hotel, Queens Square, DOLGELLAU ☎(0341) 422209 24rm(13⇨3♠)

FFESTINIOG   Map 06 SH74

Ffestiniog ☎(076676) 2637
Moorland course set in Snowdonia National Park.
9 holes, 4570yds, Par 68, SSS 66, Course record 77.
Club membership 150.

Visitors	welcome except during competitions.
Societies	must telephone in advance.
Green Fees	not confirmed.
Facilities	△
Location	Y Cefn (1m E on B4391)
Hotel	★★(red)⚑ Maes y Neuadd Hotel, TALSARNAU ☎(0766) 780200 12⇨♠Annexe4⇨♠

HARLECH   Map 06 SH53

Royal St Davids ☎(0766) 780361
Championship links, with easy walking and natural hazards.
18 holes, 6427yds, Par 69, SSS 71, Course record 64.
Club membership 750.

Visitors	must contact in advance and have an introduction from own club.
Societies	apply in writing.
Green Fees	£20 per day (£25 weekends & bank holidays).
Facilities	⊗ ℿ ⅃ ♣ ♀ △ ☎ (John Barnett.
Location	W side of town on A496
Hotel	★★62% Ty Mawr Hotel, LLANBEDR ☎(034123) 440 10⇨♠

HOLYHEAD   Map 06 SH28

Holyhead ☎(0407) 763279
Treeless, undulating seaside course which provides a varied and testing game, particularly in a south wind. The fairways are bordered by gorse, heather and rugged outcrops of rock. Accuracy from most tees is paramount as there are 43 fairway and greenside bunkers and lakes. Designed by James Braid. Indoor driving range.
18 holes, 6056yds, Par 70, SSS 70, Course record 64.
Club membership 1309.

Visitors	must have handicap certificate. Must contact in advance.
Societies	must telephone in advance.
Green Fees	£14.50 per day (£16.50 weekends & bank holidays).
Facilities	⊗ ℿ ⅃ ♣ ♀ △ ☎ ⊨ (Paul Capper.
Leisure	snooker.

Location	Trearddur Bay (1.25m S on B4545)
Hotel	★★★62% Trearddur Bay Hotel, TREARDDUR BAY ☎(0407) 860301 27rm(20⇨)

LLANDUDNO   Map 06 SH78

Llandudno (Maesdu) ☎(0492) 76450
Part links, part parkland, this championship course starts and finishes on one side of the main road, the remaining holes, more seaside in nature, being played on the other side. The holes are pleasantly undulating and present a pretty picture when the gorse is in bloom. Often windy, this varied and testing course is not for beginners.
18 holes, 6513yds, Par 73, SSS 72.
Club membership 700.

Visitors	welcome although some times are restricted. Must be member of a club with handicap certificate.
Societies	must apply in advance, must be members of a recognised golf club.
Green Fees	£17 per day (£21 weekends & bank holidays).
Facilities	⊗ ℿ ⅃ ♣ ♀ △ ☎ ♈ (Simon Boulden.
Leisure	snooker.
Location	Hospital Rd (S side of town centre on A546)
Hotel	★★★68% Imperial Hotel, The Promenade, LLANDUDNO ☎(0492) 877466 100⇨♠
Additional hotel	★★★61% Risboro Hotel, Clement Av, LLANDUDNO ☎(0492) 876343 65⇨♠

See advertisement on page 239

Nestling within 150 acres of grounds, complete with salmon river, lake and leisure complex, the Seiont Manor provides that unique blend of country house hospitality and service.

Complimentary tickets are available to residents for the nearby Caernarfon Golf Course and the local driving range adjacent to the hotel.

The Seiont Manor Hotel, Llanrug, Caernarfon, Gwynedd, LL55 2AQ
Tel: (0286) 673366 Fax: (0286) 2840

North Wales ☎(0492) 875325
Challenging seaside links with superb views of Anglesey and Snowdonia.
18 holes, 6132yds, Par 71, SSS 69, Course record 65.
Club membership 750.

Visitors	welcome, some times are restricted weekdays. Must contact in advance and have an introduction from own club.
Societies	must telephone in advance.
Green Fees	£17 per day (£22 weekends & bank holidays).
Facilities	⊗ ⅲ by prior arrangement ⮑ 🍺 ⛳ ⛳ 🏠 ⚐ 🥾 Richard Bradbury.
Leisure	snooker.
Location	72 Bryniau Rd, West Shore (W side of town on A546)
Hotel	★★(red) St Tudno Hotel, Promenade, LLANDUDNO ☎(0492) 874411 21⇒🐾

Rhos-on-Sea ☎Colwyn Bay (0492) 549641
Seaside course, with easy walking and panoramic views.
18 holes, 6064yds, Par 69, SSS 69, Course record 68.
Club membership 400.

Visitors	must contact in advance.
Societies	booking essential, telephone in advance.
Green Fees	£11 per day (£15 weekends).
Facilities	⊗ & ⅲ by prior arrangement ⮑ 🍺 ⛳ ⛳ 🏠 🛏 🥾 Mike Greenough.
Leisure	snooker.
Location	Penrhyn Bay (.5m W off A546)
Hotel	★★★64% Gogarth Abbey Hotel, West Shore, LLANDUDNO ☎(0492) 876211 40⇒🐾

LLANFAIRFECHAN   Map 06 SH67

Llanfairfechan ☎(0248) 680144
Hillside course with panoramic views of coast.
9 holes, 3119yds, Par 54, SSS 57, Course record 53.
Club membership 350.

Visitors	no restrictions.
Societies	apply in writing to the secretary.
Green Fees	£7 per day (£11 weekends).
Facilities	⛳ (7.30pm-11pm weekdays) 🏠
Location	Fford Llannerch (W side of town on A55)
Hotel	★★★65% Sychnant Pass Hotel, Sychnant Pass Rd, CONWY ☎(0492) 596868 & 596869 13⇒🐾

LLANGEFNI (ANGLESEY)   Map 06 SH47

Llangefni (Public) ☎(0248) 722193
Picturesque parkland course designed by Hawtree & Son.
9 holes, 1342yds, Par 28, SSS 28.

Visitors	no restrictions.
Societies	must contact in advance.
Facilities	🏠 ⚐ 🥾
Location	1.5m off A5
Hotel	★★65% Anglesey Arms, MENAI BRIDGE ☎(0248) 712305 17rm(10⇒6🐾)

A golf-course name printed in *bold italics* means that we have been unable to verify information with the club's management for the current year

---

MORFA NEFYN   Map 06 SH24

Nefyn & District ☎(0758) 720218
Seaside course, with parkland fairways and good views. Testing golf along cliff edge. Large clubhouse with excellent facilities. Course record holder Ian Woosnam.
18 holes, 6301yds, Par 72, SSS 71, Course record 67.
Club membership 800.

Visitors	must have a handicap certificate. Must contact in advance.
Societies	apply in writing to the secretary.
Green Fees	£17.50 per day (£25 weekends).
Facilities	⊗ ⅲ ⮑ 🍺 ⛳ 🏠 ⚐ 🥾 J R Pilkington.
Leisure	snooker.
Location	.75m NW
Hotel	★★58% Linksway Hotel, MORFA NEFYN ☎(0758) 720258 26rm(11⇒10🐾)

PENMAENMAWR   Map 06 SH77

Penmaenmawr ☎(0492) 623330
Hilly course with magnificent views across the bay to Llandudno and Anglesey. Dry-stone wall natural hazards.
9 holes, 5306yds, Par 67, SSS 66, Course record 65.
Club membership 500.

Visitors	no restrictions.
Societies	must telephone in advance.
Green Fees	£10 per day (£14 weekends & bank holidays).
Facilities	⮑ 🍺 ⛳ 🏠
Location	Cae Maen Pavilion (1.5m NE off A55)
Hotel	★★58% Lion Hotel, Y Maes, CRICCIETH ☎(0766) 522460 36rm(27⇒🐾)

PORTHMADOG   Map 06 SH53

Porthmadog ☎(0766) 512037
Seaside links, very testing but with easy walking and good views.
18 holes, 6309yds, Par 70, SSS 70, Course record 68.
Club membership 700.

Visitors	must contact in advance.
Societies	must telephone in advance.
Green Fees	£15 per day (£18 weekends).
Facilities	⊗ ⅲ ⮑ 🍺 ⛳ 🏠 ⚐ 🥾 Peter Bright.
Leisure	snooker.
Location	Morfa Bychan (1.5m SW)
Hotel	★★57% Madoc Hotel, TREMADOG ☎(0766) 512021 21rm(1⇒3🐾)

PWLLHELI   Map 06 SH33

Pwllheli ☎(0758) 612520
Easy walking on flat seaside course with outstanding views of Snowdon, Cadar Idris and Cardigan Bay.
18 holes, 6091yds, Par 69, SSS 69, Course record 67.
Club membership 650.

Visitors	restricted Tue, Thu & weekends.
Societies	must telephone in advance.
Green Fees	£16 per day (£18 weekends & bank holidays).
Facilities	⊗ ⅲ ⮑ 🍺 ⛳ 🏠 ⚐ 🥾 G D Verity.
Leisure	snooker.
Location	Golf Rd (.5m SW off A497)
Hotel	★60% Caeau Capel Hotel, Rhodfar Mor, NEFYN ☎(0758) 720240 15rm(9🐾)Annexe4⇒

RHOSNEIGR (ANGLESEY)   Map 06 SH37

Anglesey ☎Rhosneigr (0407) 811202
Links course, low and fairly level with sand dunes and tidal river.
18 holes, 5713yds, Par 68, SSS 68, Course record 66.
Club membership 400.

Visitors	welcome, some times are reserved for members.
Societies	apply in writing.
Green Fees	£10.50 per day (£12.50 weekends & bank holidays).
Facilities	⊗ 〗॥ ᇿ ▰ 〒 ⏥ 🏠 𝄃 Paul Lovell.
Location	Station Rd (NE side of village on A4080)
Hotel	★★★62% Trearddur Bay Hotel, TREARDDUR BAY ☎(0407) 860301 27rm(20⇌)

MID GLAMORGAN

ABERDARE   Map 03 SO00

Aberdare ☎(0685) 871188
Mountain course with parkland features overlooking Cynon Valley.
18 holes, 5845yds, Par 69, SSS 69, Course record 63.
Club membership 550.

Visitors	may only play on Sat with member. Must contact in advance and have an introduction from own club.
Societies	must contact in writing.
Green Fees	£13 per day (£15 weekends & bank holidays).
Facilities	⊗ 〗॥ ᇿ by prior arrangement ▰ 〒 ⏥ 🏠 𝄃 Alan Palmer.
Leisure	snooker.
Location	Abernant (.75m E)
Hotel	★★★56% Maes Manor Hotel, BLACKWOOD ☎(0495) 224551 & 220011 8⇌Annexe14⇌

BARGOED   Map 03 SO19

Bargoed ☎(0443) 830143
Mountain parkland course, testing par 4, 13th hole.
18 holes, 5836yds, Par 70, SSS 70, Course record 65.
Club membership 500.

Visitors	must play with member at weekends. Must have an introduction from own club.
Societies	must contact in advance.
Green Fees	not confirmed.
Facilities	⊗ 〗॥ by prior arrangement ᇿ ▰ 〒 ⏥
Location	Heolddu (NW side of town)
Hotel	★★★56% Maes Manor Hotel, BLACKWOOD ☎(0495) 224551 & 220011 8⇌Annexe14⇌

BRIDGEND   Map 03 SS97

Southerndown ☎(0656) 880476
Dowland Championship course with rolling fairways and fast greens. The par 3, 5th is played across a valley and the 18th, with its split level fairway, is a demanding finishing hole. Superb views.
18 holes, 6615yds, Par 70, SSS 73.
Club membership 720.

Visitors	must play with member on Sun Oct-Mar. Must contact in advance and have an introduction from own club.
Societies	must contact in advance.
Green Fees	£24 per day (£30 weekends & bank holidays).
Facilities	⊗ 〗॥ by prior arrangement ᇿ ▰ 〒 ⏥ 🏠 𝄃 Dennis McMonagle.
Leisure	snooker.
Location	Ewenny (3m SW on B4524)
Hotel	★★★65% Heronston Hotel, Ewenny, BRIDGEND ☎(0656) 668811 76⇌🐾

CAERPHILLY   Map 03 ST18

Caerphilly ☎(0222) 883481 & 86344
Undulating mountain course with woodland. Good views especially from 10th hole, 700 ft above sea level.
14 holes, 6028yds, Par 73, SSS 71, Course record 62.
Club membership 792.

Visitors	must have a handicap certificate & membership of a recognised golf club. May only play with member at weekends & bank holidays. Must contact in advance.
Societies	must contact in advance.
Green Fees	£16 per day.
Facilities	⊗ 〒 ⏥ 🏠 𝄃
Leisure	billiards/snooker.
Location	Pencapel Mountain Rd (.5m S on A469)
Hotel	★★66% Griffin Inn Motel, Rudry, CAERPHILLY ☎(0222) 869735 Annexe32⇌🐾

Castell Heights ☎(0222) 886666
'Pay as you play' parkland courses.
Castell Heights: 9 holes, 2700yds, Par 34, SSS 32, Course record 31.
Mountain Lakes: 18 holes, 6500yds, Par 72, SSS 73, Course record 69.
Club membership 700.
Visitors	no restrictions.
Societies	must contact in advance.
Green Fees	£5 per 9 holes.
Facilities	⊗ ⅲ ᴸᴸ ♨ ♀ △ 📠 ⊤ ⌞ Sion Bebb.
Location	Blaengwynlais (2m SW)
Hotel	★★66% Griffin Inn Motel, Rudry, CAERPHILLY ☎(0222) 869735 Annexe32⇔♠

CREIGIAU (CREIYIAU) Map 03 ST08

Creigiau ☎Cardiff (0222) 890263
Downland course, with small greens.
18 holes, 5979yds, Par 70, SSS 69, Course record 66.
Club membership 850.
Visitors	must be a member of a recognised golf club. Must play with member at weekends.
Societies	must contact in writing.
Green Fees	£20 per day.
Facilities	⊗ ⅲ ᴸᴸ ♨ ♀ △ 📠 ⌞ Mark Maddison.
Location	6m NW of Cardiff on A4119
Hotel	★★★65% Forte Crest Hotel, Castle St, CARDIFF ☎(0222) 388681 155⇔♠

MAESTEG Map 03 SS89

Maesteg ☎(0656) 732037
Reasonably flat hill-top course with scenic views.
18 holes, 5900yds, Par 70, SSS 69, Course record 69.
Club membership 650.
Visitors	must be a member of a recognised golf club & have a handicap certificate.
Societies	weekdays only. Must contact in advance.
Green Fees	£12 (£15 weekends & bank holidays).
Facilities	⊗ ⅲ (summer only, ex Thu) ᴸᴸ ♨ ♀ △ 📠 ⌞ Gary Hopkins.
Location	Mount Pleasant, Neath Rd (.5m W off B4282)
Hotel	★★★58% Aberavan Beach Hotel, Princess Margaret Way, PORT TALBOT ☎(0639) 884949 66⇔

MAESYCWMMER Map 03 ST19

Bryn Meadows ☎Blackwood (0495) 225590
A heavily wooded parkland course with panoramic views of the Brecon Beacons.
18 holes, 6132yds, Par 72, SSS 69, Course record 69.
Club membership 540.
Visitors	may not play Sun mornings. Must contact in advance.
Societies	Tue & Thu only.
Green Fees	£17.50 (£22.50 weekends).
Facilities	⊗ ⅲ ᴸᴸ ♨ ♀ △ 📠 ⋈ ⌞ Bruce Hunter.
Leisure	heated indoor swimming pool, sauna, gymnasium.

Location	The Bryn (on the A4048 Blackwood to Ystrad Mynach rd)
Hotel	★★★56% Maes Manor Hotel, BLACKWOOD ☎(0495) 224551 & 220011 8⇔Annexe14⇔

MERTHYR TYDFIL Map 03 SO00

Merthyr Tydfil (Cilanws) ☎(0685) 723308
Mountain-top course with good views and water hazards. Requires accuracy off the tee.
11 holes, 5808yds, Par 70, SSS 68, Course record 66.
Club membership 150.
Visitors	may not play on Sun.
Societies	must contact in writing.
Green Fees	£12 per day (£15 weekends).
Facilities	ᴸᴸ ♨ ♀
Location	Cilsanws, Cefn Coed (2m NW off A470)
Hotel	★★61% Nant Ddu Lodge, Cwm Taf, MERTHYR TYDFIL ☎(0685) 79111 15⇔♠

Morlais Castle ☎(0685) 722822
Beautiful moorland course in National Park adjacent to Brecon Beacons. Rocky terrain off the fairways makes for a testing game.
18 holes, 6320yds, Par 71, SSS 71.
Club membership 400.
Visitors	may not play noon-4pm Sat or 8am-noon Sun.
Societies	weekdays only; must telephone in advance & confirm in writing.
Green Fees	£17 per day.
Facilities	⊗ ⅲ by prior arrangement ᴸᴸ ♨ ♀ △
Location	Pant, Dowlais (2.5m N off A465)
Hotel	★★61% Nant Ddu Lodge, Cwm Taf, MERTHYR TYDFIL ☎(0685) 79111 15⇔♠

MOUNTAIN ASH Map 03 ST09

Mountain Ash ☎(0443) 472265
Mountain course.
18 holes, 5553yds, Par 69, SSS 68, Course record 63.
Club membership 800.
Visitors	must play with member at weekends. Must have an introduction from own club.
Societies	must contact in writing.
Green Fees	£16 per day.
Facilities	⊗ ⅲ ᴸᴸ & ♨ by prior arrangement ♀ △ 📠 ⌞ Jeff Sim.
Location	Cefnpennar (1m NW off A4059)
Hotel	★★61% Nant Ddu Lodge, Cwm Taf, MERTHYR TYDFIL ☎(0685) 79111 15⇔♠

NELSON Map 03 ST19

Whitehall ☎(0443) 740245
Windy hilltop course. Testing 4th hole (225 yds) par 3, and 6th hole (402 yds) par 4. Pleasant views.
9 holes, 5666yds, Par 69, SSS 68, Course record 63.
Club membership 300.
Visitors	must be a member of a recognised golf club & have a handicap certificate. Must contact in advance to play at weekends.
Societies	must contact in writing 4 weeks in advance.
Green Fees	£12 per day.
Facilities	⊗ & ⅲ by prior arrangement ᴸᴸ ♨ ♀ △

Location	The Pavilion (2m W off A470)
Hotel	★★66% Griffin Inn Motel, Rudry, CAERPHILLY ☎(0222) 869735 Annexe32⇨🏠

PENRHYS   Map 03 ST09

Rhondda ☎Tonypandy (0443) 441384
Mountain course with good views.
18 holes, 6206yds, Par 70, SSS 70, Course record 67.
Club membership 700.

Visitors	restricted Sun
Societies	must contact in advance.
Green Fees	not confirmed.
Facilities	⊗ ⅷ ⅃ 🍺 ♀ △ 🏠 ℓ Rhys Davies.
Leisure	snooker.
Location	Golf Club House (.5m W off B4512)
Hotel	★★57% Wyndham Hotel, Dunraven Place, BRIDGEND ☎(0656) 652080 & 657431 28rm(25⇨)

PONTYPRIDD   Map 03 ST09

Pontypridd ☎(0443) 402359
Well-wooded mountain course with springy turf. Good views
of the Rhondda Valleys and coast.
18 holes, 5648yds, Par 69, SSS 68.
Club membership 750.

Visitors	must play with member on weekends & bank holidays. Must have a handicap certificate. Must have an introduction from own club.
Societies	weekdays only. Must apply in writing.
Green Fees	£15 per day.
Facilities	⊗ & ⅷ (ex Thu) ⅃ 🍺 ♀ △ 🏠 ⚑ ℓ Keith Gittins.
Leisure	snooker.
Location	Ty Gwyn Rd (E side of town centre off A470)
Hotel	★★★65% Forte Crest Hotel, Castle St, CARDIFF ☎(0222) 388681 155⇨🏠

PORTHCAWL   Map 03 SS87

Royal Porthcawl ☎(0656) 782251
This championship-standard heathland/downland links
course is always in sight of the sea, and has hosted many
major tournaments.
18 holes, 6409yds, Par 72, SSS 73, Course record 65.
Club membership 800.

Visitors	must have a handicap certificate. Restricted at weekends & bank holidays. Must contact in advance and have an introduction from own club.
Societies	must contact in writing.
Green Fees	£30 per day (£45 weekends & bank holidays).
Facilities	⊗ ⅷ ⅃ 🍺 ♀ △ 🏠 ⚑ ℓ Graham Poor.
Location	1.5m NW of town centre
Hotel	★★★58% Seabank Hotel, The Promenade, PORTHCAWL ☎(0656) 782261 64⇨🏠

Entries highlighted in green identify
courses which are considered
to be particularly interesting

PYLE   Map 03 SS88

Pyle & Kenfig ☎Porthcawl (065678) 3093
Links and downland course, with sand-dunes. Easy walking.
Often windy.
18 holes, 6081mtrs, Par 71, SSS 73, Course record 68.
Club membership 1089.

Visitors	must play with member at weekends. Must have an introduction from own club.
Societies	weekdays only. Must contact in advance.
Green Fees	£25 per day; £20 per round.
Facilities	⊗ ⅷ ⅃ 🍺 ♀ △ 🏠 ℓ Robert Evans.
Location	Waun-Y-Mer (S side of Pyle off A4229)
Hotel	★★★58% Seabank Hotel, The Promenade, PORTHCAWL ☎(0656) 782261 64⇨🏠

TALBOT GREEN   Map 03 ST08

Llantrisant & Pontyclun ☎Llantrisant (0443) 222148
Parkland course.
12 holes, 5712yds, Par 68, SSS 68.
Club membership 600.

Visitors	must have a club membership card & handicap certificate. Must be accompanied by member and have an introduction from own club.
Societies	apply in writing.
Green Fees	not confirmed.
Facilities	⊗ ⅷ by prior arrangement ⅃ 🍺 ♀ △ 🏠 ⚑ ℓ Nick Watson.
Location	Llanelry Rd (N side of village off A473)
Hotel	★★57% Wyndham Hotel, Dunraven Place, BRIDGEND ☎(0656) 652080 & 657431 28rm(25⇨)

✴ POWYS ✴

BRECON   Map 03 SO02

Brecon ☎(0874) 622004
Parkland course, with easy walking. Natural hazards include
two rivers on its boundary. Good river and mountain
scenery.
9 holes, 5218yds, Par 66, SSS 66, Course record 61.
Club membership 420.

Visitors	restricted on competition days.
Societies	must contact in writing.
Green Fees	£8 per day.
Facilities	⊗ & ⅷ by prior arrangement ⅃ ♀ △
Location	Newton Park (.75m W of town centre on A40)
Hotel	★★63% Castle of Brecon Hotel, Castle Square, BRECON ☎(0874) 624611 34⇨🏠 Annexe12🏠

Cradoc ☎(0874) 623658
Parkland with wooded areas, lakes and spectacular views
over the Brecon Beacons. Challenging golf.
18 holes, 6301yds, Par 71, SSS 71, Course record 65.
Club membership 700.

Visitors	restricted on Sun. Must contact in advance.
Societies	must contact 7 days in advance.
Green Fees	£15 (£18 weekends).
Facilities	⊗ & ⅷ (ex Mon) ⅃ 🍺 ♀ △ 🏠 ℓ Douglas Beattie.

▶

Location	Penoyre Park, Cradoc (2m NW)
Hotel	★★63% Castle of Brecon Hotel, Castle Square, BRECON ☎(0874) 624611 34⇔🏠Annexe12🏠

KNIGHTON   Map 07 SO27

Knighton ☎(0547) 528646
Hill course with hard walking.
9 holes, 5320yds, Par 68, SSS 66, Course record 62.
Club membership 150.

Visitors	may not play on Sun afternoons.
Societies	must contact in advance.
Green Fees	£7 per day.
Facilities	♀ ⚲
Location	Frydd Wood (.5m S off B4355)
Hotel	★★68% Radnorshire Arms Hotel, High St, PRESTEIGNE ☎(0544) 267406 8⇔🏠Annexe8⇔🏠

LLANDRINDOD WELLS   Map 03 SO06

Llandrindod Wells ☎(0597) 822010
Moorland course, designed by Harry Vardon, with easy walking and panoramic views. One of the highest courses in Wales. (1, 100 ft above sea level).
18 holes, 5759yds, Par 68, SSS 67, Course record 63.
Club membership 650.

Visitors	no restrictions.
Societies	must telephone in advance.
Green Fees	£10 per day (£15 weekends).
Facilities	⊗ ⽊ 🍴 🍺 (no catering Tue) ♀ ⚲ 🏠🔧
Location	1m SE off A483
Hotel	★★★59% Hotel Metropole, Temple St, LLANDRINDOD WELLS ☎(0597) 823700 121⇔🏠

LLANGATTOCK   Map 03 SO21

Old Rectory ☎(0873) 810373
Sheltered course with easy walking.
9 holes, 2225yds, Par 53, SSS 54 or 53yds.
Club membership 200.

Visitors	no restrictions.
Green Fees	not confirmed.
Facilities	♀ ⚲
Leisure	swimming pool.
Location	SW of village
Hotel	★★⚑70% Gliffaes Country House Hotel, CRICKHOWELL ☎(0874) 730371 19rm(15⇔3🏠)Annexe3⇔🏠

LLANIDLOES   Map 06 SN98

St Idloes ☎(05512) 2559
Hill-course, slightly undulating but walking is easy. Good views.
9 holes, 5320yds, Par 66, SSS 66.
Club membership 350.

Visitors	may not play on Sun mornings. Must have a handicap certificate.
Societies	must contact in advance.
Green Fees	£12 per round/day.
Facilities	⊗ ⽊ 🍴 🍺 (no catering Mon) ♀ (ex Mon) ⚲

Location	Penrhallt (1m N off B4569)
Hotel	★★69% Glansevern Arms Hotel, Pant Mawr, LLANGURIG ☎(05515) 240 7⇔🏠

MACHYNLLETH   Map 06 SH70

Machynlleth ☎(0654) 702000
Lowland course with mostly natural hazards.
9 holes, 5726yds, Par 68, SSS 67, Course record 66.
Club membership 247.

Visitors	may not play during competitions & Thu 1-2pm.
Societies	must contact in advance.
Green Fees	£10 per day (£7 in winter).
Facilities	⊗ (summer only) 🍴 🍺 ♀ ⚲ 🔧
Location	Ffordd Drenewydd (.5m E off A489)
Hotel	★★64% Wynnstay Arms Hotel, Maengwyn St, MACHYNLLETH ☎(0654) 702941 20⇔🏠

NEWTOWN   Map 06 SO19

St Giles ☎(0686) 625844
Inland country course with easy walking. Testing 2nd hole, par 3, and 4th hole, par 4. River Severn skirts four holes.
9 holes, 5864yds, Par 70, SSS 68.
Club membership 250.

Visitors	restricted Thu & Sat afternoons & Sun mornings. Must have an introduction from own club.
Societies	must contact in advance.
Green Fees	not confirmed.
Facilities	⊗ ⽊ 🍴 🍺 ♀ ⚲ 🏠🔧🍷
Leisure	fishing.
Location	Pool Rd (.5m NE on A483)
Hotel	★★63% Elephant & Castle, Broad St, NEWTOWN ☎(0686) 626271 25⇔🏠Annexe11⇔🏠

WELSHPOOL   Map 07 SJ20

Welshpool ☎Castle Caerinion (0938) 83249
Undulating moorland course with bracing air. Testing holes are 2nd (par 5), 14th (par 3), 17th (par 3).
18 holes, 5708yds, Par 70, SSS 69.
Club membership 250.

Visitors	must contact in advance.
Societies	must book in advance.
Green Fees	not confirmed.
Facilities	⊗ (ex Mon) 🍺 (ex Mon) ♀ (ex Mon) ⚲ 🏠
Location	Golfa Hill (3m W off A458)
Hotel	★★64% Royal Oak Hotel, WELSHPOOL ☎(0938) 552217 24⇔🏠

SOUTH GLAMORGAN

BARRY   Map 03 ST16

Brynhill ☎(0446) 735061
Meadowland course with some hard walking. Prevailing west wind.
18 holes, 5511mtrs, Par 71, SSS 69, Course record 67.
Club membership 450.

Visitors	must have a handicap certificate. May not play on Sun. Must have an introduction from own club.
Societies	weekdays only.
Green Fees	not confirmed.
Facilities	⊗ ⅲ ᴌ ☎ ♀ ⚲ 🖿 ⚐ ⌐ ℓ P Fountain.
Leisure	snooker.
Location	Port Rd (1.25m N on B4050)
Hotel	★★★57% Mount Sorrell Hotel, Porthkerry Rd, BARRY ☎(0446) 740069 45⇨🖝Annexe4⇨

CARDIFF   Map 03 ST17

Cardiff ☎(0222) 753320
Parkland course, where trees form natural hazards.
Interesting variety of holes, mostly bunkered.
18 holes, 6016yds, Par 70, SSS 70.
Club membership 930.

Visitors	must play with member at weekends. Must have an introduction from own club.
Societies	Thu only.
Green Fees	not confirmed.
Facilities	⊗ ⅲ by prior arrangement ᴌ ☎ ♀ ⚲ 🖿 ℓ Terry Hanson.
Location	Sherborne Av, Cyncoed (3m N of city centre)
Hotel	★★★63% Forte Posthouse, Pentwyn Rd, Pentwyn, CARDIFF ☎(0222) 731212 136⇨🖝

Llanishen ☎(0222) 755078
Mountain course, with hard walking overlooking the Bristol Channel.
18 holes, 5296yds, Par 68, SSS 66.
Club membership 900.

Visitors	must play with member at weekends & bank holidays. Must contact in advance and have an introduction from own club.
Societies	Thu only.
Green Fees	£20 per day.
Facilities	⊗ ⅲ ᴌ ☎ ♀ ⚲ 🖿 ℓ R A Jones.
Leisure	snooker.
Location	Cwm Lisvane (5m N of city centre off A469)
Hotel	★★★63% Forte Posthouse, Pentwyn Rd, Pentwyn, CARDIFF ☎(0222) 731212 136⇨🖝

Radyr ☎(0222) 842408
Hillside, parkland course which can be windy. Good views.
18 holes, 6031yds, Par 69, SSS 70, Course record 63.
Club membership 870.

Visitors	must play with member at weekends. Must contact in advance and have an introduction from own club.
Societies	must contact in advance.
Green Fees	£22 per day.
Facilities	⊗ ⅲ ᴌ ☎ ♀ ⚲ 🖿 ℓ Steve Gough.
Leisure	snooker.
Location	Drysgol Rd, Radyr (4.5m NW of city centre off A4119)
Hotel	★★★★54% Park Hotel, Park Place, CARDIFF ☎(0222) 383471 119⇨🖝

If you know of a golf course which welcomes visitors and is not already in this guide, we should be grateful for information

---

St Mellons ☎(0633) 680408
This parkland course comprises quite a few par-3 holes and provides some testing golf. It is indeed a challenge to the single handicap golfer. The 12th hole runs over a stream, making an accurate drive virtually essential.
18 holes, 6080yds, Par 70, SSS 70, Course record 62.
Club membership 800.

				SCORECARD: White Tees		
Hole	Yds	Par	Hole	Yds	Par
1	333	4	10	454	4
2	421	4	11	135	3
3	199	3	12	556	5
4	320	4	13	493	5
5	172	3	14	160	3
6	470	4	15	280	4
7	477	5	16	357	4
8	186	3	17	437	4
9	361	4	18	464	4
Out	2939	34	In	3336	36
			Totals	6275	70

Visitors	must play with member at weekends. Must contact in advance and have an introduction from own club.
Societies	must telephone in advance.
Green Fees	not confirmed.
Facilities	⊗ ⅲ ᴌ ☎ ♀ ⚲ 🖿 ℓ Barry Thomas.
Location	St Mellons (5m NE off A48)
Hotel	★★★63% Forte Posthouse, Pentwyn Rd, Pentwyn, CARDIFF ☎(0222) 731212 136⇨🖝

Whitchurch ☎(0222) 620985
Well manicured parkland course, with easy walking.
18 holes, 6319yds, Par 71, SSS 70, Course record 62.
Club membership 1000.

Visitors	must have a handicap certificate. Restricted Sat (Apr-Oct), Sun (Oct-Apr). Must have an introduction from own club.
Societies	Thu only. Must contact in writing.
Green Fees	£21 (£26 weekends & bank holidays).
Facilities	⊗ ⅲ by prior arrangement ᴌ ☎ ♀ ⚲ 🖿 ⚐ ℓ E Clark.
Location	Whitchurch (4m N of city centre on A470)
Hotel	★★★★54% Park Hotel, Park Place, CARDIFF ☎(0222) 383471 119⇨🖝

DINAS POWIS   Map 03 ST17

Dinas Powis ☎(0222) 512727
Parkland/downland course with views over the Bristol Channel and the seaside resort of Barry.
18 holes, 5377yds, Par 67, SSS 66, Course record 65.
Club membership 620.

Visitors	must play with member at weekends. Must have an introduction from own club.
Societies	must contact in advance.
Green Fees	not confirmed.
Facilities	⊗ ⅲ ᴌ ☎ ♀ ⚲ 🖿 ℓ G Bennett.
Location	Old High Walls (NW side of village)
Hotel	★★★57% Mount Sorrell Hotel, Porthkerry Rd, BARRY ☎(0446) 740069 45⇨🖝Annexe4⇨

PENARTH   Map 03 ST17

Glamorganshire ☎Cardiff (0222) 701185
Parkland course, overlooking the Bristol Channel.
18 holes, 6181yds, Par 70, SSS 70, Course record 65.
Club membership 1000.

▶

Visitors	must be a member of a recognised golf club & have a handicap certificate. May not play on competition & society days. Must contact in advance and have an introduction from own club.
Societies	Mon, Wed-Fri only. Must contact in advance.
Green Fees	£22 per day (£28 weekends & bank holidays).
Facilities	⊗ ⫪ ᴸ ᴾ ♀ ⌂ 🕿 (Andrew Kerr Smith.
Leisure	squash, snooker.
Location	Lavernock Rd (S side of town centre on B4267)
Hotel	★65% Walton House Hotel, 37 Victoria Rd, PENARTH ☎(0222) 707782 13rm(10⇨3🌂)

WENVOE   Map 03 ST17

Wenvoe Castle ☎Cardiff (0222) 594371
Parkland course which is hilly for first 9 holes. Lake, situated 280 yds from tee at 10th hole, is a hazard.
18 holes, 6422yds, Par 72, SSS 71, Course record 68.
Club membership 600.

Visitors	must be a member of a recognised golf club & have a handicap certificate. Must play with member at weekends. Must contact in advance and have an introduction from own club.
Societies	must contact in writing.
Green Fees	£20 per day.
Facilities	⊗ ⫪ ᴸ ᴾ ♀ ⌂ 🕿 (R J Wyer.
Location	1m S off A4050
Hotel	★★★65% Forte Crest Hotel, Castle St, CARDIFF ☎(0222) 388681 155⇨🌂

WEST GLAMORGAN

CLYDACH   Map 03 SN60

Inco ☎(0792) 844216
Flat meadowland course.
18 holes, 5976yds, Par 71, SSS 69.
Club membership 300.

Visitors	no restrictions.
Societies	must contact in advance.
Green Fees	not confirmed.
Facilities	♀ ⌂
Location	.75m SE on B4291
Hotel	★★62% Oak Tree Parc Hotel, Birchgrove Rd, BIRCHGROVE ☎(0792) 817781 10⇨🌂

GLYNNEATH   Map 03 SN80

Glynneath ☎(0639) 720452
Attractive hillside golf overlooking the Vale of Neath. Reasonably level farmland/wooded course.
18 holes, 5560yds, Par 68, SSS 67, Course record 67.
Club membership 520.

Visitors	restricted starting times at weekend.
Societies	welcome mid-week. Must book in advance.
Green Fees	£8 per day (£16 weekends).
Facilities	ᴸ ᴾ ♀ ⌂ 🕿
Leisure	snooker.
Location	Pen-y-graig, Pontneathvaughan (2m NE on B4242)
Hotel	★★62% Oak Tree Parc Hotel, Birchgrove Rd, BIRCHGROVE ☎(0792) 817781 10⇨🌂

NEATH   Map 03 SS79

Neath ☎(0639) 643615
Mountain course, with spectacular views. Testing holes: 10th par 4; 12th par 5; 15th par 4.
18 holes, 6492yds, Par 72, SSS 72, Course record 67.
Club membership 700.

Visitors	with member only at weekends.
Societies	should either telephone or write in advance.
Green Fees	£15 per day.
Facilities	⊗ ⫪ ᴸ ᴾ ♀ ⌂ 🕿 (E M Bennett.
Leisure	snooker.
Location	Cadoxton (2m NE off A4230)
Hotel	★★64% Castle Hotel, The Parade, NEATH ☎(0639) 641119 & 643581 28⇨🌂

Swansea Bay ☎Skewen (0792) 814153
Fairly level seaside links with part-sand dunes.
18 holes, 6302yds, Par 71, SSS 70, Course record 67.
Club membership 500.

Visitors	must have an introduction from own club.
Societies	must book in advance.
Green Fees	£15 per day (£20 weekends & bank holidays).
Facilities	⊗ ⫪ by prior arrangement ᴸ ᴾ ♀ ⌂ 🕿 (Mike Day.
Leisure	snooker.
Location	Jersey Marine (4m SW off A48)
Hotel	★★64% Castle Hotel, The Parade, NEATH ☎(0639) 641119 & 643581 28⇨🌂

PONTARDAWE   Map 03 SN70

Pontardawe ☎(0792) 863118
Meadowland course situated on plateau 600 ft above sea-level with good views over Bristol Channel and Brecon Beacons.
18 holes, 6162yds, Par 70, SSS 70.
Club membership 700.

Visitors	must contact in advance.
Societies	welcome weekdays by prior arrangement.
Green Fees	not confirmed.
Facilities	⊗ ⫪ by prior arrangement ᴸ ᴾ ♀ ⌂ 🕿 (
Leisure	snooker.
Location	Cefn Llan (N side of town centre M4 junc 45 off A406)
Hotel	★★62% Oak Tree Parc Hotel, Birchgrove Rd, BIRCHGROVE ☎(0792) 817781 10⇨🌂

SOUTHGATE   Map 02 SS58

Pennard ☎Bishopston (044128) 3131
Undulating, cliff-top seaside links with good coastal views.
18 holes, 6289yds, Par 71, SSS 71, Course record 66.
Club membership 779.

Visitors	a handicap certificate is required.
Societies	welcome except weekends & bank holidays, must apply by letter.
Green Fees	£14 (£18 weekends & bank holidays).
Facilities	⊗ & ⫪ by prior arrangement ᴸ ᴾ ♀ (times vary) ⌂ 🕿 (M V Bennett.
Leisure	squash, snooker.
Location	2 Southgate Rd (NW side of village)
Hotel	★73% Windsor Lodge Hotel, Mount Pleasant, SWANSEA ☎(0792) 642158 & 652744 19rm(11⇨4🌂)

SWANSEA   Map 03 SS69

Clyne ☎(0792) 401989
Moorland course, very open to the wind and with grazing rights for local commoners.
18 holes, 6323yds, Par 70, SSS 71, Course record 64.
Club membership 800.

Visitors	must be member of a club with handicap certificate. Must contact in advance and have an introduction from own club.
Societies	must telephone in advance.
Green Fees	£18 per day (£25 weekends).
Facilities	⊗ �🍴 ㄥ 🍺 (all catering by prior arrangement) ♀ ㄥ 🏠 (Mark Bevan.
Leisure	snooker, practise facilities.
Location	120 Owls Lodge Ln, The Mayals, Blackpyl (3.5m SW on B4436 off A4067)
Hotel	★★67% Langland Court, Langland Court Rd, LANGLAND ☎(0792) 361545 16⇨(Annexe5⇨(

Langland Bay ☎(0792) 366023
Parkland course overlooking Gower coast. The par 4, 6th is an uphill dog-leg open to the wind, and the par 3, 16th (151 yds) is aptly named 'Death or Glory'.
18 holes, 5830yds, Par 70, SSS 70.
Club membership 850.

Visitors	must have an introduction from own club.
Societies	must telephone in advance.
Green Fees	not confirmed.
Facilities	⊗ �🍴 ㄥ 🍺 ♀ ㄥ 🏠 (
Location	Langland Bay (6m W on A4067)
Hotel	★★★60% Osborne Hotel, Rotherslade Rd, LANGLAND ☎(0792) 366274 36rm(32⇨()

Morriston ☎(0792) 796528
Pleasant parkland course.
18 holes, 5800yds, Par 68, SSS 68, Course record 65.
Club membership 580.

Visitors	a handicap certificate is required. Must have an introduction from own club.
Societies	apply in writing.
Green Fees	£15 per day (£21 weekend & bank holiday).
Facilities	⊗ �🍴 by prior arrangement ㄥ 🍺 ♀ ㄥ 🏠 ⚑ (Deryl Rees.
Location	160 Clasemont Rd (5m N on A48)
Hotel	★★62% Oak Tree Parc Hotel, Birchgrove Rd, BIRCHGROVE ☎(0792) 817781 10⇨(

UPPER KILLAY   Map 02 SS59

Fairwood Park ☎Swansea (0792) 203648
Championship parkland course on Gower coast with good views and easy walking.
18 holes, 6606yds, Par 72, SSS 72, Course record 67.
Club membership 720.

Visitors	welcome except when championship or club matches are being held. Must contact in advance.
Societies	must contact in advance.
Green Fees	£18 per day (£23 weekends & bank holidays).
Facilities	⊗ �🍴 ㄥ 🍺 ♀ ㄥ 🏠 ⚑ (Mark Evans.
Leisure	snooker.
Location	Blackhills Ln (1.5m S off A4118)

Hotel   ★73% Windsor Lodge Hotel, Mount Pleasant, SWANSEA ☎(0792) 642158 & 652744 19rm(11⇨4()

YSTALYFERA   Map 03 SN70

Palleg ☎(0639) 842193
Heathland course liable to become heavy going after winter rain.
9 holes, 6400yds, Par 36, SSS 72, Course record 71.
Club membership 200.

Visitors	no restrictions.
Societies	must contact two months in advance.
Green Fees	not confirmed.
Facilities	⊗ �🍴 ㄥ 🍺 (catering by arrangement) ♀ ㄥ
Location	Lower Cwm-twrch (1.5m N off A4068)
Hotel	★★62% Oak Tree Parc Hotel, Birchgrove Rd, BIRCHGROVE ☎(0792) 817781 10⇨(

SCOTLAND

BORDERS

COLDSTREAM   Map 12 NT83

Hirsel ☎(0890) 2678
Parkland course, with hard walking and sheltered trees. Testing 3rd and 6th holes.
9 holes, 5830yds, Par 70, SSS 68, Course record 64.
Club membership 400.

Visitors	restricted during competitions.
Societies	contact for details.
Green Fees	£7 per day (£12 weekends).
Facilities	⊗ ㄥ 🍺 (all catering Apr-Oct) ♀ (Apr-Oct) ㄥ 🏠 ⚑
Location	Kelso Rd (SW side of town off A678)
Hotel	★★★64% Ednam House Hotel, Bridge St, KELSO ☎(0573) 24168 32⇨(

DUNS   Map 12 NT75

Duns ☎(0361) 82717
Interesting upland course, with natural hazards of water and hilly slopes. Views south to the Cheviot Hills.
9 holes, 5826yds, Par 68, SSS 68, Course record 66.
Club membership 295.

Visitors	welcome except competition days & Tue evenings.
Societies	apply in writing.
Green Fees	£12 per day; £8 per round.
Facilities	ㄥ
Location	Longformacus Rd (1m W off A6105)
Hotel	★★★63% Turret House Hotel, Etal Rd, Tweedmouth, BERWICK-UPON-TWEED ☎(0289) 330808 13⇨(

We make every effort to ensure that our information is accurate but details may change after we go to print

EYEMOUTH   Map 12 NT96

Eyemouth ☎(08907) 50551
With the exception of a steep climb to the 1st tee, this is a
compact, flat and popular seaside course. Fast smooth greens
and fine views are typified by the 15th, played from an
elevated tee to a green on a peninsula over a North Sea inlet.
9 holes, 4608mtrs, Par 66, SSS 65, Course record 60.
Club membership 250.

Visitors	may not play before 10.30am Sat or noon Sun.
Societies	apply in writing.
Green Fees	£7 per day.
Facilities	♀ (evenings) ⚐ 🏠 ♪ Craig Maltman.
Leisure	snooker.
Location	Gunsgreen House (E side of town)
Hotel	★★★63% Turret House Hotel, Etal Rd, Tweedmouth, BERWICK-UPON-TWEED ☎(0289) 330808 13⇔♠

GALASHIELS   Map 12 NT43

Galashiels ☎(0896) 3724
Hillside course, superb views from the top; 10th hole very
steep.
18 holes, 5311yds, Par 68, SSS 67.
Club membership 250.

Visitors	no restrictions.
Societies	must contact in advance.
Green Fees	not confirmed.
Facilities	⊗ (Sun only) ⅷ (Sun only) ⅊ (Sat-Sun) ♀ ⚐
Location	Ladhope Recreation Ground (N side of town centre off A7)
Hotel	★★★67% Kingsknowes Hotel, Selkirk Rd, GALASHIELS ☎(0896) 58375 11rm(10⇔♠)

Torwoodlee ☎(0896) 2260
Parkland course with natural hazards designed by James
Braid. Testing 3rd hole (par 3).
9 holes, 5720yds, Par 68, SSS 68, Course record 64.
Club membership 300.

Visitors	may not play Sat & Thu evenings.
Societies	must contact in advance.
Green Fees	£12 per day; £10 per round (£14/£12 weekends).
Facilities	⊗ ⅷ ⅊ 🖥 (all catering by prior arrangement) ♀ ⚐ 🏠
Location	1.75m NW off A7
Hotel	★★67% Burt's Hotel, The Square, MELROSE ☎(089682) 2285 21⇔♠

HAWICK   Map 12 NT51

Hawick ☎(0450) 72293
Hill course with good views.
18 holes, 5929yds, Par 68, SSS 69.
Club membership 690.

Visitors	by arrangement at weekends.
Societies	must contact in writing.
Green Fees	not confirmed.
Facilities	⊗ ⅊ 🖥 ♀ 🏠
Location	Vertish Hill (SW side of town)
Hotel	★★71% Kirklands Hotel, West Stewart Place, HAWICK ☎(0450) 72263 6rm(2⇔1♠)Annexe7⇔♠

INNERLEITHEN   Map 11 NT33

Innerleithen ☎(0896) 830951
Moorland course, with easy walking. Burns and rivers are
natural hazards. Testing 5th hole (100 yds) par 3.
9 holes, 2910yds, Par 68, SSS 68, Course record 67.
Club membership 185.

Visitors	no restrictions.
Societies	must contact in writing.
Green Fees	£6 per day (£9 weekends).
Facilities	⅊ ♀ ⚐
Location	Leithen Water, Leithen Rd (1.5m N on B709)
Hotel	★★⚑68% Tweed Valley Hotel & Restaurant, Galashiels Rd, WALKERBURN ☎(089687) 636 15⇔♠

JEDBURGH   Map 12 NT62

Jedburgh ☎(08356) 3587
Undulating parkland course, windy, with young trees.
9 holes, 5760yds, Par 68, SSS 67, Course record 62.
Club membership 250.

Visitors	restricted at weekends during competitions.
Societies	must contact at least one month in advance.
Green Fees	£7 (£8 weekends).
Facilities	Catering Sat and Sun ♀ ⚐ 🏠
Location	Dunion Rd (1m W on B6358)
Hotel	★★71% Kirklands Hotel, West Stewart Place, HAWICK ☎(0450) 72263 6rm(2⇔1♠)Annexe7⇔♠

KELSO   Map 12 NT73

Kelso ☎(0573) 23009
Parkland course. Easy walking.
18 holes, 6061yds, Par 70, SSS 69, Course record 64.
Club membership 450.

Visitors	no restrictions.
Societies	apply in writing.
Green Fees	£12 per day; £9 per round (£15/£11 weekends).
Facilities	⚐ 🏠
Location	Racecourse Rd (N side of town centre off B6461)
Hotel	★★★63% Cross Keys Hotel, 36-37 The Square, KELSO ☎(0573) 23303 24⇔♠

MELROSE   Map 12 NT53

Melrose ☎(089682) 2855
Undulating tree-lined fairways with spendid views.
9 holes, 5579yds, Par 70, SSS 68, Course record 62.
Club membership 390.

Visitors	may not play on Sat, Apr-Oct.
Societies	must telephone in advance.
Green Fees	not confirmed.
Facilities	Catering by arrangement ♀ ⚐
Location	Dingleton (S side of town centre on B6359)
Hotel	★★67% Burt's Hotel, The Square, MELROSE ☎(089682) 2285 21⇔♠

Opening times of bar and catering facilities
vary from place to place. Please remember
to check in advance of your visit

MINTO
Map 12 NT52

Minto ☎Denholm (045087) 220
Pleasant, undulating parkland course featuring mature trees and panoramic views of Scottish Border country. Short but quite testing.
18 holes, 5460yds, Par 68, SSS 68, Course record 66.
Club membership 600.
Visitors	may not play before 10.15am & 3.15pm Sat-Sun or during a club medal competition. Must have an introduction from own club.
Societies	must contact in writing.
Green Fees	£10 per day (£15 weekends & bank holidays).
Facilities	⊗ & ∭ by prior arrangement (ex Mon) 🖺 🍽 ☕ ⌂ 🖾
Location	Denholm (S side of village)
Hotel	★★71% Kirklands Hotel, West Stewart Place, HAWICK ☎(0450) 72263 6rm(2⇨1🛏)Annexe7⇨🛏

NEWCASTLETON
Map 12 NY48

Newcastleton ☎Liddesdale (03873) 75257
Hill course.
9 holes, 5748yds, Par 70, SSS 68, Course record 64.
Visitors	no restrictions.
Societies	must contact in advance.
Green Fees	not confirmed.
Facilities	⌂
Location	Holm Hill (W side of village)
Hotel	★★56% Eskdale Hotel, Market Place, LANGHOLM ☎(03873) 80357 16rm(3⇨7🛏)

PEEBLES
Map 11 NT24

Peebles Municipal ☎(0721) 20197
Parkland course with fine views.
18 holes, 6137yds, Par 70, SSS 70.
Club membership 600.
Visitors	must contact in advance and have an introduction from own club.
Societies	must be pre-booked with deposit.
Green Fees	£14.50 per day; £10.50 per round (£22/£15.50 weekends).
Facilities	⌂ 🖾
Location	Kirkland St (W side of town centre off A72)
Hotel	★★★50% The Tontine, High St, PEEBLES ☎(0721) 20892 37⇨🛏

ST BOSWELLS
Map 12 NT53

St Boswells ☎(0835) 22359
Attractive parkland course by the banks of the River Tweed; easy walking.
9 holes, 2625yds, Par 66, SSS 65, Course record 61.
Club membership 310.
Visitors	may not play competition days.
Societies	must apply in writing.
Green Fees	£5 per day (£8 weekends).
Facilities	⌂
Leisure	fishing.

Location	N side of village off B6404
Hotel	★★69% Buccleuch Arms Hotel, The Green, ST BOSWELLS ☎(0835) 22243 19rm(17⇨🛏)

SELKIRK
Map 12 NT42

Selkirk ☎(0750) 20427
Pleasant moorland course set around Selkirk Hill. Unrivalled views.
9 holes, 5620yds, Par 68, SSS 67, Course record 61.
Club membership 364.
Visitors	may not play Mon evening, competition/match days.
Societies	must telephone in advance.
Green Fees	£9 per day.
Facilities	⌂
Location	Selkirk Hills (1m S on A7)
Hotel	★62% Heatherlie House Hotel, Heatherlie Park, SELKIRK ☎(0750) 21200 7rm(6🛏)

WEST LINTON
Map 11 NT15

West Linton ☎(0968) 60970
Moorland course with beautiful views of Pentland Hills.
18 holes, 5864yds, Par 68, SSS 68, Course record 67.
Club membership 600.
Visitors	may not play on competition days.
Societies	must contact in writing.
Green Fees	£15.50 per day; £11.50 per round.
Facilities	⊗ ∭ by prior arrangement & 🖺 (all ex Tue) 🍽 ☕ ⌂ 🖾 ✆ Nigel Burkitt.

▶

Location	NW side of village off A702
Hotel	★★★50% The Tontine, High St, PEEBLES ☎(0721) 20892 37⇌♦

CENTRAL

ABERFOYLE   Map 11 NN50

Aberfoyle ☎(08772) 493
Scenic heathland course with mountain views.
18 holes, 5210yds, Par 66, SSS 66, Course record 64.
Club membership 665.

Visitors	may not tee off before 10am Sat & Sun.
Societies	must contact in advance.
Green Fees	£12 per day; £8 per round (£15 per day; £10 per round weekends).
Facilities	⊗ ⊪ & ⅃ (summer only) ♀ (summer/winter wknd) ⌕ ☖
Location	Braeval (1m E on A81)
Hotel	★★★⚑ Roman Camp Hotel, CALLANDER ☎(0877) 30003 14rm(13⇌♦)

ALLOA   Map 11 NS89

Alloa ☎(0259) 722745
Undulating, wooded parkland course.
18 holes, 6230yds, Par 70, SSS 70, Course record 63.
Club membership 700.

Visitors	must contact in advance.
Societies	may not play at weekends.
Green Fees	£16 per day; £9 per round (£18 weekends).
Facilities	⊗ ⊪ ⅃ ⬤ ♀ ☖ ☖ ⌕ ♩
Leisure	snooker.
Location	Schawpark, Sauchie (1.5m NE on A908)
Hotel	★★★65% Royal Hotel, Henderson St, BRIDGE OF ALLAN ☎(0786) 832284 32⇌♦

Braehead ☎(0259) 722078
Attactive parkland course at the foot of the Ochil Hills, and offering spectacular views.
18 holes, 6041yds, Par 71, SSS 69, Course record 64.
Club membership 700.

Visitors	must contact in advance.
Societies	must contact in advance.
Green Fees	£12 per day; £10 per round (£20/£15 weekends).
Facilities	⊗ ⊪ ⅃ ⬤ ♀
Location	Cambus (1.5m NE on A908)
Hotel	★★59% King Robert Hotel, Glasgow Rd, Bannockburn, STIRLING ☎(0786) 811666 53⇌♦

BONNYBRIDGE   Map 11 NS88

Bonnybridge ☎(0324) 812822
Testing heathland course, with tightly guarded greens. Easy walking.
9 holes, 6060yds, Par 72, SSS 69.
Club membership 325.

Visitors	must be accompanied by member and contact in advance.
Societies	must contact in advance.
Green Fees	not confirmed.
Facilities	♀ ☖ ☖

Location	Larbert Rd (1m NE off A883)
Hotel	★★★65% Inchyra Grange Hotel, Grange Rd, POLMONT ☎(0324) 711911 33⇌♦

BRIDGE OF ALLAN   Map 11 NS79

Bridge of Allan ☎(0786) 832332
Parkland course, very hilly with good views of Stirling Castle and beyond to the Trossachs. Testing 1st hole, 221 yds (par 3) uphill 6 ft wall 25 yds before green.
9 holes, 4932yds, Par 66, SSS 65, Course record 62.
Club membership 400.

Visitors	restricted Sat.
Societies	must contact in advance.
Green Fees	£7 per round 18 holes (£10 weekends).
Facilities	Catering at weekends or by arrangement ♀ ☖
Leisure	pool table.
Location	Sunnylaw (.5m N off A9)
Hotel	★★★65% Royal Hotel, Henderson St, BRIDGE OF ALLAN ☎(0786) 832284 32⇌♦

CALLANDER   Map 11 NN60

Callander ☎(0877) 30090
Parkland course, with fairly tightly guarded greens.
Designed by Tom Morris Snr and overlooked by the Trossachs.
18 holes, 5125yds, Par 66, SSS 66, Course record 62.
Club membership 580.

Visitors	no restrictions.
Societies	apply in writing.
Green Fees	£15 per day; £10 per round (£19/£14 weekends).
Facilities	⊗ ⊪ ⅃ ⬤ ♀ ☖ ☖ ♩ ♩ William Kelly.
Location	Aveland Rd (E side of town off A84)
Hotel	★★★⚑ Roman Camp Hotel, CALLANDER ☎(0877) 30003 14rm(13⇌♦)

DOLLAR   Map 11 NS99

Dollar ☎(0259) 42400
Compact hillside course.
18 holes, 5144yds, SSS 66.
Club membership 360.

Visitors	no restrictions
Societies	must contact in advance.
Green Fees	£9 per day; £6 per round (£12 per day weekends).
Facilities	⊗ ⊪ ⅃ ⬤ (no catering Tue) ♀ ☖ ♩
Leisure	snooker.
Location	Brewlands House (.5m N off A91)
Hotel	★★59% King Robert Hotel, Glasgow Rd, Bannockburn, STIRLING ☎(0786) 811666 53⇌♦

DRYMEN   Map 11 NS48

Buchanan Castle ☎(0360) 60307
Parkland course, with easy walking and good views.
18 holes, 6086yds, Par 70, SSS 69.
Club membership 830.

Visitors	must be accompanied by member, contact in advance and have an introduction from own club.
Societies	must contact in advance.
Green Fees	not confirmed.

Facilities	⊗ by prior arrangement ⅢÎ by prior arrangement 🏊 ⬤ ♀ ⛳ 🏠 ⚑ ⚓ Charles Dernie.
Location	1m W
Hotel	★★★65% Buchanan Highland Hotel, DRYMEN ☎(0360) 60588 51⇨🐾

DUNBLANE　　　　　　　　　Map 11 NN70

Dunblane New Golf Club ☎(0786) 823711
Well maintained parkland course, with reasonably hard walking. Testing 6th and 9th holes.
18 holes, 5876yds, Par 69, SSS 68, Course record 64.
Club membership 800.

Visitors	may play 9.30am-noon & 2.30-4pm Mon-Fri. Must contact in advance.
Societies	welcome Mon & Thu, contact in advance.
Green Fees	£22 per day; £13 per round (£22 weekends).
Facilities	⊗ ⅢÎ 🏊 ⬤ ♀ ⛳ 🏠 ⚓ R M Jamieson.
Location	Perth Rd (E side of town on A9)
Hotel	★★★(red)🏌 Cromlix House Hotel, Kinbuck, DUNBLANE ☎(0786) 822125 14⇨🐾

FALKIRK　　　　　　　　　　Map 11 NS88

Falkirk ☎(0324) 611061
Parkland course with trees, gorse and streams.
18 holes, 6282yds, Par 71, SSS 69, Course record 66.
Club membership 800.

Visitors	with member only at weekends.
Societies	telephone (0324) 612219 in advance.
Green Fees	£15 per day; £8 per round.
Facilities	⊗ ⅢÎ 🏊 ⬤ ♀ ⛳ 🏠
Location	Stirling Rd, Camelon (1.5m W on A9)
Hotel	★★★62% Stakis Park Hotel, Camelon Rd, FALKIRK ☎(0324) 28331 55⇨🐾

KILLIN　　　　　　　　　　　Map 11 NN53

Killin ☎(05672) 312
Parkland course with good views. Glorious setting.
9 holes, 5200yds, Par 66, SSS 65, Course record 61.
Club membership 250.

Visitors	may not play competition days.
Societies	apply in writing.
Green Fees	£8 per round.
Facilities	⛳ 🏠 ⚑
Location	1m N on A827
Hotel	★★65% Morenish Lodge Hotel, Loch Tayside, KILLIN ☎(05672) 258 13rm(4⇨8🐾)

LARBERT　　　　　　　　　　Map 11 NS88

Falkirk Tryst ☎(0324) 562415
Moorland course, fairly level with trees and broom, well-bunkered. Winds can affect play.
18 holes, 6053yds, Par 70, SSS 69, Course record 64.
Club membership 900.

Visitors	with member only Wed, weekend & bank holidays. Must contact in advance.
Societies	apply in writing.
Green Fees	£15 per day; £10 per round.
Facilities	⊗ ⅢÎ (Sat evening only) 🏊 ⬤ ♀ ⛳ 🏠 ⚓ Donald Slicer.

Location	86 Burnhead Rd (1m NE off A88/B905)
Hotel	★★★65% Inchyra Grange Hotel, Grange Rd, POLMONT ☎(0324) 711911 33⇨🐾

Glenbervie Clubhouse ☎(0324) 562605
Parkland course with good views.
18 holes, 6469yds, Par 71, SSS 71, Course record 63.
Club membership 600.

Visitors	restricted at weekends. Must contact in advance.
Societies	apply in writing.
Green Fees	£24 per day; £18 per round.
Facilities	⊗ ⅢÎ 🏊 ⬤ ♀ ⛳ 🏠 ⚓ John Chillas.
Location	Stirling Rd (2m NW on A9)
Hotel	★★★62% Stakis Park Hotel, Camelon Rd, FALKIRK ☎(0324) 28331 55⇨🐾

MUCKHART　　　　　　　　　Map 11 NO00

Muckhart ☎(025981) 423
Scenic heathland/downland course.
18 holes, 6192yds, Par 71, SSS 70, Course record 66.
Club membership 700.

Visitors	welcome except weekends before 9.45am & between noon-2.30pm. Must contact in advance.
Societies	must telephone in advance.
Green Fees	£16 per day; £10 per round (£20/£15 weekends).
Facilities	⊗ ⅢÎ 🏊 ⬤ ♀ (all day) ⛳ 🏠 ⚓ K Salmoni.
Location	SW of village off A91
Hotel	★★★62% Green Hotel, 2 The Muirs, KINROSS ☎(0577) 63467 40⇨🐾

POLMONT　　　　　　　　　　Map 11 NS97

Grangemouth ☎(0324) 711500
Windy parkland course. Testing holes: 3rd, 4th (par 4's); 5th (par 5); 7th (par 3) 216 yds over reservoir (elevated green); 8th, 9th, 18th (par 4's).
18 holes, 6314yds, Par 71, SSS 71, Course record 67.
Club membership 700.

Visitors	must contact in advance.
Societies	must contact in writing.
Green Fees	not confirmed.
Facilities	⊗ by prior arrangement ⅢÎ by prior arrangement 🏊 ⬤ ♀ ⛳ 🏠 ⚓ Stuart J Campbell.
Leisure	pool tables.
Location	Polmont Hill (on unclass rd .5m N of M9 junc 4)
Hotel	★★★65% Inchyra Grange Hotel, Grange Rd, POLMONT ☎(0324) 711911 33⇨🐾

Polmont ☎(0324) 711277
Parkland course, hilly with few bunkers. Views of the River Forth and Ochil Hills.
9 holes, 3031yds, Par 36.
Club membership 200.

Visitors	restricted Sat.
Societies	must telephone in advance.

►

We make every effort to ensure that our information is accurate but details may change after we go to print

Green Fees not confirmed.
Location Manuelrigg, Maddiston (E side of village off A803)
Hotel ★★★65% Inchyra Grange Hotel, Grange Rd, POLMONT ☎(0324) 711911 33⇨🏠

STIRLING Map 11 NS79

Stirling ☎(0786) 64098
Undulating parkland course with magnificent views. Testing 15th, 'Cotton's Fancy', 384 yds (par 4).
18 holes, 6438yds, Par 72, SSS 71, Course record 65.
Club membership 950.
Visitors may not play Sat & restricted Sun.
Societies must telephone in advance.
Green Fees not confirmed.
Facilities ⊗ 🍴 by prior arrangement 📇 ♨ ♀ (all day) 🔥 🏠 Ⴑ Ian Collins.
Location Queens Rd (W side of town on B8051)
Hotel ★★59% King Robert Hotel, Glasgow Rd, Bannockburn, STIRLING ☎(0786) 811666 53⇨🏠

TILLICOULTRY Map 11 NS99

Tillicoultry ☎(0259) 50741/51337
Parkland course at foot of the Ochil Hills entailing some hard walking.
18 holes, 5358yds, Par 68, SSS 66, Course record 64.
Club membership 400.
Visitors welcome except during club competitions.
Societies apply in writing.
Green Fees not confirmed.
Facilities ⊗ (May-Sep) 🍴 by prior arrangement 📇 ♨ ♀
Location Alva Rd
Hotel ★★★65% Royal Hotel, Henderson St, BRIDGE OF ALLAN ☎(0786) 832284 32⇨🏠

DUMFRIES & GALLOWAY

CASTLE DOUGLAS Map 11 NX76

Castle Douglas ☎(0556) 2801
Parkland course, one severe hill.
9 holes, 2704yds, Par 34, SSS 33 or , SSS 62.
Club membership 500.
Visitors welcome except Tue & Thu after 4pm & Sun during competitions.
Societies apply by writing.
Green Fees £8 per day.
Facilities ⊗ (in season) 📇 (in season) ♨ ♀ 🔥
Location Abercromby Rd (W side of town)
Hotel ★★70% Douglas Arms, King St, CASTLE DOUGLAS ☎(0556) 2231 22rm(15⇨🏠)

A golf-course name printed in **bold italics** means that we have been unable to verify information with the club's management for the current year

---

COLVEND Map 11 NX85

Colvend ☎Rockcliffe (055663) 398
Picturesque and challenging course on Solway coast. Superb views.
9 holes, 2322yds, Par 66, SSS 63, Course record 63.
Club membership 480.
Visitors restricted Tue & Thu in summer.
Societies must telephone in advance.
Green Fees £10 per day.
Facilities ⊗ 🍴 📇 ♨ (catering daily Apr-Sep, Sat and Sun Oct-Mar) ♀ 🔥 🏌
Location Sandyhills (6m from Dalbeattie on A710 Solway Coast Rd)
Hotel ★★★🏊65% Baron's Craig Hotel, ROCKCLIFFE ☎(055663) 225 27rm(20⇨🏠)

CUMMERTREES Map 11 NY16

Powfoot ☎(04617) 227
The hills of Cumbria, away beyond the Solway Firth, and from time to time a sight of the Isle of Man, make playing at this delightfully compact semi-links seaside course a scenic treat. Lovely holes include the 2nd, the 8th and the 11th.
18 holes, 6283yds, Par 71, SSS 70, Course record 65.
Club membership 924.

SCORECARD: White Tees					
Hole	Yds	Par	Hole	Yds	Par
1	352	4	10	430	4
2	477	5	11	313	4
3	445	4	12	154	3
4	358	4	13	339	4
5	272	4	14	501	5
6	351	4	15	201	3
7	155	3	16	432	4
8	359	4	17	336	4
9	402	4	18	406	4
Out	3171	36	In	3112	35
			Totals	6283	71

Visitors may not play Sat & only after 2.45pm on Sun. Must contact in advance.
Societies must book at least one week in advance.
Green Fees £18 per day; £15 per round at weekends.
Facilities ⊗ 🍴 📇 ♨ ♀ 🔥 🏠 Ⴑ Gareth Dick.
Location .5m off B724
Hotel ★★64% Golf Hotel, Links Av, POWFOOT ☎(04617) 254 19rm(9⇨🏠)

DUMFRIES Map 11 NX97

Dumfries & County ☎(0387) 53585
Parkland course alongside River Nith, with views over the Queensberry Hills.
18 holes, 5928yds, Par 69, SSS 68, Course record 63.
Club membership 600.
Visitors may not play on Sat during Mar-Oct. Must contact in advance.
Societies apply in writing.
Green Fees £18.00 per day (£20 weekends).
Facilities ⊗ 🍴 📇 ♨ ♀ 🔥 🏠 🏌 Ⴑ Gordon Gray.
Location Edinburgh Rd (1m NE off A701)
Hotel ★★★68% Station Hotel, 49 Lovers Walk, DUMFRIES ☎(0387) 54316 32⇨🏠

Dumfries & Galloway ☎(0387) 63848
Parkland course.
18 holes, 5803yds, Par 68, SSS 68, Course record 62.
Club membership 800.
Visitors may not play on competition days.
Societies must telephone in advance.
Green Fees £14 per day (£17 per round weekends).

Facilities	🏠
Leisure	snooker.
Location	2 Laurieston Av (W side of town centre on A75)
Hotel	★★★68% Station Hotel, 49 Lovers Walk, DUMFRIES ☎(0387) 54316 32⇨🐾

GATEHOUSE-OF-FLEET   Map 11 NX55

Gatehouse ☎(0557) 814281
Set against a background of rolling hills with scenic views of Fleet Bay and the Solway Firth.
9 holes, 2398yds, Par 66, SSS 63, Course record 60.
Club membership 280.

Visitors	no restrictions.
Societies	telephone (0557) 814459 in advance.
Green Fees	£8 per day/round.
Facilities	⌣
Location	Laurieston Rd (N side of village)
Hotel	★★★62% Murray Arms Hotel, GATEHOUSE OF FLEET ☎(0557) 814207 12⇨Annexe1⇨

GLENLUCE   Map 10 NX15

Wigtownshire County ☎(05813) 420
Seaside links course on the shores of Luce Bay, easy walking.
18 holes, 5411yds, Par 70, SSS 66, Course record 66.
Club membership 310.

Visitors	may not play on Wed evenings.
Societies	must telephone (05813) 589 in advance.
Green Fees	£14 per day ; £11 per round (£16 per day; £13 per round weekends).
Facilities	⊗ 〭 🝣 ⬛ ♀ ⌣ 🏠
Leisure	pool table.
Location	Mains of Park (1.5m W off A75)
Hotel	★★★74% North West Castle Hotel, STRANRAER ☎(0776) 4413 74⇨🐾

KIRKCUDBRIGHT   Map 11 NX65

Kirkcudbright ☎(0557) 30314
Parkland course. Hilly, with hard walking. Good views.
18 holes, 5598yds, Par 67, SSS 67, Course record 63.
Club membership 500.

Visitors	welcome except during club competitions.
Societies	apply in writing.
Green Fees	£10 per day or round.
Facilities	⊗ 〭 by prior arrangement 🝣 ⬛ (no catering Mon) ♀ ⌣
Location	Stirling Crescent (NE side of town off A711)
Hotel	★★66% Selkirk Arms Hotel, Old High St, KIRKCUDBRIGHT ☎(0557) 30402 14⇨🐾Annexe1⇨

LANGHOLM   Map 11 NY38

Langholm ☎(03873) 80878
Hillside course with fine views, hard walking.
9 holes, 5744yds, Par 70, SSS 68, Course record 66.
Club membership 130.

Visitors	restricted Sat.
Societies	apply in writing or telephone in advance.
Green Fees	£6 per day/round.
Facilities	🝣 ⬛ (Sat & Sun) ♀ (Sat & Sun)

Location	Whiteside (E side of village off A7)
Hotel	★★56% Eskdale Hotel, Market Place, LANGHOLM ☎(03873) 80357 16rm(3⇨7🐾)

LOCHMABEN   Map 11 NY08

Lochmaben ☎(0387) 810552
Comfortable-walking parkland course between two lochs with fine old trees and fast greens all year round.
9 holes, 5304yds, Par 66, SSS 66, Course record 60.
Club membership 550.

Visitors	restricted weekdays & during competitions.
Societies	must contact in advance.
Green Fees	£10 per day (£12 weekends).
Facilities	⬛ (catering by prior arrangement) ♀ ⌣
Location	Castlehill Gate (S side of village off A709)
Hotel	★★★66% Dryfesdale Hotel, LOCKERBIE ☎(05762) 2427 15⇨🐾

LOCKERBIE   Map 11 NY18

Lockerbie ☎(05762) 3363
Parkland course with fine views and featuring the only pond hole in Dumfriesshire.
18 holes, 5418yds, Par 67, SSS 66, Course record 64.
Club membership 555.

Visitors	no restrictions.
Societies	apply in writing.
Green Fees	£12 (£15 weekends).
Facilities	⊗ 🝣 ⬛ ♀ ⌣

►

Location	Corrie Rd (E side of town centre off B7068)
Hotel	★★★66% Dryfesdale Hotel, LOCKERBIE ☎(05762) 2427 15⇱🛏

Moffat   Map 11 NT00

Moffat ☎(0683) 20020
Scenic moorland course overlooking the town, with
panoramic views.
18 holes, 5218yds, Par 69, SSS 66, Course record 60.
Club membership 350.

Visitors	restricted Wed afternoons.
Societies	must contact in advance.
Green Fees	£12 per day (£22 weekends).
Facilities	⊗ 🍴 🏌 💺 ♀ ⛳ 🏨 ☂
Location	Coatshill (1m SW off A701)
Hotel	★★★64% Moffat House Hotel, High St, MOFFAT ☎(0683) 20039 16⇱🛏Annexe4⇱🛏

Monreith   Map 10 NX34

St Medan ☎Port William (09887) 358
Links course with panoramic views of the Solway and Isle of
Man.
9 holes, 4552yds, Par 64, SSS 62, Course record 61.
Club membership 300.

Visitors	no restrictions.
Societies	apply in writing.
Green Fees	£15 per day; £10 per 18 holes; £5 per 9 holes.
Facilities	⊗ 🍴 🏌 💺 ♀ ⛳ ☂
Location	1m SE off A747
Hotel	★★★63% Corsemalzie House Hotel, PORT WILLIAM ☎(098886) 254 14⇱🛏

New Galloway   Map 11 NT00

New Galloway ☎(06442) 737
Set on the edge of the Galloway Hills and overlooking Loch
Ken, the course has excellent tees and first class greens.
9 holes, 4604yds, Par 63, SSS 63, Course record 66.
Club membership 215.

Visitors	restricted on competition days.
Societies	apply in writing.
Green Fees	£7.50 per day (£10 Sun).
Facilities	💺 ♀ (1200-1400 May-Sep) ⛳
Location	S side of town on A762
Hotel	★★59% Culgruff House Hotel, CROSSMICHAEL ☎(055667) 230 16rm(4⇱)

Newton Stewart   Map 10 NX46

Newton Stewart ☎(0671) 2172
Parkland course in picturesque setting. Short but quite tight.
9 holes, 5362yds, Par 68, SSS 65, Course record 64.
Club membership 300.

Visitors	telephone for details.
Societies	must contact in advance.
Green Fees	£8 per day (£11 weekends & public holidays).
Facilities	⊗ 🍴 🏌 💺 ♀ ⛳ 🏨
Leisure	pool table.
Location	Kirroughtree Av, Minnigaff (.5m N of town centre)

Hotel	★★★67% Kirroughtree Hotel, Minnigaff, NEWTON STEWART ☎(0671) 2141 20⇱🛏Annexe2⇱🛏

Portpatrick   Map 10 NX05

Portpatrick ☎(077681) 273
Seaside links-type course, set on cliffs overlooking the Irish
Sea, with magnificent views.
18 holes, 5732yds, Par 70, SSS 68, Course record 64 or 9 holes,
1442yds, Par 27, SSS 27.
Club membership 450.

Visitors	welcome except for competition days. A handicap certificate is required. Must contact in advance.
Societies	must contact in advance.
Green Fees	18 holes: £18 per day; £12 per round (£22/£15 weekends) 9 holes: £8 per day; £4 per round.
Facilities	⊗ 🍴 🏌 💺 ♀ (all day) ⛳ 🏨 ☂
Location	Golf Course Rd (NW side of village)
Hotel	★★★66% Fernhill Golf Hotel, PORTPATRICK ☎(077681) 220 15rm(14⇱🛏)Annexe 6rm(3⇱1🛏)

Sanquhar   Map 11 NS70

Sanquhar ☎(0659) 50577
Moorland course, fine views.
9 holes, 5144mtr, Par 70, SSS 68, Course record 66.
Club membership 180.

Visitors	may not play competition days.
Societies	apply in writing.
Green Fees	not confirmed.
Facilities	⊗ 🍴 🏌 💺 (all catering by prior arrangement) ⛳
Leisure	snooker.
Location	Euchan Golf Course (.5m SW off A76)
Hotel	★★64% Mennockfoot Lodge Hotel, Mennock, SANQUHAR ☎(0659) 50382 & 50477 1⇱Annexe8⇱🛏

Southerness   Map 11 NX95

Southerness ☎Kirkbean (038788) 677
Natural links, Championship course with panoramic views.
Heather and bracken abound.
18 holes, 6554yds, Par 71, SSS 72, Course record 65.
Club membership 720.

Visitors	some restricted times
Societies	must contact in advance.
Green Fees	£15 per day (£20 weekends & bank holidays).
Facilities	⊗ by prior arrangement 🍴 by prior arrangement 🏌 💺 ♀ ⛳
Location	3.5m S of Kirkbean off A710
Hotel	★★★65% Baron's Craig Hotel, ROCKCLIFFE ☎(055663) 225 27rm(20⇱)

Stranraer   Map 10 NX06

Stranraer ☎Leswalt (077687) 245
Parkland course with beautiful view of Lochryan.
18 holes, 6300yds, Par 70, SSS 71, Course record 66.
Club membership 550.

Visitors	restricted at weekends. Must contact in advance.
Societies	must telephone in advance.
Green Fees	not confirmed.
Facilities	⊗ by prior arrangement ⅲ by prior arrangement 🏌 ⬤ ♀ △ 🏠
Leisure	snooker.
Location	Creachmore by Stranraer (2.5m NW on A718)
Hotel	★★★74% North West Castle Hotel, STRANRAER ☎(0776) 4413 74↩🐾

THORNHILL   Map 11 NX89

Thornhill ☎Dumfries (0848) 30546
Moorland/parkland course with fine views.
18 holes, 6011yds, Par 71, SSS 69.
Club membership 580.

Visitors	no restrictions.
Societies	must telephone in advance.
Green Fees	not confirmed.
Facilities	🏌 ⬤ ♀ △
Location	Blacknest (1m E of town off A92)
Hotel	★★72% Trigony House Hotel, Closeburn, THORNHILL ☎(0848) 31211 9↩🐾

WIGTOWN   Map 11 NX45

Wigtown & Bladnoch ☎(09884) 3354
Slightly hilly parkland course with fine views over Wigtown Bay to Galloway Hills.
9 holes, 5462yds, Par 68, SSS 67, Course record 61.
Club membership 130.

Visitors	may not play competition days.
Societies	apply in writing.
Green Fees	£7 per day (£10 weekends per round).
Facilities	⊗ (Jun-Sep) ⅲ by prior arrangement 🏌 (Jun-Sep) ⬤ ♀ (summer & weekends) △
Location	Lightlands Ter (SW on A714)
Hotel	★★★⏣67% Kirroughtree Hotel, Minnigaff, NEWTON STEWART ☎(0671) 2141 20↩🐾Annexe2↩🐾

FIFE

ABERDOUR   Map 11 NT18

Aberdour ☎(0383) 860256
Parkland course with lovely views over Firth of Forth.
18 holes, 5001mtrs, Par 67, SSS 67, Course record 63.
Club membership 580.

Visitors	weekdays only. Must contact in advance.
Societies	must telephone in advance.
Green Fees	not confirmed.
Facilities	⊗ ⅲ 🏌 ⬤ ♀
Location	Seaside Place (S side of village)
Hotel	★★66% Woodside Hotel, High St, ABERDOUR ☎(0383) 860328 21↩🐾

Entries highlighted in green identify
courses which are considered
to be particularly interesting

ANSTRUTHER   Map 12 NO50

Anstruther ☎(0333) 310956
Seaside links course with some excellent par 3 holes; always in good condition.
9 holes, 4144mtrs, Par 62, SSS 63.
Club membership 500.

Visitors	advised to phone in advance.
Societies	welcome except Jun-Aug.
Green Fees	£6 per round (£8 weekends).
Facilities	⊗ 🏌 ⬤ (catering Jun-Sep) ♀ △
Location	Shore Rd, 'Marsfield' (SW off A917)
Hotel	★★★60% Craws Nest Hotel, Bankwell Rd, ANSTRUTHER ☎(0333) 310691 31↩🐾Annexe19↩🐾

BURNTISLAND   Map 11 NT28

Burntisland Golf House Club ☎(0592) 874093
This hill course has fine sea views.
18 holes, 5908yds, Par 69, SSS 69, Course record 65.
Club membership 780.

Visitors	must contact in advance.
Societies	apply in writing.
Green Fees	£18 per day; £13 per round (£24/£17 weekends).
Facilities	⊗ ⅲ 🏌 ⬤ ♀ △ 🏠 🥢 Jacky Montgomery.
Location	Dodhead (1m E on B923)
Hotel	★★★62% Dean Park Hotel, Chapel Level, KIRKCALDY ☎(0592) 261635 45↩🐾Annexe12🐾

CRAIL   Map 12 NO60

Crail Golfing Society ☎(0333) 50278
Perched on the edge of the North Sea on the very point of the golfing county of Fife, the Crail Golfing Society's course at Balcomie is picturesque and sporting. And here again golf history has been made for Crail Golfing Society began its life in 1786. The course is highly thought of by students of the game both for its testing holes and the stardard of its greens.
18 holes, 5720yds, Par 69, SSS 68, Course record 64.
Club membership 950.

Visitors	restricted 10am-noon & 2-4.30pm. Must contact in advance.
Societies	must telephone in advance.
Green Fees	£24 per day; £16 per round (£30/£20 weekends).
Facilities	⊗ ⅲ 🏌 ⬤ ♀ △ 🏠 🥢 🥢 Graheme Lennie.
Location	Balcomie Clubhouse, Fifeness (2m NE off A917)
Hotel	★★★60% Craws Nest Hotel, Bankwell Rd, ANSTRUTHER ☎(0333) 310691 31↩🐾Annexe19↩🐾

CUPAR   Map 11 NO31

Cupar ☎(0334) 53549
Hilly parkland course with fine views.
9 holes, 5500yds, Par 68, SSS 65, Course record 61.
Club membership 400.

Visitors	with member only weekends.
Societies	must contact in advance.

▶

Green Fees	£9 per day; £7 per round (£11/£9 weekends).
Facilities	⊗ ᒪ ⬤ (weekends only) ⚲ (weekends only) ⌂
Location	Hilltarvit (.75m S off A92)
Hotel	★★★68% Rufflets Country House & Garden Restaurant, Strathkinness Low Rd, ST ANDREWS ☎(0334) 72594 17⇨🎍Annexe3⇨🎍

DUNFERMLINE Map 11 NT08

Canmore ☎(0383) 724969
Undulating parkland course affording excellent views.
18 holes, 5474yds, Par 67, SSS 66.
Club membership 620.

Visitors	no restrictions.
Green Fees	not confirmed.
Facilities	⚲ ⌂ 🍴 🏌
Location	Venturefair Av (1m N on A823)
Hotel	★★★62% King Malcolm Thistle Hotel, Queensferry Rd, Wester Pitcorthie, DUNFERMLINE ☎(0383) 722611 48⇨🎍

Dunfermline ☎(0383) 723534
Gently undulating parkland course with interesting contours.
Sixteenth-century clubhouse.
18 holes, 6237yds, Par 72, SSS 70, Course record 65.
Par 3 course: 9 holes, 1144yds, Par 27.
Club membership 675.

Visitors	welcome Mon-Fri. Must contact in advance.
Societies	must contact in advance.
Green Fees	£25 per day; £15 per round.
Facilities	⊗ (ex Mon) ⋔ by prior arrangement ᒪ ⬤ ⚲ ⌂ 🍴 🏌 Steve Craig.
Location	Pitfirrane, Crossford (2m W on A994)
Hotel	★★★62% King Malcolm Thistle Hotel, Queensferry Rd, Wester Pitcorthie, DUNFERMLINE ☎(0383) 722611 48⇨🎍

Pitreavie ☎(0383) 722591
Picturesque woodland course with panoramic view of the River Forth Valley. Testing golf.
18 holes, 6086yds, Par 70, SSS 69, Course record 65.
Club membership 700.

Visitors	welcome except for competition days.
Societies	must write or telephone in advance.
Green Fees	£18 per day; £12 per round (£20 per day weekends).
Facilities	⊗ & ⋔ (ex Tue) ᒪ ⬤ ⚲ ⌂ 🍴 🏌 Jim Forrester.
Location	Queensferry Rd (SE side of town on A823)
Hotel	★★★62% King Malcolm Thistle Hotel, Queensferry Rd, Wester Pitcorthie, DUNFERMLINE ☎(0383) 722611 48⇨🎍

Each golf-course entry has a recommended AA-appointed hotel. For a wider choice of places to stay, consult *AA Hotels and Restaurants in Britain and Ireland* and *AA Inspected Bed and Breakfast in Britain and Ireland*

ELIE Map 12 NO40

Golf House Club
☎(0333) 330301
One of Scotland's delightful holiday courses with panoramic views over the Firth of Forth. Some of the holes out towards the rocky coastline are splendid. This is the course which has produced many good professionals, including the immortal James Braid.
18 holes, 6241yds, Par 70, SSS 70, Course record 62.
Club membership 650.

	SCORECARD				
Hole	Yds	Par	Hole	Yds	Par
1	420	4	10	267	4
2	284	4	11	120	3
3	214	3	12	466	4
4	378	4	13	380	4
5	365	4	14	414	4
6	316	4	15	338	4
7	252	4	16	407	4
8	382	4	17	439	4
9	440	4	18	359	4
Out	3051	35	In	3190	35
			Totals	6241	70

Visitors	may not play before 10am; no parties at weekends.
Societies	mid week only, except Jun-Aug.
Green Fees	not confirmed.
Facilities	⊗ by prior arrangement ᒪ ⬤ ⚲ ⌂ 🍴 🏌 Robin Wilson.
Location	W side of village off A917
Hotel	★★★60% Craws Nest Hotel, Bankwell Rd, ANSTRUTHER ☎(0333) 310691 31⇨🎍Annexe19⇨🎍

FALKLAND Map 11 NO20

Falkland ☎(0337) 57404
A flat, well-kept course with excellent greens and views of East Lomond Hill and Falkland Palace.
9 holes, 5216yds, Par 68, SSS 65, Course record 67.
Club membership 250.

Visitors	parties must make prior arrangements.
Societies	must contact in advance.
Green Fees	£6 per day (£8 weekends).
Facilities	catering by prior arrangement ⚲ (evening & WE) ⌂
Location	The Myre (N side of town on A912)
Hotel	★★★72% Balgeddie House Hotel, Balgeddie Way, GLENROTHES ☎(0592) 742511 18⇨🎍

GLENROTHES Map 11 NO20

Glenrothes ☎(0592) 758686
Testing and hilly parkland course with burn crossed four times. Good views.
18 holes, 6444yds, Par 71, SSS 71, Course record 65.
Club membership 800.

Societies	telephone one month in advance.
Green Fees	£10 per day; £7.20 per round (£12/£9.70 weekends).
Facilities	⊗ ⋔ ᒪ ⬤ ⚲ ⌂
Location	Golf Course Rd (W side of town off B921)
Hotel	★★★72% Balgeddie House Hotel, Balgeddie Way, GLENROTHES ☎(0592) 742511 18⇨🎍

A golf-course name printed in **bold italics** means that we have been unable to verify information with the club's management for the current year

KINCARDINE Map 11 NS98

Tulliallan ☎(0259) 30396
Partially hilly parkland course with testing 3rd hole (par 4).
18 holes, 5982yds, Par 69, SSS 69.
Club membership 525.
Visitors restricted at weekends.
Societies may not play on Sat; must contact in advance.
Green Fees not confirmed.
Facilities ⊗ ⅲ ⅊ ☕ ♀ △ 🏠 ⅞ ⅌ Steven Kelly.
Location Alloa Rd (1m NW on A977)
Hotel ★★★65% Inchyra Grange Hotel, Grange Rd, POLMONT ☎(0324) 711911 33⇨🐾

KINGHORN Map 11 NT28

Kinghorn ☎(0592) 890345
Municipal course, 300 ft above sea level with views over Firth of Forth and North Sea. Undulating and quite testing. Facilities shared by Kinghorn Ladies.
18 holes, 5269yds, Par 65, SSS 67.
Club membership 190.
Visitors no restrictions.
Societies must contact in writing.
Green Fees not confirmed.
Facilities ♀ △
Location Macduff Cres (S side of town on A921)
Hotel ★★★62% Dean Park Hotel, Chapel Level, KIRKCALDY ☎(0592) 261635 45⇨🐾Annexe12🐾

KIRKCALDY Map 11 NT29

Dunnikier Park ☎(0592) 261599
Parkland, rolling fairways, not heavily bunkered, views of Firth of Forth.
18 holes, 6601yds, Par 72, SSS 72, Course record 66.
Club membership 600.
Visitors no restrictions.
Societies apply in writing to the Secretary.
Green Fees not confirmed.
Facilities ⊗ ⅲ ⅊ ☕ ♀ △ 🏠 ⅌ Jack Montgomery.
Location Dunnikier Way (2m N off A988)
Hotel ★★★62% Dean Park Hotel, Chapel Level, KIRKCALDY ☎(0592) 261635 45⇨🐾Annexe12🐾

Kirkcaldy ☎(0592) 260370
Parkland course.
18 holes, 6004yds, Par 71, SSS 70, Course record 67.
Club membership 725.
Visitors may not play Sat. Must contact in advance.
Societies apply in writing to the Secretary.
Green Fees £18 per day; £12 per round (£21/£15 weekends).
Facilities ⊗ ⅲ ⅊ ☕ ♀ △ 🏠 ⅌ Paul Hodgson.
Location Balwearie Rd (SW side of town off A910)
Hotel ★★★62% Dean Park Hotel, Chapel Level, KIRKCALDY ☎(0592) 261635 45⇨🐾Annexe12🐾

If you know of a golf course which welcomes visitors and is not already in this guide, we should be grateful for information

LADYBANK Map 11 NO30

Ladybank ☎(0337) 30814
Picturesque parkland/heathland course, popular with visitors. Qualifying course for the British Open.
18 holes, 6641yds, Par 71, SSS 72, Course record 67.
Club membership 800.
Visitors must contact in advance.
Societies must telephone or write in advance.
Green Fees £29 per day; £22 per round (£32/£24 weekends).
Facilities ⊗ ⅲ ⅊ ☕ ♀ △ 🏠 ⅞ ⅌ Martin Gray.
Location Annsmuir (N side of village off B9129)
Hotel ★★62% Lomond Hills Hotel, Parliament Square, FREUCHIE ☎(0337) 57329 & 57498 25⇨🐾

LESLIE Map 11 NO20

Leslie
Challenging parkland course.
9 holes, 2470yds, Par 62, SSS 64, Course record 62.
Club membership 250.
Visitors no restrictions.
Societies must apply to the secretary.
Green Fees not confirmed.
Facilities ♀ △
Location Balsillie Laws (N side of town off A911)
Hotel ★★★72% Balgeddie House Hotel, Balgeddie Way, GLENROTHES ☎(0592) 742511 18⇨🐾

LEUCHARS Map 12 NO42

St Michaels ☎(0334) 839365
Parkland course with open views over Fife and Tayside.
9 holes, 5158yds, Par 70, SSS 66, Course record 66.
Club membership 450.
Visitors may not play on Sun mornings Mar-Oct.
Societies must telephone in advance.
Green Fees not confirmed.
Facilities ⊗ ⅊ ☕ ♀ △ ⅞
Location NW side of village on A919
Hotel ★★62% Lomond Hills Hotel, Parliament Square, FREUCHIE ☎(0337) 57329 & 57498 25⇨🐾

LEVEN Map 11 NO30

Leven Golfing Society ☎(0333) 26096
Plays over Leven Links - typical links course.
18 holes, 6435yds, Par 71, SSS 71, Course record 63.
Club membership 700.
Visitors may not play Sat.
Societies apply in writing.
Green Fees £22.50 per day ;£16 per round (£30/£20 weekends).
Facilities ⊗ ⅲ ⅊ ☕ ♀ △ 🏠 ⅌ George Finlayson.
Leisure snooker.
Location Links Rd
Hotel ★★★65% Old Manor Hotel, Leven Rd, LUNDIN LINKS ☎(0333) 320368 19rm(15⇨)

For a full list of golf courses included in the book, see the index at the end of the directory

Leven Thistle ☎(0333) 26397

Leven has the classic ingredients which make up a golf links in Scotland; undulating fairways with hills and hallows, out of bounds and a 'burn' or stream. A top class championship links course used for British Open final qualifying stages, it has fine views over Largo Bay.
18 holes, 6434yds, Par 71, SSS 71, Course record 64.
Club membership 400.

SCORECARD: Leven Links (Medal Tees)					
Hole	Yds	Par	Hole	Yds	Par
1	413	4	10	325	4
2	376	4	11	369	4
3	343	4	12	482	5
4	449	4	13	484	5
5	157	3	14	330	4
6	567	5	15	188	3
7	184	3	16	386	4
8	348	4	17	412	4
9	164	3	18	457	4
Out	3001	34	In	3433	37
			Totals	6434	71

Visitors parties may not play on Sat.
Societies must telephone 1 month in advance.
Green Fees £22.50 per day; £16 per round (£30 per day; £20 per round weekends).
Facilities ⊗ & ⅏ by prior arrangement ⓛ ⬛ ♀ △ 🏠 ℓ G Finlayson.
Leisure pool table, carpet bowls, TV, darts.
Location 3 Balfour St
Hotel ★★★65% Old Manor Hotel, Leven Rd, LUNDIN LINKS ☎(0333) 320368 19rm(15⇌)

LOCHGELLY Map 11 NT19

Lochgelly ☎(0592) 780174
Parkland course with easy walking and often windy.
18 holes, 5491yds, Par 68, SSS 67.
Club membership 600.
Visitors no restrictions.
Societies must apply in writing.
Green Fees £12 per day (£15 weekends).
Facilities ⊗ ⅏ ⓛ ⬛ (catering by prior arrangement) ♀ △
Location Cartmore Rd (W side of town off A910)
Hotel ★★★62% Dean Park Hotel, Chapel Level, KIRKCALDY ☎(0592) 261635 45⇌🏠Annexe12🏠

Lochore Meadows ☎Ballingry (0592) 860086
Lochside course with natural stream running through, and woodland nearby. Country park offers many leisure facilities.
9 holes, 5554yds, Par 72, SSS 71, Course record 68.
Club membership 200.
Visitors no restrictions.
Societies must contact in advance.
Green Fees not confirmed.
Facilities ⊗ ⓛ ⬛ △
Leisure fishing, riding.
Location Lochore Meadows Country Park, Crosshill (2m N off B920)
Hotel ★★★62% Green Hotel, 2 The Muirs, KINROSS ☎(0577) 63467 40⇌🏠

We make every effort to ensure that our information is accurate but details may change after we go to print

LUNDIN LINKS Map 12 NO40

Lundin ☎(0333) 320202
The Leven Links and the course of the Lundin Club adjoin each other. This course is part seaside and part inland. The holes, which can be described as seaside holes, are excellent. The others no less so, but of a different nature.
18 holes, 6377yds, Par 71, SSS 71, Course record 64.
Club membership 850.

SCORECARD					
Hole	Yds	Par	Hole	Yds	Par
1	424	4	10	353	4
2	346	4	11	466	4
3	335	4	12	133	3
4	452	4	13	512	5
5	140	3	14	175	3
6	330	4	15	418	4
7	273	4	16	314	4
8	364	4	17	345	4
9	555	5	18	442	4
Out	3219	36	In	3158	35
			Totals	6377	71

Visitors with member only on Sun.
Societies apply in writing.
Green Fees £24 per day; £16.50 per round (£20 Sat visitors after 2.30pm).
Facilities ⊗ ⅏ ⓛ ⬛ ♀ 🏠 ℓ D K Webster.
Location Golf Rd (W side of village off A915)
Hotel ★★★65% Old Manor Hotel, Leven Rd, LUNDIN LINKS ☎(0333) 320368 19rm(15⇌)

Lundin Ladies ☎(0333) 320022
Short, lowland course with Roman stones on the second fairway, and coastal views.
9 holes, 4730yds, Par 68, SSS 67, Course record 67.
Club membership 260.
Visitors no restrictions.
Green Fees not confirmed.
Location Woodilea Rd (W side of village off A915)
Hotel ★★★65% Old Manor Hotel, Leven Rd, LUNDIN LINKS ☎(0333) 320368 19rm(15⇌)

MARKINCH Map 11 NO20

Balbirnie Park ☎Glenrothes (0592) 752006
Scenic parkland course with several interesting holes.
Balbirnie Park Golf Club: 18 holes, 6210yds, Par 71, SSS 70, Course record 66.
Club membership 690.
Visitors must contact in advance.
Societies apply in writing.
Green Fees £24 per day; £17 per round (£30/£25 Sat, £29/£24 Sun).
Facilities ⊗ ⅏ by prior arrangement ⓛ ⬛ ♀ △
Location 2m W of Glenrothes
Hotel ★★★★⏵73% Balbirnie House, Balbirnie Park, MARKINCH ☎(0592) 610066 30⇌🏠

Each golf-course entry has a recommended AA-appointed hotel. For a wider choice of places to stay, consult *AA Hotels and Restaurants in Britain and Ireland* and *AA Inspected Bed and Breakfast in Britain and Ireland*

ST ANDREWS   Map 12 NO51

British Golf Museum ☎(0334)78880 (Situated opposite Royal & Ancient Golf Club) Tells the fascinating history of golf. Highly visual displays are complemented by the use of visitor-activated touch screens throughout the galleries. Exhibits take the visitor from the misty origins of the game to the present day. You will see amazing images, fascinating collections of clubs, balls, fashion and memorabilia, two period workshops and historic documents. An audio-visual theatre shows historic golfing moments. Shop. **Open** : Jun-Oct, daily 1000-1730; Nov, Tue-Sun 1000-1700; Dec, Tue-Sat 1000-1600. Closed 25-26 Dec. Opening hours may vary during major St Andrews Golfing events. ☎to confirm. **Admission** : ☎for details.

St Andrews Links See page 259

SALINE   Map 11 NT09

Saline ☎(0383) 852591
Hillside course with panoramic view of the Forth Valley.
9 holes, 5302yds, Par 68, SSS 66, Course record 62.
Club membership 350.

Visitors	may not play Sat.
Societies	telephone one week in advance.
Green Fees	£7 per weekday; £10 Sunday.
Facilities	ⓛ ⓦ ⓨ
Location	Kinneddar Hill (.5m E at junc B913/914)
Hotel	★★★62% King Malcolm Thistle Hotel, Queensferry Rd, Wester Pitcorthie, DUNFERMLINE ☎(0383) 722611 48⇨🔦

TAYPORT   Map 12 NO42

Scotscraig ☎Dundee (0382) 552515
A rather tight course on downland-type turf with an abundance of gorse. The sheltered position of this Open qualifying course ensures good weather throughout the year.
18 holes, 6496yds, Par 71, SSS 71, Course record 61.
Club membership 650.

Visitors	restricted at weekends. Must contact in advance.
Societies	apply in writing.
Green Fees	£27 per day; £18 per round (£34/£24 weekends).
Facilities	⊗ ⓜ ⓛ ⓦ ⓨ △ ⓐ ⓣ
Location	S side of village off B945
Hotel	★★★59% Queens Hotel, 160 Nethergate, DUNDEE ☎(0382) 22515 47⇨🔦

THORNTON   Map 11 NT29

Thornton ☎Glenrothes (0592) 771111
Undulating and fairly difficult parkland course.
18 holes, 5589yds, Par 70, SSS 69, Course record 65.
Club membership 650.

Visitors	restricted at weekends before 9.30am, also public holidays between 12.30-2pm.
Societies	apply in advance.
Green Fees	£15 per day; £10 per round (£22/£15 weekends).

▶

Facilities ⊗ ⓛ � ☕ ⛳ △ 🏠
Location Station Rd (1m E of town off A92)
Hotel ★★★72% Balgeddie House Hotel, Balgeddie Way, GLENROTHES ☎(0592) 742511 18⇨🏠

GRAMPIAN

ABERDEEN   Map 15 NJ90

Balnagask ☎(0224) 876407
Links course.
18 holes, 5486mtrs, SSS 69.
Visitors no restrictions.
Societies must contact in advance.
Facilities ⛳ △
Location St Fitticks Rd (2m E of city centre)
Hotel ★★★68% Caledonian Thistle Hotel, 10 Union Ter, ABERDEEN ☎(0224) 640233 80⇨🏠

Bon Accord ☎(0224) 633464
Links coastal course. Municipal course used by three clubs.
18 holes, 6433yds, Par 72, SSS 71, Course record 65.
Club membership 800.
Visitors no restrictions.
Societies welcome.
Green Fees £5.50 per round.
Facilities ⊗ by prior arrangement ⓛ ☕ ⛳ 🏠
Leisure snooker.
Location 19 Golf Rd (.75 NE of city centre)
Hotel ★★★68% Caledonian Thistle Hotel, 10 Union Ter, ABERDEEN ☎(0224) 640233 80⇨🏠

Deeside ☎(0224) 867697
Scenic parkland course.
18 holes, 6000yds, Par 69, SSS 69, Course record 64.
Club membership 800.
Visitors may not play on Sat before 4pm & medal days. Must contact in advance and have an introduction from own club.
Societies Thu only.
Green Fees not confirmed.
Facilities ⊗ ⧠ ⓛ (Tue-Sun) ☕ (Tue-Sun) ⛳ △ 🏠 ᵖ ꞔ
Leisure snooker.
Location Bielside (3m W of city centre off A93)
Hotel ★★★72% Ardoe House, Blairs, South Deeside Rd, ABERDEEN ☎(0224) 867355 71⇨🏠

Hazelhead Public ☎No telephone
A tree-lined course.
18 holes, 6595yds, Par 70, SSS 70.
Visitors no restrictions.
Societies must contact in advance.
Green Fees not confirmed.
Facilities △ 🏠 ᵖ
Location Hazelhead (4m W of city centre off A944)
Hotel ★★★72% Ardoe House, Blairs, South Deeside Rd, ABERDEEN ☎(0224) 867355 71⇨🏠

Murcar ☎(0224) 704370
Seaside links course, prevailing NE wind, hard-walking. Testing 4th and 14th holes.
18 holes, 5809yds, Par 69, SSS 68, Course record 65.
Club membership 830.
Visitors may not play Wed noon onwards & Sat all day. Must have either a letter of introduction or a handicap certificate. Must contact in advance.
Societies apply in writing.
Green Fees £20 per day; £13 per round before 11.30am (Sun £22 per day after 10am..
Facilities ⊗ & ⧠ (ex Tue) ⓛ ☕ ⛳ △ 🏠 ꞔ Alan White.
Location Bridge of Don (5m NE of city centre off A92)
Hotel ★★★55% Skean Dhu Dyce Hotel, Farburn Ter, DYCE ☎(0224) 723101 Annexe219⇨🏠

Nigg Bay ☎(0224) 871286
Seaside course, hard walking. Plays over Balnagask Course.
18 holes, 5984yds, Par 69, SSS 69.
Club membership 800.
Visitors must be accompanied by member.
Societies must contact in advance.
Green Fees not confirmed.
Facilities ⛳ △
Location St Fitticks Rd
Hotel ★★★55% Skean Dhu Dyce Hotel, Farburn Ter, DYCE ☎(0224) 723101 Annexe219⇨🏠

Northern ☎(0224) 636440
Exposed and windy seaside course, testing 10th hole. One of three clubs playing over King's Links municipal course.
18 holes, Par 72, SSS 72.
Club membership 1000.
Visitors no restrictions.
Societies must contact in advance.
Green Fees not confirmed.
Facilities ⛳ △
Location 22 Gold Rd (adjacent to beach)
Hotel ★★★68% Caledonian Thistle Hotel, 10 Union Ter, ABERDEEN ☎(0224) 640233 80⇨🏠

Royal Aberdeen ☎(0224) 702571
Championship links course. Windy, easy walking.
Balgownie : 18 holes, 6372yds, Par 70, SSS 71, Course record 64.
Silverburn : 18 holes, 4066yds, Par 64, SSS 60.
Club membership 640.
Visitors may not play before 3.30pm Sat. Must contact in advance and have an introduction from own club.
Societies must telephone in advance.
Green Fees not confirmed.
Facilities ⊗ ⧠ by prior arrangement ⓛ ☕ ⛳ (all day) △ 🏠 ᵖ ꞔ Ronnie MacAskill.
Location Balgownie, Bridge of Don (2.5m N of city centre off A92)
Hotel ★★★68% Caledonian Thistle Hotel, 10 Union Ter, ABERDEEN ☎(0224) 640233 80⇨🏠

Westhill ☎(0224) 740159
A highland course.
18 holes, 5921yds, Par 69, SSS 69.
Club membership 600.
Visitors restricted Mon-Fri 4pm-7pm & Sat all day. Must contact in advance.

This guide is updated annually – make sure that you use the up-to-date edition

▶

SCORE CARD: Old Course					
Hole	Yds	Par	Hole	Yds	Par
1	370	4	10	318	4
2	411	4	11	172	3
3	352	4	12	316	4
4	419	4	13	398	4
5	514	5	14	523	5
6	374	4	15	401	4
7	359	4	16	351	4
8	166	3	17	461	4
9	307	4	18	354	4
Out	3272	36	In	3294	36
			Totals	6566	72

ST ANDREWS   Map12N051

St Andrews Links ☎ (0334) 75757

John Ingham writes: If golf has a mother, then without doubt it is St Andrews, the most famous links in all the world. Sir Winston Churchill is said to have claimed golf was invented by the Devil, and if this is so then the famous Old Course must be the Devil's playground. How can one reconcile these two thoughts; the birthplace and mother of the game - and yet the very Devil of a test?

The great Bobby Jones started by hating St Andrews, and shredded his card into a hundred pieces, letting it blow in the wind. But eventually he came to love the place, and earn the affection of all golf. However you view St Andrews, you cannot ignore it. That master shot-maker from America, Sam Snead took one look and claimed they should plant cattle fodder on the bumpy acres. Gary Player once said is should be towed out to sea, and sunk. But Jack Nicklaus loved it so much that when he won an Open title here, he threw his putter into the air. And he went away, and copied several of the St Andrews features in other courses that now decorate this earth.

St Andrews is much more than an 18-hole test. It is a whole experience and a walk in history. Name the famous players of yesteryear, and they played here, taking divots from the very spot that you can take divots - merely by paying for a ticket and wandering out with your clubs to conquer some holes, maybe, and to be brought to a humbling halt by others.

Jack Nicklaus won his most remarkable victory on this course, thanks to an historic missed putt of just 3 feet 6 inches by Doug Sanders who had needed a final hole par 4 to win the 1970 Open Championship. The all-time course record is 62, shot by Curtis Strange in the 1987 Dunhill Cup. Surely nobody can ever beat that?

81 holes. Old Course 18 holes, 6566 yds, Par 72, SSS 72. New (West Sands Rd) 18 holes, 6604 yds, Par 71, SSS 72. Jubilee (West Sands Rd) 18 holes, 6284 yds, Par 69, SSS 70. Eden (Dundee Rd) 18 holes, 5971 yds, Par 69, SSS 69. Balgrove (Dundee Rd) 9 holes, 3546 yds, Par 60, SSS61

Visitors   must contact in advance.

Societies   must telephone in advance.

Green fees   Not confirmed

Facilities   ♀ ⛳ 🖼 ⛳

WHERE TO STAY AND EAT NEARBY

HOTELS:

ST ANDREWS   ★★★★ (red) St Andrews Old Course, Old Station Rd. ☎ (0334) 74371. 125 ⇆ 🦊. ♧ Scottish & French cuisine.

★★★ 71% St Andrews Golf, 40 The Scores. ☎ (0334) 72611. 23 ⇆ 🦊 . ♧ Scottish & French cuisine.

★★★ 62% Scores, 76 The Scores. ☎ (0334) 72451. 30 ⇆ 🦊 . ♧ English & French cuisine.

RESTAURANTS:

CUPAR   ✗ Ostlers Close, Bonnygate. ☎ (0334) 55574. ♧ French & Swiss cuisine.

PEAT INN   ✗✗ The Peat Inn ☎ (033484) 206. ♧ French cuisine.

ST ANDREWS   ✗ The Grange Inn, Grange Rd. ☎ (0334) 72670

See page 257 for advertisements

Societies	must contact in advance.
Green Fees	not comfirmed.
Facilities	⊗ ⅷ by prior arrangement ⅼ 🍺 ♀ △ 🏠 (
Location	Westhill Heights, Westhill, Skene (6m NW of city centre off A944)
Hotel	★★★59% Westhill Hotel, WESTHILL ☎(0224) 740388 38⇔🏋🏻 Annexe14⇔🏋🏻

ABOYNE   Map 15 NO59

Aboyne ☎(03398) 86328
Beautiful parkland with outstanding views. Two lochs on course.
18 holes, 5910yds, Par 68, SSS 68, Course record 69.
Club membership 900.

Visitors	must contact in advance.
Societies	prior booking essential.
Green Fees	£13 (£17 weekends).
Facilities	⊗ ⅼ 🍺 24 ♀ △ 🏠 ⚑ (Innes Wright.
Location	Formaston Park (E side of village, N of A93)
Hotel	★★66% Birse Lodge Hotel, Charleston Rd, ABOYNE ☎(03398) 86253 & 86254 11⇔🏋🏻 Annexe4⇔🏋🏻

AUCHINBLAE   Map 15 NO77

Auchinblae ☎Laurencekirk (05617) 8869
Picturesque, small, undulating parkland course offering good views.
9 holes, 2174yds, Par 32, SSS 30, Course record 60.
Club membership 60.

Visitors	restricted Wed & Fri evenings.
Societies	must telephone (05612) 331 in advance.
Green Fees	£6 per round (£6.50 Sun).
Location	.5m NE
Hotel	★★54% County Hotel, Arduthie Rd, STONEHAVEN ☎(0569) 64386 14⇔🏋🏻

BALLATER   Map 15 NO39

Ballater ☎(03397) 55567
Moorland course with testing long holes and beautiful scenery.
18 holes, 5638yds, Par 67, SSS 68, Course record 66.
Club membership 620.

Visitors	must contact in advance.
Societies	must telephone in advance.
Green Fees	£18 per day; £12 per round (£19/£14 weekends).
Facilities	⊗ ⅷ ⅼ 🍺 ♀ △ 🏠 ⚑ (Fraser Mann.
Leisure	hard tennis courts, fishing, snooker, bowling club & putting green.
Location	Victoria Rd (W side of town)
Hotel	★★68% Darroch Learg Hotel, Braemar Rd, BALLATER ☎(03397) 55443 15⇔🏋🏻 Annexe6⇔🏋🏻

We make every effort to ensure that our information is accurate but details may change after we go to print

BANCHORY   Map 15 NO69

Banchory ☎(03302) 2365
Sheltered parkland course situated beside the River Dee, with easy walking and woodland scenery. 11th and 12th holes are testing.
18 holes, 5245yds, Par 67, SSS 66, Course record 60.
Club membership 1000.

Visitors	must contact in advance.
Societies	must book in advance.
Green Fees	£15 per day (£17 weekends).
Facilities	⊗ ⅼ 🍺 ♀ (all day) △ 🏠 ⚑ (Douglas Smart.
Leisure	snooker.
Location	Kinneskie Rd (A93, 300 yds from W end of High St)
Hotel	★★★(red)⚐ Banchory Lodge Hotel, BANCHORY ☎(03302) 2625 23⇔🏋🏻

BANFF   Map 15 SH57

Duff House Royal ☎(0261) 812062
Well-manicured flat parkland, bounded by woodlands and River Deveron. Well bunkered and renowned for its large, two-tier greens.
18 holes, 6161yds, Par 68, SSS 69, Course record 63.
Club membership 1000.

Visitors	a handicap certificate is preferred. Some time restrictions.
Societies	must apply in writing.
Green Fees	£12 per day; £9 per round (£15/£12 weekends).
Facilities	⊗ ⅼ 🍺 ♀ △ 🏠 (R S Strachan.
Leisure	snooker.
Location	The Barnyards (.5m S on A98)
Hotel	★★★56% Banff Springs Hotel, Golden Knowes Rd, BANFF ☎(02612) 2881 30⇔🏋🏻

BRAEMAR   Map 15 NO19

Braemar ☎(03397) 41618
Flat course, set amid beautiful countryside on Royal Deeside, with River Clunie running through several holes. The 2nd hole is one of the most testing in the area.
18 holes, 5000yds, Par 65, SSS 64, Course record 61.
Club membership 400.

Visitors	are advised to book 24 hours in advance to play at weekends.
Societies	must contact in advance.
Green Fees	£12 per day; £9 per round (£15 per day; £12 per round weekends).
Facilities	⊗ ⅷ ⅼ 🍺 ♀ △ ⚑
Location	Cluniebank Rd (.5m S)
Hotel	★★69% Braemar Lodge Hotel, Glenshee Rd, BRAEMAR ☎(03397) 41627 8rm(6🏋🏻)

BUCKIE   Map 15 NJ46

Buckpool ☎(0542) 32236
Windy, seaside course, with easy walking. Overlooking Moray Firth, its fairways are lined by whin and broom.
18 holes, 6257yds, Par 70, SSS 70.
Club membership 300.

Visitors	may not play on competition days.
Societies	booking advisable.

Green Fees	£9 per day (£12 weekends).
Facilities	⊗ (May-Sep daily or by prior arrangement) ⅷ by prior arrangement ⌷ ⊞ ♀ ⌂
Leisure	squash, snooker.
Location	Barhill Rd, Buckpool (W side of town off A990)
Hotel	★★57% Cluny Hotel, 2 High St, BUCKIE ☎(0542) 32922 10➪🛏Annexe4rm

---

Strathlene ☎(0542) 31798
Windy seaside course with magnificent view, offering testing golf, including difficult 4th (par 3).
18 holes, 5925yds, Par 68, SSS 68.
Club membership 200.

Visitors	no restrictions.
Societies	must telephone in advance.
Green Fees	not confirmed.
Facilities	♀ ⌂
Location	Strathlene Rd (3m E on A942)
Hotel	★★57% Cluny Hotel, 2 High St, BUCKIE ☎(0542) 32922 10➪🛏Annexe4rm

---

CAIRNBULG   Map 15 NK06

Inverallochy ☎No telephone
Windy seaside links course with natural hazards, tricky par 3s and easy walking. Panoramic views of North Sea at every hole.
18 holes, 5137yds, Par 64, SSS 65, Course record 60.
Club membership 200.

Visitors	no restrictions
Societies	apply in writing.
Green Fees	£5.
Facilities	⌷ & ⊞ (evenings and weekends)
Location	24 Shore St (E side of village off B9107)
Hotel	★★63% Tufted Duck Hotel, ST COMBS ☎(03465) 2481 2482/3 18➪🛏

CRUDEN BAY   Map 15 NK03

Cruden Bay ☎(0779) 812285
A seaside links which provides golf of a high order. It was designed by a master architect, Tom Simpson, and although changed somewhat from his original design it is still a great golf course. Magnificent views.
Cruden Bay: 18 holes, 6370yds, Par 70, SSS 71, Course record 63.
St Olaf: 9 holes, 4710yds, Par 64, SSS 62.
Club membership 1050.

Visitors	restricted on Wed & may not play competition days. Must have an introduction from own club.
Societies	apply in writing.
Green Fees	Cruden Bay £16.50 per day (£22.50 weekends); St Olaf £9 per day (£12.50 weekends).
Facilities	⊗ ⅷ ⌷ ⊞ ♀ ⌂ 📷 ⍾ 🍴 David Symington.
Location	SW side of village on A975
Hotel	★★★67% Waterside Inn, Fraserburgh Rd, PETERHEAD ☎(0779) 71121 70➪🛏Annexe40➪🛏

For a full list of golf courses included in the book, see the index at the end of the directory

---

CULLEN   Map 15 NJ56

Cullen ☎(0542) 40685
Interesting links on two levels with rocks and ravines offering some challenging holes. Spectacular scenery.
18 holes, 4610yds, Par 63, SSS 62, Course record 58.
Club membership 580.

Visitors	no restrictions.
Societies	apply in writing.
Green Fees	£8 per day (£11 weekends).
Facilities	⊗ ⅷ ⌷ ⊞ ♀ ⌂
Location	The Links (.5m W off A98)
Hotel	★★57% Cluny Hotel, 2 High St, BUCKIE ☎(0542) 32922 10➪🛏Annexe4rm

---

DUFFTOWN   Map 15 NJ33

Dufftown ☎(0340) 20325
A short and undulating inland course with good views. Highest hole over 1000 ft above sea level.
18 holes, 5308yds, Par 67, SSS 67, Course record 68.
Club membership 150.

Visitors	Tue & Wed evening course not available until after 7pm.
Societies	must contact in advance.
Green Fees	£6-£7 per day (£7-£8 weekends).
Facilities	⊗ by prior arrangement ⌷ ⊞ ♀ ⌂
Location	.75m SW off B9009
Hotel	★★★⚑62% Rothes Glen Hotel, ROTHES ☎(03403) 254 & 255 16rm(13➪)

ELGIN
Map 15 NJ26

Elgin ☎(0343) 542338
Possibly the finest inland course in the north of Scotland, with undulating greens and compact holes that demand the highest accuracy. There are thirteen par 4's and one par 5 hole on its parkland layout.
18 holes, 6401yds, Par 69, SSS 71, Course record 64.
Club membership 906.

SCORECARD					
Hole	Yds	Par	Hole	Yds	Par
1	459	4	10	428	4
2	438	4	11	375	4
3	368	4	12	278	4
4	155	3	13	325	4
5	484	5	14	462	4
6	222	3	15	188	3
7	167	3	16	417	4
8	453	4	17	334	4
9	408	4	18	440	4
Out	3154	34	In	3247	35
			Totals	6401	69

Visitors	restricted until 10.05am at weekends. A handicap certificate is required. An advance telephone call is required if more than four people intend to play.
Societies	contact in advance.
Green Fees	£19 per day; £13 per round (£26.50/£18.50 weekends).
Facilities	⊗ ℳ by prior arrangement ⊫ ☛ ♀ ⚲ 🏠 (Ian P Rodger.
Leisure	practice area..
Location	Hardhillock, Birnie Rd, New Elgin (1m S off A941)
Hotel	★★★57% Eight Acres Hotel, Sheriffmill, ELGIN ☎(0343) 543077 57⇨🐾

ELLON
Map 15 NJ93

McDonald ☎(0358) 20576
Tight, parkland course with streams and a pond.
18 holes, 5986yds, Par 70, SSS 69.
Club membership 710.

Visitors	no restrictions.
Green Fees	not confirmed.
Facilities	♀ ⚲
Location	Hospital Rd (.25m N on A948)
Hotel	★66% Meldrum Arms Hotel, The Square, OLD MELDRUM ☎(06512) 2238 & 2505 7🐾

FORRES
Map 14 NJ05

Forres ☎(0309) 72949
An all-year parkland course laid on light, well-drained soil in wooded countryside. Walking is easy despite some hilly holes. A test for the best golfers.
18 holes, 6203yds, Par 70, SSS 70.
Club membership 950.

Visitors	welcome although club competitions take priority. Weekends may be restricted in summer.
Societies	must telephone 2-3 weeks in advance.
Green Fees	£12 (£17 weekends).
Facilities	⊗ ℳ ⊫ ☛ ♀ ⚲ 🏠 ⚑ (Sandy Aird.
Location	Muiryshade (SE side of town centre off B9010)
Hotel	★★65% Ramnee Hotel, Victoria Rd, FORRES ☎(0309) 72410 20⇨🐾

FRASERBURGH
Map 15 NJ96

Fraserburgh ☎(0346) 28287
Testing seaside course.
18 holes, 6217yds, Par 70, SSS 70.
Club membership 500.

Visitors	no restrictions.
Societies	must contact in advance.
Green Fees	not confirmed.
Facilities	⊗ ℳ ⊫ ℳ ♀ (1100-2300) ⚲ 🏠
Location	Corbie Hill (1m SE on B9033)
Hotel	★★63% Tufted Duck Hotel, ST COMBS ☎(03465) 2481 2482/3 18⇨🐾

GARMOUTH
Map 15 NJ36

Garmouth & Kingston ☎Spey Bay (034387) 388
Seaside course with several parkland holes and tidal waters. Naturally flat.
18 holes, 5656yds, Par 67, SSS 67, Course record 64.
Club membership 400.

Visitors	restricted on competition days.
Societies	must telephone in advance.
Green Fees	£10 per day; £8 per round (£12/£10 weekends).
Facilities	⊗ ℳ ⊫ ☛ (catering May-Sep or by prior booking) ♀ ⚲
Location	In village on B9015
Hotel	★★58% Gordon Arms Hotel, High St, FOCHABERS ☎(0343) 820508 13⇨🐾

HOPEMAN
Map 15 NJ16

Hopeman ☎(0343) 830578
Links-type course with beautiful views over the Moray Firth.
18 holes, 5511yds, Par 67, SSS 67, Course record 66.
Club membership 490.

Visitors	restricted Tue 5pm-6pm & weekends.
Societies	apply by letter 2 weeks in advance.
Green Fees	£10 per day (£15 weekends).
Facilities	⊗ ⊫ ☛ ♀ ⚲
Leisure	pool table.
Location	E side of village off B9012
Hotel	★★★57% Eight Acres Hotel, Sheriffmill, ELGIN ☎(0343) 543077 57⇨🐾

HUNTLY
Map 15 NJ53

Huntly ☎(0466) 2643
A parkland course lying between the Rivers Deveron and Bogie.
18 holes, 5650yds, Par 67, SSS 66, Course record 61.
Club membership 600.

Visitors	no restrictions.
Societies	must contact in writing.
Green Fees	not confirmed.
Facilities	⊗ ℳ ⊫ ☛ ♀ ⚲ 🏠
Location	Cooper Park (.25m through School Arch N side of Huntly)
Hotel	★★⚑56% Castle Hotel, HUNTLY ☎(0466) 792696 23rm(13⇨🐾)

Opening times of bar and catering facilities vary from place to place. Please remember to check in advance of your visit

INVERURIE   Map 15 NJ72

Inverurie ☎(0467) 24080
Parkland course, part of which is exposed and windy, and part through wooded area.
18 holes, 5096yds, Par 66, SSS 65.
Club membership 585.
Visitors   no restrictions.
Green Fees   £8 (£10 weekends).
Facilities   △ 🏠
Location   Davah Wood, Blackhall Rd (W side of town off A96)
Hotel   ★★57% Gordon Arms Hotel, Market Place, INVERURIE ☎(0467) 20314 11rm(6🛏)

KEITH   Map 15 NJ45

Keith ☎(05422) 2469
Parkland course, with natural hazards over first 9 holes. Testing 7th hole, 232 yds, par 3.
18 holes, 5767yds, Par 69, SSS 68.
Club membership 250.
Visitors   no restrictions.
Societies   must telephone in advance.
Green Fees   not confirmed.
Facilities   ♀ △
Location   Fife Park (NW side of town centre off A96)
Hotel   ★★58% Gordon Arms Hotel, High St, FOCHABERS ☎(0343) 820508 13🛏🛏

KEMNAY   Map 15 NJ71

Kemnay ☎(0467) 42225
Undulating parkland course with superb views. A stream crosses four holes.
9 holes, 5502yds, Par 68, SSS 67, Course record 66.
Club membership 395.
Visitors   may not play Mon, Tue & Thu evenings or before 11am on Sun.
Societies   must telephone in advance.
Green Fees   £8 (£9 weekends).
Facilities   🍴 💺 ♀ △
Location   Monymusk Rd (W side of village on B993)
Hotel   ★★★59% Westhill Hotel, WESTHILL ☎(0224) 740388 38🛏🛏 Annexe14🛏🛏

LOSSIEMOUTH   Map 15 NJ27

Moray ☎(034381) 2018
Two fine Scottish Championship links courses, known as Old and New (Moray), and situated on the Moray Firth where the weather is unusually mild.
Old Course: 18 holes, 6643yds, Par 71, SSS 72.
New Course: 18 holes, 6005yds, Par 69, SSS 69.
Club membership 1300.
Visitors   restricted at weekends. Must contact in advance.
Societies   must contact in advance.
Green Fees   not confirmed.
Facilities   ⊗ 🍴 by prior arrangement 🍴 💺 ♀ △ 🏠 ✆ Alistair Thomson.
Location   Stotfield Rd (N side of town)
Hotel   ★★★73% Mansion House Hotel, The Haugh, ELGIN ☎(0343) 548811 24🛏🛏

MACDUFF   Map 15 NJ76

Royal Tarlair ☎(0261) 32897
Seaside clifftop course, can be windy. Testing 13th, 'Clivet' (par 3).
18 holes, 5866yds, Par 71, SSS 68.
Club membership 400.
Visitors   no restrictions.
Societies   apply in writing.
Green Fees   £5-£8 per day; £7 per round (£6-£10/£8 weekends).
Facilities   ⊗ 🍴 💺 ♀
Location   Buchan St (.75m E off A98)
Hotel   ★★60% The Highland Haven, Shore St, MACDUFF ☎(0261) 32408 20🛏🛏

NEWBURGH ON YTHAN   Map 15 NJ92

Newburgh on Ythan ☎Newburgh (03586) 89438
Seaside course adjacent to bird sanctuary. Testing 550-yd dog leg (par 5).
9 holes, 6404yds, Par 72, SSS 70, Course record 69.
Club membership 300.
Visitors   restricted Tue & Sat.
Societies   must telephone in advance.
Green Fees   £8 per day (£10 weekends).
Location   E side of village on A975
Hotel   ★66% Meldrum Arms Hotel, The Square, OLD MELDRUM ☎(06512) 2238 & 2505 7🛏

NEWMACHAR Map 15 NJ81

Newmachar ☎(06517) 3002
New Championship parkland course designed by Dave
Thomas. Several lakes affect five of the holes and there are
well-developed birch and Scots pine trees.
*Hawkshill : 18 holes, 6605yds, Par 72, SSS 73, Course record
67.*
Club membership 750.

Visitors	restricted at weekends. Must contact in advance and have an introduction from own club.
Societies	apply in writing
Green Fees	£18 per day; £12 per round (£18 per round weekends).
Facilities	⊗ ⊞ ⊫ ◚ ♀ ⚲ 🏠 ⛴ ⛴ Glenn Taylor.
Location	Swailend (2m N of Dyce, off A947)
Hotel	★★★55% Skean Dhu Dyce Hotel, Farburn Ter, DYCE ☎(0224) 723101 Annexe219⇔🏶

OLD MELDRUM Map 15 NT53

Old Meldrum ☎(06512) 2648
Parkland course with tree-lined fairways and superb views.
There is a water feature at the par 3, 11th.
18 holes, 5988yds, Par 70, SSS 69, Course record 70.
Club membership 500.

Visitors	may not play during Club competitions.
Societies	apply in writing.
Green Fees	£8 per day (£10 weekends).
Facilities	⊫ ◚ ♀ ⚲
Location	E side of village off A947
Hotel	★66% Meldrum Arms Hotel, The Square, OLD MELDRUM ☎(06512) 2238 & 2505 7🏶

PETERHEAD Map 15 NK14

Peterhead ☎(0779) 72149
Natural links course bounded by the sea and the River Ugie.
*Old Course : 18 holes, 6173yds, Par 70, SSS 70, Course record
64.*
New Course : 9 holes, 2237yds, Par 62, SSS 62.
Club membership 550.

Visitors	telephone for details.
Societies	apply in writing.
Green Fees	Old Course £8 per day (£12 weekends). New Course £3.50 per day.
Facilities	⊗ & ⊞ by prior arrangement ⊫ ◚ ♀ ⚲
Location	Craigewan Links (N side of town centre off A952)
Hotel	★★★67% Waterside Inn, Fraserburgh Rd, PETERHEAD ☎(0779) 71121 70⇔🏶Annexe40⇔🏶

PORTLETHEN Map 15 NO99

Portlethen ☎Aberdeen (0224) 782575
Set in pleasant parkland, this new course features mature
trees and a stream which affects a number of holes.
18 holes, 6735yds, Par 72, SSS 72, Course record 67.
Club membership 650.

Visitors	may not play prior to 3pm Sat.
Societies	apply in writing.

Green Fees	£12.50 per day; £8.50 per round (£15.50/£10.50 weekends & bank holidays).
Facilities	⊗ ⊞ ⊫ ◚ ♀ ⚲ 🏠 ⛴ Muriel Thompson.
Leisure	snooker.
Location	Badentoy Rd
Hotel	★★★68% Maryculter House Hotel, MARYCULTER ☎(0224) 732124 12⇔🏶

SPEY BAY Map 15 NJ36

Spey Bay ☎Fochabers (0343) 820424
Seaside links course over gently undulating banks and well-
drained ground. Good views along Moray coast. Driving
range.
18 holes, 5736yds, Par 71, SSS 69, Course record 66.
Club membership 177.

Visitors	telephone for details.
Societies	must contact in advance.
Green Fees	£7 (£8.50 Sun).
Facilities	⊗ ⊞ ⊫ ◚ ♀ ⚲ 🏠 ⛴ 🏄
Leisure	hard tennis courts, fishing, caravan site.
Location	4.5m N of Fochabers on B9104
Hotel	★★58% Gordon Arms Hotel, High St, FOCHABERS ☎(0343) 820508 13⇔🏶

STONEHAVEN Map 15 NO88

Stonehaven ☎(0569) 62124
Challenging meadowland course overlooking sea with three
gullies and splendid views.
18 holes, 5103yds, Par 66, SSS 65, Course record 62.
Club membership 840.

Visitors	restricted at weekends. Must contact in advance.
Societies	must contact in advance.
Green Fees	£13 per day (£18 weekends).
Facilities	⊗ ⊞ by prior arrangement ⊫ ◚ ♀ ⚲ 🏠
Leisure	snooker.
Location	Cowie (1m N off A92)
Hotel	★★54% County Hotel, Arduthie Rd, STONEHAVEN ☎(0569) 64386 14⇔🏶

TARLAND Map 15 NJ40

Tarland ☎(03398) 81413
Difficult upland course, but easy walking.
9 holes, 5816yds, Par 66, SSS 68, Course record 69.
Club membership 240.

Visitors	welcome except for competition days. Advisable to contact in advance for weekends.
Societies	must telephone in advance.
Green Fees	£8 (£10 day ticket weekends).
Facilities	⊗ ⊫ ◚ ♀ ⚲
Location	Aberdeen Rd (E side of village off B9119)
Hotel	★★66% Birse Lodge Hotel, Charleston Rd, ABOYNE ☎(03398) 86253 & 86254 11⇔🏶Annexe4⇔🏶

A golf-course name printed in ***bold italics***
means that we have been unable to verify
information with the club's management
for the current year

TORPHINS   Map 15 NJ60

Torphins ☎(03398) 82115
Heathland/parkland course built on a hill with views of the Cairngorms.
9 holes, 4634yds, Par 64, SSS 63, Course record 64.
Club membership 370.

Visitors	may not play on competition days. Must contact in advance.
Societies	must contact in writing.
Green Fees	£8 per day (£10 weekends).
Facilities	🏴 (weekends and evenings) 🍽 🛆
Location	Golf Rd (.25m W of village off A980)
Hotel	★★★66% Tor-na-Coille Hotel, BANCHORY ☎(03302) 2242 24⇨🏴

TURRIFF   Map 15 NJ74

Turriff ☎(0888) 62982
A well-maintained parkland course alongside the River Deveron in picturesque surroundings. Friendly clubhouse.
18 holes, 6145yds, Par 69, SSS 69, Course record 67.
Club membership 808.

Visitors	may not play before 10am weekends. Must contact in advance.
Societies	apply in writing to the secretary.
Green Fees	£11 per day; £8 per round (£15/£12 weekends).
Facilities	⊗ 🍴 by prior arrangement 🏴 🍽 ♀ 🛆 🏠 ꜛ ꞓ Robin Smith.
Location	Rosehall (1m W off B9024)
Hotel	★★★56% Banff Springs Hotel, Golden Knowes Rd, BANFF ☎(02612) 2881 30⇨🏴

● HIGHLAND ●

ALNESS   Map 14 NH66

Alness ☎(0349) 883877
A short, but testing, parkland course with beautiful views over the Cromarty Firth and the Black Isle.
9 holes, 2606yds, Par 66, SSS 64, Course record 62.
Club membership 230.

Visitors	restricted during competitions.
Societies	must telephone in advance.
Green Fees	£6 per day (£7.50 weekend & bank holiday).
Facilities	🏴 🍽 ♀ 🛆 ꜛ
Location	Ardross Rd (.5m N off A9)
Hotel	★★★61% Morangie House Hotel, Morangie Rd, TAIN ☎(0862) 892281 11⇨🏴

Each golf-course entry has a recommended AA-appointed hotel. For a wider choice of places to stay, consult *AA Hotels and Restaurants in Britain and Ireland* and *AA Inspected Bed and Breakfast in Britain and Ireland*

BOAT OF GARTEN   Map 14 NH91

Boat of Garten
☎(047983) 282
This parkland course was cut out from a silver birch forest though the fairways are adequately wide. There are natural hazards of broom and heather, good views and walking is easy. A round provides great variety.
18 holes, 5765yds, Par 69, SSS 68, Course record 67.
Club membership 400.

SCORECARD					
Hole	Yds	Par	Hole	Yds	Par
1	186	3	10	265	4
2	347	4	11	369	4
3	146	3	12	339	4
4	484	5	13	432	4
5	333	4	14	323	4
6	403	4	15	305	4
7	382	4	16	167	3
8	353	4	17	346	4
9	150	3	18	435	4
Out	2784	34	In	2981	35
			Totals	5765	69

Visitors	must contact in advance and have an introduction from own club.
Societies	must telephone in advance.
Green Fees	not confirmed.
Facilities	⊗ 🏴 🍽 ♀ 🛆 🏠
Leisure	hard tennis courts.
Location	E side of village
Hotel	★★★63% Boat Hotel, BOAT OF GARTEN ☎(047983) 258 32⇨🏴

For a full range of AA guides and maps, visit your local AA shop or any good bookshop

BONAR BRIDGE   Map 14 NH69

Bonar Bridge-Ardgay ☎Invershin (054982) 248
Wooded moorland course with picturesque views of hills and loch.
9 holes, 4626yds, Par 66, SSS 63, Course record 66.
Club membership 240.
Visitors   restricted during competitions.
Green Fees   £5 per day.
Facilities   ⌳
Location   .5m E
Hotel   ★★65% Dornoch Castle Hotel, Castle St,
                 DORNOCH ☎(0862) 810216
                 4⇆♠Annexe15rm(13⇆♠)

BRORA   Map 14 NC90

Brora ☎(0408) 21417
Typical seaside links with little rough and fine views. Some testing holes.
18 holes, 6110yds, Par 69, SSS 69, Course record 61.
Club membership 450.
Visitors   welcome except for competition days.
Societies   must contact in advance.
Green Fees   £13 per day.
Facilities   ⊗ ⅏ by prior arrangement ⌸ ⌷ ♀ ⌳ ⌸ ⛟
Location   Golf Rd (E side of village)
Hotel   ★★★59% The Links Hotel, Golf Rd, BRORA
                 ☎(0408) 21225 due to change to 621225 21⇆♠

CARRBRIDGE   Map 14 NH92

Carrbridge ☎(047984) 674
Short part-parkland, part-moorland course with magnificent views of the Cairngorms.
9 holes, 5300yds, Par 71, SSS 66, Course record 67.
Club membership 400.
Visitors   restricted Sun & competition days.
Societies   must contact in advance.
Green Fees   not confirmed.
Facilities   ⌸ ⌷ (catering Jun-mid Oct) ⌳ ⛟
Location   N side of village
Hotel   ★★♨67% Muckrach Lodge Hotel, DULNAIN
                 BRIDGE ☎(047985) 257 10⇆Annexe2⇆

DORNOCH   Map 14 NH78

Royal Dornoch ☎(0862) 810219
Very challenging seaside Championship links, designed by Tom Morris and John Sutherland.
18 holes, 6591yds, Par 70, SSS 72, Course record 67 or 18 holes, 5250yds, Par 70, SSS 68.
Club membership 900.
Visitors   handicap of 24 for gentlemen (ladies 35).
                 Must contact in advance and have an
                 introduction from own club.
Societies   must telephone in advance.
Green Fees   not confirmed.
Facilities   ⊗ ⅏ by prior arrangement ⌸ ⌷ ♀ ⌳
                 ⌸ ⛟ (
Leisure   hard tennis courts, fishing, riding.
Location   Golf Rd (E side of town)

Hotel   ★★65% Dornoch Castle Hotel, Castle St,
                 DORNOCH ☎(0862) 810216
                 4⇆♠Annexe15rm(13⇆♠)

DURNESS   Map 14 F1

Durness ☎(097181) 364
A 9-hole course set in tremendous scenery overlooking Balnakeil Bay. Part links and part inland with water hazards. Off alternative tees for second 9 holes giving surprising variety. Tremendous last hole played across the sea to the green over 100 yards away.
9 holes, 5545yds, Par 70, SSS 68.
Club membership 100.
Visitors   restricted 10am-noon on Sun.
Societies   must telephone in advance.
Green Fees   £6 per day.
Facilities   ⌸ ⌷ (catering Jun-Sep) ⌳ ⛟
Location   Balnakeil (1m W of village)
Hotel   ★★★63% Kinlochbervie Hotel,
                 KINLOCHBERVIE ☎(097182) 275 14⇆♠

FORT AUGUSTUS   Map 14 NH30

Fort Augustus ☎(0320) 6460
Moorland course, with narrow fairways and good views. Bordered by the tree-lined Caledonian Canal.
9 holes, 5454yds, Par 67, SSS 68, Course record 69.
Club membership 150.
Visitors   no restrictions.
Societies   welcome.
Green Fees   £6 per day.
Facilities   ⌸ ⌷
Location   Markethill (1m SW on A82)
Hotel   ★★61% Lovat Arms Hotel, FORT AUGUSTUS
                 ☎(0320) 6206 21⇆♠

FORTROSE   Map 14 NH75

Fortrose & Rosemarkie ☎(0381) 20733
Seaside links course, set on a peninsula with sea on three sides. Easy walking, good views. Designed by James Braid; the club was formed in 1888.
18 holes, 5973yds, Par 71, SSS 69.
Club membership 750.
Visitors   restricted Sat & Sun 8.45-10.15am & 12.45-
                 1.15pm.
Societies   must telephone (0381) 20529 in advance.
Green Fees   £12.50 per day; £9 per round (£12 per round
                 weekends). Nov-Mar £6 per round (£8 weekends).
Facilities   ⊗ ⌸ ⌷ ♀ ⌳ ⌸ ⛟ (
Location   Ness Rd East (W side of town centre)
Hotel   ★★68% Priory Hotel, The Square, BEAULY
                 ☎(0463) 782309 12⇆♠

FORT WILLIAM   Map 14 NN17

Fort William ☎(0397) 4464
Moorland course with fine views. Tees and greens very good, but fairways can be very soft in wet weather.
18 holes, 5640yds, Par 70, SSS 68.
Club membership 200.
Visitors   no restrictions.
Societies   must contact in writing.

Green Fees not confirmed.
Facilities ⊗ ⅃ 🔟 ♀ 🏌 ♈
Location 3m NE on A82
Hotel ★★★71% Moorings Hotel, Banavie, FORT
WILLIAM ☎(0397) 772797 21⇾🏳Annexe3🏳

GAIRLOCH   Map 14 NG87

Gairloch ☎(0445) 2407
Fine seaside course running along Gairloch Sands with good
views over the sea to Skye.
9 holes, 4577yds, Par 62, SSS 63, Course record 59.
Club membership 350.
Societies must telephone in advance.
Green Fees £8 per day.
Facilities 🔟 ⅄ ♈
Location 1m S on A832
Hotel ★★62% The Old Inn, Flowerdale, GAIRLOCH
☎(0445) 2006 14⇾🏳

GOLSPIE   Map 14 NH89

Golspie ☎(0408) 633266
Founded in 1889, Golspie's seaside course offers easy
walking and natural hazards including beach heather and
whins. Spectacular scenery.
18 holes, 5836yds, Par 68, SSS 68, Course record 65.
Club membership 480.
Visitors restricted on competition days.
Societies must telephone in advance.
Green Fees not confirmed.
Facilities ⊗ ⑭ by prior arrangement ⅃ 🔟 ♀ (Apr-Oct)
⅄ 🖼
Location Ferry Rd (.5m S off A9)
Hotel ★★57% Golf Links Hotel, GOLSPIE ☎(04083)
3408 9⇾🏳

GRANTOWN-ON-SPEY   Map 14 NJ02

Grantown-on-Spey ☎(0479) 2079 (summer)
Parkland and woodland course. Part easy walking,
remainder hilly. The 7th to 13th really sorts out the golfers.
18 holes, 5745yds, Par 70, SSS 67, Course record 60.
Club membership 430.
Visitors restricted 8am-10am Sat & Sun.
Societies telephone in advance, or write in winter.
Green Fees £11 per day (£14 weekends).
Facilities ⊗ ⑭ by prior arrangement ⅃ 🔟 (Clubhouse
closed Nov-Mar) ♀ (Apr-Oct) ⅄ 🖼 ♈ ♛ W
Mitchell.
Location Golf Course Rd (E side of town centre)
Hotel ★★63% Seafield Lodge Hotel, Woodside Av,
GRANTOWN-ON-SPEY ☎(0479) 2152 14⇾🏳

HELMSDALE   Map 14 ND01

Helmsdale ☎(04312) 240
Sheltered, undulating course following the line of the
Helmsdale River.
9 holes, 1825yds, Par 62, SSS 62.
Club membership 137.
Visitors no restrictions.
Societies apply in writing.
Green Fees £3 per day; £10 weekly.

▶

Facilities	⌂
Location	Golf Rd (NW side of town on A896)
Hotel	★★★59% The Links Hotel, Golf Rd, BRORA ☎(0408) 21225 due to change to 621225 21⇨🏠

INVERGORDON   Map 14 NH76

Invergordon ☎(0349) 852715
Fairly easy but windy parkland course, with good views over
Cromarty Firth. Very good greens. Clubhouse situated 1m
from course close to middle of town.
9 holes, 6028yds, Par 68, SSS 69, Course record 65.
Club membership 300.

Visitors	no restrictions.
Societies	must telephone in advance.
Green Fees	not confirmed.
Facilities	🍴 (Sat only) 🍽 (Sat only) ⚑ (Sat, Tue & Thu eve) ⌂
Location	King George St (W side of town centre on B817)
Hotel	★★66% Royal Hotel, Marine Ter, CROMARTY ☎(03817) 217 10rm(5⇨2🏠)

INVERNESS   Map 14 NH64

Inverness ☎(0463) 239882
Fairly flat parkland course with burn running through it.
Windy in winter.
18 holes, 6226yds, Par 69, SSS 70.
Club membership 1050.

Visitors	restricted at weekends. Must have an introduction from own club.
Societies	must telephone in advance.
Green Fees	£18 per day; £13.50 per round (£20/£16.50 weekends & public holidays.
Facilities	⊗ 🍴 🍽 ⚑ ⌂ 🏠 🚩 ⚏ A P Thomson.
Location	Culcabock (1m S of town centre on B9006)
Hotel	★★★★66% Kingsmills Hotel, Culcabock Rd, INVERNESS ☎(0463) 237166 73⇨🏠Annexe6⇨🏠

Torvean ☎(0463) 237543
Municipal parkland course, easy walking, good views.
18 holes, 5784yds, Par 69, SSS 68.
Club membership 403.

Visitors	restricted on competition days. Must contact in advance.
Societies	must telephone in advance.
Green Fees	£8.70.
Facilities	⊗ 🍴 & 🍴 by prior arrangement 🍽 ⚑ (Apr-Oct) ⌂ 🏠 🚩
Location	Glenurquhart Rd (1.5m SW on A82)
Hotel	★★(red)🍴 Dunain Park Hotel, INVERNESS ☎(0463) 230512 12rm(10⇨🏠)

KINGUSSIE   Map 14 NH70

Kingussie ☎(0540) 661374
Hilly upland course with natural hazards and magnificent
views. Stands about 1,000ft above sea level at its highest
point, and the River Gynack comes into play on five holes.
18 holes, 5555yds, Par 66, SSS 67, Course record 64.
Club membership 700.

Visitors	no restrictions.

Societies	must telephone (0540) 661600 to book.
Green Fees	£11.25 per day; £8.25 per round.
Facilities	⊗ 🍽 ⚑ ⌂ 🏠 🚩
Location	Gynack Rd (.25m N off A86)
Hotel	★64% Osprey Hotel, Ruthven Rd, KINGUSSIE ☎(0540) 661510 8rm(4⇨🏠)

LYBSTER   Map 15 ND23

Lybster
Picturesque, short heathland course, easy walking.
9 holes, 1896yds, Par 62, SSS 62.
Club membership 80.

Visitors	no restrictions.
Societies	must contact in advance.
Green Fees	not confirmed.
Facilities	⌂ 🚩
Location	Main St (E side of village)
Hotel	★★60% Portland Arms, LYBSTER ☎(05932) 208 19⇨🏠

MUIR OF ORD   Map 14 NH55

Muir of Ord ☎(0463) 870825
Old established (1875), heathland course with tight fairways
and easy walking. Testing 11th, 'Castle Hill' (par 3).
18 holes, 5202yds, Par 67, SSS 65.
Club membership 700.

Visitors	not permitted during specified draw times for medal tees.
Societies	apply in writing.
Green Fees	£9 per day (£10 weekends) summer.
Facilities	⌂ 🏠 🚩 ⚏ J Hamilton.
Leisure	snooker.
Location	Great North Rd (S side of village on A862)
Hotel	★★68% Priory Hotel, The Square, BEAULY ☎(0463) 782309 12⇨🏠

NAIRN   Map 14 NH85

Nairn ☎(0667) 53208
Championship, seaside links founded in 1887 and
extended by Tom Morris and James Braid. Opening holes
stretch out along the shoreline with the turn for home at
the 10th. Regularly chosen for national championships.
18 holes, 6722yds, Par 72, SSS 71, Course record 65.
Club membership 1037.

Visitors	restricted until 1030 Sat & Sun.
Societies	telephone at least 2 weeks in advance.
Green Fees	£25 per day; £18 per round (£30/£22 weekends).
Facilities	⊗ 🍴 🍴 🍽 ⚑ ⌂ 🏠 🚩 ⚏ Robin Fyfe.
Location	Seabank Rd
Hotel	★★★★65% Golf View Hotel, Seabank Rd, NAIRN ☎(0667) 52301 48⇨🏠

Nairn Dunbar ☎(0667) 52741
Links course with sea views and testing gorse and whin-lined
fairways. Breezy at holes 6, 7 and 8. Testing hole: 'Long
Peter' (529yds).
18 holes, 6431yds, Par 71, SSS 71.
Club membership 700.

Visitors	must contact in advance and have an introduction from own club.

Societies	must contact in advance.
Green Fees	£15 per day (£20 weekends).
Facilities	⊗ ⤴ 💺 ♀ ⚐ 🏠 ⍑ 𝄐 Brian Mason.
Location	Lochloy Rd (E side of town off A96)
Hotel	★★62% Carnach House Hotel, Delnies, NAIRN ☎(0667) 52094 14rm(12⇨🏶)

NETHY BRIDGE   Map 14 NH02

Abernethy ☎(047982) 305
Picturesque moorland course.
9 holes, 4986yds, Par 66, SSS 66, Course record 61.
Club membership 300.

Visitors	restricted during club matches.
Societies	must telephone in advance.
Green Fees	£8 per day (£10 weekends).
Facilities	⊗ snacks 💺 ⚐ ⍑
Location	N side of village on B970
Hotel	★★♨67% Muckrach Lodge Hotel, DULNAIN BRIDGE ☎(047985) 257 10⇨Annexe2⇨

NEWTONMORE   Map 14 NN79

Newtonmore ☎(05403) 328
Inland course beside the River Spey. Beautiful views and easy walking. Testing 17th hole (par 3).
18 holes, 5880yds, Par 70, SSS 68, Course record 64.
Club membership 450.

Visitors	must contact in advance.
Societies	apply in writing.
Green Fees	£12 per day (£15 weekend).

Facilities	⊗ ⍈ 💺 ⚐ (all catering Mar-Oct ex Tue) ♀ ⚐ 🏠 𝄐 Robert Henderson.
Location	Golf Course Rd (E side of town off A9)
Hotel	★★67% Columba House Hotel, Manse Rd, KINGUSSIE ☎(0540) 661402 7⇨🏶

PORTMAHOMACK   Map 14 NH98

Tarbat ☎(086287) 236
Picturesque links course with magnificent views.
9 holes, 4658yds, Par 66, SSS 63.
Club membership 180.

Visitors	no restrictions.
Societies	must telephone in advance.
Green Fees	£4 per day (£5 weekends).
Facilities	⚐
Location	E side of village
Hotel	★★★56% Royal Hotel, High St, TAIN ☎(0862) 892013 25rm(9⇨13🏶)

REAY   Map 15 NC96

Reay ☎(084781) 288
Picturesque seaside links with natural hazards, following the contours of Sandside Bay. Tight and testing.
18 holes, 5865yds, Par 69, SSS 68, Course record 65.
Club membership 350.

Visitors	restricted competition days.
Societies	apply in writing.
Green Fees	£10 per day.
Facilities	⊗ (weekdays in summer)

▶

Location	.5m E off A836
Hotel	★★62% Pentland Hotel, Princes St, THURSO ☎(0847) 63202 53rm(28⇨11♠)

STRATHPEFFER   Map 14 NH45

Strathpeffer Spa ☎(0997) 421219
Upland course with many natural hazards (no sand bunkers), hard walking and fine views. Testing 3rd hole (par 3) across loch.
18 holes, 4792yds, Par 65, SSS 65, Course record 60.
Club membership 550.

Visitors	may not play during club competition times or until after 10am on Sun.
Societies	apply in writing.
Green Fees	£15 per day; £10 per round (£15 per round weekends).
Facilities	⊗ ㋺ ☙ (no catering Mon) ♀ ⌂ 🏠 ㋨
Location	.25m N of village off A834
Hotel	★★64% Holly Lodge Hotel, STRATHPEFFER ☎(0997) 21254 7rm(3⇨3♠)

TAIN   Map 14 NH78

Tain ☎(0862) 892314
Heathland/links course with river affecting 3 holes; easy walking, fine views.
18 holes, 6238yds, Par 70, SSS 70.
Club membership 500.

Visitors	may not play on competition days. Must contact in advance.
Societies	must book in advance.
Green Fees	£13 per day; £8.50 per round (£15/£10 weekends).
Facilities	⊗ ㋺ ☙ ♀ ⌂ 🏠
Location	Golf Links (E side of town centre off B9174)
Hotel	★★★56% Royal Hotel, High St, TAIN ☎(0862) 892013 25rm(9⇨13♠)

THURSO   Map 15 ND16

Thurso ☎(0847) 63807
Parkland course, windy, but with fine views of Dunnet Head and the Orkney Islands.
18 holes, 5818yds, Par 69, SSS 69, Course record 63.
Club membership 366.

Visitors	no restrictions.
Societies	must telephone in advance.
Green Fees	not confirmed.
Facilities	⊗ & ㎳ (summer only) ㋺ ☙ ♀ ⌂ 🏠 ㋨
Location	Newlands of Geise (2m SW on B874)
Hotel	★★62% Pentland Hotel, Princes St, THURSO ☎(0847) 63202 53rm(28⇨11♠)

WICK   Map 15 ND35

Wick ☎(0955) 2726
Typical seaside links course, windy, easy walking.
18 holes, 5976yds, Par 69, SSS 69, Course record 63.
Club membership 250.

Visitors	no restrictions.
Societies	apply in writing or telephone in advance.
Green Fees	£8 per day (£10 weekends).
Facilities	㋺ ☙ ♀ (restricted times)

Location	Reiss (3.5m N off A9)
Hotel	★★58% Mackay's Hotel, Union St, WICK ☎(0955) 2323 26rm(23⇨1♠)

◦ LOTHIAN ◦

ABERLADY   Map 12 NT47

Kilspindie ☎(08757) 358
Seaside course, short but tight and well-bunkered. Testing holes: 2nd, 3rd, 4th and 7th.
18 holes, 5410yds, Par 69, SSS 66.
Club membership 600.

Visitors	no restrictions.
Societies	must contact in advance.
Green Fees	not confirmed.
Facilities	⊗ high tea (Apr-Oct) ㋺ ☙ ♀ ⌂ 🏠 ㋦ Graham J Sked.
Location	W side of village off A198
Hotel	★★66% Kilspindie House Hotel, Main St, ABERLADY ☎(08757) 682 26⇨♠

Luffness New ☎Gullane (0620) 843336
Seaside course.
18 holes, 6122yds, Par 69, SSS 69, Course record 63.
Club membership 700.

Visitors	may not play at weekends & bank holidays. Must contact in advance and have an introduction from own club.
Societies	must contact in writing.
Green Fees	not confirmed.
Facilities	⊗ ㎳ by prior arrangement㋺ ☙ ♀ ⌂ 🏠
Location	1m E on A198
Hotel	★★★(red)🏰 Greywalls Hotel, Muirfield, GULLANE ☎(0620) 842144 17⇨♠ Annexe5⇨♠

BATHGATE   Map 11 NS96

Bathgate ☎(0506) 630505
Moorland course. Easy walking. Testing 11th hole, par 3.
18 holes, 6328yds, Par 71, SSS 70, Course record 64.
Club membership 650.

Visitors	may not play on competition days. Must contact in advance.
Societies	must contact in advance.
Green Fees	£10 per day; £12 per round (£20 per day weekends).
Facilities	⊗ ㎳ (Wed & Fri-Sun only) ㋺ ☙ ♀ ⌂ 🏠 ㋦ Sandy Strachan.
Location	Edinburgh Rd (E side of town off A89)
Hotel	★★★🏰65% Houstoun House Hotel, UPHALL ☎(0506) 853831 28⇨♠ Annexe2⇨

BONNYRIGG   Map 11 NT36

Broomieknowe ☎031-663 9317
Easy walking, mature parkland course laid out by Ben Sayers and extended by James Braid. Elevated site with excellent views.
18 holes, 5754yds, Par 68, SSS 68, Course record 64.
Club membership 450.

Visitors	restricted Wed, weekends & bank holidays; a handicap certificate is preferred.
Societies	must contact in writing and pay a deposit.
Green Fees	£14 per round; £20 per day (£20 per round weekends).
Facilities	⊗ & ㄥ (ex Mon) ● ♀ ᐃ 🏠 ⫟ (Mark Patchett.
Location	36 Golf Course Rd (.5m NE off B704)
Hotel	★★★60% Donmaree Hotel, 21 Mayfield Gardens, EDINBURGH ☎031-667 3641 17⇨🏠

DALKEITH   Map 11 NT36

Newbattle ☎031-663 2123
Undulating parkland course on three levels, surrounded by woods.
18 holes, 6012yds, Par 69, SSS 69.
Club membership 650.

Visitors	restricted before 4pm on weekdays; may not play at weekends. Must have an introduction from own club.
Societies	must contact in advance.
Green Fees	not confirmed.
Facilities	ㄥ ● ♀ ᐃ 🏠 (David Torrance.
Location	Abbey Rd (SW side of town off A68)
Hotel	★★66% Eskbank Motor Hotel, 29 Dalhousie Rd, DALKEITH ☎031-663 3234 16⇨🏠

DUNBAR   Map 12 NT67

Dunbar ☎(0368) 62317
Another of Scotland's old links. It is said that it was some Dunbar members who first took the game of golf to the North of England. The club dates back to 1856. The wind, if blowing from the sea, is a problem.
18 holes, 6426yds, Par 71, SSS 71, Course record 64.
Club membership 650.

SCORECARD: White Tees

Hole	Yds	Par	Hole	Yds	Par
1	477	5	10	202	3
2	494	5	11	417	4
3	172	3	12	459	4
4	349	4	13	378	4
5	148	3	14	433	4
6	350	4	15	343	4
7	386	4	16	166	3
8	369	4	17	339	4
9	507	5	18	437	4
Out	3252	37	In	3174	34
			Totals	6426	71

Visitors	must contact in advance.
Societies	must contact in advance.
Green Fees	not confirmed.
Facilities	⊗ ⫟ ㄥ ● ♀ (all day) ᐃ 🏠 (
Location	East Links (.5m E off A1087)
Hotel	★★64% Bayswell Hotel, Bayswell Park, DUNBAR ☎(0368) 62225 13⇨🏠

Winterfield ☎(0368) 63562
Seaside course with superb views.
18 holes, 5220yds, SSS 64.
Club membership 200.

Visitors	must contact in advance.
Green Fees	not confirmed.
Facilities	♀ ᐃ 🏠 ⫟
Location	North Rd (W side of town off A1087)
Hotel	★★64% Bayswell Hotel, Bayswell Park, DUNBAR ☎(0368) 62225 13⇨🏠
Additional hotel	★★66% Redheugh Hotel, Bayswell Park, DUNBAR ☎(0368) 62793 10⇨🏠

EDINBURGH   Map 11 NT27

Baberton ☎031-453 4911
Parkland course.
18 holes, 6098yds, Par 69, SSS 69, Course record 64.
Club membership 800.

Visitors	may not play at weekends.
Societies	must contact in advance.
Green Fees	£22 per day; £15 per round.
Facilities	⊗ ⫟ by prior arrangement ㄥ ● ♀ ᐃ 🏠 (Ken Kelly.
Location	Juniper Green (5m W of city centre off A70)
Hotel	★★★68% Bruntsfield Hotel, 69/74 Bruntsfield Place, EDINBURGH ☎031-229 1393 50⇨🏠

Braid Hills ☎031-447 6666
Municipal heathland course with good views of Edinburgh and the Firth of Forth.
18 holes, 5731yds, Par 70, SSS 68.

Visitors	may not play on Sat mornings or evenings.
Green Fees	not confirmed.
Facilities	♀ ᐃ 🏠 ⫟ (
Location	Braid Hills Approach (2.5m S of city centre off A702)
Hotel	★★★55% Braid Hills Hotel, 134 Braid Rd, Braid Hills, EDINBURGH ☎031-447 8888 68⇨🏠

For an explanation of symbols and abbreviations, see page 32

AA ★★
Les Routiers

STB 🏵🏵🏵🏵 Commended

Redheugh Hotel

Bayswell Park, Dunbar
East Lothian

Small private licenced hotel set in the Heart of "Golf Country". Tee times arranged on 14 different courses within ½ hour drive, 2 in Dunbar itself. Emphasis on personal attention and home cooking. Special golf breaks and group rates from £36.50 D/B/B per person per night based on 2 people sharing twin or double room.

Telephone (0368) 62793
FOR MORE INFORMATION.

Bruntsfield Links Golfing Society ☎031-336 1479
Parkland course with good views of Forth Estuary. 4th and 14th holes testing.
18 holes, 6407yds, Par 71, SSS 71.
Club membership 1000.

Visitors	may not play at weekends. Must contact in advance and have an introduction from own club.
Societies	must contact in advance.
Green Fees	not confirmed.
Facilities	⊗ ⅷ by prior arrangement ⬛ ♀ ⌂ 🖼 (
Location	32 Barnton Av, Davidsons-Mains (4m NW of city centre off A90)
Hotel	★★★67% Barnton Thistle Hotel, Queensferry Rd, Barnton, EDINBURGH ☎031-339 1144 50⇨🐾

Carrick Vale ☎031-337 1096
Flat parkland course.
18 holes, 6299yds, Par 71, SSS 70, Course record 64.
Club membership 450.

Visitors	must have an introduction from own club.
Green Fees	£4 per round (£5 weekends).
Location	Carricknowe Municipal, Glendevon Park (3m W of city centre, S of A8)
Hotel	★★★65% Forte Posthouse, Corstorphine Rd, EDINBURGH ☎031-334 0390 200⇨🐾

Craigmillar Park ☎031-667 0047
Parkland course, with good views.
18 holes, 5859yds, Par 70, SSS 68, Course record 65.
Club membership 520.

Visitors	must play with member at weekends & before 3pm on weekdays. Must have an introduction from own club.
Societies	must contact in writing.
Green Fees	on application.
Facilities	♀ ⌂ 🖼 ⅃ (Brian McGhee.
Location	1 Observatory Rd (2m S of city centre off A7)
Hotel	★★★60% Donmaree Hotel, 21 Mayfield Gardens, EDINBURGH ☎031-667 3641 17⇨🐾

Dalmahoy Country ☎031-333 1845
Two upland courses, one Championship.
18 holes, 6664yds, Par 72, SSS 72.
Club membership 700.

Visitors	must contact in advance.
Societies	must telephone for details.
Facilities	♀ ⌂ 🖼 ⅃ 🍴 (
Leisure	squash.
Location	Kirknewton (7m W of city centre on A71)
Hotel	★★★65% Forte Posthouse, Corstorphine Rd, EDINBURGH ☎031-334 0390 200⇨🐾

Duddingston ☎031-661 7688
Parkland, semi-seaside course with burn as a natural hazard. Testing 11th hole. Easy walking and windy.
18 holes, 6647yds, Par 72, SSS 72.
Club membership 700.

Visitors	may not play at weekends.
Societies	Tue & Thu only. Must contact in advance.
Green Fees	£24 per day; £18 per round.

Facilities	⊗ ⅷ by prior arrangement ⬛ ⬛ ♀ ⌂ 🖼 ⅃ (Alastair McLean.
Location	Duddingston Rd West (2.5m SE of city centre off A1)
Hotel	★★★60% Donmaree Hotel, 21 Mayfield Gardens, EDINBURGH ☎031-667 3641 17⇨🐾

Kingsknowe ☎031-441 1145
Hilly parkland course with prevailing southwest winds.
18 holes, 5979yds, Par 69, SSS 69.
Club membership 705.

Visitors	must contact in advance.
Societies	must contact in advance.
Green Fees	£16.50 per day; £11.50 per round (£16.50 weekends).
Facilities	⊗ ⬛ ⬛ ♀ ⌂ 🖼 ⅃ (William Bauld.
Leisure	snooker.
Location	326 Lanark Rd (4m SW of city centre on A70)
Hotel	★★★68% Bruntsfield Hotel, 69/74 Bruntsfield Place, EDINBURGH ☎031-229 1393 50⇨🐾

Liberton ☎031-664 3009
Undulating, wooded parkland course.
18 holes, 5299yds, Par 67, SSS 67, Course record 61.
Club membership 650.

Visitors	may only play before 5pm on Tue & Thu Apr-Sep. Must contact in advance.
Societies	must contact in writing.
Green Fees	£18 per day; £12.50 per round.
Facilities	⊗ ⬛ ⬛ ♀ ⌂ 🖼 (John Murray.
Location	297 Gilmerton Rd (3m SE of city centre on A7)
Hotel	★★60% Suffolk Hall Hotel, 10 Craigmillar Park, EDINBURGH ☎031-668 4333 12rm(11⇨🐾)

Lothianburn ☎031-445 2206
Hillside course with a 'T' shaped wooded-area, situated in the Pentland foothills. Sheep on course. Testing in windy conditions.
18 holes, 5750yds, Par 71, SSS 69, Course record 63.
Club membership 700.

Visitors	may not play on competition days.
Societies	must contact in writing.
Green Fees	£12 per day; £8 per round (£15 per day; £11 per round weekends).
Facilities	⊗ ⅷ ⬛ ⬛ (no catering Wed) ♀ (ex Wed) ⌂ 🖼 ⅃ (Paul Morton.
Location	106A Biggar Rd, Fairmilehead (4.5m S of city centre on A702)
Hotel	★★★55% Braid Hills Hotel, 134 Braid Rd, Braid Hills, EDINBURGH ☎031-447 8888 68⇨🐾

Merchants of Edinburgh ☎031-447 1219
Testing hill course.
18 holes, 4889mtrs, Par 64, SSS 64, Course record 61.
Club membership 700.

Visitors	must play with member at weekends.
Societies	must contact in writing.
Green Fees	£12 per day; £8 per round.
Facilities	⊗ & ⅷ (ex Wed and Thu) ⬛ ♀ ⌂ 🖼 (Craig Imlah.
Leisure	snooker.
Location	10 Craighill Gardens (2m SW of city centre off A702)

Hotel	★★★55% Braid Hills Hotel, 134 Braid Rd, Braid Hills, EDINBURGH ☎031-447 8888 68⇔ 🏃

Mortonhall ☎031-447 6974
Moorland course with views over Edinburgh.
18 holes, 6557yds, Par 72, SSS 71, Course record 66.
Club membership 650.

Visitors	must have an introduction from own club.
Societies	may not play at weekends. Must contact in advance.
Green Fees	£35 per day; £25 per round (£40 per day; £30 per round weekends).
Facilities	⊗ (ex Mon and Sat) 🦺 🍺 ♀ ⚐ 📷 ⚐ (D B Horn.
Location	Braid Rd (3m S of city centre off A702)
Hotel	★★★55% Braid Hills Hotel, 134 Braid Rd, Braid Hills, EDINBURGH ☎031-447 8888 68⇔ 🏃

Murrayfield ☎031-337 1009
Parkland course on the side of Corstorphine Hill, with fine views.
18 holes, 5725yds, Par 70, SSS 68, Course record 64.
Club membership 775.

Visitors	may not play at weekends. Must be accompanied by member, contact in advance and have an introduction from own club.
Green Fees	£21 per day; £15 per round.
Facilities	⊗ ⚐ by prior arrangement 🦺 🍺 ♀ ⚐ 📷 ⚐ (James Fisher.
Location	43 Murrayfield Rd (2m W of city centre off A8)
Hotel	★★★65% Forte Posthouse, Corstorphine Rd, EDINBURGH ☎031-334 0390 200⇔ 🏃

Portobello ☎031-669 4361
Public parkland course, easy walking.
9 holes, 2400yds, Par 32, SSS 32.
Club membership 70.

Visitors	may not play Sat 8.30-10am & 12.30-2pm.
Societies	must contact in advance.
Green Fees	not confirmed.
Facilities	⚐
Location	Stanley St (3m E of city centre off A1)
Hotel	★★★60% Donmaree Hotel, 21 Mayfield Gardens, EDINBURGH ☎031-667 3641 17⇔ 🏃

Prestonfield ☎031-667 1273
Parkland course with beautiful views.
18 holes, 6216yds, Par 70, SSS 70, Course record 62.
Club membership 800.

Visitors	may not play between noon-1pm Sat & before 11.30am Sun.
Societies	must contact in advance.
Green Fees	£22 per day; £15 per round (£22 per round; £30 per day weekends).
Facilities	⊗ ⚐ by prior arrangement 🦺 🍺 ♀ ⚐ 📷 (Brian M Commins.
Location	Priestfield Rd North (1.5m S of city centre off A68)
Hotel	★★★60% Donmaree Hotel, 21 Mayfield Gardens, EDINBURGH ☎031-667 3641 17⇔ 🏃

Ravelston ☎031-332 2486
Parkland course.
9 holes, 5322yds, Par 66, SSS 66, Course record 66.
Club membership 610.

Visitors	may not play at weekends & bank holidays. Must contact in advance and have an introduction from own club.
Green Fees	not confirmed.
Facilities	🦺 🍺 ⚐
Location	24 Ravelston Dykes Rd (3m W of city centre off A90)
Hotel	★★★65% Forte Posthouse, Corstorphine Rd, EDINBURGH ☎031-334 0390 200⇔ 🏃

Royal Burgess ☎031-339 2075
No mention of golf clubs would be complete without mention of the Royal Burgess, which was instituted in 1735, thus being the oldest golfing society in the world. Its course is a pleasant parkland, and one with much variety. A club which all those interested in the history of the game should visit.
18 holes, 6111yds, Par 68, SSS 69.
Club membership 620.

Visitors	must contact in advance and have an introduction from own club.
Societies	must contact in advance.
Green Fees	not confirmed.
Facilities	⊗ 🦺 🍺 ♀ ⚐ 📷 ⚐ (George Yuille.
Location	181 Whitehouse Rd, Barnton (5m W of city centre off A90)
Hotel	★★★67% Barnton Thistle Hotel, Queensferry Rd, Barnton, EDINBURGH ☎031-339 1144 50⇔ 🏃

Silverknowes ☎031-336 3843
Public links course on coast overlooking the Firth of Forth.
18 holes, 6216yds, Par 71, SSS 70, Course record 67.
Club membership 500.

Visitors	no restrictions.
Green Fees	£5 per day.
Facilities	⚐
Location	Silverknowes, Parkway (4m NW of city centre N of A902)
Hotel	★★★65% Murrayfield Hotel, 18 Corstorphine Rd, EDINBURGH ☎031-337 1844 23⇔ 🏃 Annexe10 🏃

Swanston ☎031-445 2239
Hillside course with steep climb at 12th & 13th holes.
18 holes, 5024yds, Par 66, SSS 65, Course record 63.
Club membership 500.

Visitors	may not play on competition days. Must contact in advance.
Societies	telephone for details.
Green Fees	not confirmed.
Facilities	⊗ 🦺 🍺 ♀ ⚐ 📷 (Ian Seith.
Location	111 Swanston Rd, Fairmilehead (4m S of city centre off B701)
Hotel	★★★55% Braid Hills Hotel, 134 Braid Rd, Braid Hills, EDINBURGH ☎031-447 8888 68⇔ 🏃

This guide is updated annually – make sure that you use the up-to-date edition

For a full range of AA guides and maps, visit your local AA shop or any good bookshop

Torphin Hill ☎031-441 1100
Beautiful hillside, heathland course, with fine views of
Edinburgh and the Forth Estuary.
18 holes, 4597mtrs, Par 67, SSS 66, Course record 62.
Club membership 410.

Visitors	may not play on competition days. Must contact in advance.
Societies	must contact in advance.
Green Fees	not confirmed.
Facilities	⊗ & ⊞ by prior arrangement (ex Tue) ⅃ ⬛ ♀ 🛆 🏠 ⫪
Location	Torphin Rd, Colinton (5m SW of city centre S of A720)
Hotel	★★★55% Braid Hills Hotel, 134 Braid Rd, Braid Hills, EDINBURGH ☎031-447 8888 68⇨🏠

Turnhouse ☎031-339 5937
Hilly, parkland/heathland course, good views.
18 holes, 4171yds, Par 69, SSS 69, Course record 64.
Club membership 750.

Visitors	may not play at weekends or on competition days. Must be accompanied by member and contact in advance.
Societies	must contact in writing.
Green Fees	£18 per day; £12 per round.
Facilities	⊗ by prior arrangement ⊞ ⅃ ⬛ ♀ 🛆 🏠 ⫪ ⫪ Kevin Whitson.
Location	Turnhouse Rd (6m W of city centre N of A8)
Hotel	★★★67% Barnton Thistle Hotel, Queensferry Rd, Barnton, EDINBURGH ☎031-339 1144 50⇨🏠

GIFFORD   Map 12 NT56

Gifford ☎(062081) 267
Parkland course, with easy walking.
9 holes, 6138yds, Par 71, SSS 69.
Club membership 450.

Visitors	restricted Tue, Wed & weekends.
Green Fees	not confirmed.
Facilities	🛆
Location	Calroust (1m SW off B6355)
Hotel	★★69% Tweeddale Arms Hotel, GIFFORD ☎(062081) 240 15⇨🏠

GULLANE   Map 12 NT48

Gullane ☎(0620) 843115
Gullane is a delightful village and one of Scotland's great
golf centres. Gullane club was formed in 1882. There are
three Gullane courses and the No 1 is of championship
standard. It differs from most Scottish courses in as much
as it is of the downland type and really quite hilly. The
first tee is literally in the village. The views from the top
of the course are magnificent and stretch far and wide in
every direction - in fact, it is said that 14 counties can be
seen from the highest spot.
Course No 1 : : 18 holes, 6466yds, Par 71, SSS 71.
Course No 2 : : 18 holes, 6219yds, Par 70, SSS 70.
Course No 3 : : 18 holes, 5128yds, Par 65, SSS 65.
Club membership 1200.

Visitors	must contact in advance.
Societies	must contact in writing.

Green Fees	£14-£46 per day; £10-£31 per round (£17-£49 per day; £12-41 per round weekends).
Facilities	⊗ ⊞ ⅃ ⬛ ♀ 🛆 🏠 ⫪ ⫪ J Hume.
Location	On A198
Hotel	★★★(red)⬛ Greywalls Hotel, Muirfield, GULLANE ☎(0620) 842144 17⇨🏠 Annexe5⇨🏠

Muirfield (Honourable Company of Edinburgh Golfers)
See page 275

HADDINGTON   Map 12 NT57

Haddington ☎(062082) 3627
Inland course, tree-lined and bunkered, but not hilly.
18 holes, 6280yds, Par 71, SSS 70.
Club membership 500.

Visitors	may not play between 7am-10am & noon-2pm at weekends. Must contact in advance.
Societies	must contact in advance; deposits required.
Green Fees	not confirmed.
Facilities	⊗ ⊞ ⅃ ⬛ ♀ 🛆 🏠 ⫪ John Sandilands.
Leisure	pool table.
Location	Amisfield Park (E side off A613)
Hotel	★★69% Tweeddale Arms Hotel, GIFFORD ☎(062081) 240 15⇨🏠

LINLITHGOW   Map 11 NS97

Linlithgow ☎(0506) 842585
Slightly hilly parkland course in beautiful setting.
18 holes, 5800yds, Par 70, SSS 68.
Club membership 400.

Visitors	may not play Sat. Must book in advance Sun. Must contact in advance.
Societies	must contact in writing.
Green Fees	not confirmed.
Facilities	⊗ ⅃ ⬛ ♀ 🛆 🏠 ⫪ Derek Smith.
Location	Braehead (1m S off Bathgate Road off A803)
Hotel	★★★65% Inchyra Grange Hotel, Grange Rd, POLMONT ☎(0324) 711911 33⇨🏠

West Lothian ☎(0506) 826030
Hilly parkland course with superb views of River Forth.
18 holes, 6578yds, Par 71, SSS 71.
Club membership 500.

Visitors	must contact in advance.
Societies	must telephone in advance.
Green Fees	not confirmed.
Facilities	♀ 🛆
Location	Airngath Hill (1m S off A706)
Hotel	★★★65% Inchyra Grange Hotel, Grange Rd, POLMONT ☎(0324) 711911 33⇨🏠

LIVINGSTON   Map 11 NT06

Deer Park ☎(0506) 38843
Long testing course, fairly flat, championship standard.
18 holes, 6636yds, Par 71, SSS 72.
Club membership 500.

Visitors	no restrictions.
Green Fees	not confirmed.
Facilities	♀ 🛆 🏠 ⫪ ⫪

▶

SCORE CARD					
Hole	Yds	Par	Hole	Yds	Par
1	444	4	10	471	4
2	345	4	11	350	4
3	374	4	12	376	4
4	174	3	13	146	3
5	506	5	14	442	4
6	436	4	15	391	4
7	151	3	16	181	3
8	439	4	17	501	5
9	460	4	18	414	4
Out	3329	35	In	3272	35
			Totals	6601	70

GULLANE   Map 12 NT48

Muirfield (Honourable Company of Edinburgh Golfers). ☎ (062084) 2123

John Ingham writes: Ask an American superstar to name the best golf course in Great Britain, or maybe even in the world, and the likely answer will be Muirfield. It certainly features in the top ten of any meaningful selection.

Purely on shape and balance, the course has everything. Ask competitors in the Open Championship what they think of the last nine holes, and they will tell you it can wreck the stoutest heart. But ask Isoa Aoki of Japan what he thinks, and he will smile and maybe tell of his course record 63 here.

Established in 1744, it is just ten years older than the R&A itself but not as old as Royal Blackheath. However, these dates show that Muirfield certainly has seniority and tradition. Quite simply, it is exclusive and entirely excellent, and has staged some outstanding Open Championships with one, I suspect, standing out in people's minds more than any other.

Back in 1972, Tony Jacklin was Europe's best player and looked set to prove it again at Muirfield when he had appeared to wear down Lee Trevino, the defending champion. At the 71st hole, Trevino seemed to be frittering away strokes as he mishit a shot downwind through the dry, fast, green. In the next few minutes, hair stood on end. 'I was mad' recalled Trevino. 'My next shot from the bank was strictly a give-up one. And the ball went straight in the hole.' Jacklin had chipped up, well short. Then he missed his put, turned for the return putt, and missed again. We all did mental arithmetic. Jacklin had blown it and when he bogeyed the last, furious at himself, he suddenly wasn't the winner - Trevino was.

Those of us there recall Trevino has holed one bunker shot, and chipped in three times. Muirfield looked on his brilliance with favour and sad Jacklin never won an Open again.

18 holes, 6610 yards, Par 70, SSS73.

Visitors	only on Tuesdays, Thursdays and Friday morning. Must contact in advance and have a letter of introduction from home club.
Societies	telephone in advance. But also restricted to Tuesdays, Thursdays and Friday morning.
Green fees	£60 per day; £45 per round
Facilities	⊗ ■ ⚲ ⛳
Location	Duncur Rd (off A98 on NE side of village).

WHERE TO STAY AND EAT NEARBY

HOTELS:

ABERLADY ★★ 64% Kilspindie House, Main St. ☎ (08757) 682. 26 ⇨♠. ⚲ European cuisine.

GULLANE ★★★⚑ Greywalls, Muirfield. ☎ (0620) 842144. 17 ⇨♠, Annexe 5 ⇨♠

NORTH BERWICK ★★★ 64% The Marine, Cromwell Rd. ☎ (0620) 2406. 83 ⇨♠. ⚲ International cuisine.

★★ 61% Nether Abbey, 20 Dirleton Ave. ☎ (0620) 2802. 16rm (4 ⇨6 ♠)

★★ 56% Point Garry, West Bay Rd. ☎ (0620) 2380. 16rm (12 ⇨♠). ⚲ International cuisine.

RESTAURANT:

GULLANE ✕ La Potinière, Main St. ☎ (0620) 843214. ⚲ French cuisine.

| Location | Carmowdean (N side of town off A809) |
| Hotel | ★★★♨65% Houstoun House Hotel, UPHALL ☎(0506) 853831 28⇨🛏Annexe2⇨ |

Pumpherston ☎(0506) 32869
Undulating parkland course with testing 6th hole (par 3), and view of Pentland Hills.
9 holes, 5154yds, Par 64, SSS 65, Course record 61.
Club membership 350.

Visitors	must be accompanied by member.
Green Fees	not confirmed.
Facilities	⊗ 🖫 💻 ♀ 🛆
Location	Drumshoreland Rd, Pumpherston (1m E between A71 & A89)
Hotel	★★★♨65% Houstoun House Hotel, UPHALL ☎(0506) 853831 28⇨🛏Annexe2⇨

LONGNIDDRY   Map 12 NT47

Longniddry ☎(0875) 52141
Undulating seaside links and partial parkland course. One of the numerous courses which stretch east from Edinburgh right to Dunbar. The inward half is more open and less testing than the wooded outward half.
18 holes, 6219yds, Par 68, SSS 70, Course record 63.
Club membership 950.

| SCORECARD: White Tees ||||||
Hole	Yds	Par	Hole	Yds	Par
1	398	4	10	364	4
2	416	4	11	333	4
3	461	4	12	381	4
4	199	3	13	174	3
5	314	4	14	403	4
6	168	3	15	425	4
7	430	4	16	145	3
8	367	4	17	434	4
9	374	4	18	433	4
Out	3127	34	In	3092	34
			Totals	6219	68

Visitors	must have a handicap certificate; must play with member at weekends but may not play on bank holidays or competition days. Must contact in advance.
Societies	must contact in writing.
Green Fees	£30 per day; £20 per round.
Facilities	⊗ & 🍴 (ex Fri) 🖫 💻 ♀ (Apr-Sep) 🛆 🏠 ⚑ ⚐ John Gray.
Location	Links Rd (W side of village off A198)
Hotel	★★66% Kilspindie House Hotel, Main St, ABERLADY ☎(08757) 682 26⇨🛏

MUSSELBURGH   Map 11 NT37

Musselburgh ☎031-665 2005
Testing parkland course with natural hazards including trees and a burn, easy walking.
18 holes, 6614yds, Par 71, SSS 72, Course record 65.
Club membership 500.

Visitors	must contact in advance.
Societies	must contact in advance.
Green Fees	not confirmed.
Facilities	⊗ 🖫 💻 ♀ 🛆 🏠 ⚑ ⚐ Tom Stangoe.
Location	Monktonhall (1m S on B6415)
Hotel	★★★60% Donmaree Hotel, 21 Mayfield Gardens, EDINBURGH ☎031-667 3641 17⇨🛏

Musselburgh Old Course ☎031-655 2005
A links type course.
9 holes, 2371yds, Par 33, SSS 33, Course record 67.
Club membership 70.

| Visitors | may not play at weekends. |
| Societies | must contact in advance. |

Green Fees	not confirmed.
Facilities	♀ 🛆
Location	Millhill (1m E of town off A1)
Hotel	★★★60% Donmaree Hotel, 21 Mayfield Gardens, EDINBURGH ☎031-667 3641 17⇨🛏

NORTH BERWICK   Map 12 NT58

East Links ☎(0620) 2726
Coastal course on the south shores of Firth of Forth, opposite the famous Bass Rock Island.
18 holes, 6086yds, Par 69, SSS 69.
Club membership 500.

Visitors	no restrictions.
Societies	must contact in advance.
Green Fees	not confirmed.
Facilities	⊗ 🖫 💻 ♀ 🛆 🏠 ⚑
Location	E side of town off A198
Hotel	★★61% Point Garry Hotel, West Bay Rd, NORTH BERWICK ☎(0620) 2380 16rm(12⇨🛏)

Glen ☎(0620) 2221
An interesting course with a good variety of holes. The views of the town, the Firth of Forth and the Bass Rock are breathtaking.
18 holes, 6079yds, Par 69, SSS 69, Course record 65.
Club membership 500.

Visitors	no restrictions.
Societies	must telephone in advance.
Green Fees	not confirmed.
Facilities	⊗ 🖫 💻 ♀ 🛆 🏠 ⚑
Location	East Links, Tantallon Ter (E side of town centre)
Hotel	★★61% Nether Abbey Hotel, 20 Dirleton Av, NORTH BERWICK ☎(0620) 2802 16rm(4⇨6🛏)

North Berwick ☎(0620) 2135
Another of East Lothian's famous courses, the links at North Berwick is still popular. A classic championship links, it has many hazards including the beach, streams, bunkers, light rough and low walls. The great hole on the course is the 15th, the famous 'Redan', selected for televisions best 18 in the UK.
18 holes, 6315yds, Par 71, SSS 70.
Club membership 500.

| SCORECARD: White Tees ||||||
Hole	Yds	Par	Hole	Yds	Par
1	328	4	10	161	3
2	431	4	11	499	5
3	460	4	12	389	4
4	171	3	13	365	4
5	373	4	14	376	4
6	160	3	15	192	3
7	354	4	16	381	4
8	488	5	17	421	4
9	492	5	18	274	4
Out	3257	36	In	3058	35
			Totals	6315	71

Visitors	may not play on Sat. Must contact in advance.
Societies	must contact in advance.
Green Fees	not confirmed.
Facilities	⊗ 🍴 by prior arrangement 🖫 💻 ♀ 🛆 🏠 ⚑ ⚐
Location	New Clubhouse, Beach Rd (W side of town on A198)
Hotel	★★★64% The Marine Hotel, Cromwell Rd, NORTH BERWICK ☎(0620) 2406 83⇨🛏

PENICUIK   Map 11 NT25

Glencorse ☏(0968) 77177
Picturesque parkland course with burn affecting ten holes.
Testing 5th hole (237 yds) par 3.
18 holes, 5205yds, Par 64, SSS 66, Course record 61.
Club membership 650.

Visitors	restricted at weekends. Must contact in advance.
Societies	Tue-Thu only; must contact in advance.
Green Fees	£12 per round (£16 per day/round weekends).
Facilities	⊗ ∭ by prior arrangement ⌂ 🍺 ♀ △ 🏠 ⛳ ⏃ Cliffe Jones.
Location	Milton Bridge (1.5m N on A701)
Hotel	★★★55% Braid Hills Hotel, 134 Braid Rd, Braid Hills, EDINBURGH ☏031-447 8888 68⇨🛏

PRESTONPANS   Map 11 NT37

Royal Musselburgh ☏(0875) 810276
Tree-lined parkland course overlooking Firth of Forth.
18 holes, 6237yds, Par 70, SSS 70, Course record 66.
Club membership 900.

Visitors	restricted Fri afternoons & weekends. Must contact in advance.
Societies	must contact in writing.
Green Fees	not confirmed.
Facilities	⊗ ∭ by prior arrangement ⌂ 🍺 ♀ △ 🏠 ⛳ ⏃ John Henderson.
Leisure	snooker.
Location	Prestongrange House (W side of town centre off A59)
Hotel	★★66% Kilspindie House Hotel, Main St, ABERLADY ☏(08757) 682 26⇨🛏

RATHO   Map 11 NT17

Ratho Park ☏031-333 1252
Flat parkland course.
18 holes, 5900yds, Par 69, SSS 68, Course record 61.
Club membership 720.

Visitors	must contact in advance.
Societies	must contact in writing.
Green Fees	£24 per day; £16 per round (£30 weekends).
Facilities	⊗ ∭ ⌂ 🍺 ♀ △ 🏠 ⏃ Alan Pate.
Leisure	snooker.
Location	.75m E, N of A71
Hotel	★★★65% Forte Posthouse, Corstorphine Rd, EDINBURGH ☏031-334 0390 200⇨🛏

SOUTH QUEENSFERRY   Map 11 NT17

Dundas Parks ☏031-331 1601
Parkland course situated on the estate of Lady Jane Stewart-Clark, with excellent views. For 18 holes, the 9 are played twice. Driving bay and practice ground.
9 holes, 6024yds, Par 70, SSS 69, Course record 65.
Club membership 500.

Visitors	must be accompanied by member and contact in advance.
Societies	must contact in advance.
Green Fees	not confirmed.
Facilities	△
Location	3 Loch Place (1m S on B8000)
Hotel	★★★61% Forth Bridges Moat House, Forth Bridge, SOUTH QUEENSFERRY ☏031-331 1199 108⇨🛏

UPHALL   Map 11 NT07

Uphall ☏(0506) 852414
Windy parkland course, easy walking.
18 holes, 5567yds, Par 69, SSS 67.
Club membership 500.

Visitors	restricted weekends until 11am.
Green Fees	not confirmed.
Facilities	♀ △
Location	W side of village on A899
Hotel	★★★♨65% Houstoun House Hotel, UPHALL ☏(0506) 853831 28⇨🛏 Annexe2⇨

WEST CALDER   Map 11 NT06

Harburn ☏(0506) 871256
Moorland, reasonably flat.
18 holes, 5853yds, Par 69, SSS 68, Course record 62.
Club membership 600.

Visitors	may not play after 2.30pm.
Societies	must contact in writing.
Green Fees	£12.50 per day; £9 per round (£17.50 per day; £12.50 per round weekends).
Facilities	⊗ ⌂ 🍺 ♀ △ 🏠 ⏃
Hotel	★★★♨65% Houstoun House Hotel, UPHALL ☏(0506) 853831 28⇨🛏 Annexe2⇨

WHITBURN   Map 11 NS96

Polkemmet Country Park ☏(0501) 43905
Public parkland course surrounded by mature woodland and rhododendron bushes. 15-bay floodlit driving range.
9 holes, 2969mtrs, Par 37.

Visitors	no restrictions.
Societies	must contact in advance.
Green Fees	£1.90 per round (£2.45 Sun).
Facilities	⊗ ∭ ⌂ 🍺 ♀
Location	2m W off B7066
Hotel	★★★♨65% Houstoun House Hotel, UPHALL ☏(0506) 853831 28⇨🛏 Annexe2⇨

STRATHCLYDE

AIRDRIE   Map 11 NS76

Airdrie ☏(0236) 762195
Picturesque parkland course with good views.
18 holes, 6004yds, Par 69, SSS 69, Course record 64.
Club membership 450.

Visitors	with member only weekends & bank holidays. Must contact in advance and have an introduction from own club.
Societies	apply in writing.
Green Fees	£25 per day; £12 per round.

▶

Facilities	⊗ ⍟ ⌐ ☙ ♀ ⌂ ⋒ ⎰ A McCloskey.
Leisure	snooker.
Location	Rochsoles (1m N on B802)
Hotel	★★★64% Garfield House Hotel, Cumbernauld Rd, STEPPS ☎041-779 2111 27⇨⤺

Easter Moffat ☎(0236) 842878
Moorland/parkland course.
18 holes, 6221yds, Par 72, SSS 70, Course record 67.
Club membership 450.

Visitors	may only play on weekdays.
Societies	must contact in advance.
Green Fees	not confirmed.
Facilities	⊗ ⍟ by prior arrangement ⌐ and ☙ (all day) ♀ ⌂ ⋒ ⎰ Brian Dunbar.
Location	Mansion House, Plains (2m E on old Edinburgh-Glasgow road)
Hotel	★★★64% Garfield House Hotel, Cumbernauld Rd, STEPPS ☎041-779 2111 27⇨⤺

AYR   Map 10 NS32

Belleisle ☎(0292) 41258
Parkland course with beautiful sea views. First-class conditions.
Belleisle Course: 18 holes, 6540yds, Par 70, SSS 71.
Seafield Course: 18 holes, 5244yds, Par 66, SSS 66.

Visitors	must contact in advance.
Societies	must contact in advance.
Green Fees	not confirmed.
Facilities	♀ ⌂ ⋒ ⎰ ⋒ ⎰
Location	Belleisle Park (2m S on A719)
Hotel	★★★60% Pickwick Hotel, 19 Racecourse Rd, AYR ☎(0292) 260111 15⇨⤺

Dalmilling ☎(0292) 263893
Meadowland course, with easy walking.
18 holes, 5752yds, Par 69, SSS 68.
Club membership 140.

Visitors	must contact in advance.
Societies	must contact in advance.
Green Fees	not confirmed.
Facilities	⊗ ⍟ ⌐ ☙ (no catering Tue) ♀ ⌂ ⋒ ⎰ ⋒
Location	Westwood Av (1.5m W of town centre off A719)
Hotel	★★★60% Carlton Toby Hotel, PRESTWICK ☎(0292) 76811 39⇨⤺

Seafield ☎(0292) 41258
Public self-starting course of parkland type.
18 holes, 5457yds, Par 66, SSS 66, Course record 64.

Visitors	no restrictions.
Societies	must contact in writing.
Green Fees	not confirmed.
Facilities	⊗ ⍟ ⌐ ☙ ♀ ⌂ ⋒ ⎰ ⋒ ⎰ J S Easey.
Location	Doonfoot Rd (2m S on A719)
Hotel	★★★64% Caledonian Hotel, Dalblair Rd, AYR ☎(0292) 269331 114⇨⤺

For a full list of golf courses included in the book, see the index at the end of the directory

BALMORE   Map 11 NS57

Balmore ☎(0360) 20240
Parkland course with fine views.
18 holes, 5516yds, Par 66, SSS 67.
Club membership 700.

Visitors	must be accompanied by member and contact in advance.
Societies	must contact in advance.
Green Fees	not confirmed.
Facilities	⊗ ⍟ ⌐ ☙ ♀ ⌂ ⋒
Location	N off A807
Hotel	★★★65% Black Bull Thistle Hotel, Main St, MILNGAVIE ☎041-956 2291 27⇨⤺

BARASSIE   Map 10 NS33

Kilmarnock (Barassie) ☎Troon (0292) 313920
A magnificent seaside course, relatively flat with much heather. The turf and greens are quite unequalled. The 15th is a testing par 3 at 220 yards.
18 holes, 6473yds, Par 71, SSS 71, Course record 63.
Club membership 500.

Visitors	with member only Wed & weekends. After noon Mon, Tue, Thu & Fri. Must contact in advance.
Societies	bookings to Club Secretary.
Green Fees	£35 per day.
Facilities	⊗ ⍟ by prior arrangement ⌐ ☙ ♀ ⌂ ⋒ ⎰ ⋒ W R Lockie.
Location	29 Hillhouse Rd (E side of village on B746)
Hotel	★★★★67% Marine Highland Hotel, TROON ☎(0292) 314444 72⇨⤺

BARRHEAD   Map 11 NS45

Fereneze ☎041-881 1519
Hilly moorland course, with a good view at the end of a hard climb to the 3rd, then levels out.
18 holes, 5821yds, Par 70, SSS 68, Course record 64.
Club membership 700.

Visitors	may not play at weekends. Must be accompanied by member, contact in advance and have an introduction from own club.
Societies	apply in writing.
Green Fees	£16 per round/day.
Facilities	⊗ ⍟ ⌐ ☙ (no catering Mon) ♀ ⌂ ⋒ ⎰
Location	Fereneze Av (NW side of town off B774)
Hotel	★★64% Dalmeny Park Hotel, Lochlibo Rd, BARRHEAD ☎041-881 9211 18rm(3⇨10⤺)

BEARSDEN   Map 11 NS57

Bearsden ☎041-942 2351
Parkland course, with 16 greens and 11 teeing grounds. Easy walking and views over city.
9 holes, 6020yds, Par 68, SSS 69, Course record 67.
Club membership 550.

Visitors	must be accompanied by member and contact in advance.
Societies	apply by letter at least 1 mth prior.
Green Fees	£2 (£4 weekends).
Facilities	⊗ ⌐ ☙ ♀ ⌂ ⋒

Location	Thorn Rd (1m W off A809)
Hotel	★★★65% Black Bull Thistle Hotel, Main St, MILNGAVIE ☎041-956 2291 27⇨🐾

Douglas Park ☎041-942 2220
Parkland course with wide variety of holes.
18 holes, 5957yds, Par 69, SSS 69, Course record 64.
Club membership 900.

Visitors	may not play Mon & Fri. Must be accompanied by member and contact in advance.
Societies	must telephone in advance.
Green Fees	£18 per day; £14 per round.
Facilities	⊗ ⅢⅡ ⅃ ■ ♀ ⚎ 🖻 ⛳ ⌿ David Scott.
Location	Hillfoot (E side of town on A81)
Hotel	★★★65% Black Bull Thistle Hotel, Main St, MILNGAVIE ☎041-956 2291 27⇨🐾

Glasgow ☎041-942 2011
One of the finest parkland courses in Scotland.
18 holes, 5968yds, Par 70, SSS 69, Course record 63.
Club membership 760.

Visitors	must be accompanied by member, contact in advance and have an introduction from own club.
Green Fees	£30 per round/day.
Facilities	♀ (members guests only) ⚎ 🖻 ⌿ J Steven.
Location	Killermont (SE side off A81)
Hotel	★★★65% Black Bull Thistle Hotel, Main St, MILNGAVIE ☎041-956 2291 27⇨🐾

Windyhill ☎041-942 2349
Hard walking parkland/moorland course; testing 12th hole.
18 holes, 6254yds, Par 71, SSS 70, Course record 66.
Club membership 675.

Visitors	may not play at weekends. Must contact in advance.
Societies	must apply to secretary in writing.
Green Fees	£15 per day.
Facilities	⊗ ⅢⅡ ⅃ ■ (no catering Tue) ♀ ⚎ 🖻 ⌿ R Collinson.
Location	Windyhill (2m NW off B8050)
Hotel	★★★65% Black Bull Thistle Hotel, Main St, MILNGAVIE ☎041-956 2291 27⇨🐾

BEITH

Map 10 NS35

Beith ☎(05055) 3166
Hilly course, with panoramic views over 7 counties.
9 holes, 2559yds, Par 68, SSS 67, Course record 63.
Club membership 400.

Visitors	may not play at weekends.
Societies	apply in writing.
Green Fees	£12 per day; £7 per round.
Facilities	⅃ ■ ♀ ⚎
Location	Threepwood Rd (1.5m NE off A737)
Hotel	★★★⅃75% Chapeltoun House Hotel, STEWARTON ☎(0560) 82696 8⇨🐾

BELLSHILL

Map 11 NS76

Bellshill ☎(0698) 745124
Parkland course.
18 holes, 6205yds, Par 70, SSS 70, Course record 68.
Club membership 600.

Visitors	may not play between 4-7pm May-Aug.
Societies	apply in writing in advance.
Green Fees	£11 per day (£15 weekends & public holidays).
Facilities	⊗ & ⅢⅡ by prior arrangement ⅃ ■ ♀ ⚎
Location	Community Rd, Orbiston (1m SE off A721)
Hotel	★★58% Silvertrees Hotel, Silverwells Crescent, BOTHWELL ☎(0698) 852311 7⇨Annexe19⇨🐾

BIGGAR

Map 11 NT03

Biggar Municipal ☎(0899) 20618
Flat parkland course, easy walking and fine views.
18 holes, 5229yds, Par 67, SSS 65, Course record 65.
Club membership 200.

Visitors	must contact in advance.
Societies	telephone (0899) 20319 to book in advance.
Green Fees	£4.30 per round.
Facilities	⊗ ⅢⅡ ⅃ ■ ♀ ⚎ 🖻
Leisure	hard tennis courts, caravan park.
Location	The Park, Broughton Rd (S side of town)
Hotel	★★★67% Peebles Hydro Hotel, PEEBLES ☎(0721) 20602 137⇨🐾

BISHOPBRIGGS

Map 11 NS67

Bishopbriggs ☎041-772 1810
Parkland course with views to Campsie Hills.
18 holes, 6041yds, Par 69, SSS 69, Course record 63.
Club membership 600.

▶

Visitors	must be accompanied by member, contact in advance and have an introduction from own club.
Societies	apply in writing to the Committee one month in advance.
Green Fees	not confirmed.
Facilities	⊗ 𝕸 ﹦ ⬛ ♀ (1100-2300) ⛳ 🏠
Leisure	snooker.
Location	Brackenbrae Rd (.5m NW off A803)
Hotel	★★★65% Black Bull Thistle Hotel, Main St, MILNGAVIE ☎041-956 2291 27⇄🐾

Cawder ☎041-772 5167
Two parkland courses; Cawder Course hilly, with 5th, 9th, 10th, 11th-testing holes. Keir Course flat.
Cawder Course: 18 holes, 6295yds, Par 70, SSS 71, Course record 65.
Keir Course: 18 holes, 5877yds, Par 68, SSS 68.
Club membership 1150.

Visitors	may play on weekdays only. Must contact in advance.
Societies	must contact in writing.
Green Fees	not confirmed.
Facilities	⊗ 𝕸 ﹦ ⬛ ♀ ⛳ 🏠 ⚐ (
Location	Cadder Rd (1m NE off A803)
Hotel	★★★65% Black Bull Thistle Hotel, Main St, MILNGAVIE ☎041-956 2291 27⇄🐾

BISHOPTON   Map 10 NS47

Erskine ☎(0505) 862302
Parkland course.
18 holes, 6287yds, Par 71, SSS 70.
Club membership 700.

Visitors	must be accompanied by member, contact in advance and have an introduction from own club.
Societies	apply in writing.
Green Fees	not confirmed.
Facilities	⊗ ﹦ ⬛ ♀ ⛳ 🏠 (Peter Thomson.
Location	.75 NE off B815
Hotel	★★★67% Forte Posthouse Glasgow, North Barr, ERSKINE ☎041-812 0123 166⇄🐾

BONHILL   Map 10 NS37

Vale of Leven ☎Alexandria (0389) 52351
Hilly moorland course, tricky with many natural hazards - gorse, burns, trees. Overlooks Loch Lomond.
18 holes, 5162yds, Par 67, SSS 66, Course record 60.
Club membership 640.

Visitors	may not play Sat Apr-Sep.
Societies	apply to the secretary.
Green Fees	£11 per day; £7.50 per round (£15/£10 weekends & holidays.
Facilities	⊗ 𝕸 ﹦ ⬛ ♀ ⛳ 🏠
Location	North Field Rd (E side of town off A813)
Hotel	★★65% Dumbuck Hotel, Glasgow Rd, DUMBARTON ☎(0389) 34336 22⇄🐾

A golf-course name printed in ***bold italics***
means that we have been unable to verify
information with the club's management
for the current year

BOTHWELL   Map 11 NS75

Bothwell Castle ☎(0698) 853177
Flat parkland course in residential area.
18 holes, 6243yds, Par 71, SSS 70, Course record 64.
Club membership 1200.

Visitors	Mon-Fri 8am-3.30pm.
Societies	apply in writing.
Green Fees	£18 per day, £12 per round.
Facilities	⊗ 𝕸 (Fri, Sat & Sun) ﹦ ⬛ ♀ ⛳ 🏠 (W Walker.
Location	Blantyre Rd (NW of village off B7071)
Hotel	★★58% Silvertrees Hotel, Silverwells Crescent, BOTHWELL ☎(0698) 852311 7⇄Annexe19⇄🐾

BURNSIDE   Map 11 NS51

Blairbeth ☎041-634 3355
Parkland course.
18 holes, 5481yds, Par 70, SSS 67, Course record 64.
Club membership 400.

Visitors	introduced by a member or by arrangement with Secretary. Must be accompanied by member.
Societies	apply in writing.
Green Fees	not confirmed.
Facilities	⊗ 𝕸 ﹦ ⬛ ♀ ⛳
Location	S off A749
Hotel	★★★63% Macdonald Thistle Hotel, Eastwood Toll, GIFFNOCK ☎041-638 2225 56⇄🐾

Cathkin Braes ☎041-634 6605
Moorland course, prevailing westerly wind, small loch hazard at 5th hole.
18 holes, 6208yds, Par 71, SSS 71.
Club membership 890.

Visitors	may not play at weekends. Must contact in advance and have an introduction from own club.
Societies	apply in writing.
Green Fees	£25 per day; £16 per round.
Facilities	⊗ 𝕸 by prior arrangement ﹦ ⬛ ♀ ⛳ 🏠 (Stephen Bree.
Location	Cathkin Rd (1m S on B759)
Hotel	★★61% Royal Hotel, 1 Glaisnock St, CUMNOCK ☎(0290) 20822 11rm(2⇄1🐾)

CAMBUSLANG   Map 11 NS66

Cambuslang ☎041-641 3130
Parkland course.
9 holes, 6072yds, Par 70, SSS 69, Course record 65.
Club membership 200.

Visitors	must contact in advance and have an introduction from own club.
Societies	weekdays only; must contact in writing.
Green Fees	not confirmed.
Facilities	⊗ ﹦ ⬛ ♀ ⛳
Location	Westburn Dr (.25m N off A724)
Hotel	★★58% Silvertrees Hotel, Silverwells Crescent, BOTHWELL ☎(0698) 852311 7⇄Annexe19⇄🐾

CARDROSS   Map 10 NS37

Cardross ☎(0389) 841213
Undulating parkland course, testing with good views.
18 holes, 6496yds, Par 71, SSS 71, Course record 65.
Club membership 800.

Visitors	may not play at weekends unless introduced by member.
Societies	must contact in writing.
Green Fees	not confirmed.
Facilities	⊗ ⅏ by prior arrangement ⌫ ☛ ♀ ⌂ 🏠 ⛴ ℓ Robert Craig.
Location	Main Rd (In centre of village on A814)
Hotel	★★★58% Commodore Toby Hotel, 112 West Clyde St, HELENSBURGH ☎(0436) 76924 45⇨

CARLUKE   Map 11 NS85

Carluke ☎(0555) 71070
Parkland course with views over the Clyde Valley. Testing 11th hole, par 3.
18 holes, 5811yds, Par 70, SSS 68, Course record 64.
Club membership 460.

Visitors	until 4.30pm weekdays only. Must contact in advance and have an introduction from own club.
Societies	apply in writing.
Green Fees	£15 per day; £10 per round.
Facilities	⊗ ⅏ ⌫ ☛ ♀ ⌂ 🏠 ⛴ ℓ Andrew Brooks.
Location	Mauldslie Rd, Hallcraig (1m W off A73)
Hotel	★★★63% Popinjay Hotel, Lanark Rd, ROSEBANK ☎(055586) 441 36⇨🐾Annexe4⇨🐾

CARNWATH   Map 11 NS94

Carnwath ☎(0555) 840251
Picturesque parkland course slightly hilly, with small greens calling for accuracy. Panoramic views.
18 holes, 5953yds, Par 70, SSS 69, Course record 65.
Club membership 470.

Visitors	restricted after 5pm, no visitors Sat.
Societies	apply in writing or telephone.
Green Fees	£15 per day (£18 Sun & bank holidays).
Facilities	⊗ ⅏ (only Tue) ⌫ (Thu) ☛ ♀ (all day) ⌂ 🏠
Location	1 Main St (W side of village on A70)
Hotel	★★★63% Popinjay Hotel, Lanark Rd, ROSEBANK ☎(055586) 441 36⇨🐾Annexe4⇨🐾

CARRADALE   Map 10 NR83

Carradale ☎(05833) 387
Pleasant seaside course built on a promontory overlooking the Isle of Arran. Natural terrain and small greens are the most difficult natural hazards. Described as the most sporting 9-hole course in Scotland. Testing 7th hole (240 yds), par 3.
9 holes, 2387yds, Par 66, SSS 63, Course record 62.
Club membership 300.

Societies	welcome.
Green Fees	£4 per day.
Location	S side of village
Hotel	★★65% Carradale Hotel, CARRADALE ☎(05833) 223 12rm(10⇨🐾)Annexe5⇨🐾

CLARKSTON   Map 11 NS55

Cathcart Castle ☎041-638 0082
Tree-lined parkland course, with undulating terrain.
18 holes, 5832yds, Par 68, SSS 68, Course record 62.
Club membership 990.

Visitors	must be accompanied by member.
Societies	Tue & Thu only must apply in writing.
Green Fees	with member £2-£3.
Facilities	All catering by prior arrangement. ♀ ⌂ 🏠 ℓ David Naylor.
Location	Mearns Rd (.75m SW off A726)
Hotel	★★★63% Macdonald Thistle Hotel, Eastwood Toll, GIFFNOCK ☎041-638 2225 56⇨🐾

CLYDEBANK   Map 11 NS56

Clydebank Municipal ☎041-952 6372
Hilly, compact parkland course with tough finishing holes.
18 holes, 5349yds, Par 67, SSS 67, Course record 63.

Visitors	no restrictions.
Societies	welcome.
Green Fees	£3.20 (£3.60 Sun & public holidays).
Facilities	Cafeteria ⌂ 🏠 ℓ Richard Bowman.
Location	Overtoun Rd, Dalmur (2m NW of town centre)
Hotel	★★★66% Stakis Normandy Hotel, Inchinnan Rd, Renfrew, RENFREW ☎041-886 4100 141⇨🐾

COATBRIDGE   Map 11 NS76

Drumpellier ☎(0236) 24139
Parkland course.
18 holes, 6227yds, Par 71, SSS 70, Course record 63.
Club membership 700.

Visitors	may not play weekends or public holidays. Must contact in advance.
Societies	telephone for details.
Green Fees	not confirmed.
Facilities	⊗ ⅏ ⌫ ☛ ♀ ⌂ 🏠 ℓ Kenneth Hutton.
Leisure	pool table.
Location	Drumpellier Av (.75m W off A89)
Hotel	★★★60% Bothwell Bridge Hotel, 89 Main St, BOTHWELL ☎(0698) 852246 41⇨🐾

CUMBERNAULD   Map 11 NS77

Dullatur ☎(0236) 723230
Parkland course, with natural hazards and wind. Testing 17th hole, par 5.
18 holes, 6219yds, Par 70, SSS 70, Course record 65.
Club membership 656.

Visitors	may not play on competition days & must play with member at weekends. Must contact in advance.
Societies	must contact in writing.

▶

Green Fees	£16 per day; £10 per round after 1.30pm.
Facilities	⊗ ⅢL by prior arrangement ⌁ ⚑ ♀ ⚐ 🛍 ✗ (Duncan Sinclair.
Leisure	snooker.
Location	Dullatur (1.5m N)
Hotel	★★★62% Stakis Park Hotel, Camelon Rd, FALKIRK ☎(0324) 28331 55➪🐾

Palacerigg ☎(0236) 734969
Parkland course.
18 holes, 6444yds, Par 72, SSS 71, Course record 66.
Club membership 400.

Visitors	may not play at weekends. Must contact in advance and have an introduction from own club.
Societies	must contact in advance.
Green Fees	not confirmed.
Facilities	⊗ Ⅲ ⌁ ⚑ (catering Wed-Sun) ♀
Location	Palacerigg Country Park (2m S)
Hotel	★★★62% Stakis Park Hotel, Camelon Rd, FALKIRK ☎(0324) 28331 55➪🐾

Westerwood Hotel Golf & Country Club ☎(0236) 457171
Undulating parkland/woodland course designed by Dave
Thomas and Seve Ballesteros. Holes meander through silver
birch, firs, heaths and heathers, and the spectacular 15th,
'The Waterfall', has its green set against a 40ft rockface.
Buggie track. Hotel facilities.
18 holes, 6721yds, Par 73, SSS 72, Course record 69.
Club membership 250.

Visitors	no restrictions.
Societies	by prior arrangement.
Green Fees	£20-£30 weekdays (£25-£40 weekends).
Facilities	⊗ Ⅲ ⌁ ⚑ ♀ ⚐ 🛍 ✗ ⋈ (Tony Smith.
Leisure	hard tennis courts, heated indoor swimming pool, snooker, solarium, gymnasium.
Location	St Andrews Dr (adjacent to A80)
Hotel	★★★62% Stakis Park Hotel, Camelon Rd, FALKIRK ☎(0324) 28331 55➪🐾
Additional hotel	★★★★69% Westerwood Hotel Golf And Country Club, 1 St Andrews Dr, Westerwood, CUMBERNAULD ☎(0236) 457171 47➪🐾 **See advertisement on page 285**

DUMBARTON Map 10 NS37

Dumbarton ☎(0389) 32830
Flat parkland course.
18 holes, 5992yds, Par 71, SSS 69, Course record 65.
Club membership 500.

Visitors	may not play weekends & public holidays.
Societies	advance booking with secretary.
Green Fees	£12 per round.
Facilities	⊗ & Ⅲ by prior arrangement ⌁ ⚑ ♀ ⚐
Location	Broadmeadow (.25m N off A814)
Hotel	★★65% Dumbuck Hotel, Glasgow Rd, DUMBARTON ☎(0389) 34336 22➪🐾

DUNOON Map 10 NS17

Cowal ☎(0369) 5673
Moorland course. Panoramic views of Clyde Estuary and
surrounding hills.
18 holes, 6251yds, Par 70, SSS 70, Course record 64.
Club membership 550.

Visitors	handicap certificate preferred or club membership.
Societies	must telephone in advance.
Green Fees	not confirmed.
Facilities	⊗ Ⅲ by prior arrangement ⌁ ⚑ ♀ ⚐ 🛍 ✗ (Russell D Weir.
Location	Ardenslate Rd (1m N)
Hotel	★★76% Enmore Hotel, Marine Pde, Kirn, DUNOON ☎(0369) 2230 11➪🐾

EAGLESHAM Map 11 NS55

Bonnyton ☎(03553) 2781
Windy, moorland course.
18 holes, 6255yds, Par 72, SSS 71.
Club membership 950.

Visitors	must contact in advance.
Societies	must telephone in advance.
Green Fees	£20.
Facilities	⊗ Ⅲ ⌁ ⚑ ♀ ⚐ 🛍 ✗ (Robert Crerar.
Location	.25m SW off B764
Hotel	★★★62% Bruce Swallow Hotel, Cornwall St, EAST KILBRIDE ☎(03552) 29771 79➪🐾

EAST KILBRIDE Map 11 NS65

East Kilbride ☎(03552) 20913
Parkland and hill course.Very windy. Testing 7th, 9th and
14th holes.
18 holes, 6419yds, Par 71, SSS 71, Course record 64.
Club membership 800.

Visitors	must be a member of recognised golfing society. Must be accompanied by member.
Societies	must telephone in advance.
Green Fees	£18 per day; £12 per round.
Facilities	⊗ Ⅲ ⌁ ⚑ ♀ ⚐ 🛍 ✗ (Alastair R Taylor.
Location	Chapelside Rd, Nerston (.5m N off A7)
Hotel	★★★62% Bruce Swallow Hotel, Cornwall St, EAST KILBRIDE ☎(03552) 29771 79➪🐾

Torrance House ☎(03552) 48638
A parkland course.
18 holes, 6415yds, Par 72, Course record 64.
Club membership 1000.

Visitors	must contact 6 days in advance.
Green Fees	not confirmed.
Facilities	Catering by prior arrangement ♀ 🛍 (John D Dunlop.
Location	Calderglen Country Park, Strathaven Rd (1.5m SE of Kilbride on A726)
Hotel	★★★62% Bruce Swallow Hotel, Cornwall St, EAST KILBRIDE ☎(03552) 29771 79➪🐾

GALSTON Map 11 NS53

Loudoun ☎(0563) 821993
Pleasant, testing parkland course.
18 holes, 5800yds, Par 67, SSS 68, Course record 61.
Club membership 750.

Visitors	may not play at weekends. Must contact in advance.
Societies	must contact in advance.
Green Fees	not confirmed.

Facilities	⊗) by prior arrangement 🛒 💷 ⛳ (times vary) ⚲ 🏠
Location	Edinburgh Rd (NE side of town on A71)
Hotel	★★★57% Howard Park Hotel, Glasgow Rd, KILMARNOCK ☎(0563) 31211 46⇨🏠

GARTCOSH   Map 11 NS66

Mount Ellen ☎(0236) 872277
Downland course with 73 bunkers. Testing hole: 10th ('Bedlay'), 156 yds, par 3.
18 holes, 5525yds, Par 68, SSS 68, Course record 60.
Club membership 500.

Visitors	may play Mon-Fri 9am-4pm. Must contact in advance.
Societies	must contact in advance.
Green Fees	not confirmed.
Facilities	⊗) (Fri and Sat) 🛒 💷 ⛳ ⚲ 🏠 (Gary Brooks.
Location	.75m N off A752
Hotel	★★★64% Garfield House Hotel, Cumbernauld Rd, STEPPS ☎041-779 2111 27⇨🏠

GIRVAN   Map 10 NX19

Girvan ☎(0465) 4272
Municipal seaside and parkland course. Testing 17th hole (223-yds) uphill, par 3. Good views.
18 holes, 5098yds, Par 64, SSS 65.
Club membership 175.

Visitors	no restrictions.
Societies	may not play Jul & Aug.
Green Fees	not confirmed.
Facilities	⛳ ⚲
Location	Golf Course Rd (N side of town off A77)
Hotel	★★63% King's Arms Hotel, Dalrymple St, GIRVAN ☎(0465) 3322 25⇨🏠

GLASGOW   Map 11 NS56

Alexandra ☎041-556 3211
Parkland course, hilly with some woodland.
9 holes, 2800yds, Par 34.
Club membership 250.

Visitors	no restrictions.
Societies	no prior arrangement required.
Green Fees	£1.65 per day.
Facilities	⚲
Leisure	gymnasium.
Location	Alexandra Park, Alexandra Pde (2m E of city centre off M8/A8)
Hotel	★★★★64% Stakis Grosvenor Hotel, 1/10 Grosvenor Ter, Great Western Rd, GLASGOW ☎041-339 8811 95⇨🏠

Cowglen ☎041-632 0556
Parkland course with good views over Clyde valley to Campsie Hills.
18 holes, 5976yds, Par 69, SSS 69, Course record 63.
Club membership 775.

Visitors	play on shorter course. Must contact in advance and have an introduction from own club.
Societies	must telephone in advance.
Green Fees	£21 per day; £14 per round.

Facilities	⊗) 🛒 💷 ⛳ ⚲ 🏠 (John McTear.
Location	Barrhead Rd (4.5m SW of city centre on B762)
Hotel	★★★63% Macdonald Thistle Hotel, Eastwood Toll, GIFFNOCK ☎041-638 2225 56⇨🏠

Haggs Castle ☎041-427 0480
Wooded, parkland course where Scottish National Championships and the Glasgow and Scottish Open have been held. Quite difficult.
18 holes, 6464yds, Par 72, SSS 71, Course record 65.
Club membership 960.

Visitors	may not play at weekends. Must be accompanied by member, contact in advance and have an introduction from own club.
Societies	apply in writing in advance.
Green Fees	£33 per day; £22 per round.
Facilities	⊗) 🛒 💷 ⛳ ⚲ 🏠 ⚑ (Jim McAlister.
Location	70 Dumbreck Rd, Dumbreck (2.5m SW of city centre on B768)
Hotel	★★★61% Sherbrooke Hotel, 11 Sherbrooke Av, Pollokshields, GLASGOW ☎041-427 4227 10⇨🏠 Annexe11⇨🏠

Kirkhill ☎041-641 8499
Meadowland course designed by James Braid.
18 holes, 5889yds, Par 69, SSS 69, Course record 63.
Club membership 650.

Visitors	must play with member at weekends. Must contact in advance.
Societies	must contact in advance.
Green Fees	not confirmed.

▶

Facilities	⊗ (ex Mon) 🍴 by prior arrangement 🎱 (ex Mon and Thu) 💺 ♀ ⚘
Location	Greenless Rd, Cambuslang (5m SE of city centre off A749)
Hotel	★★★60% Stuart Hotel, 2 Cornwall Way, EAST KILBRIDE ☎(03552) 21161 39⇔🐾

Knightswood Park ☎041-959 2131
Parkland course within easy reach of city. Two dog legs.
9 holes, 2700yds, Par 33, SSS 33.
Club membership 60.

Visitors	no restrictions.
Societies	welcome.
Green Fees	not confirmed.
Location	Lincoln Av (4m W of city centre off A82)
Hotel	★★★60% Jurys Pond Hotel, Great Western Rd, GLASGOW ☎041-334 8161 134⇔🐾

Lethamhill ☎041-770 6220
Municipal parkland course.
18 holes, 5859yds, Par 70, SSS 68.

Visitors	must have an introduction from own club.
Societies	must contact in advance.
Facilities	⚘
Location	1240 Cumbernauld Rd, Millerston (3m NE of city centre on A80)
Hotel	★★★64% Garfield House Hotel, Cumbernauld Rd, STEPPS ☎041-779 2111 27⇔🐾

Linn Park ☎041-637 5871
Municipal parkland course with six par 3's in outward half.
18 holes, 4952yds, Par 65, SSS 65, Course record 61.
Club membership 80.

Visitors	no restrictions.
Green Fees	not confirmed.
Facilities	⚘
Location	Simshill Rd (4m S of city centre off B766)
Hotel	★★★62% Bruce Swallow Hotel, Cornwall St, EAST KILBRIDE ☎(03552) 29771 79⇔🐾

Pollok ☎041-632 1080
Parkland course with woods and river.
18 holes, 6257yds, Par 71, SSS 70.
Club membership 460.

Visitors	must play with member at weekends. Must contact in advance and have an introduction from own club.
Societies	Mon-Fri only; must contact in writing.
Green Fees	not confirmed.
Facilities	⊗ 🍴 by prior arrangement 🎱 💺 ♀ ⚘
Location	90 Barrhead Rd (4m SW of city centre on A762)
Hotel	★★★66% Tinto Firs Thistle Hotel, 470 Kilmarnock Rd, GLASGOW ☎041-637 2353 28⇔🐾

Williamwood ☎041-637 1783
Inland course, fairly hilly with wooded areas, a small lake and pond.
18 holes, 5878yds, SSS 68, Course record 61.
Club membership 450.

We make every effort to ensure that our information is accurate but details may change after we go to print

---

Visitors	must be accompanied by member and have an introduction from own club.
Green Fees	not confirmed.
Facilities	🖃 (J Gardner.
Location	Clarkston Rd (5m S of city centre on B767)
Hotel	★★★63% Macdonald Thistle Hotel, Eastwood Toll, GIFFNOCK ☎041-638 2225 56⇔🐾

GOUROCK   Map 10 NS27

Gourock ☎(0475) 31001
Moorland course with hills and dells. Testing 8th hole, par 5.
Magnificent views over Firth of Clyde.
18 holes, 6492yds, Par 73, SSS 71, Course record 64.
Club membership 720.

Visitors	by introduction or with member.
Societies	welcome weekdays, must contact in advance.
Green Fees	£15 per day; £10 per round.
Facilities	⊗ 🍴 🎱 💺 ♀ ⚘ 🖃 (Robert Collinson.
Location	Cowal View (SW side of town off A770)
Hotel	★★★⚑60% Manor Park Hotel, SKELMORLIE ☎(0475) 520832 10⇔🐾 Annexe13⇔🐾

GREENOCK   Map 10 NS27

Greenock ☎(0475) 20793
Testing moorland course with panoramic views of Clyde Estuary.
18 holes, 5838yds, Par 68, SSS 68, Course record 64.
Club membership 730.

Visitors	may not play Sat. Must contact in advance and have an introduction from own club.
Societies	must telephone in advance.
Green Fees	£13 per day (£17 Sun & bank holidays).
Facilities	⊗ 🍴 🎱 💺 ♀ ⚘ 🖃 (Graham Ross.
Location	Forsyth St (SW side of town off A770)
Hotel	★★★⚑60% Manor Park Hotel, SKELMORLIE ☎(0475) 520832 10⇔🐾 Annexe13⇔🐾

Whinhill ☎(0475) 21064
Picturesque heathland public course.
18 holes, 5454yds, Par 66, SSS 68.

Visitors	may only use club facilities with member.
Green Fees	not confirmed.
Location	Beith Rd (1.5m SW off B7054)
Hotel	★★★⚑60% Manor Park Hotel, SKELMORLIE ☎(0475) 520832 10⇔🐾 Annexe13⇔🐾

HAMILTON   Map 11 NS75

Hamilton ☎(0698) 282872
Beautiful parkland course.
18 holes, 6281yds, Par 70, SSS 70.
Club membership 480.

Visitors	must be accompanied by member.
Green Fees	not confirmed.
Facilities	♀ ⚘ 🖃 (
Location	Riccarton, Ferniegair (1.5m SE on A72)

Hotel	★★58% Silvertrees Hotel, Silverwells Crescent, BOTHWELL ☎(0698) 852311 7⇄Annexe19⇄🐾

Strathclyde Park ☎(0698) 66155
Municipal parkland course.
9 holes, 3147yds, Par 36, SSS 70.
Club membership 120.

Visitors	no restrictions.
Societies	must contact in advance.
Green Fees	not confirmed.
Facilities	⊗ �𝍷 🝙 🍺 ♀ ⌂ 🛏 (Ken Davidson.
Location	Mote Hill (N side of town off B7071)
Hotel	★★58% Silvertrees Hotel, Silverwells Crescent, BOTHWELL ☎(0698) 852311 7⇄Annexe19⇄🐾

HELENSBURGH   Map 10 NS28

Helensburgh ☎(0436) 74173
Sporting moorland course with superb views of Loch Lomond and River Clyde.
18 holes, 6058yds, Par 69, SSS 69, Course record 64.
Club membership 850.

Visitors	may not play at weekends. Must contact in advance.
Societies	must contact in writing.
Green Fees	£15 per day; £12 per round.
Facilities	�𝍷 by prior arrangement 🝙 🍺 ♀ ⌂ 🛏 ⚑ (Robert Farrell.

Location	25 East Abercromby St (NE side of town off B832)
Hotel	★★★58% Commodore Toby Hotel, 112 West Clyde St, HELENSBURGH ☎(0436) 76924 45⇄

IRVINE   Map 10 NS33

Glasgow ☎(0294) 311347
A lovely seaside links. The turf of the fairways and all the greens are truly glorious and provide tireless play. Established in 1787, this is the ninth oldest course in the world and is a qualifying course for the Open Championship.
18 holes, 6493yds, Par 71, SSS 71, Course record 62.
Club membership 1150.

Visitors	may not play at weekends & bank holidays. Must contact in advance and have an introduction from own club.
Societies	must contact in writing.
Green Fees	£30 per day; £25 per round.
Facilities	⊗ �𝍷 🝙 🍺 ♀ ⌂ 🛏 (J Steven.
Location	2m S off A737
Hotel	★★★★55% Hospitality Inn, Annick Rd, Annickwater, IRVINE ☎(0294) 74272 128⇄🐾

Irvine ☎(0294) 78139
Testing links course; only two short holes.
18 holes, 6400yds, Par 71, SSS 71, Course record 65.
Club membership 450.

Visitors	may not play before 3pm Sat & Sun. Must contact in advance.

▶

Societies	are welcome weekdays, telephone (0294) 75979 to book in advance.
Green Fees	£26 per day; £21 per round.
Facilities	⊗ ⊞ ㋹ ☕ ♀ 🛆 🛏 (Keith Erskine.
Location	Bogside (N side of town off A737)
Hotel	★★★★55% Hospitality Inn, Annick Rd, Annickwater, IRVINE ☎(0294) 74272 128↩🐾

Irvine Ravenspark ☎(0294) 79550
Parkland course.
18 holes, 6702yds, Par 71, SSS 71, Course record 66.
Club membership 400.

Visitors	ex Sat 7-10am & 12-2pm
Societies	telephone
Green Fees	not confirmed.
Facilities	⊗ ⊞ ㋹ ☕ (no catering Tue and Thu) ♀ 🛆 🛏 (Peter Bond.
Location	N side of town on A737
Hotel	★★★♨75% Chapeltoun House Hotel, STEWARTON ☎(0560) 82696 8↩🐾

Western Gailes ☎(0294) 311649
A magnificent seaside links with glorious turf and wonderful greens. The view is open across the Firth of Clyde to the neighbouring islands. It is a well-balanced course crossed by 3 burns. There are 2 par 5's, the 6th and 14th, and the 11th is a testing 445-yd, par 4, dog-leg.
18 holes, 6664yds, Par 71, SSS 72.

Visitors	welcome Mon, Tue, Wed & Fri. Must contact in advance.
Societies	must contact in advance.
Green Fees	£33 per round; £40 per day.
Facilities	⊗ ⊞ ㋹ ☕ ♀ 🛆
Location	Gailes by Irvine (2m S off A737)
Hotel	★★★★67% Marine Highland Hotel, TROON ☎(0292) 314444 72↩🐾

JOHNSTONE   Map 10 NS46

Cochrane Castle ☎(0505) 20146
Fairly hilly parkland course, wooded with two small streams running through it.
18 holes, 6226yds, Par 70, SSS 70, Course record 66.
Club membership 580.

Visitors	may not play at weekends. Must contact in advance.
Societies	may not play at weekends.
Green Fees	£18 per day; £12 per round.
Facilities	⊗ ⊞ (ex Mon and Thu) ㋹ ☕ ♀ 🛆 🛏 (Stuart Campbell.
Location	Scott Av (.5m W off A737)
Hotel	★★★62% Glynhill Hotel & Leisure Club, Paisley Rd, RENFREW ☎041-886 5555 125↩🐾

Elderslie ☎(0505) 22835
Parkland course, undulating, with good views.
18 holes, 6037yds, Par 70, SSS 69.
Club membership 700.

Visitors	may not play at weekends & bank holidays. Must contact in advance and have an introduction from own club.
Societies	must contact in writing.
Green Fees	not confirmed.

Facilities	♀ 🛆 🛏 (
Leisure	snooker.
Location	63 Main Rd, Elderslie (E side of town on A737)
Hotel	★★★62% Glynhill Hotel & Leisure Club, Paisley Rd, RENFREW ☎041-886 5555 125↩🐾

KILBIRNIE   Map 10 NS35

Kilbirnie Place ☎(0505) 684444
Easy walking parkland course.
18 holes, 5400yds, Par 69, SSS 67.
Club membership 300.

Visitors	no restrictions.
Green Fees	not confirmed.
Facilities	♀ 🛆
Location	Largs Rd (1m W on A760)
Hotel	★★67% Elderslie Hotel, John St, Broomfields, LARGS ☎(0475) 686460 25rm(9↩4🐾)

KILMACOLM   Map 10 NS36

Kilmacolm ☎(050587) 2139
Moorland course, easy walking, fine views. Testing 7th, 13th and 14th holes.
18 holes, 5964yds, Par 69, SSS 68, Course record 64.
Club membership 800.

Visitors	restricted at weekends. Must contact in advance.
Societies	apply in writing.
Green Fees	£20 per day; £15 per round.
Facilities	⊗ ㋹ ☕ ♀ 🛆 🛏 (David Stewart.
Location	Porterfield Rd (SE side of town off A761)
Hotel	★★★♨72% Gleddoch House Hotel, LANGBANK ☎(047554) 711 33↩🐾

KILMARNOCK   Map 10 NS43

Annanhill ☎(0563) 21644
Municipal, tree-lined parkland course played over by private clubs.
18 holes, 6269yds, Par 71, SSS 70, Course record 64.
Club membership 280.

Visitors	restricted at weekends.
Societies	must telephone in advance.
Green Fees	not confirmed.
Facilities	⊗ (ex Tue & Thu) ⊞ ㋹ ☕ ♀
Location	Irvine Rd (1m W on A71)
Hotel	★★★57% Howard Park Hotel, Glasgow Rd, KILMARNOCK ☎(0563) 31211 46↩

Caprington ☎(0563) 23702
Municipal parkland course.
18 holes, 5718yds, Par 69, SSS 68.
Club membership 400.

Visitors	may not play on Fri afternoons. Must contact in advance and have an introduction from own club.
Green Fees	not confirmed.
Facilities	♀ 🛆 🛏 (
Location	Ayr Rd (1.5m S on B7038)
Hotel	★★★57% Howard Park Hotel, Glasgow Rd, KILMARNOCK ☎(0563) 31211 46↩

KILSYTH
Map 11 NS77

Kilsyth Lennox ☎(0236) 822190
Hilly moorland course, hard walking.
9 holes, 5944yds, Par 70, SSS 69, Course record 65.
Club membership 400.

Visitors	must play with member at weekends.
Societies	must contact in writing.
Green Fees	not confirmed.
Facilities	﹅ ﹅ ♀ ﹅ ﹅
Location	Tak Ma Doon Rd (N side of town off A803)
Hotel	★★69% Kirkhouse Inn, STRATHBLANE ☎(0360) 70621 15⇔﹅

KIRKINTILLOCH
Map 11 NS67

Hayston ☎041-776 1244
An undulating, tree-lined course with a sandy subsoil.
18 holes, 6042yds, Par 70, SSS 69.
Club membership 440.

Visitors	must be accompanied by member, contact in advance and have an introduction from own club.
Societies	apply in writing.
Green Fees	£18 per day; £12 per round.
Facilities	⊗ ﹅ ﹅ ﹅ ♀ (restricted winter) ﹅ ﹅ ﹅ Steven Barnett.
Location	Campsie Rd (1m NW off A803)
Hotel	★★★65% Black Bull Thistle Hotel, Main St, MILNGAVIE ☎041-956 2291 27⇔﹅

Kirkintilloch ☎041-776 1256
Parkland course in rural setting.
18 holes, 5269yds, Par 70, SSS 66, Course record 61.
Club membership 650.

Visitors	must be accompanied by member.
Societies	apply in writing.
Green Fees	£17 per day; £12 per round.
Facilities	﹅ ﹅ ♀ ﹅ ﹅
Location	Campsie Rd (1m NW off A803)
Hotel	★★★65% Black Bull Thistle Hotel, Main St, MILNGAVIE ☎041-956 2291 27⇔﹅

LANARK
Map 11 NS84

Lanark ☎(0555) 3219
Chosen as one of the pre-qualifying tests for the Open Championship held at Lanark from 1977 to 1983. The address of the club, 'The Moor', gives some indication as to the kind of golf to be found there. Golf has been played at Lanark for well over a century and the Club dates from 1851.
18 holes, 6423yds, Par 70, SSS 71, Course record 65 or 9 holes, 1562yds, Par 32.
Club membership 850.

Visitors	restricted until 4pm weekdays only. Must contact in advance and have an introduction from own club.

SCORECARD					
Hole	Yds	Par	Hole	Yds	Par
1	360	4	10	152	3
2	467	4	11	397	4
3	409	4	12	362	4
4	457	4	13	362	4
5	318	4	14	399	4
6	377	4	15	470	4
7	141	3	16	337	4
8	530	5	17	309	4
9	360	4	18	216	3
Out	3419	36	In	3004	34
			Totals	6423	70

Societies	may not play at weekends. Telephone in advance.
Green Fees	£24 per day; £16 per round. 9 hole £1.50-£3.50.
Facilities	⊗ ﹅ by prior arrangement ﹅ ﹅ ♀ ﹅ ﹅ ﹅ Ron Wallace.
Location	The Moor (E side of town centre off A73)
Hotel	★★★63% Popinjay Hotel, Lanark Rd, ROSEBANK ☎(055586) 441 36⇔﹅ Annexe4⇔﹅

LANGBANK
Map 10 NS37

Gleddoch Golf and Country Club ☎(047554) 304
Parkland and heathland course with other sporting facilities available to temporary members. Good views over Firth of Clyde.
18 holes, 5661yds, Par 68, SSS 67.
Club membership 300.

Visitors	with member only at weekends. Must contact in advance and have an introduction from own club.
Societies	welcome.
Green Fees	£20.
Facilities	⊗ ﹅ ﹅ ﹅ ♀ ﹅ ﹅ ﹅ Keith Campbell.
Leisure	heated indoor swimming pool, squash, riding, sauna.
Hotel	★★★⚑72% Gleddoch House Hotel, LANGBANK ☎(047554) 711 33⇔﹅

LARGS   Map 10 NS25

Largs ☎(0475) 673594
A parkland, tree-lined course with views to the Clyde coast and Arran Isles.
18 holes, 6220yds, Par 70, SSS 70, Course record 64.
Club membership 850.
Visitors	may not play weekends & competition days. Must contact in advance.
Societies	apply in writing.
Green Fees	£24 per day.
Facilities	⊗ ⍿ ⊾ ⬤ ♀ 🖾 ⵗ ℂ Robbie Stewart.
Location	Irvine Rd (1m S of town centre on A78)
Hotel	★★67% Elderslie Hotel, John St, Broomfields, LARGS ☎(0475) 686460 25rm(9⇄4🌰)

Routenburn ☎(0475) 673230
Heathland course with fine views over Firth of Clyde.
18 holes, 5675yds, Par 68, SSS 67.
Club membership 350.
Visitors	no restrictions.
Green Fees	not confirmed.
Facilities	♀ △ 🖾
Location	Routenburn Rd (1m N off A78)
Hotel	★★★♨60% Manor Park Hotel, SKELMORLIE ☎(0475) 520832 10⇄🌰Annexe13⇄🌰

LARKHALL   Map 11 NS75

Larkhall ☎(0698) 881113
Small, inland parkland course.
9 holes, 6700yds, Par 72, SSS 71, Course record 69.
Club membership 250.
Visitors	restricted Tue & Sat.
Green Fees	£2.50 per 9 holes.
Facilities	⊾ (weekends only) ♀
Location	Burnhead Rd (E side of town on B7019)
Hotel	★★★63% Popinjay Hotel, Lanark Rd, ROSEBANK ☎(055586) 441 36⇄🌰Annexe4⇄🌰

LEADHILLS   Map 11 NS81

Leadhills ☎(0659) 74222
Testing, hilly course with high winds. It is the highest 9-hole course in Great Britain (1, 500ft above sea level).
9 holes, 4354yds, Par 66, SSS 64, Course record 59.
Club membership 80.
Visitors	no restrictions.
Societies	must telephone in advance.
Green Fees	£4.50 per day.
Facilities	⬤
Location	E side of village off B797
Hotel	★★64% Mennockfoot Lodge Hotel, Mennock, SANQUHAR ☎(0659) 50382 & 50477 1⇄Annexe8⇄🌰

This guide is updated annually – make sure that you use the up-to-date edition

LENNOXTOWN   Map 11 NS67

Campsie ☎(0360) 310244
Scenic hillside course.
18 holes, 5515yds, Par 70, SSS 67, Course record 65.
Club membership 560.
Visitors	restricted after 4pm.
Societies	must contact one month in advance.
Green Fees	not confirmed.
Facilities	⊗ ⍿ ⊾ ⬤ ♀ △ 🖾
Location	Crow Rd (.5m N on B822)
Hotel	★★69% Kirkhouse Inn, STRATHBLANE ☎(0360) 70621 15⇄🌰

LENZIE   Map 11 NS67

Lenzie ☎041-776 1535
Pleasant moorland course.
18 holes, 5984yds, Par 69, SSS 69, Course record 64.
Club membership 750.
Visitors	must have introduction by member or by prior arrangement with secretary. Must be accompanied by member and contact in advance.
Societies	apply in writing.
Green Fees	£18 per day; £11 per round.
Facilities	⊗ ⍿ ⊾ ⬤ ♀ △ 🖾 ℂ Jim McCallum.
Location	19 Crosshill Rd (S side of town on B819)
Hotel	★★★64% Garfield House Hotel, Cumbernauld Rd, STEPPS ☎041-779 2111 27⇄🌰

LESMAHAGOW   Map 11 NS83

Holland Bush ☎(0555) 893484
Fairly difficult, tree-lined municipal parkland and moorland course. First half is flat, while second is hilly. No bunkers.
18 holes, 6110yds, Par 72, SSS 70, Course record 63.
Club membership 500.
Visitors	no restrictions.
Societies	must contact in advance.
Green Fees	not confirmed.
Facilities	⊗ ⍿ ⊾ ⬤ ♀ △ 🖾 ⵗ ℂ Ian Rae.
Location	Acretophead
Hotel	★★★63% Popinjay Hotel, Lanark Rd, ROSEBANK ☎(055586) 441 36⇄🌰Annexe4⇄🌰

LOCHWINNOCH   Map 10 NS35

Lochwinnoch ☎(0505) 842153
Parkland course, slightly hilly in middle, with testing golf. Overlooks bird sanctuary and boating loch.
18 holes, 6202yds, Par 70, SSS 70, Course record 67.
Club membership 500.
Visitors	may not play at weekends & restricted during competition days.
Societies	apply in writing to club administrator.
Green Fees	£12 per day.
Facilities	♀ △ 🖾 ℂ Gerry Reilly.
Location	Burnfoot Rd (W side of town off A760)
Hotel	★★67% Elderslie Hotel, John St, Broomfields, LARGS ☎(0475) 686460 25rm(9⇄4🌰)

MACHRIHANISH   Map 10 NR62

Machrihanish ☎(058681) 213
Magnificent seaside links of championship status. The
1st hole is the famous drive across the Atlantic. Sandy soil
allows for play all year round. Large greens, easy walking,
windy.
18 holes, 6228yds, Par 70, SSS 70.
Club membership 850.
Visitors no restrictions.
Societies apply in writing.
Green Fees £18 per day Mon-Sun; £13.50 per round
Mon-Fri.
Facilities ⊗ & ⅢⅡ by prior arrangement ⅃ ⬤ ♀ △
🏠 ℓ Kenneth Campbell.
Location 5m W of Campbeltown on B843
Hotel ★★64% Seafield Hotel, Kilkerran Rd,
CAMPBELTOWN ☎(0586) 54385
3🦅Annexe6🦅

MAUCHLINE   Map 11 NS42

Ballochmyle ☎(0290) 50469
Wooded parkland course.
18 holes, 5952yds, Par 70, SSS 69, Course record 65.
Club membership 840.
Visitors may not play on Sat.
Societies apply in writing.
Green Fees £20 per day; £12 per round (£25 per day Sun).
Facilities ⊗ ⅢⅡ ⅃ ⬤ (seasonal variations) ♀ △ 🏠
Leisure squash, snooker.
Location Ballochmyle (1m SE on B705)
Hotel ★★61% Royal Hotel, 1 Glaisnock St,
CUMNOCK ☎(0290) 20822 11rm(2⇨1🦅)

MAYBOLE   Map 10 NS20

Maybole Municipal
Hilly parkland course.
9 holes, 2635yds, Par 33, SSS 65, Course record 64.
Club membership 100.
Visitors no restrictions.
Societies must contact in advance.
Green Fees not confirmed.
Location Memorial Park
Hotel ★★★66% Malin Court, TURNBERRY
☎(0655) 31457 8🦅

MILNGAVIE   Map 11 NS57

Clober ☎041-956 1685
Parkland course. Testing 5th hole, par 3.
18 holes, 5042yds, Par 65, SSS 65, Course record 61.
Club membership 600.
Visitors before 4.30pm.
Societies must contact in advance.
Green Fees not confirmed.
Facilities ⊗ ⅢⅡ ⅃ ⬤ ♀ 🏠
Location Craigton Rd (NW side of town)
Hotel ★★★65% Black Bull Thistle Hotel, Main St,
MILNGAVIE ☎041-956 2291 27⇨🦅

Dougalston ☎041-956 5750
Tree-lined with water features.
18 holes, 6683yds, Par 72, SSS 71.
Visitors must contact in advance.
Societies must contact in advance.
Green Fees not confirmed.
Facilities ⊗ ⅢⅡ ⅃ ⬤ ♀ △ ⟟
Location Strathblane Rd (NE side of town on A81)
Hotel ★★★65% Black Bull Thistle Hotel, Main St,
MILNGAVIE ☎041-956 2291 27⇨🦅

Hilton Park ☎041-956 4657
Moorland courses set amidst magnificent scenery.
Hilton: 18 holes, 6007yds, Par 70, SSS 70, Course record 65.
Allander: 18 holes, 5374yards, Par 69, SSS 67, Course record 66.
Club membership 1200.
Visitors may not play at weekends. Must contact in advance.
Societies weekdays only.
Green Fees £16.50 per round; £22.50 two rounds.
Facilities ⊗ ⅢⅡ ⅃ ⬤ ♀ △ 🏠 ⟟ ℓ
Location Stockiemuir Rd (3m NW on A809)
Hotel ★★★65% Black Bull Thistle Hotel, Main St,
MILNGAVIE ☎041-956 2291 27⇨🦅

Milngavie ☎041-956 1619
Moorland course, hard walking, sometimes windy, good
views. Testing 1st and 4th holes (par 4).
18 holes, 5818yds, Par 68, SSS 68, Course record 64.
Club membership 700.
▶

Visitors	must be accompanied by member, contact in advance and have an introduction from own club.
Societies	apply in writing.
Green Fees	£22 per day; £15 per round.
Facilities	⊗ 〗 ⓛ ☕ ♀ 👟
Location	Laigh Park (1.25m N)
Hotel	★★★65% Black Bull Thistle Hotel, Main St, MILNGAVIE ☎041-956 2291 27⇨🐦

MOTHERWELL   Map 11 NS75

Colville Park ☎(0698) 63017
Parkland course. First nine, tree-lined, second nine, more exposed. Testing 10th hole par 3, 16th hole par 4.
18 holes, 6265yds, Par 71, SSS 70, Course record 65.
Club membership 790.

Visitors	with member only except for parties. Must contact in advance.
Societies	weekdays only, apply in writing.
Green Fees	£12 per day (party booking).
Facilities	⊗ 〗 ⓛ ☕ ♀ 👟 🏠
Leisure	2 bowling greens, sailing, fishing club.
Location	New Jerviston House, Jerviston Estate (1.25m NE on A723)
Hotel	★★58% Silvertrees Hotel, Silverwells Crescent, BOTHWELL ☎(0698) 852311 7⇨Annexe19⇨🐦

MUIRHEAD   Map 11 NS66

Crow Wood ☎041-779 2011
Parkland course.
18 holes, 6249yds, Par 71, SSS 70, Course record 62.
Club membership 600.

Visitors	may not play at weekends. Must contact in advance.
Societies	maximum 32, apply in writing.
Green Fees	£15 per day; £10 per round.
Facilities	⊗ 〗 by prior arrangement ⓛ ☕ ♀ 👟 🏠 (Stephen Forbes.
Leisure	snooker.
Location	Garnkirk House (.5m W on A80)
Hotel	★★★64% Garfield House Hotel, Cumbernauld Rd, STEPPS ☎041-779 2111 27⇨🐦

NEW CUMNOCK   Map 11 NS61

New Cumnock ☎(0290) 20822
Parkland course.
9 holes, 2365yds, Par 66, SSS 63.

Visitors	no restrictions.
Green Fees	not confirmed.
Location	Lochhill (.75m N on A76)
Hotel	★★61% Royal Hotel, 1 Glaisnock St, CUMNOCK ☎(0290) 20822 11rm(2⇨1🐦)

If you know of a golf course which welcomes visitors and is not already in this guide, we should be grateful for information

NEWTON MEARNS   Map 11 NS55

East Renfrewshire ☎Loganswell (03555) 258
Undulating moorland with loch; prevailing SW wind.
18 holes, 6097yds, Par 70, SSS 70.
Club membership 500.

Visitors	must contact in advance.
Societies	must contact in advance.
Green Fees	not confirmed.
Facilities	⊗ 〗 ⓛ ☕ ♀ 👟 🏠 (
Location	Pilmuir (3m SW on A77)
Hotel	★★★63% Macdonald Thistle Hotel, Eastwood Toll, GIFFNOCK ☎041-638 2225 56⇨🐦

Eastwood ☎Loganswell (03555) 261
Moorland course.
18 holes, 5864yds, Par 68, SSS 68, Course record 62.
Club membership 950.

Visitors	welcome by appointment. Must contact in advance.
Societies	must contact in advance.
Green Fees	£18 per day; £12 per round.
Facilities	⊗ & 〗 (ex Tue & Thu) ⓛ ☕ ♀ 👟 🏠 (Kendal McWade.
Leisure	pool table.
Location	Muirshield (2.5m S on A77)
Hotel	★★★63% Macdonald Thistle Hotel, Eastwood Toll, GIFFNOCK ☎041-638 2225 56⇨🐦

Whitecraigs ☎041-639 4530
Beautiful parkland course.
18 holes, 6230yds, Par 70, SSS 70.
Club membership 1150.

Visitors	must be accompanied by member and have an introduction from own club.
Societies	apply in writing.
Green Fees	£23 per round.
Facilities	⊗ 〗 ⓛ ☕ ♀ 👟 🏠 (W Watson.
Location	72 Ayr Rd (1.5m NE on A77)
Hotel	★★★63% Macdonald Thistle Hotel, Eastwood Toll, GIFFNOCK ☎041-638 2225 56⇨🐦

OBAN   Map 10 NM83

Glencruitten ☎(0631) 62868
There is plenty of space and considerable variety of hole on this downland course - popular with holidaymakers. In a beautiful, isolated situation, the course is hilly and testing, particularly the 1st and 12th, par 4's, and 10th and 15th, par 3's.
18 holes, 4250yds, Par 61, SSS 63, Course record 55.
Club membership 620.

SCORECARD: Medal Tees					
Hole	Yds	Par	Hole	Yds	Par
1	445	4	10	150	3
2	170	3	11	238	3
3	167	3	12	410	4
4	271	4	13	185	3
5	163	3	14	318	4
6	228	3	15	178	3
7	219	3	16	313	4
8	263	4	17	180	3
9	197	3	18	357	4
Out	2123	30	In	2329	31
			Totals	4452	61

Visitors	restricted Thu & Sat.
Societies	must contact in writing.
Green Fees	not confirmed.
Facilities	⊗ 〗 by prior arrangement ⓛ ☕ ♀ 👟 🏠

Location	Glencruitten Rd (NE side of town centre off A816)
Hotel	★★★56% Caledonian Hotel, Station Square, OBAN ☎(0631) 63133 70⇨

PAISLEY

Map 11 NS46

Barshaw ☎041-889 2908
Municipal parkland course.
18 holes, 5703yds, Par 68, SSS 67.
Club membership 77.
Visitors   no restrictions.
Green Fees not confirmed.
Facilities ⌣
Location   Barshaw Park (1m E off A737)
Hotel   ★★★62% Glynhill Hotel & Leisure Club, Paisley Rd, RENFREW ☎041-886 5555 125⇨

Paisley ☎041-884 3903
Moorland course, windy but with good views.
18 holes, 6220yds, Par 70, SSS 70.
Club membership 700.
Visitors   must have handicap certificate. Must be accompanied by member, contact in advance and have an introduction from own club.
Societies   apply in writing.
Green Fees £16.35 per day; £12.25 per round.
Facilities ⊗ � ⌣ ⌣ (catering by prior arrangement) ♀ ⌣ ⌣ (Grant Gilmour.
Leisure   snooker.
Location   Braehead (S side of town off B774)
Hotel   ★★★62% Glynhill Hotel & Leisure Club, Paisley Rd, RENFREW ☎041-886 5555 125⇨

Ralston ☎041-882 1349
Parkland course.
18 holes, 6071yds, Par 71, SSS 69.
Club membership 750.
Visitors   must be accompanied by member.
Green Fees not confirmed.
Facilities ♀ ⌣ ⌣
Location   Strathmore Av, Ralston (2m E off A737)
Hotel   ★★★62% Swallow Hotel, 517 Paisley Rd West, GLASGOW ☎041-427 3146 119⇨

PORT GLASGOW

Map 10 NS37

Port Glasgow ☎(0475) 704181
A moorland course set on a hilltop overlooking the Clyde, with magnificent views to the Cowal hills.
18 holes, 5712yds, Par 68, SSS 68, Course record 63.
Club membership 390.
Visitors   may not play on Sat. Must contact in advance.
Societies   apply in writing.
Green Fees £12 per day; £8 per round.
Facilities ⊗ ⌣ ⌣ ⌣ (catering on request) ♀
Location   Devol Rd (1m S)
Hotel   ★★★‡72% Gleddoch House Hotel, LANGBANK ☎(047554) 711 33⇨

PRESTWICK

Map 10 NS32

Prestwick ☎(0292) 77404
Seaside links with natural hazards and fine views.
18 holes, 6544yds, Par 71, SSS 72.
Club membership 590.
Visitors   restricted Thu; may not play at weekends. Must contact in advance and have an introduction from own club.
Societies   must contact in writing.
Green Fees not confirmed.
Facilities ⊗ ⌣ ⌣ ♀ ⌣ ⌣ ⌣ (Frank Rennie.
Location   2 Links Rd (In town centre off A79)
Hotel   ★★60% Parkstone Hotel, Esplanade, PRESTWICK ☎(0292) 77286 15⇨

Prestwick St Cuthbert ☎(0292) 77101
Parkland course with easy walking, natural hazards and sometimes windy.
18 holes, 6470yds, Par 71, SSS 71, Course record 66.
Club membership 820.
Visitors   may not play at weekends & bank holidays. Must contact in advance.
Societies   apply in writing.
Green Fees £20 per day; £15 per round.
Facilities ⊗ ⌣ by prior arrangement ⌣ ⌣ ♀ ⌣
Location   East Rd (.5m E of town centre off A77)
Hotel   ★★60% St Nicholas Hotel, 41 Ayr Rd, PRESTWICK ☎(0292) 79568 17rm(13⇨)

Prestwick St Nicholas ☎(0292) 77608
Seaside course with whins, heather and tight fairways. It provides easy walking and has an unrestricted view of the Firth of Clyde.
18 holes, 5926yds, Par 68, SSS 68.
Club membership 700.
Visitors   except weekends & public holidays. Must contact in advance.
Societies   must contact in advance.
Green Fees £28 per day; £18 per round.
Facilities ⊗ ⌣ ⌣ ⌣ ♀ ⌣ ⌣ ⌣ (Stewart Smith.
Location   Grangemuir Rd (S side of town off A79)
Hotel   ★★60% Parkstone Hotel, Esplanade, PRESTWICK ☎(0292) 77286 15⇨

RENFREW

Map 11 NS46

Renfrew ☎(041886) 6692
Tree-lined parkland course.
18 holes, 6818yds, Par 72, SSS 73, Course record 67.
Club membership 700.
Visitors   must be accompanied by member, contact in advance and have an introduction from own club.
Green Fees not confirmed.
Facilities ⊗ ⌣ ⌣ ⌣ ♀ ⌣ ⌣
Location   Blythswood Estate, Inchinnan Rd (.75m W off A8)
Hotel   ★★★66% Stakis Normandy Hotel, Inchinnan Rd, Renfrew, RENFREW ☎041-886 4100 141⇨

For an explanation of symbols and abbreviations, see page 32

For a full range of AA guides and maps, visit your local AA shop or any good bookshop

SHOTTS Map 11 NS86

Shotts ☎(0501) 20431
Moorland course.
18 holes, 6125yds, Par 70, SSS 70, Course record 62.
Club membership 900.

Visitors welcome weekdays. Must contact in advance.
Societies apply by letter, weekdays only.
Green Fees £12 per day (£15 weekends); Low season £8 per round (£10 weekends).
Facilities ⊗ 🍴 🥪 ☕ 🍷 (all day) ⌂ 🏠 🏌 Gordon Graham.
Location Blairhead (2m from M8 off Benhar Road)
Hotel ★★★63% Popinjay Hotel, Lanark Rd, ROSEBANK ☎(055586) 441 36⇨🚿 Annexe4⇨🚿

SKELMORLIE Map 10 NS16

Skelmorlie ☎(0475) 520152
Parkland/moorland course with magnificent views over Firth of Clyde. Designed by James Braid, the club celebrated its centenary in 1991. The first five holes are played twice.
18 holes, 5056yds, Par 64, SSS 65, Course record 62.
Club membership 400.

Visitors restricted Sat. Must contact in advance.
Societies apply in writing to the secretary.
Green Fees £10.50 per day; £7.50 per round (£14/£10 weekends).
Facilities ⊗ 🍴 🥪 ☕ (no catering Tue & Thu) 🍷 ⌂
Leisure fishing.
Location Beithglass (E side of village off A78)
Hotel ★★★🏰60% Manor Park Hotel, SKELMORLIE ☎(0475) 520832 10⇨🚿 Annexe13⇨🚿

SOUTHEND Map 10 NR60

Dunaverty ☎No telephone
Undulating, seaside course.
18 holes, 4597yds, SSS 63.
Club membership 250.

Visitors no restrictions.
Societies apply in writing.
Green Fees not confirmed.
Facilities ⊗ by prior arrangement ☕ ⌂
Location 10m S of Campbeltown on B842
Hotel ★★64% Royal Hotel, Main St, CAMPBELTOWN ☎(0586) 52017 16rm(8⇨4🚿)

STEVENSTON Map 10 NS24

Ardeer ☎(0294) 64542
Parkland course, with natural hazards.
18 holes, 6500yds, Par 72, SSS 72, Course record 67.
Club membership 560.

Visitors may not play Sat.
Societies must contact in advance.
Green Fees £10 per day; £6 per round (£14/£8 Sun).
Facilities ⊗ 🍴 🥪 ☕ 🍷 🏠 🏌 Bob Rodgers.
Leisure snooker.
Location Greenhead (.5m N off A78)
Hotel ★★★★55% Hospitality Inn, Annick Rd, Annickwater, IRVINE ☎(0294) 74272 128⇨🚿

STRATHAVEN Map 11 NS64

Strathaven ☎(0357) 20421
Gently undulating, tree-lined, Championship parkland course with panoramic views over town and Avon valley.
18 holes, 6206yds, Par 71, SSS 70, Course record 63.
Club membership 950.

Visitors welcome weekdays only. Must contact in advance.
Societies Tue only.
Green Fees £20 per day; £15 per round.
Facilities ⊗ 🍴 🥪 ☕ 🍷 ⌂ 🏠 🏌 M McCrorie.
Location Overton Av, Glasgow Rd (NE side of town on A726)
Hotel ★★★60% Stuart Hotel, 2 Cornwall Way, EAST KILBRIDE ☎(03552) 21161 39⇨🚿

TARBERT Map 10 NR86

Tarbert ☎(0880) 820565
Beautiful moorland course. Four fairways crossed by streams.
9 holes, 4460yds, Par 66, SSS 64, Course record 61.
Club membership 110.

Visitors may not play competition days.
Societies apply in writing.
Green Fees £6 per 18 holes; £4 per 9 holes.
Facilities 🍷 (Sat & Sun)
Location 1m W on B8024
Hotel ★★★61% Stonefield Castle Hotel, TARBERT ☎(0880) 820836 33rm(30⇨2🚿)

TIGHNABRUAICH Map 10 NR97

Kyles of Bute ☎(0700) 811601
Moorland course which is hilly and exposed to wind. Good views of the Kyles of Bute.
9 holes, 4778yds, Par 66, SSS 64 or 47 holes.
Club membership 160.

Visitors no restrictions.
Societies must give 3 weeks prior notice.
Green Fees not confirmed.
Facilities ⌂
Location 1.25m S off B8000
Hotel ★★76% Kilfinan Hotel, KILFINAN ☎(070082) 201 11⇨

TROON Map 10 NS33

Royal Troon ☎(0292) 311555
Famous Championship Links. The current course record holder on the Old Course is Greg Norman with a 64 (1989).
Old Course: 18 holes, 7067yds, Par 73, SSS 74, Course record 64.
Portland: 18 holes, 6386yds, Par 71, SSS 71, Course record 65.
Club membership 500.

Visitors may not play Wed, Fri, weekends & public holidays. Must have handicap certificate. Must contact in advance and have an introduction from own club.
Societies apply in writing.

Green Fees	Old Course £65 inc lunch; Portland £40 inc lunch.
Facilities	⊗ ⅏ ㆔ ⅏ ♀ ⅄ 🖿 ⅏ ⅃ B R Anderson.
Location	Craigend Rd (S side of town on B749)
Hotel	★★★★67% Marine Highland Hotel, TROON ☎(0292) 314444 72⇆🛏

Troon Municipal ☎(0292) 312464
Three links courses, two Championship.
Lochgreen Course: 18 holes, 6785yds, Par 74, SSS 73, Course record 66.
Darley: 18 holes, 6501yds, Par 71, SSS 71, Course record 65.
Fullerton: 18 holes, 4822yds, Par 64, SSS 63, Course record 59.
Club membership 3000.

Visitors	must contact in advance.
Societies	apply in writing.
Green Fees	Lochgreen/Darley £16.40 per day; £10.20 per round. Fulverton £14.40 per day; £8.20 per round.
Facilities	⊗ ⅏ 🝆 ㆔ ⅏ ♀ ⅄ 🖿 ⅏ ⅃ Gordon McKinley.
Location	Harling Dr (100yds from railway station)
Hotel	★★60% Ardneil Hotel, 51 Saint Meddans St, TROON ☎(0292) 311611 9rm(3⇆4🛏)

TURNBERRY   Map 10 NS20

Turnberry Hotel Golf Courses See page 295

UDDINGSTON   Map 11 NS66

Calderbraes ☎(0698) 813425
Parkland course with good view of Clyde Valley. Testing 4th hole (par 4), hard uphill.
9 holes, 5046yds, Par 66, SSS 67, Course record 65.
Club membership 230.

Visitors	weekdays before 5pm.
Societies	welcome.
Green Fees	not confirmed.
Facilities	⊗ ⅏ 🝆 ㆔ ⅏ ♀ ⅄
Location	57 Roundknowe Rd (1.5m NW off A74)
Hotel	★★62% Redstones Hotel, 8-10 Glasgow Rd, UDDINGSTON ☎(0698) 813774 & 814843 18rm(16⇆🛏)

UPLAWMOOR   Map 10 NS45

Caldwell ☎(050585) 329
Parkland course.
18 holes, 6046yds, Par 71, SSS 69.
Club membership 600.

Visitors	restricted weekends & bank holidays.
Societies	apply in writing.
Green Fees	not confirmed.
Facilities	⊗ ⅏ 🝆 ㆔ ⅏ ♀ ⅄ 🖿 ⅃ Keith Baxter.
Location	.5m SW A736
Hotel	★★64% Dalmeny Park Hotel, Lochlibo Rd, BARRHEAD ☎041-881 9211 18rm(3⇆10🛏)

WEST KILBRIDE   Map 10 NS24

West Kilbride ☎(0294) 823911
Seaside links course on Firth of Clyde, with fine view of Isle of Arran from every hole.
18 holes, 6247yds, Par 71, SSS 70, Course record 63.
Club membership 960.

Visitors	may not play at weekends. Must have an introduction from own club.
Societies	Tue & Thu only must contact in advance.
Green Fees	not confirmed.
Facilities	⊗ ⅏ by prior arrangement 🝆 ㆔ ♀ ⅄ 🖿 ⅃ Gregor Howie.
Location	Fullerton Dr (W side of town off A78)
Hotel	★★67% Elderslie Hotel, John St, Broomfields, LARGS ☎(0475) 686460 25rm(9⇆4🛏)

WISHAW   Map 11 NS75

Wishaw ☎(0698) 372869
Parkland course with many tree-lined areas. Bunkers protect 17 of the 18 greens.
18 holes, 6051yds, Par 69, SSS 69, Course record 63.
Club membership 1003.

Visitors	welcome midweek before 5pm, Sun after 10.30am, not Sat.
Societies	apply by letter 4 weeks in advance.
Green Fees	£8.50 per round; £12.50 per day (mid week) (£19 Sun) no visitors Sat.
Facilities	⊗ ⅏ 🝆 ㆔ ⅏ ♀ ⅄ 🖿 ⅃ John Campbell.
Location	55 Cleland Rd (NW side of town off A721)
Hotel	★★★63% Popinjay Hotel, Lanark Rd, ROSEBANK ☎(055586) 441 36⇆🛏 Annexe4⇆🛏

Opening times of bar and catering facilities vary from place to place. Please remember to check in advance of your visit

TAYSIDE

ABERFELDY Map 14 NN84

Aberfeldy ☎(0887) 20535
Flat, parkland course, situated by River Tay near the famous Wade Bridge and Black Watch Monument.
9 holes, 5466yds, Par 67, SSS 67, Course record 65.
Club membership 250.

Visitors	are advised to book in advance and must do so at weekends Jun-Aug.
Societies	must contact in advance.
Green Fees	£12 per day; £8 per 18 holes.
Facilities	⊗ ⅷ ⅼ Ⅼ ⅼ ♀ ⚊ ⚌
Location	Taybridge Rd (N side of town centre)
Hotel	★★63% Weem Hotel, Weem, ABERFELDY ☎(0887) 20381 14⇨⚊

ALYTH Map 15 NO24

Alyth ☎(08283) 2268
Windy, heathland course with easy walking.
18 holes, 6226yds, Par 70, SSS 70, Course record 66.
Club membership 850.

Visitors	must contact in advance.
Societies	must contact in advance.
Green Fees	not confirmed.
Facilities	⊗ high tea ⅷ by prior arrangement ⅼ ⅬⅬ ♀ ⚊ ⚌ ⚌ Tom Melville.
Location	Pitcrocknie (1m E on B954)
Hotel	★★♨62% Lands of Loyal Hotel, Loyal Rd, ALYTH ☎(08283) 3151 11⇨

ARBROATH Map 12 NO64

Arbroath Artisan ☎(0241) 75837
Municipal seaside links course, with bunkers guarding greens. Played upon by Arbroath Artisan Club.
18 holes, 6090yds, Par 70, SSS 69.
Club membership 600.

Visitors	no restrictions.
Societies	must telephone in advance; deposit required.
Green Fees	£15 weekday ticket; £10 per round (£20 per day; £13 per round weekends).
Facilities	⊗ ⅼ ⅬⅬ ♀ ⚊ ⚌ ⚌ ⚌ Lindsay Ewart.
Location	Elliot (2m SW on A92)
Hotel	★★59% Hotel Seaforth, Dundee Rd, ARBROATH ☎(0241) 72232 20⇨

Letham Grange ☎(024189) 373
Two courses of great variety. Old Course is set in wooded estate with attractive lochs and burns. New Course is shorter and less arduous but deceptive.
Old Course: 18 holes, 6939yds, Par 73, SSS 73, Course record 72.
New Course: 18 holes, 5528yds, Par 68, SSS 68.
Club membership 780.

Visitors	restricted Tue & weekends on Old Course. Must contact in advance.
Societies	must contact in advance.
Green Fees	Old Course: £22.50 per day; £15 per round (£18 per round weekends). New Course: £12 per day; £8 per round (£10 weekends).
Facilities	⊗ ⅷ ⅼ ⅬⅬ ♀ ⚊ ⚊ ⚌ ⚌ David F G Scott.
Location	Colliston (4m N on A993)
Hotel	★★★65% Letham Grange Hotel, Colliston, ARBROATH ☎(024189) 373 19⇨

AUCHTERARDER Map 11 NN91

Auchterarder ☎(0764) 62804
Parkland course with easy walking.
18 holes, 5757yds, Par 69, SSS 68, Course record 65.
Club membership 650.

Visitors	restricted on competition days. Must contact in advance.
Societies	must contact 2 months in advance.
Green Fees	£15 per day; £10 per round (£20 per day; £15 per round weekends).
Facilities	⚊ ⚊ ⚌ ⚌ Keith Salmoni.
Location	Orchil Rd (.75m SW on A824)
Hotel	★★★★★(red) The Gleneagles Hotel, AUCHTERARDER ☎(0764) 62231 236⇨⚊

Gleneagles Hotel ☎(0764) 63543
Famous moorland courses designed by James Braid. The King's has heather and gorse threatening wayward shots; The Queen's is more heavily wooded with a variety of dog-leg holes and the Loch-an-Eerie to negotiate. Sumptuous hotel offers unrivalled sports and leisure activities. Course record holder on King's Course is Ian Woosnam. The new championship Monarchs Course, designed by Jack Nicklaus, will be opening at the end of 1992.
Kings Course: 18 holes, 6471yds, Par 70, SSS 71, Course record 62.
Queens Course: 18 holes, 5965yds, Par 68, SSS 69.
Wee Course: 9 holes, 1481yds, Par 27.

Visitors	must be hotel residents. Must be accompanied by member and contact in advance.
Societies	must be resident in the hotel.
Green Fees	not confirmed.
Facilities	⊗ ⅷ ⅼ ⅬⅬ (catering available to hotel guests) ♀ ⚊ ⚊ ⚌ ⚌ ⚌ Ian Marchbank.
Leisure	hard and grass tennis courts, heated indoor swimming pool, squash, fishing, riding, snooker, sauna, solarium, gymnasium, croquet, bowls, pitch & putt & cycling.
Location	2m SW of A823
Hotel	★★★★★(red) The Gleneagles Hotel, AUCHTERARDER ☎(0764) 62231 236⇨⚊

BARRY Map 12 NO53

Panmure ☎(0241) 53120
A nerve-testing, adventurous course set amongst sandhills - its hazards belie the quiet nature of the opening holes. This tight links has been used as a qualifying course for the Open Championship, and features Ben Hogan's favourite hole, the dog-leg 6th, which heralds the toughest stretch, around the turn.
18 holes, 6317yds, Par 70, SSS 70, Course record 62.
Club membership 500.

Visitors	must play with member on Sat.
Societies	must contact secretary in advance.
Green Fees	£30 per day; £20 per round.

▶

SCORE CARD: Old Course					
Hole	Yds	Par	Hole	Yds	Par
1	370	4	10	318	4
2	411	4	11	172	3
3	352	4	12	316	4
4	419	4	13	398	4
5	514	5	14	523	5
6	374	4	15	401	4
7	359	4	16	351	4
8	166	3	17	461	4
9	307	4	18	354	4
Out	3272	36	In	3294	36
			Totals	6566	72

TURNBERRY   Map10NS20

Turnberry Hotel Golf Courses ☎ (0655) 31000

John Ingham writes: The hotel is sumptuous, the Ailsa and Arran courses beneath it are total magic. The air reaches down into your inner lung and of all places in Scotland, Turnberry has to be among the finest.

You are not obliged to stay at the superb hotel, and if you wish to fly in, then Prestwick Airport is only seventeen miles from the first tee.

What makes the place so desirable is the warmness of the welcome and, on occasions, local professional Bob Jamieson will tell you, this is literally so as the links is on the friendliest of gulf streams.

It was here that in the 1977 Open, Jack Nicklaus put up such a brave fight against Tom Watson. Then, a few years later, we had a wondrous victory from Greg Norman who loved the place so much that a few hours after the prize-giving he sat with his wife on the edge of the great links, drinking champagne, and watching the moon roll round the pure white lighthouse out by the ninth green.

Without any doubt, Turnberry is the stuff of dreams and you must go there if you possible can.

36 holes. Ailsa Course 18 holes, 6408 yds, Par 69, SSS 72, course record 63 (Greg Norman & Mark Hayes). Arran Course 18 holes, 6249 yds, Par 69, SSS 70, course record 66.

Visitors   must contact in advance. The golf courses are principally for residents of the hotel.

Societies   residents only.

Green fees   Ailsa Course £36 per round; Arran £18 per round. Residents £30.50, includes a round on Ailsa Course with an optional round on the Arran if played on the same day.

Facilities   ⊗ ⍊ ㄴ ▰ ♀ ⋈ 🖆 ⚲ ⏾ (R S Jamieson)

Leisure   tennis (hardcourt), indoor-heated swimming pool, squash, snooker, sauna, solarium, gymnasium, treatment rooms.

Location   N side of village, on A719.

WHERE TO STAY AND EAT NEARBY

HOTELS:

GIRVAN   ★★ 63% King's Arms, Dalrymple St
              ☎ (0465) 3322. 25 ⇌🏾 .
              ♧ Scottish & French cuisine.

MAYBOLE   ★★ ⚐ Ladyburn
              ☎ Crosshill (06554) 585.
              8rm (4 ⇌ 3 🏾).
              ♧ Scottish & French cuisine.

TURNBERRY   ★★★★★ 68% Turnberry Hotel and
              Golf Courses
              ☎ (0655) 31000.
              132 ⇌🏾 .
              ♧ Scottish & French cuisine.
              ★★★ 66% Malin Court
              ☎ (0655) 31457.
              8 🏾

Facilities	⊗ ⅷ 🎽 ➡ ⏚ 🛇 📤 ᙅ T Shiel.
Location	Burnside Rd (S side of village off A930)
Hotel	★★62% Glencoe Hotel, Links Pde, CARNOUSTIE ☎(0241) 53273 11rm(3⇄5🐾)

BLAIR ATHOLL   Map 14 NN86

Blair Atholl ☎(079681) 407
Parkland course, river runs alongside 3 holes, easy walking.
9 holes, 5710yds, Par 70, SSS 69.
Club membership 200.
Visitors	no restrictions.
Societies	must contact in advance.
Green Fees	not confirmed.
Facilities	⏚ 🛇 ᙅ
Location	.5m S off B8079
Hotel	★★60% Atholl Arms Hotel, BLAIR ATHOLL ☎(079681) 205 30⇄🐾

BLAIRGOWRIE   Map 15 NO14

| Blairgowrie ☎(0250) 2622 |
| Two 18-hole heathland courses, also a 9-hole course. |
| *Rosemount Course: 18 holes, 6588yds, Par 72, SSS 72.* |
| *Lansdowne Course: 18 holes, 6895yds, Par 72, SSS 73.* |
| *Wee Course: 9 holes, 4654yds, Par 64, SSS 63.* |
| *Club membership 1200.* |
Visitors	restricted Wed, Fri & weekends. Must contact in advance and have an introduction from own club.
Societies	must contact in writing.
Green Fees	on application.
Facilities	⊗ ⅷ 🎽 ➡ ⏚ 🛇 📤 ᙅ ᙅ Gordon Kinnoch.
Location	Rosemount (2m S off A93)
Hotel	★★★⚑77% Kinloch House Hotel, BLAIRGOWRIE ☎(025084) 237 21⇄🐾

BRECHIN   Map 15 NO56

Brechin ☎(03562) 2383
Rolling parkland course, with easy walking and good views
of Strathmore Valley and Grampian Mountains.
18 holes, 5287yds, Par 65, SSS 66.
Club membership 650.
Visitors	may not play at weekends when competitions are being held.
Societies	must contact in advance.
Green Fees	not confirmed.
Facilities	⊗ ⅷ 🎽 ➡ ⏚ 🛇 📤 ᙅ ᙅ S Crookston.
Leisure	squash, pool table.
Location	Trinity (1m N on B966)
Hotel	★★57% Northern Hotel, Clerk St, BRECHIN ☎(03562) 2156 & 5505 17rm(4⇄11🐾)

CARNOUSTIE   Map 12 NO53

Carnoustie Golf Links See page 297

This guide is updated annually – make
sure that you use the up-to-date edition

COMRIE   Map 11 NN72

Comrie ☎(0764) 70055
Scenic highland course.
9 holes, 5250yds, Par 70, SSS 69.
Club membership 400.
Visitors	restricted Mon & Tue evenings.
Societies	must contact in advance.
Green Fees	£6 per day (£10 weekends).
Facilities	🎽 ➡ 🛇 ᙅ
Location	E side of village off A85
Hotel	★★64% Royal Hotel, Melville Square, COMRIE ☎(0764) 70200 9rm(8⇄)

CRIEFF   Map 11 NN82

Crieff ☎(0764) 2909
This course is what you might
call 'up and down' but the turf
is beautiful and the highland
air fresh and invigorating.
There are views from the
course over Strathearn. Of the
two courses the Ferntower is
the more challenging. Both
parkland, the Dornock has
one water hazard.
*Ferntower: 18 holes, 6402yds,
Par 71, SSS 71, Course record
66.*
Dornock: 9 holes, 4772yds, Par 64, SSS 63.
Club membership 570.

SCORECARD: Ferntower Course (Medal Tees)						
Hole	Yds	Par	Hole	Yds	Par	
1	163	3	10	414	4	
2	380	4	11	379	4	
3	418	4	12	467	4	
4	124	3	13	191	3	
5	532	5	14	353	4	
6	482	5	15	377	4	
7	454	4	16	412	4	
8	303	4	17	139	3	
9	511	5	18	303	4	
Out	3367	37	In	3035	34	
			Totals	6402	71	

Visitors	must have a handicap certificate. Must contact in advance and have an introduction from own club.
Societies	must contact in advance.
Green Fees	Ferntower £25 per day; £15 per round (£16 weekends); Dornock £10 per round (£11 weekends).
Facilities	⊗ ⅷ by prior arrangement 🎽 ➡ 🛇 ᙅ 📤 ᙅ ᙅ D Murchie & J M Stark.
Location	Perth Rd (.5m NE on A85)
Hotel	★★68% Murray Park Hotel, Connaught Ter, CRIEFF ☎(0764) 3731 13⇄

DUNDEE   Map 11 NO43

Caird Park ☎(0382) 453606
Municipal parkland course.
18 holes, 6281yds, Par 72, SSS 70.
Club membership 400.
Visitors	no restrictions.
Green Fees	not confirmed.
Facilities	🛇 📤 ᙅ
Location	Mains Loan (1.5m N of city centre off A972)
Hotel	★★★59% Queens Hotel, 160 Nethergate, DUNDEE ☎(0382) 22515 47⇄🐾

Camperdown ☎(0382) 621145
Parkland course. Testing 2nd hole.
18 holes, 5999yds, Par 71, SSS 69.
Club membership 600.
Visitors	must contact in advance.
Societies	must contact in advance.
Green Fees	not confirmed.

▶

SCORE CARD: Old Course					
Hole	Yds	Par	Hole	Yds	Par
1	370	4	10	318	4
2	411	4	11	172	3
3	352	4	12	316	4
4	419	4	13	398	4
5	514	5	14	523	5
6	374	4	15	401	4
7	359	4	16	351	4
8	166	3	17	461	4
9	307	4	18	354	4
Out	3272	36	In	3294	36
			Totals	6566	72

CARNOUSTIE Map12NO53

Carnoustie Golf Links ☎ (0241) 53789

John Ingham writes: You love it, or hate it. But you respect it. Back in 1953 they came to see Ben Hogan play in the Open Championship. This little man from Texas had a magic about him, and the huge terrifying links, the dread of any short hitter, would certainly be a platform on which to examine the finest golfer of his day, and maybe of any day.

Carnoustie could be the graveyard for even the best players. If the wind blew, and it was chilly, some said it was hellish. Simply standing up to the buffeting was bad enough, but on those closing holes, across the Barry Burn (or into it) was a prospect which would gnaw at the mind, because it twists through the links like an angry serpent and has to be crossed no fewer than seven times.

Hogan came to this awesome place and not since 1860 had any golfer won the Open on his first attempt. Certainly he hadn't come for the money which, in those days, was a pittance. He had come to prove he was the best player in the world. That was pressure, but when he saw the 'Stone Age' course, dating back to the birth of the game, he was shocked because it lacked trees and colour, and looked drab.

All in all, the 7200 yard monster course came as a cultural shock to Mr Hogan. But the one Hogan beat for the 1953 Championship was, as they say, something else. 'Winning the British Open at Carnoustie gave me my greatest pleasure' he told the Fort Worth Star-Telegram. 'Certainly the other victories were pleasurable, but none gave me the feeling, the desire to perform, that gripped me in Scotland'. Sadly, Hogan never returned and then the great links was taken from the Open Championship rota.

54 holes. Championship Course 18 holes, 6936 yds, Par 72, SSS74, Course record 65 (Tom Watson). Burnside Course 18 holes, 6020 yds, Par 68, SSS69. Buddon Links 18 holes, 5196 yds, Par66, SSS66. Membership 1200.

Visitors must contact club in advance. Restricted hours during week.

Societies prior arrangement required either in writing or by telephone.

Green fees Championship: £54 per day; £31 per round. Burnside: £20 per day; £12 per round. Buddon Links: £10 per day; £7 per round. Combination day tickets: Championship & Burnside £37; Championship & Buddon Links £34.50; Burnside & Buddon Links £15.50.

Facilities ⊗ 𝍲 ☕ 🍷 👚 🏠 ⛳

Location Links Parade (SW side of town, off A930).

WHERE TO STAY AND EAT NEARBY

HOTELS:

ARBROATH ★★★ 65% Letham Grange, Colliston ☎ Gowanbank (024189) 373. 19 🛁 ☙ International cuisine.

CARNOUSTIE ★★ 60% Carlogie House, Carlogie Rd. ☎ (0241) 53185. 11 🛁 🚿. ☙ Scottish & French cuisine.

★★ 59% Glencoe, Links Pde ☎ (0241) 53273. 11rm (3 🛁 5 🚿). ☙ Scottish & French cuisine.

GLAMIS ★★★ 🏛 71% Castleton House ☎(030784) 340. 6 🛁 🚿. ☙ European cuisine.

LETHAM ★★★ 🏛 66% Idvies House ☎ (030781) 787. 10 🛁 🚿.

RESTAURANT:

INVERKEILOR ✕ Gordon's, Homewood House, Main St ☎ (02413) 364. ☙ Scottish & French cuisine.

Facilities	⌂ 🎒 (
Leisure	hard tennis courts, riding.
Location	Camperdown House, Camperdown Park (3m NW of city centre off A923)
Hotel	★★★62% Angus Thistle Hotel, 10 Marketgait, DUNDEE ☎(0382) 26874 58⇨🏠

Downfield ☎(0382) 825595
A fine inland course of recent Championship rating set in undulating woodland to the north of Dundee. The Gelly burn provides a hazard for several holes.
18 holes, 6804yds, Par 73, SSS 73.
Club membership 776.

Visitors	must play with member at weekends. Must contact in advance.
Societies	must contact in advance.
Green Fees	£30 per day; £20 per round.
Facilities	⊗ ⑪ ⓛ 🍺 ♀ ⌂ 🎒 ⑂ (Colin Waddell.
Leisure	snooker.
Location	Turnberry Av (N of city centre off A923)
Hotel	★★★62% Angus Thistle Hotel, 10 Marketgait, DUNDEE ☎(0382) 26874 58⇨🏠

DUNKELD   Map 11 NO04

Dunkeld & Birnam ☎(03502) 524
Interesting heathland course with spectacular views of surrounding countryside.
9 holes, 5240yds, Par 68, SSS 66, Course record 64.
Club membership 300.

Visitors	may not play on competition days.
Societies	must telephone in advance.
Green Fees	on application.
Facilities	⊗ ⓛ 🍺 ♀ ⌂ 🎒 ⑂
Location	Fungarth (1m N of village on A923)
Hotel	★★★★67% Stakis Dunkeld House Hotel, DUNKELD ☎(03502) 771 92⇨

DUNNING   Map 11 NO01

Dunning ☎(076484) 312
Parkland course.
9 holes, 4836yds, Par 66, SSS 64, Course record 63.
Club membership 530.

Visitors	may not play on Sat before 4pm or Sun after 1pm.
Green Fees	not confirmed.
Facilities	🍺 ⌂
Location	Rollo Park (Off A9 NW)
Hotel	★★★56% Stakis City Mills Hotel, West Mill St, PERTH ☎(0738) 28281 78⇨🏠

EDZELL   Map 15 NO66

Edzell ☎(03564) 7283
This delightful course is situated in the foothills of the Scottish Highlands and provides good golf as well as conveying to everyone who plays there a feeling of peace and quiet. The village of Edzell is one of the most picturesque in Scotland.
18 holes, 6281yds, Par 71, SSS 70, Course record 65.
Club membership 910.

Visitors	restricted at certain times. Must have an introduction from own club.
Societies	must contact in advance.
Green Fees	£21 per day; £14 per round (£22 per day; £18 per round weekends & bank holidays).
Facilities	⊗ ⑪ by prior arrangement ⓛ 🍺 ♀ ⌂ 🎒 ⑂ (A J Webster.
Location	S side of village on B966
Hotel	★★★60% Glenesk Hotel, High St, EDZELL ☎(03564) 319 25rm(23⇨🏠)

FORFAR   Map 15 NO45

Forfar ☎(0307) 62120
Moorland course with wooded, undulating fairways and fine views.
18 holes, 5522mtr, Par 69, SSS 69.
Club membership 850.

Visitors	no restrictions.
Societies	must contact in advance.
Green Fees	not confirmed.
Facilities	⊗ by prior arrangement ⑪ by prior arrangement ⓛ 🍺 ♀ ⌂ 🎒 (Peter McNiven.
Location	Cunninghill, Arbroath Rd (1m E on A932)
Hotel	★★★🏌66% Idvies House Hotel, LETHAM ☎(030781) 787 10⇨🏠

GLENSHEE (SPITTAL OF)   Map 15 NO16

Dalmunzie ☎Glenshee (025 085) 224
Well-maintained Highland course with difficult walking. Testing 5th hole. Small but good greens.
9 holes, 2035yds, Par 30, SSS 30, Course record 32.
Club membership 49.

Visitors	restricted Sun 10.30-11.30am.
Societies	must contact by telephone.
Green Fees	£7 per day.
Facilities	⊗ ⑪ by prior arrangement 🍺 ♀ ⑂ 🏌
Leisure	hard tennis courts, fishing, stalking & shooting.
Location	Dalmunzie Estate (2m NW of Spittal of Glenshee)
Hotel	★★🏌64% Dalmunzie House Hotel, GLENSHEE ☎(025085) 224 17rm(15⇨🏠)

KENMORE   Map 14 NN74

Taymouth Castle ☎(08873) 228
Parkland course set amidst beautiful mountain and loch scenery. Easy walking.
18 holes, 6066yds, Par 69, SSS 69, Course record 63.
Club membership 200.

Visitors	must contact in advance.
Societies	must telephone in advance.
Green Fees	not confirmed.
Facilities	⊗ ⓛ 🍺 ♀ ⌂ 🎒 ⑂ (Alex Marshall.
Leisure	fishing.
Location	1m E on A827
Hotel	★★63% Fortingall Hotel, FORTINGALL ☎(08873) 367 9rm(8⇨🏠)
Additional hotel	★★(red)🏌Farleyer House Hotel, ABERFELDY ☎(0887) 20332 11rm(9⇨🏠)

Entries highlighted in green identify courses which are considered to be particularly interesting

KINROSS   Map 11 N010

Green Hotel ☎(0577) 63467
Two interesting and picturesque parkland courses, with easy
walking.
Red Course: 18 holes, 6257yds, Par 72, SSS 70.
Blue Course: 18 holes, 6456yds, Par 71, SSS 71.
Club membership 450.

Visitors	must contact in advance.
Societies	must contact in advance.
Green Fees	£18 per day; £12 per round (£25 per day; £18 per day weekends).
Facilities	⊗ ﹃ ⸜ ◪ ♀ ⚘ ⌂ ⚑ ⋈ ⫯ Stuart Geraghty.
Leisure	heated indoor swimming pool, squash, fishing, sauna, solarium, gymnasium.
Location	NE side of town on B996
Hotel	★★★62% Green Hotel, 2 The Muirs, KINROSS ☎(0577) 63467 40⊸⋔
Additional hotel	★★66% Bridgend Hotel, High St, KINROSS ☎(0577) 63413 15⊸⋔

Kinross Beeches Park ☎(0577) 62237
Parkland course on the banks of Loch Leven.
18 holes, 6124yds, Par 70, SSS 70.
Club membership 540.

Visitors	no restrictions.
Green Fees	not confirmed.
Facilities	♀ ⸜ ⌂ ⫯ ⋔
Location	NE side of town on B996
Hotel	★★★62% Green Hotel, 2 The Muirs, KINROSS ☎(0577) 63467 40⊸⋔

KIRRIEMUIR   Map 15 NO35

Kirriemuir ☎(0575) 73317
Parkland and heathland course set at the foot of the Angus
glens, with good views.
18 holes, 5553yds, Par 68, SSS 67, Course record 62.
Club membership 600.

Visitors	must play with member at weekends.
Societies	must telephone in advance.
Green Fees	£14.50 per day; £8 per round after 4pm.
Facilities	⊗ ﹃ ⸜ ◪ ♀ ⸜ ⌂ ⫯ A Caira.
Location	Northmuir (1m N off B955)
Hotel	★★★⚑71% Castleton House Hotel, GLAMIS ☎(030784) 340 6⊸⋔

MILNATHORT   Map 11 NO10

Milnathort ☎Kinross (0577) 64069
Undulating parkland course.
9 holes, 5969yds, Par 71, SSS 69.
Club membership 400.

Visitors	must contact in advance.
Societies	must contact in writing; deposit required.
Green Fees	£8 per day (£12 weekends).
Facilities	⊗ & ﹃ by prior arrangement ⸜ ◪ ♀ ⸜
Location	South St (S side of town on A922)
Hotel	★★★62% Green Hotel, 2 The Muirs, KINROSS ☎(0577) 63467 40⊸⋔

For a full list of golf courses included in the
book, see the index at the end of the directory

MONIFIETH
Map 12 NO43

Monifieth ☎(0382) 532767
The chief of the two courses at Monifieth is the Medal Course. It has been one of the qualifying venues for the Open Championship on more than one occasion. A seaside links, but divided from the sand dunes by a railway which provides the principal hazard for the first few holes. The 10th hole is outstanding, the 17th is excellent and there is a delightful finishing hole. The other course here is the Ashludie, and both are played over by a number of clubs who share the links.
Medal Course: 18 holes, 6651yds, Par 71, SSS 72, Course record 63.
Ashludie Course: 18 holes, 5123yds, SSS 64.
Club membership 1500.

Visitors	must contact in advance.
Societies	must contact in advance.
Green Fees	Medal Course: £22.50 per day; £15 per round (£25.50 per day; £22.50 per round Sun). Ashludie Course: £12 per day; £9 per round (£14 per day; £10 per round Sun).
Facilities	♀ ⏶ 🖴 ⛳ ⟨ Ron McLeod.
Location	The Links (NE side of town on A930)
Hotel	★★60% Carlogie House Hotel, Carlogie Rd, CARNOUSTIE ☎(0241) 53185 11⇥👣

MONTROSE
Map 15 NO75

Montrose Links Trust
☎(0674) 72932
The links at Montrose like many others in Scotland are on commonland and are shared by three clubs. The Medal Course at Montrose - the fifth oldest in the world - is typical of Scottish seaside links, with narrow, undulating fairways and problems from the first hole to the last. The Broomfield Course is flatter and easier.

SCORECARD: Medal Tees					
Hole	Yds	Par	Hole	Yds	Par
1	391	4	10	379	4
2	391	4	11	444	4
3	154	3	12	150	3
4	365	4	13	320	4
5	292	4	14	414	4
6	479	5	15	524	5
7	368	4	16	235	3
8	329	4	17	418	4
9	444	4	18	346	4
Out	3213	36	In	3230	35
			Totals	6443	71

Medal Course: 18 holes, 6443yds, Par 71, SSS 71, Course record 64.
Broomfield Course: 18 holes, 4815yds, Par 66, SSS 63.
Club membership 920.

Visitors	may not play on the Medal Course on Sat & before 10am on Sun. Must have a handicap certificate for medal play. Must contact in advance.
Societies	must telephone at least 7 in advance.
Green Fees	Medal Course: £16 per day; £10 per round (£21 per day; £13.50 per round weekends). Broomfield Course: £9 per day; £6 per round (£11.50 per day; £9 per round weekends).
Facilities	⊗ ⧆ ᛚ ⏴ ♀ ⏶ 🖴 ⛳ ⟨ Kevin Stables.
Location	Traill Dr (NE side of town off A92)
Hotel	★★★59% Park Hotel, 61 John St, MONTROSE ☎(0674) 73415 59rm(48⇥55👣)

This guide is updated annually – make sure that you use the up-to-date edition

MUTHILL
Map 11 NN81

Muthill ☎(076481) 523
Parkland course with fine views. Not too hilly, tight with narrow fairways.
9 holes, 4700yds, Par 66, SSS 63, Course record 61.
Club membership 400.

Visitors	restricted on match nights.
Green Fees	£7 per day (£10 weekends).
Facilities	⏴ ⏶
Location	Peat Rd (W side of village off A822)
Hotel	★★68% Murray Park Hotel, Connaught Ter, CRIEFF ☎(0764) 3731 13⇥

PERTH
Map 11 NO12

Craigie Hill ☎(0738) 24377
Slightly hilly, parkland course. Good views over Perth.
18 holes, 5379yds, Par 66, SSS 66, Course record 63.
Club membership 610.

Visitors	may not play on Sat. Must contact in advance.
Societies	must contact in writing.
Green Fees	not confirmed.
Facilities	⊗ (ex Tue) ⧆ (ex Mon & Tue, Sun high tea only) ᛚ ⏴ ♀ ⏶ 🖴 ⟨ Frank Smith.
Location	Cherrybank (1m SW of city centre off A952)
Hotel	★★★56% Stakis City Mills Hotel, West Mill St, PERTH ☎(0738) 28281 78⇥👣

King James VI ☎(0738) 25170
Parkland course, situated on island in the middle of River Tay. Easy walking.
18 holes, 6026yds, Par 70, SSS 69, Course record 62.
Club membership 600.

Visitors	may not play on Sat. Must contact in advance.
Societies	may not play on Sat. Must contact in writing.
Green Fees	£17 per day; £11.50 per round (£23 per day Sun; £12 per round after 4pm).
Facilities	ᛚ ⏴ ♀ ⏶ 🖴 ⟨ Tony Coles.
Location	Moncrieffe Island (SE side of city centre)
Hotel	★★★60% Queens Hotel, Leonard St, PERTH ☎(0738) 25471 50rm(40⇥39👣)

Murrayshall Country House Hotel
☎New Scone (0738) 51171
This course is laid out in 130 acres of parkland with tree-lined fairways. Hotel and driving range.
18 holes, 6446yds, Par 73, SSS 71, Course record 68.
Club membership 300.

Visitors	must contact in advance.
Societies	must contact in advance.
Green Fees	£30 per day; £20 per round (£40 per day; £25 per round weekends).
Facilities	⊗ ⧆ ᛚ ⏴ ♀ ⏶ 🖴 ⛳ 🏌 ⟨ Neil Macintosh.
Leisure	hard tennis courts, putting green, croquet.
Location	Murrayshall, Scone (E side of village off A94)
Hotel	★★★59% The Royal George, Tay St, PERTH ☎(0738) 24455 42⇥

A golf-course name printed in *bold italics* means that we have been unable to verify information with the club's management for the current year

PITLOCHRY   Map 14 NN95

Pitlochry ☎(0796) 2792
A varied and interesting heathland course with fine views
and posing many problems. Its SSS permits few errors in
its achievement.
18 holes, 5811yds, Par 69, SSS 68, Course record 63.
Club membership 300.
Visitors   may not play before 9.30am.
Societies   must contact in writing.
Green Fees   £12 per day (£15 weekends).
Facilities   ⊗ ⅏ by prior arrangement 🏌 ⬤ ♀ ⏃
                  🛋 ⬥ ⏃ George Hampton.
Location   Pitlochry Estate Office (N side of town off
                  A924)
Hotel   ★★★⁴⁹69% Pine Trees Hotel, Strathview
                  Ter, PITLOCHRY ☎(0796) 2121
                  18rm(17⇨🌂)

ST FILLANS   Map 11 NN62

St Fillans ☎(076485) 312
Fairly flat, beautiful parkland course. Wonderfully rich in
flora, animal and bird life.
9 holes, 5680yds, Par 69, SSS 68, Course record 66.
Club membership 400.
Visitors   may not play on Sat mornings.
Societies   may not play in Jul & Aug. Booking fee required.
Green Fees   £12 per day (£14 weekends & bank holidays).
Facilities   ⊗ 🏌 ⬤ ⏃ 🛋 ⏃
Leisure   fishing.
Location   E side of village off A85
Hotel   ★★★65% The Four Seasons Hotel, ST
                  FILLANS ☎(076485) 333 12⇨🌂

SCOTTISH ISLANDS

ARRAN, ISLE OF

BLACKWATERFOOT   Map 10 NR82

Shiskine ☎Shiskine (077086) 226
Unique 12-hole links course with gorgeous outlook to the
Mull of Kintyre.
12 holes, 2990yds, Par 42, SSS 42.
Visitors   no restrictions.
Societies   must contact in writing.
Green Fees   not confirmed.
Facilities   ⊗ ⬤ ⏃ 🛋
Leisure   hard tennis courts, all weather bowling green.
Location   Shore Rd (W side of village off A841)
Hotel   ★★63% The Lagg Hotel, Kilmory, BRODICK
                  ☎(077087) 255 15⇨🌂

For a full list of golf courses included in the
book, see the index at the end of the directory

BRODICK   Map 10 NS03

Brodick ☎(0770) 2349
Short seaside course, very flat.
18 holes, 4405yds, Par 62, SSS 62, Course record 60.
Club membership 520.
Visitors   may not play on competition days. Must contact
                  in advance.
Societies   must contact in advance.
Green Fees   £9 per day.
Facilities   🏌 ⬤ ♀ ⏃ 🛋 ⏃ Peter McCalla.
Location   N side of village
Hotel   ★★★72% Auchrannie Country House Hotel,
                  BRODICK ☎(0770) 2234 & 2235 28⇨🌂

CORRIE   Map 10 NS04

Corrie ☎(077081) 223
A heathland course on the coast with beautiful mountain
scenery.
9 holes, 3896yds, Par 62, SSS 61, Course record 60.
Club membership 220.
Visitors   restricted Sat when medal games played.
Societies   must contact in advance.
Green Fees   not confirmed.
Facilities   ⊗ (Apr-Oct) ⅏ ⬤ 🛋 ⏃
Location   Sannox (2m N on A841)
Hotel   ★★★72% Auchrannie Country House Hotel,
                  BRODICK ☎(0770) 2234 & 2235 28⇨🌂

LAMLASH   Map 10 NS03

Lamlash ☎(07706) 296
Undulating heathland course with magnificent views of the mountains and sea.
18 holes, 4611yds, Par 64, SSS 63, Course record 62.
Club membership 400.
Visitors   no restrictions.
Societies   must contact in writing.
Green Fees   £8 per day (£9 weekends).
Facilities   ⊗ ⅊ ☍ ♀ ♨ ☏ ⴲ
Location   .75m N on A841
Hotel   ★58% Cameronia Hotel, Shore Rd, WHITING BAY ☎(07707) 254 5⬧

LOCHRANZA   Map 10 NR95

Lochranza ☎(077083) 273
Level parkland course by the sea. River crosses four holes. Nine large greens, 18 tees.
9 holes, 5569yds, Par 69, SSS 70, Course record 78.
Visitors   no restrictions; course closed Oct-mid May.
Societies   must telephone in advance.
Green Fees   £9.50 per day; £7 for 18 holes.
Facilities   ⊗ ☍ ⴲ
Hotel   ★★63% The Lagg Hotel, Kilmory, BRODICK ☎(077087) 255 15⬧⬧

MACHRIE   Map 10 NR83

Machrie Bay ☎Brodick (077084) 261
Fairly flat seaside course. Designed at turn of century by William Fernie.
9 holes, 2143yds, Par 32.
Club membership 225.
Visitors   no restrictions.
Societies   must contact in advance.
Green Fees   £3 per day/round.
Facilities   ☍
Leisure   hard tennis courts.
Location   9m W of Brodick via String Rd
Hotel   ★★63% The Lagg Hotel, Kilmory, BRODICK ☎(077087) 255 15⬧⬧

WHITING BAY   Map 10 NS02

Whiting Bay ☎(07707) 51607
Heathland course.
18 holes, 4405yds, Par 63, SSS 63.
Club membership 290.
Visitors   no restrictions.
Green Fees   not confirmed.
Facilities   ♀
Location   NW side of village off A841
Hotel   ★★63% The Lagg Hotel, Kilmory, BRODICK ☎(077087) 255 15⬧⬧

We make every effort to ensure that our information is accurate but details may change after we go to print

BUTE, ISLE OF

KINGARTH   Map 10 NS05

Kingarth ☎Kilchattan Bay (070083) 648
Flat seaside course with good fenced greens.
9 holes, 2497yds, Par 64, SSS 64, Course record 65.
Club membership 120.
Visitors   restricted Sat.
Green Fees   not confirmed.
Facilities   ☍
Location   Kingarth, Rothesay (1m W off A844)
Hotel   ★54% St Ebba Hotel, 37 Mountstuart Rd, Craigmore, ROTHESAY ☎(0700) 502683 11⬧⬧

PORT BANNATYNE   Map 10 NS06

Port Bannatyne ☎(0700) 2009
Seaside hill course with panoramic views. Difficult hole: 4th (par 3).
13 holes, 4730yds, Par 68, SSS 63, Course record 61.
Club membership 200.
Visitors   no restrictions.
Societies   must telephone in advance.
Green Fees   £6.50 per day.
Facilities   ☍
Location   Bannatyne Mains Rd (W side of village off A844)
Hotel   ★54% St Ebba Hotel, 37 Mountstuart Rd, Craigmore, ROTHESAY ☎(0700) 502683 11⬧⬧

COLONSAY, ISLE OF

SCALASAIG   Map 10 NR39

Colonsay ☎Colonsay (09512) 316
Traditional links course on natural Machair (hard wearing short grass), challenging, primitive. Colonsay Hotel, 2 miles away, is the headquarters of the club, offering accommodation and facilities.
18 holes, 4775yds, Par 72, SSS 72.
Club membership 120.
Visitors   no restrictions.
Societies   apply in writing.
Green Fees   not confirmed.
Facilities   ⴲ
Location   2m W on A870
Hotel   ★73% Colonsay Hotel, SCALASAIG ☎(09512) 316 10rm(1⬧7⬧)Annexe1rm

---

Each golf-course entry has a recommended AA-appointed hotel. For a wider choice of places to stay, consult *AA Hotels and Restaurants in Britain and Ireland* and *AA Inspected Bed and Breakfast in Britain and Ireland*

ISLAY, ISLE OF

PORT ELLEN   Map 10 NR34

Machrie Hotel ☎(0496) 2310
Championship links course opened in 1891, where golf's first
£100 Open Championship was played in 1901. Fine turf and
many blind holes.
18 holes, 6226yds, Par 71, SSS 70, Course record 66.

Visitors	must be member of a recognised golf club and have a handicap certificate.
Societies	must contact in advance.
Green Fees	£30 per day; £20 per round.
Facilities	⊗ ⍫ 🍴 🌆 🎯 ♀ 🏠 🥾 🛶
Leisure	fishing, riding, snooker, clay pigeon shooting.
Location	Machrie (4m N off A846)
Hotel	★★58% Lochside Hotel, 19 Shore St, BOWMORE ☎(049681) 244 & 265 7rm(2⇄🛏)

LEWIS, ISLE OF

STORNOWAY   Map 13 NB43

Stornoway ☎(0851) 702240
Picturesque, tree-lined parkland course, fine views. The 11th
hole, 'Dardanelles' - most difficult par 5.
18 holes, 5178yds, Par 68, SSS 66, Course record 62.
Club membership 200.

Visitors	may not play on Sun.
Societies	must contact in writing.
Green Fees	£10 per day; £7 per round.
Facilities	⊗ by prior arrangement 🌆 🏠 by prior arrangement ♀ 🥾 🏠 🛶
Location	Lady Lever Park (N side of town centre off A857)
Hotel	★★★66% Caberfeidh Hotel, STORNOWAY ☎(0851) 702604 46⇄🛏

MULL, ISLE OF

CRAIGNURE   Map 10 NM73

Craignure ☎(06802) 370
A flat links course, overlooking the sea.
9 holes, 2218mtrs, Par 64, SSS 64.
Club membership 70.

Visitors	may not play on competition days.
Societies	must contact in advance.
Green Fees	£6 per day.
Facilities	🥾
Location	Scallastle (1m N on A849)

For a full range of AA guides and maps, visit
your local AA shop or any good bookshop

TOBERMORY   Map 13 NM55

Tobermory ☎(0688) 2020
Hilly seaside cliff-top course. No sand-bunkers, hard
walking, superb views over the Sound of Mull. Testing 3rd
hole (par 3).
9 holes, 4474yds, Par 64, SSS 64, Course record 70.
Club membership 100.

Visitors	no restrictions.
Societies	must contact in advance.
Green Fees	£7 per day/round.
Facilities	🥾 🛶
Location	.5m N off A848
Hotel	★56% Mishnish Hotel, Main St, TOBERMORY ☎(0688) 2009 12rm(7⇄2🛏)

ORKNEY

KIRKWALL   Map 16 HY41

Orkney ☎(0856) 2457
Open parkland course with few hazards and superb views
over Kirkwall and Islands.
18 holes, 5406yds, Par 70, SSS 68, Course record 65.
Club membership 320.

Visitors	may not play on competition days.
Societies	advance contact preferred.
Green Fees	£8 per day.
Facilities	♀ (Apr-Sep) 🥾
Location	Grainbank (.5m W off A965)
Hotel	★★61% Ayre Hotel, Ayre Rd, KIRKWALL ☎(0856) 3001 32rm(4⇄6🛏)

STROMNESS   Map 16 HY20

Stromness ☎(0856) 850772
Testing parkland/seaside course with easy walking. Beautiful
holiday course with magnificent views of Scapa Flow.
18 holes, 4762yds, Par 65, SSS 64, Course record 62.
Club membership 150.

Visitors	no restrictions.
Societies	must contact in advance.
Green Fees	not confirmed.
Facilities	♀ (evenings only) 🥾 🏠 🛶
Leisure	hard tennis courts, bowls & putting.
Location	S side of town centre off A965
Hotel	★★61% Ayre Hotel, Ayre Rd, KIRKWALL ☎(0856) 3001 32rm(4⇄6🛏)

WESTRAY   Map 16 HY44

Westray ☎(0856) 2197
Interesting, picturesque seaside course, easy walking.
9 holes, 2405yds, Par 33.

Visitors	may not play on Sun.
Green Fees	not confirmed.
Facilities	🛶
Location	1m NW of Pierowall off B9066
Hotel	★★61% Ayre Hotel, Ayre Rd, KIRKWALL ☎(0856) 3001 32rm(4⇄6🛏)

SHETLAND

LERWICK   Map 16 HU44

Dale ☎Gott (059584) 369
Challenging moorland course, hard walking. A burn runs the
full length of the course and provides a natural hazard.
Testing holes include the 3rd (par 4), 5th (par 4).
18 holes, 5776yds, Par 68, SSS 70, Course record 69.
Club membership 370.

Visitors	restricted on competition days.
Societies	must contact in advance.
Green Fees	£5 per day.
Facilities	⛳ (Sat & Sun) ♀ ⌂
Location	PO Box 18 (4m N on A970)
Hotel	★★★57% Lerwick Hotel, South Rd, LERWICK ☎(0595) 2166 31⇔🏕

WHALSAY, ISLAND OF   Map 16 HU56

Whalsay ☎Symbister (08066) 452
The most northerly golf course in Britain, with a large part of
it running round the coastline, offering spectacular holes in
an exposed but highly scenic setting. There are no cut
fairways as yet, these are defined by marker posts, with
preferred lies in operation all year round.
18 holes, 6116yds, Par 71, SSS 70.
Club membership 90.

Visitors	are advised to telephone, and on arrival on Whalsay call at the shop by the harbour.
Societies	welcome.
Green Fees	£5 per day.
Facilities	⌂
Location	Skaw Taing

SKYE, ISLE OF

SCONSER   Map 13 NG53

Isle of Skye
Seaside course, often windy, splendid views.
9 holes, 4796yds, Par 66, SSS 63, Course record 62.
Club membership 100.

Visitors	welcome except Wed 6-6.30pm & Sat 10-10.30am.
Societies	welcome.
Green Fees	not confirmed.
Facilities	⌂
Location	.5m E of village on A850
Hotel	★★54% Broadford Hotel, BROADFORD ☎(04712) 204 20⇔🏕Annexe9⇔🏕

Each golf-course entry has a recommended
AA-appointed hotel. For a wider choice of
places to stay, consult *AA Hotels and
Restaurants in Britain and Ireland* and
*AA Inspected Bed and Breakfast in
Britain and Ireland*

SOUTH UIST, ISLE OF

ASKERNISH   Map 13 NF72

Askernish ☎No telephone
Golfers play on machair (hard-wearing short grass), close to
the Atlantic shore.
9 holes, 5312yds, Par 68, SSS 67.
Club membership 20.

Visitors	no restrictions.
Societies	must contact in advance.
Facilities	⛴
Location	Lochboisdale (5m NW of Lochboisdale off A865 via ferry)
Hotel	★★57% Lochboisdale Hotel, LOCHBOISDALE ☎(08784) 332 20rm(11⇔)

NORTHERN IRELAND

CO ANTRIM

ANTRIM   Map 01 D5

Massereene ☎(08494) 28096
The first nine holes are parkland, while the second, adjacent to the shore of Lough
Neagh, have more of a links
character with sandy ground.
*18 holes, 6614yds, Par 72, SSS
71, Course record 68.*
Club membership 800.

SCORECARD: Medal Tees					
Hole	Yds	Par	Hole	Yds	Par
1	374	4	10	510	5
2	400	4	11	205	3
3	130	3	12	341	4
4	363	4	13	415	4
5	376	4	14	135	3
6	460	4	15	392	4
7	554	5	16	496	5
8	196	3	17	436	4
9	329	4	18	502	5
Out	3182	35	In	3432	37
			Totals	6614	72

Visitors	welcome except for Sat which is competition day.
Societies	apply in writing.
Green Fees	£15 per day (£18 weekends).
Facilities	⊗ 🍴 ⛳ 🍺 ♀ ⌂ 🛏 ⛴ 🏌 ⟨ Jim Smyth.
Leisure	snooker, indoor bowling in winter.
Location	51 Lough Rd (1m SW of town)
Hotel	★★★62% Adair Arms Hotel, Ballymoney Rd, BALLYMENA ☎(0266) 653674 39⇔🏕

BALLYCASTLE   Map 01 D6

Ballycastle ☎(02657) 62536
An unusual mixture of terrain beside the sea, with
magnificent views from all parts. The first five holes are
inland type; the middle holes on the Warren are links type
and the rest, on high ground, are heath type.
18 holes, 5177mtrs, Par 71, SSS 68, Course record 66.
Club membership 784.

Visitors	are welcome during the week.
Societies	apply in writing.
Green Fees	£10 per day (£14 per round weekends).
Facilities	🍺 (catering by arrangement) ♀ ⌂ 🛏 ⟨ Trevor Stewart.

Leisure	snooker.
Location	Cushendall Rd
Hotel	★★58% Thornlea Hotel, 6 Coast Rd, CUSHENDALL ☎(02667) 71223 13◁◈

BALLYCLARE   Map 01 D5

Ballyclare ☎(09603) 22696
Parkland course with lots of trees and shrubs and water hazards provided by the river, streams and lakes.
18 holes, 5764mtrs, Par 71, SSS 72.
Club membership 980.

Visitors	may not play on Thu or weekends before 3pm.
Societies	must contact in writing.
Green Fees	£11 per round (£16 weekends & bank holidays).
Facilities	⊗ ⓛ ☐ ⴹ △
Leisure	snooker.
Location	25 Springdale Rd (1.5m N)
Hotel	★★★66% Stormont Hotel, 587 Upper Newtonards Rd, BELFAST ☎(0232) 658621 67◁◈

BALLYGALLY   Map 01 D5

Cairndhu ☎Larne (0574) 583248
Built on a hilly headland, this course is both testing and scenic, with wonderful coastal views.
18 holes, 5598mtrs, Par 70, SSS 69, Course record 64.
Club membership 875.

Visitors	may not play on Sat. Must have an introduction from own club.
Societies	must contact in writing.
Green Fees	£10 (£15 weekends & bank holidays).
Facilities	⊗ & ⴷ (Sat/Sun only) ⓛ ☐ ⴹ △ ⌂ ⴀ ⴺ Robert Walker.
Leisure	snooker.
Location	192 Coast Rd (4m N of Larne on coast road)
Hotel	★★★57% Ballygally Castle Hotel, 274 Coast Rd, BALLYGALLY ☎(0574) 83212 30◁

BALLYMENA   Map 01 D5

Ballymena ☎(0266) 861487
Parkland course of level heathland with plenty of bunkers.
18 holes, 5654yds, Par 68, SSS 67.

Visitors	may not play on Tue or Sat.
Societies	must contact in advance.
Green Fees	£9.50 (£12 Sun & bank holidays).
Facilities	⊗ ⴷ ⓛ ⴹ ⴺ ⴀ James Gallagher.
Leisure	snooker, bowling green.
Location	128 Raceview Rd (2m E on A42)
Hotel	★★★62% Adair Arms Hotel, Ballymoney Rd, BALLYMENA ☎(0266) 653674 39◁◈

CARRICKFERGUS   Map 01 D5

Carrickfergus ☎(09603) 63713
Parkland course, fairly level but nevetheless demanding, with a notorious water hazard at the 1st. Well maintained and with nice views.
18 holes, 5759yds, Par 68, SSS 68.

Visitors	no restrictions.

Societies	must contact in advance.
Green Fees	£12 (£17 Sun).
Facilities	⊗ ⴷ ⓛ ⴹ ⴀ ⴺ Raymond Stevenson.
Leisure	snooker.
Location	25 North Rd (9m NE of Belfast on A2)
Hotel	★★★59% Chimney Corner Hotel, 630 Antrim Rd, NEWTOWNABBEY ☎(0232) 844925 63◁◈

CUSHENDALL   Map 01 D6

Cushendall ☎(02667) 71318
Scenic course with spectacular views over the Sea of Moyle and Red Bay to the Mull of Kintyre. The River Dall winds through the course, coming into play in seven of the nine holes.
9 holes, 4386mtrs, Par 66, SSS 63.
Club membership 714.

Visitors	restricted on Sun.
Societies	must contact in writing.
Green Fees	£8 per day (£10 weekends & bank holidays).
Facilities	⊗ (summer only) ⴷ by prior arrangement ☐ ⴹ △
Location	21 Shore Rd
Hotel	★★58% Thornlea Hotel, 6 Coast Rd, CUSHENDALL ☎(02667) 71223 13◁◈

LARNE   Map 01 D5

Larne ☎Islandmagee (09603) 82228
An exposed part links, part heathland course offering a good test, particularly on the last three holes along the sea shore.
9 holes, 6066yds, Par 70, SSS 69, Course record 66.
Club membership 450.

Visitors	may not play on Sat.
Societies	apply in writing.
Green Fees	£8 (£12 Sun & public holidays).
Facilities	ⓛ by prior arrangement ⴹ △
Leisure	snooker.
Location	54 Ferris Bay Rd, Islandmagee
Hotel	★★★57% Ballygally Castle Hotel, 274 Coast Rd, BALLYGALLY ☎(0574) 83212 30◁

LISBURN   Map 01 D5

Lisburn ☎(0846) 677216
Meadowland course, fairly level, with plenty of trees and shrubs. Challenging last three holes.
18 holes, 6572yds, Par 72, SSS 72.
Club membership 1000.

Visitors	must play with member at weekends.
Societies	must contact in writing.
Green Fees	£15.
Facilities	⊗ ⴷ ☐ ⴹ △ ⌂ ⴀ ⴺ B R Campbell.
Leisure	snooker.
Location	Blaris Lodge, 68 Eglantine Rd (2m from town on A1)
Hotel	★★★66% Stormont Hotel, 587 Upper Newtonards Rd, BELFAST ☎(0232) 658621 67◁◈

PORTRUSH   Map 01 C6

Royal Portrush See page 307

WHITEHEAD   Map 01 D5

Whitehead ☎(09603) 53631
Undulating parkland course with magnificent sea views.
18 holes, 6426yds, Par 72, SSS 71.

Visitors	may not play on Sat. Must play with member on Sun.
Societies	must contact in advance.
Green Fees	£10 (£15 Sun & bank holidays).
Facilities	⊗ ⫪ ♀
Leisure	snooker.
Location	McCrae's Brae (0.5m N)
Hotel	★★★59% Chimney Corner Hotel, 630 Antrim Rd, NEWTOWNABBEY ☎(0232) 844925 63⇨♠

❖ CO ARMAGH ❖

ARMAGH   Map 01 C5

County Armagh ☎(0861) 522501
Mature parkland course with excellent views of Armagh city and its surroundings.
18 holes, 5641mtrs, Par 70, SSS 69, Course record 65.
Club membership 1000.

Visitors	may not play noon-3pm on Sat or noon-2pm on Sun. Must contact in advance.
Societies	must contact in writing.
Green Fees	£10 (£15 weekends).
Facilities	⊗ ⫪ ⅃ & ■ (all ex Mon) ♀ ⌂ ▦ ⌇ Alan Rankin.
Leisure	snooker.
Location	The Demesne (On the Newry road)
Hotel	★★★66% Stormont Hotel, 587 Upper Newtonards Rd, BELFAST ☎(0232) 658621 67⇨♠

LURGAN   Map 01 D5

Craigavon Golf & Ski Centre ☎(0762) 326606
Parkland course with a lake and stream providing water hazards. Putting green and floodlit driving range.
18 holes, 6496yds, Par 72, SSS 72.

Visitors	no restrictions.
Societies	must contact in advance.
Green Fees	£6 (£8 weekends).
Facilities	⊗ ⫪ ⌇ ⌇ Des Paul.
Location	Turmoyra Ln (2m N at Silverwood off the M1)
Hotel	★★★66% Stormont Hotel, 587 Upper Newtonards Rd, BELFAST ☎(0232) 658621 67⇨♠

Lurgan ☎(0762) 322087
Testing parkland course bordering Lurgan Park Lake with a need for accurate shots.
18 holes, 5836mtrs, Par 70, SSS 70, Course record 65.
Club membership 800.

Visitors	may not play Wed & Sat.
Societies	must contact in writing.
Green Fees	not confirmed.

Facilities	⊗ ⫪ ⅃ ■ ♀ ⌂ ▦ ⌇ D Paul.
Location	The Demense (0.5m from town centre near Lurgan Park)
Hotel	★★★66% Stormont Hotel, 587 Upper Newtonards Rd, BELFAST ☎(0232) 658621 67⇨♠

PORTADOWN   Map 01 D5

Portadown ☎(0762) 355356
Well wooded parkland course on the banks of the River Bann, which features among the water hazards.
18 holes, 5621mtrs, Par 70, SSS 70, Course record 67.
Club membership 1014.

Visitors	may not play on Tue & Sat.
Societies	must contact in advance.
Green Fees	£12 per round (£15 weekends & bank holidays).
Facilities	⊗ ⫪ ⅃ ■ (no catering Mon) ♀ ⌂ ▦ ⌇ ⌇ Paul Stevenson.
Leisure	squash, snooker, indoor bowling.
Location	192 Gilfrod Rd (SE via A59)
Hotel	★★★66% Stormont Hotel, 587 Upper Newtonards Rd, BELFAST ☎(0232) 658621 67⇨♠

TANDRAGEE   Map 01 D5

Tandragee ☎(0762) 841272
Pleasant hilly parkland with mature trees.
18 holes, 5519mtrs, Par 69, SSS 67.
Club membership 987.

Visitors	may not play Thu & Fri afternoon or on Sat & Sun. Must contact in advance.
Societies	Mar-Sep; must contact in writing.
Green Fees	£9 (£12 weekends).
Facilities	⊗ ⫪ ⅃ & ■ (ex Mon) ♀ ⌂ ▦ ⌇ ⌇ John Black.
Leisure	snooker, sauna, gymnasium.
Location	Markethill Rd
Hotel	★★★⚑67% Ballynahinch Castle, BALLYNAHINCH ☎(095) 31006 & 31086 28⇨♠

❖ BELFAST ❖

BELFAST   Map 01 D5

Balmoral ☎(0232) 381514
Parkland course, almost level, with tree-lined fairways and a stream providing a water hazard.
18 holes, 6238yds, Par 69, SSS 70.

Visitors	preferably Mon & Thu.
Societies	must contact in advance.
Green Fees	£11 (£13 Wed; £16.50 weekends).
Facilities	⊗ ⫪ ♀ ⌇ ⌇ Geoff Bleakley.
Location	518 Lisburn Rd (3m SW)
Hotel	★★★66% Stormont Hotel, 587 Upper Newtonards Rd, BELFAST ☎(0232) 658621 67⇨♠

This guide is updated annually – make sure that you use the up-to-date edition

SCORE CARD: DUNLUCE LINKS (Blue Tees)					
Hole	Yds	Par	Hole	Yds	Par
1	389	4	10	480	5
2	509	5	11	166	3
3	159	3	12	395	4
4	455	4	13	371	4
5	384	4	14	213	3
6	193	3	15	366	4
7	432	4	16	432	4
8	376	4	17	517	5
9	478	5	18	479	4
Out	3375	36	In	3419	36
			Totals	6794	72

PORTRUSH   Map01D4

Royal Portrush ☎ (0265) 822311

John Ingham writes: It was more than thirty years ago that I first saw Royal Portrush, but the memory lingers on. That week, the great Joe Carr won the British Amateur championship for his third, and last, time. But everyone there was a winner.

What a splendid seaside paradise this is, I wrote for a London evening newspaper, keen to follow players such as Carr and Michael Bonallack. There among the gallery was the late Fred Daly, winner of the 1947 Open. The sun shone, and the course glistened as the foaming ocean was almost blown inland on to the briar roses which dotted the rough.

The man who designed this course was Harry S Colt, a name that appears as a creator of many fine courses. This one is considered among the six best in the United Kingdom. It is spectacular, breathtaking, but one of the tightest driving tests known to man because if you get in the long stuff, you may stay there. While the greens have to be 'read' from the start, on a clear day, you have a fine view of Islay and the Paps of Jura - seen from the third tee. Then there's the Giant's Causeway, from the 5th, as good a downhill dogleg hole as you'll find anywhere.

There are fairways up and down valleys, and holes are called Calamity Corner and Purgatory for good reason. The second hole, called, Giant's Grave, is 509 yards but there's an even longer one waiting for you at the 17th, while the last hole, a 479-yarder, nearly cost Max Faulkner his 1951 Open title. He hit a crooked drive, and had to bend his second shot with a wooden club. Dressed in primrose-coloured slacks, his colourful plumage and out-going attitude attracted most of the small crowd. The Open did not return to Portrush and championship golf is the loser because the place is a gem.

You'll love it.

45 holes. Dunluce Links 18 holes, 6794 yds, Par 72, SSS 73, course record 66. Valley Links 18 holes, 6273 yds, Par 70, SSS 70, course record 65. Skerries Course 9 holes, 1187 yds. Membership 1300.

Visitors	must contact in advance, and have a letter of introduction from their own club. Restricted Saturday and Sunday morning.
Societies	must apply in writing.
Green fees	Dunluce Links £20-£25 per day (£25-£30 weekends). Valley Links £12 per day (£16 weekends). Skerries Course £1.
Facilities	⊗ ⅲ ⧠ 🍽 ⅊ (all day) ⛳ 🛍 ⚑ ⅃ (Dai Stevenson)
Leisure	snooker
Location	Bushmills Rd (0.5m from Portrush town on main road to Bushmills)

WHERE TO STAY AND EAT NEARBY

HOTELS:
PORTBALLINTRAE ★★ 68% Bayview, 2 Bayhead Rd.
☎ (02657) 31453. 16 ⇌.
★★ 60% Beach House, The Sea Front.
☎ (02657) 31214. 32 ⇌ 📱. ♧ French cuisine.

RESTAURANT:
PORTRUSH   ✕✕ Ramore, The Harbour. ☎ (0265) 824313.
♧ French cuisine.

Cliftonville ☎(0232) 744158
Parkland course with rivers bisecting two fairways.
9 holes, 5672mtrs, Par 70, SSS 70, Course record 66.
Club membership 430.
Visitors	may not play on Sat or Sun mornings.
Societies	must contact in writing.
Green Fees	£11 (£14 weekends & bank holidays).
Facilities	⊗ ⅃ & ● (Tue, Thu & Sat) ♀ △ 🖀
Leisure	snooker.
Location	44 Westland Rd (Between Cavehill Rd & Cliftonville Circus)
Hotel	★★★66% Stormont Hotel, 587 Upper Newtonards Rd, BELFAST ☎(0232) 658621 67⇌🝙

Dunmurry ☎(0232) 610834
Maturing very nicely, this tricky parkland course has several memorable holes which call for skilfull shots.
18 holes, 5348mtrs, Par 69, SSS 68.
Club membership 840.
Visitors	may not play Tue, Thu & Sat after 5pm & 11.30-12.30 Sun.
Societies	must contact in writing.
Green Fees	£11 (£15 weekends).
Facilities	⊗ Ⅲ⅃ ● (no catering Mon) ♀ △ 🖀 🏌 ⸾ Paul Leonard.
Leisure	snooker.
Location	91 Dunmurry Ln
Hotel	★★★66% Stormont Hotel, 587 Upper Newtonards Rd, BELFAST ☎(0232) 658621 67⇌🝙

Fortwilliam ☎(0232) 370770
Parkland course in most attractive surroundings. The course is bisected by a lane.
18 holes, 5771yds, Par 69, SSS 68.
Visitors	preferred weekday mornings.
Societies	preferred Thu. Must contact in advance.
Green Fees	£12 (£17 weekends).
Facilities	⊗ Ⅲ ♀ ⸾ Peter Hanna.
Leisure	snooker, practice fairway.
Location	Downview Ave (Off Antrim road)
Hotel	★★★66% Stormont Hotel, 587 Upper Newtonards Rd, BELFAST ☎(0232) 658621 67⇌🝙

Knockbracken Golf & Ski Club ☎(0232) 401811
Inland parkland course which has recently been refurbished.
18 holes, 5391yds, Par 67, SSS 68, Course record 64.
Club membership 400.
Visitors	must contact in advance at weekends & bank holidays.
Societies	must contact in writing.
Green Fees	£7.75 (£9.75 weekends).
Facilities	⊗ Ⅲ⅃ ● ♀ △ 🖀 🏌 ⸾ D Jones.
Leisure	snooker, driving ranges, bowls, ski slope.
Location	24 Ballymaconaghy Rd
Hotel	★★★66% Stormont Hotel, 587 Upper Newtonards Rd, BELFAST ☎(0232) 658621 67⇌🝙

For a full list of golf courses included in the book, see the index at the end of the directory

Malone ☎(0232) 612758
Two parkland courses, extremely attractive with a large lake, mature trees and flowering shrubs and bordered by the River Lagan. Very well maintained and offering a challenging round.
Course 1: 18 holes, 6433yds, Par 71, SSS 71.
Course 2: 9 holes, 5784yds, SSS 68.
Visitors	may not play on 18 hole course on Tue, Wed & Sat.
Green Fees	£19 per 18 holes; £8 per 9 holes (£22 per 18 holes; £9 per 9 holes weekends & bank holidays).
Facilities	⊗ Ⅲ Ⅼ ♀ ⸾ P M O'Hagan.
Location	240 Upper Malone Rd, Dunmurry (4.5m S)
Hotel	★★★66% Stormont Hotel, 587 Upper Newtonards Rd, BELFAST ☎(0232) 658621 67⇌🝙

Shandon Park ☎(0232) 701799
Fairly level parkland offering a pleasant challenge.
18 holes, 6261yds, Par 70, SSS 70.
Club membership 1100.
Visitors	may not play on competition days. Must contact in advance and have an introduction from own club.
Societies	may play weekdays only.
Green Fees	£16 (£20 weekends & bank holidays).
Facilities	⊗ Ⅲ⅃ ● ♀ △ 🖀 🏌 ⸾ Barry Wilson.
Leisure	snooker.
Location	73 Shandon Park (Off Knock road)
Hotel	★★★66% Stormont Hotel, 587 Upper Newtonards Rd, BELFAST ☎(0232) 658621 67⇌🝙

DUNDONALD Map 01 D5

Knock ☎Belfast (0232) 483251
Parkland course with huge trees, deep bunkers and a river cutting across several fairways. This is a hard but fair course and will test the best of golfers.
18 holes, 6407yds, Par 70, SSS 71, Course record 67.
Club membership 850.
Visitors	may not play on Sat.
Societies	must contact in advance.
Green Fees	£15 per day (£20 weekends).
Facilities	⊗ (ex pm in winter) Ⅲ Ⅼ (ex pm in winter) ● ♀ △ 🖀 🏌 ⸾ Gordon Fairweather.
Leisure	snooker.
Location	Summerfield
Hotel	★★★★70% Culloden Hotel, HOLYWOOD ☎(02317) 5223 91🝙

A golf-course name printed in **bold italics** means that we have been unable to verify information with the club's management for the current year

NEWTOWNBREDA   Map 01 D5

The Belvoir Park ☎Belfast (0232) 491693
This undulating parkland course is not strenuous to walk, but is certainly a test of your golf, with tree-lined fairways and a particularly challenging finish at the final four holes.
18 holes, 6501yds, Par 71, SSS 71, Course record 66.
Club membership 1076.

SCORECARD: Medal Tees

Hole	Yds	Par	Hole	Yds	Par
1	284	4	10	480	5
2	398	4	11	181	3
3	428	4	12	462	4
4	190	3	13	370	4
5	517	5	14	167	3
6	393	4	15	507	5
7	440	4	16	204	3
8	140	3	17	449	4
9	484	5	18	407	4
Out	3274	36	In	3227	35
			Totals	6501	71

Visitors   may not play between 1 & 2pm or on Sat.
Societies   must contact in writing.
Green Fees £20 per day (£25 Wed & weekends).
Facilities ⊗ ⊯ ⅃ ⅃ ♀ △ ⌂ ⛛ (Mike Kelly.
Leisure   snooker.
Location   73 Church Rd (3m from centre off Saintfield/ Newcastle rd)
Hotel   ★★★66% Stormont Hotel, 587 Upper Newtonards Rd, BELFAST ☎(0232) 658621 67⇥↰

CO DOWN

ARDGLASS   Map 01 D5

Ardglass ☎(0396) 841219
A scenic cliff-top seaside course with spectacular views and some memorable holes.
18 holes, 5515mtrs, Par 70, SSS 69.
Club membership 762.
Visitors   must contact in advance.
Societies   must contact in advance.
Green Fees £10.50 (£15.50 weekends & bank holidays).
Facilities ⊗ ⊯ & ⅃ (ex Mon) ♀ △ ⌂ (Kevin Dorrian.
Leisure   snooker.
Location   Castle Pl
Hotel   ★★★60% Slieve Donard Hotel, NEWCASTLE ☎(03967) 23681 120⇥

ARDMILLAN   Map 01 D5

Mahee Island ☎Killinchy (0238) 541234
An undulating parkland course, almost surrounded by water, with magnificent views of Strangford Lough and its islands, with Scrabo Tower in the background.
9 holes, 5588yds, Par 68, SSS 67, Course record 65.
Club membership 490.
Visitors   may not play on Wed after 4pm or Sat before 5pm.
Societies   restricted Wed evenings, Sat & some Sun ,st contact in advance.
Green Fees £8 per round (£12 weekends & bank holidays).
Facilities ⊗ ⊯ & ♀ by prior arrangement △ ⌂
Leisure   pool table.
Location   Comber (On Comber/Killyleagh road 0.5m from Comber)

Hotel   ★★★66% Stormont Hotel, 587 Upper Newtonards Rd, BELFAST ☎(0232) 658621 67⇥↰

BALLYNAHINCH   Map 01 D5

Spa ☎(0238) 562365
Parkland course with tree-lined fairways and scenic views of the Mourne Mountains.
18 holes, 5938mtrs, Par 72, SSS 72, Course record 67.
Club membership 550.
Visitors   may not play on Sat; must play with member on Sun. Must contact in advance.
Societies   must contact in advance.
Green Fees £10 (£12.50 weekends & bank holidays).
Facilities ⅃ ♀ (all day) △
Leisure   snooker.
Location   20 Grove Rd
Hotel   ★★★67% Ballynahinch Castle, BALLYNAHINCH ☎(095) 31006 & 31086 28⇥↰

BANBRIDGE   Map 01 D5

Banbridge ☎(08206) 62211
A picturesque course with excellent views of the Movene mountains. The holes are not long, but are tricky, and six new holes opening in 1992 will complete the 18.
18 holes, Par 69.
Club membership 700.
Visitors   may not play Tue, Sat or before 11am on Sun.
Societies   must contact in writing.
Green Fees £7 (£12 weekends).
Facilities ⅃ (Sat only) ♀ △
Location   116 Huntly Rd (0.5m along Huntly road)
Hotel   ★★★60% Slieve Donard Hotel, NEWCASTLE ☎(03967) 23681 120⇥

BANGOR   Map 01 D5

Bangor ☎(0247) 270922
Undulating parkland course in the town. It is well maintained and pleasant and offers a challenging round, particularly at the 5th.
18 holes, 6490yds, Par 71.
Visitors   preferred on Mon & Wed.
Societies   Mon & Wed. Must contact in advance.
Green Fees £14 (£20 weekends).
Facilities ⊗ ⊯ ⅃ ♀ (N V Drew.
Location   Broadway (1m from town on Donaghadee road)
Hotel   ★★★68% Old Inn, 15 Main St, CRAWFORDSBURN ☎(0247) 853255 32⇥↰

Carnalea ☎(0247) 465004
A scenic course on the shores of Belfast Lough.
18 holes, 5550yds, Par 68, SSS 67, Course record 63.
Club membership 1100.
Visitors   no restrictions.
Societies   must contact in writing.
Green Fees £9 (£12 weekends & bank holidays).
Facilities ⊗ ⊯ ⅃ ♀ △ ⌂ ⛛ (Michael McGee.
Location   Station Rd
Hotel   ★★★68% Old Inn, 15 Main St, CRAWFORDSBURN ☎(0247) 853255 32⇥↰

Clandeboyle ☎(0247) 271767
Parkland/heathland courses. The Dufferin is the
championship course and offers a tough challenge.
Nevertheless, the Ava has much to recommend it, with a
notable 2nd hole.
Dufferin Course : 18 holes, 6469yds, Par 72.
Ava Course : 18 holes, 5656yds, Par 67.

Visitors	must play with member at weekends.
Societies	Mon-Wed & Fri, Apr-Sep; Mon & Wed, Oct-Mar. Must contact in advance.
Green Fees	Dufferin: £13 (£18 weekends); Ava: £11 (£14 weekends).
Facilities	⊗ ⅢⅢ ᒪ ᵖ ℓ Peter Gregory.
Location	Tower Rd, Conlig, Newtownards (2m S on A21)
Hotel	★★★68% Old Inn, 15 Main St, CRAWFORDSBURN ☎(0247) 853255 32⊶⚲

CLOUGHEY   Map 01 D5

Kirkistown Castle ☎Portavogie (02477) 71233
Popular with visiting golfers because of its quiet location, the
course is exceptionally dry and remains open when others in
the area have to close.
18 holes, 6167yds, Par 69, SSS 70, Course record 66.
Club membership 837.

Visitors	must contact in advance.
Societies	must contact in advance.
Green Fees	£9 per day (£15 weekends).
Facilities	⊗ ⅢⅢ ᒪ ▬ 里 ⚞ 🏠 ℓ J Peden.
Leisure	snooker.
Location	142 Main Rd, Cloughey
Hotel	★★★68% Old Inn, 15 Main St, CRAWFORDSBURN ☎(0247) 853255 32⊶⚲

DONAGHADEE   Map 01 D5

Donaghadee ☎(0247) 883624
Undulating seaside course requiring a certain amount of
concentration. Splendid views.
18 holes, 6098yds, Par 71, SSS 69.

Visitors	preferred on Mon & Wed.
Green Fees	£10 (£12.50 weekends).
Facilities	ᒪ 里 ᵖ ℓ Gordon Drew.
Location	Warren Rd
Hotel	★★★68% Old Inn, 15 Main St, CRAWFORDSBURN ☎(0247) 853255 32⊶⚲

DOWNPATRICK   Map 01 D5

Bright Castle ☎(0396) 841319
Parkland course in elevated position with views of the
Mountains of Mourne. A good challenge for the energetic
golfer.
18 holes, 7300yds, Par 74, SSS 74.

Visitors	no restrictions.
Societies	must contact in advance.
Green Fees	£6 (£7 weekends).
Facilities	ᒪ
Location	14 Coniamstown Rd, Bright (5m S)
Hotel	★★★60% Slieve Donard Hotel, NEWCASTLE ☎(03967) 23681 120⊶

Downpatrick ☎(0396) 612152
This undulating parkland course has recently been extended,
with Hawtree & Son as architects. It provides a good
challenge.
18 holes, 6400yds, Par 70, SSS 69, Course record 64.
Club membership 800.

Visitors	must contact in advance for groups of 20 or more. May not play 7.30-10.30am at weekends & bank holidays.
Societies	must telephone in advance.
Green Fees	£12 per day (£15 weekends & bank holidays).
Facilities	⊗ ⅢⅢ ᒪ ▬ (normally Apr-Sep) 里 ⚞ 🏠 ᵖ
Leisure	snooker, putting green.
Location	43 Saul Rd (1.5m from town centre)
Hotel	★★★♨67% Ballynahinch Castle, BALLYNAHINCH ☎(095) 31006 & 31086 28⊶⚲

HOLYWOOD   Map 01 D5

Holywood ☎(02317) 2138
Hilly parkland course with some fine views and providing an
interesting game.
18 holes, 5425mtrs, Par 69, SSS 68, Course record 64.
Club membership 800.

Visitors	may not play between 1.30-2.15pm or on Sat.
Societies	must contact in writing.
Green Fees	£12.30 per round (£17.50 weekends).
Facilities	⊗ ⅢⅢ ᒪ ▬ 里 ⚞ 🏠 ᵖ ℓ Michael Bannon.
Leisure	snooker.
Location	Nuns Wall, Demesne Rd
Hotel	★★★★70% Culloden Hotel, HOLYWOOD ☎(02317) 5223 91⚲

The Royal Belfast ☎Belfast (0232) 428165
On the shores of Belfast Lough, this attractive course
consists of wooded parkland on undulating terrain which
provides a pleasant, challenging game.
18 holes, 5963yds, Par 70, SSS 69, Course record 65.
Club membership 1200.

Visitors	may not play on Thu or Sat before 4.30pm; must be accompanied by a member or present a letter of introduction from their own golf club. Must contact in advance.
Societies	must contact in writing.
Green Fees	£20 per round (£25 weekends & bank holidays).
Facilities	ⅢⅢ & ▬ by prior arrangement ⊗ 里 ⚞ 🏠 ᵖ ℓ D H Carson.
Leisure	hard tennis courts, squash, snooker.
Location	Station Rd, Craigavad (2m E on A2)
Hotel	★★★★70% Culloden Hotel, HOLYWOOD ☎(02317) 5223 91⚲

This guide is updated annually – make sure that
you use the up-to-date edition

KILKEEL   Map 01 D4

Kilkeel ☎(0693) 62296
A very good parkland course, picturesquely situated at the foot of the Mourne Mountains. A further nine holes are under construction.
9 holes, 6760yds, Par 70, SSS 69, Course record 59.
Club membership 500.

Visitors	restricted Sun mornings & Tue & Sat. Must contact in advance.
Societies	must contact in writing.
Green Fees	£10 per day (£12 weekends & bank holidays).
Facilities	⊗ (Sat & Sun) 🏌 & 🍺 (summer) ♀ 🏌
Location	Mourne Park, Ballyardle (On Newry road)
Hotel	★★★60% Slieve Donard Hotel, NEWCASTLE ☎(03967) 23681 120⇌

NEWCASTLE   Map 01 D5

Royal County Down ☎(03967) 23314
The remoteness of the links of the Royal County Down and the backdrop of the Mountains of Mourne make this a particularly exhilarating course to play, and there is a wide variety in the challenges it presents. The greens, always in good condition, can be tricky to read and some of the tee shots are blind. The natural terrain of sand dunes and gorse bushes may add to the hazards, but they also contribute to the scenic beauty of the course.
Championship Course: 18 holes, 4968yds, Par 71, SSS 73, Course record 66.
No 2 Course: 18 holes, 4087yds, Par 65, SSS 60.

Visitors	may not play on Sat; may not play on Championship Course Sat, Sun & Wed.
Societies	must contact in advance.
Green Fees	Championship: £35-£40 (summer), £25-£30 (winter); No 2: £7-£9.
Facilities	⊗ 🏌 🍺 ♀ 🏌 🏠 🏌 ℾ Kevan Whitson.
Hotel	★★★60% Slieve Donard Hotel, NEWCASTLE ☎(03967) 23681 120⇌

NEWTOWNARDS   Map 01 D5

Scrabo ☎(0247) 812355
Hilly and picturesque, this course offers a good test of golf.
18 holes, 5699mtrs, Par 71, SSS 71, Course record 65.
Club membership 840.

Visitors	may not play on Sat.
Societies	must telephone in advance.
Green Fees	£9.50 (£13.50 weekends & bank holidays).
Facilities	⊗ 🍴 🏌 🍺 ♀ 🏌 🏠 🏌 ℾ Billy Todd.
Leisure	snooker.
Location	233 Scrabo Rd
Hotel	★★★66% Stormont Hotel, 587 Upper Newtonards Rd, BELFAST ☎(0232) 658621 67⇌🐾

For a full list of golf courses included in the book, see the index at the end of the directory

WARRENPOINT   Map 01 D4

Warrenpoint ☎(06937) 53695
Parkland course with marvellous views and a need for accurate shots.
18 holes, 6288yds, Par 71, SSS 70.

Visitors	preferred Mon, Thu & Fri.
Societies	must contact in advance.
Green Fees	£11 (£16 weekends).
Facilities	⊗ 🍴 🏌 ♀ 🏌 ℾ Nigel Shaw.
Leisure	squash, snooker.
Location	Lower Dromore Rd (1m W)
Hotel	★★★60% Slieve Donard Hotel, NEWCASTLE ☎(03967) 23681 120⇌

◉ CO FERMANAGH ◉

ENNISKILLEN   Map 01 C5

Enniskillen ☎(0365) 325250
Meadowland course in Castle Coole estate.
18 holes, 5476yds, Par 71, SSS 69.

Visitors	preferred on weekdays.
Societies	must contact in advance.
Green Fees	£7.50.
Facilities	⊗ & 🍴 by prior arrangement ♀ 🏌
Leisure	snooker.
Location	Castle Coole (1m E)
Hotel	★★★52% Killyhevlin Hotel, ENNISKILLEN ☎(0232) 323481 22⇌🐾Annexe26rm

◉ CO LONDONDERRY ◉

AGHADOWEY   Map 01 C6

Brown Trout Golf & Country Inn ☎Coleraine (0265) 868209
A challenging course with two par 5s. During the course of the 9 holes, players have to negotiate water 7 times and all the fairways are lined with densely packed fir trees.
9 holes, 2519mtrs, Par 70, SSS 68.
Club membership 150.

Visitors	no restrictions.
Societies	must contact by telephone.
Green Fees	£6 per day (£8.50 weekends & bank holidays).
Facilities	⊗ (Sun only) 🍴 🏌 🍺 ♀ 🏌 🏌 ℾ Ken Revie.
Leisure	riding.
Location	209 Agivey Rd (junc of A54 & B66)
Hotel	★★68% Bayview Hotel, 2 Bayhead Rd, PORTBALLINTRAE ☎(02657) 31453 16⇌

CASTLEDAWSON   Map 01 C5

Moyola Park ☎(0648) 68468
Parkland course with some difficult shots, calling for length and accuracy. The Moyola River provides a water hazard at the 8th.
18 holes, 6517yds, Par 71, SSS 71.

Visitors	no restrictions.

▶

Societies	must contact in advance.
Green Fees	£11 (£14 weekends & bank holidays).
Facilities	⊗ �𝄪 ⤵ ♀ ⫛ ⟮ Vivian Teague.
Leisure	snooker.
Location	Shanemullagh (3m NE of Magherafelt)
Hotel	★★★62% Adair Arms Hotel, Ballymoney Rd, BALLYMENA ☎(0266) 653674 39⇥🏠

CASTLEROCK — Map 01 C6

Castlerock ☎Coleraine (0265) 848314
A most exhilarating course with three superb par 4s, four testing short holes and two par 5s. After an uphill start, the hazards are many, including the river and a railway, and both judgement and accuracy are called for. A challenge in calm weather, any trouble from the elements will test your golf to the limits.
Mussenden: 18 holes, 6687yds, Par 73, SSS 72, Course record 68.
Bann: 9 holes, 2457mtrs, Par 35, SSS 33.
Club membership 960.

Visitors	may not play at weekends.
Societies	must contact in advance.
Green Fees	£13 per 18 holes (£25 weekends & bank holidays); £5 per 9 holes (£7 weekends & bank holidays).
Facilities	�𝄪 by prior arrangement ⤵ ⬛ ♀ ⚱ 🖼 ⫛ ⟮ Bobby Kelly.
Leisure	snooker.
Location	65 Circular Rd (6m from Coleraine on A2)
Hotel	★★68% Bayview Hotel, 2 Bayhead Rd, PORTBALLINTRAE ☎(02657) 31453 16⇥

LONDONDERRY — Map 01 C5

City of Derry ☎(0504) 46369
Two parkland courses on undulating parkland with good views and lots of trees. The 9-hole course will particularly suit novices.
Prehen: 18 holes, 6406yds, Par 71.
Dunhugh Course: 9 holes, 4708yds, Par 63.

Visitors	must make a booking to play on Prehen Course at weekends or before 4.30pm on weekdays.
Societies	must contact in advance.
Green Fees	Prehen: £11 (£13 weekends & bank holidays); Dunhugh: £5.
Facilities	⊗ �𝄪 ⤵ ♀ ⟮ Michael Doherty.
Leisure	snooker.
Location	49 Victoria Rd (2m S)
Hotel	★★★66% Everglades Hotel, Prehen Rd, LONDONDERRY ☎(0504) 46722 52⇥🏠

PORTSTEWART — Map 01 C6

Portstewart ☎(026583) 2015
Three links courses with spectacular views, offering a testing round on the Strand course in particular.
Strand: 18 holes, 6784yds, Par 72, SSS 72.
Town: 18 holes, 4733yds, Par 64, SSS 62.
3: 9 holes, 2622yds, Par 32.

Visitors	preferred on weekdays.
Societies	must contact in advance.
Green Fees	Strand: £15 (£20 weekends); Town: £6 (£8 weekends); 3: £9 (£12 weekends).
Facilities	⊗ �𝄪 ♀ ⫛ ⟮ Alan Hunter.
Leisure	snooker, indoor bowling.
Location	117 Strand Rd
Hotel	★★68% Bayview Hotel, 2 Bayhead Rd, PORTBALLINTRAE ☎(02657) 31453 16⇥

CO TYRONE

COOKSTOWN — Map 01 C5

Killymoon ☎(06487) 63762
Parkland course on elevated, well drained land.
18 holes, 5498mtrs, Par 70, SSS 68, Course record 64.
Club membership 650.

Visitors	may not play on Sat afternoons. Must have a handicap certificate. Must contact in advance.
Societies	must contact in advance.
Green Fees	£11.50 (£15.50 weekends).
Facilities	⊗ �𝄪 ⤵ ⬛ (no catering Mon) ♀ ⚱ 🖼 ⟮ Barry Hamill.
Location	200 Killymoon Rd
Hotel	★★63% Royal Arms Hotel, 51 High St, OMAGH ☎(0662) 243262 21⇥🏠

DUNGANNON — Map 01 C5

Dungannon ☎(08687) 22098 or 27338
Parkland course with five par 3s and tree-lined fairways.
18 holes, 5433mtrs, Par 71, SSS 68, Course record 62.
Club membership 480.

Visitors	may not play on Sat.
Societies	must contact secretary in advance.
Green Fees	£7 per round (£9 Sun & bank holidays).
Facilities	♀ ⚱
Location	34 Springfield Ln (0.5m outside town on Donaghmore road)
Hotel	★★★66% Stormont Hotel, 587 Upper Newtonards Rd, BELFAST ☎(0232) 658621 67⇥🏠

NEWTOWNSTEWART — Map 01 C5

Newtownstewart ☎(06626) 61466 & 61829
Parkland course bisected by a stream.
18 holes, 5468mtrs, Par 70, SSS 69, Course record 66.
Club membership 500.

Visitors	restricted at weekends.
Societies	must contact in writing.
Green Fees	£6 (£8 weekends & bank holidays).
Facilities	�𝄪 by prior arrangement ⬛ ♀ ⚱ 🖼 ⫛
Leisure	snooker.
Location	38 Golf Course Rd (2m SW on B84)
Hotel	★★★62% Fir Trees Hotel, Melmount Rd, STRABANE ☎(0504) 382382 26⇥🏠

For an explanation of symbols and abbreviations, see page 32

OMAGH   Map 01 C5

Omagh ☎(0662) 243160
Undulating parkland course beside the River Drumnagh.
18 holes, 5774yds, Par 70, SSS 68.

Visitors	may not play on Tue & Sat.
Societies	must contact in advance.
Green Fees	£7 (£10 weekends & bank holidays).
Facilities	⬜ ♀
Leisure	snooker.
Location	83a Dublin Rd (On S outskirts of town)
Hotel	★★63% Royal Arms Hotel, 51 High St, OMAGH ☎(0662) 243262 21⇨♦

STRABANE   Map 01 C5

Strabane ☎(0504) 382271 & 382007
Testing parkland course with the River Mourne running
alongside and creating a water hazard.
18 holes, 5552mtrs, Par 69, SSS 69, Course record 63.
Club membership 550.

Visitors	may not play on Sat.
Societies	must contact in writing.
Green Fees	£6 (£10 weekends).
Facilities	⊗ �𝍇 ⬜ ♀ ⌂
Leisure	snooker.
Location	Ballycolman Rd
Hotel	★★★62% Fir Trees Hotel, Melmount Rd, STRABANE ☎(0504) 382382 26⇨♦

REPUBLIC OF IRELAND

⊛ CO CARLOW ⊛

CARLOW   Map 01 C3

Carlow ☎(0503) 31695
Created in 1922 to a design by Tom Simpson, this testing
and enjoyable course is set in a wild deer park, with
beautiful dry terrain and a varied character. With sandy
subsoil, the course is playable all year round. There are
water hazards at the 2nd, 10th and 11th and only two par
5s, both offering genuine birdie opportunities.
18 holes, 5599mtrs, Par 70, SSS 69, Course record 65.
Club membership 1000.

Visitors	are welcome, although play is limited on Tue and difficult on Sat & Sun. Must contact in advance.
Societies	must book in advance.
Green Fees	IR£13 per day (IR£17 weekend & bank holidays).
Facilities	⊗ ⟒ ⬜ ♀ ⌂ ⌂ ☂ ℓ Andrew Gilbert.
Location	Deerpark (2m N of Carlow)
Hotel	★★★64% Royal Hotel, CARLOW ☎(0503) 31621 34⇨♦

This guide is updated annually – make sure that
you use the up-to-date edition

⊛ CO CAVAN ⊛

BELTURBET   Map 01 C4

Belturbet ☎Cavan (049) 22287
Beautifully maintained parkland course with predominantly
family membership and popular with summer visitors.
9 holes, 5480yds, Par 68, SSS 65, Course record 64.
Club membership 150.

Visitors	restrictions the same as for members.
Societies	must contact secretary or captain in advance.
Green Fees	IR£5 per day (due to be increased).
Facilities	⊗ & ⟒ by prior arrangement ⬜ ⬛ ♀ ⌂
Leisure	snooker.
Location	Erne Hill
Hotel	Slieve Russell Hotel, BALLYCONNELL ☎(049) 26444 140⇨♦

BLACKLION   Map 01 C5

Blacklion ☎(0772) 53024
Parkland course established in 1962, with coppices of
woodland and mature trees. The lake comes into play on two
holes and there are some magnificent views of the lake,
islands and surrounding hills. It has been described as one of
the best maintained nine-hole courses in Ireland.
9 holes, Par 72, SSS 69, Course record 64.
Club membership 200.

Visitors	may not play on Sun mornings & occasional competition days.
Societies	must contact in advance.
Green Fees	IR£5 per day (IR£10 weekends & bank holidays).
Facilities	⬜ & ⬛ (afternoons only) ♀ ⌂
Leisure	fishing.
Location	Toam
Hotel	★★★52% Killyhevlin Hotel, ENNISKILLEN ☎(0232) 323481 22⇨♦Annexe26rm

⊛ CO CLARE ⊛

ENNIS   Map 01 B3

Ennis ☎(065) 24074
On rolling hills, this immaculately manicured course presents
an excellent challenge to both casual visitors and aspiring
scratch golfers, with tree-lined fairways and well protected
greens.
18 holes, 5318mtrs, Par 69, SSS 68, Course record 63.
Club membership 965.

Visitors	must be a member of a golf club. Must contact in advance.
Societies	apply in writing.
Green Fees	IR£14 per day.
Facilities	⊗ ⟒ by prior arrangement ⬜ ⬛ ♀ ⌂ ⌂ ☂ ℓ Martin Ward.
Leisure	snooker.
Location	Drumbiggle
Hotel	★★★65% Auburn Lodge Hotel, Galway Rd, ENNIS ☎(065) 21247 75⇨♦

For a full range of AA guides and maps, visit
your local AA shop or any good bookshop

KILKEE   Map 01 A3

Kilkee ☎(065) 56048
Well-established course on the cliffs of Kilkee Bay, with beautiful views.
9 holes, 6185yds, Par 69, SSS 68.
Club membership 600.

Visitors	may not play on certain competition days.
Societies	must contact in writing.
Green Fees	IR£10 per day (IR£12 weekends).
Facilities	⊗ ⓛ 📠 ♀ △ ⋔
Leisure	squash, fishing, sauna.
Location	East End
Hotel	★ Halpin's Hotel, Erin St, KILKEE ☎(065) 56032 11rm(7⇨🐾)

LAHINCH   Map 01 B3

Lahinch ☎(065) 81003
Originally designed by Tom Morris and later modified by Dr Alister Mackenzie, Lahinch has hosted every important Irish amateur fixture and the Home Internationals. The par five 5th - The Klondike - is played along a deep valley and over a huge dune; the par three 6th may be short, but calls for a blind shot over the ridge of a hill to a green hemmed in by hills on three sides.
Old Course: 18 holes, 6702yds, Par 72, SSS 73.
Castle Course: 18 holes, 4786mtrs, Par 67, SSS 66.

Visitors	no restrictions.
Green Fees	IR£25.
Facilities	⊗ ⫫ ⓛ ♀ 🏠 ⋔ ♪ R McCavery.
Location	2m W of Ennisstymon on N67
Hotel	★★★ Aberdeen Arms Hotel, LAHINCH ☎(065) 81100 48⇨🐾

SHANNON AIRPORT   Map 01 B3

Shannon ☎(061) 61849
Superb parkland course with tree-lined fairways, strategically placed bunkers, water hazards and excellent greens, offering a challenge to all levels of players - including the many famous golfers who have played here.
18 holes, 6874yds, Par 72, SSS 74, Course record 65.
Club membership 700.

Visitors	must contact in advance and have an introduction from own club.
Societies	must contact in writing.
Green Fees	IR£20 per day (IR£24 weekends & bank holidays).
Facilities	⊗ ⫫ ⓛ 📠 ♀ △ 🏠 ⋔ ♪ Artie Pyke.
Leisure	pool table.
Location	2m from Shannon Airport
Hotel	★★★60% Fitzpatrick Shannon Shamrock Hotel, BUNRATTY ☎(061) 361177 115⇨🐾

A golf-course name printed in ***bold italics*** means that we have been unable to verify information with the club's management for the current year

---

CO CORK

BANDON   Map 01 B2

Bandon ☎(023) 41111
Lovely parkland course in pleasant rural surroundings.
18 holes, 5663mtrs, Par 70, SSS 69, Course record 66.
Club membership 800.

Visitors	welcome but may not play during club competitions. Must be accompanied by member and contact in advance.
Societies	must apply in writing.
Green Fees	IR£12 (IR£15 weekends).
Facilities	⊗ ⫫ ⓛ 📠 ♀ △ 🏠 ⋔ ♪ Paddy O'Boyle.
Leisure	hard tennis courts.
Location	Castlebernard
Hotel	★★ Inishannon House Hotel, INISHANNON ☎(021) 775121 13⇨🐾

BANTRY   Map 01 A2

Bantry Park ☎(027) 50579
An undulating 9-hole course with some magnificent sea views.
9 holes, 5882mtrs, Par 72, SSS 70, Course record 68.
Club membership 230.

Visitors	course is restricted only during competition times.
Societies	must apply in writing .
Green Fees	IR£10 per day.
Facilities	⊗ ⓛ 📠 ♀ △ ⋔
Location	Donemark
Hotel	★★(red)⚑ Sea View Hotel, BALLYLICKEY ☎(027) 50073 & 50462 17⇨🐾 Annexe5rm

BLARNEY   Map 01 B2

Muskerry ☎(021) 385297
An adventurous game is guaranteed at this course, with its wooded hillsides and the meandering Shournagh River coming into play at a number of holes. The 15th is a notable hole - not long, but very deep - and after that all you need to do to get back to the clubhouse is stay out of the water.
18 holes, 6327yds, Par 71, SSS 70.

Visitors	may not play Wed afternoon & Thu morning. Must play with member at weekends.
Green Fees	IR£16.
Facilities	⊗ & ⫫ by prior arrangement ⓛ ♀ 🏠 ⋔ ♪ Martin Lehane.
Location	Carrigrohane (2m W)
Hotel	★★★71% Blarney Park Hotel, BLARNEY ☎(021) 385281 76⇨🐾

CASTLETOWNBERE   Map 01 A2

Berehaven ☎(027) 70039
Seaside links founded in 1902.
9 holes, 2380mtrs, Par 69, SSS 66, Course record 65.
Club membership 200.

Visitors	no restrictions.
Societies	must telephone (027) 70469 in advance.

Green Fees	IR£7.
Facilities	⚒ ⛳
Leisure	hard tennis courts, outdoor swimming pool, fishing.
Location	Millcove (2m E on Glen Garriff Rd)
Hotel	★★(red)⚑ Sea View Hotel, BALLYLICKEY ☎(027) 50073 & 50462 17⇨🐾Annexe5rm

CHARLEVILLE   Map 01 B2

Charleville ☎(063) 81257
Wooded parkland course offering not too strenuous walking.
18 holes, 6434yds, Par 71, SSS 70, Course record 68.
Club membership 700.

Visitors	may not play at weekends. Must contact in advance.
Societies	must telephone in advance.
Green Fees	IR£10.
Facilities	⊗ �🍴 🛏 🛋 ♀ ⚒
Location	Ardmore
Hotel	★★★⚑72% Longueville House Hotel, MALLOW ☎(022) 47156 47306 17⇨🐾

CORK   Map 01 B2

Cork ☎(021) 353451
This championship-standard course is always kept in superb condition and is playable all year round. It has many memorable and distinctive features including holes at the water's edge and holes in a disused quarry.
18 holes, 6115mtrs, Par 72, SSS 72.
Club membership 705.

Visitors	may not play 12.30-2pm or on Thu (Ladies Day), and only after 2.30pm Sat & Sun. Must have an introduction from own club.
Societies	must contact in advance.
Green Fees	IR£20 per day (IR£22 weekends).
Facilities	⊗ 🍴 🛏 🛋 ♀ ⚒ 🏠 ⛳ ⚑ David Higgins.
Location	Little Island (5m E, on N25)
Hotel	★★★★65% Jurys Hotel, Western Rd, CORK ☎(021) 276622 185⇨🐾

Mahon Municipal ☎(021) 362480
Municipal course which stretches alongside the river estuary, with some holes across water.
18 holes, 4818mtrs, Par 67, SSS 66.

Visitors	may not play mornings at weekends.
Green Fees	IR£6.50 (IR£7.50 weekends & bank holidays).
Facilities	⊗ 🍴 🛏 ♀ 🏠 ⛳
Location	Blackrock (2m from city centre)
Hotel	★★★64% Fitzpatrick Silver Springs Hotel, Tivoli, CORK ☎(021) 507533 109⇨🐾

DOUGLAS   Map 01 B2

Douglas ☎Cork (021) 36255
Level inland course overlooking the city of Cork. Suitable for golfers of all ages and abilities.
18 holes, 5664mtrs, Par 70, SSS 69, Course record 65.
Club membership 750.

Visitors	may not play Tue or Sat & Sun before 2.30pm.
Societies	must contact in advance.
Green Fees	IR£15 per day (IR£16 weekends).

Facilities	⊗ 🍴 🛏 🛋 ♀ ⚒ 🏠 ⛳ ⚑ Garry Nicholson.
Leisure	snooker.
Hotel	★★★★65% Jurys Hotel, Western Rd, CORK ☎(021) 276622 185⇨🐾

FERMOY   Map 01 B2

Fermoy ☎(025) 31472
Rather exposed heathland course, bisected by a road.
18 holes, 6370yds, Par 70, SSS 69.

Visitors	preferred on weekdays.
Green Fees	IR£10 (IR£12 weekends).
Facilities	⊗ 🍴 🛏 ♀ ⛳
Location	Corrin Cross (2m SW)
Hotel	★★★⚑72% Longueville House Hotel, MALLOW ☎(022) 47156 47306 17⇨🐾

MALLOW   Map 01 B2

Mallow ☎(022) 21145
A well-wooded parkland course overlooking the Black-water Valley, Mallow is straightforward, but no less of a challenge for it. The front nine is by far the longer, but the back nine is demanding in its call for accuracy and the par 3 18th provides a tough finish.
18 holes, 6640yds, Par 72, SSS 70.

Visitors	preferred on Mon, Wed, Thu & Fri.
Green Fees	IR£10 (IR£12 weekends).

▶

Facilities	⊗ �𝍓 🛏 ♀ 🏠 ⚑ ⚲ Sean Lonway.
Location	Ballyellis
Hotel	★★★♨72% Longueville House Hotel, MALLOW ☎(022) 47156 47306 17⇨🐾

MIDLETON   Map 01 B2

East Cork ☎(021) 631687
A well-wooded course calling for accuracy of shots.
18 holes, 5207mtrs, Par 69, SSS 67, Course record 66.
Club membership 511.

Visitors	may not play Sun mornings.
Societies	must apply in writing.
Green Fees	IR£12 per day.
Facilities	⊗ 🛏 🛏 ♀ 🏠 ⚑
Leisure	squash, fishing, riding, snooker.
Location	Gortacrue (on the A626)
Hotel	★★62% Ashbourne House Hotel, GLOUNTHAUNE ☎(021) 353319 & 353310 26⇨🐾

MONKSTOWN   Map 01 B2

Monkstown ☎(021) 841376
Undulating parkland course with five tough finishing holes.
18 holes, 5669mtrs, Par 70, SSS 69, Course record 66.
Club membership 800.

Visitors	restricted Tue & busy weekends. Must contact in advance.
Societies	must apply in writing.
Green Fees	IR£15-IR£16.
Facilities	⊗ ⍓ 🛏 🛏 ♀ 🏠 ⚑ ⚲ Batt Murphy.
Location	Parkgariffe
Hotel	★★★79% Rochestown Park Hotel, CORK ☎(021) 892233 39⇨🐾

YOUGHAL   Map 01 C2

Youghal ☎(024) 92787
For many years the host of various Golfing Union championships, Youghal offers a good test of golf and is well maintained for year-round play. There are panoramic views of Youghal Bay and the Blackwater estuary.
18 holes, 5700mtrs, Par 70, SSS 69, Course record 67.
Club membership 600.

Visitors	may not play Wed (Ladies Day) and should contact in advance for weekends.
Societies	must apply in writing a few months in advance.
Green Fees	IR£12 per day.
Facilities	⊗ ⍓ by prior arrangement 🛏 🛏 ♀ 🏠 ⚑ ⚲ Ciaran Carroll.
Location	Knockaverry
Hotel	★★ Devonshire Arms Hotel, Pearse Square, YOUGHAL ☎(024) 92827 & 92409 10⇨🐾

For a full range of AA guides and maps, visit your local AA shop or any good bookshop

CO DONEGAL

BALLINTRA   Map 01 B5

Donegal ☎(073) 34054
This massive links course was opened in 1973 and provides a world-class facility in peaceful surroundings. It is a very long course with some memorable holes, including five par 5s, calling for some big hitting. Donegal is the home club of former Curtis Cup captain, Maire O'Donnell.
18 holes, 6712mtrs, Par 73, SSS 73.

Visitors	no restrictions.
Green Fees	IR£12 (IR£15 weekends).
Facilities	⍓ 🛏 ♀ ⚑
Location	Murvagh (6m S of Donegal on Ballyshannon road)
Hotel	★★★78% Sand House Hotel, ROSSNOWLAGH ☎(072) 51777 42⇨🐾

BALLYBOFEY   Map 01 C5

Ballybofey & Stranorlar ☎(074) 31093
A most scenic course incorporating pleasant valleys backed by mountains with three of its holes bordered by a lake. There are three par 3s on the first nine and two on the second. The most difficult hole is the long uphill par 4 16th. The only par 5 is the 7th.
18 holes, 5328mtrs, Par 68, SSS 69.

Visitors	may play on weekdays.
Green Fees	IR£8.
Facilities	🛏 ♀
Location	Stranorlar (0.25m from Stranorlar)
Hotel	★★★54% Kee's Hotel, Stranorlar, BALLYBOFEY ☎(074) 31917 27⇨🐾

BUNCRANA   Map 01 C6

North West ☎(077) 61027
A traditional-style links course on gently rolling sandy terrain with some long par 4s. Good judgement is required on the approaches and the course offers a satisfying test coupled with undemanding walking.
18 holes, 6203yds, Par 69, SSS 69, Course record 65.
Club membership 500.

Visitors	no restrictions.
Societies	must contact in advance.
Green Fees	IR£8 (IR£13 weekends).
Facilities	⊗ ⍓ 🛏 🛏 (catering Wed & weekends only) ♀ 🏠 ⚲ Seamus McBriarty.
Leisure	snooker.
Location	Lisfannon, Fahan
Hotel	★★71% Strand Hotel, BALLYLIFFEN ☎(077) 76107 12⇨🐾

If you know of a golf course which welcomes visitors and is not already in this guide, we should be grateful for information

BUNDORAN
Map 01 B5

Bundoran ☎(072) 41302
This popular course, acknowledged as one of the best in the country, runs along the high cliffs above Bundoran beach and has a difficult par of 69. Designed by Harry Vardon, it offers a challenging game of golf in beautiful surroundings and has been the venue for a number of Irish golf championships.
18 holes, 5785mtrs, Par 70, SSS 71.
Club membership 400.
Visitors   must contact in advance.
Societies   must contact in advance.
Green Fees   IR£10 (IR£12 weekends).
Facilities   🍔 by prior arrangement 💪 ♀ ⛴ 🏠 ⛵ (David Robinson.
Hotel   ★★72% Dorrians Imperial Hotel, BALLYSHANNON ☎(072) 51147 26⇨🐾

DUNFANAGHY
Map 01 C6

Dunfanaghy ☎Letterkenny (074) 36335
Overlooking Sheephaven Bay, the course has a flat central area with three difficult streams to negotiate. At the Port-na-Blagh end there are five marvellous holes, including one across the beach, while at the Horn Head end, the last five holes are a test for any golfer.
18 holes, 5066mtrs, Par 68, SSS 66, Course record 65 or , Par 6.
Club membership 300.
Visitors   restricted on Sat & Sun mornings.
Societies   must telephone in advance.
Green Fees   IR£7 (IR£8 weekends & bank holidays).
Facilities   ♀ ⛴ 🏠 ⛵ (Doug Hennessy.
Location   Kill (On N56)
Hotel   ★★67% Arnold's Hotel, DUNFANAGHY ☎(074) 36208 & 36142 34⇨

GREENCASTLE
Map 01 C6

Greencastle ☎(077) 81013
A typical links course along the shores of Lough Foyle, surrounded by rocky headlands and sandy beaches. In 1992 the club is celebrating its centenery and increasing its size from 9 to 18 holes.
18 holes, 5118mtrs, Par 69, SSS 67.
Club membership 400.
Visitors   no restrictions.
Societies   must apply in writing in advance.
Green Fees   IR£8 (IR£12 weekends & bank holidays).
Facilities   💪 ♀ ⛴
Location   Moville
Hotel   ★★ McNamara's Hotel, MOVILLE ☎(077) 82010 15rm(5⇨)

A golf-course name printed in ***bold italics*** means that we have been unable to verify information with the club's management for the current year

LETTERKENNY
Map 01 C5

Letterkenny ☎(074) 21150
The fairways are wide and generous, but the rough, when you find it, is short, tough and mean. The flat and untiring terrain on the shores of Lough Swilly provides good holiday golf. Many interesting holes include the intimidating 1st with its high tee through trees and the tricky dog-leg of the 2nd hole.
18 holes, 5756mtrs, Par 70.
Visitors   preferred Mon-Fri.
Green Fees   IR£8.
Facilities   🍔 ♀
Location   Barnhill (2m from town on Rathmelton road)
Hotel   ★★★54% Kee's Hotel, Stranolar, BALLYBOFEY ☎(074) 31917 27⇨🐾

NARIN
Map 01 B5

Narin & Portnoo ☎(075) 45107
Seaside links with every hole presenting its own special feature. The par 4 5th, for instance, demands a perfectly placed drive to get a narrow sight of the narrow entrance to the elevated green. Cross winds from the sea can make some of the par 4s difficult to reach with two woods.
18 holes, 5225mtrs, Par 69, SSS 68.
Visitors   preferred on weekdays.
Green Fees   IR£8 (IR£10 weekends).
Facilities   🍔 ♀
Location   6m from Ardara
Hotel   ★★★55% The Hyland Central Hotel, The Diamond, DONEGAL ☎(073) 21027 & 21090 72⇨🐾

PORTSALON
Map 01 C6

Portsalon ☎(074) 59459
Another course blessed by nature. The three golden beaches of Ballymastocker Bay lie at one end, while the beauty of Lough Swilly and the Inishowen Peninsula beyond is a distracting but pleasant feature to the west. Situated on the Fanad Peninsula, this lovely links course provides untiring holiday golf at its best.
18 holes, 5050mtrs, Par 69, SSS 68.
Visitors   may not play at weekends.
Green Fees   IR£8.
Facilities   ⊗ 🍔 ♀
Hotel   ★ Pier Hotel, RATHMULLAN ☎(074) 58178 16rm(11⇨🐾)

ROSAPENNA
Map 01 C6

Rosapenna ☎Letterkenny (074) 55301
Dramatic links course offering a challenging round. Originally designed by Tom Morris and later modified by James Braid and Harry Vardon, it includes such features as bunkers in mid fairway. The best part of the links runs in the low valley aong the ocean.
18 holes, 6271yds, Par 70, SSS 71, Course record 64.
Club membership 200.

Visitors	no restrictions.
Societies	must contact in advance.
Green Fees	IR£12 (IR£15 Fri-Sun & bank holidays).
Facilities	⫟ 🕍 ➌ ♀ ⟁ 🏠 🍴 🏌 ℂ Simon Byrne.
Leisure	hard tennis courts, snooker.
Location	Downings
Hotel	★★67% Arnold's Hotel, DUNFANAGHY ☎(074) 36208 & 36142 34↩

CO DUBLIN

BALBRIGGAN

Map 01 D4

Balbriggan ☎Dublin (01) 412229
A parkland course with great variations and good views of the Mourne and Cooley mountains.
18 holes, 5881mtrs, Par 71, SSS 71.
Club membership 600.

Visitors	no restrictions.
Societies	must apply in writing.
Green Fees	IR£14 per day (IR£16 weekends).
Facilities	⊗ ⫟ 🕍 ➌ ♀ ⟁
Location	Blackhall

BRITTAS

Map 01 D3

Slade Valley ☎(01) 582183
This is a course for a relaxing game, being fairly easy and in pleasant surroundings.
18 holes, 5345mtrs, Par 69, SSS 69.

Visitors	preferred on Mon, Thu & Fri.
Green Fees	IR£12.
Facilities	⊗ ⫟ 🕍 ♀ 🏠 🏌 ℂ Gerry Egan.
Location	Lynch Park (9m SW of Dublin on N81)
Hotel	★★★63% Downshire House Hotel, BLESSINGTON ☎(045) 65199 14↩🐾Annexe11↩🐾

CLOGHRAN

Map 01 D4

Forrest Little ☎(01) 401183
Testing parkland course.
18 holes, 5865mtrs, Par 70, SSS 70.

Visitors	preferred weekday mornings.
Green Fees	IR£16.
Facilities	🕍 ♀ 🏠 🏌 ℂ Tony Judd.
Location	6m N of Dublin on N1
Hotel	★★★ Marine Hotel, Sutton, DUBLIN ☎(01) 322613 27↩

A golf-course name printed in ***bold italics*** means that we have been unable to verify information with the club's management for the current year

DONABATE

Map 01 D4

Beaverstown ☎Dublin (01) 436439
Well-wooded course with water hazards at more than half of the holes.
18 holes, 5855mtrs, Par 71, SSS 71, Course record 67.
Club membership 800.

Visitors	may not play 12.30-2pm daily & must contact in advance to play on Wed, Sat or Sun.
Societies	must contact in writing.
Green Fees	IR£12 (IR£15 weekends).
Facilities	⊗ ⫟ 🕍 ➌ ♀ ⟁
Leisure	snooker.
Location	Beaverstown (5m from Dublin Airport)
Hotel	★★★54% Grand Hotel, MALAHIDE ☎(01) 450633 100↩🐾

Corballis Public ☎(01) 436583
Well-maintained coastal course with excellent greens.
18 holes, 4971yds, Par 65, SSS 64.

Visitors	no restrictions.
Green Fees	IR£6 (IR£7 weekends).
Facilities	🕍 ➌
Location	Corballis
Hotel	★★★54% Grand Hotel, MALAHIDE ☎(01) 450633 100↩🐾

Donabate ☎(01) 436346
Level parkland course.
18 holes, 5704yds, Par 70, SSS 69.

Visitors	may not play on Wed or at weekends.
Green Fees	IR£15.
Facilities	⊗ ⫟ 🕍 ♀ 🏠 🏌 ℂ Hugh Jackson.
Hotel	★★★54% Grand Hotel, MALAHIDE ☎(01) 450633 100↩🐾

The Island ☎(01) 436104
Links course on a promontary, with sea inlets separating some of the fairways. Accuracy as well as length of shots are required on some holes and sand hills provide an additional challenge.
18 holes, 5760mtrs, Par 71, SSS 70.

Visitors	preferred on Mon, Tue & Fri.
Green Fees	IR£21.
Facilities	⊗ ⫟ 🕍 ♀
Location	Corballis
Hotel	★★★54% Grand Hotel, MALAHIDE ☎(01) 450633 100↩🐾

DUBLIN

Map 01 D4

Castle ☎(01) 904207
A tight, tree-lined parkland course which is very highly regarded by all who play there.
18 holes, 5653mtrs, Par 70, SSS 69, Course record 63.
Club membership 1150.

Visitors	restricted at weekends.
Societies	must apply in writing.
Green Fees	IR£25.

For an explanation of symbols and abbreviations, see page 32

Facilities	⊗ ⅷ Ⅼ ⬛ ♀ ⚲ 🛅 ʃ David Kinsella.
Location	Woodside Dr, Rathfarnham
Hotel	★★★★ Jurys Hotel & Towers, Ballsbridge, DUBLIN ☎(01) 605000 300⇌🛏 Annexe100⇌🛏

Clontarf ☎(01) 331892

The nearest golf course to Dublin city, with a historic building as a clubhouse, Clontarf is a parkland type course bordered on one side by a railway line. There are several testing and challenging holes including the 12th, which involves playing over a pond and a quarry.
18 holes, 5459mtrs, Par 69, SSS 68, Course record 65.
Club membership 1000.

Visitors	may not play on Tue & Fri after 3.30pm; must play with member at weekends. Must contact in advance.
Societies	Tue & Fri. Must contact in writing.
Green Fees	IR£18 per day.
Facilities	Ⅼ ⬛ ♀ ⚲ 🛅 ⛳ ʃ Joe Craddock.
Leisure	snooker, bowling green.
Location	Donnycarney House, Malahide Rd
Hotel	★★★63% Central Hotel, 1-5 Exchequer St, DUBLIN 2 ☎(01) 6797302 70⇌🛏

Deer Park Hotel & Golf Course ☎(01) 322624

Claiming to be Ireland's largest golf/hotel complex, be warned that its popularity makes it extremely busy at times and only hotel residents can book tee-off times.
St Fintans: 18 holes, 6647yds, Par 72.
Old 9: 9 holes, 3130yds, Par 35.
Par 3: 12 holes, 1810yds, Par 36.

Visitors	no restrictions.
Societies	must contact by telephone.
Green Fees	IR£5.50 (IR£7.50 weekends).
Facilities	⊗ ⅷ Ⅼ ⬛ ♀ ⚲ 🛅 ⛳ 🍴
Leisure	snooker.
Location	Howth
Hotel	★★★53% Howth Lodge Hotel, HOWTH ☎(01) 321010 17🛏

Edmonstown ☎(01) 931082

A popular and testing parkland course situated at the foot of the Dublin Mountains in the suburbs of the city. An attractive stream flows in front of the 4th and 6th greens calling for an accurate approach shot.
18 holes, 5663mtrs, Par 70, SSS 69, Course record 69.
Club membership 600.

Visitors	must contact in advance and have an introduction from own club.
Societies	must contact in writing.
Green Fees	IR£18 per round (IR£22 weekends & bank holidays).
Facilities	⊗ ⅷ Ⅼ ⬛ ♀ ⚲ 🛅 ʃ Andrew Crofton.
Leisure	snooker.
Location	Edmonstown Rd, Rathfarnham
Hotel	★★★63% Hotel Montrose, Stillorgan Rd, DUBLIN ☎(01) 2693311 190⇌🛏

Elm Park Golf & Sports Club ☎(01) 2694505

Interesting parkland course requiring a degree of accuracy, particularly as half of the holes involve crossing the stream.
18 holes, 5422mtrs, Par 69, SSS 68.

Visitors	must contact in advance.
Green Fees	IR£27 (IR£30 weekends).
Facilities	⊗ ⅷ Ⅼ ⬛ ♀ ⚲ 🛅 ʃ Seamus Green.
Location	Nutley House (3m from city centre)
Hotel	★★★★ Jurys Hotel & Towers, Ballsbridge, DUBLIN ☎(01) 605000 300⇌🛏 Annexe100⇌🛏

Grange ☎(01) 932889

Wooded parkland course which provides both interest and challenge.
18 holes, 5517mtrs, Par 68, SSS 69.

Visitors	preferred on weekdays.
Green Fees	IR£22 (IR£25 weekends).
Facilities	⊗ ⅷ Ⅼ ♀ 🛅 ʃ W Sullivan.
Location	Rathfarnham (6m from city centre)
Hotel	★★★63% Hotel Montrose, Stillorgan Rd, DUBLIN ☎(01) 2693311 190⇌🛏

Howth ☎(01) 323055

A moorland course with scenic views of Dublin Bay. It is very hilly and presents a good challenge for the athletic golfer.
18 holes, 5618mtrs, Par 71, SSS 69.
Club membership 1257.

Visitors	may not play on Wed. Contact in advance if more than 4 in party.
Societies	must apply in writing.
Green Fees	IR£15 weekdays.
Facilities	Ⅼ ⬛ ♀ ⚲ 🛅 ʃ John McGuirk.
Location	St Fintan's, Carrickbrack Rd, Sutton
Hotel	★★★ Marine Hotel, Sutton, DUBLIN ☎(01) 322613 27⇌

Milltown ☎(01) 976090

Level parkland course on the outskirts of the city.
18 holes, 5638mtrs, Par 71, SSS 69, Course record 68.
Club membership 1200.

Visitors	with member only on Sun and after 5pm daily. Must contact in advance.
Societies	welcome
Green Fees	IR£25.
Facilities	⊗ ⅷ Ⅼ ⬛ ♀ ⚲ 🛅 ʃ Christy Greene.
Leisure	snooker.
Location	Lower Churchtown Rd
Hotel	★★★★ Jurys Hotel & Towers, Ballsbridge, DUBLIN ☎(01) 605000 300⇌🛏 Annexe100⇌🛏

Newlands ☎(01) 593157

Mature parkland course offering a testing game.
18 holes, 5473mtrs, Par 71, SSS 69.
Club membership 1000.

Visitors	may play weekdays only. Must contact in advance.
Societies	must contact in writing.
Green Fees	IR£20 per round.
Facilities	⊗ ⅷ Ⅼ ⬛ ♀ ⚲ 🛅 ⛳ ʃ Paul Heeney.
Location	Clondalkin
Hotel	★★★56% Green Isle Hotel, Clondalkin, DUBLIN ☎(01) 593406 50⇌🛏 Annexe34rm

---

This guide is updated annually – make sure that you use the up-to-date edition

Rathfarnham ☎(01) 931201
Parkland course designed by John Jacobs in 1962.
9 holes, 5833mtrs, Par 71, SSS 70, Course record 70.
Club membership 554.

Visitors	may not play Tue, Sat, or Thu pm.
Societies	must apply in writing.
Green Fees	IR£13 (IR£15 Sun).
Facilities	🏊 ⬛ ♀ ⛳ 🏠 (Brian O'Hara.
Location	Newtown
Hotel	★★★★ Jurys Hotel & Towers, Ballsbridge, DUBLIN ☎(01) 605000 300⇨🛏Annexe100⇨🛏

Royal Dublin ☎(01) 336346
A popular course with visitors, for its design subtleties, for the condition of the links and the friendly atmosphere. Founded in 1885, the club moved to its present site in 1889 and received its Royal designation in 1891. A notable former club professional was Christie O'Conner, who was appointed in 1959 and immediately made his name. Along with its many notable holes, Royal Dublin has a fine and testing finish. The 18th is a sharply dog-legged par 4, with out of bounds along the right-hand side. The decision to try the long carry over the 'garden' is one many visitors have regretted.
18 holes, 6262mtrs, Par 71, SSS 73, Course record 63.
Club membership 800.

Visitors	green fees not accepted on Wed or Sat. Must contact in advance and have an introduction from own club.
Societies	must apply in writing.
Green Fees	not confirmed.
Facilities	⊗ ∭ (ex Mon) 🏊 ⬛ ♀ ⛳ 🏠 (Leonard Owens.
Location	Dollymount
Hotel	★★★63% Central Hotel, 1-5 Exchequer St, DUBLIN 2 ☎(01) 6797302 70⇨🛏

St Anne's ☎(01) 336471
Links course, recently extended from 9 holes to 18.
18 holes, 5660mtrs, Par 70, SSS 69.
Club membership 500.

Visitors	telephone for restrictions. Must have an introduction from own club.
Societies	must apply in writing.
Green Fees	IR£15 (IR£20 weekends & bank holidays).
Facilities	⊗ ∭ 🏊 ⬛ ♀ (Paddy Skerritt.
Location	North Bull Island, Dollymount
Hotel	★★★63% Central Hotel, 1-5 Exchequer St, DUBLIN 2 ☎(01) 6797302 70⇨🛏

Stackstown ☎(01) 942338
Pleasant course in scenic surroundings.
18 holes, 5925mtrs, Par 72, SSS 72.

Visitors	preferred Mon-Fri.
Green Fees	IR£12 (IR£15 weekeknd).
Facilities	⊗ ∭ 🏊 ♀ (Michael Kavanach.
Location	Kellystown Rd, Rathfarnham (9m S of city centre)
Hotel	★★★63% Hotel Montrose, Stillorgan Rd, DUBLIN ☎(01) 2693311 190⇨🛏

For an explanation of symbols and abbreviations, see page 32

DUN LAOGHAIRE   Map 01 D4

Dun Laoghaire ☎Dublin (01) 2803916
This is a well-wooded parkland course, not long, but requiring accurate placing of shots.
18 holes, 5478mtrs, Par 70, SSS 69, Course record 66.
Club membership 1050.

Visitors	with member only on Sun. Must contact in advance.
Societies	must apply in writing.
Green Fees	IR£20 per day.
Facilities	⊗ ∭ (Apr-Oct) 🏊 ⬛ ♀ ⛳ 🏠 ⛴ (Owen Mulhall.
Location	Eglinton Park, Tivoli Rd
Hotel	★★★61% Victor Hotel, Rochestown Av, DUN LAOGHAIRE ☎(01) 2853555 & 2853102 64⇨🛏

KILLINEY   Map 01 D3

Killiney ☎Dublin (01) 2851983
The course is on the side of Killiney Hill with picturesque views over south Dublin and the Wicklow Mountains.
9 holes, Par 69.
Club membership 480.

Visitors	welcome Thu, Sat & Sun am.
Green Fees	IR£15 (IR£18 bank holidays & weekends).
Facilities	🏊 ⬛ ♀ ⛳ 🏠 ⛴ (P O'Boyle.
Leisure	snooker.
Location	Ballinclea Rd
Hotel	★★★61% Fitzpatrick Castle Hotel, KILLINEY ☎(01) 2840700 92⇨🛏

KILTERNAN   Map 01 D4

Kilternan ☎(01) 955559
Interesting and testing course overlooking Dublin Bay.
18 holes, 4914mtrs, Par 68, SSS 67.

Visitors	may not play mornings at weekends.
Green Fees	IR£13 (IR£16 weekends).
Facilities	⊗ ∭ 🏊 ♀ 🏠 ⛴ (Bryan Malone.
Location	Kilternan Hotel, Enniskerry Rd
Hotel	★★★61% Fitzpatrick Castle Hotel, KILLINEY ☎(01) 2840700 92⇨🛏

LUCAN   Map 01 D4

Hermitage ☎(01) 6265049
Part level, part undulating course bordered by the River Liffey and offering some surprises.
18 holes, 6034mtrs, Par 71, SSS 70, Course record 65.
Club membership 1100.

Visitors	must contact in advance and have an introduction from own club.
Societies	must telephone well in advance.
Green Fees	IR£20 per round (IR£30 weekends).
Facilities	⊗ ∭ (times vary with season) 🏊 ⬛ ♀ ⛳ 🏠 ⛴ (David Daly.
Leisure	snooker.
Location	Ballydowd
Hotel	★★★ Finnstown House, Newcastle Rd, LUCAN ☎(01) 6280644 25⇨🛏

Lucan ☎Dublin (01) 6282106
Founded in 1902 as a 9-hole course and only recently
extended to 18 holes, Lucan involves playing across both the
main road and a lane which bisects the course.
18 holes, 5958mtrs, Par 71, SSS 71, Course record 68.
Club membership 780.

Visitors	with member only Sat & Sun, after 1pm Wed. Must contact in advance.
Societies	must apply in writing.
Green Fees	IR£15.
Facilities	⊗ 🏌 🛒 🍺 ♀ ⚲
Location	Celbridge Rd
Hotel	★★★ Finnstown House, Newcastle Rd, LUCAN ☎(01) 6280644 25⇦🏠

MALAHIDE   Map 01 D4

Malahide ☎(01) 461611
Parkland courses with water hazards at a number of holes.
Blue Course: 9 holes, 2888mtrs, Par 71, SSS 70.
Red Course: 9 holes, 20mtrs, Par 71, SSS 70 or 28 holes.
Yellow Course: 9 holes, 2632mtrs, Par 70, SSS 69.
Club membership 800.

Visitors	may not play on Sat & Sun mornings. Must contact in advance and have an introduction from own club.
Societies	must contact in advance.
Green Fees	IR£21 (IR£31 weekends).
Facilities	⊗ 🏌 🛒 🍺 ♀ ⚲ 🏠 🛎 (David Barton.
Leisure	snooker.
Location	Beechwood, The Grange (1m from coast road at Portmarnock)
Hotel	★★★54% Grand Hotel, MALAHIDE ☎(01) 450633 100⇦🏠

PORTMARNOCK   Map 01 D4

Portmarnock See page 323

RATHCOOLE   Map 01 C4

Beech Park ☎Dublin (01) 580100
Relatively flat parkland with heavily wooded fairways.
18 holes, 5730mtrs, Par 72, SSS 70, Course record 67.
Club membership 750.

Visitors	restricted on some days, telephone in advance.
Societies	apply in writing.
Green Fees	IR£13 per round.
Facilities	⊗ 🏌 🛒 🍺 ♀ ⚲
Leisure	snooker.
Location	Johnstown
Hotel	★★★ Finnstown House, Newcastle Rd, LUCAN ☎(01) 6280644 25⇦🏠

SKERRIES   Map 01 D4

Skerries ☎(01) 491567
Tree-lined parkland course on gently rolling countryside,
with sea views from some holes. The 1st and 18th are
particularly challenging. The club can be busy on some days,
but is always friendly.
18 holes, 5994mtrs, Par 73, SSS 72.
Club membership 500.

Visitors	must contact in advance and have an introduction from own club.
Societies	must contact well in advance in writing.
Green Fees	IR£15 (IR£18 weekends).
Facilities	⊗ 🏌 🛒 🍺 ♀ ⚲ 🏠 🛎 (Jimmy Kinsella.
Hotel	★★★54% Grand Hotel, MALAHIDE ☎(01) 450633 100⇦🏠

CO GALWAY

BALLINSLOE   Map 01 B4

Ballinasloe ☎Ballinasloe (0905) 42126
Well-maintained parkland course, recently extended from a
par 68 to a par 72.
18 holes, 6445yds, Par 72, SSS 70.
Club membership 800.

Visitors	may not play on Sun.
Societies	welcome on weekdays, apply in writing.
Green Fees	IR£10 per day.
Facilities	⊗ (when required) 🛒 🍺 ♀ ⚲
Location	Rossgloss
Hotel	★★★64% Hayden's Hotel, BALLINSLOE ☎(0905) 42347 55⇦🏠

BALLYCONNEELY   Map 01 A4

Connemara ☎Clifden (095) 23502
This championship links course is situated on the verge
of the Atlantic Ocean in a most spectacular setting, with
the Twelve Bens Mountains in the background. Established as recently as 1973, it is a tough challenge, due in
no small part to its exposed location, with the back 9 the
equal of any in the world. The last six holes are
exceptionally long.
18 holes, 6173mtrs, Par 72, SSS 73, Course record 69.
Club membership 800.

Visitors	must have a handicap certificate. Must contact in advance.
Societies	must contact in writing.
Green Fees	IR£10-IR£16 per round.
Facilities	⊗ 🏌 & 🛒 (summer only) 🍺 ♀ ⚲ 🏠 🛎
Leisure	snooker.
Location	9m SW of Clifton
Hotel	★★★53% Abbeyglen Castle Hotel, CLIFDEN ☎(095) 21201 40⇦🏠

GALWAY   Map 01 B4

Galway ☎(091) 22169
Designed by Dr Alister Mackenzie, this course is inland
by nature, although some of the fairways run close to the
ocean. The terrain is of gently sloping hillocks with plenty
of trees and furze bushes to catch out the unwary.
Although not a long course, it provided a worthy challenge
as the venue of the Celtic International Tournament in
1984 and continues to delight the visiting golfer.
18 holes, 6376yds, Par 70, SSS 70.

Visitors	preferred on weekdays, except Tue.
Green Fees	IR£20.

▶

Facilities	⊗ ⫴ ⛳ ♀ 🍴 ⛳ ✦ Don Wallace.
Location	Blackrock, Salthill (2m W in Salthill)
Hotel	★★★★64% Great Southern Hotel, Eyre Square, GALWAY ☎(091) 64041 120⇨🛏

GORT

Map 01 B3

Gort ☎(091) 31336
A 9-hole course, bisected by a railway line and with out of bounds on most holes, six of which are bunkered.
9 holes, 2587mtrs, Par 34, SSS 67, Course record 67.
Club membership 220.

Visitors	may not play on Sun mornings or Wed evenings.
Societies	must contact club secretary in advance.
Green Fees	IR£6-IR£8 per day.
Facilities	⛳ (summer) ⛳ ♀ (Apr-Sep) 🏌 ⛳
Location	Laughtyshaughnessy
Hotel	★★★ Corrib Great Southern Hotel, Dublin Rd, GALWAY ☎(091) 55281 178⇨🛏

LOUGHREA

Map 01 B3

Loughrea ☎Galway (091) 41049
An excellent parkland course with good greens. Nine new holes opening in August 1992 will increase the variety and attraction of a game here.
9 holes, 5860yds, Par 68, SSS 67, Course record 65.
Club membership 290.

Visitors	may not play Sun mornings.
Societies	must contact in advance.
Green Fees	IR£10 per day.
Facilities	⛳ ⛳ ♀ 🏌
Location	Bullaun Rd
Hotel	★★64% Westpark Hotel, PORTUMNA ☎(0509) 41121 & 41112 29⇨🛏

ORANMORE

Map 01 B3

Athenry ☎(091) 94466
Wooded parkland course, recently extended to 18 holes.
18 holes, 6100yds, Par 70, SSS 69.
Club membership 400.

Visitors	may not play on Sun.
Societies	must telephone in advance.
Green Fees	IR£10 per round.
Facilities	⊗ ⛳ ⛳ ♀ 🏌 ⛳
Location	Palmerstown
Hotel	★★★ Corrib Great Southern Hotel, Dublin Rd, GALWAY ☎(091) 55281 178⇨🛏

OUGHTERARD

Map 01 B4

Oughterard ☎(091) 82131
Well-maintained parkland course with mature trees and shrubs. Some very challenging holes.
18 holes, 6060yds, Par 70, SSS 69.

Visitors	preferred Mon-Fri.
Green Fees	IR£12 (IR£15 weekends).
Facilities	⊗ ⫴ ⛳ ♀ 🍴 ⛳ ✦ Michael Ryan.
Location	1m from town on Galway road
Hotel	★★★ Connemara Gateway Hotel, OUGHTERARD ☎(091) 82328 62⇨🛏

PORTUMNA

Map 01 B3

Portumna ☎(0509) 41059
Parkland course with mature trees.
18 holes, 5205mtrs, Par 68, SSS 69, Course record 64.
Club membership 500.

Visitors	must contact in advance to play on Sun.
Societies	must contact in writing.
Green Fees	IR£10 (IR£12 weekends).
Facilities	⊗ by prior arrangement ⛳ ⛳ ♀ 🏌 ⛳
Location	1m from town on Scarriffe road
Hotel	★★64% Westpark Hotel, PORTUMNA ☎(0509) 41121 & 41112 29⇨🛏

TUAM

Map 01 B4

Tuam ☎(093) 24354
Interesting course with plenty of trees and bunkers.
18 holes, 6377yds, Par 73, SSS 70.

Visitors	preferred Mon-Fri.
Green Fees	IR£10.
Facilities	⛳ ♀ 🍴 ⛳
Location	Barnacurragh (0.5m from town on Athenry road)

CO KERRY

BALLYBUNION

Map 01 A3

Ballybunion See page 325

BALLYFERRITER

Map 01 A2

Ceann Sibeal ☎(066) 56255
This most westerly golf course in Europe has a magnificent scenic location. It is a traditional links course with beautiful turf, many bunkers, a stream that comes into play on 14 holes and, usually, a prevailing wind.
18 holes, 6440yds, Par 72, SSS 71.
Club membership 300.

Visitors	no restrictions.
Societies	must telephone in advance.
Green Fees	IR£15 per round.
Facilities	⊗ ⫴ ⛳ ⛳ (catering Apr-Oct) ♀ (Apr-Oct) 🏌 🍴 ⛳ 🛏 ✦ Dermot O'Connor.
Leisure	heated outdoor swimming pool, sauna.
Hotel	★★★ Benner's, Main St, DINGLE ☎(066) 51638 25⇨🛏

A golf-course name printed in **bold italics** means that we have been unable to verify information with the club's management for the current year

SCORE CARD: Championship Course (Blue Tees)					
Hole	Ms	Par	Hole	Ms	Par
1	358	4	10	341	4
2	346	4	11	389	4
3	351	4	12	136	3
4	407	4	13	516	5
5	364	4	14	359	4
6	550	5	15	191	3
7	161	3	16	484	5
8	368	4	17	423	4
9	404	4	18	381	4
Out	3309	36	In	3220	36
			Totals	6529	72

PORTMARNOCK   Map01D4

Portmarnock ☎ Dublin (01) 323082

John Ingham writes: The night before our fourball tackled Portmarnock was spent, as I recall, in Dublin. Guinness in that city seems smoother while the conversation, with locals, ranged from why no southern Irish player ever won the Open to how such a small nation can boast the great writers, wits and actors.

This preparation, prior to facing one of the world's great golfing monsters, is recommended by me - providing you only intend playing eighteen holes in one day. Frankly, you will have to reach into the base of your golf bag to pull out every shot if you want to play to your handicap on this superb links.

An opening birdie, downwind, made me wonder what the fuss was about. Two hours later, with a backswing too fast and the breeze now something near a gale, I decided that a test of 7,182 yards off the back tees was too man-size for me. Maybe it would be more enjoyable on a calm, summer evening!

I remember the course not for the way it humiliated me, but for the 1960 Canada Cup where I watched Sam Snead and Arnold Palmer play with such skill to win. Even so, both took 75 in one round while scores by the mighty Gary Player ranged from 65 to 78.

There are no blind shots, unless you drive into sandhills. This is natural golf with no unfair carries off the tee and the only damage to your card is self-inflicted. True, there are a couple of holes of 560 yards and the 522 yard 16th is frightening, as you tee up in a fierce wind.

It's incredible to think that in 1893 Portmarnock was 'discovered' almost by accident by a Mr Pickeman and architect Ross, when they rowed a boat from Sutton to the peninsula where they came across a wilderness of bracken, duneland and natural-looking bunkers made by God.

They created the course, built a shack for a clubhouse and talked about the only real hazard left - a cow which devoured golf balls. Today it's so very different with a modern clubhouse filled with members delighted to belong to such an internationally well-known establishment.

27 holes. Old Course 18 holes, 7182 yds, Par 72, SSS 74, course record 74 (Sandy Lyle). New Course 9 holes, 3478 yds, Par 37. Membership 1100.

Visitors	must contact in advance, and have a letter of introduction from their own club. Restricted Saturday, Sunday and Public Holidays.
Societies	must apply in writing.
Green fees	not confirmed
Facilities	⊗ ⫻ 🍴 🍺 ♀ (all day) 🛋 📷 ⛳ ☍ (Joey Purcell)

WHERE TO STAY AND EAT NEARBY

HOTELS:

HOWTH   ★★★ Howth Lodge. ☎ (01) 321010. 17 ☍ .
         ⊊ Irish & French cuisine.

MALAHIDE ★★★ Grand. ☎ (01) 450633. 110 ⇔☍ .
         ⊊ European cuisine.

RESTAURANT:

HOWTH   King Sitric, East Pier, Harbour Rd.
         ☎ (01) 325235 & 326729.
         ⊊ Fish

GLENBEIGH Map 01 A2

Dooks ☎Tralee (066) 68205
Old-established course on the sea shore between the Kerry mountains and Dingle Bay. Sand dunes are a feature (the name Dooks is a derivation of the Gaelic word for sand bank) and the course offers a fine challenge in a pretty Ring of Kerry location.
18 holes, 6010yds, Par 70, SSS 68.
Club membership 580.

SCORECARD: White Tees					
Hole	Yds	Par	Hole	Yds	Par
1	419	4	10	406	4
2	131	3	11	531	5
3	300	4	12	370	4
4	344	4	13	150	3
5	194	3	14	375	4
6	394	4	15	213	3
7	477	5	16	348	4
8	368	4	17	313	4
9	183	3	18	494	5
Out	2810	34	In	3200	36
			Totals	6010	70

Visitors   no restrictions.
Societies   must apply in writing.
Green Fees   IR£15 per round.
Facilities   ⊗ ⑾ 🏔 🛒 ♀ ⚓
Hotel   ★★★54% Gleneagle Hotel, KILLARNEY ☎(064) 31870 177⇨🏠

KENMARE Map 01 A2

Kenmare ☎(064) 41291
Parkland course situated at the head of Kenmare Bay in very picturesque surroundings.
9 holes, 4410mtrs, Par 66, SSS 63, Course record 64.
Club membership 250.
Visitors   may not play Wed or Sun.
Societies   must contact secretary in writing.
Green Fees   IR£10 per day.
Facilities   🛒 ♀ ⚓ 🏠 ⚲
Location   Kilgarvan Rd
Hotel   ★★★★(red)🏨 Park Hotel, KENMARE ☎(064) 41200 48⇨🏠

KILLARNEY Map 01 A2

Killarney Golf & Fishing Club ☎(064) 31034
Both of the courses are parkland with tree-lined fairways, many bunkers and small lakes which provide no mean challenge. Mahoney's Point Course has a particularly testing 5, 4, 3 finish and both courses call for great skill from the tee. Killarney has been the venue for many important events, including the Irish Open in 1991, and is a favourite of many famous golfers
Mahony's Point : 18 holes, 6152mtrs, Par 72, Course record 68.
Killeen : 18 holes, 6475mtrs, Par 72, Course record 65.
Club membership 1400.
Visitors   must have a handicap certificate. Must contact in advance.
Societies   must telephone in advance.
Green Fees   not confirmed.
Facilities   ⊗ ⑾ 🏔 🛒 ♀ ⚓ 🏠 ⚲ ⚔ Tony Coveney.
Leisure   sauna, gymnasium.
Location   O'Mahony's Point (On Ring of Kerry road)
Hotel   ★★★★74% Aghadoe Heights Hotel, KILLARNEY ☎(064) 31766 61⇨🏠

▶

For a full list of golf courses included in the book, see the index at the end of the directory

PARKNASILLA Map 01 A2

Parknasilla ☎(064) 45122
Short, tricky 9-hole course, with 18 different tees which make the second 9 more interesting.
9 holes, 2447yds, Par 35, SSS 65, Course record 64.
Club membership 40.
Visitors   may not play on competition days.
Societies   must conatct in advance.
Green Fees   IR£10 per day.
Facilities   ⑾ 🏔 🛒 ♀ ⚓ 🏠 ⚲ ⚔ ⚔ Charles McCarthy.
Leisure   hard tennis courts, heated indoor swimming pool, riding, snooker, sauna.
Hotel   ★★★★70% Great Southern Hotel, PARKNASILLA ☎(064) 45122 25⇨🏠Annexe59⇨🏠

TRALEE Map 01 A2

Tralee ☎(066) 36379
The first Arnold Palmer designed course in Europe, the magnificent 18-hole links are set in spectacular scenery on the Barrow peninsula. Perhaps the most memorable hole is the par four 17th which plays from a high tee, across a deep gorge to a green perched high against a backdrop of mountains.
18 holes, 6252mtrs, Par 73, Course record 66.
Club membership 1000.
Visitors   may play before 4.30pm on weekdays but only 10.30am-12.15pm on Wed & 11am-12.30pm at weekends & bank holidays. Must have a handicap certificate. Must contact in advance.
Societies   weekdays only; must contact in writing.
Green Fees   IR£25 per round (IR£30 weekends).
Facilities   ⊗ ⑾ 🏔 🛒 ♀ ⚓ 🏠
Location   West Barrow (8m W of Tralee on Spa-Fenit road)
Hotel   ★★★63% The Brandon Hotel, TRALEE ☎(066) 23333 160⇨🏠

WATERVILLE Map 01 A2

Waterville ☎(0667) 4102
On the western tip of the Ring of Kerry, this course is highly regarded by many top golfers. The feature holes are the par five 11th, which runs along a rugged valley between towering dunes, and the par three 17th, which features an exceptionally elevated tee. Needless to say, the surroundings are beautiful.
18 holes, 6549yds, Par 72, SSS 74, Course record 65.
Club membership 300.
Visitors   must have a handicap certificate. May not play on Sun 8.30-9.30am & 2-3.30pm. Must contact in advance and have an introduction from own club.
Societies   must contact in advance.
Green Fees   IR£30 per round.
Facilities   ⊗ ⑾ 🏔 🛒 ♀ ⚓ 🏠 ⚲ ⚔ Liam Higgins.
Leisure   fishing, riding.
Hotel   ★★ Derrynane Hotel, CAHERDANIEL ☎(0667) 5136 62⇨

Tom Watson paid annual visits here to remind himself of the flavour of golf's essence.

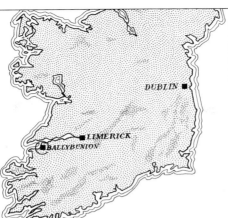

Hole	Yds	Par	Hole	Yds	Par
1	392	4	10	359	4
2	445	4	11	453	4
3	220	3	12	192	3
4	520	5	13	484	5
5	524	5	14	131	3
6	364	4	15	216	3
7	423	4	16	499	5
8	153	3	17	385	4
9	454	4	18	379	4
Out	3495	36	In	3098	35
			Totals	6593	71

SCORE CARD: Old Course (Championship Tees)

BALLYBUNION

Map01A3

Ballybunion ☎ (068) 27146

John Ingham writes: Since golf is a state of mind over muscle and a great day on the links is exhilarating, it is my view that memorable fairways tend not to be decorated with artificial lakes which are fun only for ducks and golf ball manufacturers.

Some of the best courses look natural even though they have, maybe, been helped along by skilful architects such as Colt, Hawtree or Mackenzie. And in the Emerald Isle it is entirely appropriate that a Mr Murphy built Ballybunion on the West Coast of Ireland, back in 1906.

Believe me, there are few greater adventures waiting to be tackled and not to play this old course is a crime. In an American list of the world's top 100 courses, Ballybunion is in there at number eight and the reason is simple: it probably represents the ultimate links on as wild a stretch as you will find.

The Atlantic waves crash into the shore and no golfer will ever feel closer to nature as he hunts his ball and flights it through crosswinds and breathtaking views. The experience of taking on this classic will be remembered as long as you live.

There are now two courses at Ballybunion, separated only by a 19th hole, which has heard all the wondrous stories before as well as hosting such great names as Tom Watson, five times winner of the Open. Likeable Tom can't speak highly enough of the place and claims that before anyone builds a golf course, they should play Ballybunion in a part of Ireland that is wall-to-wall golf courses of the highest calibre.

36 holes. Old Course 18 holes, 6593 yds, Par 71, SSS 72. New Course 18 holes, 6130 yds, Par 71, SSS 72.

Visitors must contact in advance, and have a handicap certificate (maximum handicap 24; women 36).

Societies must book in advance.

Green fees Old Course £30 per round. New Course £20 per round. Day ticket £40 (but Old Course cannot be played twice).

Facilities ⊗ ᛟ ᛚ ♨ ♀ ⌂ ⛳ ⸙ (Ted Higgins)

Location Sandhill Rd.

WHERE TO STAY AND EAT NEARBY

HOTEL:
BALLYBUNION ★★ Marine.
☎ (068) 27522 & 27139. 13 ⇄↑ .
Irish & French cuisine.

CO KILDARE

DONADEA
Map 01 C4

Knockanally Golf & Country Club ☎(045) 69322
Home of the Irish International Professional Matchplay
championship, this parkland course is set in a former estate,
with a Palladian-style clubhouse.
18 holes, 6485yds, Par 72, SSS 72, Course record 66.
Club membership 250.

Visitors	may not play on Sun 8.30-11am.
Societies	must contact in writing.
Green Fees	IR£13 (IR£16 weekends).
Facilities	⅏ by prior arrangement 🏌 ⚐ ♀ ⚒ 🏠 ☂ ⚑ Peter Hickey.
Location	3m off main Dublin-Galway road
Hotel	★★ Curryhills House Hotel, PROSPEROUS ☎(045) 68150 10⇨🏠

KILDARE
Map 01 C3

Curragh ☎(045) 41238
A particularly challenging course, well wooded and with
lovely scenery all around.
18 holes, 6003mtrs, Par 72, SSS 71.

Visitors	preferred on Mon, Thu & Fri.
Green Fees	IR£12 (IR£15 weekends & bank holidays).
Facilities	⊗ ⅏ 🏌 ♀ 🏠 ☂ ⚑ Phil Lawlor.
Location	Curragh (Off N7 between Newbridge & Kildare)
Hotel	★★ Curryhills House Hotel, PROSPEROUS ☎(045) 68150 10⇨🏠

KILL
Map 01 D3

Killeen ☎(045) 66003
Set in pleasant countryside, the attractive course is
characterised by its many lakes. It provides a challenge to
test the skills of the moderate enthusiast and the more
experienced golfer.
18 holes, 4979mtrs, Par 69, SSS 66, Course record 71.
Club membership 300.

Visitors	may not play at weekends before 11am.
Societies	must contact by telephone.
Green Fees	IR£8 per round (IR£10 per round weekends & bank holidays).
Facilities	⊗ ⅏ by prior arrangement 🏌 ⚐ ♀ ⚒ 🏠 ☂
Leisure	snooker, putting green.
Hotel	The Kildare Hotel & Country Club, STRAFFAN ☎(01) 6273333 42⇨🏠

Each golf-course entry has a recommended
AA-appointed hotel. For a wider choice of
places to stay, consult *AA Hotels and
Restaurants in Britain and Ireland* and
*AA Inspected Bed and Breakfast in
Britain and Ireland*

NAAS
Map 01 C3

Bodenstown ☎(045) 97096
The old course in Bodenstown has ample fairways and large
greens, some of which are raised, providing more than a fair
test of golf. The Ladyhill course is a little shorter and tighter,
but still affords a fair challenge.
Bodenstown: 18 holes, 5788mtrs, Par 72, SSS 70.
Ladyhill: 18 holes, 5278mtrs, Par 71, SSS 68.
Club membership 650.

Visitors	may not play on Bodenstown course at weekends.
Societies	must contact by telephone.
Green Fees	IR£8 (IR£6 on Ladyhill course at weekends).
Facilities	⊗ 12 🏌 ⚐ ♀ 🏠
Leisure	snooker.
Location	Sallins (4m from town near Bodenstown grave-yard)
Hotel	The Kildare Hotel & Country Club, STRAFFAN ☎(01) 6273333 42⇨🏠

Naas ☎(045) 97509
Scenic parkland course with different tees for the return 9.
9 holes, 3000mtrs, Par 36, SSS 70, Course record 68.
Club membership 800.

Visitors	may not play on Sun, Tue or Thu.
Societies	must contact in advance.
Green Fees	IR£10 per round (IR£12 weekends & bank holidays).
Facilities	🏌 ⚐ ♀ 🏠
Leisure	snooker.
Location	Kerdiffstown (1m from town on Sallins-Johns-town road)
Hotel	The Kildare Hotel & Country Club, STRAFFAN ☎(01) 6273333 42⇨🏠

CO KILKENNY

KILKENNY
Map 01 C3

Kilkenny ☎(056) 22125
One of Ireland's most pleasant inland courses, noted for
its tricky finishing holes and its par threes. Features of
the course are its long 11th and 13th holes and the
challenge increases year by year as thousands of trees
planted over the last 30 years or so are maturing. As host
of the Kilkenny Scratch Cup annually, the course is
permanently maintained in championship condition. The
Irish Dunlop Tournament and the Irish Professional
Matchplay Championship have also been held here.
18 holes, 5824mtrs, Par 71, SSS 70, Course record 65.
Club membership 1000.

Visitors	restricted weekends & Tue. Must contact in advance.
Societies	must contact in advance.
Green Fees	IR£12 per day (IR£15 weekends).
Facilities	⊗ ⅏ 🏌 ⚐ ♀ 🏠 ☂ ⚑ Noel Leahy.
Leisure	snooker.
Location	Glendine (1m from centre on Castlecomer road)
Hotel	★★★70% Hotel Kilkenny, College Rd, KILKENNY ☎(056) 62000 60⇨🏠

CO LAOIS

MOUNTRATH   Map 01 C3

Mountrath ☎(0502) 32558
Small picturesque course at the foot of the Slieve Bloom
Mountains in central Ireland. At the time of going to press,
the course was in the process of being extended to 18 holes.
9 holes, 4634mtrs, Par 68, SSS 66, Course record 65.
Club membership 300.

Visitors	no restrictions.
Societies	must contact in advance.
Green Fees	IR£6 per day.
Facilities	ⓧ ⛳ 🍴 🏌
Location	Knockanina (1.5m from town on Dublin-Limerick road)
Hotel	★★★60% Killeshin Hotel, Dublin Rd, PORTLAOISE ☎(0502) 21663 44

PORTARLINGTON   Map 01 C3

Portarlington ☎Portlaoise (0502) 23115
Lovely parkland course beside the River Barrow and
surrounded by 10, 000 trees.
9 holes, 5264mtrs, Par 68, SSS 68.
Club membership 400.

Visitors	must be accompanied by member, contact in advance and have an introduction from own club.
Societies	must contact in writing.
Green Fees	£IR8 (£IR10 weekends).
Facilities	ⓧ ⛳ & 🍴 by prior arrangement ♀ 🏌
Location	Garryhinch (4m from town on Mountmellick road)
Hotel	★★★59% Hotel Montague, EMO ☎(0502) 26154 80

PORTLAOISE   Map 01 C3

The Heath ☎(0502) 46533
One of the oldest clubs in Ireland. The course is set in pretty
countryside and offers a good challenge.
18 holes, 5721mtrs, Par 71, SSS 70.

Visitors	preferred on weekdays.
Green Fees	IR£8 (IR£12 weekends).
Facilities	ⓧ ⛳ ♀ 🍴 Eddie Doyle.
Location	5m NE
Hotel	★★★60% Killeshin Hotel, Dublin Rd, PORTLAOISE ☎(0502) 21663 44

CO LEITRIM

BALLINAMORE   Map 01 C4

Ballinamore ☎(078) 44346
A very dry and very testing 9-hole parkland course along the
Ballinamore/Ballyconnell Canal.
9 holes, 5680yds, Par 68, SSS 66, Course record 68.
Club membership 100.

Visitors	restricted occasionally. Must contact in advance.

Societies	must contact in writing.
Green Fees	IR£5 per day.
Facilities	⛳ 🍴 ♀ 🏌
Leisure	fishing.
Hotel	Slieve Russell Hotel, BALLYCONNELL ☎(049) 26444 140

CO LIMERICK

LIMERICK   Map 01 B3

Castletroy ☎(061) 335753
Parkland course with out of bounds on the left of the first two
holes. The long par five 10th features a narrow entrance to a
green guarded by a stream. The par three 13th has a
panoramic view of the course and surrounding countryside
from the tee and the 18th is a daunting finish, with the drive
played towards a valley with the ground rising towards the
green which is protected on both sides by bunkers. In recent
years the club has hosted the finals of the Irish Mixed
Foursomes and the Senior Championships.
18 holes, 5793mtrs, Par 71, SSS 71.
Club membership 1020.

Visitors	may not play Sun or 1-2.30pm weekdays. Must contact in advance and have an introduction from own club.
Societies	must contact in advance.
Green Fees	IR£20 per day.
Facilities	ⓧ ⛳ 🍴 ♀ 🏌 📷 ⚑ Noel Cassidy.
Leisure	snooker.
Location	Castletroy (3m from city on Dublin road)
Hotel	★★★ Jurys Hotel, Ennis Rd, LIMERICK ☎(061) 327777 95

Limerick ☎(061) 414083
Tree-lined parkland course which hosted the 1991 Ladies
Senior Interprovincial matches. The club are the only Irish
winners of the European Cup Winners Team Championship.
18 holes, 5890mtrs, Par 72, SSS 71, Course record 69.
Club membership 1067.

Visitors	may not play after 4pm or on Tue & weekends.
Societies	must contact in writing.
Green Fees	IR£20.
Facilities	ⓧ ⛳ 🍴 ♀ 🏌 📷 ⚑ John Cassidy.
Leisure	snooker.
Location	Ballyclough (3m S on Fedamore road)
Hotel	★★★ Jurys Hotel, Ennis Rd, LIMERICK ☎(061) 327777 95

CO LOUTH

ARDEE   Map 01 C4

Ardee ☎(041) 53227
Pleasant parkland course with mature trees and a stream.
18 holes, 6100yds, Par 69, SSS 69.

Visitors	may normally play on weekdays (except Wed).
Green Fees	IR£12.
Facilities	⛳ ⛳ ♀

►

Location	Townparks
Hotel	★★★68% Ballymascanlon House Hotel, DUNDALK ☎(042) 71124 36⇄

Facilities	⊗ ⅷ ㏇ ▣ ♀ ⏚
Hotel	★★★68% Ballymascanlon House Hotel, DUNDALK ☎(042) 71124 36⇄

BALTRAY — Map 01 D4

County Louth ☎Drogheda (041) 22329

Generally held to have the best greens in Ireland, this links course was designed by Tom Simpson to have well guarded and attractive greens without being overly dependant on bunkers. It provides a good test for the modern champion, notably as the annual venue for the East of Ireland Amateur Open.

18 holes, 6577yds, Par 73, SSS 72, Course record 65.
Club membership 870.

	SCORECARD: White Tees				
Hole	Yds	Par	Hole	Yds	Par
1	423	4	10	388	4
2	476	5	11	476	5
3	534	5	12	410	4
4	334	4	13	408	4
5	148	3	14	322	4
6	521	5	15	142	3
7	153	3	16	375	4
8	397	4	17	169	3
9	409	4	18	492	5
Out	3395	37	In	3182	36
			Totals	6577	73

Visitors	must have a handicap certificate. Must contact in advance.
Societies	must contact in writing.
Green Fees	IR£25 (IR£35 weekends).
Facilities	⊗ ⅷ ㏇ ▣ ♀ ⏚ 🗄 ⋈ ℓ Paddy McGuirk.
Leisure	snooker.
Location	5m NE of Drogheda
Hotel	★★★63% Boyne Valley Hotel, DROGHEDA ☎(041) 37737 35⇄🏌

DUNDALK — Map 01 D4

Dundalk

A tricky course with extensive views.
18 holes, 6115mtrs, Par 72, SSS 68.

Visitors	may not play Tue or Sun. Must contact in advance.
Green Fees	IR£15 (IR£18 weekends).
Facilities	⊗ ⅷ ▣ ♀
Leisure	sauna.
Location	4km S on coast road
Hotel	★★★68% Ballymascanlon House Hotel, DUNDALK ☎(042) 71124 36⇄

GREENORE — Map 01 D4

Greenore ☎Dundalk (042) 73212

Situated amidst beautiful scenery on the shores of Carlingford Lough, the trees here are an unusual feature on a links course. There are quite a number of water facilities, tight fairways and very good greens.
18 holes, Par 71, SSS 71, Course record 68.
Club membership 500.

Visitors	must contact in advance at weekends. A letter of introduction is desirable, but not essential.
Societies	must contact in writing well in advance.
Green Fees	IR£8 per round (IR£14 weekends & bank holidays).

✤ CO MAYO ✤

BALLINROBE — Map 01 B4

Ballinrobe ☎(092) 41448

Mainly flat terrain with some very interesting features. Although no other club plays on the course, its landlords, The Ballinrobe Race Company, hold races there five or six times a year.
9 holes, 5790yds, Par 72, SSS 68, Course record 67.
Club membership 250.

Visitors	may not play on Tue after 5pm or on Sun.
Societies	must contact in advance.
Green Fees	IR£6 per day.
Facilities	ⅷ ㏇ & ▣ (summer only) ♀ (summer only) ⏚
Leisure	snooker.
Location	Castlebar Rd
Hotel	★★★ Breaffy House Hotel, CASTLEBAR ☎(094) 22033 40⇄

BALLYHAUNIS — Map 01 B4

Ballyhaunis ☎(0907) 30014

Undulating parkland course with 9 holes, 10 greens and 18 tees.
18 holes, 5393mtrs, Par 69, SSS 68.
Club membership 185.

Visitors	may not play Thu & Sun. Must contact in advance.
Societies	must contact in advance.
Green Fees	IR£5 per day.
Facilities	catering & bar by arrangement ⏚
Location	Coolnaha
Hotel	★★★ Breaffy House Hotel, CASTLEBAR ☎(094) 22033 40⇄

CASTLEBAR — Map 01 B4

Castlebar ☎(094) 21649

Pleasant parkland course with a particularly interesting 9th hole.
18 holes, Par 71.

Visitors	are preferred to play on weekdays.
Green Fees	IR£10.
Facilities	⊗ ㏇ ♀ 🍴
Location	Rocklands (1m from town on Belcarra road)
Hotel	★★★ Breaffy House Hotel, CASTLEBAR ☎(094) 22033 40⇄

We make every effort to ensure that our information is accurate but details may change after we go to print

KEEL   Map 01 A4

Achill ☎(098) 43202
Seaside links in a scenic location on the edge of the Atlantic Ocean.
9 holes, 2723yds, Par 70, SSS 66, Course record 58.
Club membership 50.
Visitors	no restrictions.
Societies	must telephone in advance.
Green Fees	IR£3 per day.
Facilities	⬛ 🏌 ⛳
Location	Achill, Westport
Hotel	★★★♨75% Newport House Hotel, NEWPORT ☎(098) 41222 & 41154 24⇨📶Annexe10⇨📶

SWINFORD   Map 01 B4

Swinford ☎(094) 51378
A pleasant parkland course with good views of the beautiful surrounding countryside.
9 holes, 5901yds, Par 70, SSS 68, Course record 70.
Club membership 137.
Visitors	no restrictions.
Societies	must contact in writing.
Green Fees	IR£5 per day.
Facilities	⬛ (evenings only) ♈ (evenings only) 🏌
Leisure	squash, fishing, riding, snooker.
Location	Brabazon Park
Hotel	★★★ Breaffy House Hotel, CASTLEBAR ☎(094) 22033 40⇨

WESTPORT   Map 01 A4

Westport ☎(098) 25113
This is a beautiful course with wonderful views of Clew Bay, with its 365 islands, and the holy mountain called Croagh Patrick, famous for the annual pilgrimage to its summit. Golfers indulge in a different kind of penance on this challenging course with many memorable holes. Perhaps the most exciting is the par five 15th, 580 yards long and featuring a long carry from the tee over an inlet of Clew Bay.

SCORECARD: White Tees					
Hole	Yds	Par	Hole	Yds	Par
1	348	4	10	517	5
2	343	4	11	433	4
3	162	3	12	220	3
4	501	5	13	455	4
5	356	4	14	189	3
6	453	4	15	580	5
7	524	5	16	363	4
8	468	4	17	316	4
9	202	3	18	520	5
Out	3357	36	In	3593	37
			Totals	6950	73

18 holes, 6959yds, Par 73, SSS 73, Course record 68.
Club membership 650.
Visitors	may not play Wed 1.45-3pm, or Sat & Sun 8-10am & 1-3pm. Must have an introduction from own club.
Societies	must write for application form.
Green Fees	Apr-1 Oct: IR£15 (IR£18 weekends);2 Oct-Mar: IR£12 (IR£15 weekends).
Facilities	⊗ �𝄆 🏌 ⬛ ♈ 🏌 📶 🏌 ⎩ Alex Mealia.
Location	Carrowholly
Hotel	★★★61% Hotel Westport, WESTPORT ☎(098) 25122 49⇨📶

CO MEATH

BETTYSTOWN   Map 01 D4

Laytown & Bettystown ☎(041) 27170
A very competitive and trying links course, home of famous golfer, Des Smyth.
18 holes, 5652mtrs.
Club membership 950.
Visitors	may not play 1-2pm. Must contact in advance.
Societies	must contact in writing.
Green Fees	IR£15 per day (IR£20 weekends).
Facilities	⊗ �𝄆 🏌 ⬛ ♈ 🏌 📶 🏌 ⎩ Robert J Browne.
Leisure	tennis courts, snooker.
Hotel	★★★63% Boyne Valley Hotel, DROGHEDA ☎(041) 37737 35⇨📶

DUNSHAUGHLIN   Map 01 C4

Black Bush ☎(01) 250021
Recently constructed 18-hole course in lovely parkland, with a lake providing a hazard at the 1st. The 9-hole course is less of a challenge.
18 holes, 6930yds, Par 72, SSS 73.
Visitors	may not play Tue afternoons.
Green Fees	IR£12 (IR£14 weekends).
Facilities	⊗ �𝄆 🏌 ♈
Location	Thomastown (1.5m from village on Dublin-Navan road)
Hotel	★★★71% Ashling Hotel, Parkgate St, DUBLIN 8 ☎(01) 772324 56⇨📶

KELLS   Map 01 C4

Headfort ☎(046) 40146
A delightful parkland course which is regarded as one of the best of its kind in Ireland. There are ample opportunities for birdies, but even if these are not achieved, Headfort provides for a most pleasant game.

SCORECARD: White Tees					
Hole	Yds	Par	Hole	Yds	Par
1	479	5	10	187	3
2	189	3	11	537	5
3	389	4	12	374	4
4	488	5	13	384	4
5	433	4	14	187	3
6	419	4	15	296	4
7	477	5	16	409	4
8	158	3	17	357	4
9	348	4	18	369	4
Out	3380	37	In	3100	35
			Totals	6480	72

18 holes, 6480yds, Par 72, SSS 70, Course record 65.
Club membership 650.
Visitors	must contact in advance.
Societies	must contact in writing.
Green Fees	IR£10 (IR£15 weekends).
Facilities	🏌 ⬛ ♈ 🏌 📶 ⎩ Brendan McGovern.
Hotel	★★ Conyngham Arms Hotel, SLANE ☎(041) 24155 16rm(15⇨📶)

Opening times of bar and catering facilities vary from place to place. Please remember to check in advance of your visit

NAVAN   Map 01 C4

Royal Tara ☎(046) 25244
Pleasant parkland course offering plenty of variety. Situated close to the Hill of Tara, the ancient seat of the Kings of Ireland.
18 holes, 5757mtrs, Par 71, SSS 70.

Visitors	preferred Mon, Thu & Fri.
Green Fees	IR£12 (IR£15 weekends & bank holidays).
Facilities	⊗ ⊪ ⊾ ♀ 🖿 ⚐ ⚑ Adam Whiston.
Location	Bellinter (6m from town on N3)
Hotel	★★ Conyngham Arms Hotel, SLANE ☎(041) 24155 16rm(15⇨🛏)

CO MONAGHAN

CARRICKMACROSS   Map 01 C4

Nuremore ☎Dundalk (042) 61438
Picturesque parkland course of championship length which offers an excellent test of golf.
18 holes, 6246mtrs, Par 72, SSS 73, Course record 69.
Club membership 275.

Visitors	restricted for short periods at weekends.
Societies	must contact in advance.
Green Fees	IR£12 per day (IR£15 weekends & bank holidays).
Facilities	⊗ ⊪ ⊾ ⚐ ♀ 🛆 🖿 ⚐ 🖛 ⚑ Maurice Cassidy.
Leisure	grass tennis courts, heated indoor swimming pool, squash, fishing, snooker, sauna, solarium, gymnasium.
Location	S on Dublin road
Hotel	★★★68% Ballymascanlon House Hotel, DUNDALK ☎(042) 71124 36⇨

CASTLEBLAYNEY   Map 01 C4

Castleblayney ☎(042) 40197
Scenic course on Muckno Park estate, adjacent to Muckno Lake and Blayney Castle.
9 holes, 5345yds, Par 68, SSS 66, Course record 68.
Club membership 175.

Visitors	may not play during competitions.
Societies	must contact in advance.
Green Fees	IR£4 per day (IR£5 weekends & bank holidays).
Facilities	🛆
Leisure	hard tennis courts.
Location	Onomy
Hotel	★★★68% Ballymascanlon House Hotel, DUNDALK ☎(042) 71124 36⇨

Each golf-course entry has a recommended AA-appointed hotel. For a wider choice of places to stay, consult *AA Hotels and Restaurants in Britain and Ireland* and *AA Inspected Bed and Breakfast in Britain and Ireland*

MONAGHAN   Map 01 C5

Rossmore ☎(047) 81316
An undulating parkland course amidst beautiful countryside. At the time of going to press the course was being extended from 9 to 18 holes, the design commissioned from Des Smyth Golf Design.
18 holes, 6000yds, Par 70, SSS 68, Course record 66.
Club membership 350.

Visitors	may not play on competition days.
Societies	must contact in writing.
Green Fees	IR£8 (IR£10 weekends).
Facilities	⊗ ⊪ ⊾ ⚐ ♀ 🛆
Leisure	snooker.
Location	Rossmore Park (2m S on Cootehill road)
Hotel	★★51% Ortine Hotel, LISNASKEA ☎(03657) 21206 18⇨🛏

CO OFFALY

BIRR   Map 01 C3

Birr ☎(0509) 20082
The course has been laid out over undulating parkland utilising the natural contours of the land, which were created during the ice age. The sandy sub-soil means that the course is playable all year round.
18 holes, 6262yds, Par 70, SSS 70, Course record 64.
Club membership 450.

Visitors	may not play on Sun except 11am-noon; some restrictions on Sat.
Societies	must contact in writing.
Green Fees	IR£10 per day (IR£10 per round weekends).
Facilities	⊗ & ⊪ by prior arrangement ⊾ ⚐ ♀ 🛆
Location	Glenns
Hotel	★★65% County Arms Hotel, BIRR ☎(0509) 20791 20193 18⇨🛏

EDENDERRY   Map 01 C4

Edenderry ☎(0405) 31072
A most friendly club which offers a relaxing game in pleasant surroundings. At the time of going to press, the course was being extended to 18 holes and it is expected to be ready, albeit with temporary greens, by mid 1992.
9 holes, 6047yds, Par 71, SSS 69, Course record 64.
Club membership 350.

Visitors	restricted Thu & weekends.
Societies	may not play on Thu & Sun; must contact the secretary in writing.
Green Fees	IR£5 (IR£6 weekends).
Facilities	⊗ ⊪ ⊾ ♀ 🛆
Leisure	pool table.
Hotel	★★ Curryhills House Hotel, PROSPEROUS ☎(045) 68150 10⇨🛏

For a full range of AA guides and maps, visit your local AA shop or any good bookshop

TULLAMORE   Map 01 C4

Tullamore ☎(0506) 21439
Well-wooded parkland course.
18 holes, 6314yds, Par 71, SSS 70, Course record 64.
Club membership 950.
Visitors   restricted on Tue & at weekends. Must contact in advance.
Societies   must contact in writing.
Green Fees   IR£10 (IR£12 weekends).
Facilities   ⊗ & ⊪ by prior arrangement ⌧ ⬛ ♀ ♨ 🏠 ⊪ (John E Kelly.
Location   Brookfield (2.5m SW on Kinnity road)
Hotel   ★★★63% Prince Of Wales Hotel, ATHLONE ☎(0902) 72626 72⇥🛏

CO ROSCOMMON

ATHLONE   Map 01 C4

Athlone ☎(0902) 92073
A picturesque course with a panoramic view of Lough Ree. Overall, it is a tight, difficult course with some outstanding holes and is noted for its magnificent greens.
18 holes, 5529mtrs, Par 69, SSS 67, Course record 63.
Club membership 750.
Visitors   may not play on Sun & competition days.
Societies   must contact in advance.
Green Fees   IR£10 per round.
Facilities   ⊗ ⊪ ⌧ ⬛ ♀ ♨ 🏠 ⊪ (Martin Quinn.
Leisure   snooker.
Location   Hodson Bay (4m from town beside Lough Ree)
Hotel   ★★★63% Prince Of Wales Hotel, ATHLONE ☎(0902) 72626 72⇥🛏

BOYLE   Map 01 B4

Boyle
Situated on a low hill and surrounded by beautiful scenery, this is an undemanding course where, due to the generous fairways and semi-rough, the leisure golfer is likely to finish the round with the same golf ball.
9 holes, 5324yds, Par 67, SSS 66, Course record 65.
Club membership 260.
Visitors   no restrictions.
Societies   must contact in writing.
Green Fees   IR£6-10.
Facilities   ⌧ ⬛ ♀ ♨ ⊪
Location   Roscommon Rd
Hotel   ★★62% Royal Hotel, BOYLE ☎(079) 62016 16⇥🛏

CARRICK-ON-SHANNON   Map 01 B4

Carrick-on-Shannon ☎(079) 67015
A pleasant 9-hole course overlooking the River Shannon.
9 holes, 5545mtrs, Par 70, SSS 68.
Club membership 200.
Visitors   restricted on competition days & some Sun.
Societies   must contact in advance.
Green Fees   IR£6 per day.
Facilities   ⌧ ⬛ ♀ ♨ ⊪
Leisure   snooker.

Location   Woodbrook (4m W beside N4)
Hotel   ★★62% Royal Hotel, BOYLE ☎(079) 62016 16⇥🛏

CO SLIGO

ENNISCRONE   Map 01 B5

Enniscrone ☎(096) 36297
In a magnificent situation with breathtaking views of mountain, sea and rolling countryside, this course offers some unforgettable golf. It has been designated by the Golfing Union of Ireland as suitable for major national and provincial championships and offers an exciting challenge among its splendid sandhills. A particularly favourite hole is the tenth, with a marvellous view from the elevated tee and the chance of a birdie with an accurate drive.

SCORECARD: White Tees					
Hole	Yds	Par	Hole	Yds	Par
1	551	5	10	338	4
2	525	5	11	430	4
3	395	4	12	510	5
4	524	5	13	202	3
5	170	3	14	368	4
6	356	4	15	412	4
7	359	4	16	373	4
8	165	3	17	147	3
9	345	4	18	400	4
Out	3390	37	In	3180	35
			Totals	6570	72

18 holes, 6570yds, Par 72, SSS 72.
Club membership 700.
Visitors   may not play before 10.30am or between 1.30 & 3pm on Sun.
Societies   must telephone (096) 36335 in advance.
Green Fees   IR£15 per day Apr-Oct; IR£12 per day Nov, Feb & Mar; IR£10 per day Dec-Jan.
Facilities   ⊗ ⊪ ⌧ ⬛ ♀ ♨ 🏠 ⊪
Location   0.5m S on Ballina road
Hotel   ★★★59% Downhill Hotel, BALLINA ☎(096) 21033 51⇥🛏

SLIGO   Map 01 B5

County Sligo ☎(071) 77134
Now considered to be one of the top links courses in Ireland, County Sligo is host to a number of competitions, including the West of Ireland Championships. Set in an elevated position on cliffs above three large beaches, the prevailing winds provide an additional challenge.
18 holes, 6003mtrs, Par 71, SSS 72, Course record 66.
Club membership 930.
Visitors   must contact in advance.
Societies   must contact in writing & pay a deposit.
Green Fees   IR£20 per round.
Facilities   ⊗ ⊪ ⌧ ⬛ ♀ ♨ 🏠 ⊪ (Leslie Robinson.
Location   Rosse Point
Hotel   ★★★68% Ballincar House Hotel, Rosses Point Rd, SLIGO ☎(071) 45361 26⇥🛏

Strandhill ☎(071) 68188
This scenic course is situated between Knocknarea Mountain and the Atlantic, offering golf in its most natural form amid the sand dunes of the West of Ireland. The 1st, 16th and 18th are par 4 holes over 364 metres in length; the 2nd and 17th are testing par 3s which vary according to the prevailing wind; the par 4 13th is a testing dog-leg right. This is a course where accuracy will be rewarded.
18 holes, 5045mtrs, Par 69, SSS 68.

▶

Visitors	preferred on weekdays, except Thu.
Green Fees	IR£10 (IR£12 weekends).
Facilities	⊗ �𝕝 by prior arrangement ⿱ ⵧ
Location	Strandhill (5m from town)
Hotel	★★★68% Ballincar House Hotel, Rosses Point Rd, SLIGO ☎(071) 45361 26⇔⋔

CO TIPPERARY

CLONMEL   Map 01 C2

Clonmel ☎(052) 24050
Set in the scenic, wooded slopes of the Comeragh Mountains, this is a testing course with lots of open space and plenty of interesting features. It provides an enjoyable round in exceptionally tranquil surroundings.
18 holes, 5806mtrs, Par 71, SSS 70, Course record 64.
Club membership 650.

Visitors	may not play at weekends & bank holidays. Must contact in advance.
Societies	must contact in writing.
Green Fees	IR£10 per day (IR£12 weekends).
Facilities	⊗ �𝕝 ⿱ ⬛ ⵧ △ ⿴ ⵧ ₡ Robert Hayes.
Leisure	snooker, pool table, table tennis.
Location	Lyreanearla, Mountain Rd
Hotel	★★★75% Minella Hotel, CLONMEL ☎(052) 22388 & 22717 43⇔⋔

NENAGH   Map 01 B3

Nenagh ☎(067) 31476
Interesting gradients call for some careful approach shots. Some magnificent views.
18 holes, 5996yds, Par 69, SSS 68.

Visitors	preferred weekdays.
Green Fees	IR£12 (IR£10 Sat & Wed; IR£15 Sun & bank holidays).
Facilities	⿱ ⵧ ⿴ ⵧ ₡ John Coyle.
Location	Graigue (At Beechwood, 5m from town)
Hotel	★★★63% Castle Oaks House Hotel, CASTLECONNELL ☎(061) 377666 11⇔⋔

TEMPLEMORE   Map 01 C3

Templemore ☎(0504) 31400
Parkland course with newly planted trees which offers a pleasant test to visitors without being too difficult. Walking is level too.
9 holes, Par 68, SSS 67, Course record 68.
Club membership 220.

Visitors	may not play on Sun during Special Events & Open weeks.
Societies	must contact in advance.
Green Fees	IR£6 per day.
Facilities	⬛ by prior arrangement ⵧ △
Location	Manna South (0.5m S)
Hotel	★★69% Leix County Hotel, BORRIS-IN-OSSORY ☎(0505) 41213 19⇔

If you know of a golf course which welcomes visitors and is not already in this guide, we should be grateful for information

THURLES   Map 01 C3

Thurles ☎(0504) 21983
Superb parkland course with a difficult finish at the 18th.
18 holes, 6456yds, Par 71, SSS 71.

Visitors	preferred on Mon, Wed, Thu & Fri.
Green Fees	IR£10 (IR£13 weekends).
Facilities	⊗ ⿱ ⵧ ⿴ ⵧ ₡ Sean Hunt.
Location	1m from town on Cork road
Hotel	★★★★66% Cashel Palace Hotel, CASHEL ☎(062) 61411 20⇔

CO WATERFORD

LISMORE   Map 01 C2

Lismore ☎(058) 54026
Scenic inland parkland course with mature deciduous trees.
9 holes, 5196mtrs, Par 69, SSS 67, Course record 65.
Club membership 250.

Visitors	may not play Wed & Sun.
Societies	must telephone in advance to play on weekdays (contact in writing for weekends).
Green Fees	IR£8 per day.
Facilities	⿱ & ⬛ (summer & weekends only) ⵧ (summer/weekends) △
Location	Ballyin
Hotel	★★50% Ballyrafter House Hotel, LISMORE ☎(058) 54002 12rm(4⇔)

TRAMORE   Map 01 C2

Tramore ☎(051) 86170
This course has matured nicely over the years to become a true championship test and has been chosen as the venue for the Irish Professional Matchplay Championship and the Irish Amateur Championship. Most of the fairways are lined by evergreen trees, calling for accurate placing of shots, and the course is continuing to develop.
18 holes, 6660yds, Par 72, SSS 71.

Visitors	preferred on weekdays.
Green Fees	IR£16 (IR£20 weekends).
Facilities	⊗ ⿱ ⵧ ⿴ ⵧ ₡ Paul McDaid.
Location	Newtown Hill
Hotel	★★★★79% Waterford Castle Hotel, The Island, WATERFORD ☎(051) 78203 19⇔⋔

WATERFORD   Map 01 C2

Waterford ☎(051) 78489
Undulating parkland course in pleasant surroundings.
18 holes, 6237yds, Par 71, SSS 70.

Visitors	preferred on weekdays.
Green Fees	IR£14 (IR£17 weekdays & bank holidays).
Facilities	⊗ ⿱ ⵧ ⿴ ⵧ ₡ E Condon.
Location	Newrath (1m N)
Hotel	★★★59% Jurys Hotel, Ferrybank, WATERFORD ☎(051) 32111 98⇔⋔

CO WESTMEATH

MULLINGAR
Map 01 C4

Mullingar ☎(044) 48366
The wide rolling fairways between mature trees provide parkland golf at its very best. The course, designed by the great James Braid, offers a tough challenge and annually hosts one of the most important amateur events in the British Isles - the Mullingar Scratch Cup. It has also been the venue of the Irish Professional Championship. One advantage of the layout is that the clubhouse is never far away.
18 holes, 6451yds, Par 72, SSS 71.

Visitors	preferred on weekdays, except Wed.
Green Fees	IR£12 (IR£8 weekends).
Facilities	⊗ ⅲ ⅙ ♀ ⌂ ⅎ Ⅽ John Burns.
Location	3m W
Hotel	★★★63% Prince Of Wales Hotel, ATHLONE ☎(0902) 72626 72⇔🏠

CO WEXFORD

ENNISCORTHY
Map 01 D3

Enniscorthy ☎(054) 33191
A pleasant course suitable for all levels of ability.
18 holes, 5382mtrs, Par 70.
Club membership 650.

Visitors	preferred on weekdays. Must contact in advance.
Societies	must book in advance.
Green Fees	IR£8 (IR£10 weekends).
Facilities	⊗ ⅲ ⅙ ⅃ ♀ △ ⅎ
Leisure	snooker.
Location	Knockmarshall (2m from town on New Ross road)
Hotel	★★ Murphy-Flood's Hotel, ENNISCORTHY ☎(054) 33413 21rm(5⇔13🏠)

GOREY
Map 01 D3

Courtown ☎(055) 25166
A pleasant parkland course which is well wooded and enjoys views across the Irish Sea near Courtown Harbour.
18 holes, 5852mtrs, Par 71, SSS 70, Course record 67.
Club membership 700.

Visitors	may not play on major competition days or 5-7pm in Jul & Aug.
Societies	must contact in advance.
Green Fees	IR£11 (IR£15 weekends).
Facilities	⊗ & ⅲ (Jun-Aug) ⅙ ⅃ ♀ △ ⌂ ⅎ Ⅽ John Coone.
Location	Kiltennel (Off Courtown Road)
Hotel	★★★(red)🏠 Marlfield House Hotel, GOREY ☎(055) 21124 19⇔🏠

For an explanation of symbols and abbreviations, see page 32

ROSSLARE
Map 01 D2

Rosslare ☎(053) 32113
This traditional links course is within minutes of the ferry terminal at Rosslare, but its popularity is not confined to visitors from Fishguard or Le Havre. It is a great favourite with the Irish too. Many of the greens are sunken and are always in beautiful condition, but the semi-blind approaches are among features of this course which provide a healthy challenge.
18 holes, 6502yds, Par 74, SSS 71.

Visitors	preferred on weekdays, except Tue.
Green Fees	IR£15 (IR£20 weekends).
Facilities	⊗ ⅲ ⅙ ♀ ⌂ ⅎ Ⅽ Austin Skerrit.
Location	Rosslare Strand (Near the ferry terminal)
Hotel	★★★(red) Kelly's Strand Hotel, ROSSLARE ☎(053) 32114 Annexe96⇔🏠

A golf-course name printed in ***bold italics*** means that we have been unable to verify information with the club's management for the current year

WEXFORD   Map 01 D2

Wexford ☎(053) 42238
Parkland course with panoramic view of the Wexford
coastline and mountains.
18 holes, 6100yds, Par 71, SSS 69.
Club membership 800.

Visitors	may not play Thu & weekends. Must contact in advance.
Societies	must contact in writing.
Green Fees	IR£12 per day (IR£15 weekends).
Facilities	⬛ 🍺 🏌 🛎 (Gerry Royane.
Location	Mulgannon
Hotel	★★★70% Talbot Hotel, Trinity St, WEXFORD ☎(0530 22566 100⇨🛏
Additional hotel	★★64% Wexford Lodge Hotel, WEXFORD ☎(053) 23611 19⇨🛏

CO WICKLOW

ARKLOW   Map 01 D3

Arklow ☎(0402) 32492
Scenic links course.
18 holes, 5404mtrs, Par 68, SSS 67.

Visitors	may play Mon-Fri.
Green Fees	IR£10 (IR£12 weekends & bank holidays).
Facilities	⊗ 🏌 ⬛ 🍺
Location	Abbeylands (0.5m from town centre)
Hotel	★★★(red)🏵 Marlfield House Hotel, GOREY ☎(055) 21124 19⇨🛏

BLAINROE   Map 01 D3

Blainroe ☎(0404) 68168
Parkland course overlooking the sea on the east coast,
offering a challenging round to golfers of all abilities.
18 holes, 6159mtrs, Par 72, SSS 72.
Club membership 600.

Visitors	must contact in advance.
Societies	must apply in writing.
Green Fees	IR£14 (IR£19 weekends).
Facilities	⊗ 🏌 ⬛ 🍺 🛎 (John McDonald.
Hotel	★★★🏵74% Tinakilly House Hotel, RATHNEW ☎(0404) 69274 29⇨🛏

BLESSINGTON   Map 01 C3

Tulfarris Hotel & Country Club ☎Naas (045) 64574
Designed by Eddie Hachett, this course is on the Blessington
lakeshore with the Wicklow Mountains as a backdrop.
9 holes, 2806mtrs, Par 36, SSS 69, Course record 78.
Club membership 150.

Visitors	tee booking advisable; may not play Sun. Must contact in advance.
Societies	must contact in writing.
Green Fees	IR£10 per round (IR£12 weekends & bank holidays).
Facilities	⊗ 🏌 ⬛ 🍺 🏌 🛎 🏁
Leisure	hard tennis courts, heated indoor swimming pool, fishing, sauna, gymnasium.

Hotel	★★★63% Downshire House Hotel, BLESSINGTON ☎(045) 65199 14⇨🛏 Annexe11⇨🛏

BRAY   Map 01 D3

Old Conna ☎(01) 2826055
Fairly young but interesting course with a number of shots
across water.
18 holes, 6551yds, Par 72, SSS 71, Course record 72.
Club membership 550.

Visitors	may not play 12.30-2pm or at weekends. Must contact in advance.
Green Fees	IR£15.
Facilities	⊗ 🏌 ⬛ 🍺 🏌 🛎 🏁 (Niall Murray.
Leisure	snooker.
Location	Ferndale Rd
Hotel	★★63% Royal Hotel, Main St, BRAY ☎862935 70⇨🛏 Annexe70⇨🛏

Woodbrook ☎Dublin (01) 2824799
Pleasant parkland with magnificent views and bracing sea
breezes which has hosted a number of events, including the
Irish Close and the Irish Open Championships. A testing
finish is provided by an 18th hole with out of bounds on both
sides.
18 holes, 5996mtrs, Par 72, SSS 71, Course record 65.
Club membership 960.

Visitors	must contact in advance and have an introduction from own club.
Societies	must contact in advance.
Green Fees	IR£25 (IR£35 weekends).
Facilities	⊗ 🏌 ⬛ 🍺 🏌 🛎 🏁 (Billy Kinsella.
Leisure	snooker.
Location	Dublin Rd (11m S of Dublin on N11)
Hotel	★★63% Royal Hotel, Main St, BRAY ☎862935 70⇨🛏 Annexe70⇨🛏

DELGANY   Map 01 D3

Delgany ☎(01) 2874536
An undulating parkland course amidst beautiful scenery.
18 holes, 5414mtrs, Par 69, SSS 67.

Visitors	preferred on Mon, Thu & Fri.
Green Fees	IR£15 (IR£20 weekends & bank holidays).
Facilities	⊗ 🏌 ⬛ 🍺 🛎 🏁 (E Darcy.
Location	Greystones (0.75m from village)
Hotel	★★63% Royal Hotel, Main St, BRAY ☎862935 70⇨🛏 Annexe70⇨🛏

GREYSTONES   Map 01 D3

Greystones ☎(01) 876624
A part level and part hilly parkland course.
18 holes, 5401mtrs, Par 69, SSS 68, Course record 66.

Visitors	must contact in advance.
Green Fees	IR£16 (IR£20 weekends).
Hotel	★★★63% Downshire House Hotel, BLESSINGTON ☎(045) 65199 14⇨🛏 Annexe11⇨🛏

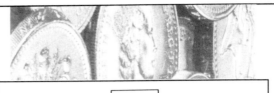

AA
BUDGET GUIDE
BRITAIN

In this new series, the AA's Budget Guide Britain breaks entirely fresh ground. Practical budgeting advice on planning your holiday is combined with a voyage of discovery.

The book covers eight regions, from the Scottish Highlands in the north to the Cornish peninsula in the far south-west. Insider information reveals unusual places to visit as well as familiar tourist attractions such as the Shakespeare country of the Midlands and the Georgian elegance of Bath.

Good value accommodation and eating out, money-saving tips, getting around by bus and train, local specialities and events, specially drawn location maps - all these and more are included in this wide-ranging guide which gives you all the information you need to plan and enjoy a stay in Britain.

Available at good bookshops and AA shops.

Another great guide from the AA

INDEX
TO COUNTIES
AND
GOLF COURSES

INDEX
TO COUNTIES

INDEX
TO COURSES

The first name is the name of the course or club; the second (*in italic*) is the name of the town under which the course or club appears in the gazetteer.

COMMENTS PLEASE

We try to tailor our books to meet our readers' needs. Your comments would help us keep in touch with what you find useful and interesting. Listed below are a few suggested headings under which you may like to comment. However, if you have any other observations or ideas please mention these too.

1 Are there any courses that we do not list at present which you feel warrant inclusion?

2 Are there any courses included in the book that you feel do not warrant listing and why?

3 If you stayed at a hotel we recommended with the course entry, did you find it convenient for the course, and of the expected standard?

4 Would you find it helpful for the distance between the recommended hotel and course to be shown?

5 Are there any further club facilities you would like to see mentioned?

_____

_____

_____

_____

_____

6 Are the course descriptions adequate or would you like to see more detail given?

_____

_____

_____

_____

7 Please indicate your usage of this guide

Usually linked to a business trip ☐

When holidaying ☐

General leisure ☐

8 How often do you play?

_____

9 Did you find the feature articles interesting?

Are there any further feature subjects which you would like to read about in the Guide?

_____

_____

_____

_____

▶

Follow the Country Code

Enjoy the countryside and
respect its life and work.

Guard against all risk of fire.

Fasten all gates.

Keep your dogs under close control.

Keep to public paths across farmland.

Use gates and stiles to cross
fences, hedges and walls.

Leave livestock, crops
and machinery alone.

Take your litter home.

Help to keep all water clean.

Protect wildlife, plants and trees.

Take special care on country roads.

Make no unnecessary noise.

10 If you have any further improvements that you would like to see incorporated in this book please list these below.

Name

Address

Signature

Date

The Editor
AA Guide to Golf Courses in Britain
The Automobile Association
Guidebooks Unit
Fanum House
Basingstoke
Hants
RG21 2EA

Opening doors to the World of books

**Book Tokens
can be bought and
exchanged at most bookshops**

Acknowledgements

The Automobile Association wishes to thank
the following for their assistance:

Paul Sheldon Photo Library for:-
St Andrews, pages 6 & 7
Doug Sanders, page 8
Max Faulkner, page 13
Alison Nicholas, page 26
Nick Faldo & Fanny Sunnesson,
page 26 & 27
Laura Davies, page 27
Dale Reid, page 28

Peter Dazeley Photo Library for:-
Sunningdale, page 5

Matthew Harris for:-
St Andrews, pages 8 & 9
Ballybunion, pages 10 & 11
Royal Troon, page 12

Northern Ireland Tourist Board for:-
Royal Portrush, pages 12 & 13

Mansell Collection Ltd for:-
Winston Churchill, page 9

John Ingham for:-
Bobby Jones, page 6

KEY TO ATLAS

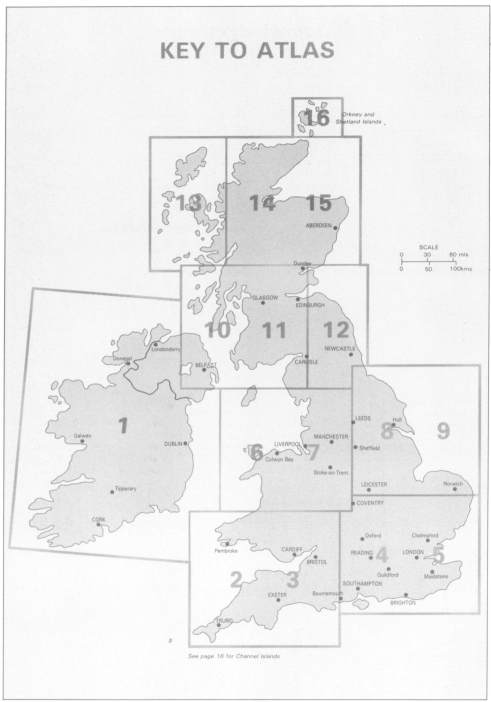

SCALE

| 0 | 30 | 60 mls |
| 0 | 50 | 100kms |

16 Orkney and Shetland Islands

13

14

15

ABERDEEN

Dundee

Glasgow

EDINBURGH

10

11

12

NEWCASTLE

Londonderry

Donegal

BELFAST

CARLISLE

LEEDS

Hull

8

9

Galway

1

MANCHESTER

Sheffield

Liverpool

6

7

DUBLIN

Colwyn Bay

Stoke-on-Trent

LEICESTER

Norwich

Tipperary

COVENTRY

CORK

Oxford

Chelmsford

Pembroke

CARDIFF

READING

4

LONDON

5

BRISTOL

Guildford

Maidstone

2

3

SOUTHAMPTON

EXETER

Bournemouth

BRIGHTON

TRURO

See page 16 for Channel Islands

© The Automobile Association

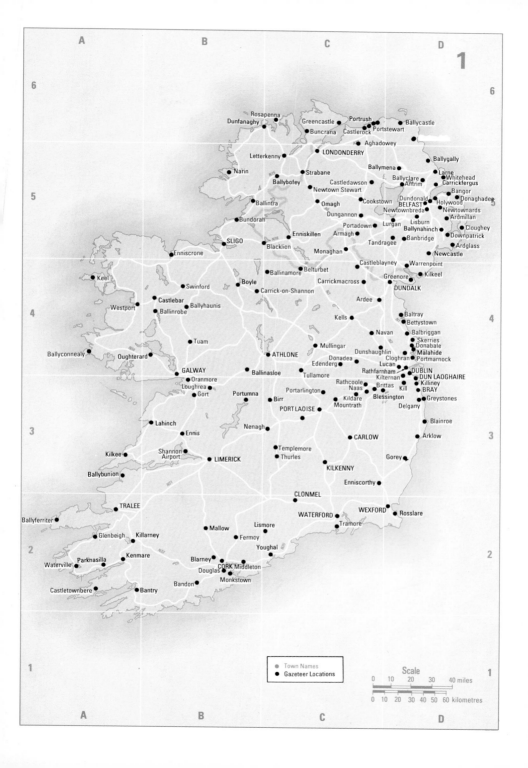

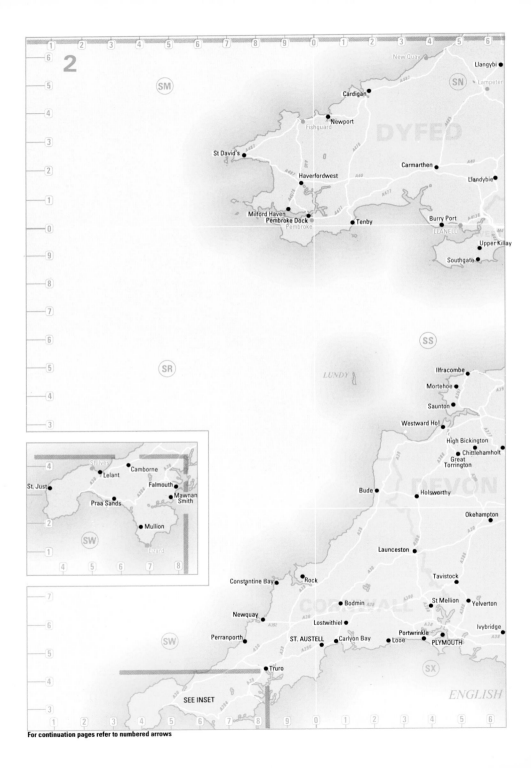

2

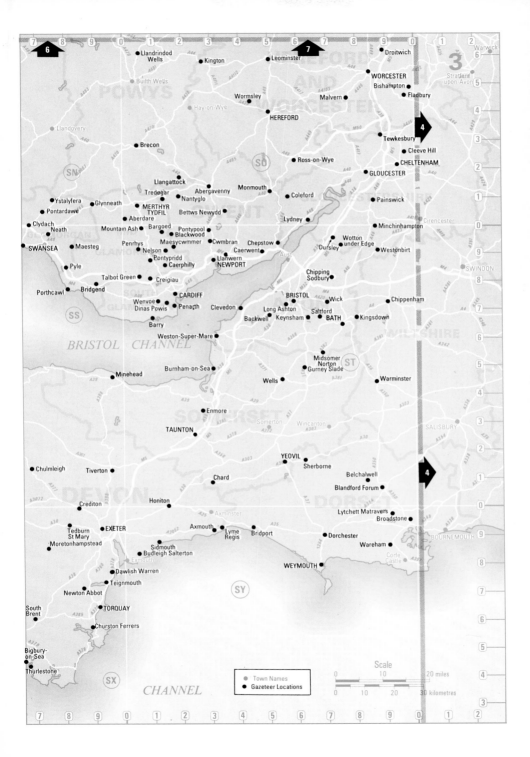

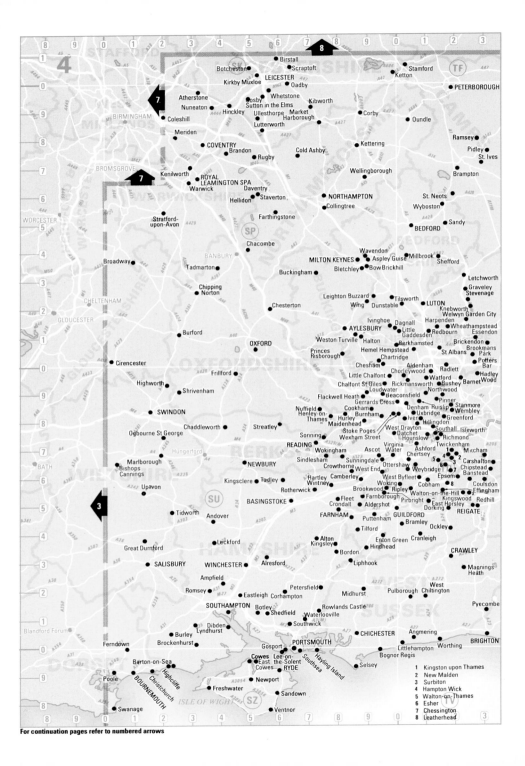

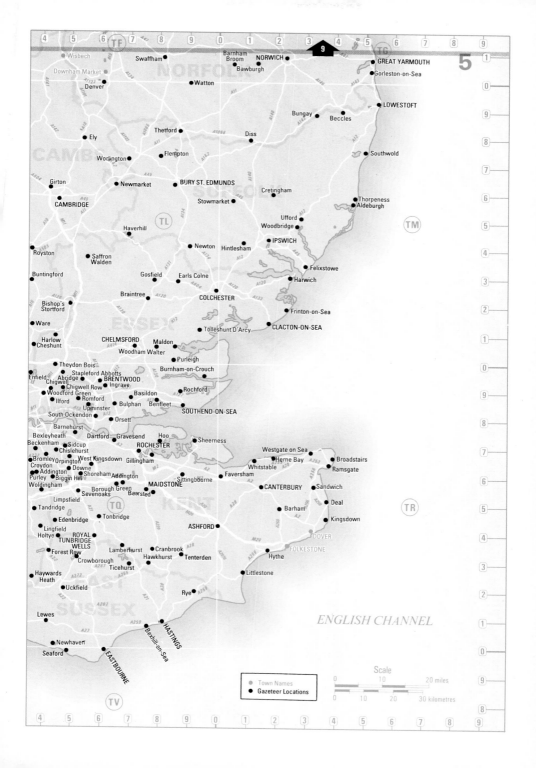

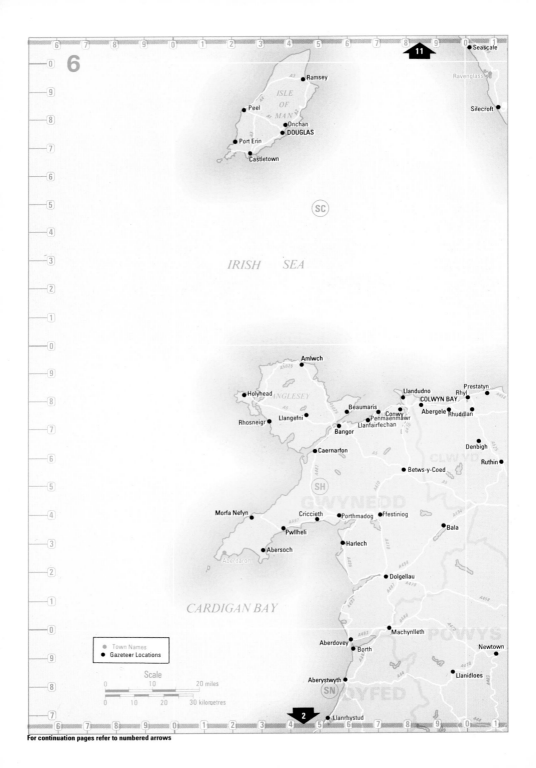

Seascale

11

Ravenglass

RAMSEY

A3

ISLE
OF
MAN

Peel

Silecroft

Onchan
DOUGLAS

A1

Port Erin

Castletown

SC

IRISH   SEA

Amlwch

A5025

Holyhead

ANGLESEY

A5

Llandudno

Prestatyn

COLWYN BAY

Rhyl

Beaumaris

Conwy

Abergele

Rhuddlan

Rhosneigr

Llangefni

Penmaenmawr

Bangor

Llanfairfechan

Denbigh

Caernarfon

CLWYD

Ruthin

A487

Betws-y-Coed

A5

SH

GWYNEDD

A494

Morfa Nefyn

Criccieth

Porthmadog

Ffestiniog

A4085

Pwllheli

A497

Harlech

A470

Bala

Abersoch

Aberdaron

Dolgellau

A470

A458

CARDIGAN   BAY

A493

Machynlleth

A470

POWYS

Aberdovey

Newtown

A483

Borth

SN

Llanidloes

Aberystwyth

A483

DYFED

2

Llanrhystud

A44

A4120

A470

Town Names
Gazeteer Locations

Scale
0   10   20 miles
0   10   20   30 kilometres

For continuation pages refer to numbered arrows

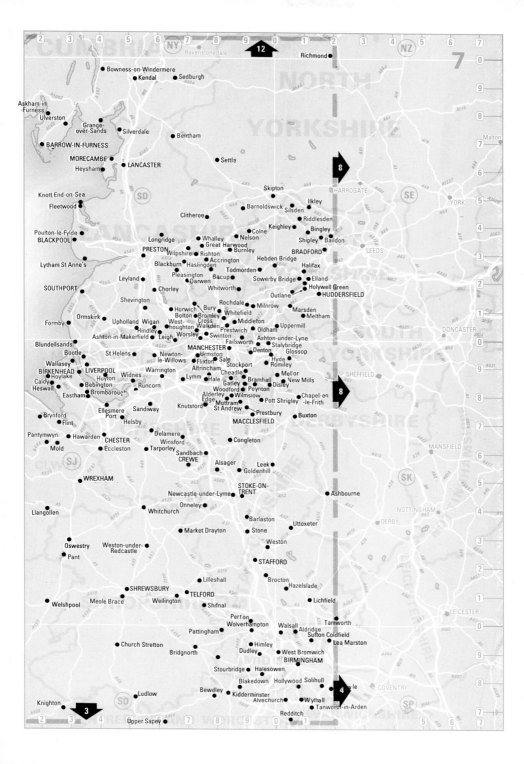

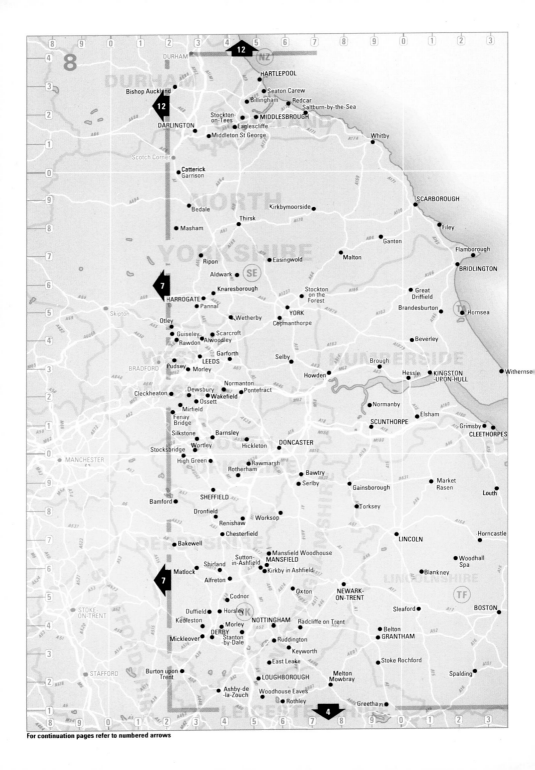

For continuation pages refer to numbered arrows

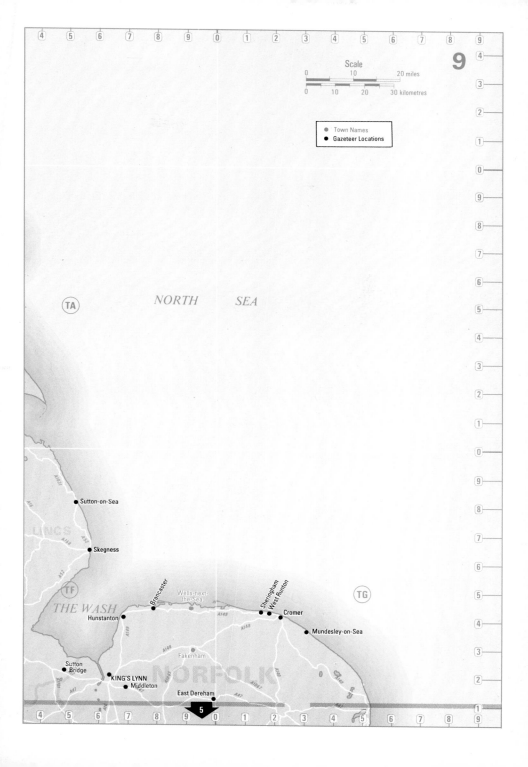

9

Scale

0   10   20 miles

0   10   20   30 kilometres

● Town Names
● Gazeteer Locations

TA

NORTH   SEA

● Sutton-on-Sea

● Skegness

THE WASH

TF

LINCS

● Brancaster

Wells-next-the-Sea

● Sheringham
● West Runton

● Cromer

TG

● Hunstanton

● Mundesley-on-Sea

Fakenham

Sutton
● Bridge

● KING'S LYNN
● Middleton

NORFOLK

● East Dereham

5

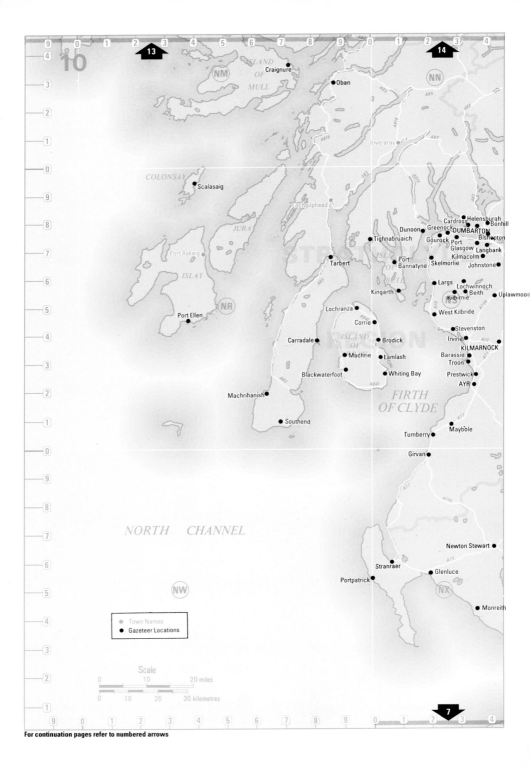

Town Names
Gazeteer Locations

Scale

0   10   20 miles
0   10   20   30 kilometres

For continuation pages refer to numbered arrows

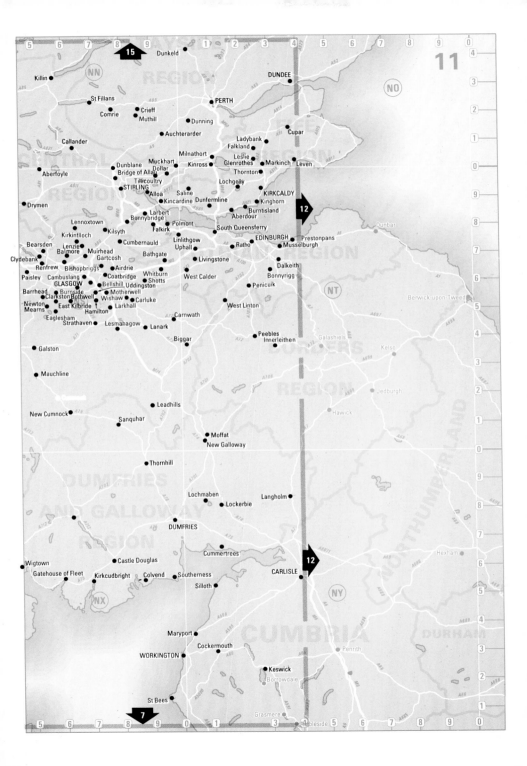

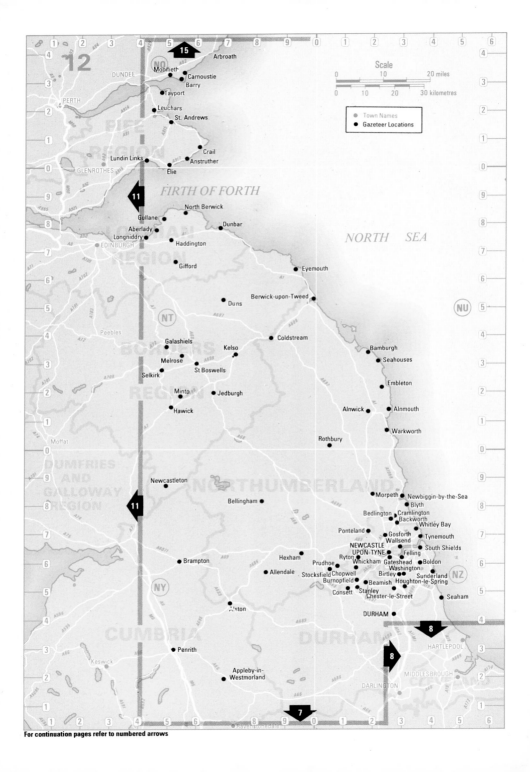

12

Scale

Town Names
Gazeteer Locations

NO
15
Arbroath
Monifieth
Carnoustie
Barry
Tayport
Leuchars
St. Andrews
DUNDEE
PERTH
FIFE
REGION
GLENROTHES
Lundin Links
Crail
Anstruther
Elie

11
FIRTH OF FORTH

North Berwick
Gullane
Aberlady
Longniddry
Dunbar
Haddington
EDINBURGH
REGION
Gifford
NORTH SEA
NU

Eyemouth

Peebles
NT
Duns
Berwick-upon-Tweed

BORDERS
Galashiels
Melrose
Selkirk
Kelso
St Boswells
Coldstream
Bamburgh
Seahouses

REGION
Minto
Jedburgh
Hawick
Embleton

Moffat
Alnwick
Alnmouth

Warkworth
DUMFRIES
AND
Rothbury

Newcastleton
GALLOWAY
REGION
NORTHUMBERLAND
Bellingham
Morpeth
Newbiggin-by-the-Sea
Blyth
Bedlington
Cramlington
Backworth
11
Ponteland
Whitley Bay
Gosforth
Tynemouth
Wallsend
NEWCASTLE
UPON-TYNE
Felling
South Shields
Brampton
Hexham
Ryton
Whickham
Gateshead
Prudhoe
Boldon
Allendale
Stocksfield
Chopwell
Birtley
Washington
NY
Burnopfield
Beamish
Houghton-le-Spring
Sunderland
NZ
Consett
Stanley
Chester-le-Street
Seaham
Alston
DURHAM
Penrith
8
HARTLEPOOL
8
Appleby-in-
Westmorland
DURHAM
MIDDLESBROUGH
CUMBRIA
DARLINGTON
CLEVELAND
Keswick
7
Ravenstonedale

For continuation pages refer to numbered arrows

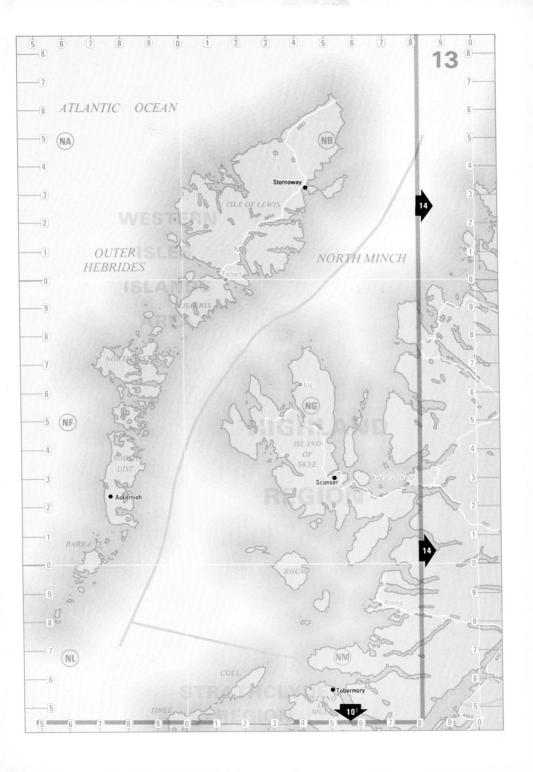

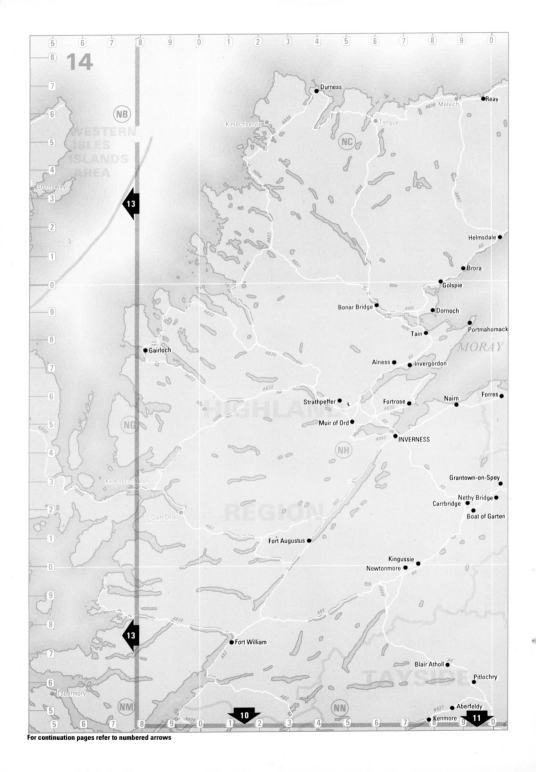

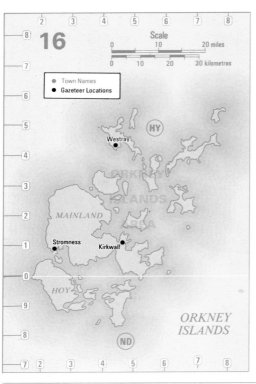

Scale

0   10   20 miles

0   10   20   30 kilometres

- Town Names
- Gazeteer Locations

HY

Westray

LARKIN
ISLANDS
AREA

MAINLAND

Stromness

Kirkwall

HOY

ND

*ORKNEY
ISLANDS*

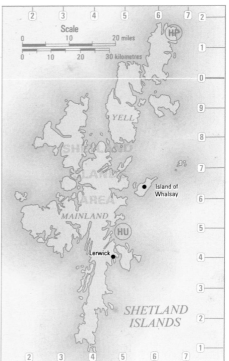

Scale

0   10   20 miles

0   10   20   30 kilometres

HP

YELL

SHETLAND
ISLAND
AREA

MAINLAND

Island of
Whalsay

HU

Lerwick

*SHETLAND
ISLANDS*

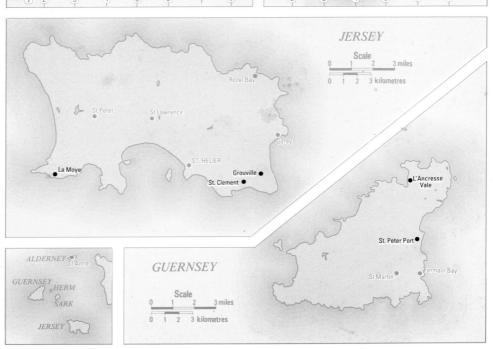

JERSEY

Scale

0   1   2   3 miles

0   1   2   3 kilometres

Rozel Bay

St Peter

St Lawrence

Gorey

ST. HELIER

La Moye

Grouville

St. Clement

L'Ancresse
Vale

St. Peter Port

St Martin

Fermain Bay

ALDERNEY
St Anne

GUERNSEY

HERM

SARK

JERSEY

GUERNSEY

Scale

0   1   2   3 miles

0   1   2   3 kilometres